P9-DTA-153

OSWALD AND THE CIA

Also by John Newman

JFK and Vietnam

OSWALD AND THE CIA

John Newman

Carroll & Graf Publishers, Inc.
New York

First Carroll & Graf edition 1995

Carroll & Graf Publishers, Inc.
260 Fifth Avenue
New York, NY 10001

All photographs, unless otherwise indicated, are courtesy of the National Archive and Dan Wolf/Photo Concepts.

Library of Congress Cataloging-in-Publication Data

Newman, John, 1942–
Oswald and the CIA / John Newman. — 1st Carroll & Graf ed.
p. cm.
ISBN 0-7867-0131-5 :
1. Kennedy, John F. (John Fitzgerald), 1917–1963—Assassination.
2. Oswald, Lee Harvey. 3. United States. Central Intelligence Agency. 4. Intelligence service—United States. I. Title.
E842.9.N47 1995
364.1'524—dc20 94-22392
CIP

Manufactured in the United States of America

2 4 6 8 10 9 7 5 3 1

To the men and women who served the CIA with distinction and made possible the Agency's greatest accomplishments; and to the courageous citizens who dared to investigate the Agency's greatest failures.

Acknowledgments

I would like to thank the JFK Assassination Records Review Board, especially the staff, which went out of their way to ensure that I was informed of the latest releases, no matter how small. I enjoyed meeting and speaking with some of the staff as they set about the daunting task of studying the large bureaucracies whose documents they would be working with. My manuscript and all my files have been available to the staff from early on. I hope this work will assist the board in the difficult choices it faces in prioritizing its work.

How is it that we suddenly have so much to study? The reason that the case has survived so long is the same reason that Congress finally decided to declassify it: lack of trust. American citizens have worked tirelessly to free the documents in the government's possession. Erroneously ridiculed by the national media as the lunatic fringe, most of these people are mainstream Americans who have always understood the wisdom of working within the system. Many of them spent years using the Freedom of Information Act (FOIA) to pry loose documents. Harold Weisberg, Mark Allen, Gary Shaw, Paul Hoch, Bernard Fensterwald, Jr., James Lesar, Gordon Winslow, and Bill Adams are a few among many who have worked within the lethargic constraints of the FOIA over the past several decades. Eventually their efforts and the efforts of many more people resulted in the bipartisan passage of the 1992 JFK Records Act.

Some thanks to specific researchers are in order. First of all to Mary Ferrell. I sent her many thousands of pages of new documents which she added to her database, which I then used as the cross-grid between the new releases and prior government investigations. Mary has always been a tireless and selfless research assistant for everyone who has asked her help. A special thanks also to Scott Malone, whose contacts and comments aided greatly in the early phases of this work. Scott also made his documents and interview notes available, materials I found useful further down the line. A special thanks is also due to David Lifton. I had the benefit of David's early thinking on several issues important to this book—as he did to my early views and documents. For the most part, however, our two projects have been conducted separately, and it will be interesting to see the result. Norman Mailer and I spoke twice briefly as his book was finished and this book entered the final chapters. Norman suggested then that we were staking out "base camps on opposite sides of the mountain."

Thanks also go to Larry Haapanen, who has been a "reliable and highly sensitive source" in Idaho. Larry helped on several points and made available his valuable documentary collection. Paul Hoch also made his documents available, along with his prolific notes and correspondence. Bill Adams, Peter Vea, Bill Davy, Jim Di Eugenio, Steve Vetter, Lamar Waldron, and Mike Willman made available hundreds of documents, rare manuscripts, and other materials that were used in this book.

Peter Dale Scott gave generous amounts of time and energy to document acquisition, processing, cross-referencing, and analysis and discussion. I am especially grateful to Anthony and Robbyn Summers for the generous assistance they gave on several occasions, including the interview with Silvia Duran. Several volunteers from the community and interns from the University of Maryland helped in the long and tedious assembling and cross-filing of data necessary for a work like this. Debbie Drucker, Suzanne Adamko, Nassir Khan, David Vivian, Tracy Vaughn, and Adrienne Freda permitted far more ground to be covered than would otherwise have been possible. John Taylor and John Harvey, in particular, spent many nights copying and filing documents. Without their efforts this book would not have been possible. Melissa Burneston was particularly helpful in the preparation of the footnotes.

To Richard Helms, Jane Roman, June Cobb, Ray Rocca, Scotty Miler, Russell Holmes, Robert Bannerman, Paul Garbler, Otto Otepka, Richard Snyder, John McVickar, Priscilla Johnson, Ned Kenan, Silvia Duran, Gerry Hemming, James Hosty, Larry Keenan, Nicholas Anikeeff, and the many others with whom I conducted formal interviews or background discussion, I thank you for taking the time to run yet another gauntlet of questions.

A special thanks to Ed Jeunovitch, whose many decades of experience in the CIA's Clandestine Services made him uniquely qualified to discuss some of the tougher issues these documents raise. Ed earned my admiration for his openness, honesty, and willingness to engage in genuine give-and-take discussion. I do not mean to imply that anything in this book has Ed's approval or reflects his views, but his persuasiveness and his willingness to give credit where it is due went a long way in convincing me that many among the Agency's mainstream have no desire to stand in the way of the truth.

To all of the dedicated National Archives employees who put up with the researchers and the national media, I take my hat off. Especially to Steve Tilley, who took time from the heavy demands of his schedule to go the extra mile in giving support to this project. Two of the largest logistical problems recently faced by the Archives occurred back to back: the quick processing of an enormous volume of new JFK documents and then the move of the entire collection to the new Archives II location in College Park, Maryland. The discipline and organization of the Archives staff made it possible to keep the records open nearly the entire time before and after the move.

During the work on this, my second book, my family once again made great sacrifices. Ally, my daughter, a science student at the University of Maryland, did several independent research projects in support of this work. My wife, Sue, filled in on all sorts of tasks, from typing to proofreading and editing, and endless discussions about the content. She was a constant source of strength. I want to acknowledge the care and support of my parents, who have always been an inspiration for my work. Thanks also to my children, Mary and John, who pitched in wherever they could. I would also like to thank my friend and colleague Dick Thornton, whose incisive writings on American foreign policy have for years served as my guideposts.

To Jennifer Prior, Henry Lincoln, Janet, Failey, and others at my publisher, Carroll & Graf, thanks for bearing with me. Thanks to Herman Graf, who managed to keep me (more or less) on schedule, and especially to Kent Carroll, from whom I learned more about direct writing and active voice than I did when I was in the Army. Kent's contribution to this text was invaluable. Thanks also to Abby Bardi, who gave up many evenings and weekends to edit much of this book. To Rich, Lou, and Krystal, thanks for being good listeners.

To my many friends and former colleagues in the National Security Agency, the Central Intelligence Agency, the Defense Intelligence Agency, and the Army Intelligence and Security Command, and you know who you are: Thanks for your words of encouragment or constructive criticism, whatever they happened to be. Buck, Tom, and Bill, I wish I could put your comments in a book and ship it to everyone in the research community so that they might see the wide range of opinions but nevertheless intense interest in these matters that exists in the federal workforce—especially in the intelligence agencies. To Pete, Ray, and Cookie from the "keyhole," who spent many lunches working over specific problems: Some of those points turned out to be key indicators, such as the espionage element in Oswald's defection and the anomalous aspects of his Cuban activities.

To the faculty and students at the University of Maryland—College Park and University College—I hope this work will stimulate greater use of the amazing resource that has moved to our campus: the National Archives. There can be no greater acknowledgment than that to the American tradition which produced these archives. It is up to us to use them.

The mistakes in this book are mine alone.

Contents

FOREWORD

A Crisis of Confidence

We no longer question whether there have been government excesses, lies, and cover-ups. Rather, the issue is what to do about them. The key question is this: Can citizens work within the system to root out corruption and, when necessary, reform the government? The answer to that is yes, with a big "if." Yes, if those in power are courageous enough to let the people have all the facts. Upon that "if" hangs the essence of our democracy.

The steady decline of faith in government has intensified political conflict. What has caused this decline? The controversy surrounding the Kennedy assassination has played its part. Along with the Vietnam War, the Watergate scandal, and the ascension of the politics of hate, the JFK case has fed the public's disaffection with their government. The purpose of the JFK Assassination Records Act was to take a step in the direction of restoring faith. The premise underlying this step is simple: Opening up all the government's files will demonstrate that our institutions work today.

The bureaucratic urge to protect sources and methods still moves intelligence agencies to ask that not everything be released. Here the government is its own worst enemy. The failure to open all the files will undermine the promise of Congress. It is inevitable that there will be debate about this. The Assassination Records Review Board has the power to fulfill the spirit and the letter of the Records Act. These five American citizens have been invested with a sacred mission: Open up the government's secrets. Only the president may overrule their decisions. If he has to face such a decision, the purpose of the Records Act will already be in jeopardy. The stakes are high not only because of the crisis of confidence but also because the mandate of the Records Act is so clear. Rarely has a government had to pass a law to force itself to tell the truth and appoint private citizens as guardians of that process.

Such full-scale disclosure will inevitably threaten the well-being of some people and the reputations of others. For these people we feel sympathetic, but they are far from alone. Their sacrifice will be added to the suffering of the hundreds of others who have been drawn into the vortex of this case. What the country gains from full disclosure, however, is incomparably greater. In order for the Act to work, there can be no compromise on the fundamental requirement: the whole truth.

In opening all the files related to the Kennedy assassination Americans should seek not to destroy the government or the intelligence agencies but to reform them. In the course of researching this work, I have learned about the people who work in CIA operations. Most of the men and women who have served the Agency in the past and do so today are decent, honorable Americans. When laying out the Agency's mistakes, we should not lose sight of the integrity with which most served. If I have been critical in the pages that follow, it was not with malice.

The CIA has had its bad apples, and has made mistakes—sometimes terrible ones. All large bureaucracies have such problems, but the secrecy that protects intelligence organizations from external threats is itself the main obstacle to healthy change and reform. I know a former Agency employee whose conscience so troubled him about something secret he had learned that he resigned. Today he is a respected officer in another large intelligence organization, where he does superb intelligence work. I also know a man—who became famous for his analytic skills and accomplishments—who left the Defense Intelligence Agency because of principled dissent. He took a lower-paying position with the CIA. Today he teaches ethics in intelligence work.

The thread that ties these two Americans together is that neither was willing to live a lie. That one joined the CIA and one left the CIA to escape that fate seems noteworthy. Both felt compelled to leave their organizations, but neither opted out of the system. They continued to work for their country. We have the same responsibility, and opportunity.

April 19, 1995

Introduction

The thesis of this work holds that the CIA had a keen operational interest in Lee Harvey Oswald from the day he defected to the Soviet Union in 1959 until the day he was murdered in the basement of the Dallas city jail. From this thesis flow two conclusions: first, that the Agency used sensitive sources and methods to acquire intelligence on Oswald. Secondly, whether witting or not, Oswald became involved in CIA operations.

The scope of this project is as follows: We will follow the trails in Oswald's CIA, FBI, DOD, Navy, Army, and American Embassy files from the time of his defection up to the assassination; and we will follow segments of his files from the State Department, the Immigration and Naturalization Service, and selected Navy and FBI field offices. This work also seeks to address that part of American Cuban policy and covert operations that are either fundamentally or reasonably relevant to the Oswald who emerges in these files. We will not address the assassination of President Kennedy. We will not discuss Dealey Plaza. This book is content to explore the subject of Oswald and the CIA without regard to who is right and who is wrong in the larger debate about the Kennedy assassination.[1]

We will employ a two-track methodology. On one line we will tell the story through a chronological arrangement of evidence and findings. There are self-imposed limitations on this track: First, we will not attempt to describe Lee Harvey Oswald "the man," but concern ourselves instead with Oswald "the file"—the subject of records maintained by intelligence agencies. On the other line we will develop continuity in several historical areas. These areas emerge and clarify through the disclosure of what the government knew about Oswald.

Oswald's was a ponderous case from the beginning. This book is about the people and organizations who had access to and contributed to Oswald's intelligence files before the Kennedy assassination. What was the nature of their interest in Oswald? Who in the CIA had access to Oswald's files? What were their operations?

The official CIA position on its relationship with Oswald has always been that there was no relationship of "any kind." That is what the Agency told the Warren Commission in 1964, and it is what they told the House Select Committee on Assassinations (HSCA) in 1978. CIA director John A. McCone stated this in his 1964 testimony to the Warren Commission:

> Oswald was not an agent, employee, or informant of the Central Intelligence Agency. The Agency never contacted him, interviewed him, talked with him, or solicited any reports or information from him, or communicated with him indirectly or in any other manner. Oswald was never associated or connected directly or indirectly in any way whatsoever with the Agency.[2]

According to the HSCA Report, "The record reflects that once these assurances had been received, no further efforts were made by the Warren Commission to pursue the matter."[3]

A diametrically opposing view of Oswald and the CIA came from James Wilcott, who served as a CIA finance officer in Japan at the time Oswald served there in the Marines. Wilcott claimed that a CIA case officer told him—the day after Kennedy was assassinated—that Oswald was an agent. In 1978 Wilcott told the HSCA that "Oswald was a CIA agent who had received financial disbursements under an assigned cryptonym." Wilcott could only cite informal conversations as evidence, and after talking with Wilcott's coworkers, the HSCA "concluded that Wilcott's allegation was not worthy of belief."[4]

The record suggests that neither the Agency's official story nor Wilcott's characterization is accurate. The truth lies in between. The Agency appears to have had serious operational interest in Oswald and there probably was a relationship, though not that of an "agent" or "informant." While Oswald wasn't James Bond, it is increasingly apparent that the Agency's operational interest may have led to his use or manipulation. For its part, the *HSCA Report* accepted the CIA official position:

> There was no indication in Oswald's CIA file that he had ever had contact with the Agency. . . . This finding, however, must be placed in context, for the institutional characteristics—in terms of the Agency's strict compartmentalization and the complexity of its enormous filing system—that are designed to prevent penetration by foreign powers have the simultaneous effect of making congressional inquiry difficult.[5]

The HSCA said they tried to overcome "the Agency's security-oriented institutional obstacles that potentially impede effective scrutiny of the CIA." But the CIA withheld an important key to Oswald's CIA files: the internal dissemination records for those files. In the absence of those records, the HSCA was unable to resolve the most glaring deficiencies in the Agency's account of the Oswald files.[6]

We have those internal dissemination records and other information not shared with the Warren Commission, Church Committee, or HSCA investigations. This information indicates, at the least, that Oswald was probably involved in CIA operations. No attempt is made in this book to evaluate this material with respect to any conspiracy theory. Beyond the scope of this book, that discussion is already under way with several new works, such as Norman Mailer's *Oswald's Tale: An American Mystery* (New York: Random House, 1995); Ray and Mary La Fontaine's *Oswald Talked: The New Evidence in the JFK Assassination* (New Orleans: Pelican, scheduled for publication in 1995); and David Lifton's *Oswald* (New York: Dutton, scheduled for publication in 1995).

Some useful information has been drawn from previous government investigations, but the vast majority of research for this work was conducted in the newly released files, especially those made available in 1993 through 1995. The two million pages that have been added to the National Archives will take years to process, and the references to these materials in the footnotes reflect the shape and size of the "chunks" of records as they were initially released from contributing agencies. For example, if the footnote states "CIA January 1994 (5 brown boxes) release," researchers will know to go to the five large brown boxes that became available on that date. The Record Identification Form (RIF) numbering system used by the Archives was used in this book whenever possible, but some of the early RIF numbers may no longer be valid. With few exceptions, however, all of the CIA and FBI documents referred to in this book should be easily retrievable at the Archives.

There is something to be said for going first. It is humbling to look at two million pieces of paper. Several disciplines in the social sciences will have enough case study material to last for decades. Pulled forward by our curiosity for the unknown, yet unsettled by the fear of what we might find, we can enter these boxes and finally discover for ourselves. No matter our convictions about the case, to finally look inside those boxes in pursuit of the truth is a liberating experience.

Oswald and the CIA

CHAPTER ONE

Defection in Moscow

"There's a man here and he wants to renounce his citizenship," Jean Hallett announced to American Consul Richard Snyder.[1] Jean, the receptionist for the American Embassy in Moscow on this particular Saturday morning in October 1959, then produced the man's passport and laid it down on Snyder's brown wooden desk. Snyder looked up; it was a little after eleven A.M., and on Saturdays the embassy always closed at noon. "Well, send him on in, then," Snyder replied.

Meanwhile, out in the lobby, an interesting group of people bumped into each other. The lobby at the entrance to the building was the only way to the elevator that ascended to the other sections of the embassy and the living quarters for the Americans working there. Twelve-year-old Carolyn Hallett had come out of the elevator and down the three steps into the lobby after her mother had disappeared into Snyder's office to announce Oswald's arrival. Carolyn found her mother's chair empty, but not so the couch—two young men were sitting on it. The one that fascinated twelve-year-old Carolyn was Lee Harvey Oswald. His countenance seemed to be anything but normal, and a curious little girl was probably the last thing he wanted to see before carrying out his plan to defect. At this particular moment he was working himself up for what he later referred to as a "showdown" with the American consul.[2]

Sitting on the couch next to Oswald was Ned Keenan, an American graduate student based in Leningrad who was there that day seeking the embassy's assistance on visa matters.[3] "I saw him sitting on the sofa when I arrived," Keenan recalls, "and I sat down next to him." Like Carolyn, Keenan also thought Oswald looked odd. "He was a memorable character," Keenan says. "He was strangely dressed—I remember him being lightly dressed above [i.e. on top].'' Jean Hallett came back out from Snyder's office and found there were now two visitors on the couch as well as her daughter staring at Oswald, who was undoubtedly happy to be extricated from this scene.

As Lee Harvey Oswald confidently strode across the old wooden office floor behind Jean, he passed the other American consul, John McVickar, on his way to Snyder's desk. Oswald was dressed immaculately, in a dark suit with a white shirt and tie—''very businessman-looking,'' Snyder later recalled.[4] But Snyder soon noticed odd things, like the fact that the man had no coat or hat on this brisk October thirty-first morning in Moscow. And then there were those thin, dressy white gloves that he wore into the room and removed rather deliberately as he came to a halt in front of Snyder's desk. Snyder, who was typing a report, was struck by the ''humorless and robotic'' quality of Oswald's demeanor. ''Please sit down,'' Snyder said, still typing.[5]

Oswald, perhaps annoyed at being put off, complied with this invitation to sit. He later wrote a one-page essay about the visit which contains this recollection:

> I do so, selecting an armchair to the front left side of Snyder's desk. . . . I wait, crossing my legs and laying my gloves in my lap. He finishes typing, removes the letter from his typewriter, and adjusting his glasses looks at me. ''What can I do for you,'' he asks, leafing through my passport.[6]

This passage is nearly identical to Snyder's account of this scene. Of course, Oswald's perspective of himself was quite different from Snyder's, whose attention was distracted by those little white gloves.

Jean returned to her reception desk to find her daughter bursting with curiosity. ''Mommy, who was that weird man at your desk?'' Jean replied, ''I got rid of him.''[7]

Richard Snyder studied the scrawny, nervous young man sitting next to him as he posed the question, ''What can I do for you?''[8] Oswald responded with what appeared to be a carefully prepared statement: ''I've come to give up my American passport and renounce my citizenship,'' he said firmly but without emotion. With a dignified hand movement, he then gave Snyder a note which formally announced his intention to defect to the Soviet Union.[9]

Oswald continued talking. ''I've thought this thing over very carefully and I know what I'm doing. I was just discharged from the Marine Corps on September eleventh,'' he said, ''and I have been planning to do this for two years.''[10] That remark really caught Snyder's attention. Even McVickar, the other consular official, who was across the room, began to listen more closely, and Oswald later remembered noticing McVickar look up from his work.[11] ''I know what you're going to say,'' Oswald said matter-of-factly to Snyder, ''but I don't want any lectures or advice. So let's save my time and yours, and you just give me the papers to sign and I'll leave.'' By ''papers'' Oswald meant the forms to formally renounce his American citizenship. Snyder was struck by Oswald's ''cocksure'' and even arrogant attitude, and remarked later, ''This was part of a scene he had rehearsed before coming into the embassy. It was a preplanned speech.''[12]

Indeed, Oswald had planned well—exceptionally well. ''Since he arrived in Moscow in mid-October 1959 and was discharged from the Marine Corps in September 1959,'' McVickar told the State Department in 1964, ''he would have to have made a direct and completely arranged trip.''[13] In addition, Oswald had entered the Soviet Union through Helsinki, not the customary route for Americans, but an ideal place to apply for an exception to the rules and get a quick entry visa. ''It [Helsinki as an entry point] is a well enough known fact among people who are working in the Soviet Union and undoubtedly people who are associated with Soviet matters,'' McVickar later told the Warren Commission, ''but I would say it was not a commonly known fact among the ordinary run of people in the United States.''[14] In fact, even in Helsinki, the average turnaround time for a visa was still seven to fourteen days at that time, something which the Warren Commission checked into carefully after the Kennedy assassination.[15] However, the point is that exceptions were often made—perhaps more often than anyplace else—in Helsinki. That Oswald had managed to go from the U.S. straight to the ideal site where such exceptions were sometimes made—and succeeded in becoming just such an exception—suggests that his defection had been well planned and was intended to be speedy.

Oswald tried to remain calm during the scene in the embassy, "but he was wound up inside tighter than a clockspring," Snyder said later, "hoping he could keep control of the conversation."[16] Oswald's diary corroborates this, describing the meeting as a "showdown."[17] Oswald told Snyder he had not applied for a Soviet tourist visa until he reached Helsinki on October 14, and that in doing so he had purposely not told the Soviet Embassy of his plan to remain in the Soviet Union. Oswald then described how he had implemented the next phase of his game plan upon reaching Moscow: On October 16 he had applied for Soviet citizenship by letter to the Supreme Soviet.[18]

Oswald paused here for Snyder's reaction. The consul searched for a way to knock the young man off his prepared script. Snyder recalls that there was a brief moment of silence while Oswald, still clutching those little white gloves in one hand, calculated his next move. The sunlight shone through the wall of glass to Snyder's left, painted opaque so that the Soviets could not see the classified work that went on in the office.

Snyder, a seasoned diplomat, was drawn to the olive-green passport that lay on the desk between the two of them. Picking it up and examining it carefully, he was immediately able to deduce that he was speaking with a minor, a twenty-year-old young ex-marine. Snyder noticed that Oswald had deliberately scratched out his address.[19] That gave the consul some leverage. "Well, I'm afraid that to complete the papers for renunciation I will need some basic information," Snyder said at last, "including an address in the U.S. and an address of your closest living relative." Oswald, upset at the prospect of involving his mother, Marguerite, in the extraordinary move he was undertaking, was suddenly out of his game plan. He began to protest, but Snyder would not budge: no address, no papers. Finally, Oswald gave Snyder Marguerite Oswald's address in Forth Worth.

Snyder knew that Oswald had lost control of the exchange, and the consul therefore decided to press his advantage. "Why do you want to defect to the Soviet Union?" Snyder probed. The "principal reason," Oswald said, thinking on his feet, was because he was a "Marxist." Of course, this answer left open the possibility that he might have other reasons for defecting, too.[20] Snyder then tested Oswald with a barb that was subtle but aggressive: "Life will be lonely as a Marxist.'' However, this cleverly worded inference that the Soviet Union was anything but Marxist seemed to go right over Oswald's head.[21] He had no pat answer, and was clearly unprepared for a verbal duel about Marxism with Snyder. The consul was not as easy to bamboozle with Marxist quips as his marine colleagues had been in Japan, where he had been assigned. There, Private Oswald had especially enjoyed outwitting officers on political, especially left wing, subjects.

Now, however, Oswald was clearly out of his depth, and so he returned to what he had come prepared to say. Oswald declared he wanted the matter to conclude ''quickly,'' Snyder recalls. In a feeble attempt to stop Snyder's questions, Oswald made what appears to be a slip-up. Snyder recalls that Oswald then blurted out, ''I was warned you would try to talk me out of defecting.''[22]

The significance of Oswald's remark is worth considering. Who could have forewarned Oswald about what the American consul in Moscow would say or try to do? It stands to reason—unless Oswald was lying—that someone had helped Oswald plan his defection. But who could that have been? This possibility was so startling that it would later occupy the attention of many people—including Snyder. As it turned out, Oswald had an even bigger surprise in store that morning.

The most extraordinary development during the defection occurred when Snyder—on a roll—asked Oswald if he was willing to serve the Soviet state. Whether or not Oswald had prepared for this question is intriguing, for his answer could not have been worse from the standpoint of eliciting Snyder's cooperation in getting his defection papers. Oswald's reply, McVickar later wrote, ''tended to extinguish any sympathy one may have felt for a confused and unhappy young man.''[23] It also led to an interesting start to the paper trail on Oswald back in Washington, especially at the CIA, a subject to which we will shortly return. Snyder's contemporaneous written account of the duel with Oswald contains this passage:

> Oswald offered the information that he had been a radar operator in the Marine Corps and that he had voluntarily stated to unnamed Soviet officials that as a Soviet citizen he would make known to them such information concerning the Marine Corps and

> his specialty as he possessed. He intimated that he might know something of special interest.[24]

Here again Oswald's remarks seem laden by significance. Special interest? What "special interest" information did Oswald know beyond what he had learned as a radar operator? Perhaps Oswald had in mind something he had learned because of his assignment to Atsugi Naval Air Station, Japan, where an extremely sensitive CIA program had been—and still was—ongoing.

McVickar also recalls that Oswald said he was going to turn over "classified things" to "Soviet authorities."[25] Snyder later theorized that what Oswald may have had in mind by using the words "something of special interest" was the supersecret American U-2 spy plane that was based at Atsugi.[26] If so, this question then arises: Why drop the hint in the American Embassy? After all, was not Oswald's purpose simply to obtain the defection papers? Snyder's hypothesis was that Oswald assumed the KGB had bugged the American Embassy, and "was speaking for Russian ears in my office."[27]

By this time it was after noontime. "We are closed now," Snyder said, "and I can't get all the papers typed up right now. If you want, you can come back in a couple days when we are open and get them."[28] At this point, Oswald simply turned around and left. "He came storming out," Keenan—who was still sitting on the couch outside Snyder's office—recalls. "It was enough to catch my attention."[29]

In spite of this ending to the defection scene, however, Oswald followed up Snyder's stalling tactics in a curious way. He complained bitterly about Snyder's treatment during an interview with a news reporter in his hotel room but never returned to the embassy to sign the papers. "Perhaps he heard a little voice," Snyder now muses, "[which said] don't burn that bridge." By not executing the renunciation papers, Oswald had, in effect, left open a way to return to America.[30]

Room 233, the Metropole

Oswald left the American Embassy interpreting the outcome not as a defeat but as a victory. This seems strange given that he had failed to get the paperwork for renunciation of U.S. citizenship, the ostensible purpose for his visit that morning. But not if his real objective, as Snyder had guessed, was to impress the KGB, whom he had to assume was bugging the American Embassy. Support for this interpretation comes from Oswald's diary, which records his exuberance after his return to his hotel room:

> I leave Embassy, elated at this showdown, returning to my hotel I feel now my enorgies [sic] are not spent in vain. I'm sure Russians will except [sic] me after this sign of my faith in them.[31]

Still wrapped up in his thoughts about his encounter with Snyder, Oswald returned to his hotel room. He had not had time to sort much out, when he was surprised by a knock on his door.

The hand knocking on Oswald's door belonged to the Moscow bureau chief of United Press International (UPI), Robert J. Korengold, whom Snyder had immediately notified by telephone after alerting Washington—in his cable 1304—about the defection request. "I called on Korengold fairly quickly," Snyder explains, "to try and get another line on Oswald."[32] Snyder encouraged Korengold by telling him that an interview with Oswald might prove "interesting" for the UPI. Snyder may even have told Korengold the room in which Oswald was staying at the Metropole.[33] Korengold wasted no time in following up Snyder's lead, and arrived at the door of Room 233 at two P.M.[34]

When Oswald opened his door, Korengold requested an interview. "How did you find out?" Oswald asked in response, flabbergasted at the speed with which events were unfolding.[35] (Korengold might even have beaten Oswald back to his room, a possibility suggested by Korengold's recollection that his contact with Oswald came "after several unsuccessful attempts."[36]) It was rare that a chance to interview a defector came around, and it began to look as though his persistence had paid off. "The embassy called us," Korengold replied hopefully. Caught off guard, Oswald flatly refused to give Korengold an interview. Korengold recalled, "Oswald stated he knew what he was doing and insisted he did not wish to talk to anyone."[37]

After ten minutes of getting nowhere with Oswald, the intrepid UPI bureau chief left the Metropole, disappointed but not about to give up. When Oswald shut the door, he felt Korengold was part of a plot. Oswald later wrote of his feelings: "This is one way to bring pressure on me. By notifing [sic] my relations in U.S. through the newspapers."[38] Meanwhile, Korengold went back to his office and spoke with a correspondent for the UPI, Aline Mosby. As we will discuss in a later chapter, Mosby led a colorful life in the Soviet Union, including being "drugged" in a Moscow restaurant and victimized in the Soviet press for her "drink and debauchery."[39]

Within minutes of talking to her bureau chief, Mosby was on her way to Room 233 in the Metropole. She told the FBI in 1964 that she had learned of Oswald in the fall of 1959 "from a source she can no longer recall,"[40] but the source was probably Korengold. Mosby recounts her journey to Oswald this way:

> I went up in the creaky elevator to the second floor and down the hall, past the life-sized nude in white marble, the gigantic painting of Lenin and Stalin and the usual watchful clerk in her prim navy blue dress with brown braids around her head. An attractive fellow answered my knock on the door of Room 233.[41]

For Oswald, life was getting more interesting by the moment. Oswald was surprised at the attention he was getting: two American reporters in less than half an hour.[42]

"I am Lee Oswald," he said with a "hesitant smile" to Aline, who recalls that she then "murmured some pleasantry" in reply. Oswald, still off guard and unsure, refused her a formal interview, but Mosby, it seems, was far more successful than Korengold in loosening Oswald's tongue. "I think you may understand and be friendly because you're a woman," Oswald told her.[43] He then agreed to answer Mosby's questions.

Oswald informed Mosby that he had applied to renounce his American citizenship and become a Soviet citizen. He did so, he said, "for purely political reasons."[44] Mosby successfully elicited enough personal details from Oswald to rush back to her office and put all of this into a report for the wires, adding, "The slender, unsmiling Oswald refused to give any other reasons for his decision to give up his American citizenship and live in the Soviet Union. He would not say what he is planning to do here."[45]

There was, of course, someone else who was listening to what Oswald said to Mosby. An internal 1964 CIA memorandum that commented on a draft paper entitled ''KGB operations against foreign tourists'' contained the following useful entry: ''Rm 233, Hotel Metropole, Moscow—equipped with infra-red camera for observation of occupants.''[46] Thus the Soviet KGB office in Moscow was presumably busy writing a report of the conversation between Aline Mosby and Lee Oswald, as Mosby's UPI ticker of the same event burned across the wires of the U.S., including those in Texas.

The reporters of the *Star Telegram* in Forth Worth were probably still drinking their first cup of coffee when Mosby's UPI report popped out of their ticker. The second line read,''Lee Harvey Oswald, of Fort Worth, Tex., told United Press International in his room at the Metropole Hotel, 'I will never return to the United States for any reason.' ''[47]

Halloween in Fort Worth

''The first time I was aware he was in Russia,'' Robert Oswald testified in 1964 about his brother Lee Harvey Oswald, ''was on Halloween Day 1959, October 31.''[48] Within hours after Oswald's defection, three or four Forth Worth reporters were at the home of Robert Oswald, pestering him for information about his brother. Robert Oswald initially resisted but then yielded to the pressure tactics of the reporters, who suggested that he cooperate because he might be ''the only source of information'' about what brother Lee was doing in Russia.

When the interview was over, another man appeared at Robert Oswald's house. Robert does not recall who he was other than that he identified himself as a reporter for the Fort Worth *Star Telegram*. This man not only asked questions but had suggestions as well. He told Robert Oswald he should send two telegrams, one to Secretary of State Christian Herter, and the other to Lee Oswald in Russia. With the man still in his home, Robert immediately called Western Union and sent both telegrams, and then advised the reporter of the contents. Even though Robert ''did not receive confirmation of these telegrams from Western Union'' while the reporter was still present, they both appeared in full in the Sunday, November 1, edition of the *Star Telegram*.[49]

Thus Robert Oswald sent two messages to his brother, one directly and the other through the U.S. State Department. The first one to arrive in Moscow was the latter, a State cable arriving at 6:34 P.M. Sunday evening at the American Embassy in Moscow. The embassy was requested to "pass following message if possible." The message read, "For Lee Harvey Oswald from Robert Lee Oswald. QUOTE Contact me as soon as possible through the fastest means available. UNQUOTE." The photostatic copy of this cable extant in the National Archives today bears the signature of then Secretary of State Christian Herter,[50] who had either come into his office at the State Department or received the cable via an aide early that Sunday morning. In any event, arriving at the embassy communications center at 6:34 P.M., the cable would have to wait until Monday morning for someone to attempt to deliver it to Oswald.

That same Sunday, Oswald's mother attempted to call him at his hotel room. Kent Biffle, a Fort Worth newspaper reporter, had arranged a three-way telephone conversation between his office, Marguerite Oswald, and her son at the Metropole hotel. Seth Kantor, another Fort Worth newspaperman at the time, recalls what happened:

> [I]t took several hours to arrange the call trans-Atlantically and trans-continentally and get the call into Russia to where Oswald was. At times it seemed it would be impossible to get the call through, but at last the call was ready and Mrs. Oswald was on her line in her home and Kent Biffle, sitting right across from me at the Press city desk, was on his phone, and here came Oswald on the phone from Russia. As soon as Oswald found out that it was his mother on the phone in Fort Worth and it was a newspaperman who had set this thing up, so she could talk to her son, Oswald hung up. All those hours down the drain.[51]

Oswald was evidently offended at the thought that newspaper reporters would use his mother as a means of getting the story on his defection.

On Monday, Richard Snyder asked his secretary, Marie Cheatham, who also served as the administrative assistant for the consular section, to telephone Oswald, tell him that the embassy had received a telegram from his brother, and ask him to stop by the office to pick it up.[51] When he took Cheatham's call at 9:30 A.M., Oswald, not keen on the idea of returning to the embassy, refused Cheatham's request. Snyder told his secretary to try a different approach. She wrote a memo to Snyder afterward to explain what happened:

> I again called Mr. Oswald immediately thereafter, as instructed by you, to ask him if I could read the message to him over the telephone. His room did not answer. At 11:05 I contacted Mr. Oswald at his hotel and asked him if I could read the message from his brother, that I now had two telegrams for him. Mr. Oswald replied, "No, not at the present time," and hung up.[53]

This passage makes it clear that the second of the two Robert Oswald telegrams arrived in the consular office between the second and third of Marie Cheatham's phone calls to Oswald's hotel room—that is, between 9:30 and 11:05 A.M. that Monday morning in Moscow.

The situation of the Oswalds in Dallas was unenviable. All immediate efforts to reach Lee in Russia had failed, and the local press in Texas did not look favorably upon defectors. There had been one press report in the *Corpus Christi Times* a week earlier profiling a string of defections to the Soviet Union. The article said:

> As far as we are concerned, any American citizen, male or female, who renounces his citizenship in favor of the Soviet Union, is entitled to the protection of this government in two particulars only. The State Department should ask him two questions: Was he drunk or sober when he did it? Did he seem to have all his marbles with him at the time?
>
> Having settled these questions to its own satisfaction, the government and people of the United States should wave him goodbye and see to it that his name is wiped off our national books forever, and he never be allowed to set foot in this country again, dead or alive.[54]

This newspaper clipping, which had been sparked by the recent defection of other Americans, would, by mid-November 1959, become the first official record in Oswald's FBI headquarters file—105-82555.[55] By that time there would be more than the *Corpus Christi Times* complaint to put in Oswald's file.

An "Intelligence Matter"

Snyder recorded the details of Oswald's defection, fully documenting his bizarre performance in the embassy that day. Snyder's complete account was typed by his secretary, Vera Brown, and sent to the State Department in a lengthy dispatch two days later, Monday, November 2. It included this assessment:

> Throughout the interview Oswald's manner was aggressive, arrogant, and uncooperative. He appeared to be competent. . . . He was contemptuous of any efforts by the interviewing officer in his interest, made clear that he wanted no advice from the embassy. He stated that he knew the provisions of U.S. law on loss of citizenship and declined to have them reviewed by the interviewing officer. In short, he displayed all the airs of a new sophomore party-liner.[56]

These observations weighed heavily in Snyder's abiding impression that Oswald's defection had been carefully planned.

In a November 1963 memorandum, Snyder's colleague McVickar said it was possible that Oswald had read books he did not understand. Nevertheless, McVickar argued,

> . . . it seemed that it could also have been that he had been taught to say things which he did not really understand. In short, it seemed to me that there was a possibility that he had been in contact with others before or during his Marine Corps tour who had guided him and encouraged him in his actions.[57]

McVickar argued that there seemed the possibility that Oswald "was following a pattern of behavior in which he had been tutored by person or persons unknown."[58]

Who were these "persons unknown," and how did they know what Snyder would or would not do? Something about the way Oswald was using pat phrases about Marxism along with his reference to "papers to sign" led Snyder and McVickar to conclude that Oswald had only incomplete knowledge of such intellectual and legal matters. Snyder says he retains a "strong impression" that Oswald "used simple Marxist stereotypes without sophistication or independent formulation."[59]

Both Snyder and McVickar thought at the time that Oswald might have been "tutored" before appearing at the consulate, and both today continue to believe that Oswald's performance that October Saturday in 1959 was carefully planned. Oswald's stated intent to turn over military secrets should be considered in this context. If someone did help Oswald plan his defection, this someone might also have told Oswald to threaten to reveal military secrets.

Oswald's statements about radar secrets and "something special" were the most significant part of the defection event. Such behavior is difficult to imagine of an ex-marine. "I certainly did not expect anyone in his position to make a statement that he was disloyal to the U.S.," Snyder explained.[60] McVickar told Oswald biographer Edward J. Epstein that it was the part of the conversation where Oswald said he was going to turn over classified radar information that "raised hackles."[61] McVickar summed up his recollection for the Warren Commission in this way:

> He [Oswald] mentioned that he knew certain classified things in connection with having been, I think, a radar operator in the Marine Corps, and that he was going to turn this information over to the Soviet authorities. And, of course, we didn't know how much he knew or anything like that, but this obviously provoked a rather negative reaction among us Americans in the consulate section.[62]

Again, both witnesses to this performance by Oswald emphasize its unusual nature, especially with regard to military secrets.

Part of what made Oswald's stated intent to reveal state secrets so remarkable is that it had not been solicited. Snyder had made no attempt to probe for intelligence or espionage-related information. "He volunteered this statement," Snyder testified before the Warren Commission in 1964. "It was rather peculiar."[63] Peculiar indeed—to walk into an American Embassy anywhere in the world, let alone Moscow at the height of the Cold War, and to announce, in the presence of American consular officials, one's intent to commit a deliberate act of espionage is an extraordinary act. However, perhaps because Oswald did not specifically "claim to possess knowledge or information of [a] highly classified nature," Snyder was content to get out of the embassy that Saturday afternoon and deal with the mess the following week. Nevertheless, Snyder knew without question that, at the very least, Oswald was "declaring [his] intention [to] commit a disloyal act."[64] Before going home that same Saturday afternoon, Snyder cabled this news to Washington.[65]

The serious nature of Oswald's threats and their consequences may be the reason he chose not to return for his renunciation papers after that Saturday morning. If his speech was for the Soviets, it had served its purpose, and Oswald could not be sure how the Americans would react. If he had thought this part of it through, he would have to have realized that the Defense Department and the CIA would treat his situation not as a simple defection but as a security matter requiring a careful investigation. Oswald could not rule out the possibility that if he returned, the marine guard on duty, rather than ushering him in to see Snyder, might instead take him into custody for questioning.

On Tuesday, November 3, Oswald wrote a letter to the U.S. embassy protesting his treatment in Snyder's office the previous Saturday. "I appeared in person, at the consulate office of the United States embassy, Moscow, on Oct. 31st, for the purpose of signing the formal papers" for the revocation of his American citizenship. "This legal right I was refused at that time."[66] He protested this and the "conduct of the official," i.e., Richard Snyder. The letter arrived at the embassy on Friday, November 6, and Snyder sent a reply on the following Monday, November 9,[67] having informed the State Department about it in the meantime.[68] In his reply to Oswald, Snyder invited him to come back "anytime during normal business hours."

Snyder was not the only person in Moscow sending cables to Washington about Oswald's espionage intentions. While Oswald sat in his hotel room writing his letter of protest to the embassy, the naval attaché in the embassy was also writing a confidential cable, in this case to the chief of Naval Operations in the Pentagon. The determination that this ex-marine was no simple defector but in truth a self-declared saboteur arrived at the Navy Department the next morning, November 3, 1963. Like Snyder's October 31 cable, the navy attaché's cable was very short. It invited attention to the embassy's reporting on the defections of Oswald and another ex-navy man, and added only one thing: that Oswald had offered to furnish the Soviets information on U.S. radar.[69]

Whatever Oswald's thinking might or might not have been, there is little question about the thinking in Washington, D.C. It did not take long for the naval attaché's message from Moscow to set off alarm bells at the Navy Department. There the cable was routed by a person named Hamner in the Navy Department and checked by ''RE/Hediger.''[70] The meaning of the letters ''RE'' is not clear, but it is interesting—as we will discuss in a later chapter—that they also belong to a person connected to a very sensitive CIA monitoring operation. Just twenty-seven hours after being notified that an ex-marine had stated his intent to give up radar secrets, Navy Headquarters replied to Moscow.[71] The final sentence of the navy cable underlines the importance that Washington attached to the news of Oswald's defection. The cable requested updates of developments on Oswald because of ''CONTINUING INTEREST OF HQ, MARINE CORPS, AND US INTELLIGENCE AGENCIES.'' Centered underneath the bottom of these words were two more: ''INTELLIGENCE MATTER.''

Chapter Two

Paper Trail in Washington

At 7:59 A.M., October 31, 1959, a teletype printer at the State Department began its thumping clackety-clack, typing out Snyder's Confidential cable 1304 from the embassy in Moscow.[1] The news that Oswald's defection included an intent to commit espionage was now in the nation's capital, but it was Saturday morning, so official Washington was asleep or perhaps just getting up to go shopping or work in their gardens. The children were probably thinking about their costumes for an American pastime—it was Halloween. At the State Department message center, the personnel were probably changing over from the mid[night] shift to the day shift as Moscow cable 1304 was copied and assigned an initial internal distribution. It would have to wait until Monday for anyone to look at it.

At 9:20 A.M., Aline Mosby's UPI report flashed across the Washington news tickers, indicating that Oswald had spoken publicly about his defection in his Metropole hotel room a few hours earlier.[2] Oswald had not told Mosby of his intention to hand over military secrets to the Soviets. That part of the story was classified, and was still sitting in a distribution box over in the State Department. The UPI story told only of Oswald's attempt to renounce his American citizenship and become a Soviet citizen.

It was the unclassified version of the defection that set off the alarm bell at the FBI. At 10:19 A.M., the stamp "RECEIVED DIRECTOR FBI" was placed on the back side of the Mosby UPI ticker and her story was handed to E. B. Reddy, who was on duty that morning.[3] Perhaps the ex-marine's announcement, "I will never return to the United States for any reason'' grabbed Reddy's attention, or perhaps his FBI training led his eyes to rest on the sentence that stated that Oswald ''would not say what he was planning to do here.'' The way the UPI ticker was worded led Reddy to conclude incorrectly that Oswald had held a ''press conference'' in his hotel room.[4] Reddy immediately decided to check out just who this defector was.

Reddy grabbed a standard FBI questionnaire for the records branch of the Identification Division and filled it out. In the ''subject'' box he wrote ''Lee Harvey Oswald,'' placing a check in the block requesting ''all references (subversive and nonsubversive)'' and another check in the block ''return to,'' where he added ''Reddy [room] 1742.''[5] By lunchtime Paul Kupferschmidt of the records branch had managed to locate only Oswald's fingerprints. They had been taken when he entered the Marine Corps, a standard procedure for everyone entering the military, and the prints are always sent to the FBI. These fingerprints did not lead to much in the FBI's files. Kupferschmidt was able to advise Reddy only that ''Oswald, a white male, born on October 18, 1939, at New Orleans, Louisiana, enlisted in the U.S. Marine Corps on October 24, 1956, at Dallas, Texas, and holds U.S. Marine Corps Number 1653230.''

Using this information and the details of Mosby's UPI ticker, Reddy prepared a memorandum and attached a copy of the UPI report to his memo. He addressed this memo to Alan H. Belmont, head of the FBI's Intelligence Division. Either Belmont or, more likely, someone from his office came into the FBI that Saturday afternoon, because the back of the ticker also bears the stamp ''REC'D BELMONT FBI-JUSTICE Oct 31 3:18 PM '59.''[6]

Moscow: Sunday, November 1

On Sunday, the American press began to report a few more details about the defection in Moscow. Based on Saturday's UPI story, the New York office of the Associated Press (AP) called its Moscow correspondent, A. I. Goldberg, and asked him to verify the story. It was still Sunday in Moscow when Goldberg made the by then well-traveled journey to Oswald's hotel room, whereupon Oswald identified himself but refused to grant an interview. Goldberg pressed for something, asking Oswald why he was going to remain in Russia. "I've got my reasons," Oswald responded, but refused to elaborate further. Goldberg then tried to dissuade Oswald from staying, and inquired whether Oswald knew Russian or had any particular skill he could use in the Soviet Union. According to Goldberg, Oswald replied that he did not know Russian, but that he could learn and that he could "make out."[7]

Goldberg apparently contacted someone in the American Embassy, for when he sent his story back to AP headquarters in New York on Sunday, it included the sentence, "The embassy urged him [Oswald] not to sign papers renouncing his American citizenship until he was sure the Soviet Union would accept him."[8] Meanwhile, by Sunday, UPI bureau chief Bob Korengold had done some more calling as well, both to Oswald and to the American Embassy. The Sunday UPI story out of Moscow contained this new sentence attributed to Oswald: "I cannot make any statement until after I receive my Soviet citizenship. It might jeopardize my position—I mean the Soviet authorities might not want me to say anything."[9]

Korengold also was successful in reaching Richard Snyder and gleaning from him some of the details of what had occurred inside the embassy on Saturday morning. The Sunday UPI story also contained this paragraph:

> The U.S. Embassy official [Snyder] said that he had advised Oswald to wait for the Soviet reply to his application for citizenship before giving up his American passport. He said Oswald would retain his full U.S. citizenship until he formally signed a document of renunciation and before he officially accepted Soviet citizenship.[10]

The UPI Sunday story also contained one other interesting item buried in between parentheses: "His [Oswald's] sister-in-law in Fort Worth said: 'He said he wanted to travel a lot and talked about going to Cuba.' "

Oswald had often talked about Cuba when he served in the marines at Atsugi. "I know that Cuba interested him more than most other situations," Oswald's marine commander from Atsugi Naval

Air Station later told the Warren Commission.[11] While at Atsugi, Oswald used to ''dream'' about joining Castro's forces with his fellow marine Nelson Delgado.[12] Four years later Oswald would try—and fail—to go to Cuba.

Washington: Monday, November 2

''A file concerning Oswald was opened,'' FBI Director J. Edgar Hoover wrote to the Warren Commission in 1964, ''at the time newspapers reported his defection to Russia in 1959, for the purpose of correlating information inasmuch as he was considered a possible security risk in the event he returned to this country.''[13] Hoover explained that the Bureau's ''first interest'' was a direct result of the October 31 UPI story, the story that E. B. Reddy had checked into that same day and prepared a memorandum about. Mosby's UPI news ticker was attached to Reddy's memo and waiting at FBI headquarters Monday morning, when the brass arrived for work.

At 10:07 A.M. on Monday, November 2, the second most powerful man in the FBI and close friend of Director Hoover's, Clyde Anderson Tolsen, looked over Reddy's Saturday November 1 memorandum and UPI attachment.[14] Not a skilled FBI investigator, Tolsen had been hired by Hoover in 1928 on the recommendation of then Secretary of War Dwight F. Davis, and within three years Hoover had promoted Tolsen from rookie agent to assistant director. There is little reason to conclude that Tolsen's immediate concern would have been much more than to make sure Hoover was aware of the Reddy memo and then pass it on. Tolsen initialed Reddy's memo and quickly sent it to the next most powerful man in the FBI—Cartha De Loach.

It is likely that Hoover and Tolsen had already seen the expanded UPI coverage that had appeared in the Sunday edition of the *Washington Post*.[15] That expanded coverage included the results of UPI Bureau Chief Korengold's calls to Oswald and Snyder: Oswald saying he feared the Soviets wanted him to remain silent, and Snyder saying he had advised Oswald to get his Soviet citizenship before renouncing his American citizenship. The UPI ticker attached to Reddy's memo was, of course, from the Saturday wires, and Reddy's memo added a few more odds and ends such as Oswald's birth date, his New Orleans roots, and his entrance into the marines.

Mosby's UPI ticker became the second item in Oswald's FBI file numbered 105-82555, and the Reddy memo became the third document.[16] The honor of being the first item in the Oswald FBI file was reserved for a document that was not about Oswald. It was the *Corpus Christi Times* article (mentioned in Chapter One) of October 13, 1959.[17] Whoever put it in Oswald's file may have sardonically thought that such an article, with its title "Goodbye," and its broadside attack against Americans who defected to the Soviet Union, was the most fitting capstone for Oswald's headquarters file anyway. The first part of Oswald's file number—the "105" serial—was used exclusively for files on "Foreign Counterintelligence Matters."[18]

At 10:36 A.M., the assistant director for Crime Records, Cartha "Deke" De Loach, began reading about the Halloween defection in Moscow. De Loach had far more experience working in the FBI bureaucracy than Tolsen, who was purely a creature of Hoover's. DeLoach, who would shortly become Lyndon Johnson's favorite man in the FBI, had previously worked in the group that handled liaison with the CIA and Office of Naval Intelligence (ONI). Such liaison duties were sensitive given Hoover's suspicion of other intelligence agencies.

The FBI man who handled liaison with the CIA in November 1959 was Sam Papich. At some point during the workday on that Monday, someone at the FBI notified Papich about the Bureau's interest in the Oswald defection. If the date-time stamps on the back of Reddy's memo are an indicator, DeLoach was probably the person in FBI headquarters who had the memo most of the day and who, therefore, either contacted Papich or gave the order to do so—perhaps to Alan Belmont.[19] Papich liked Belmont and disliked DeLoach, especially with respect to their views on CIA–FBI liaison on surveillance matters.[20] Extant CIA and FBI records indicate that Sam Papich telephoned just one CIA element that Monday, and it was not the Office of Security, the Records Integration Division, the Contacts Division, or the Soviet Russia Division. He phoned someone on the liaison staff of the CIA counterintelligence czar, James Jesus Angleton.

"Mr. Papich would like to know about this ex-marine who recently defected in the U.S.S.R.," wrote someone in Angleton's Counterintelligence Liaison (CI/LI) Office—probably Jane Roman, whose handwritten initials often appear on CIA cover sheets for documents concerning Lee Harvey Oswald.[21] As it happened, the CI/LI Office had no quick answer for Papich, and would not get back to him until midweek. Meanwhile, back at FBI headquarters, at 3:32 P.M., the Reddy memo wound up in the office of Alan Belmont. Belmont, like Tolsen and De Loach, was an assistant director to Hoover, and head of the Bureau's Intelligence Division. (Belmont will probably long be remembered for his 1953 internal memo in which he argued that existence of the Mafia in the U.S. was "doubtful."[22])

At some point on November 2, there was contact between the FBI and the Office of Naval Intelligence about the Oswald defection. J. M. Barron of ONI authored a memo on Oswald that same day and directed that it be transmitted "by hand" to Mr. Wells at the FBI.[23] Barron's memo begins by noting Saturday's Mosby UPI story and then stating that ONI files "contain no record" of Oswald. Two days later, a subordinate of Belmont's, W. A. Brannigan, wrote, "On 11/2/59, it was determined through Liaison with the Navy Department that the files of ONI contained no record of the subject [Oswald]."[24] On the other hand, Barron observed that Oswald's file at Marine Corps Headquarters did have information,[25] including the fact that his address upon entering the Marine Corps was 4936 Collinswood Street, Fort Worth, Texas. Handwriting, now faint, on Reddy's memo appears to say "4936 Collinswood St. Fort Worth, Texas,"[26] information not available at the FBI (at that time) except from the Barron ONI memo or from Marine headquarters by telephone.

Barron's ONI memo ended with the comment "No action contemplated by this office."[27] The Reddy memo on Monday, November 2 appeared headed toward the same dead end. Reddy's original memo was returned again to De Loach at 4:58 P.M., and then traveled yet again back to Belmont, at 6:31 P.M. At the bottom of this popular memo, Reddy entered this notation: "ACTION: None. For Information."

Someone, however, possibly Belmont, was not finished with Reddy's memo. The next morning, Reddy's memo was on its way again, this time to the FBI's Counterintelligence Branch. More specifically, it went to the Espionage Section in that Branch. Before proceeding to Counterintelligence, however, it is safe to say that Aline Mosby's little fragment of a story, along with Reddy's unspectacular and rather empty memo, had made the rounds of the entire upper echelon of the FBI. The more sinister and classified part of the Oswald story—that he had offered to give the Soviets radar secrets and "something of special interest"—was still inside the State Department, and would remain classified until after the Kennedy assassination. It was, however, about to wind its way through the most sensitive elements of the American intelligence community.

Washington: Tuesday, November 3

By Tuesday morning, November 3, counterintelligence officers in both the CIA and FBI were examining the Oswald defection. Their interest had been sparked almost entirely by the few words Aline Mosby had pried from Oswald's lips at the door to his hotel room in the Moscow Metropole. No one in the FBI or CIA yet knew the darker details of Oswald's Halloween performance in the American Embassy in Moscow. No one in the FBI, CIA, or Navy Department yet knew that Snyder's classified cable alerting Washington to this part of the Oswald story was still trapped somewhere on a State Department desk in Foggy Bottom. No one in official Washington outside the State Department was yet aware that the "confidential" aspect of Snyder's cable was a piece of news so startling that any newspaper would properly have led with it: Ex-marine Lee Harvey Oswald intended to turn over classified material to the Soviet Union.

At four minutes past noon on November 3, a teletype at the Navy Department in the Pentagon began to print out a troublesome message from Moscow. The words "Attention invited to AMEMB Moscow dispatches 234 DTD 2 November and 224 DTD 26 October" began the cable from the U.S. naval attaché in Moscow, Captain John Jarret Munsen. The dispatches Munsen referred to concerned the defections of Lee Harvey Oswald and Robert Edward Webster, another ex-navy man. Webster had defected in Moscow while working for an American company, the Rand Development Corporation, on July 11, 1959. Dispatch 234 on Oswald was in a diplomatic pouch in an aircraft somewhere between Moscow and Washington and would not arrive at the State Department until Thursday, November 5. Munsen's cable, therefore, was alerting the navy to ask for it as soon as it arrived. Munsen concluded: "OSWALD STATED HE WAS [A] RADAR OPERATOR IN MARCORPS AND HAS OFFERED TO FURNISH SOVIETS INFO HE POSSESSES ON US RADAR."[28]

At 3:37 P.M., the FBI Reddy memo was date-stamped into the Espionage Section of the FBI's Counterintelligence Branch.[29] By this time, it is virtually certain that Wells had delivered Barron's brief ONI memo on Oswald's headquarters Marine Corps file, and that it was now attached to the Reddy memo along with the Mosby UPI story. The Navy Liaison cable from Moscow was still in the Pentagon and would not arrive at the FBI until the next day, and there was still no word from the CIA's Counterintelligence Liaison on what, if anything, they knew about Oswald.

It was at this point, late on Wednesday afternoon, November 6, 1959, that the official paper trail in Washington on Lee Harvey Oswald took on a completely different character. At this moment the classified cables out of Moscow—Snyder's to the State Department and Munsen's to the Navy Department—began to wind their way into the espionage and counterintelligence worlds of the FBI and CIA.

At 6:40 P.M., FBI Assistant Director Belmont got his first look at what was to become the fourth item in the FBI file on Lee Harvey Oswald: the confidential Snyder cable from Moscow.[30] To be sure, this cable, like most cables, was brief. It mentioned Oswald's appearance at the embassy to defect, his arrogant and aggressive attitude, and his recent discharge from the Marine Corps. Then came the bottom line: It told of Oswald's stated intention to give military secrets to the Soviet Union. Snyder closed by asking the State Department for permission to delay allowing Oswald's formal renunciation until word was received on what action the Soviets were prepared to take.[31]

That evening, someone in the FBI who read the Snyder cable took his pen and made double hash marks in both margins next to the words "SAYS HAS OFFERED SOVIETS ANY INFORMATION HE HAS ACQUIRED AS ENLISTED RADAR OPERATOR." Someone, probably the same individual, then underlined those same words.[32] Meanwhile, across the Potomac River in the CIA, someone was reading a copy of the Snyder cable there too. The CIA reader focused on precisely the same words as the anonymous FBI reader. On the extant CIA copy of the Snyder cable are handwritten markings. These markings circle the words "LEE HARVEY OSWALD" and underline the words "SAYS HAS OFFERED SOVIETS ANY INFORMATION HE HAS ACQUIRED AS ENLISTED RADAR OPERATOR."

The State Department almost certainly sent Snyder's cable to the CIA at the same time they sent it to the FBI. Today, the exact date of the cable's entry to the CIA still cannot be confirmed, and is a matter that deserves close attention. The Agency itself cannot account for the details of its receipt and handling of Snyder's cable.[33] In 1964 the Warren Commission asked then–CIA Director Richard Helms to account for a number of crucial Oswald documents. Helms could not explain when the Agency had received several of the 1959–1960 files on Oswald. Incredible though it may seem in view of the amount of press coverage of Oswald's defection, the beginning of the Oswald file in the CIA is the story of a hidden file inside a black hole. It was a file so sensitive that almost no one in the Agency knew of its existence.

The "Black Hole" in Oswald's CIA Files

"The Commission would appreciate a letter or memorandum from the Central Intelligence Agency," wrote Warren Commission chief counsel J. Lee Rankin to CIA Director Helms in 1964, "acknowledging that it received the following communications from the Department of State." Rankin listed several communications, including Snyder's cable 1304 of October 31. Helms replied that the date of receipt "cannot be determined," but that this cable was in the CIA's possession four years later.[34] That the CIA had no idea when it received one of the most important documents pertaining to Lee Harvey Oswald seems incredible. Yet the fact is that after the Kennedy assassination, the CIA was unable to find out when and to whom these first State Department cables on Oswald were sent in the Agency.

At the time of Oswald's defection, however, someone in the CIA did have those Oswald documents. Since the 1992 passage of the JFK Records Act, a public law mandating the release of all assassination-related records, Oswald's CIA files at the time of his defection have been coming to light, as well as later Agency reviews of Oswald's records for official investigations of the JFK assassination. In two lists of files on Oswald that the CIA prepared in response to the HSCA in 1978 and released to the public in 1993, one gives no date of receipt for the Snyder cable at all, while the other acknowledges only that it was in the Agency's possession by February 20, 1964.[35] By 1978, then, the CIA could not even confirm Helms's inadequate 1964 answer that the Agency had possessed it by the time Kennedy was assassinated. In other words, instead of straightening out what was obviously an embarrassing problem for the CIA in 1964, the Agency has let the problem of its first paperwork on Oswald fester over time. Even the most casual observer would be justified in wondering whether the CIA is wholly incompetent in its paperwork or whether dark secrets remain about Oswald's CIA file.

On November 4, the Navy Department sent a copy of the November 3 Moscow Naval Attaché cable to both the FBI and the CIA.[36] Again, this cable, like Snyder's cable 1304, contained the disturbing news about Oswald's stated intent to give up radar secrets. And again, this confidential cable, like Snyder's, also disappeared into the CIA black hole on Oswald, and did not show up again until after the assassination. It is therefore not surprising that the CIA element originally contacted by the FBI's liaison, Sam Papich—the counterintelligence staff liaison element—replied two days later that they had no information on Oswald.[37]

The FBI had already heard from the ONI that it was contemplating no action when the negative trace—spy jargon for having no information—on Oswald from the CIA came in.[38] Perhaps this combination seemed justification enough to shut off the alarm bell in the Bureau that Mosby's story had set off the previous Saturday. On November 4, W. A. Brannigan wrote a memo to Belmont, noting the ONI decision not to act and also arguing, "Since subject's defection is known to Department of the Navy, and since subject apparently has no knowledge of any strategic information which would be of benefit to the Soviets, it does not appear that any action is warranted by the Bureau in this matter."[39] Brannigan recommended, however, that "a stop be placed against the [finger]prints to prevent subject's [Oswald's] entering the U.S. under any name." Brannigan advised that the FBI's Espionage Section stay on the lookout for Oswald's reentry to the U.S. Brannigan's recommendation was approved, possibly by Belmont, and on November 4 the FBI issued a "FLASH" against Oswald's fingerprints, asking that "Any information or inquiry received [please] notify Espionage Section, Div 5, Bu[reau]."[40]

Brannigan's analysis of the navy's position—that Oswald knew nothing important and therefore no action was necessary—was flawed. The fact that ONI had decided against action did not mean that such a decision had been made at the chief of Naval Operations level. Similarly, the CIA Counterintelligence Liaison section's claim that they knew nothing about Oswald did not necessarily mean that this was true for the CIA as a whole. In fact, the wording of Brannigan's memo seems to invite questions. His contention that Oswald "apparently has no knowledge of any strategic information" still leaves open the possibility he might have had other useful information. Moreover, the word "apparently" did not foreclose the possibility that Oswald might have indeed possessed strategic information of value to the Soviets.

It is obvious that the navy was very concerned about Oswald. We know this from the record of the same day that the FBI was deciding against taking any further action. At 11:59 A.M. Lieutenant D. E. Sigsworth of ONI drafted, and Captain F. A. Klaveness released—for the chief of Naval Operations, Admiral Arleigh Burke—a cable to Moscow asking to be kept abreast of new developments on Oswald.[41] The Sigsworth cable said "no record" of Oswald's clearance at Marine Corps headquarters had been found, but that Oswald had been an aviation electronics operator and "may have had access to confidential info." Actually, Oswald had access, at a minimum, to secret information while stationed at Atsugi as a consequence of his radar duties there. This much could have been ascertained by no more than a simple phone call to Oswald's former commander at Atsugi, John E. Donovan. "He [Oswald] must have had [a] secret clearance to work in the radar center," Donovan testified to the Warren Commission in 1964, "because that was a minimum requirement for all of us."[42]

The November 4 cable from the chief of Naval Operations to Moscow makes it abundantly clear that the navy, at a high level, far from putting the matter to bed, wanted to know more. The cable concluded: "REQUEST SIGNIFICANT DEVELOPMENTS IN VIEW OF CONTINUING INTEREST OF HQ, MARINE CORPS

AND U.S. INTELLIGENCE AGENCIES. 'INTELLIGENCE MATTER.' '' Besides being routed to Moscow and many other navy addresses, the cable was also sent to army and air force intelligence, and to the FBI and the CIA. At the same time there were some curious details missing from the initial navy report on Oswald, details to which we will shortly turn.

Setting aside the defects in the November 4 chief of Naval Operations cable, what happened to the CIA copy of it after it entered the Agency? Again, the answer is that Oswald's early CIA files were sensitive security and counterintelligence matters. We know from the CIA's Oswald document lists prepared for the HSCA that the navy cable arrived in the Special Investigation Group (SIG) of Angleton's counterintelligence staff on December 6.[43] The question is: In whose possession in the CIA had that cable been for the previous thirty-one days? The answer is that for those thirty-one days—November 4 through December 6—the CNO cable had crawled into the same dark corner of the Agency that the Snyder and Navy Liaison cables from Moscow had. This same fate befell the newspaper clippings as well. These clippings, three of them, along with a cable from Tokyo concerning Oswald's half brother, John Pic, and Snyder's first cable on Oswald, were buried in a Security Office file and did not circulate to the Soviet Russia division where, presumably, they should have been looked at by a wide array of the branches.[44]

The date that Moscow cable 1304, the new stories, and Tokyo cable 1448 entered the Security Office file is uncertain, for the documents lists released in 1993 contain nothing that would help us to pin down the precise dates. It is possible these documents were in the CI/SIG file first and then later moved to the security office. We will return to these arcane early CIA files on Oswald in Chapter Four, but here it is sufficient to point out that some hungry black hole in the CIA seemed to be consuming every scrap of paper on Oswald in the days immediately following his defection, a black hole that kept the Oswald files away from the spot we would expect them to go—the Soviet Russia division. At the end of the black hole stands the date December 6 and a place: the Counterintelligence Special Investigation Group—CI/SIG—where, according to the information released by the CIA in 1993, the CNO memo and two *Washington Star* newspaper articles were originally located.

Is it possible the documents described above, whether in the CI/SIG files or the Office of Security, were shown to the Soviet Russia Division until after the Kennedy assassination? It seems unlikely that a newspaper article that mentioned that the Russians were considering sending Oswald to a Soviet "institute" would not be shared with the appropriate analysts in the Soviet Russia Division unless the entire body of material on Oswald was considered too sensitive to share outside of OS and CI. It is conceivable that the Oswald black hole in the CIA *was* caused by a very sensitive Agency program, a program imperiled by Oswald's defection. Unless the CIA was wholly incompetent, it would have to have been in the throes of an investigation of Oswald's defection at this time. Moreover, that investigation, like the program Oswald's defection endangered, would have been known by only a handful of people in the CIA.

Finally, as mentioned above, the navy's apparent check into Oswald's past had some curious omissions. There is only one early document that qualifies as a sketch of what the navy knew about Oswald's past, and even this document is most noteworthy for what it leaves out—the sensitive part. We might do well to remember that this document was the November 4 CNO cable to Moscow.[45] It is reasonable to assume that if the navy had found something troubling, they might not have wanted to send it via cable to Moscow. If the navy had looked carefully into Oswald's past, what sensitive nuggets would they have seen?

The answer is shocking, and all the more so if navy intelligence missed it. Oswald and his marine companions had walked patrol to guard a supersecret espionage weapon hidden in an airplane hanger. As a radar operator, he had also tracked this dark object with advanced height-finding radar equipment. This particular espionage weapon was then the single most important intelligence asset available to the United States. It was the one that produced the most critical intelligence on the Soviet ballistic missile program at the height of the missile bluff (1957–1960) crisis with Khrushchev: the U-2.

Chapter Three

Top Secret Eider Chess

''It was a beautiful sight to watch,'' recalls Sam Berry, ''when the U-2s would land—their final approach to the runway would sometimes be at less than fifty miles an hour.'' Sam was a coworker of Lee Harvey Oswald's at Atsugi, and remembers how the sleek U-2s made their effortless landings and how, when the pilots would disembark, ''a crew would rush to throw a black sheet over their heads'' to conceal who they were.[1] ''We had sometimes bumped noses with them,'' Berry says of the U-2 pilots. ''We couldn't avoid it. And we'd talk to the guys from the U-2 squadron and they'd say it was just local recon, but we knew better.'' Indeed, everyone in Oswald's radar squadron knew better. They saw these incredible planes being fueled for hours, then departing early in the morning and not returning until late afternoon or evening.

''We were in a controlled squadron, and our barracks were right there adjacent to the airstrip at Atsugi,'' Donald Athey recalls of his stay at Atsugi Naval Air Station.[2] He was a lieutenant in Oswald's marine unit, Marine Air Corps Station-1 (MACS-1), of Marine Air Group-11 (MAG-11), 1st Marine Air Wing (MAW). Athey, too, remembers how the U-2s ''would take off and land right there, usually in the daytime. Our compound was adjacent to the airstrip, and the control center too.'' While the U-2 program had its own CIA control center, the marines that worked in the marine control center often watched these planes using their height-finding radar. ''We could track the U-2, sometimes up to 100,000 feet,'' recalls Berry, ''and then we lost them.''[3] Berry remembers hearing the U-2 pilots speak to the control tower. Athey recalled that on rare occasions the pilots ''would check in with us at 60,000 feet and then check out as they reached 80,000 and kept climbing.''[4]

The U-2 program was TOP SECRET and more, but it was no secret to the marines in Oswald's unit. They saw the planes, they tracked them, and they even communicated with them. That is, until Oswald defected to the Soviet Union, which was the target of the U-2s' espionage mission. The ballistic missile information these dark planes from Atsugi collected as they overflew the Communist giant was vital intelligence for U.S. estimates of the Soviet Union's ability to wage nuclear war.[5] What Oswald knew of the U-2 program before his defection is therefore a matter that deserves close attention.

Detachment C

The newly released JFK files contain a small set of documents on the U-2 program.[6] What the Agency has not blacked out are some of the details on the history of a U-2 operation called "Detachment C." The reason we have these documents is that someone from the House Select Committee on Assassinations (HSCA) asked questions about it. The CIA's deputy director for science and technology (DDS&T) answered them. Even what little we have in these new documents is revealing.

"Detachment C advance party of security and communication personnel," a 1978 CIA memo to the HSCA began, "departed the U.S. for Atsugi, Japan, on 20 February 1957, the second echelon of administrative personnel departed on 4 March, and the main body of the detachment with two U-2 aircraft and equipment began deployment on 15 March."[7] Detachment C was operational by the week of April 8, 1957, and "operating procedures and liaison" had been accomplished with the Atsugi Naval Air Station.

Detachment C was a CIA U-2 operation producing data vital to U.S. strategic intelligence, and Oswald, a trained radar operator, had a bird's-eye view of the operation from the runway to his radar bubble. The classification level of the U-2's intelligence information was very high. The CIA's (DS&T) answers to U-2 questions posed by the HSCA in 1978 were top secret with a further restrictive caveat. The top secret classification remains on all the pages of these documents, but the additional caveat for the intelligence associated with the program has been excised—almost.

In an apparent attempt to prevent the public from knowing the name of this intelligence "compartment" (intelligence jargon for a category of information, usually tied to a particular technical system), the CIA removed this part of the classification from the top and bottom of every page of the two separate but nearly identical documents which the Agency released in January 1994—except for one page. Just one slipped by. There, on the top and bottom of the page is the rest of the classification: "EIDER CHESS." How much did Oswald know about Detachment C? What did he know that could betray what the Americans had learned through EIDER CHESS intelligence channels?

". . . It's Moving over China!"

Atsugi was a "closed base," Special Agent Berlin noted in his March 10, 1964, Naval Investigative Service report, and "at the time, was the base for the Joint Technical Advisory Group, which maintained and flew recon[naissance] U-2 flights." Berlin had located and interviewed Eugene J. Hobbs, a marine hospital corpsman who had been stationed at Atsugi Naval Air Station while Oswald was there. During the interview, Corpsman Hobbs stated that it was "gossip around the base that the U-2s were taking recon flights over Russia." He also described a series of conversations he overheard about the U-2s flying over China, and stated that a naval commander had said "the flights would be the same as the ones the U-2s were making over Russia." Hobbs told Berlin that the U-2 missions over the Soviet Union were "common knowledge around the [Atsugi] base."[8]

From November 20, 1957, through March 6, 1958, Oswald's unit, MACS-1, joined other marine units for maneuvers—code-named OPERATION STRONGBACK—in the South China Sea and the Philippines. MACS-1 left for the Philippines aboard the *Terrell County*, LST 1157, on November 20, 1957.[9] The purpose of this operation was to prepare for American intervention in the Indonesian crisis in late 1957. This planned action in the Far East was paralleled by a crisis in the Middle East that featured a U.S.–backed force of 50,000 Turkish soldiers set to invade Iraq. Overlaying both situations was the larger context of the Soviet launch of a satellite—

Sputnik—in October 1957, on the top of an intercontinental ballistic missile (ICBM). This event publicly dramatized the ongoing race to deploy ICBMs tipped with nuclear warheads, and *Sputnik*'s success sparked U.S. fears that the Soviet Union was well ahead in this lethal new arms race.

MACS-1 landed and stayed a week on an island at the northern end of the Philippine archipelago, reboarded only to sail to Subic Bay, where they waited for another week, then returned to sea to join an invasion flotilla off Indonesia for a month. They returned to the Philippines, landing at Cubi Point just before January 1, 1958.[10] They set up their radar bubble at Cubi Point Air Base, next to a special hangar. Inside it, the CIA often stored a U-2 reconnaissance plane. ''I saw it take off, saw it on radar, and saw it land,'' recalls Oswald's commander, John Donovan, ''and I saw it hand-pushed into the hanger.''[11] On this assignment, Oswald's unit had an additional mission with a direct connection to the U-2: sentry duty to guard the U-2 hangar.[12]

That rather inglorious task which Oswald, like the other enlisted men, performed, did not curtail his interest in the U-2 when he was at his favorite place—drawing traces of aircraft trails with his grease pencil on the plotting board inside the radar bubble. Oswald's unit had not been operational very long before he noticed something interesting. Donovan describes what happened:

> One time we were watching the radar there at Cubi Point and Oswald said, ''Look at this thing.'' He had a trail in grease mark and he said, ''This thing just took off from Clark and it's moving over China!'' And I said, ''You can't be right,'' and he agreed. A week later he saw it again, so several of us began looking hard and we saw it. Oswald was right, and we saw it so regularly that we started clocking them. I even called the duty officer about them and he said, ''Look, fella, there's no planes flying over China.'' We knew better. We saw them all the time, mostly flying out of Cubi Point, but sometimes they flew out of Clark.[13]

This story confirms what Hospital Corpsman Hobbs told the ONI in 1964 about the gossip at Atsugi in 1958. The CIA was flying U-2s over China as well as over the Soviet Union.

Oswald's unit later deployed (September 14 through October 6,

1958) to Ping Tong on the north side of Taiwan, and Donovan was his commander there too. Donovan recalls: "In Formosa [Taiwan] we were near the U-2 as well."[14] There, Oswald spent many hours drawing traces of the U-2's tracks over the People's Republic of China.

The deployment of Oswald's unit occurred as a series of international crises escalated the U.S.–Soviet Cold War toward the brink of confrontation. The Chinese Communists, perhaps to embarrass Khrushchev,[15] provoked a crisis by shelling Nationalist islands in the Taiwan Straits, taking advantage of an already simmering crisis in the Middle East. Eisenhower intervened in Lebanon and brushed aside the Chinese provocation. Khrushchev upped the ante by threatening Berlin, demanding an end to Western control of that encircled German city. Eisenhower forced Khrushchev to back down. Throughout this sequence, Eisenhower's toughness was more than bravado. He knew something—as we will shortly discuss in more detail—that made these decisions easier: The Soviet ballistic missile testing program had ground to a halt. The president knew this, in part, because of intelligence collected by the very U-2s Oswald was watching. It is reasonable, therefore, to try to determine if the CIA ever investigated what Oswald knew about the U-2 program.

Claims of an Investigation at El Toro

One day in November 1959—shortly after Oswald's defection—a group of strangers are alleged to have visited Oswald's former unit at the El Toro Marine Base. One of Oswald's marine coworkers, Nelson Delgado, recalled the experience to Oswald biographer Edward J. Epstein. Delgado told Epstein he "remembers a group of civilians in dark suits arriving in November with stenographers and literally taking over their headquarters company to question marines about Oswald." Delgado explained that "one by one" Oswald's marine associates "were ushered into their captain's office."[16] According to Delgado, none of the marines were told who their interrogators were. That was and is most unusual. El Toro was a marine base, and it would have been natural for Naval Investigative Service (NIS) agents to come and ask questions, but such agents must—and always do—identify themselves when questioning military personnel in any official capacity.

Epstein recorded Delgado's vivid account of how the interrogation at El Toro proceeded:

> When his turn came, Delgado recalls, he was asked his name, rank and serial number. Then one of the civilians shot quick questions at him concerning his job in the radar bubble, his knowledge of Oswald's activities and especially his opinion of the sorts of classified information to which Oswald had had access. A number of other marines in the unit recalled being asked the same questions as a stenographer typed away at her machine.[17]

Researchers have been unable to identify the origin of this interrogation unit. Neither the FBI nor the Marine Corps has any record of this investigation, and both the OSI and the CIA have denied ever conducting it. The ONI and the NIS response to Epstein's Freedom of Information Act request was similarly uneventful: They told Epstein that "the report of the investigation was not in their files."

If Delgado's account of this investigation is true, who were these men in dark suits? It is not unreasonable to assume they were from the intelligence agency that had the most at risk with respect to U-2 operations when Oswald defected: the CIA. It would not have been abnormal for the Office of Security, which was the most likely element to be charged with protecting the overall security of the U-2 program, to have been conducting what, in military intelligence parlance, could be called a quiet "damage control" assessment. Oswald had worked at three locations in Asia, where one of the most sensitive CIA programs in the world was in progress, and he had then traveled directly to the very country against which this supersecret program was targeted. American intelligence methods and the lives of American U-2 pilots were potentially at stake.

Whether or not such an investigation—perhaps at a much higher level of classification than the confidential Navy and State Department cables on Oswald—was conducted, it *should* have been. The situation called for quick and accurate answers to the questions. Who was Oswald? What did he know? What damage could he do to the program? If such an investigation did not exist, it is reasonable to begin wondering why not. In this vein, one would be justified in asking if there had been some terrible lapse in U.S. counterintelligence or if Oswald's defection may have been planned by American intelligence.[18] We know little about the November 1959 El Toro interrogation Delgado claims to have been part of. If it did occur, it fell into the same black hole that the confidential Navy and State Department cables from Moscow fell into at the CIA. The possibility that those cables—which described Oswald's stated intent to disclose secrets to the Soviets—were somehow lost in the CIA is close to zero. The State and Navy cables eventually surfaced, but no documents on an Agency damage assessment of Oswald's defection have yet emerged. Nevertheless, Donovan argues that Delgado would not tell a lie about an investigation such as this. Donovan is more cautious in the way he recalls the event. He recalls that there might have been a "light investigation." Interviews, such as they were, were conducted at Santa Ana, California, he says today.[19]

The couple-of-civilians-snoop-around scenario led investigator-lawyer Mark Lane to argue that this investigation "was a cover investigation so it could be said there had been an investigation."[20] This is but one of many possibilities. Given the sensitive nature of the U-2 program, one might advance the counterargument that resources would more likely be used in covering up an embarrassing internal investigation than leaving a deliberate trail to advertise it. For our purposes, however, we may proceed by observing that given Oswald's extensive knowledge of U-2 operations in Japan, Taiwan, and the Philippines, the Soviets could be expected to be interested in him. Therefore, any American files on Oswald after his defection should have been carefully examined, stored, and controlled. As we shall see, they were.

Whether we look at Oswald as a "lone nut" or a "fall guy" in the assassination of John Kennedy, we know that he knew a lot about the CIA's U-2 program. Thus, it would have been odd for the CIA not to have pursued an investigation into the possible consequences of his defection to the Soviet Union. It would not have been unusual for a U-2 damage assessment to have been so highly classified that only a few people in the Agency knew about it. The program itself was restricted to those few people who had a legitimate "need to know," and these same restrictions would have applied to any security investigation of the program. The disclosure of information relating to the location of the U-2s, their personnel, logistical and security support, the frequency of their missions, and the countries against which they were targeted—all subjects upon which Oswald could offer the Soviets information—would reasonably be considered damaging to the national security.

Moreover, an assessment of the potentialities in the Oswald case would have been a security embarrassment to the CIA, whose U-2 program was facing stiffening competition from other technological innovations. The U-2 gave the Agency a major voice in the strategic debate at a seminal moment of the arms race. We still lack, however, hard evidence of any Oswald damage assessment—and this will likely remain the case. Even a ''light'' investigation into the potential damage if it fell into the KGB's hands would have been alarming enough to prompt a quick and quiet burial of the matter.

It seems prudent for the sake of analysis, however, that we should not proceed without at least examining what it was that the CIA would have discovered and likely concluded had it looked into the U-2 information in Oswald's past. These questions naturally arise: First, who would have been concerned about this in the CIA? And second, just how sensitive was Oswald's knowledge of the U-2 program?

Who Should Have Examined Oswald's U-2 Background?

Even though the U-2 operations at Atsugi, Cubi Point, and Taiwan were very ''closely held'' (intelligence jargon meaning very limited distribution), Oswald obviously knew a great deal about the program. Thus it is only natural to wonder if the CIA was, as it properly should have been, aghast at the dangers presented by Oswald's defection to the Soviet Union. It seems probable that the CIA counterintelligence vacuum cleaner—which sucked in many of Oswald's early documents—was also the resting place for any Security Office files generated by the defection, including any assessment of the damage to EIDER CHESS.

The CIA could reasonably expect the KGB to be interested in Oswald, and the counterintelligence staff would have been a natural collection point in the Agency for his files at that time. The counterintelligence implications of the Oswald case were there from the very beginning and, as we will discover, would grow more acute right until the murders of Kennedy and Oswald. Quite apart from the U-2 considerations of Oswald's defection in 1959, the CI staff and its controversial leader, James Jesus Angleton, should have had many concerns. For example, they should have wanted to know about the defection's implications for the KGB's capability against CIA operations in Japan and every other place Oswald had been stationed. If Angleton and his staff were to get involved in a secret damage investigation in the wake of any defection to the Soviet Union, the logical person for him to call upon would be the chief of his own mole-hunting section, the Counterintelligence Special Investigation Group. That person at the time was Birch D. O'Neal. Therefore we should ask the question: Is there any evidence of O'Neal's interest in Oswald during the initial "black hole" period in November 1959?

The answer is yes.[21] On Friday, November 6, 1959, Snyder's lengthier dispatch on Oswald's defection arrived at State Department headquarters in Washington.[22] This document was in the possession of the FBI no later than the following Thursday, November 12, and was at the CIA, where fifteen copies were sent, no later than Friday, November 13. We can confirm that it was physically located at the CIA by this date because of a parenthetical entry on the CIA's document lists on Oswald prepared for the HSCA.[23] The original CIA cover sheet is missing, which still prevents an authoritative determination on the precise office and person to whom it first went in the CIA.

We at least know, however, that this document was in fact in the CIA during the mysterious, or "black hole," period of November 3 through December 6. In fact, it falls nearly in the middle of this period. A kind soul to whom historians shall forever be indebted typed a bracketed note about this document on a CIA document list, which reads "[Received in CIA on 13 Nov 59]."[24] Moreover, upon close examination there is some handwriting in the upper right-hand corner of the copy in the National Archives. We can easily read it because it was written so neatly. It says "O'Neal," almost certainly the very man we are looking for—chief of CI/SIG. That writing appears to be identical to O'Neal's writing elsewhere in the collection, and is thus hard evidence that Angleton's mole-hunting chief was scrutinizing these earliest of materials on Oswald.

The disheveled nature of Oswald's early CIA files makes it impossible to understand as much as we might otherwise, but the foregoing is clear evidence of CI/SIG receipt of several Oswald documents on December 6, 1959. This information was not publicly available until 1993, and much additional research will be necessary just to ensure all related records have been located. We now know that somebody in the CIA was examining a key Oswald document on November 13, and so we should consider whether the content of that document could help illuminate the threat posed to the U-2 program by Oswald's defection. The contents of Snyder's November 2 dispatch confirmed what those in the Agency who knew of the U-2 program should have feared the most—that Oswald had threatened to talk about more than radar. As previously discussed, in this dispatch Snyder offered a more complete version of the threat Oswald made in the American Embassy on October 31:

> Oswald offered the information that he had been a radar operator in the Marine Corps and that he had voluntarily stated to unnamed Soviet officials that as a Soviet citizen he would make known to them such information concerning the Marine Corps and his specialty as he possessed. He intimated that he might *know something of special interest* [emphasis added].

Snyder's later theory that by "something of special interest" Oswald may have meant the U-2 program seems reasonable. The question is, how could the CIA possibly avoid drawing the same conclusion?

Among the concerns the Agency might have had about Oswald's intentions would certainly be the possibility of revelations about the U-2 in the media. Fortunately, from the Agency's perspective, this did not happen even after a U-2 was shot down in May 1960 in the Soviet Union. The American Embassy in Moscow had not notified the press of Oswald's threats at the time of his defection. Moreover, the only reporter who knew about it did not, for reasons we will examine in Chapter Five, use it. Oswald's threat to give up secrets to the Soviets remained classified until after the Kennedy assassination.

We may not find out any time soon—at least as far as hard documentary evidence is concerned—what the CIA concluded about Oswald's possible role in the May 1960 U-2 shootdown and about the related question of what else he might have compromised about

American U-2 operations. In one sense, however, we don't have to. Something that Captain Donovan said right after the Kennedy assassination goes straight to the heart of the matter. Donovan explained that he "did not know whether Oswald actually turned over secrets to the Russians. But for security's sake it had to be assumed that he did."[25] What Donovan said then is still the standard operating procedure for any intelligence organization today, and it was certainly true with respect to the U-2 program in 1959. Corpsman Hobbs pointed out to the ONI in 1964 that "one year after Oswald visited Russia, J. F. Powers [sic] was captured."[26] ONI Agent Berlin's report concluded: "Since it was common knowledge around the base that the U-2s were being utilized for recon flights, Hobbs now believes that Oswald could have given that information to Russia."

It is reasonable to assume that someone at the CIA might have concluded the same thing that Corpsman Hobbs did. From the newly released files come fresh hints that someone took a hard look at what damage Oswald might have done to the U-2 program after he defected. This new detail has emerged: By August 19, 1960—three and a half months after U-2 pilot Francis Gary Powers was shot down in the Soviet Union—all CIA personnel and every piece of their equipment at Atsugi had "cleared the base and turned the facilities back to the Navy."[27] The Oswald defection in October 1959 must be considered in the context of his knowledge of the U-2 program. That this is so can readily be seen from examining how sensitive the U-2 program and Oswald's knowledge really were.

Oswald and the U-2: How Sensitive?

The Soviet ballistic missile program began in spring 1957. Detachment C, the CIA U-2 spy mission at Atsugi Naval Air Station, Japan, was operational by the week of April 8, 1957. By March 1958, ten to fifteen Soviet ICBMs had been launched to distances of up to 3700 miles. Thus, Atsugi was an ideal location from which to launch espionage flights to collect the Far East end—presumably impact areas—of the evidence of these test launches. The first American intelligence report on a successful Soviet test launch of an ICBM landed on President Eisenhower's desk in late August 1957.

Lee Harvey Oswald arrived at the Atsugi Naval Air Station on September 12, 1957. Twenty-two days later, the Soviet Union launched the Soviet satellite *Sputnik* on the tip of an intercontinental ballistic missile.

The Soviets followed with more launches, and an American attempt failed. This series of events jolted America's sense of its own preeminence in science and technology, and a top secret report by the Gaither Committee recommended that the United States engage in an all-out effort to close the "missile gap." Khrushchev fed these American fears by hinting at an intercontinental capability and his willingness to use it. The missile gap, however, was not—nor would it ever be—concrete. The deployments were anticipated, and CIA intelligence estimates in 1958 and 1959 projected the early prospects for Soviet ICBMs in the hundreds. Senator Stuart Symington predicted that the Soviets would have 3000 ICBMs by 1959.

The only reassuring factor in the rising hysteria about the perceived imminent missile gap was the U-2 program. Given the size of the Soviet Union, an assessment of the missile program required a global strategy. Allen Dulles, writing in 1963, recalled how it was in 1957 to 1958: "When the Soviets started testing their missiles, they chose launching sites in their most remote and unapproachable wastelands."[28] The location of the U-2s at Atsugi was crucial in getting at these remote areas.

The U-2 was destined to lie at the heart of the U.S. intelligence debate over the nature and extent of the Soviet strategic threat. Difficulties developed in the Soviet test program, difficulties identified by the U-2 that led to an interruption of their missile testing program between April 1958 and March 1959.[29] This negative intelligence provided by U-2 coverage vitiated against the doomsday predictions of Soviet ICBM deployments, allowing President Eisenhower to privately discount the missile gap threat. Publicly, however, Eisenhower faced newspaper journalists like the Alsop brothers, who wrote articles under such titles as "After Ike, the Deluge" and "Our Gamble with Destiny." Khrushchev attempted to cover for the slippage in the Soviet test program with threatening nuclear signals during the Lebanese and Berlin crises of 1958.

To counter Khrushchev's bullying tactics, Secretary of State John Foster Dulles proposed to make the U-2 program public after the launch of *Sputnik*, but Eisenhower declined to publicize the most important means of verification he had. Eisenhower, not wanting to give the Russians—who had been vigorously protesting the U-2 violations of their airspace—any diplomatic leverage, refused to declassify the program. So the U-2 program continued under tight security, and its missions in 1958 and 1959 were increasingly influential in steering the intelligence community toward a more realistic assessment of the Soviet threat. Based on U-2 coverage, U.S. intelligence had concluded that the expected Soviet ICBM deployments would take place in late 1959 instead of early 1959.[30] By early 1960 a national intelligence estimate predicted that the Soviet Union would deploy thirty-five ICBMs by mid-1960, and 140 to 200 by 1961. In the end they deployed only four by 1961.[31]

The critical intelligence provided by the U-2 program influenced the U.S. strategic calculus in the major crisis of 1957 to 1959. U.S. behavior changed from constrained to emboldened—notwithstanding the highly publicized missile gap myth—as the truth about the Soviet missile program emerged at the top secret level. An American-backed Turkish invasion of Syria to topple the pro-Soviet leadership was preempted by *Sputnik* and its aftermath, and the American invasion force poised to invade Indonesia in December 1957 was never sent in. Then, at this important junction, the Soviet launch program hit the rocks. Publicly, Khrushchev continued to brandish his missiles during the ensuing Middle East crisis of May to August 1958. For his part, Eisenhower, in a speech to the U.N. charged Khrushchev with "ballistic blackmail,"[32] but gave the order to intervene in Lebanon with American ground forces.

The Soviet reaction to the American and British troop landings in Lebanon was muted, but the unfolding crisis soon widened to the Far East. With the Americans in Lebanon, Chinese leader Mao Zedong, in a struggle with Khrushchev and wanting to embarrass him, saw an opportunity. He provoked a crisis of his own by shelling Chinese Nationalist islands in the Taiwan Straits in August. With the geopolitical initiative slipping away, Khrushchev launched an aggressive strategy by triggering a major crisis over Berlin.[33] This crisis, in turn, created favorable conditions for a revolutionary success in Cuba. In the protracted Berlin crisis that ensued during the winter of 1958 to 1959, Khrushchev's renewed claims to strategic supremacy were the crucial linchpin in his attempt to deter the West while making demands.

The terms of Khrushchev's Berlin ultimatum included the demand that the city be internationalized and its ties severed with Bonn and the West. Distracted by the Berlin crisis, Washington did not effectively counter the unfolding situation in Cuba, a subject to which we will return in a later chapter because of its importance to Oswald. The Eisenhower administration's stand in the Berlin crisis, however, was resolute. This firmness surprised Khrushchev, who, in the end, backed down. The U-2 flights provided consistent evidence that Khrushchev's missile claims were a bluff, a crucial factor in Eisenhower's calculus in not letting the perceived missile gap soften his resistance to Khrushchev's pressures.

In short, the intelligence provided by this high-flying spy plane was the most important single source in the U.S. perception of the Soviet threat. This makes Lee Harvey Oswald's movements in the Far East all the more important, since they dovetail with the salient points of the U-2's contribution to the strategic debate in Washington. Oswald was at Atsugi from early September through late November 1957, a period that precisely overlays the launching of *Sputnik* and the early active phase of the Soviet ICBM test program. His participation in Operation Strongback maneuvers (November 1957 to March 1958) were part of the abortive U.S. invasion of Indonesia. During his short shore deployment at Cubi Point during the early weeks of 1958, he tracked U-2 overflights of China.

The "tracks" (routes) of these Chinese overflights, which Oswald personally plotted with his grease pencil, would have given the U.S. useful intelligence on Chinese military intentions, Sino-Soviet relations, and the unfolding politicomilitary struggle in the Chinese leadership. Similarly, Oswald's stationing in Taiwan paralleled the Taiwan Straits crisis in the fall of 1958, and Oswald's knowledge of U.S. military reactions would have been helpful to the KGB. In between the Cubi Point and Taiwan deployments Oswald was back at Atsugi. This period, from March to August 1958, was when the Soviet ballistic missile testing program ground to a halt, and the U-2 missions flown from Atsugi provided critical intelligence on this significant development in U.S.–Soviet strategic relations. After Taiwan, Oswald was back in Atsugi again, in October to November 1958, in the months leading up to Khrushchev's ultimatum over Berlin, when, again, flights from Atsugi could show only one thing: that Moscow had not resumed its testing program.

Unless the CIA never varied its flight activity, Oswald's general knowledge of the frequency of missions would have been useful to the KGB. The KGB would want to know what the Americans had learned of Soviet capabilities. Oswald also possessed knowledge of the U-2 flights over China—territory out of the range of Soviet radar—knowledge that would have been very valuable to the KGB.

There is circumstantial evidence that Oswald gave away something the Soviets used. The U-2 flew thirty penetration flights over Soviet territory between June 1956 and May 1960.[34] Twenty-eight flights occurred prior to Oswald's defection in October 1959. After his defection, the next U-2 flight, on April 9, 1960, was successful, but the one after that, on May 1, was shot down.[35] The pilot, Francis Gary Powers, survived, and his own analysis suggests that Oswald betrayed the height at which the U-2 flew. In Powers's view, Oswald's work with the new MPS 16 height-finding radar looms large. If the pilot reached this conclusion, the CIA should have, at the very least, considered it. Whether or not the CIA looked into the U-2 background of Lee Harvey Oswald, the Warren Commission should have as a routine part of their investigation. They did not, an omission that deserves closer attention.

A Warren Omission: Oswald and the U-2

The Kennedy assassination led newspaper reporters to ask where the accused assassin had been stationed. It was not hard to find out that Oswald had served with the marines in Japan, the Philippines, and Taiwan, and that his former commander, John E. Donovan, was living at 2009 Belmont Road, N.W., in Washington, D.C. It is not surprising, then, that within a week of the Kennedy assassination, reporters had located Donovan. The possibility that the alleged assassin of Kennedy might also have been a traitor or saboteur was a story newspapers could hardly resist. What is surprising is that when called to testify at the Warren Commission hearings, Oswald's marine colleages were not questioned about the U-2.

''Oswald was a very unpopular man that month [November 1959],'' Donovan told the *Washington Evening Star* in December 1963.[36] As the former commander of Oswald's radar unit, Donovan knew Oswald's ability to handle radar equipment and radar-related information. "Clearly, for dealing with aircraft going from 500 to 2,000 miles an hour, you don't fool with nitwits," Donovan said on December 3. "He [Oswald] was a good man on radar, there's no denying it."[37] According to Donovan, Oswald's defection "compromised all our secret radio frequencies, call signs, and authentication codes." Oswald "knew the location of every unit on the West Coast and the radar capability of every installation. We had to spend thousands of man-hours changing everything, all the tactical frequencies, and verify the destruction of the codes."[38]

On May 5, 1964, Donovan told the Warren Commission the same story about how the military codes, call signs, and authentication procedures had to be changed once "we received word that he [Oswald] had showed up in Moscow."[39] Donovan added,

> He had the access to the location of all the bases in the west coast area, all radio frequencies for all squadrons, all tactical call signs, and the relative strength of all squadrons, number and type of aircraft in a squadron, who was the commanding officer, the authentication code of entering and exiting the ADIZ, which stands for Air Force [Defense] Identification Zone. He knew the range of our radar. He knew the range of our radio. And he knew the range of the surrounding units' radio and radar. . . . There are some things he knew on which he received instruction that there is no way of changing, such as the MPS 16 height-finder radar gear. That had recently been integrated into the Marine Corps system. It had a height-finding range far in excess of our previous equipment, and it has certain limitations. He had been schooled on those limitations. . . . He had been schooled on a piece of machinery called the TPX-1, which is used to transfer radio—radar and radio signals over a great distance. Radar is very susceptible to homing missiles, and this piece of equipment is used to put your radar antenna several miles away, and relay the information back to your site which you hope is relatively safe. He had been schooled on this.

All of Oswald's knowledge would have been valuable to the KGB and the Soviet military. It is interesting that this level of detail was not routinely available at Marine Corps headquarters or at the ONI and thus had not been provided to the FBI in the immediate wake of Oswald's defection in 1959.

In view of the public knowledge of the 1960 U-2 shootdown and the fact that President Eisenhower had lied about the program, it is noteworthy that there is not one reference to the U-2 in Donovan's testimony to the Warren Commission. Asked about this now, Donovan recalls:

> I was briefed by the Warren Commission attorneys, and they were very hospitable, but they said, don't wander off the topic. These investigators know what you know and just need to fill in a couple of points. So I went in there and it was over so fast you wouldn't believe it. And when I came out there was one thing on my mind, and I said to one of them, "Don't you want to know anything about the U-2?" And he said, "We asked you exactly what we wanted to know from you and we asked you everything we wanted for now and that is all. And if there is anything else we want to ask you, we will." And I asked another friend of mine who had testified, "Did they ask you about the U-2?" And he said, "No, not a thing."[40]

At least one member of the Warren Commission knew all about the U-2 program, as he might also have known what steps, if any, the agency took after Oswald's defection. Allen Dulles had been CIA director at the time of Oswald's marine service, and he remained director until Kennedy fired him at the end of 1961.

Shortly after the Kennedy assassination, Donovan made a phone call to the CIA. An internal CIA "incident report" written on December 1, 1963—eight days after the Kennedy assassination and the day before Donovan's interviews with the newspapers—recorded this call.[41] This would suggest that before he talked to the media, Donovan told the CIA that he had known and worked with Oswald in 1959, and that he could provide "names and etc., of Oswald's intimate acquaintances during this period."[42] Furthermore, Donovan told the CIA he had not previously related this information to the FBI or the Secret Service.

Donovan recalls how he came to talk with the CIA and the FBI just after the assassination. "A guy who had been in our unit was [then] a CIA agent," Donovan explains, "and I spoke with him and he said, 'You should call the Agency,' which I did, and I called the FBI too."[43] On December 2 Jerome Vacek of the U.S. Marine

Corps telephoned the Office of Naval Intelligence (ONI) to pass along that John Donovan ''may be able to furnish information'' on Oswald.[44] An internal ONI memo of the following date noted, ''The Federal Bureau of Investigation and the United States Secret Service were made cognizant of the foregoing on 2 December 1963.''

''The thing that interested me,'' Donovan recalls, ''was that all of these agencies asked a lot of questions, but only the CIA was interested in the U-2.'' Asked specifically if the CIA had posed questions to him about the U-2 program, Donovan responded, ''You bet.'' Asked when the Agency posed these questions, he replied, ''The CIA asked me questions about the U-2 seven to ten days after the *Washington Star* article, but no one else was interested.''[45] It is not surprising that the CIA was asking questions about Oswald and the U-2 in 1963—no more surprising than was their decision to close down U-2 operations at Atsugi after Gary Powers was shot down. Powers did not fly out of Atsugi. The only link between Atsugi and the shootdown of Powers was Lee Harvey Oswald.

Whether or not the CIA investigated the damage that Oswald could have done to the U-2 program, the point is that the Agency could presume that the KGB would be interested in Oswald's U-2 knowledge. Clearly, Oswald thought he had something of ''special interest.'' According to information from the Soviets, Oswald said he was ''prepared to offer something of interest. He knew about airplanes; he mentioned something about devices.''[46]

Chapter Four

"I Am Amazed"

"Why the delay in opening Oswald's 201 file?" the House Select Committee on Assassinations (HSCA) asked the CIA in 1978.[1] This was a valid and penetrating question. According to the February 1960 Agency *Clandestine Services Handbook*, 201 files were then opened on persons "of active operational interest at any given point in time."[2] *Operational interest* is a broad phrase, and the *Handbook* spelled out three specific types it intended for 201 files: "subjects of extensive reporting and CI [counterintelligence] investigation, prospective agents and sources, and members of groups and organizations of continuing interest." In addition, the *Handbook* added a fourth category of individual:

> It has become apparent that the 201 machine listings should include the identities of persons of operational interest because of their connection with a target group or organization even though there may not be sufficient information or specific interest to warrant opening a file.

Oswald fit these criteria, but the fact is that Oswald's CIA 201 file was not opened for over a year after his defection. The delay was not noticed by the Warren Commission, which paid scant attention to Oswald's CIA files. The HSCA, however, tried to find out why this delay occurred.

In order to study the early portion of Oswald's CIA records, we must understand why Oswald would have a 201 file at all; this perspective is necessary to appreciate the implications of his not having one. Oswald's 201 file was not opened until December 8, 1960, but its shadow reaches back into the events of October to

December 1959 and presents us with one of the great quandaries of the Oswald case. The Agency's explicit reason for opening Oswald's 201 file in December 1960 was that he was a defector, a condition that had been clear from October 1959. Because no 201 file followed Oswald's defection, it seems reasonable to wonder how the Agency interpreted his defection. Abnormalities in Oswald's files like this one raise questions about his possible role in U.S. intelligence operations.

The Late Opening of Oswald's 201 File: Part I[3]

The HSCA investigators justifiably felt they had discovered something important when they learned that there was no proximate post-defection 201 file in the CIA on Lee Harvey Oswald. The HSCA began by searching for the person who finally opened the 201 at the end of 1960. HSCA investigator Dan Hardaway located and spoke with the enigmatic Ann Egerter, who had the fortune of having first Birch D. O'Neal, and second James Jesus Angleton, in her immediate chain of command. She was inside the most sensitive counterintelligence operation in the Agency: the mole-hunting CI/SIG. Hardaway's notes of that encounter are more memorable than most such HSCA contact reports:

> I contacted Ms. Egerter for an interview. Ms. Egerter said she had no knowledge of the assassination of John Kennedy and that she did not wish to submit to an interview. I told her we wished to talk about her knowledge of Lee Oswald. She said that she did not know anything about Oswald that was not in the papers, and really had nothing to tell us and would not talk to us. I informed Ms. Egerter that if she did not submit to an interview that I was afraid we would have to subpoena her.[4]

Ann Egerter handled Oswald's files for the last three years of his life. For most of that time, nothing could go in or out of his file and no one could see it without Ann Egerter's permission. Hardaway was therefore justified in threatening to subpoena her testimony. Though she is no longer alive today, Ann Egerter changed her mind and eventually testified before the HSCA. The verbatum record of her testimony is still classified.

Fortunately, the HSCA did paraphrase a few important items from her testimony and put them into their final report. We know that on June 27, 1978, the doors in a room in the Rayburn Building of the House of Representatives were closed to the public so that the HSCA could take the "classified deposition of a CIA employee."[5] The Agency's "201 files are opened when a person is considered to be of potential intelligence or counterintelligence significance," the anonymous "employee" testified, and the Oswald file was opened "because, as an American defector, he was considered to be of continuing intelligence interest."

We know that the "employee" doing the talking is Egerter because the Final Report read: "The Committee was able to determine the basis for opening Oswald's file on December 9, 1960, by interviewing and deposing the Agency employee who was directly responsible for initiating the opening action." Because of the CIA's 1992–1994 files release, we can be certain that person was Ann Egerter. All the House Select Committee could get out of Egerter was that she had opened the file after she saw Oswald's name on a list of defectors received from the State Department.[6] This reply, while perhaps technically correct, is only remotely helpful. It begs this troubling question: If the CIA was willing to open a 201 file on Oswald for this reason in December 1960, why not open it in October 1959, when he actually defected?

In the end, and after much testimony, the HSCA resorted to a statistical analysis and found that for the period 1958 to 1963, a 201 was opened on a person immediately after that person's defection only twenty-five percent of the time. In the other seventy-five percent of the cases, the HSCA noted, the 201 opening was "triggered by some event independent of the defection." Based on this superficial analysis, the committee concluded that such a delay in 201 openings on defectors "was not uncommon."[7] However, this analysis only confounded the issue, because it did not state if those seventy-five percent were cases like Oswald's, where the defection was known when it occurred. Put another way, in a quarter of all cases, defection led to a 201 opening, and might well have in the other cases were it not that other events came to light first. This statistical study did not consider whether the defectors without 201s were known defectors, and thus the study ignored the main question:

Would a defection—once known and verified by the Agency—lead to a 201 file opening?

The committee's reasoning also seems flawed because defection itself is a ''trigger'' event—all the more so when supplemented with cable traffic from American Embassies in Moscow and Tokyo, military and civilian intelligence cables and memoranda, and considerable national and international press reporting. All of this and a lot more were loaded into the same shell when the Oswald ''trigger'' was pulled in November 1959. Much, much more.

There was a far deeper omission in the HSCA's analysis of the late 201 opening. Defection is a legal act, but espionage is illegal. It defies reason that a known defector who had threatened—in front of a U.S. Embassy official—to commit espionage would be the object of a 201 opening a year later just because his name appeared on a list of defectors. This is simply too great a flaw in the landscape of Oswald's CIA files to dismiss. It prompts suspicion that his files were deliberately handled in some special way. Otherwise, one would have to say that CIA was derelict.

In the 201 opening form filled out by Egerter, Oswald's defection is mentioned but not his threat to give up military secrets. Actually, Oswald's CIA 831A [Field Personality (201) Request] looks pretty threatening without the espionage information, with comments such as ''Defected to USSR'' and ''Radar operator,'' and a check mark in the box for ''Restricted File.'' But the failure to mention his threat to talk about radar to the Soviets is extraordinary. Thus, unless there is more to the CIA's relationship with Oswald than we are being told, one can argue that the failure of the CIA's mole-hunting experts to open a 201 file in 1959—when they knew that Oswald had defected and offered to give up radar secrets along with ''something of special interest''—was a conspicuous breakdown of the Agency's security and counterintelligence functions.

So that there should be no question about the paramount importance of the timing and circumstances of Oswald's 201 file opening, it is worth revisiting what happened in 1978, when the HSCA deposed the director of Central Intelligence, Richard Helms, specifically on the question of the delay in the opening of Oswald's 201 file. The following exchange between HSCA questioner Michael Goldsmith and Mr. Helms took place:

MR. GOLDSMITH: . . . Why did it take more than one year to open a 201 file on Oswald? I might add, this is an issue which is somewhat controversial in the case.

MR. HELMS: I can't imagine why it would have taken an entire year. I am amazed. Defect to the USSR [in] October 1959. This [201 opening] is December 1960. There wasn't a 201 file already in existence, I am amazed. Are you sure there wasn't?

MR. GOLDSMITH: The opening of the file, according to the record, is 9 December 1960.

MR. HELMS: Yes, [approximately 1/2 a line still classified] but [2-4 words still classified] had they not opened a file a lot earlier?

MR. GOLDSMITH: According to the record that the committee has seen, the first opening of any file on Oswald was 9 December 1960.

MR. HELMS: I can't explain that.[8]

Indeed he could not explain it, because it makes no sense at all. We will return shortly to the clue in Helms's statement—the section still partially censored—because it fits with other evidence of pre-201 file activity at the CIA on Oswald.

There is more to the HSCA probe, which refused to let this important question die. The HSCA insisted that the CIA indicate "where documents pertaining to Oswald had been disseminated internally and stored prior to the opening of his 201 file."[9] The answer is disturbing. The CIA argued that "none of these documents were classified higher than confidential," and, further, that "because document dissemination records of a relatively low national security interest are retained for only a 5-year period, they were no longer in existence for the years 1959 to 63."[10] None of this was close to the truth. The HSCA threw its hands up and resigned with the statement that "in the absence of dissemination records, the [late 201] issue could not be resolved."[11]

It is unfortunate the CIA made such misleading statements to a congressional investigation. We have most of those records today, along with the internal dissemination documents the HSCA asked for—but did not get—back in 1978. What these documents show is eye-opening. The old argument that Oswald's pre-201 files were not important enough to keep turned out to be untrue in a particularly embarrassing way. The truth is that part of Oswald's pre-201 CIA files were classified SECRET EYES ONLY. This sort of mischief compromises not just the Agency's integrity on this issue, but also on the entire gamut of surrounding issues. Not surprisingly, there are more problems with the Agency's story about Oswald's pre-201 files, especially the claim that Confidential files had been destroyed. This, too, turns out to be wrong. The truth is that the CIA kept Oswald's Confidential files. We have them today. These files were stored in some sensitive and revealing places, places we will visit at the end of this chapter.

So why the bogus story about missing documents? Perhaps we should have a whole new subdiscipline for contemporary historians who try to wade through the deceitful maze of Cold War counterintelligence. In practice, this story functioned as a smoke screen preventing further disclosure of Oswald's CIA files—especially the early ones. The idea is this: We have nothing because we destroyed what we had. At the same time, this story reinforced the fictitious notion that the Agency's preassassination interest in Lee Harvey Oswald was superficial: We got rid of his files because we were not interested in him. Problems with this begin, however, the moment you think about it.

The story that a marine who defected and threatened to give military secrets to the enemy was judged to be of only ''relatively low national security interest'' is dubious. The fact that the HSCA was misled to adds a dramatic and tragic perspective to this cover-up, and impresses one with the lengths to which the CIA was prepared to go to protect the secrets that lay in Oswald's files. Spinning tales is not done for sport, but rather to protect secrets. Oswald's early files are astonishing to read. They establish beyond any doubt that the CIA had a keen interest in him from the very day of his defection.

CI/PROJECT/RE

CIA Director Helms's testimony contained this partial—because some words were redacted—question: ''Had they not opened a file a lot earlier?'' This question is worth exploring based upon the internal record now available to us. Let us revisit the paper trail inside the CIA in the immediate wake of Oswald's defection to the Soviet Union.

We must begin with what we have previously labeled the documentary "black hole" in the CIA's Oswald files, the period from November 4 to December 6, 1959. During this time, the arrival and movement of all incoming documents on Oswald—even news clippings—are seemingly impossible to trace. To this day, the Agency has not properly accounted for the internal distribution of these documents. We now know that these documents entered the CIA, and we have fragmentary but growing evidence of early files that were both substantial and intriguing. At the end of this chapter we will offer additional specific examples of these files. Now we will focus on one such file and pick up the trail where three documents told a troublesome story about Oswald, a story the public would not learn about until after JFK's death.

These three documents are the two Moscow cables, one from Snyder on October 31 and one from the Navy Liaison on November 2, which told of Oswald's intent to reveal radar secrets. The third is the November 2 dispatch from Snyder that included the additional detail about "something of special interest." How can we find out how the Agency reacted to these startling cables? Remarkably, answers are in the newly released JFK files. In spite of the obstacles presented by the CIA's record-keeping on Oswald, we can now reconstruct the path these crucial documents took inside the Agency. Moreover, what we find in these documents is not only the classified story of Oswald's threat to commit espionage, but also what the CIA decided to do about it.

Here is the sequence from the time of the defection. The CIA acknowledged it received the Snyder cable, probably on Wednesday, November 4, because that is when the State Department also sent it to the FBI. The CIA acknowledges it received the Navy Liaison cable, and it is likely this also happened on November 4, because we know from Navy records that is the date the Navy sent it. The CIA's records show it received the "something of special interest" dispatch and we know that it was received on Friday, November 13[12] probably by chief mole-hunter Birch O'Neal, whose signature is on the dispatch. These documents must therefore have formed a file with identifying numbers or letters, at least in CI/SIG. Evidence of these files is still accumulating, and we will return to them in a later section of this chapter, where we will examine some of Oswald's early Security and Counterintelligence records.

For the moment, we need to focus on what the CIA actually did after Oswald defected and threatened to commit espionage. What the documents show is hard evidence of keen CIA interest in Oswald during the November 4 to December 6 "black hole" period. A single document which has emerged is significant. The CIA did not share this document with the Warren Commission in 1964, possibly because its existence suggests that the Agency's projection of only trivial preassassination interest was misleading. This document shows that on Monday, November 9, 1959, someone in the CIA put Lee Harvey Oswald on the "Watch List:" meaning that as of that date the CIA authorized the illegal opening of his mail.[13]

"SECRET EYES ONLY," someone in a supersecret compartment of James Angleton's counterintelligence staff wrote on the notecard which put Oswald on the Watch List. In 1975, the CIA explained to the Senate the criteria for putting someone on this list:

> Individuals or organizations of particular intelligence interest [one should also add *counter*-intelligence] interest [sic] were specified in Watch Lists provided to the mail project by the Counterintelligence Staff, by other CIA components, and the FBI. The total number of names on the Watch List varied, from time to time, but on the average, the list included approximately 300 names including about 100 furnished by the FBI. The Watch List included the names of foreigners and of United States citizens.[14] [First brackets and underline in original]

Thus, this SECRET EYES ONLY document proves that in November 1959 Lee Harvey Oswald joined a select set of 300 people whose mail was opened by a highly sensitive, and very illegal, CIA program: HT/LINGUAL

What is more, this piece of evidence proves Oswald's status and makes the late 201 issue all the more controversial. The talk about needing a "trigger" for a 201 on Oswald is silly because of his presence on the Watch List. The absence of a 201 file was a deliberate act, not an oversight. Moreover, this particular configuration of being on the Watch List without a 201 is another anomaly that encourages speculation about whether Lee Harvey Oswald's defection could have been designed as part of a U.S. operation from the beginning, or if an operation was built around his defection after the fact.

While the Warren Commission never knew about the mail intercept program or Oswald's entry on the HI/Lingual list, the House Select Committee on Assassinations did find out. Naturally, the HSCA wanted to know who put Oswald on it. On August 15, 1978, the CIA responded to the HSCA's request.

The CIA had much to explain. To begin with, on the top right-hand corner of the notecard is typed "CI/PROJECT/RE." Under this is a date—November 9, 1959—which is also typed, and underneath the date is handwritten "7-305." Finally, underneath that number is handwritten "N/R-RI 20 Nov. 59." The CIA explained these notations in this way:

> The office within the CIA staff responsible for the exploitation of the material produced by mail intercept in New York was known as the "CI/Project," a cover title to hide the true nature of its functions. . . .
>
> "RE" represents the initials of a CIA employee now retired under cover. The presence of the initials indicates that on 9 November 1959, RE placed Oswald's name on the "Watch List" for the reason given on the card, to wit, "Recent defector to the USSR—Former Marine."
>
> The number 7-305 indicates the communication (not necessarily written) to the Office of Security informing the latter of the Staff's interest in seeing any mail either coming from or going to Lee Harvey Oswald in the Soviet Union.
>
> N/R-RI, 20 Nov. 59—this notation indicates that a name trace run in central files resulted in a no record on 20 November 1959.

This response, in the CIA's view, was sufficient to explain both the significance of "CI/PROJECT/RE" and the handwritten notations on the November 9, 1959, Watch List card.

A closer analysis of the two handwritten entries is fascinating. The "N/R-RI," upon further reflection, would appear to mean "No Record, Records Integration Division." This is suitably close to the Agency's explanation, and so there seems no need to focus on semantic differences between "central files" and "Records Integration Division." The number 7-305, however, is worth a closer pass. The Agency says it is only a reference to a communication between the counterintelligence staff and the Office of Security.

According to the Agency's 1978 explanation of how the HT-

LINGUAL program worked, the Office of Security played an important role:

> From the beginning until its end, the Agency's Office of Security controlled and operated the mechanics of procurement with members of the Post Office. The Counterintelligence Staff assumed the responsibility for the translation and analysis of the material both as consumer and for dissemination to selected officers in the Agency.[15]

Thus, it would make sense for the person working in CI/PROJECT who filled out the opening Lingual index card to enter some number or designator—such as 7-305—right on the card which referred to a communication with the Office of Security.

What is fascinating about the number 7-305 is what the Agency did not say about it. It would appear that this number has two parts. Moreover, it is possible that the number "7" refers to the communication, perhaps a request, written or verbal, while the number "305" is the date. It is not uncommon in intelligence work to refer to dates by their ordinal number on the Julian calendar. If this is true, the number "305" would be the same as saying November 1, which is the 305th day of the year 1959.

It seems more than a coincidence that a number possibly referring to the day after Oswald's defection appears on his first HT-LINGUAL index card. Oswald has one other HT-LINGUAL index card, dated August 7, 1961, which has three similar handwritten references to communications with the Office of Security. The first is illegible, but can be partially read as 9-2?0, while the other two are clearly 10-288 and 11-323. All these numbers could refer to days in 1961.[16] There are still difficulties with this analysis, and there may be another explanation for these numbers. For the time being we will note that someone in the CI/PROJECT office called or sent a note to the Office of Security very soon after Oswald's defection to the Soviet Union.

Oswald's Early CIA Files: OS-351-164, "CI/SI," and 74-500

The large new release of documents directed by the JFK Assassination Records Act allows us to fill in considerable detail about Oswald's early CIA files. One of the earliest files associated with Oswald is OS-351-164, the "OS" being an acronym for the Agency's Office of Security.[17] Cables and news clippings on Oswald that were put into the file beginning as far back as Oswald's defection in 1959 were in this file. The first document is Snyder's[18] cable from Moscow reporting Oswald's defection and his threat to give up radar secrets. The second is a *Washington Post* clipping entitled "Ex-Marine Asks Soviet Citizenship."[19]

Documents were also put into Oswald's counterintelligence file, now referred to variously in CIA documents as Oswald's "CI/SI" file or CI "soft file." What these letters tell us is that the CI/SIG mole-hunting unit, like the Security Office, had an early file on Oswald. Newspaper articles about Oswald's defection that first weekend were placed in both these files in an interesting way. The *Star* coverage (two articles) was put in his CI/SI file and the *Post* coverage (one article) was put in OS-351-164. Beyond who read which newspaper, that distinction tells us little. The prudent way to look at these documents registers is as incomplete records. We cannot even be sure that 351-164 was a security number exclusively for Oswald. It has yet to appear on a document under Oswald's name on the subject line. While it would be startling, it is not impossible that 351-164 belonged to another person. For our purposes, however, it appears to function as a security number for Oswald, as documents are periodically added to this file up to the time of the assassination.

Robert L. Bannerman was the Deputy Director of Security in 1959. In a recent interview he responded to this question: How did the Office of Security react to Oswald's defection? "Jim Angleton was in on this," Bannerman replied, and he emphasized how OS cooperated with Angleton's Counterintelligence Staff and others after the news of the defection arrived.[20] "We were calling in all the people in all the areas," Bannerman recalled, "who might have something." As to who in OS was privy to this effort, Bannerman stated, "We had a certain amount—most of my staff—Paul Gaynor, on my staff, was one who was very active in handling that end of the business, along with Bruce Solie.''

Bannerman recalls nothing else about Oswald's defection. It is fair to point out that the event was over thirty-five years ago and that, as the number-two person in the Office of Security, he may have been too senior to have been absorbed in the details of whatever the ''business'' was. At least Bannerman remembered who was in on it. We would be even more fortunate if Angleton's mole-hunting lieutenant, Birch O'Neal, would tell us what he remembers. O'Neal is possibly the person most knowledgeable about Oswald's CIA files alive today. Now in his eighties, O'Neal has so far refused to comment.

A key document is conspicuously absent from the OS-351-164 and CI/SI files as described in the 1978 lists provided to the HSCA. It is Snyder's dispatch #234. What a strange coincidence that the document with the most foreboding piece of information—Oswald's threat to give the Soviets ''something of special interest''—is one whose initial resting place in the CIA cannot be determined. This does not inspire confidence in the Agency's capability to monitor, let alone control itself. The 1978 CIA Oswald document lists have a column titled ''Location of Original,'' and for Snyder's #234 it says ''201-0748009,'' which is not an Oswald file at all. It is the 201 number for the American Consul in Moscow, Richard Snyder. Moreover, a close look at the copy in the National Archives suggests that it is possible that the original number might have been excised and Snyder's 201 number typed in over it at some later point.

Snyder's 201 number did not exist at the time the original document was created. Not even close to it. Snyder earned the honor of a CIA 201 file after the Kennedy assassination when Angleton's mole-hunting activities intensified. It is difficult to escape the conclusion that the original location designator was Oswald's. A bracketed comment under the entry for this document (Moscow dispatch 234) in a CIA document register states, ''Received in CIA on 13 Nov 59.''[21] The document was there all along, right from the beginning. The lack of the correct file number invites attention. This means the loss of the chain of possession and therefore our ability to determine responsibility. Nevertheless, it would make sense if it were either OS or CI—or both, because there is no doubt that the document describes Oswald's threat to commit espionage, and that this threat should have been taken seriously.

So far we have said nothing about the Soviet Russia (SR) Division. Oswald had defected to Russia. Was SR informed? If not, why not? Wouldn't SR have had a keen interest in the Oswald defection? We are still acquiring the information with which to begin answering these questions. Another early number associated with Oswald was ''74-500,'' a number that would be put on an FBI report in May 1960, which we will discuss in Chapter Ten. This number, however, meant ''Russia-miscellaneous,'' and was maintained by the Soviet Russia Division.

If Oswald was just a normal tourist or legitimate traveler to the Soviet Union, the SR/10 branch, known as the ''Legal Travelers'' branch, would have been interested in him. ''We would piggy-back on their perfectly legal reasons for going there,'' Paul Garbler explained, ''tourists, visiting professor, etc.''[22] Garbler was chief of SR/10 in 1959. ''We would brief them to be passively aware,'' he states. ''They were not supposed to take specific actions, but sometimes this rule was violated.'' Garbler has no recollection of Oswald, however, until much later. Garbler does not recall seeing Snyder's cable or the Navy Liaison cable from Moscow. This seems unusual.

Even more unusual is this: When a major FBI report on Oswald arrived in May 1960, it was routed to SR/10, but Garbler says it was not sent to him. Garbler's memory could be faulty, but if he is correct, then the first FBI report on Oswald passed through SR/10 without coming to the attention of the branch chief. ''I do not recall having heard about Oswald,'' Garbler maintains, ''until after I had been in the Soviet Union'' two years later.

The 74-500 number was not put on any other Oswald documents, although ''74'' would turn up on his 201 opening sheet because it is the CIA country code for Russia. A branch chief in the Soviet Russia Division who was watching Oswald worked in SR/6, the ''Soviet Realities'' branch. In that branch someone was keeping a ''soft file'' on Oswald, a subject to which we will return in Chapter Eleven.

Meanwhile, we still have some loose ends to cover in Moscow, where Oswald's defection was still in progress.

Chapter Five

The American Girls in Moscow

"She was quite a good-looking woman," Snyder remembers of Aline Mosby. "I saw her naked once."[1] That moment had been innocent on Snyder's part, for he had really had no choice in the matter. Under the circumstances, Mosby had probably been extremely happy to see Snyder. The attractive UPI reporter had made the mistake of getting involved with a young Soviet man who, Snyder believes, "was either KGB or had come under KGB control." The KGB was ever present in the lives of the American journalists in Moscow, always lurking in the background and constantly devising schemes to entrap and recruit them.

"Aline had met him downtown," Snyder recalls, "at the Aragvi Restaurant," a popular Georgian restaurant and hangout in Moscow. "He put a pill in her champagne, and the drink went to her head. She went outside to get air, and that is the last thing she remembers. She passed out right there on the curb." Snyder was in his office when the Soviet Foreign Ministry called on the telephone. They explained there was an American who had gotten into trouble, and that the Moscow police had taken her to a *vytrezvitel*, which is Russian for a "sobering-up station."

"I went down there," Snyder says, "and they took me up to the women's ward. Aline was lying on a cot, and a big Soviet woman was standing there who looked more imposing than a German soldier from a World War Two movie." The large woman glared at Snyder and yanked away the blanket that had been covering Aline. "She had been stripped naked," Snyder recalls, and was still woozy from being drugged. The Soviet woman jerked Aline off the cot like a rag doll and shoved her into Snyder's arms. "You hold her," the woman ordered Snyder, who put one hand under each arm to balance Aline.

So there the American consul was, holding the naked Mosby in his arms. It was an unusual role for a diplomat, but he had no choice but to help as the Soviet woman, piece by piece, dressed the drugged American reporter. Mosby could not be accused of leading a dull life in Moscow. While she enjoyed the diplomats, defectors, and tourists she moved among in Moscow, Aline Mosby was not a CIA informant and had never applied to work for the Agency. The same was not true for another woman, Priscilla Johnson, the only journalist besides Aline Mosby who succeeded in getting an interview with Lee Harvey Oswald.

The Case of the Two Priscillas

"Screwball," said a CIA employee who had known Priscilla Johnson at Harvard. "Goofy," and "mixed up," said an April 1958 CIA message characterizing Johnson at the time she had applied for CIA employment in 1952.[2] These unkind, condescending words were accompanied, however, by "excellent scholastic rating" and "thought [to be] liberal, international-minded, and anti-Communist."

Priscilla Johnson came from a wealthy Long Island family and had a master's degree from Radcliffe College. Perhaps the general political inquisitiveness of this intelligent girl rendered her insufficiently malleable for work with the CIA, but it was her associations with left wing organizations like the United World Federalists (UFW) which, in the end, became the red flag that made her unattractive to the CIA.

"Security disapproved," wrote Sheffield Edwards, CIA security officer in 1953, at the end of an investigative process that lasted more than six months.[3] By this time—April 13—the point was moot because Priscilla had withdrawn her application. In fact, in April 1953 she was working for Senator John Kennedy.

While membership in organizations like the UFW were an obstacle to Priscilla Johnson's application for CIA employment, the same was not true for someone else she met in the UFW. He was Cord Meyer, a man whom Johnson says eventually went on to become "the brains behind the CIA program to fund left wing publications."[4] The umbrella organization for these publications, according to Johnson, was the Congress for Cultural Freedom, and the CIA was the "covert" source for its funds. Its publications were "respected Cold War liberal" journals, she recalls, like *Encounter* and *Survey*, which I did some writing for."

CIA interest in Priscilla Johnson was reopened in 1956. On August 8, Chief, CI/Operational Approval and Support Division (CI/OA) submitted a new request to a Mr. Rice in the deputy director for security's office.[5] This was a standard CIA form asking for approval of operational use of Johnson, and it was accompanied by a CIA standard form 1050, Personal Record Questionnaire. The questionnaire listed Priscilla's previous work in 1955 and 1956 as a translator for the U.S. Embassy in Moscow, and also her "freelance" writing for several publications, including the *New York Times* and the North American Newspaper Alliance.

On August 23—and in spite of the 1953 security disapproval—a CIA Security Office and FBI records check was completed without adverse comment.[6] This information was passed in a Security Office memo from Robert Cunningham back to the requesting counterintelligence element, CI/OA. The Cunningham memo partially illuminates the original CI/OA request. For example, it said, "Pursuant to your request, no other action is being taken at this time." In other words, the chief of CI/OA had specifically requested that no further action, which presumably included further investigation, about Johnson be carried out. It also said this about Johnson: "who is of potential interest [approximately four to five words redacted]." The redacted words were probably a name or element in the CIA's Soviet Russia Division, most likely SR/10, the branch that handled "legal travelers" to the Soviet Union.

We may surmise that SR/10 was behind the request for operational approval because of a CIA document five months later. On January 25, 1957, SR/10 sent a standard form to Chief CI/OA asking for cancellation of the approval for Johnson's operation use.[7] In Form 937's box "Reason for Cancellation" was this typed note: "SR/10 has no further operational interest in subject [Johnson]. Please cancel."

To understand the significance of this form, we must return to the 1956 Cunningham memo of August 23. There is something terribly wrong about the contents of this CIA document. It said that Security Office files showed Priscilla's middle initial was "L for Livingston and is not R."[8] That the Security Office had uncovered this kind of error is perhaps understandable, but the next sentence was extraordinary: "She was apparently born 23 September 1922 in Stockholm, Sweden, rather than 19 July 1928 at Glen Cove, New York." The Cunningham memo made no attempt to explain this transformation. Instead, the memo rather matter-of-factly proceeded to explain the new history of Priscilla this way:

> She was utilized by OSO in 1943 and 1944. Clearance was based on Civil Service Commission rating of eligibility which in turn was based on a favorable investigation and record checks. An FBI record check completed 21 August 1956 was returned NIS [Naval Investigative Service].

The 1928 birth date carried in Priscilla Johnson's CIA records for the preceding four years could not be reconciled with this new data unless a fifteen-year-old girl, not yet out of high school, had been working for the Office of Special Operations during World War Two.

The Cunningham memo is all the more incredible because it makes no attempt whatsoever to reconcile the incongruity between these two seemingly different Priscilla Johnsons, one an OSO veteran at the time the other was a child. Moreover, this time there was no mention of adverse information about Priscilla's left wing activities. There appears to be too many egregious errors by the Office of Security, and therefore this story does not sound believable.

The bizarre story of the CIA's 1956 renewed scrutiny of Priscilla Johnson does not end with the Cunningham memo. If we back up one step for a closer look at the August 8 request for operational approval, we notice something weird about the CIA standard form 1050, Personal Record Questionnaire, which accompanied it. The questionnaire's contents purport to be about the Priscilla born in New York on July 19, 1928. Yet it is strange that Priscilla's memberships in professional and social organizations, her political affiliations, contacts, acquaintances, brothers, sisters, and relatives, were all listed as unknown. The form did manage to correctly name her parents, Stuart and Eunice Johnson. Priscilla's alleged signature, however, is now too faint to read, as are the date and the city and state where she supposedly signed it. Moreover, it was witnessed by someone who lived in Somerville, Massachusetts. Priscilla was in New York during August 1956.

Perhaps the Office of Security has an excuse for why it failed in 1956 to furnish CI/OA with the same "derogatory" information on Priscilla that it furnished in 1953. That excuse might be that the second, Swedish-born, Priscilla Johnson—whether she was a real person or a cover story—had a good security record. Historians now have the unenviable task of trying to figure out whether the CIA was inventing a false Priscilla Johnson or whether it was incapable of telling the difference between two people born five years and three thousand miles apart—not to mention possessing different middle names. The Central Intelligence Agency owes the American public an explanation for the case of the two Priscillas, if for no other reason than because a Priscilla Johnson—whom we know to be real—did in fact conduct the longest interview on record with the accused assassin of President Kennedy.

The most important question is this: What was the real Priscilla Johnson doing that led the CIA to reopen its interest in her in 1956? The answer might lie in an Agency interest about her 1955 to 1956 sojourn in the Soviet Union. It would not be unusual for the Agency to want to debrief someone who had recently returned from there. But why do two Priscillas then appear in the CIA's files? To proceed logically here, from Priscilla's return from Russia in April 1956 to the emergence in August of the CIA two-Priscillas problem requires more information than we have in the files. One new lead comes from a heretofore unconnected recollection of Priscilla's. It concerns a neighbor, who was a close friend and regular tennis partner of Stuart Johnson's, Priscilla's father. Sometime soon after her return from the Soviet Union, this friend asked Stuart if he might speak with Priscilla about her experiences in Moscow. The meeting took place, and Priscilla told the man what she could remember about her stay in Moscow. That man, who had known her since she was a small child, was F. Trubee Davidson. He worked for the CIA.[9]

Looking back on her experience now, Priscilla believes it is possible that Davidson "was waiting for me to grow up to recruit me." It is an intriguing thought, and one that she has had about one other person too. "The other person who was waiting for me to grow up," she recalls, "was Cord Meyer."[10] While we do not know the extent of Cord Meyer's knowledge or interest in Johnson up to the time that the CIA closed out its interest in her in January 1957, he does show up the next time they become interested.

More than a year after this close-out, the CIA again reopened its interest in Priscilla Johnson. On April 10, 1958, CIA headquarters sent a cable to a place that is still classified but which, from all indications, was one of its stations in Western Europe. It contained this detailed and condescending description of Johnson referred to earlier. It is worth repeating in full:

> Subj DOB July 1928. MA Radcliffe 1952. From wealthy Long Island Famil[y]. Excellent scholastic rating. Application [for] KUBARK [CIA] employment 1952 rejected because some associates and memberships would have required more investigation than thought worthwhile. Once [a] member of United World Federalists; thought liberal, international-minded, anti-communist. Translator, current Digest of Soviet Press, New York, 1954. Considered by present KUBARK employee [who] knew her [at] Harvard to have been "screwball" then; considered "goofy, mixed up" when applied KUBARK employment. No recent data. No Headquarters record [of] prior KUBARK use.[11]

The releasing official listed on the bottom left of this cable was then the CIA's chief of Investigations and Operational Support. His name was Cord Meyer, Jr.

Again the question is: Why the renewed CIA interest in Priscilla? The answer: Because she was planning to return to the Soviet Union. Cord Meyer's cable in April occurred after her visa application, during the period she was waiting for it to be approved. "I went to Cairo in February 1958," Priscilla remembers, "to see a boyfriend. Then in March of 1958 I went to Paris, and did a little translating in a building on Haussmann Boulevard."[12] There she worked for "someone I knew either for Radio Liberty or the Congress for Cultural Freedom." While in Paris she applied to the Soviet consulate to go to the U.S.S.R. It "took a couple of months" for the Soviets to approve it, and Priscilla arrived in Moscow for the third time on July 4, 1958.

On May 6, 1958—again, possibly on behalf of SR/10—Chief, CI/OA submitted a request for an operational approval on Johnson. The operation for which she was being considered is still classified, but we may presume that SR/10 wished to take advantage of her as a "legal traveler" to the Soviet Union in some sort of passive collection role. This time the Security Office furnished a "summary of derogatory information."[13] Whereas in 1956 the Office of Security failed to furnish CI/OA the 1953 "derogatory" information on Priscilla, there was no problem finding this information in 1958. The April 10 Cord Meyer cable, for example, made clear reference to her earlier security rejection.

The story after the Cord Meyer "screwball" cable is intriguing. There is evidence to suggest that the CIA, in June 1958, discovered the problem of the two Priscilla Johnsons. A June 6, 1958, internal CIA handwritten note "for the record" on SO 71589, which is definitely one of the real Priscilla's CIA numbers, reads:

> SO stated this date that which had been previously written was being revised and should be coming down today. In addition [name redacted] stated that [name or office redacted], who is handling the memo, doubted if subject would be utilized because of the record.[14]

This may indicate that the Stockholm Priscilla, whose Security Office and FBI records checks had been favorable, was being revised to reflect the real Glen Cove, New York, Priscilla. The author of this June 6 memo and office from which it came are still classified, but it is clear that the author, whoever it was, felt that a request to use Johnson in an operational role in the summer of 1958 had been or was about to be killed.

The ax came three weeks later, on June 27, as the result of a memorandum from an office whose identity is still classified. In fact, the June 27 memo itself is still entirely classified, and we know of its existence only because of a passing reference to it in another CIA memorandum almost six years later.[15] The possibility exists that while SR/10 had again initiated a request to use Johnson, it was a different office that killed the plan. This is at least suggested by the fact that SR/10 did not submit a Form 937 canceling their interest until August 28.[16]

Fourteen and a half months later, Priscilla Johnson was on her way back to Moscow again, as a reporter for the North American News Alliance (NANA). While she was in an airplane somewhere over the Atlantic, another reporter, Aline Mosby, managed to land the first formal interview with Lee Harvey Oswald.

''We Never Got Together for Dinner''

The day Oswald defected, many reporters tried to pry his story loose from him. However, it was not until the attractive Aline Mosby ''murmured some pleasantry'' to Oswald that he not only spoke more than two sentences to a reporter but also flattered her because she was ''a woman.''[17] UPI Bureau Chief Bob Korengold probably sent Mosby to Oswald's room with that very thought in mind. After Mosby's brief but successful encounter that Saturday, Korengold explained that ''I subsequently telephoned Mr. Oswald, who finally agreed to give an interview with Miss Mosby.''[18] (Mosby recalls that it was she who arranged over the telephone for the interview.[19]) *Newsweek* war correspondent Albert Newman interviewed Mosby in Paris in 1964, and fixed the date of her two-hour interview with Oswald as Friday, November 13, 1959.[20]

''I speculated whether he was flattering me,'' Mosby later wrote, ''because he was eager for publicity, or if he preferred to talk to women because he resented men and the authority they stood for.'' For her part, Mosby said she found Oswald ''attractive,'' and noted how he was ''neatly dressed in a suit, white shirt and tie, that had the air of his 'Sunday best.' '' Aline Mosby noticed a lot more about defectors than their politics. She classified them into different categories, tried to psychoanalyze them, and seemed to enjoy the personal interaction with them more than their stories.

Mosby triumphantly entered Oswald's room that Friday, the first reporter to succeed in doing so. ''I selected a red plus[h] chair by the window,'' Mosby later wrote, and ''he sat opposite me in another chair in the baroque room resplendent with gilt clocks and chandeliers.'' Mosby was soon disappointed, however. ''He talked almost nonstop,'' she complained. ''He sounded smug and self-important. And so often was that small smile, more like a smirk . . .''

Oswald's self-absorption was frustrating for Mosby. ''I felt we were not carrying out a conversation,'' she said, and remarked how she had difficulty getting ''a word in edgewise.'' Oswald droned on and on about his ideology and the Soviet Union, while Mosby ''tried to steer his conversation back to his mother and his early childhood.'' Oswald, only too happy to talk about himself, disclosed information freely about his past, until Mosby asked him what his mother thought about his decision to defect. Mosby recalls this anxious response:

> ''She doesn't know,'' he said. ''She's rather old. I couldn't expect her to understand. I guess it wasn't quite fair of me not to say anything, but it's better that way. I don't want to involve my family in this. I think it would be better if they would forget about me. My brother might lose his job because of this.''

Clearly, Oswald was sensitive about his family, and especially about his mother, Marguerite Oswald, whose address he only reluctantly gave to Snyder the day of the defection.

Other aspects of Oswald's behavior similar to what both Snyder and McVickar noticed during the defection scene in the embassy caught Mosby's attention. When Oswald spoke about his plans for the Soviet Union, it ''sounded to me as if he had rehearsed these sentences,'' Mosby said. As Oswald's monologue progressed, her attention drifted from listening to the words he was saying to analyzing the person behind them. Her 1964 retrospective essay of the interview contains this passage:

> As he spoke he held his mouth stiffly and nearly closed. His jaw was rigid. Behind his brown eyes I felt a certain coldness. He displayed neither the impassioned fever of a devout American Communist who at last had reached the land of his dreams, nor the wise-cracking informality and friendliness of the average American.

This description fit nicely with Snyder's dispatch, in which he said Oswald put on the ''airs of a new sophomore party-liner.[21]

There was one very big difference between what Oswald told Snyder and Mosby. When, in his discourse with Mosby, Oswald spoke about what he had done in the Marine Corps, he mentioned he had been a "radar operator" but said nothing of his intention to give radar data to the Soviets. Mosby did not find out this crucial detail until more than four years later. Her essay, written in Paris well after the assassination, makes clear the fact that she learned about this from what "American embassy officials" had said of the defection.[22]

One is struck by a peculiar irony of that Friday the thirteenth in November 1959. On one side of the planet Oswald spoke for hours with Mosby, and not once did he let slip the darkest detail of his defection. After the sun rose on the other side of the planet, Birch O'Neal, chief of the mole-hunting CI/SIG unit in the CIA, got an eyeful of that dark detail when he read Snyder's dispatch. That was the first official document that fully described Oswald's threat to turn over both radar secrets and something "special" to the Soviets.[23]

Unlike Snyder, who had engaged Oswald in verbal combat, Mosby wanted Oswald to like her. Her failure to bring Oswald out of his defector role frustrated her. When, after what had seemed an eternity of monologue, he once again launched into the "ebb and flow of communism," Mosby decided it was time to leave. "I was tired of listening," she wrote later, "to what sounded like recitations from *Pravda*."[24]

Oswald had been sitting with Mosby for more than two hours and, although he sometimes looked at her, had not once given her a signal that he might be interested in her. Mosby got up to leave. "As I put on my coat," she wrote, "I thought about how Oswald had appeared totally disinterested in anything but himself." When reading Mosby's essay, one detects the possibility that this might have hurt her feelings. "He never once asked what I was doing in Moscow," she complained.

Yet the resourceful Mosby had not given up. As she moved toward the door she was struck by the idea that she might still get to Oswald through his stomach. Mosby asked Oswald to come to her apartment for dinner. Oswald did not say yes or give her an opening to set a date. He simply said, "Thank you." Mosby interpreted this as a polite rebuff. "It was obvious," she said, "he had no intention of seeing me again."

One senses in Aline Mosby's essay a lingering disappointment—perhaps even bitterness—at having been rejected by Oswald. "I had known other men of Oswald's type," she wrote, "they worked as cowhands . . . married casually or not at all, got drunk and into fights, always seeking recognition and some way of expressing their frustrations." Oswald added insult to injury when, after reading Mosby's coverage of the interview, he called her up. "The defector immediately telephoned me," she wrote derisively, "not to suggest dinner, but to complain." Oswald was angry with Mosby because she had "stressed that he was affected by his mother's plight."

"We never got together for dinner," Mosby lamented. Indeed, for Mosby, that little detail, which she recorded almost as if it were a statistic, seemed to be the bottom line of the entire episode.

A Monday Meeting at Mail Call

It was Monday, November 16, and Priscilla Johnson, probably still feeling the effects of jet lag from arrival the day before from America, got up late. It was already dark by the time she made it to the mail room at the American Embassy. It was about four thirty P.M., but that was still half an hour before closing—plenty of time to get her mail. She walked through the lobby past Jean Hallett's desk to the corridor where the mail was kept. This path took Priscilla past the door to the consul's office, where Snyder and John McVickar were working. McVickar, whose desk was closer to the door, noticed Priscilla when she walked by.

Priscilla was busy looking through several days of mail. "Hello," John said with genuine enthusiasm, "I'm glad you're back."[25] The two were good friends, and John had undoubtedly missed her in the oppressive and hermetic environment of the Moscow Mission. At this particular moment, however, McVickar's attention was focused on a serious bit of business, and he wasted no time in getting straight to the point. "Oh, by the way," he added as if it were an afterthought, "there's a guy in your hotel who wants to defect, and he won't talk to any of us here. He might talk to you because you're a woman."

Priscilla thought McVickar was giving her a break. She had not done stories on the other big defector cases because she was with the North American News Agency, a shoestring operation consisting of her and her hotel room at the Metropole. ''I couldn't compete with the [other press] agencies,'' she later told the Warren Commission, but she was immediately interested in Oswald. ''John McVickar said he was refusing to talk to journalists. So I thought that it might be an exclusive, for one thing, and he was right in my hotel, for another.''[26]

By this time McVickar probably knew that Mosby had interviewed Oswald but, at the same time, felt constrained in passing the details of a rival reporter's interview to Priscilla. So he gave her a clue instead, dropping the name of Bob Korengold, the UP bureau chief. The following extract from her 1964 testimony to the Warren Commission clarifies this part of Priscilla's encounter with McVickar in the embassy that day;

MISS JOHNSON: I had been told he wasn't talking to people, and I hoped that he hadn't talked to anyone else.

MR. SLAWSON: Did you ever learn from Oswald that he had spoken to Miss Mosby earlier?

MISS JOHNSON: No; I never heard from anyone until November the 22nd, 1963, although Mr. McVickar had said I could ask Mr. Korengold about him [Oswald]. That was a tip that perhaps he had talked to somebody at UPI, but I didn't want to tip the UPI that I was on to it because I thought that would reinvigorate their efforts.[27]

''John may have been doing me a favor,'' Priscilla recalls. ''However, John also had in mind it was not in the U.S. interest for Oswald to defect.'' McVickar wanted Priscilla to handle Oswald in a special way, one that she might not have used if she were treating the situation as if she were purely a journalist. ''John wanted me to 'cool off' Oswald so he would not defect,'' Priscilla remembers of her coaching session in the hall that afternoon. ''He felt that Snyder had mishandled Oswald and that Oswald was heated up and angry. John's concern was that Dick need not have responded in such an ascerbic way to Oswald's ugly remarks.''

Snyder was the senior man in the consular office and Oswald was, after all, his case. McVickar, for reasons which we will have cause to examine further, was taking events into his own hands when he sent Priscilla on this mission of mercy to Oswald. McVickar was very insistent with Priscilla that day. In her 1978 testimony in executive session of the HSCA, "she recalled that as she was leaving, McVickar told her to remember that she was an American."[28]

We now know even more about this last remark. McVickar told Priscilla that "there was a thin line somewhere between her duty as a correspondent and as an American," and "mentioned Mr. Korengold as a man who seemed to have known this difference pretty well." There was also a thin line between taking actions approved by the responsible consular official and taking matters into one's own hands, and McVickar was stepping over this line. We will return to this "thin line" remark and how it applied to Korengold shortly. For the moment, we will leave this scene with a comment by Richard Snyder. "I have a recollection of being annoyed at John McVickar," Snyder recalls, "for having told Priscilla to interview Oswald without having asked if I had any objection to it."[29]

Room 319, the Metropole

"So I went back to the hotel, mail in hand, and I asked the lady at the end of the hall on the second floor if there was an Oswald there," Priscilla recalls. "Yes, he is in Room 233," the lady answered. "And I went to his room and knocked on his door, and there he was." It was about five-twenty P.M. Priscilla describes what happened next this way:

> So the door opens and Oswald came out, and he stood in the door, not letting me in his room but talking to me. I said, "My name is Priscilla Johnson and I work for the North American News Alliance. I am a reporter here and I live in your hotel, and I wonder if I could talk with you. He said "Yes," and I said, "Well, when can I come and see you?" He said, "Nine tonight. I'll come to your room."[30]

Oswald showed up on time. He talked with Priscilla until one or two in the morning.

In December 1963 Priscilla wrote her recollections of the interview. Oswald began, she recalled, by saying he had dissolved his American citizenship, "as much as they would let me at that time," and he then complained that "they refused to allow me to take the oath at that time."[31] Priscilla says she next put a question to him about "the official Soviet attitude," and he responded that the Russians had "confirmed" that he would not have to leave the country. Oswald then added, "They have said they are investigating the possibilities of my continuing my education at a Soviet institute." This 1963 description of the way the interview opened matches almost precisely her 1959 notes written during the interview with Oswald.[32]

Oswald explained that since the embassy had "released"[33] the story of his defection, he was granting this interview "to give my side of the story—I would like to give people in the United States something to think about." He continued. "Once having been assured by the Russians that I would not have to return to the United States, come what may, I assumed it would be safe for me to give my side of the story" [the underline was in Priscilla's contemporaneous notes and may have been Oswald's emphasis].[34] Again, Priscilla's 1963 account matched her 1959 notes, but what did Oswald mean by "safe"?

The answer is in Oswald's diary, and it concerns a visit he received over the weekend. His diary records that the day after his interview with Mosby,[35] "A Russian official comes to my room [and] asks how I am. [He] notifies me I can stay in the U.S.S.R. till some solution is found with what to do with me." This visit occurred on Saturday, November 14, twenty-four hours *after* his interview with Mosby and a little more than forty-eight hours *before* his "safe" remark to Johnson. This sequence is crucial, and it provokes a new question: What was it in Oswald's "side of the story" about his episode in the embassy that was not safe to tell Mosby on Friday?

Indeed, there was a detail that Oswald withheld from Mosby: his brazen declaration to tell the Russians about radar and something "special." It would have been reasonable for Oswald to think it was not "safe" to tell this to a reporter *before* receiving the assurance he could stay. There is no escaping the question that this leads to: Did Oswald feel it was "safe" for him to unburden himself about this with Priscilla *after* he received Soviet assurance? This overriding question strikes at the very heart of the entire story of Oswald's defection in Moscow.

Neither Priscilla Johnson's 1959 contemporaneous notes nor her 1963 written recollection mentions that Oswald told her he had threatened to reveal radar secrets. Her book *Marina and Lee* makes no mention of radar secrets. Her newspaper articles then and since make no mention of radar secrets. Under oath, however, she told a very different story. Here is the bombshell she dropped during her sworn testimony to the Warren Commission:

MR. SLAWSON: Miss Johnson, I wonder if you would search your memory with the help of your notes and make any comments you could on what contacts Lee Oswald had had with Soviet officials before you saw him, any remarks he made or things you could read between the lines, and so on.

MISS JOHNSON: I had the impression, *in fact he said*, he hoped his experience as a radar operator would make him more desirable to them [the Soviets]. That was the only thing that really showed any lack of integrity in a way about him, a negative thing. That is, he felt he had something he could give them, something that would hurt his country in a way, or could, and that was the one thing that was quite negative, that he was holding out some kind of bait.[36] [Emphasis added]

In a 1994 interview with the author, Priscilla McMillan found the contradiction between her Warren Commission testimony and other writings troubling.

How could Priscilla not have written about such a startling part of her interview with Oswald? "I know, that it is terrible," she remarked in 1994, "that is so unprofessional." Her recollection was at first indecisive, and she wondered if it had not been "wrong to tell the Warren Commission that." At length, however, she stuck with her testimony.[37] Not surprisingly, Priscilla's revelation about radar secrets startled her Warren Commission interrogator, W. David Slawson. This is what happened next:

MR. SLAWSON: Could you elaborate a little bit on that radar point. Had you been informed by the American Embassy at the time that he had told Richard Snyder that he had already volunteered to the Soviet officials that he had been a radar operator in the Marine Corps, and would give the Russian government any secrets he had possessed?

MISS JOHNSON: I had no idea that he had told Snyder that, *but he did tell me*—I got the impression, I am not sure that it is in the notes or not, *I certainly got the impression* that he was using his radar training as a come-on to them, hoped that that would make him of some value to them, and I—

MR. SLAWSON: This was something then that he must have volunteered to you, because you would not have known to ask about it?

MISS JOHNSON: Well, again I am not very military minded, and I couldn't have cared less, you know. But somehow along the line, if it is not in my notes then it is a memory, then it is one of the things I didn't write—well, one thing is you know I tend to write what I thought I might use in the story. But I wasn't going to write a particularly negative story about him. I wasn't going to write that he was using it as a come-on so I might not have transcribed it simply for that reason, that it wasn't a part of my story.

But it definitely was an impression that he—*and it was from him, certainly not from the embassy*, that he was using that as a come-on, and I sure didn't like that. But it didn't occur to me he might have military secrets. I just felt, well hell, he didn't have much as a radar operator that they need, although even there I didn't know. Maybe there was some little twist in our radar technique that he might know. It showed a lack of integrity in his personality, and that I remembered. What he might or might not have to offer them I didn't know[38] [emphasis added].

What emerges from this testimony is that Priscilla was predisposed against doing a critical story on Oswald, so much so that contrary to a reporter's instincts to get the most dramatic story, she deliberately ignored Oswald's stated intent to commit a disloyal act.

"I felt very sorry for him," Priscilla says now.[39] "We were both comparatively young and up against it alone." In a 1994 interview with the author, Priscilla elaborated on this feeling in the following words:

> Oswald was the only believer I met and I respected him for it. Also he and I were in the same boat: I was the least credentialed reporter in Moscow—lowest on the totem pole. So we were sort of alone together. I was interested in the Soviet Union, and he was there because he believed in it.

Again we have to believe that this "same boat" psychology would override good journalistic sense. This Priscilla herself admits, but insists she wanted to be Oswald's friend:

> There again I was not very professional; I wanted him to know that he had somebody there, because I thought he was going to get stuck out in the provinces and have a hard time. So I said to him . . . let me know before you leave Moscow." He said, "Yes I will." I said, "I will be writing my story tomorrow, and would be glad to show it to you for mistakes, and he said, "No. I trust you."

Perhaps it is helpful to think—as Priscilla might have then—what the impact might have been had she printed the story about radar secrets. It might well have angered Oswald and would have led to no more interviews.[40]

This exercise quickly becomes too speculative, for we must begin making assumptions about why Oswald told Johnson about radar secrets in the first place. There is, however, another dimension to Priscilla's interview with Oswald that needs to be further explored. That dimension concerns someone who was her friend and whose story was as mysterious then as it is now. That person was John McVickar.

CHAPTER SIX

The Thin Line of Duty

''I took a typed copy of the message from Pic,'' John McVickar wrote in a memo on November 9, 1959, ''down to the Metropole Hotel today to deliver to Oswald.''[1] John Edward Pic was a twenty-eight-year-old staff sergeant in the U.S. Air Force, stationed at Tachigawa Air Base, Japan. He was also the son of Marguerite Oswald from her first marriage to Edward J. Pic, Jr.,[2] and thus a half brother to Oswald. Sergeant Pic's message read, ''Please reconsider your intentions. Contact me if possible. Love. John.''[3] The message arrived early Monday morning in Moscow, and Snyder asked McVickar to ''contact Oswald''[4] and deliver it. ''I went directly to the room (233) and knocked several times,'' McVickar said in his memo afterward, ''but no one answered.'' McVickar checked with the hotel staff on the second floor, only to find conflicting stories about whether or not Oswald was in the room. ''On the way out I phoned from downstairs,'' McVickar said, ''but no answer.''

''He might talk to you because you're a woman,'' McVickar told Priscilla Johnson the following Monday.[5] ''I did ask John to go over,'' Richard Snyder later recalled regarding McVickar's November 9 trip to Oswald's hotel room, ''but I didn't ask him to talk to Priscilla.''[6] When McVickar approached Priscilla as she collected her mail on November 16, he was distinctly out of bounds. ''I definitely remember being upset with John,'' Snyder says. ''I was annoyed, particularly because it was at the beginning of the case when I was sort of feeling my way along.'' Oswald was Snyder's case, and Snyder was naturally upset that McVickar had decided—without permission or consultation—to take matters into his own hands.

McVickar's contemporaneous accounts of his actions are as troubling as the actions themselves. ''I also pointed out to Miss Johnson that there was a thin line somewhere between her duty as a correspondent and as an American,'' he wrote of his November 17 dinner conversation with Priscilla. But that was the day *after* her interview with Oswald, and the truth is that he had issued this ''reminder'' four hours *before* the interview. Today McVickar claims he does not remember what he meant by this ''thin line'' of duty. One can reasonably excuse a memory lapse thirty-five years after an event. But we may be justifiably skeptical of such a convenient loss of memory about the timing of this patriotic exhortation just twenty-four hours after it was given. Such an oddity in the written record—made at the time of the events themselves—invites one to compare Priscilla's account of the November 17 dinner with the McVickar memo which followed it.

Dinner at a shashlichnaya

''I wrote up the story of my interview the next day,'' Priscilla recalls, ''and I called Snyder because I wanted to get his version too, because Oswald was so critical of him. I probably talked to Snyder between 12:00 and 1:00 p.m. on Tuesday, the 17th.'' She finished the piece ''and then took it to the Central Telegraph at 2:00 or 3:00. The Soviet censor did not cut a word from my story. I took it there, to the Central Telegraph, on the afternoon of the 17th—it was on Gorky Street.''

''I probably went to a store on the ground floor of the Moscow Hotel and bought some cheese or milk and took it back to my room.'' Sometime that afternoon after she returned, John McVickar called, ''probably around 2:30 to 3,'' she thinks. ''It would surprise me if Snyder hadn't reported on my talk with him at lunchtime.

''McVickar invited me out. He had known my brother and sister in the past, in Cold Spring Harbor, New York. John remembered dancing with my sister, and my brother's manner on the dance floor.'' Sometime between 6 and 7 p.m. on November 17, Johnson and McVickar met for the second time in as many days. ''I had supper with John that evening, and we went to an ordinary restaurant. Not a fancy one. It was also in keeping with our pocketbooks. It was a *shashlichnaya*—lamb-on-a-skewer type restaurant—sort of cafeteria style. No waiter. It was very informal. It was a kind of eating that had just started in Moscow under Khrushchev.

If it had not been for Khrushchev, the two of them would not have been eating dinner together at the *shashlichnaya* that night. In fact, Priscilla would not have been allowed to return to the Soviet Union. She had been the victim of a familiar Soviet technique, which involved giving her visa extensions for only a thirty-to-ninety-day period, at the end of which the KGB would attempt to recruit her. But Cord Meyer's "mixed up" girl from Long Island refused to cave in, and her reward at the end of a year was expulsion by fiat—Soviet officials told her in the summer of 1959 that her visa would no longer be renewed. Her friends in the Moscow press corps complained to Mikoyan, the Soviet foreign minister, at American Ambassador Thompson's Fourth of July reception. They asked the minister to let Johnson stay to cover the upcoming Nixon visit.

"With a snap of the fingers," Mikoyan ordered it done, but when the Nixon visit was over and Priscilla left for America to cover Khrushchev's return visit, she went with the idea that she might not be coming back anytime soon. Ambassador Thompson accompanied Khrushchev on his American journey, and during the trip confronted Khrushchev about the harassment of Priscilla Johnson and another American journalist in Moscow, McGraw Hill. Khrushchev said he "didn't believe in that kind of thing and sent a message back to Moscow ordering it stopped." Priscilla later heard from Soviet journalists in Moscow: "We knew you'd be back." It took two months for her visa to be processed by the Soviet Consulate in Washington, D.C., but she returned on November 15, and forty-eight hours later was able to share lamb-on-a-skewer with McVickar at the *shashlichnaya*.

"We had a lot to catch up on," Priscilla says of her dinner engagement. Indeed they did. "He took me there because he figured it wasn't bugged," she remembers. There was so much to talk about, and none of it fit for KGB ears. "There was the embassy gossip, who was doing what to who," and "we bitched about Snyder, who was giving him a hard time, the usual." Then there was the incredible saga of the Khrushchev trip, how she had managed to get into his hotel room in Iowa and how surprised she was that she had gotten a Soviet reentry visa. And there was also the problem of Lee Harvey Oswald.

"We talked about Oswald's personality and how the Embassy had handled him. John and I, out of sympathy for Oswald, were talking about how Snyder goaded Oswald. To tell you the truth," Priscilla says of Snyder, "I did not like him at the time—he could be very snide. I like him very well now," she says today. As that evening with McVickar progressed, the two of them sat there in the little cafeteria-style restaurant, with its damp cement floor, no waiters to bother them, and relaxed with the comforting thought that they were alone and free to speak candidly.

"We felt that Snyder had mishandled Oswald," Priscilla recalls, "and this got Oswald heated up and angry. John's concern was that Dick need not have responded in such an ascerbic way to Oswald's ugly remarks." For his part, Snyder says he "was told at some point that John had criticized my handling of the case." Snyder recalls that McVickar's actions with Priscilla were "very unprofessional," and that this kind of information "should not have been given to the press." In a recent interview Snyder further elaborated:

> It you give out specific information of this kind it does help the [Soviet] decryptors if you give a clue to the content, the name, or especially something really specific, it helps a lot for the decoders. So that's one reason alone you're not going to give out any hard specifics; it's part of your security briefing before you go there.[7]

Security considerations aside, Snyder also thinks that the reason John told Priscilla about Oswald was largely because of their "relationship." That may be true. It was also true that, like it or not, Priscilla's relationship with Oswald had become a part of the official story.

That part of the story is an important document written by McVickar after the dinner with Johnson. This document deserves our close attention because it is one of the first major stumbling blocks in the Oswald files.

A "Memo for the Files"

It was after 9:30, when Priscilla Johnson returned to her room in the Metropole, now fully caught up on the Oswald affair and the rest of the embassy gossip. John McVickar, however, still had work to do. He went back to the embassy to find a typewriter. Unless he postdated what he typed that evening and used the word "today" when it was "yesterday" or before, John McVickar had to have worked late that night on November 17, for he could not have begun much before 10:30. Whatever the time, McVickar wrote "A Memo for the Files."[8]

There would, over the next four years, be memos for the files written by various CIA and FBI observers, many of them interesting because of the element of intrigue they add. The McVickar memo is no exception. "Priscilla Johnson of NANA asked me today," McVickar's opening sentence began, "about Oswald." This was misleading, because it gave the impression that the subject of Oswald came up because Johnson initiated it. Which of the two mentioned it first during dinner is less important than the fact that McVickar had, the day before, approached Johnson about Oswald. The dinner only provided an opportunity for McVickar to learn about the outcome of her interview.

The second sentence of McVickar's memo was equally misleading. It read:

> I gave her a general rundown of the outlines of the case, as I knew they were known to the public, suggesting that she also check with Korengold for any factual details I might have omitted and which were already generally known.[9]

If McVickar did make these comments at dinner, they were not helpful since Johnson's story was already filed. This sentence fits perfectly with the information—as recalled by Johnson—that McVickar had passed on to her the previous afternoon. That encounter in the embassy was on Monday, November 16.

The third sentence contained an error which is inexplicable under the circumstances. The sentence states: "She told me that on Sunday, November 15, she had spent several hours talking with Oswald and that she had left it with him that she was available if he wanted somebody to talk to again." This, of course, is impossible, since she arrived back in Moscow on Sunday, November 15, and learned about Oswald from McVickar only on the sixteenth. Because McVickar specified the day of the week as well as the numeric day of the month, a typographical mistake is out of the question. For whatever reason, McVickar placed Johnson's interview with Oswald *before* his meeting with her in the embassy.

The next two paragraphs contain the sort of information we would expect Johnson to have passed on to McVickar at their dinner. She told him of her impression of Oswald as naive, and how this impression agreed with "ours," presumably an impression from their discussion in the embassy before Priscilla's interview. McVickar's report after the dinner with Priscilla included these two sentences:

> He [Oswald] told her [Johnson] that his Soviet citizenship was still under consideration, but that the Soviets had already assured him that he could stay here as a resident alien if he so desired. They are also looking into the possibility of getting him into a school.[10]

This was all true, and tracks well with the notes Johnson made during her interview with Oswald. McVickar wrote that Oswald "had also told her that he did not intend to come back to the embassy, yet he seemed very much annoyed at the embassy for having prevented him from formally giving up his citizenship." This should have been good news, for it meant Oswald would not renounce his citizenship and, therefore, that Snyder's handling of Oswald might not have been so bad after all.

Then McVickar's memo again superimposes events and dialogue from Monday afternoon on to the Tuesday evening dinner conversation. The memo states this:

> I also pointed out to Miss Johnson that there was a thin line somewhere between her duty as a correspondent and as an American. I mentioned Mr. Korengold as a man who seemed to have known this difference pretty well. I asked that if someone could persuade Oswald at least to delay before taking the final plunge on his American citizenship, or for that matter Soviet citship [citizenship], they would be doing him a favor and doubtless the USA as well. She seemed to understand this point. I beleive [sic] that she is going to try and write a story on what prompts a man to do such a thing.[11]

We have discussed these lines previously, but they are reprinted here in full and we reexamine them because there is something very wrong about McVickar's memo: He presents his adjuration to Johnson as if he did it *after* her interview with Oswald. Of course, this was not true. At the time McVickar gave her this charge, she had never met Oswald; indeed, she was learning of Oswald for the first time from McVickar himself. Moreover, it makes no sense for McVickar to say such a thing to Johnson after the interview. It does make sense, however, if, as Johnson recalls, they spoke on Monday afternoon before the interview when the suggestion that Oswald might open up to her because she was a woman had some value.

The November 17 McVickar memo was not finished. Two days later, he added the following OFFICIAL USE ONLY postscript to the bottom of the second page:

> PS (11/19/59) Priscilla J. told me since: that O. has been told he will be leaving the hotel at the end of this week; that he will be trained in electronics; that she has asked him to keep in touch with her; that he has showed some slight signs of disillusionment with the USSR, but that his ''hate'' for the US remains strong although she cannot fathom the reason.[12]

The last three items of the five contained in this postscript—that she asked him to keep in touch, that he showed signs of disillusionment, and that she could not fathom his ''hate'' for the U.S.—were fully consistent with Johnson's notes and recollections. The first two, however, probably did not happen.

Oswald had not told her he was ''leaving the hotel at the end of the week,'' and there was no reason she would make up a story about this. As previously discussed, all Oswald had said in the interview was that he felt ''safe in the knowledge that I can have a prolonged stay.'' Johnson does recall, however, that a few days after the interview she asked the *dezhurnaya*, the lady on duty on Oswald's floor, ''and what about number 233, is he there?'' ''No, he's gone,'' the hall monitor replied. ''I thought she meant he had left for good,'' Johnson explains, ''but he hadn't.'' This is hardly a clean fit with McVickar's claim in the postscript that Oswald had been told anything, let alone when he would be leaving the hotel.

McVickar's memo leaves the reader with the impression that Johnson had met again with Oswald. She had not.

We need not parse the hotel departure issue further, as there is something far more enigmatic—and troubling—about the McVickar postscript. That is his claim that Johnson said Oswald "would be trained in electronics." Oswald did not say this to Johnson, and she has no recollection of saying this or anything like it to McVickar. Oswald had mentioned "studying" and "education," but not "training" or "electronics." Johnson's notes recorded his remarks that the Soviets were investigating the possibility of his studying in the U.S.S.R. and that "they have said they are investigating [the] possibilities of my continuing my education at [an] Institute." Johnson combined the two notes in her statement after the Kennedy assassination into this: "And he [Oswald] repeated 'they are investigating the possibility of my studying.' "[13]

What is absorbing is that Oswald did go to work in an electronics factory. How could McVickar have known about that beforehand? At the time of Johnson's interview, Oswald did not yet know he would be going to Minsk, let alone receive any specific "training" or do any work in "electronics." Oswald had not so much as mentioned the word "electronics" in his interview with Johnson. All he said was that he had been a radar operator in the Marines. For McVickar's postscript to be true, Johnson would have to have imagined this intriguing detail all on her own, and then told McVickar at dinner, and then forgot all about it in all of her subsequent testimony.

The references in McVickar's November 19 postscript to Oswald's departure date from the hotel and his upcoming assignment in an electronics capacity are crucial evidence that raise the possibility that information from Oswald or from a Soviet source had come into McVickar's possession. After studying the postscript again today, Snyder finds it "fascinating," and has this to say: "How did McVickar find it out? It wasn't known to me. Since he purported to get it from Priscilla, where did she get it from? And if she didn't tell him, where the hell did John get it from?" All are important questions.

It is interesting to observe how, during the Warren Commission investigation, it appeared that Snyder's career, not McVickar's, might suffer because of the entire episode. Johnson recalls that "behind the scenes'' the Warren Commission didn't want McVickar to be too critical of Snyder. ''The Warren Commission lawyers seemed to know,'' she adds, ''and they did not put me on the record to say something that might have been damaging to his career, they made it clear to me that they knew.'' By this she meant that McVickar's view that Snyder had mishandled the Oswald case would be damaging to Snyder.[14]

The same pattern occurred when Johnson testified to the HSCA, whose Final Report included this passage:

> She believed that McVickar called her on November 17, the day after the interview, and asked her to supper. That evening they discussed the interview. McVickar indicated a general concern about Oswald and believed that the attitude of another American consular official might have pushed Oswald further in the direction of defection.[15]

The reference is unmistakably to Richard Snyder, whose anonymity in this passage supports Johnson's recollection that the Warren Commission and HSCA agreed that McVickar's views might damage Snyder's career.

It is now apparent that more attention need be paid to McVickar's role in the story. In the previous chapter we discussed Johnson's testimony to the Warren Commission that she knew—and had not written about—Oswald's threat to give up radar secrets. When asked directly if she told this story to McVickar at their dinner, this was her spontaneous response:

> I can't remember. If he knew it and I knew it then I know we discussed it. My guess is that I was wrong to tell the Warren Commission that. With what I now know and thinking back on it, my guess would be that Oswald did not tell me and that I learned it from John McVickar.[16]

If true, that would explain how she could have learned of Oswald's threat without it appearing in her story. She had already filed her story by the time she had dinner with McVickar.

When and how Johnson found out about the radar story is important, but speculative. What is a fact is McVickar's knowledge—

before he should have known—that Oswald was to leave Moscow for electronics training. That he attributed it to information obtained from Johnson troubles her, as does the fact that he wrote this report at all: "If I thought he was going to write it up I would not have said anything to him about the interview. I would not have liked the idea that it was going out as a report from me."[17]

"I definitely remember being upset with John," Snyder says today. "I was annoyed, particularly because it was at the beginning of the case when I was sort of feeling my way along."[18] Snyder's inference here is that McVickar had no business interfering in Snyder's handling of the case. Indeed, by getting Johnson to do the interview, then inviting her to dinner to talk about it, and then writing it in a memo as if Oswald had continued to speak with Johnson, McVickar had muscled his way into the case. His actions affected the official record beyond his own "memo for the files."

On December 1, Snyder sent a cable to the State Department to update them on Oswald, who, Snyder said, was "believed departed from the Metropole Hotel within the last few days."[19] This may not have been true, but the source was McVickar's November 17 postscript. Snyder said an American "correspondent" had "maintained contact" with Oswald. This was not true either, and was also based on the McVickar postscript. "Correspondent states that Oswald appeared in last conversation last week" not to have changed his position, said the cable, leaving the impression that a second Johnson-Oswald discussion had been the source of this information. This was again not true. The source was the November 19 postscript.

Johnson was recently asked whether she had ever knowingly discussed Oswald with the CIA. "No, I did not," she responded.[20] The McVickar postscript raised the possibility that someone else had access to Oswald in Moscow. Could that someone have been working for U.S. intelligence? We will return to this question in Chapter Eleven. But before leaving Oswald's defection in Moscow, it is pertinent to recall that the CIA's Counterintelligence Staff and, in particular, the mole-hunting CI/SIG office, was interested in Oswald at this point. Therefore, we need to ask: What about the Counterintelligence Chief himself? What might James Angleton's interest in Oswald have been?

Angleton's Molehunt in the Soviet Russia Division

By the time of Oswald's defection to the Soviet Union, Angleton was obsessed by a traitor, a mole who might have penetrated deep enough to have acquired and betrayed secrets about the U-2 program to the Soviet Union. James Jesus Angleton was the chief of the Agency's Counterintelligence Staff, and he had created the Special Investigations Group, SIG, principally for finding double agents inside the CIA. The origin of Angleton's molehunt goes back to an event in 1958, but the hunt focused on and narrowed to the Soviet Russia Division in October 1959. Both events intersect with the Oswald story and so it is safe to say that Angleton noticed the confluence.

The first revelation of a possible KGB mole came from the Agency's top defector-in-place* in the Soviet Union, Petr Popov. Code-named ATTIC, Popov had been silently funneling high-quality intelligence to the CIA since 1952, including the Soviet Field Army Table of Organization, and Soviet battlefield tactics developed during nuclear tests with live troops.[21] This time, however, Popov's news was about an American espionage asset: the CIA's sensitive U-2 program. According to a study of FBI-CIA rivalry by Mark Riebling:

> In April 1958, Popov had reported hearing a drunken colonel boast that the KGB had many technical details on a new high-altitude spycraft America was routing over the Soviet Union. Details of this revolutionary plane had been tightly held within the U.S. government; the leak could only have come from somewhere within the project itself.[22]

As discussed in Chapter Three, Oswald had been posted at several U-2 sites and knew quite a bit about the program. The Soviet reaction to Oswald could help confirm or deny Popov's intelligence tip. For example, if the Soviets showed no interest whatsoever in Oswald, it would help to confirm Popov's tip that they already had a high-level source on the project.

Popov had been in Berlin when he passed the U-2 leak to the

---

*A defector-in-place is an agent who not only defects, but remains in and feigns loyalty to the target country, in this instance, the former Soviet Union.

CIA. He returned to Moscow for duty in November 1958. Then, on the very day that Oswald set foot in Moscow, October 16, 1959, Popov was arrested while riding on a bus and attempting to receive a note from his CIA contact, Russell Langelle. According to Angleton biographer Tom Mangold, this event accelerated Angleton's mole-hunt for an incorrect reason.

> Popov could only have been betrayed by a mole buried deep within Soviet Division. . . . "The betrayal of Popov was the key—*the key* to our belief that we had been penetrated." . . . Popov was actually lost to the Soviets because of a slipshod CIA operation; there was no treachery.[23]

Angleton thus erroneously believed that Popov—who was later executed—had been betrayed by a mole, an impression in which Golitsin, another Soviet who defected a year later, indulged the Counterintelligence Chief. Angleton's belief was reinforced in 1964, when another Soviet defector, Yuriy Nosenko, came over to the CIA.[24]

When he did defect, Golitsin told Angleton that back in May 1959 he and two thousand other Soviet intelligence officers attended a conference in Moscow, convened by the new KGB chief, Alexander Shelepin. Shelepin presented the KGB plan to "affect the fundamental reasoning power" of the U.S. government. According to Kim Philby—a British intelligence officer who became a mole for the KGB—biographer Anthony Brown:

> As evidence that such a grand plan was already in effect, that the monster plot had begun, Golitsin stated that the split between Russia and China was a fake, meant in part to cause the United States to miscalculate militarily and politically. In due course he revealed more: to effect Shelepin's grand scheme, the KGB had placed a mole inside the Soviet Division of the CIA—an assertion that touched upon Angleton's greatest nightmare, that there was a Philby in the CIA.[25]

Golitsin reportedly had documents to back up his claims, among which was one describing Department D, a new KGB organization for disinformation, which was to implement the Soviet grand strategy for winning without fighting.[26] The Sino-Soviet split, however, was no fake. By 1961, relations between the two nation's leaders, Mao Zedong and Nikita Khrushchev, had deteriorated beyond repair.

Yet a third series of events was in motion which suggested a mole in the CIA: a series of letters to the CIA written by another Soviet informant, Michal Goleniewski, beginning in 1959, under the name ''Sniper.'' According to another of Angleton's molehunters, Clare Petty, this is why some people in the CIA began to suspect there was a mole:

> This case was extremely closely held, as much as anything I can remember. Yet, within a matter of just a few weeks, the Soviets were aware that somebody had come to us with valuable information—and they knew the nature of it. This is an indicator, if you adopt my solution, as to where the penetration was. Eliminate everyone who didn't know about Goleniewski, and you end up with the fingers of one hand.[27]

Angleton was said to be suspicious of Goleniewski from the beginning, but he could not casually dismiss the argument that Goleniewski might have been manipulated by the KGB after being blown by the same alleged mole in the CIA he apparently warned against. Lewis Carroll would have appreciated this.

It was the Goleniewski episode that gave credence within the Agency to the idea of a mole, an idea Angleton would shortly turn into a crusade. David Martin's CIA chronicle, *Wilderness of Mirrors,* has this incisive comment:

> Goleniewski, with or without the knowledge of the KGB, had planted a germ within the body of the CIA that would become a debilitating disease, all but paralyzing the Agency's clandestine operations against the Soviet Union. The germ was the suspicion that the CIA itself had been penetrated by the KGB, that a Soviet mole had burrowed to the Agency's core. ''Goleniewski was the first and primary source on a mole,'' a CIA officer said.[28]

Could that germ from 1959, along with the U-2 compromise of the previous year, have led to a counterintelligence ''dangle'' of Oswald in the Soviet Union? We will return to this question in Chapter Eleven, when we examine Oswald's decision to return to America.

Chapter Seven

Early Cuban Connections

"Cuba interested him more than most other situations," said Oswald's former marine commander, John Donovan.[1] In his 1964 testimony before the Warren Commission, Donovan explained that Oswald "was fairly well informed about Batista." When speaking of Batista, Oswald talked about how he was opposed to atrocities in general and how he was opposed to Batista's sort of "dictatorship" in particular. Fulgencio Batista y Zaldivar had been president of Cuba until January 1, 1959, when Castro seized power. Oswald's expressed support for Castro and his comment that "it was a godsend that somebody had overthrown Batista," did not alarm Donovan at the time because such sympathetic views of Castro were common in *Time* magazine and at Harvard.

Oswald's apparent interest in Castro began while he was still in the armed forces and continued during the two and a half years he was in Russia. By this time, the United States had launched a covert war against Cuba and, in particular, against Castro. Shortly after Oswald left the marines, the CIA began to seriously consider how to assassinate Castro. By the time Oswald returned from Russia, the CIA had hired Mafia boss Sam Giancana to do the deed.

Oswald's Cuban capers in New Orleans and Mexico City in the summer of 1963 occurred during a particularly dangerous episode of the Cold War. The Lee Harvey Oswald who emerges in these newly released files was under FBI and CIA surveillance as he walked into a deadly web of deceit, woven from the anti-Castro Cuban underworld, organized crime interests, and the clandestine side of the CIA. It behooves us, therefore, to retrace the Cuban trails along which Oswald and the CIA traveled to their inevitable collision in the weeks before the Kennedy assassination. These trails take us back to the very time we have been considering: 1959 to 1960. What evidence is there of Oswald's interest in Cuba and Castro then, and what was the nature of the CIA's Cuban operations at that time?

The Warren Commission's 1964 investigation into the Kennedy assassination failed to consider the CIA's anti-Castro operations in any capacity at all. In the many controversies surrounding other shortcomings of the Warren Commission's work, this particular failure is often overlooked. There could be no more profound omission to any study of Oswald's activities in the months before the murder of Kennedy than that of the CIA's anti-Cuban operations.

The Warren Commission's aversion to examining espionage leads in Oswald's past was alluded to in a 1975 secret CIA report. Written by Angleton subordinate Ray Rocca, the report focused on the testimony of a marine associate of Oswald's, Nelson Delgado. Delgado had told the Warren Commission that Oswald had been in contact with Cuban diplomats while he was still in the Marine Corps and stationed at El Toro. The commission was not interested. The "implications do not appear to have been run down or developed by investigation," Rocca's report said. This was more than a veiled criticism of the Warren Commission; Rocca is pointing the finger of blame in the Kennedy assassination at Fidel Castro. "The beginning of Oswald's relationship with the Cubans," Rocca's report declared darkly, "starts with a question mark."

There were many Cuban question marks in 1959 and 1960 from Havana to Miami and the White House.

In Fort Worth and Minsk

Oswald's interest in Cuba was well documented in his early FBI and CIA files. Reporting on Oswald that contained information about statements by Oswald hinting at this interest reached the CIA as early as May 1960. When he visited his mother, Marguerite, on his way to the Soviet Union, Oswald reportedly said he wanted to go to Cuba. Six months later Marguerite told an FBI agent that Lee "had mentioned something about his desire to travel and said something about the fact that he might go to Cuba." The FBI man, Dallas special agent John Fain, put the details of this and more in a report. Fain also said, "Mrs. Oswald stated she would not have been surprised to learn that Lee had gone to say South America or Cuba, but that it never crossed her mind that he might go to Russia or that he might try to become a citizen there."[2]

The Oswald we see in the newspapers behaves the same way as the Oswald that develops in the CIA's files. Oswald's 1959 comments to his relatives about his interest in the Cuban revolution were well documented in the press at the time. Wire service coverage the day after Oswald's October 31, 1959, defection reported that "His [Oswald's] sister-in-law in Fort Worth said: 'He said he wanted to travel a lot and talked about going to Cuba.' "[3] Over two and a half years later, after Oswald returned to America, his 1959 comments again surfaced. "When he visited his family shortly after his release from the marines," a 1962 Fort Worth newspaper recalled of Oswald's 1959 visit with his family, "he talked optimistically about the future. Some of his plans had included going to college, writing a book, or joining Castro's Cuban army."[4]

Oswald's oral and written remarks refer to interest in Cuba and Cubans during his stay in Minsk. In his diary, Oswald wrote that Anita Ziger had a "Hungarian chap for a boyfriend named 'Alferd.' (Alfred)"[5] Oswald had met him, but Alfred might have been a Cuban. Anita did know a Hungarian chap, but his name was Frederick. After Oswald returned to America, Anita wrote a letter to him about how the relationship ended. "Concerning my love life," Anita said disappointedly, "nothing nice is happening. I was telling you about Alfred from Cuba. They sent him to Moscow to study." Anita recalled the "very nice" time she had spent vacationing with Alfred in Odessa, but lamented, "happiness cannot be extended for as long as one likes."[6] Anita also mentioned she had told Alfred about her friend named Frederick, but added that "it doesn't affect him."

Marina knew about Frederick and Alfred. She described the latter to the FBI as "a young man from Cuba who is apparently an admirer of Anita Ziger, who is a member of the Ziger family from Argentina who were friends of the Oswalds in Minsk." Alfred and Anita, Marina recalled, "both spoke Spanish."[7] On another occasion Marina provided the FBI with additional details about Alfred. Dallas FBI Special Agent Wallace B. Heitman wrote this afterward:

> Marina stated "Alfred," whose last name she did not know, is a Cuban citizen and a resident of Cuba who for some time has

> been studying in Russia. He studied at the University of Minsk for about six months and later studied at the University of Moscow, where he is believed to presently be studying. Marina said ''Alfred's'' parents have visited him in Russia both in Minsk and Moscow. She said although she did not personally know ''Alfred,'' Lee Harvey Oswald had known him as he had met ''Alfred'' at Minsk through Anita Ziger on one occasion when they visited at the University of Minsk to attend some social or scholastic affair. Marina also related ''Alfred'' had wanted to marry Anita but the latter had not wanted to marry him.

''Frederick,'' Marina told Special Agent Heitman, was a young man whom Oswald had met in the radio factory where they both worked. ''Frederick,'' Marina added, ''is a Hungarian.''[8]

When he was serving as a member of the Warren Commission, former CIA Director Allen Dulles felt it was noteworthy that Oswald and Marina had ''Cuban friends'' in Minsk. ''Marina told me about them,'' Dulles said. ''They played the guitar.''[9] In her testimony to the commission, Marina said that there were Cuban students studying in Minsk, and mentioned that one was a boyfriend of ''this Argentinean girl,'' meaning Anita Ziger. ''Do you know where the Cuban students were studying, what particular school?'' Dulles asked Marina. ''They study in various educational institutions in Minsk'' and elsewhere, Marina replied. Marina then added this comment:

> From what I could tell from what Lee said, many of these Cuban students were not satisfied with life in the Soviet Union, and this Argentinean girl told me the same thing. Many of them thought that, they were not satisfied with the conditions in the Soviet Union and thought if Castro were to be in power that the conditions in Cuba would become similar to those in the Soviet Union and they were not satisfied with this. They said it wasn't worthwhile carrying out a revolution just to have the kind of life that these people in the Soviet Union had.[10]

Representative Ford asked Marina how many Cubans were in school in Minsk. ''I heard the figure of 300,'' Marina replied, ''but I never knew even a single one.''

Whether Alfred was a Cuban or Soviet national, it is noteworthy that Allan Dulles, and probably the CIA, thought Alfred was a Cuban. In that view, Alfred might easily have been the son of a Cuban diplomat serving in the Soviet Union. On the other hand, after FBI reports and Warren Commission testimony had decided that Frederick, not Alfred, was the Hungarian, the Warren Report published a photo of Oswald and Alfred with the caption describing Alfred as ''a Hungarian friend'' of Anita Ziger's.[11] At a minimum, this is sloppiness. At the same time, such mistakes often serve as guideposts, especially where they concern Oswald's contacts with Cubans. Marina had said Oswald knew a ''Cuban family'' in the Soviet Union. Is it possible that Alfred, or Frederick may have been the son of Carlos Olivares or Faure Chomon? Both had been Cuban diplomats in the Soviet Union during the period when Oswald knew Alfred in Minsk. An anti-Castro Cuban academic, Dr. Herminio Portell-Vila, told the FBI that he had heard through the Cuban underground that these Cuban diplomats had a file on Oswald in Moscow which they turned over to the ''Castro brothers'' two days after the Kennedy assassination.[12]

From one of the most dramatic moments of Oswald's FBI and CIA files in the summer of 1963 comes information that refers to the time Oswald was in Minsk, and is suggestive of his continuing interest in Cuba and Castro. The 1963 event was an important propaganda event, a live radio debate featuring Oswald and Cubans, staged by a CIA-backed exile group, the Cuban Student Directorate (DRE). The part of the debate that concerns us now is a segment[13] in which Oswald comments on Cuban matters during his Russian sojourn, including his views in 1960:

STUCKEY: What particular event in your life made you decide that the Fair Play for Cuba Committee had the correct answers about Cuban–United States relations?

OSWALD: Well, of course, *I have only begun to notice Cuba since the Cuban revolution,* that is true of everyone, I think. I became acquainted with it about the same time as everybody else, in 1960. In the beginning of 1960. I always felt that the Cubans were being pushed into the Soviet bloc by American policy [emphasis added].

Oswald's marine associates and his family in Texas knew the truth about the origin of Oswald's ideas. He had noticed Cuba before his early days in Minsk in the beginning of 1960. His "notice" started when he was stationed in Japan and might have included contact with Cuban officials at his following assignment at El Toro, California. When he applied for travel to the Soviet Union in the summer of 1959, Oswald listed several countries he wanted to travel to, including the Soviet Union. The country he listed first was Cuba.[14]

When he defected to the Soviet Union in October 1959, and again, when he returned to the United States in June 1962, his pre-defection interest in going to Cuba was discussed in newspaper articles. The November 1, 1959, *Washington Post* article entitled "Ex-Marine Asks Soviet Citizenship" was placed in Oswald's CIA security file, OS-351-164.[15] Early 1960 was when FBI special agent Fain's interview of Marguerite took place, during which she told of Oswald's early (pre-defection) interest in going to Cuba. On May 25, 1960, the FBI transmitted Fain's report of that interview over to the CIA. Oswald's murder foreclosed any chance of knowing for sure why he would have neglected to mention in the debate his interest in Cuba during his last year in the marines.

Also significant is the fact that early 1960 was the time when the Fair Play for Cuba Committee (FPCC) was created—a pro-Castro organization destined to be destroyed by its association with Oswald. The April 6, 1960, *New York Times* carried a full-page ad announcing the formation of the FPCC, an ad paid for by Castro.[16] Until its demise on December 31, 1963, the FPCC was a pawn in a power struggle between the Communist Party USA and the Socialist Workers Party, both of which were considered by the FBI as subversive.[17] With headquarters at 1799 Broadway in New York City, by November 20, 1960, the FPCC claimed 5,000 members.[18] The CIA's Security Office then launched—under the orders of James McCord—a counterintelligence operation in the United States against the FPCC without the FBI's permission. That is a subject to which we will return later.

Oswald's Cuban Question Mark

"We had quite many [sic] discussions regarding Castro," said a marine who had befriended Oswald at Atsugi, Japan, and returned with him to El Toro, California. In his 1964 testimony to the Warren Commission, Nelson Delgado explained that it was their views on

Cuba that had solidified their friendship in the first place. Delgado explained,

> At the time I was in favor of Castro, I wholeheartedly supported him, and made it known that I thought he was a pretty good fellow, and that was one of the main things [reasons why] Oswald and I hit it off so well, we were along the same lines of thought. Castro at the time showed all possibilities of being a freedom-loving man, a democratic sort of person that was going to do away with all tyranny and finally give the Cuban people a break.[19]

Delgado was referring to the period just after Castro had seized power in Cuba, a time when Castro's plans for a communist Cuba were not widely known or understood. Even so, the idea of two marine privates discussing the Cuban revolution in these terms is, at the very least, unusual. Angleton's deputy, Ray Rocca, felt that Delgado's assertions were "of germinal significance to any review of the background of Lee Harvey Oswald's feeling toward and relations with Castro's Cuba." Delgado, in Rocca's view, "was probably the closest peer group member to Oswald during his specialist training period at El Toro Marine Corps Base December 1958 to September 1959."[20]

The Warren Commission Report noted that "Oswald told Delgado that he was in touch with Cuban diplomatic officials in this country, which Delgado at first took to be 'one of his lies, but later believed.' "[21] The question is this: Did the commission believe Delgado? The report leaves us without an answer to this essential question. Something Delgado said during his testimony about Oswald's plans gave Warren Commission lawyer Wesley Liebeler quite a surprise. This is what happened:

MR. DELGADO: . . . And we talked [about] how we would like to go to Cuba and—

MR. LIEBELER: You and Oswald did?

MR. DELGADO: Right. We were going to beome officers, you know, enlisted men. We are dreaming now, right? So we were going to become officers. So we had a head start, you see. We were getting honorable discharges. . . . So we were all thinking, well, honorable discharge, and I speak Spanish and he's [Oswald] got his ideas of how a government should be run, you know, the same line as Castro did at that time.

MR. LIEBELER: Oswald?

MR. DELGADO: Right. So we could go over there and become officers and lead an expedition to some of these other islands and free them too, you know, from—this was really weird, you know, but—

MR. LIEBELER: That is what you and Oswald talked about?

MR. DELGADO: Right, things like that; and how we would go to take over, to make a republic. . . . And we would talk about how we would do away with Trujillo, and things like that, but never got no farther than the speaking stage.[22]

Generalissimo Rafael B. Trujillo was commander-in-chief of the Dominican Republic Armed Forces, and dictator of that tiny Caribbean country for more than thirty years when he was finally assassinated in May 1961. Latin American nations were pressing the U.S. to take action against Trujillo, whose harsh dictatorial methods were unpopular but whose obedience to Washington had long since assured his survival. At the time Oswald and Delgado discussed Trujillo, Washington could count on the unpopular dictator not to follow Castro's lead.[23]

There came a time, however, when things began to progress beyond the "speaking stage," things that put distance between Delgado and Oswald. Delgado recounted that part of the story for the Warren Commission in these words:

> But then when he started, you know, going along with this, he started actually making plans, he wanted to know, you know, how to get to Cuba and things like that. I was shying away from him. He kept asking me questions like "how can a person in his category, an English [speaking] person, get with a Cuban, you know, people, be part of that revolution movement?"[24]

Oswald's dream of joining Castro's forces with his fellow marine Nelson Delgado was never realized. However, another ex-marine, Gerry Patrick Hemming, did manage to get into Castro's army, a story we will shortly turn to.

By far the most provocative detail in Delgado's recollection concerned Oswald's contact with Cuban diplomats.

MR. DELGADO: Oh, yes, then he kept on asking me about how about—how he could go helping the Castro government. I didn't know what to tell him, so I told him the best thing that I know was to get in touch with a Cuban Embassy, you know. But at that time that I told him this we were on friendly terms with Cuba, you know, so this wasn't no subversive or malintent [sic], you know. I didn't know what to answer him. I told him go see them.

MR. LIEBELER: With the Cuban Embassy?

MR. DELGADO: Right. And I took it to be just a—one of his, you know, lies, you know, saying he was in contact with them, until one time I had the opportunity to go into his room, I was looking for—I was going over for the weekend, I needed a tie, he lent me the tie, and I seen this envelope in his footlocker, and as far as I could recollect that was mail from Los Angeles, and he was telling me there was a Cuban Consul. And just after he started receiving these letters—you see, he would never go out, he'd stay near the post all the time. He always had money. That's why.[25]

''Delgado's testimony has the cast of credibility,'' Ray Rocca wrote in his 1975 report.[26] Whether or not Rocca is right, it is difficult to believe that the Warren Commission accidentally overlooked this or forgot to follow it up. This failure casts suspicion on the integrity of the commission's work.

Just how glaring their failure was can be seen from Liebeler's amazement as he took Delgado's testimony. When Delgado mentioned Oswald's comment about the Cuban Consul, this is what took place:

MR. LIEBELER: What did you just say?

MR. DELGADO: He always had money, you know, he never spent it. He was pretty tight. So then one particular instance, I was in the train station in Santa Ana, California, and Oswald comes in, on a Friday night. I usually make it every Friday night to Los Angeles and spend the weekend. And he is on the same platform, so we talked, and he told me he had to see some people in Los Angeles. I didn't bother questioning him. We rode into Los Angeles, nothing eventful happened, just small chatter, and once we got to Los Angeles I went my way and he went his. I came to find out later on he had come back Saturday. He didn't stay like we did, you know, come back Sunday night, the last train. Very seldom did he go out. At one time he went with us to Tijuana, Mexico.[27]

Liebeler knew better than to let Delgado wander before finishing his account of Oswald's Cuban contacts. So Liebeler interrupted Delgado and the following exchange occurred:

MR. LIEBELER: Before we get into that, tell me all you can remember about Oswald's contact with the Cuban Consulate.

MR. DELGADO: Well, like I stated to these FBI men, he had one visitor; after he started receiving letters he had one visitor. It was a man, because I got the call from the MP guard shack, and they gave me a call that Oswald had a visitor at the front gate. This man had to be a civilian, otherwise they would have let him in. So I had to find somebody to relieve Oswald, who was on guard, to go down there to visit with this fellow, and they spent about an hour and a half, two hours talking, I guess, and he came back. I don't know who the man was or what they talked about, but he looked nonchalant about the whole thing when he came back. He never mentioned who he was, nothing.[28]

Liebeler asked Delgado if he connected the stranger's visit with the Cuban Consulate and Delgado replied that he had because of the lateness of the visit—around nine P.M., and also because Oswald hardly ever received mail. Mail to Oswald, Delgado recalled, began "after he started to get in contact with these Cuban people."

"Actually," wrote the CIA's Ray Rocca in his 1975 report, "Delgado's testimony says a lot more of possible <u>operational</u> significance than is reflected by the language of the [Warren] report, and its implications do not appear to have been run down or developed by investigation [emphasis his]." Rocca explained the importance of the man at the gate at El Toro in this way:

> . . . It is of basic importance to focus attention on the male visitor who contacted Oswald at El Toro Camp and talked with him for between one and a half to two hours. The event was unique in Delgado's recollections, and actually there is nothing like it—on the record—in everything else we know about Oswald's activity before or after his return to the United States. The record reflects no identification of the El Toro contact. Delgado's presumption is that he was from the Cuban Consulate in Los Angeles. Assuming that, the questions are: Who was it, and was

> there reporting from Los Angeles to Washington and Havana that could, in effect, represent the opening of a Cuban file on Oswald?[29]

In the decades since, the mysterious visitor has never been identified. Did the CIA know of anyone else who visited the Cuban Consulate in Los Angeles in 1959? Indeed they did, but his story is as murky and intriguing as Oswald's. If, as Ray Rocca put it, Cuba was an early "question mark" for Oswald, the same can be said of another ex-marine who did manage to get into Castro's army. His name was Gerry Patrick Hemming.

Hemming's Cuban Question Mark

One ex-marine who did manage to get into Castro's army was Gerry Patrick Hemming. That his marine service is less well known than Oswald's may be a reflection of the fact that Hemming was not investigated for the murder of President Kennedy. The shadowy nature of Hemming's marine past may also be the result of his association with the CIA. Hemming's CIA files tell us that he, like Oswald, became interested in Cuba during his service in the marines. A 1963 Hemming letter contains the following description of his marine service and interest in Cuba:

> While attending the U.S. Navy Academy Prep School, I became interested in the Cuban situation and upon graduation I decided to separate from the service and travel to Cuba. I received my Honorable Discharge at the U.S. Naval Academy in October, 1958. Total service time was 4½ years (active).[30]

CIA files show that Hemming's background was remarkably similar to Oswald's. His security file, OS-429-229, appears to have been generated after Oswald's OS-351-164. It is possible that these two numbers reflect the November 1959 and October 1960 time frames, respectively, for Oswald's defection and Hemming's debriefing by the CIA in Los Angeles.[31]

On the other hand, what if Hemming's OS number was created at the time of an earlier, February 1959 CIA debriefing in Costa Rica? This might indicate an earlier date for Oswald's OS file number. It is possible, though less likely, that both numbers go as far back as early

1959. A 1977 document in Hemming's CIA Office of Security file has this revealing observation:

> [The] Hemming file reflects that he served in the U.S. Marine Corps from 19 April 1954 to 17 October 1958. (The 201 File concerning Hemming reflects that he served in Japan with a U.S. Marine Air Wing.) He then returned to the Los Angeles area for discharge and then left for Cuba circa 18 February 1959 and joined Castro's forces.[32]

In view of the sparseness of information in CIA documents on Hemming's Marine Corps history, the above document is intriguing in its claim that Hemming, too, had served in a Marine Air Wing in Japan. This would open the possibility that both men were assigned together to Marine Air Squadron One (MACS-1) at Atsugi. However, this did not happen, according to Hemming, who should be familiar with his own service record. If he is right, when the Marine Corps and Navy release his entire service record, we will find he served with the Third Marine Air Wing in Hawaii, not the First Marine Air Wing, which was the only air wing in Japan.

This particular piece of incorrect information on Hemming—that Hemming had been assigned to Oswald's air wing in Japan—is arresting. It moves us to ask this question: What other incorrect information was in CIA files about Hemming? The answer is best illustrated by this 1976 CIA internal memo describing Hemming in this way:

> Gerald Patrick Hemming is well known to this Agency, the Office of Security Miami Field Office, and JMWAVE. On numerous occasions since at least the early 1960's, Hemming had claimed Agency affiliation when in fact there had been none. The most recent incident wherein Hemming claimed such affiliation was in May 1975 when he volunteered his services to the Drug Enforcement Administration. Gerald Patrick Hemming is a long-time cohort of Frank Anthony Sturgis (SF#353459), aka Frank Fiorini, of Watergate notoriety who also has a long-time record of falsely claiming Agency affiliation. In the late 1950's Hemming and Sturgis, both former U.S. Marines, joined Fidel Castro in Cuba but returned shortly thereafter, claiming disillusionment with the Castro cause.[33]

The problem with this is that Hemming had long been associated with the CIA, from Los Angeles to Costa Rica, Guantanamo, Cuba, and eventually Miami and New Orleans. "We do wish to call to your attention," said a 1967 CIA report, "that statement in the chart that there was no relationship between Subject [Hemming] and the Agency. This statement is not correct." Traces from a "review of Hemming's file," the Report said, "indicate that Gerald Patrick Hemming Jr. was probably telling the truth about furnishing reports to the Los Angeles office." While we do not have this chart, we do have the 1967 Report. It describes "other memoranda" in Hemming's CIA 201 file which discuss Hemming's early contact with the CIA and his move to Miami. According to the Report, the October 1960 "contact" alone produced "14 reports on Cuba."[33]

These extensive CIA debriefings of Hemming after his sojourn in Castro'a army and return to the U.S. included details of his February 1959 visit to the Cuban Consulate in Los Angeles.[34] A 1977 memo by the CIA's Security Office which described the October 11–21, 1960, debriefing sessions by the "Contact Division/Los Angeles Office," included this information:

> Henning [Hemming] returned to California in October 1958. . . . He left for Cuba by air via Miami on or about 18 February 1959, arriving in Havana on 19 February 1959. He claimed to have contacted the officials in the Cuban Consul's office in Los Angeles prior to his departure.[35]

The 1977 CIA memo suggested that the importance of this and other escapades by Hemming was their possible relevance to Oswald's files. The memo described the intersection between Oswald's and Hemming's files in this way:

> The pertinence of the foregoing is that Lee Harvey Oswald served with a U.S. Marine Air Wing in Japan, and when Oswald returned to the United States, he was assigned to Santa Ana, California (Los Angeles area). Extensive testimony contained in the Warren Commission hearings by Oswald's fellow Marines at Santa Ana contain the theme that Oswald was interested in going to Cuba to join Castro (upon his discharge) in early 1959 and that in early 1959 Oswald allegedly made some contact with the Cuban Consul's Office in Los Angeles.[36]

This document is strangely silent on a key question: Did Hemming corroborate Delgado's story about Oswald's contacts with the Cuban Consulate?

This question really separated into two: Did Hemming meet Oswald? If so, what, if anything, did he tell the CIA about it in October 1960? If Hemming did speak about such a meeting with Oswald, the implications are quite interesting. For example, that might help us understand the sudden interest in defectors in October 1960, a subject to which we will return in Chapter Eleven. As we have seen, in the 1970s the CIA had some trouble coming to grips with Hemming's claims of association with the CIA, let alone his claims of having met Oswald. A 1977 routing sheet on Hemming said, "From a perusal of Agency files, which are meager, I have been unable to corroborate a possible relationship between Oswald and Hemming. A comparison of their (limited) records did not produce any matches."[37]

The Man at the Gate

Hemming's Agency association in early 1959 casts a shadow over the entire issue of whether he met with Oswald at that time. From elsewhere in the CIA's files come hints of links between Hemming and Oswald, such as in this sentence from a 1977 CIA Security Office memo:

> [The] Office of Security file concerning Hemming which is replete with information possibly linking Hemming and his cohorts to Oswald was brought to the attention of Mr. John Leader and Mr. Scott Breckinridge, Inspector General, on 6 April 1977. Mr. Leader advised he would pursue the matter.[38]

This passage suggests there was more in Hemming's CIA files "possibly linking" him to Oswald than the 1959 story. As we will see in later chapters, this is indeed the case.

The story of an Oswald-Hemming meeting in the Cuban Consulate took a new turn in April 1976. An interview with Hemming, published that month in the magazine *Argosy,* contained the following account by Hemming of his encounter with Oswald:

ARGOSY: You've said you believe Oswald was a patsy. Did you ever have contact with Oswald?

HEMMING: I ran into Oswald in Los Angeles in 1959, when he showed up at the Cuban Consulate. The coordinator of the 26th of July Movement [a Cuban organization] called me aside and said a Marine officer had showed up, intimating that he was prepared to desert and go to Cuba to become a revolutionary. I met with the Marine and he told me he was a noncommissioned officer. He talked about being a radar operator and helping the Cubans out with everything he knew. He turned out to be Oswald.

ARGOSY: What was your impression of him? Was he sincere?

HEMMING: I thought he was a penetrator (of pro-Castro forces). I told the 26th of July leadership to get rid of him. I thought he was on the Naval Intelligence payroll at the time.[39]

Hemming should have been good at spotting penetrators because he was a penetrator himself. When he formed his own group in Miami in 1961, he named it Intercontinental Penetration Forces. "Hemming maintains that the U.S. should utilize a number of Special Forces types," said a CIA biographic summary of Hemming, who could "penetrate" revolutionary movements "at an early stage," gain influential positions, and then "channel" them into more "favorable areas."[40]

That was what Hemming had been doing in Cuba and in Miami. Moreover, he did so at a time when the Cuban problem became a crisis in the White House. Just before he left to penetrate Castro's army in February 1959, Hemming entered the Cuban Consulate in Los Angeles. In a 1995 interview Hemming made an extraordinary claim which will be interesting to watch stand the test of time. This is the pertinent part of the exchange:

NEWMAN: Did you tell CIA in October 1960 about seeing Oswald in the Cuban Consulate?

HEMMING: Sure I did.

NEWMAN: Did you bring it up or did they?

HEMMING: I brought it up.

NEWMAN: Did they want to know other information about the consulate?

HEMMING: Yes. But when I saw Oswald in the Consulate I called up Jim Angleton and he passed me on to his number one guy. I was angry, I was mad at being stuck with him, wanted to know whether

> it was ONI or whoever put him on me. Oswald was like a rabbit. I figured these guys were putting snitches on me.[41]

Directly afterward, Hemming left for Cuba via Washington, D.C., he says, and departed from the airfield at El Toro. Oswald was stationed at El Toro at that time. In the same interview, Hemming explained what happened while he waited a few days to catch a military plane to Washington:

> I was raising hell that I needed to get back into Cuba. I got back into my uniform, and packed up to go. The night before I went down to look for Oswald and told the guard, "I have some documents for PFC Oswald." It was really bothering me. In the Consulate Oswald had known who I was. He knew I was a marine, and he knew I had been in an air wing. So naturally I figured they had put a snitch on me or something. But I had just heard back from Washington there was no one that had been inserted on me, no backstop had been assigned or anything like that. So I had to straighten this thing out with Oswald. I thought maybe he was trying to set me up. I wanted to clear things up with him. Afterward, I went to the other side of El Toro that night and put my name on the list for a hop. I was there staying on fourth floor of the control tower for a couple of days waiting for the hop. Sam Bass, an old friend of mine, woke me up around four A.M. and said, "An R-4Y [2-star general's plane] is here to pick you up and take you back to Anacostia. What are you into?" This was a flight from El Toro to NAX Anacostia [Maryland], at the end of the first week of February 1959.[42]

In other words, Hemming now claims that he met Oswald in the Cuban Consulate in Los Angeles and then confronted him about it outside the gate at El Toro. Hemming says he is the man at the gate to whom Delgado referred in his Warren Commission testimony.

Hemming says he told his 1960 CIA debriefers in Los Angeles that he had met Oswald in the Cuban Consulate. When Ray Rocca wrote his 1975 memo about Oswald's Cuban question mark, presumably he had access to Hemming's debriefs.

We have taken time to acquaint ourselves with Oswald's interest in Castro and the Cuban Revolution because we know that he is destined to be swallowed up in their politics during the eight months before President Kennedy's death. During the HSCA investigation, information surfaced about this involvement, some of which concerned an intriguing informant: June Cobb. Because her path crosses the Oswald paper trail, we get to look into her CIA files. The result is extraordinary because of who June Cobb was, and because it illuminates a section or two of our journey along the Oswald trail.

June Cobb, Castro, and the CIA

"On May 24, 25, and 26, the undersigned located and met June Cobb," wrote Harry Hermsdorf, "an American woman employed at the Ministry Office of Fidel Castro in Havana, Cuba."[44] In 1960 Hermsdorf worked in WH/4, which handled Cuban matters, and he was writing about the biggest catch of his CIA career:

> On 3 June Miss June Cobb, Aide to Fidel Castro in the Prime Minister's office, will arrive in New York City ostensibly for medical treatment. Money for her trip was given to her by the undersigned in Havana on 27 May 1960. No mention of [2-3 words redacted] intelligence implication was made to her, although I have felt that she is probably aware that my purpose for talking with her in New York goes a little beyond normal routine employment.[45]

It was rare that the CIA was able to arrange a meeting with someone who worked directly for Castro. And, at this time, the CIA department in which Hermsdorf worked was involved in plans to invade Cuba and assassinate Castro.

In one of his Cuban trip reports, Hermsdorf boasted how he had flattered and bribed the bell captain at the Havana Hilton Hotel into giving up June Cobb's address, how he then visited and "aroused her curiosity in me" by mentioning the names of her friends in New York, and how he then pitched her with the line that "she had been highly recommended to me by a person in New York and I was giving thought to the use of her services for an interesting, long-range employment project that I had in mind."[46] Cobb had accepted his offer for a talk outside of Cuba. They settled on New York, where she had a legitimate excuse to go for medical treatment. "I will hold a series of meetings with her in New York," Hermsdorf announced, "and [2-3 words redacted] I will evaluate her motivations and potential usefulness in a little greater detail." Hermsdorf also commented that Cobb needed "a little more indoctrination." She needed convincing that Castro was involved in "Communist intrigue."[47]

June Cobb went to New York via Washington, D.C. On June 6, 1960, a CIA officer—whose identity is still classified—working in the counterintelligence staff, arranged for the surveillance of her hotel room. The surveillance was thorough, as the following CIA memo makes clear:

> [redacted material] surveillance was established in three rooms of the Raleigh Hotel in Washington D.C., on 6 June 1960 and also included monitoring of a polygraph of subject[Cobb]. From 21 to 29 September [redacted material] coverage was maintained on Subject at her hotel in New York City. This coverage included a [redacted]. Also at least one surreptitious entry into Subject's hotel room was conducted during this time. Physical surveillance was conducted on Subject during the period 10 to 13 October 1960 when she was in Boston, Massachusetts, as well as [redacted] coverage of a second polygraph in Boston.[48]

From another memo we know the name of the counterintelligence officer who requested this surveillance: William P. Curtin, and also that he made the request on behalf of Joseph P. Langan, security officer for WH/4.[49]

Curtin's memo indicated that WH/4 had a keen operational interest in Cobb:

> At first Mr. Langan requested that we determine our potential for conducting a "black bag" job on the Subject's hotel room at the Blackstone during the time that she was to be FLUTTERED [given a lie detector test]. This was explored with the SAC/WFO [special agent in charge/Washington field office] who indicated that he could accomplish this task but that the operation would have to be completed by 4 p.m. since his contact left the hotel at that time.[50]

This "black bag job" (generic term for illegal operations) was canceled, but, as previously mentioned, Cobb was subjected to such "a job'' in September in New York. Obviously the Agency was going to do whatever it felt necessary to get the information it wanted.

CIA documents indicate interest in Cobb by both CI/OPS and CI/SIG, the operations and molehunting elements of counterintelligence.[51] These are the same two elements that appear on many of Oswald's CIA documents. And there is another document that reveals high-level interest in Cobb. Dated June 6, 1960—less than a week after she left Cuba—it is from the office of the vice president. It was placed in Cobb's 201 file, with the name ''R. E. Cushman'' handwritten on it. Lieutenant Colonel Cushman, U.S. Marine Corps, was Richard Nixon's national security assistant. As we will see in Chapter Eight, Cushman was ''hands on'' when it came to the Agency's Cuban operations.

Cobb did not know there was a CIA technician on the other side of the wall in her various hotel rooms. These eavesdroppers kept logs of the activities taking place in her room, such as this one from October 23, 1960:

> 8:03 P.M. Radio turned up. Announcement of Nixon's acceptance of 5th debate with Kennedy.
>
> 8:13 P.M. Other woman on phone. ''Wanna say hello to June.'' June on phone, in Spanish.[52]

''One would have thought that the CIA could have found someone who could speak Spanish in New York,'' Cobb remarks wryly today. She has a point: In this and other logs, it is apparent that the snoopers did not speak Spanish. With White House–backed plots to assassinate Castro afoot, and a subject who had access to his inner sanctum, it seems odd to go to the expense of this elaborate surveillance without the benefit of an on-site linguist.

A surveillance log turned in on October 25 said that among the phone calls of the previous six days, one had been to ''AC 2-7190; Alexander I. Rorke, Jr., 7 West 96 Street, Apt. 2-A.[53] Rorke was another Hemming, a soldier of fortune caught up in the Cuban vortex. Unlike Hemming, however, Rorke did not survive to tell his war stories. On September 24, 1963, he and a colleague, Geoffrey Sullivan, disappeared on a flight somewhere in the Caribbean. Rorke's right wing politics did not mix with Cobb's liberalism, and his call was not as a friend but in connection with one Marita

Lorenz. ''Marita and he had called me,'' Cobb recalls, ''and I called him back, it it would have been to politely end the conversation.'' The name Marita Lorenz is well known to students of the Kennedy assassination case. For example, in his book *Plausible Denial,* investigator-lawyer Mark Lane narrates her remarkable claim to have been recruited by the CIA to assassinate Castro, and to have met with Howard Hunt and Jack Ruby in Dallas just before the assassination.[54]

After the disappearance of Rorke and Sullivan, Rorke's in-laws became involved. Sherman Billingsley's daughter Jackie was married to Rorke. Hoover was a regular at Billingsley's famous restaurant, the Stork Club. Billingsley's hopes were fueled by persistent but unproven rumors of Rorke's capture and imprisonment. Billingsley became angry with the administration and the CIA for ransoming Cubans and not doing the same for Rorke. He collected documents he thought embarrassing to JFK and the CIA and stored them in bank vaults. There was a second Billingsley daughter who had handled some of the material. She disclosed their content to her boyfriend, Douglas K. Gentzkow, a West Point cadet.

Gentzkow skipped his chain of command and Army security, went straight to the New York office of the CIA's Domestic Contacts Division (DCD), and turned over the documents in his possession. Mayo Stuntz, chief of support for DCD, wrote this on Gentzkow's file: ''We wondered why a [West Point cadet] would risk his career on such a deal.'' The person from Cuban operations who handled the file, someone named ''Ladner,'' recommended turning over the information to Army security. Decades later, Gentzkow was surprised to learn this.[55]

In one of the New York DCD reports on Gentzkow, the story of June Cobb and Marita Lorenz surfaced:

> The name of June Cobb as a double agent appears in the Rorke papers. . . . According to the Rorke notes, June Cobb forced, in the fall of 1960, a cousin of Ambassador Henry Cabot Lodge to have an abortion when ''Lodge's'' cousin was six months pregnant with Fidel Castro's child. [About three years ago, we saw a copy of *Confidential* magazine giving details about this alleged abortion.][56]

Gentzkow's papers also surfaced in William Pawley's files, a part of the JFK records long withheld by the CIA. Pawley had helped organize the Flying Tigers with Claire Chennault in 1940,[57] had served as U.S. ambassador to Brazil and Peru under Eisenhower, was appointed to the Doolittle Commission to investigate covert operations, engaged in petroleum and mining activites in the Dominican Republic, and owned transportation and sugar assets in Cuba which he lost as a result of Castro's revolution. He was wealthy, and raised money for the Eisenhower and Nixon campaigns of 1956 and 1960.[58] Pawley had been used by the CIA in 1952–1954,[59] and was used again, beginning in 1959, in Miami for gathering intelligence on Cuba.[60] Why Gentzkow's papers were mixed in with Pawley's is unclear, unless some of the Cubans whose names were in the documents were associated with Pawley.

The appearance of the story about Cobb forcing Lorenz to abort Castro's child may seem to confirm at least part of the *Confidential* article. Cobb insists, however, that the father was Captain Jesus Yanez Pelletier, military aide to Castro. Yanez's enemies later succeeded in jailing him when his friendship with Castro—and therefore Castro's protection—was destroyed in the wake of the scandal surrounding the Marita Lorenz case. The CIA became interested in the Lorenz story and June Cobb as the result of earlier FBI reporting. This reporting concerned an alleged rape of Marita by Castro. That story ended up in a CIA memorandum that quoted Cobb as saying "she would hardly call it rape." This report, apparently based on FBI intelligence, also said, "The girl involved was amorous with several of the entourage and willingly submitted to their attentions."[61] Cobb is adamant that this accusation a lie.[62] The CIA did question Cobb during one of her 1960 trips to New York "in connection with one Marita Lorenz case."[63]

Here is the story of Marita's abortion in June Cobb's own words today:

> Raul Castro had been trying to distance Yanez from Fidel—for example, by sending him on a mission to Italy. Marita became pregnant and that was a big problem. She was looking forward to having the baby. Yanez was separated but not divorced from his wife. Yanez wanted Marita to have an abortion. I suggested that she didn't have to have an abortion—we could just hide her. Unfortunately, before I could discuss this with Yanez, the abortion was performed. I learned of it when she called me from a room in the Hilton where Yanez had brought her after the operation.

When she was living in New York, Castro arranged for her to travel to Cuba. To save money she cashed the Cubana Airlines ticket and went by bus to Florida and cheap flight on over to Havana. When she got there she could not get a call through to Fidel. So she went to an inexpensive hotel in old Havana and, after a few days, was about to give up and go home. She was in her hotel room with the top half of the door open for ventilation when, suddenly, the head of this tall handsome Captain appeared. He took her to the Havana Riviera, where Fidel did visit her several times. She said that Fidel lay on the bed with her and talked a blue streak, but he never made love to her.

Fidel asked Yanez to take her out and show her around so that she could see Cuba; on a trip to one of the two beautiful beaches in Havana, she said he became her first love. She went home to New York. At the time of Fidel's April [1959] visit, she said, she was able to spend some time alone with Yanez in her mother's apartment on the Upper West Side of Manhattan. Unbeknownst to Fidel, she and Yanez arranged for her return to Havana. Yanez had limited funds, so he put her up at a little hotel, the Hotel de la Colina near the university; that's where she was staying when I met her in August; Fidel didn't even know she was back in Cuba.

We considered the possibility that she would need to go to a doctor after she got home to New York. She did not want to go to her mother's doctor because her mother would find out about the abortion; so I recommended an excellent physician who, I was sure, would treat her. After she returned to the States, at some time in the winter, Castro's Executive Secretary, Conchita Fernandez, and I both began receiving calls from Marita's mother threatening scandal.[64]

Thus Cobb opposed the abortion and had planned to intercede with Yanez to prevent it. The effect of the *Confidential* story undermined the bond between Castro and his aide and friend, Yanez. Yanez was arrested by the FBI in New York when he went there to ask Marita to marry him. Released, he returned to Cuba, where he was arrested a few days later under suspicion of being involved in mob-CIA plots against Castro. Yanez served eleven years in prison, and is a human rights activist in Cuba today.

Meanwhile, back in 1960, a call from Cobb to Rorke was not all that the eavesdroppers recorded in their logs. This passage is from November 3:

> 5:10 P.M. Outgoing Call—talking to Joan? Subject telling someone to look someone up in Cuba. Subject asking person if they read something. Subject thought it was very good. Believe Subject was referring to Drew Pearson's column. Subject is reading excerpts from the column. Subject mentions Senator [John] Kennedy and his "get tough" with the Cubans policy. Subject mentions a woman named Taylor (phonetic). Subject also mentions going back to Cuba.
>
> 6:25 P.M. Subject turns on television. Governor Dewey talking for Nixon-Lodge, Channel #4.[65]

During this stay in Boston, Cobb recalls being interviewed by a CIA man who asked her this direct question: "Would you consider going to bed with a man for the good of your country?" June Cobb's response is worth noting. "Not if Nixon gets elected," she said.

Chapter Eight

Nixon, Dulles, and American Policy in Cuba in 1960

The Eisenhower administration had not paid close enough attention to Cuba.[1] Preoccupied with Khrushchev's secret speech,[2] the missile gap, and crises in Hungary, Suez, Syria, Lebanon, Indonesia, China, and Berlin in the years 1956 to 1958, the United States was caught off guard when the insurgency in Cuba, having quietly grown beyond the capability of President Batista to control it, exploded with Castro's sudden seizure of power in January 1959.

While U.S.–Cuban relations deteriorated and the CIA began to consider "eliminating" Castro, Soviet-Cuban relations improved dramatically, culminating in a visit to Cuba, from February 2 to 13, 1960, by Soviet Foreign Minister Anastas Mikoyan. Mikoyan signed trade agreements covering sugar, oil, loans, and Soviet technical experts.[3] The Soviet loan extended to the Cubans was $100 million in trade credits. The visit sparked grave concerns in Washington over Soviet intentions. Secretary of State Christian Herter said this about the Mikoyan visit:

> Within Cuba he [Herter] found a change in attitude at the time of the Mikoyan visit. Prior to that time the Cubans had made offers of settlement [with respect to foreign assets in Cuba]. We have information that he [Mikoyan] advised them to confiscate the holdings of U.S. business people, adding that Russia would stand behind them.[4]

This trend continued on May 7, 1960, when Cuba resumed diplomatic relations with Russia. On May 18, Assistant Secretary of State for Inter-American Affairs Roy R. Rubottom was brooding over a memo stating that "there is considerable anxiety in the Pentagon lest the U.S.S.R. openly or secretly install an electronic tracking station in Cuba."[5] During early summer of 1960, the Soviet-Cuban connection began to take on an ominous character: the first Soviet arms arrived in Cuba.[6]

The summer of 1960 was the point of no return in Soviet-Cuban and U.S.–Cuban relations. In a month Castro seized U.S. oil assets. By September 1960, Castro and Khrushchev were able to laugh about this together in New York City, where both men were attending a U.N. meeting.[7] This passage by E. Howard Hunt, a veteran of the CIA's anti-Cuban operations, illustrates the developing Soviet military intelligence threat in Cuba:

> On July 6 [1960] no less a personage than Sergei M. Kudryavtsev arrived in Havana as the Soviet Union's first ambassador to Castro's Cuba. As Embassy First Secretary in Ottawa in 1946, Kudryavtsev had left hurriedly following the disclosures of Igor Gouzenko that resulted in rounding up Canada's atom spy ring. Gouzenko had been military intelligence code clerk and identified Kudryavtsev as chief of the GRU *rezidentura*. Though personally unprepossessing, Kudryavtsev had a keen mind and was an accomplished linguist. Following departure from Canada, the Soviet appeared in Vienna as Deputy High Commissioner, then in Paris as Minister-Counselor. Cuba was Kudryavtsev's first ambassadorial post, and he filled it as representative of the international section of the Communist Party of the Soviet Union. This high-echelon sponsorship indicated profound political interest in Cuba, the nature of which did not become apparent until two years later, when the installation of Soviet missiles in Cuba became chillingly known to the world.[8]

By the end of 1959 the Cuban problem had reached the crisis stage in Washington. As the Republican Party prepared to nominate Richard Nixon for president at the end of July 1960, Eisenhower wrote to British Prime Minister Macmillan, "As it appears to us, the Castro government is now fully committed to the bloc."[9] The same day, July 11, Secretary of State Herter sent this word to selected U.S. diplomatic posts: "Developments of last several days, especially Khrushchev's threat missiles can reach U.S. in event 'aggression' against Cuba, have placed early solution Cuban problem among imperatives of U.S. foreign policy and offers most fundamental challenge to date to Inter-American System."[10] The solution, however, was out of Herter's hands. The man who grasped the reins of Cuban policy was Vice President Nixon. The centerpiece of the policy he implemented was a covert operation to overthrow Castro. That plan was put together by Allen Dulles and his team at the CIA.

"We regard the situation in Cuba as a crisis . . ."

As Oswald waited in his Moscow hotel room in December 1959 for his Russian saga in Minsk to begin, Cuba had become a critical issue in the White House. The Cuban story was sensitive because the measures adopted to handle the problem were covert ways to overthrow Castro, including plans to "eliminate" him. This dark aspect to the Cuban problem led Vice President Nixon to suggest to his colleagues at a National Security Council in that same December that they should keep quiet about the fact that the situation with Cuba had reached the crisis stage.[11]

In the White House, Vice President Nixon actively participated in many of the important policy discussions. On December 10, 1959, during the discussion on Cuba at the 428th Meeting of the National Security Council (NSC), Vice President Nixon asked, "What was the Communist line toward Cuba? He gathered that the Russians did not object to a tough line on the part of Cuba." Richard Bissell, the CIA's Deputy Director of Plans, replied that "the Soviets encouraged a tough anti–U.S. line in Cuba under the guise of nationalism."[12] In other words, the Cuban problem was, from its inception, fundamentally linked to the larger U.S.–Soviet power struggle in the minds of U.S. decisionmakers. At the following 429th meeting of the NSC on December 16, Nixon told those present he "did not believe that Cuba should be handled in a routine fashion through normal diplomatic channels."[13]

The Soviet dimension of the Cuban situation raised the stakes to what was already a serious problem. Just how serious is evident from what followed the day after the 428th NSC meeting. On December 11, 1959, Allen Dulles approved a recommendation that "thorough consideration be given to the elimination of Fidel Castro." Over the years we have learned much about the Castro assassination planning that Dulles approved on that December day, including this detail from the 1975 final report of the Select Committee to Study Governmental Operations With Respect to Intelligence Activities United States Senate (SSCIA—known as the "Church Committee."):

> On December 11, 1959, J. C. King, head of CIA's Western Hemisphere Division, wrote a memorandum to Dulles observing that a "far left" dictatorship now existed in Cuba which, "if" permitted to stand, will encourage similar actions against U.S. holdings in other Latin American countries. One of King's four "Recommended Actions" was: "Thorough consideration be given to the elimination of Fidel Castro."[14]

J. C. King was not alone in believing that Castro's leadership was a cancer so malignant as to warrant assassination. His mindset was no less ethical than that of many of the Cold Warrior cowboys who set aside morality in pursuit of a "higher good." Richard M. Bissell agreed with King's recommendation to consider assassinating Castro. Bissell was a powerful man in the CIA's covert world: He was in charge of all the Agency's clandestine services, then called the "Directorate of Plans."

Over the years, we have gradually learned of Bissell's role in the CIA's original planning to assassinate Castro. First, there is the CIA's own Inspector General's Report, written in 1967 after a Jack Anderson broadcast leaking details of the CIA's links to the Mafia and assassination plots.[15] The IG Report contains this sentence:

> Bissell recalls that the idea originated with J. C. King, then Chief of the Western Hemisphere Division, although King now recalls having only had limited knowledge of such a plan and at a much later date—about mid-1962.[16]

Obviously Bissell was right and King was wrong, but this sentence is fascinating to reflect upon.[17] It was written for a secret internal CIA investigation, and its creators had not envisaged their work being released to the public. When Director Helms saw the report, he ordered all copies except his own destroyed.[18]

A better source of information about Bissell's role in the development of the CIA's plans to assassinate Castro is a report written by the SSCIA, also known as the Church Committee. Its November 20, 1975 "interim report," entitled *Alleged Assassination Plots Involving Foreign Leaders*, is still one of the best and most thorough reports on the history of these plans. Bissell's testimony to the Church Committee contains details such as this:

> I remember a conversation which I would have put in early autumn or late summer between myself and Colonel Edwards [director of the Office of Security], and I have some dim recollection of some earlier conversation I had had with Colonel J. C. King, chief of the Western Hemisphere Division, and the subject matter of both these conversations was a capability to eliminate Castro if such action should be decided upon.[19]

During the summer of 1960, apparently, coincident with the Bissell-Edwards conversations, such action was decided on. J. C. King's name appeared as the directing officer on a cable authorizing the CIA station in Havana to arrange for Castro's brother, Raul Castro, to have an "accident." We will return to that matter shortly. The revealing detail in the above passage from Bissell's testimony to the Church Committee is this: He refers to two distinct time periods during which discussions with King about assassinating Castro took place.

We can date both of these moments with some degree of confidence. The first conversation likely took place just before Dulles approved King's recommendation to study killing Castro, on December 11, 1959. The first Bissell-King conversation may have contained ideas similar to the one below, which was in the memorandum by King:

> None of those close to Fidel, such as his brother Raul or his companion Che Guevera, have the same mesmeric appeal to the masses. Many informed people believe that the disappearance of Fidel would greatly accelerate the fall of the present government.[20]

King's reasoning was based on the "belief" of "informed people" rather than hard evidence. In retrospect, the logic of singling out Castro's "mesmeric appeal" as the factor that added a high value to him as a target for assassination seems dubious. However, King's CIA chain of command never questioned this logic. Bissell's concurrence and Dulles's approval are recorded in the handwritten note that accompanied J. C. King's extraordinary document.[21]

Bissell states that the second conversation with King was in the "late summer or early autumn" of 1960. It likely occurred as a result of King's work in support of the Cuban project Allen Dulles had assigned to Bissell. According to Dulles biographer Peter Grose, Dulles had a plan to replace Castro with a moderate leadership. The CIA director is reported to have told his "closest associates" that the Agency had to "start working with the left." Dulles then set up a special Cuban task force outside of J. C. King's Western Hemisphere Division. Leading that task force were Richard Bissell, and Tracy Barnes, a veteran of CIA covert operations in Guatemala. King, functioning in a support role, told the task force that failure to eliminate Raul Castro and Che Guevera along with Castro would only draw out the "affair." As we will see, King thought it would be better to get rid of all three leaders "in one package."[22]

Nixon: "We need . . . a few dramatic things"

In 1959, Nixon and Dulles had cooperated to defeat the State Department recommendations to recognize the Castro regime. "Castro's actions when he returned to Cuba," Nixon wrote twenty years later, "convinced me he was indeed a Communist, and I sided strongly with Allen Dulles in presenting this view in NSC and other meetings."[23] The Vice President's performance at the next NSC meeting was memorable, even though it did not mention the ongoing discussion about assassinating Castro. As we have seen, Nixon chose this moment to articulate a new American policy toward Cuba, as recorded in the minutes of the December 16, 1959, NSC meeting:

> The Vice President did not believe that Cuba should be handled in a routine fashion through normal diplomatic channels. Congress was an important element in the situation. The Administration

> must try to guide Congress and not simply react to proposals which may be made in Congress. He urged that between now and January 6 supplementary studies of U.S. strategy toward Cuba must be taken.[24]

This was an important new policy statement coming from Vice President Nixon, who was expected soon to be President Nixon. It was also an attack on the current Cuban policy which, up to that point, had been largely under the control of the State Department. Nixon was openly challenging the State Department's way of ''handling'' Cuban matters.

Nixon defined the Cuban problem in such a way as to take the initiative away from the State Department. The NSC minutes under the signature of Marion W. Boggs, the deputy executive secretary of the National Security Council, contain a verbatim transcript of a lengthy admonition of the State Department by Nixon, excoriating the department for the political cost of its failure in Cuba. Here are some pertinent parts of the minutes:

> The Vice President said that when Congress reconvened there would be a great assault on the Administration's Latin American policy. Heavy criticism of that policy was coming from the Republican and Democratic members of Congress. In his view, a discussion of Cuba could not be avoided. The problem would soon have far-flung implications beyond the control of the Department of State; and any tendency of State Department officials to attempt to delay action would not be appropriate. . . . The Vice President recalled that some State Department officials had earlier taken the position that we would be able to live with Castro.[25]

This was a particularly damning assessment for the State Department officials who, like Assistant Secretary of State for Latin-American Affairs Roy C. Rubottom, had held to a softer line toward Cuba.

Nixon had a large personal stake in the unfolding events in Cuba because the next presidential election, which it seemed likely he would win, was less than eleven months away. Those listening to the vice president might also have been thinking about how to keep their positions if he became the president. It did not appear that things were going to work out very well for Assistant Secretary Rubottom. On July 27, Nixon received the Republican nomination for president, and in August 1960 Rubottom found himself promoted out of the way into the post of ambassador to Argentina.[26]

At the December 16, 1959, NSC meeting, Nixon gave some hints about what changes he foresaw in Cuban policy:

> No doubt that radical steps with respect to Cuba would create an adverse reaction through Latin America, but we need to find a few dramatic things to do with respect to the Cuban situation in order to indicate that we would not allow ourselves to be kicked around completely. . . . He repeated his fear that the problem was getting beyond the normal diplomatic province.[27]

The use of the words "dramatic things" to solve the problem "beyond the normal diplomatic province" goes hand in hand with Dulles's approval five days earlier of the King memo planning Castro's elimination. The imagery evoked by Nixon's choice of words—being "kicked around" by Cuba—was a clear indication that Nixon had something major in mind for Castro. Nixon and Dulles's capture of Cuban policy after that December 16, 1959, NSC meeting is evident from the "dramatic things" that followed: the Bay of Pigs invasion and attempts to assassinate Castro and other Cuban leaders. The original plan was for both things to happen together, culminating in the first week of November 1960, to give Nixon a boost in the presidential election.

The vice president's remarks, as we have seen, to the same December 1959 NSC meeting included his announcement that "we should not advertise the fact that we regard the situation in Cuba as a crisis situation." The reason for this reticence was the covert nature of the measures being planned. CIA Director Dulles was at the same NSC meeting, and he responded to Nixon's comment this way:

> Mr. Dulles felt the question of whether anti-Castro activities should be permitted to continue or should be stopped depended on what the anti-Castro forces were planning. We could not, for example, let the Batista-type elements do whatever they wanted to do. However, *a number of things in the covert field* could be done which might help the situation in Cuba [emphasis added].[28]

A number of things were indeed under way: "In early 1960 Eisenhower became convinced that we were right," Nixon later wrote of his and Dulles's struggle with the State Department over Cuban policy, "and that steps should be taken to support the anti-Castro forces inside and outside of Cuba."[29]

Dulles, the Special Group, and the "Package Deal"

Allen Dulles lost no time in orchestrating the new covert Cuban policy within the Special Group. The first discussion at a Special Group meeting about a plan to overthrow Fidel Castro took place on January 13, 1960.[30] This was a landmark meeting, in which CIA Director Allen Dulles laid down a chain of command that excluded the State Department for how the new covert war would be waged. That chain ran directly from the White House to the Special Group. The record of their meetings contains this entry:

> Mr. Dulles notes the possibility that over the long run the U.S. will not be able to tolerate the Castro regime in Cuba, and suggested that covert contingency planning to accomplish the fall of the Castro government might be in order. He emphasized that details of plans of this kind would be properly aired at the Special Group meetings and with the President but not necessarily with the NSC.[31]

A chain of command running from the president to a committee outside the regular institutions of government was unusual—even novel. It was also a power move to exclude the State Department from U.S. Cuban policy in Cuba. That policy was now the "elimination" of Castro and the overthrow of the Cuban government.

Declassified portions of the minutes of the January 13 Special Group meeting[32] suggest that Livingston T. Merchant, who had just been promoted the month before to Undersecretary of State for Political Affairs, disagreed with Dulles. When the CIA director "suggested that covert contingency planning to accomplish the fall of the Castro government might be in order," Merchant injected his view that timing was important to permit a solid opposition base to develop. He feared that "Raol [Raul] Castro and Che Guevara would succeed Fidel and this could be worse."[33]

What happened next was vintage Allen Dulles, whose domain of covert operations made him sensitive to any implication that the Agency might have overlooked something important. His smooth reply left the impression that the CIA's covert plans had taken Merchant's concern into account. Dulles "emphasized that we do not have in mind a quick elimination of Castro, but rather actions designed to enable responsible opposition leaders to get a foothold." Notes from minutes preserved by the Church Committee show that Dulles then added this finishing touch:

> Mr. Dulles said that the CIA would pull together the threads of this problem and would inventory and assess all possible assets, and that this might take several months. He said that this is all the action in this connection that he plans for the immediate future.[34]

The threads were pulled together by March in a report entitled "A Program of Covert Action Against the Castro Regime," a document to which we will return shortly.

Dulles's remarks to Merchant at the January 13 Special Group meeting have given rise to the notion that Dulles "specifically rejected" King's proposal on "the assassination of Fidel."[35] This interpretation is wrong. Dulles's comment that the CIA did not have Castro's "quick elimination" in mind left unsaid the fact that the CIA was planning to develop this capability for use several months down the road, in conjunction with a guerrilla-instigated uprising. In barring Castro's "quick elimination," Dulles had not rejected King's proposal "specifically" or in any other way. We know this because the fact that the Agency was planning Castro's elimination and the fact that Dulles had approved this planning in December 1959 have both long been in the public record.

At an NSC meeting the next day, January 14, Undersecretary Merchant said he viewed "the Cuban problem as the most difficult and dangerous in all the history of our relations with Latin America, possibly in all our foreign relations."[36] That comment set off this exchange between President Eisenhower, his assistant Mr. Gray, and CIA Director Dulles:

> Mr. Gray said the Attorney General had frequently wondered what our policy was with respect to stopping anti-Castro elements preparing some action against Cuba from American territory. The President said it was perhaps better not to discuss this subject. The anti-Castro agents who should be left alone were being indicated.
>
> Mr. Dulles felt we should not stop any measures we might wish to take in Cuba because of what the Soviets might do. From our point of view, it would be desirable for the U.S.S.R. to show its hand in Cuba; if Soviet activity in Cuba becomes evident, then we will have a weapon against Castro.
>
> Mr. Gray asked whether discussion of this subject should not be treated with the utmost secrecy. At the suggestion of the Vice President, it was agreed that the Planning Board would not be debriefed on the foregoing discussion.

This passage makes clear the importance the administration attached to the secrecy of its mission to topple Castro. The NSC was no longer the place to discuss Cuban operations.

Dulles's remarks suggest that he anticipated—even hoped—that Soviet Premier Khrushchev would cut a deal with Castro. Such a move by the Kremlin would only provide stronger justification for the assassination and insurrection his operatives were planning for Cuba. On March 9, 1960, J. C. King, chief of CIA's Western Hemisphere Division, attended a meeting of Bissell's new Cuban task force. The Church Committee released this part of a memorandum describing the meeting:

> That the DCI is presenting a special policy paper to the NSC 5412 [Special Group] representatives. He mentioned growing evidence that certain of the ''Heads'' in the Castro government have been pushing for an attack on the U.S. Navy installation at Guantanamo Bay and said that an attack on the installation is in fact possible.
>
> 3. Col. King stated * * * that unless Fidel and Raul Castro and Che Guevara could be *eliminated in one package*—which is highly unlikely—this operation can be a long, drawn-out affair and the present government will only be overthrown by the use of force'' [emphasis added].[37]

Thus the idea of assassinating Castro was broadened to include eliminating other Cuban leaders as well. Once assassination is considered an acceptable tool of policy, the list of targets ultimately becomes impossible to control.

A lengthy meeting of the National Security Council on March 10 involved a discussion of American policy to "bring another government to power in Cuba." The minutes of that meeting report that:

> Admiral Burke thought we needed a Cuban leader around whom anti-Castro elements could rally. Mr. Dulles said some anti-Castro leaders existed, but they are not in Cuba at present. The President said we might have another Black Hole of Calcutta in Cuba, and he wondered what we could do about such a situation * * * Mr. Dulles reported that a plan to effect the situation in Cuba was being worked on. Admiral Burke suggested that any plan for the removal of Cuban leaders should be a *package deal*, since many of the leaders around Castro were even worse than Castro [emphasis added).[38]

It seems that the "package" concept was contagious, Admiral Burke using it in an NSC meeting only a day after King used it in a CIA Cuban task force meeting.[39]

By mid-March all the threads, as Dulles had promised, had been pulled together and were ready for the Special Group. It met on March 15, 1960, and Cuba was the exclusive subject of the gathering. All present read a paper entitled "General Covert Action Plan for Cuba." The President's Assistant for National Security Affairs, Gordon Gray, "expressed concern over the time stipulated in the paper before trained Cubans would be ready for action, and asked what were the capabilities for a crash program."[40]

The Program document has been released with some deletions, but Gray's concern over the timetable was likely a reference to this subparagraph of the Summary Outline, which said:

> b. Preparations have already been made for the development of an adequate paramilitary force outside Cuba together with mechanisms for the necessary logistic support of covert military operations on the island. Initially a cadre of leaders will be recruited after careful screening and trained as paramilitary instructors. In a second phase a number of paramilitary cadres will be trained at

> secure locations outside of the U.S. so as to be available for immediate deployment into Cuba to organize, train and lead resistance forces recruited there both before and after the establishment of one or more active centers of resistance. The creation of this capability will require a minimum of six months and probably closer to eight.[41]

The six-to-eight-month time projection fell conveniently just before the election, obviously timed to give the Republicans a boost at the polls.

The minutes of the March 15 Special Group meeting preserved in the Church Committee index include this passage:

> 2. "There was a general discussion as to what would be the effect on the Cuban scene if Fidel and Raol Castro and Che Guieverra should disappear simultaneously [sic]." Admiral Burke feared that since the Communists were the only organized group in Cuba "there was therefore the danger that they might move into control. *Mr. Dulles felt this might not be disadvantageous because it would facilitate a multilateral action by OAS* [emphasis added].[42]

On January 14 Dulles had opined that it would be helpful if the Soviets showed their hand in Cuba. Now, on March 15, he felt that Communist control would provide a pretext to justify intervention.

Gordon Gray ended the March 15 Special Group meeting by remarking that he would "like to submit later this week to his associate (apparently the president) the paper entitled *General Covert Action Plan for Cuba* but modified on the basis of [the Special Group meeting's] discussion."[43] Two days later, on March 17, Eisenhower saw the Covert Program, and he assembled those advisers he wanted for a special meeting in the White House. After a brief opening by Secretary of State Herter, CIA Director Dulles briefed the president on the Special Group's plan for "covert operations to effect a change in Cuba." The first steps, Dulles said, would be to form a "moderate opposition group" in exile whose slogan would be to "restore the revolution" betrayed by Castro, to begin operating a radio station on Swan Island for "gray or black broadcasts into Cuba," and to establish a "network of disaffected elements within Cuba.'' Dulles said it would take ''something like eight months'' to train a paramilitary force outside of Cuba.[44]

The minutes of the White House meeting, prepared by White House Staff Secretary Brigadier General Andrew J. Goodpasture, show that Eisenhower had this exchange with Dulles and Bissell:

> The President said that he knows of no better plan for dealing with this situation.[45] The great problem is leakage and breach of security. Everyone must be prepared to swear that he had not heard of it. He said we should limit American contacts with the groups involved to two or three people, getting Cubans to do most of what must be done. Mr. Allen Dulles said [1½ lines not declassified]. The President indicated some question about this, and reiterated that there should be only two or three governmental people connected with this in any way. He understood that the effort will be to undermine Castro's position and prestige. Mr. Bissell commented that the opposition group would undertake a money-raising campaign to obtain funds on their own—in the United States, Cuba and elsewhere.[46]

After some discussion of the danger to Americans in Cuba, Eisenhower approved the plan: ''The president told Mr. Dulles he thought he should go ahead with the plan and the operations.'' Eisenhower also directed that the CIA and other agencies involved ''take account of all likely Cuban reactions and prepare the actions that we would take in response to these.''

When Dulles returned to the point that American businessmen in Cuba wanted guidance, the president said ''we should be very careful about giving this. Essentially they will have to make their own decisions.'' Nixon took exception to this, and flatly contradicted the president. The vice president boldly announced what he thought: ''We should encourage them to come out. Particularly if they think they should get out and are simply staying there to help the U.S. Government, we should disillusion them on that score immediately.''[47] Bissell ended the meeting by saying it was his ''sense of the meeting'' that work could get under way. Indeed it did, on its path toward the eventual disaster that would befall the Kennedy administration in its first weeks.[48]

Marine Lieutenant Colonel Cushman, Jacob "Jake," Engler, and E. Howard Hunt

Though the president's approval had never really been in doubt, such formalities permitted the final go-ahead on commitment of funds and personnel to begin implementation of the new measures against Cuba. E. Howard Hunt, working at the CIA station in Guatemala in March 1960, was urgently recalled to headquarters to "discuss a priority assignment" by a cable that had been signed by Bissell and his new assistant on the Cuban task force, Tracy Barnes.[49] Hunt had worked before with Barnes on the CIA team which had successfully overthrown Jacobo Arbenz in Guatemala in 1954.[50]

When Hunt arrived, Barnes told him he would be "Chief of Political Action in a project just approved by President Eisenhower: to assist Cuban exiles in overthrowing Castro." In his book *Give Us This Day*, Hunt recalls that things were well under way by the time he arrived:

> The nucleus of the project was already in being—a cadre of officers I had worked with against Arbenz. This time, however, all trace of U.S. official involvement must be avoided, and so I was to be located not in the Miami area, but in Costa Rica. . . . We shook hands on it, and Tracy directed me to the project offices which were in Quarters Eye, a wartime WAVE barracks facing Ohio Drive and the Potomac River.[51]

Once in Quarters Eye, Hunt was escorted into the office of the "project chief, a burly ex-ballplayer named Jake whom I had not seen for several years." "Jake" and "Jake Engler" were pseudonyms used by Jack Esterline, who had just taken over Branch 4 in Western Hemisphere (WH) Division. WH/4 handled Cuba.[52]

Hunt met with Esterline and another man involved in Cuban operations, Gerry Droller. Droller used the pseudonyms "Bender" and "Drecher." Hunt later recalled these details:

> As we discussed the project in his office, he outlined the project organization and timetable . . . "Now go around and see Drecher. He'll back you up at Headquarters." . . . Drecher greeted me effu-

> sively, said things were rolling at a great rate and I was needed urgently to take over field management of the Cuban group. We discussed my cover in Costa Rica. . . . Drecher then told me he had adopted the operational alias of Frank Bender in his dealings with the Cubans whom he told he was the representative of a private American group made up of wealthy industrialists who were determined not to let communism gain a foothold in Cuba. . . . As we talked, secretaries entered and left, Bender dictated cables, read incoming messages, and informed me that our project enjoyed its own communications center, enabling us to communicate rapidly with any part of the world while by-passing the rest of the Agency. I also learned from him that the project's chain of command began with Bissell and descended through Tracy Barnes to Jake. Colonel King, the division chief, was somewhere on the sidelines, and so far as Bender knew, Richard Helms, then Chief of Operations for Clandestine Services, had not been cut in.

"This was a radical departure from standard Agency procedure," Hunt observed, "but the system had been foreshadowed by the semi-autonomous status of our Guatemalan operation."[53] The entire covert side of the CIA was becoming a semi-autonomous operation.

Droller sketched out the project organization for Hunt, dividing it into three basic functions: political action, propaganda, and paramilitary action. Hunt was put in charge of political action, and he met the other two chiefs. First he met "Knight," who handled the propaganda component. Knight was probably David Atlee Phillips. Next he met "Ned," a retired marine officer, who handled the paramilitary component. Hunt recalls:

> He eyed me with suspicion and distaste, and muttered that he was going to lead the boys ashore himself, and that the troops, not the politicians, would decide who Cuba's next president would be. Substantively he told me that a recruiting program was getting underway among Cuban refugees who would be polygraphed and checked at Useppa Island, off Fort Myer[s], Florida. At the same time, a training area was being hacked out the mountain coffee finca owned by Roberto ("Bobby") Alejos, brother of Carlos Alejos, Guatemalan ambassador to Washington. All this had the consent of President Idigoras Fuentes. A semi-abandoned airstrip at Retalhulehu in southern Guatemala was being refurbished at

> considerable expense to handle our heavy C-46 troop and cargo-carrying aircraft. Procurement teams were scouting the U.S. and elsewhere for World War II B-25 and B-26 aircraft that would compose the exile Air Force. Small arms and machine guns were enroute from European ordnance dumps and dealers. If all went according to schedule, Ned said, we could expect to be in Havana by next Christmas.[54]

As Ned briefed the invasion plans, Hunt thought the ex-marine was crazy. Ned had not spent enough time with real troops, a perennial problem with the Agency's paramilitary operations, according to Hunt.

As March turned into April, "there were numerous cable exchanges with project headquarters having to do with my cover and activities," Hunt recalls, and then "came a message telling me that Costa Rica was out; Figueres had been unable to secure government assent, and so my Cuban government-in-exile group would be based in Mexico City." Hunt resigned his cover position in the foreign service and told his friends he was quitting the State Department and moving to Mexico "where I could live relatively well on a recent inheritance." After a detour of several days in Spain, Hunt delivered his recommendations to the Cuban task force in April. He listed four:

> 1. Assassinate Castro before or coincident with the invasion (a task for Cuban patriots);
> 2. Destroy the Cuban radio and television transmitters before or coincident with the invasion;
> 3. Destroy the island's microwave relay system just before the invasion begins;
> 4. Discard any thought of a popular uprising against Castro until the issue has already been militarily decided.

Hunt believed that, without Castro, the Cuban army would "collapse in leaderless confusion." Barnes and Bissell read Hunt's report and told him it "would weigh in the final planning."[55]

It was not long until a plot was hatched to assassinate, not Castro, but his brother Raul. This happened in July 1960, but the level at which it was approved is still murky. The CIA's 1967 Inspector General's Report concluded it could "find no evidence that any of the schemes were approved at any level higher than division, if that.''[56] The outlines of how the plot unfolded for Raul Castro to have an ''accident'' were reconstructed by the Church Committee investigation. According to its report, *Alleged Assassination Plots*, the first CIA-sanctioned attempt on the life of a Cuban leader took place in July 1960. A Cuban informant working for the CIA case officer in Havana had said he might be able to meet with Castro's brother, Raul. On July 20, the CIA Havana station issued a cable requesting intelligence requirements that the Cuban might fulfill.[57] Summoned to headquarters from his home, the duty officer contacted the director of plans, Bissell, his deputy, Barnes, and the chief of the Western Hemisphere Division, J. C. King.[58]

Bissell and Barnes gave King ''their instructions,'' which King relayed in a cable to the Havana station the next day, July 21, which said: ''Possible removal top three leaders is receiving serious consideration at HQS.'' If that sentence did not wake up the case officer, the rest of the cable did. The Church Committee investigation summarized the cable's contents:

> The cable inquired whether the Cuban was sufficiently motivated to risk ''arranging an accident'' involving Raul Castro and advised that the station could ''at discretion contact subject to determine willingness to cooperate and his suggestions on details.'' Ten thousand dollars was authorized as payment ''after successful completion,'' but no advance payment was permitted because of the possibility that the Cuban was a double agent.[59]

The case officer told the Church Committee in 1975 that this cable represented ''quite a departure from the conventional activities'' of the station, but he dutifully sought out the Cuban and told him that the CIA contemplated an ''accident to neutralize this leader's [Raul's] influence.''[60] The Cuban demanded, in the event of his own death, a college education for his sons in return for taking a ''calculated risk'' in arranging the apparent accidental death of Raul Castro.

When the Havana case officer returned to the station on July 22, he received a shocking piece of news. Another cable from CIA headquarters had just arrived. This one, signed by Tracy Barnes, said: ''Do not pursue ref [i.e. previous cable authorizing the elimination of Raul]. Would like to drop matter.'' It was, however, too late to "drop the matter" since the Cuban had already left to contact Raul Castro, who at that time was probably returning from the Soviet Union via Egypt.[61] Fortunately, the Cuban was unable to establish quick contact with Raul, and the matter was finally dropped.

It is interesting, in retrospect, to ask: Who authorized the elimination of Raul Castro? The documentary trail leads no higher than a division chief, J. C. King, who says his instructions came from Bissell, head of the Clandestine Services. The authorizing cable from CIA headquarters was sent on July 21, just days before Nixon's nomination as the Republican candidate for president. Is there any evidence that Nixon might have known about the "accident plot"? As it turns out, there is one intriguing piece of evidence from July 1960, and it concerns a meeting someone from Nixon's office had with Hunt.

In July, Esterline invited Howard Hunt to lunch with the vice president's assistant for National Security Affairs (and chief of Nixon's personal staff), Robert E. Cushman, Jr. Hunt described what transpired:

> I reviewed for Cushman my impressions of Cuba under Castro and my principal operational recommendations, then went into the specifics of my mission: form and guide the Cuban government-in-exile, accompany its members to a liberated Havana, and stay on as a friendly adviser until after the first post-Castro elections. In Mexico I was to work independently of the station, though drawing on it for communications and logistical support. Policy was to be transmitted to me by Tracy Barnes, who was at once in touch with Bissell and Allen Dulles, the higher echelons at State, and the Project Chief. Cushman's reaction was to tell me that the Vice President was the project's action officer within the White House, and that Nixon wanted nothing to go wrong. To that end, Cushman was responsible for clearing bottlenecks and resolving differences that might arise among State, CIA, and the National Security Council. He gave me his private telephone numbers and asked that I call him night or day whenever his services might be needed.[62]

While this does not prove that Nixon knew of the accident plot, it does demonstrate that his chief lieutenant, Cushman, was in close contact with the CIA operational elements involved at approximately the same time. Did Cushman also meet the other component chiefs on Bissell's task force? The idea is intriguing, but the evidence is so far lacking.

Of course Nixon and Cushman would not be around when their services were needed for the invasion of Cuba. The planned invasion did not occur before the election, which Nixon lost to Kennedy. Hunt says this about Cushman's generous offer of twenty-four-hour assistance from the vice president's office:

> I found general's [colonel's] confirmation of high-level interest and good will reassuring. Unfortunately, when I was later to need them, Nixon and Cushman had been supplanted by a new administration.[63]

Cushman was thus unable to help in 1960. Hunt would meet Colonel Cushman again a decade later, however, this time as General Cushman, whom Nixon installed as the deputy director of the CIA. This time Hunt was after materials for the break-in to the Watergate complex in Washington, D.C.

CHAPTER NINE

Lost in Minsk

"Dear Robert," Lee Oswald wrote to his brother at the end of 1959, "I will be moving from this hotel, so you need not write me here." In fact, he did not want any letters at all. Lee said good-bye to Robert in these three sentences:

> I have chosen to remove all ties with my past, and so I will not write again, nor do I wish you to try and contact me, I'm sure you understand that I would not like to receive correspondence from people in the country which I have fled. I am starting a new life and I do not wish to have anything to do with the old life.
>
> I hope you and your family will always be in good health. Lee[1]

Besides this terse farewell, the only other thing Marguerite and Robert received from Lee was a note on a scrap of paper asking for cash instead of checks. The "dear Robert" note arrived in late December and the scrap of paper arrived on January 5. They did not hear a word after that.

While Lee Harvey Oswald vanished into Russia, what happened next at home was itself a lost chapter in his history, a chapter in which his mother, worried about his fate, was a central figure. In the events that unfolded in 1960, the actions of Marguerite Oswald loom large. Except for an action by the marine reserves to process Oswald for an undesirable discharge, virtually everything in the 1960 Oswald files is directly attributable to the actions of his mother.

"When did you first hear from Lee?" U.S. Secret Service Special Agent John M. Howard asked Marguerite after the Kennedy assassination. "Did you hear from him while he was in Russia?" It was just three days after the assassination and one day after Ruby murdered Oswald, and the Secret Service had hidden Marguerite and Robert in the Six Flags Inn Motel in Arlington, Texas. "Now we will get to the very important part of the story," Marguerite replied to Howard. Indeed, what Marguerite was getting ready to tell the Secret Service about the FBI has never been acknowledged by the Bureau. On the contrary, the FBI has no record of this "important part of the story."

Mr. "Fannan": FBI Mystery Man

"Mrs. Oswald, it looks like he wanted to go there [to Russia]," the FBI man said grimly to Marguerite in February 1960. This is just one of the details Marguerite remembers from their meeting. She recalled the entire story of how the FBI contacted her just after Oswald's disappearance inside Russia in January 1960. "I had no contact with Lee at all," Marguerite told the Secret Service in the November 25, 1963, tape-recorded interview, referring to her son's disappearance from Moscow and the fact that, other than the December scrap of paper with his request for cash, she had heard nothing from him. Marguerite explained that she had gathered, by "reading the [news] stories again," that there was an investigation of "the family background as in the service." From this is it would seem that someone was looking into the military service background of Lee Oswald and possibly that of other family members. We do know that the Air Force Office of Special Investigation (OSI) conducted an interview of Oswald's half brother, John Pic, who was an air force staff sergeant in Japan.

In the transcript of this taped interview, Marguerite claimed to have read about the background investigation in the papers. She added this confusing but engaging detail: "But it was the State Department that *they had said* was investigating his background, so I called the FBI in Fort Worth and wanted to know" [emphasis added]. It would be helpful if these words were specific, for this statement leaves open the possibility that Marguerite had checked with the newspapers about the investigation story. What is certain is that she claims to have called the FBI, whether or not there was earlier contact with someone else.

''Mr. Fannan (phonetic) [sic] is the FBI agent I talked to,'' Marguerite told the Secret Service about the call to the FBI. ''What did he tell you?'' Secret Service Agent Howard asked next. The transcript of the Secret Service interview shows how Marguerite responded:

> Mr. Fannan (phonetic) came out to the house, and I had all these newspaper clippings and everything. He said, ''Mrs. Oswald, it looks like the boy wanted to go there [to Russia],'' and since I had no contact, he recommended that I get in touch with some senators and congressmen and people who could help me because we had extenuating circumstances in the case by now.

Who was this Agent ''Fannan'' who visited Marguerite at her home? And what was the FBI's purpose in suggesting she ask for high-level help?

Even more curious than the identity of Mr. ''Fannan'' was the date of this contact: ''This was February,'' Marguerite said about the visit to her house. The FBI has never acknowledged any contact with Marguerite Oswald prior to April 28, 1960, when Special Agent Fain of the Dallas FBI office interviewed her. There was no Fannan in Texas or anywhere else, and the phonetic resemblance of ''Fannan'' to Fain makes it likely that Fain was the FBI agent who visited Marguerite in February. The possibility that the letters Marguerite Oswald wrote in search of her son were actually prompted by the FBI is interesting. An element of intrigue is added by the FBI's failure to acknowledge this lost chapter in its own investigation of Oswald.

Marguerite's Search for Her Son

''Mrs. Oswald,'' Special Agent Fain said to her, ''things do not look right.''[1] The intent of this dark prognosis was evidently to cause Marguerite to worry about her son. ''I recommend that you get in touch with someone,'' Fain offered as a solution. ''Would you help me there please?'' Marguerite predictably replied. Fain suggested Congressmen Jim Wright and Sam Rayburn, as well as Secretary of State Christian Herter.

"I am very much concerned," Marguerite wrote to Herter, "because I have no contact with him now." Some researchers have noted how the Oswalds had a penchant for going straight to the top with a complaint or a request. In this case, Marguerite was doing exactly what FBI Special Agent Fain had suggested she do, and the result sparked a spectacular amount of paper for the rest of the year. Marguerite was justifiably worried because Lee had tried to renounce his American citizenship while the Soviets had refused his request for citizenship. She summed up her concerns in a March 7 letter to the State Department:

> I am writing to you because I am under the impression that Lee is probably stranded and even if he now realizes that he has made a mistake he would have no way of financing his way home. He probably needs help.
>
> I also realize that he might like Russia. That he might be working and be quite content. In that case, feeling very strongly that he has a right as an individual to make his own decisions I would in no way want to hinder or influence him in any way.
>
> If it is at all possible to give me any information concerning my son I would indeed be very grateful.[2]

Marguerite did not include the fact that she had written the previous day to Congressman Jim Wright to appeal for his help as well.[3]

The involvement of a congressman made prompt action a must. On March 21, the State Department sent copies of Marguerite's letter and Congressman Wright's follow-up letter to the American Embassy in Moscow.[4] The operations memorandum to which these letters were attached asked the embassy to report back on Oswald's "circumstances" so that "the Department may reply to Congressman Wright." No concern was expressed about a reply to the worried mother, but the memorandum did authorize, "If feasible, the substance of Mrs. Oswald's letter should be made available to her son." The same day, the department wrote to Congressman Wright, telling him about the cable to Moscow. It was signed by Assistant Secretary of State for Congressional Relations, William Macomber.[5]

Having disposed of Congressman Wright's inquiry, the bureaucracy at the State Department was free to return to its lethargy. Oswald's file landed on Henry Kupiec's desk in the passport office.[6]

Kupiec passed it to the head of the adjudication section, G. W. Masterton, who passed it, with a quickly scrawled note, to his subordinate, Bernice Waterman. In classic bureaucratese, the note said, "Miss Waterman—I think [the] Embassy should not take any action in the case at this time. If you agree, please draft something for clearance through [the] PT/F [Passport Office]."[7] Masterson evidently thought that Oswald's brazen actions precluded any routine reentry to the U.S. and, further, that the embassy should not go out of its way to help him. Waterman, the most experienced adjudicator in the section, prepared a red refusal sheet requesting a lookout card for Oswald and put it on top of his file.[8] By taking this action, Waterman intended to "avoid the issuance of a passport routinely in the event Oswald should apply in the future."[9]

Marguerite's letter had raised the possibility that Oswald "might want to return to the United States," Waterman later testified, and "it was customary to make this red refusal sheet in our office. . . . In the adjudication part of the office, to put a flag on the case for future reference."[10] The refusal sheet would normally have been indexed by another person and a red "lookout" card put in a file so that Oswald could not come back into the United States without the State Department's Passport Office knowing about it. But a lookout card was not filled out on Oswald. "Someone else was looking at it," Bernice Waterman later testified about the Oswald file's status in late March 1960. "It looks to me as if someone started to handle this for the refusal card, or lookout card as you call it," she explained. What Waterman was not saying was that she too had handled her part of the processing in an unusual way: She had failed to put the standard "disregard" mark on the red refusal sheet, a mark that would have given the authority to remove the lookout card if someone else decided that Oswald had not expatriated himself.[11]

A "Very Surprising" Case

"All I could say is it is very surprising," Waterman testified, looking back on the Oswald case. Indeed, it was an unusual case from the start. She explained, "We had been requested not to forward any kind of classified files to the usual place for having these cards made—we should forward them to the Classified Files Section, which would take it up from there, and give them to the proper person to handle.''[12] Of course the Oswald file was classified and, when it went to Classified Files Section, the normal procedure for indexing the refusal sheet—typing the person's name along the right-hand margin preceded by the number 130—was not followed. Instead, Oswald's name was handwritten and the number 130 was not entered. Six people were questioned about this, and the person who recognizes the handwriting as hers, Dorothy Carter, said that ''it could safely be concluded that a lookout card *was prepared* and filed'' [emphasis added].[13] But the trouble with Carter's story is that she does not remember writing the notation she claims is in her own handwriting. A 1964 internal State Department investigation of this episode illustrates the problem:

> Carter had no personal recollection of preparing or filing a lookout card in the Oswald case nor had she any recollection of removing the Oswald card from the file. With regard to the fact that the number 130 did not precede Oswald's name, Carter could offer no explanation other than the possibility the refusal sheet may have been indexed when the number 130 was dropped by the Passport Office. In interviewing the various Passport Office personnel, none could offer any explanation as to what may have happened to the lookout card had one been prepared. The majority of the persons interviewed were of the opinion that a card was never prepared because, among other reasons, the refusal sheet was not indexed. Mrs. Waterman, among others, offered the possible explanation that the refusal sheet was buried under subsequent correspondence and, as a result, missed when the file reached the Passport files.[14]

Thus we do not know for sure whether a lookout card was prepared on Oswald in March 1960. However, contemporaneous State Department cables suggest that *something like* a lookout card—or a flag which functioned in much the same manner—had been prepared. Take, for example, this passage in a March 28 operations memorandum from the State Department to the embassy in Moscow:

> Unless and until the Embassy comes into possession of information or evidence upon which to base the preparation of a certificate

> or loss of nationality in the case of Lee Harvey Oswald, there appears to be no further action possible in this case.
>
> An appropriate notice has been placed in the lookout card section of the Passport Office in the event that Mr. Oswald should apply for documentation at a post outside the Soviet Union.[15]

This communication crossed in the mail with an operations memorandum from the embassy in Moscow which was also written on March 28. Both messages arrived at their respective destinations on April 5.

A close look at these two operations memorandums in the light of Waterman's 1964 testimony suggests an unusual journey for Oswald's file in the Adjudication Section and Classified Files Section of the State Department's Passport Office. It appears that the final leg of that journey—the filling out of the lookout card itself—was interrupted by this "new communication coming in from our Embassy in Moscow." This March 28 Moscow operations memorandum stated, "The Embassy has no evidence that Oswald had expatriated himself other than his announced intention to do so," a technicality which the embassy felt left its options open.[16] In essence, they felt free to give Oswald his passport back at their own discretion. That same logic—that Oswald was still technically an American citizen—might also explain why the final step of creating a lookout card was never completed back at the State Department in Washington.

Far from setting up roadblocks to Oswald's routine access to his passport should he want to reclaim it, the American Embassy in Moscow was thinking of ways to locate him. The March 28 memorandum from Moscow floated a plan for the State Department's consideration, a plan which they said had been "effective" in previous cases. The plan was to have Marguerite Oswald write a personal letter to her son which the embassy would then forward to the Soviet Foreign Ministry on her behalf. Such a tactic would almost certainly have led the Soviets to provide a mailing address for Oswald. But the State Department did not respond to the plan until May 10, at which time they rejected it. They changed their minds a year later when Marguerite flew to Washington, but during all of the intervening months of her dealings with the FBI, the Marine

Corps, and the State Department, Marguerite had no idea what fate had befallen her son.

"No Clew as to His Present Whereabouts"

The State Department finally sent a short letter to Marguerite, who was, after all, the distraught mother who had started all of the paperwork in the first place.[17] George Haselton, the chief of the Protection and Representation Division, explained to Marguerite that her March 7 letter had been forwarded to the embassy in Moscow with a request that they "endeavor to obtain a report concerning your son's present welfare and inform him of your continuing desire to help him." Haselton's letter was mailed to Mrs. Oswald on March 30. To confound matters, Marguerite also received a strange letter about her son from, of all places, Switzerland. A Professor Hans Casparis had written Oswald on March 22, asking him to make an adjustment to his "travel plans."[18] Professor Casparis was an administrator at the Albert Schweitzer College in Churwalden, Switzerland, and his letter indicated that Oswald was due to attend the college from April 19 through July 20. Marguerite, relieved to know something about Lee's plans, immediately sent an inquiry to Professor Casparis to find out more. She sent the letter on April 6 and, not knowing if Lee wanted this trip kept secret, did not tell the State Department what she had discovered.[19]

Meanwhile, the State Department had learned nothing in its rather lackluster search for Oswald. When the operations memorandum from Moscow arrived at the Department on April 5, it said, "The Embassy has had no contact with Oswald since his departure from the Metropole Hotel in Moscow in November 1959, and has no clew as to his present whereabouts."[20] The State Department did not pass on this disappointing detail to Mrs. Oswald, nor did they inform her of the embassy's suggestion that she write a letter to Lee which the embassy could use as a lever with the Soviet Foreign Ministry. For her part, Marguerite's attention was trained on her mailbox, but not for a new plan of attack from the State Department. She was eagerly awaiting a response from the Albert Schweitzer College. However, the next person who contacted her was not from Switzerland or the State Department. He was Special Agent John

W. Fain of the FBI's field office in Dallas. He had just finished interviewing Robert Oswald the day before, and had tracked Marguerite down to ask her some questions about that $25 money order she had sent Lee in January.

When Fain interviewed Marguerite on April 28, three weeks had passed since her letter to the Schweitzer College. She told Fain more than the details of the money order. She told him all about Lee Harvey Oswald's family background, his service in the marines, and his recent defection to the Soviet Union. She told Fain she had written her congressman and the State Department because she was "very much alarmed for fear that something might have happened to Lee." Marguerite told Fain about the letter from the Albert Schweitzer College, and how "the receipt of this letter had raised her hopes to cause her to feel that he might actually be en route to this college in Switzerland and that she intends to write this college to see if they have received any word from Lee."[21]

Marguerite avoided mentioning the fact that she had written that letter several weeks before. After all, the April 20 date for Oswald's arrival at the college had come and gone, and still there was no word from Professor Casparis. Fain asked Marguerite if she had been asked to send "any items of personal identification" to Oswald in Russia. The answer was no, but she added that Oswald had taken his birth certificate with him when he left Fort Worth. Ironically, the very day that Fain interviewed Marguerite, Professor Casparis mailed a letter to her with bad news. While that letter was on an airplane over the Atlantic, another government organization with bad news intruded into Marguerite's life. A letter would arrive shortly in her mail, and it would not be from the Schweitzer College, the State Department, or the FBI. It was from the Marines Corps Reserve, in which Lee Harvey Oswald was still a private with obligated duty.

"Due to your recent activities," Oswald's Marine Reserve commander wrote on April 26, "this headquarters will convene a board of officers, to determine your fitness for retention in the U.S. Marine Corps Reserve."[22] The notification said there were just two options to choose from: retention in the reserves or "undesirable discharge." Oswald was invited to appear at the board or have someone appear for him within forty-five days. Marguerite, with no way of contacting Oswald, did not know how to respond, and so she did not react immediately. She had until June 10 to decide what to do about this threat, and in any case had still not heard back from Switzerland, where she had a reason—albeit a long shot—to hope that Oswald might be at that very moment. There was also the possibility that the embassy might locate him in time for the board. It must have been an awful moment for Marguerite, who had been embarrassed to ask the government for help and now learned that the marines were holding a board to give him the boot.

While Marguerite was holding out for the news from Switzerland, the State Department sent a new operations memorandum to Moscow saying they were not going to do anything at all unless they received something "specific" from Oswald's family. Therefore, the department said on May 10 that Moscow's suggested plan to prompt Mrs. Oswald to write a personal letter to her son would not be "pursued further."[23] This foreclosed any real possibility of finding Oswald in Russia unless he broke his own silence by writing. The State Department search was thus effectively over unless Marguerite forced a new move by some action of her own. With the days ticking away toward the imminent convening of the Marine Corps board on Oswald's undesirable discharge, news finally arrived from the Albert Schweitzer College in Switzerland.

"It is with great regret that we have to tell you," Professor Casparis wrote Marguerite, "that we have not had any word from your son Lee since his application for the third term of a few months ago." This could mean only that Lee had, for his own reasons, decided to excommunicate himself from his family. With no way of contacting Oswald before the Marine Corps hearing, Marguerite had to handle the matter alone. She decided to act, but elected to wait until the very last moment to do so. "I am writing you on behalf of my son Lee Harvey Oswald," she wrote to the Marine Corps on June 10. "He is out of the country at present and since I have no contact with him I wish to request a stay of action concerning his discharge. Also I desire to be informed of the charges against him."[24] At the same time, she wrote a letter to the State Department on June 8, asking for a determination as to whether Lee had in fact "signed the necessary papers renouncing his citizenship," and adding her own analysis that he had not and that he was in Russia as a "resident alien."[25] This was an excellent question that had bearing on the circumstances under which he might return to the U.S., but it would be of little use in preventing an unfavorable decision by the marine board.

The Marine Corps responded first, with a letter on June 17 saying that the investigation into Oswald "was prompted by his request for Soviet citizenship." This letter said that sending a certified letter to Oswald's last known address announcing the date of the board was all the marines needed to do, and added, "It is regretted that action of this nature must be taken in your son's case."[26] The Marine Corps did not tell Marguerite that they had already read the FBI report of her April 28 interview with Special Agent Fain.[27] The June 17 Marine Corps letter to Marguerite also did not tell her what else they had learned from the FBI. It was an FBI suspicion which would have added considerably to Marguerite's anxiety about her son had she known about it. The FBI had concluded—based on Fain's interview with Marguerite and a general analysis of the situation—that there might be an impostor using Oswald's birth certificate.

The Oswald-impostor idea began in the New York field office of the FBI when they read the report of Fain's April 28 interview with Marguerite. In its May 23 air telegram to Bureau headquarters, the New York field office said this:

> She [Marguerite] stated that Lee Oswald had taken his birth certificate with him when he left home. The fact that she had sent three letters to her son in Moscow since 1/22/60, which were returned undelivered, has caused her to fear for his safety.
>
> There appears to be a possibility of locating Lee Oswald outside the USSR at the Albert Schweitzer College in Switzerland.
>
> Furthermore, since Oswald had his birth certificate in his possession, another individual may have assumed his identity.
>
> The info furnished by Mrs. Oswald may be of interest to the US State Department and it is suggested for the consideration of the Bureau, that a copy of her interview be furnished to the State Department for any action they deem appropriate.[28]

A handwritten entry on the Bureau copy of the New York telegram indicates that the FBI relayed Fain's report to the State Department on May 24.

The Oswald-impostor thesis led the Bureau to go beyond the

advice of its New York field office. On June 3, J. Edgar Hoover sent a letter to the State Department's Office of Security, asking them to look into the matter. "Since there is the possibility that an impostor is using Oswald's birth certificate," Hoover said, "any current information the Department of State has concerning subject [Oswald] will be appreciated."[29] Emery J. Adams of the Security Office, presumably after checking with the Passport Office, checked with the Soviet Desk on June 6. "SOV has received no information concerning a possible trip by Subject to Switzerland or the possible use by Subject of his birth certificate," replied D. Anderson of the Soviet Desk.[30]

Meanwhile, the State Department had sent a short operations memorandum to the American Embassy in Moscow on June 22, saying, "Please inform the Department whether the Embassy has been successful in communicating with Mr. Oswald as requested" in its previous memorandums.[31] This seems a bit disingenuous, since we know that the department had already decided against the plan the embassy had proposed, namely, to present letters from Marguerite to her son at the Soviet Foreign Ministry. The same day, V. Hardwood Blocker, deputy director of the Office of Special Consular Services, wrote a perfunctory letter to Mrs. Oswald saying the department had again asked the embassy to send notice "as soon as further information is available."[32] Blocker also said, "With regard to your questions about your son's citizenship it will be necessary that they be answered by another office in the Department. Your questions have been referred to the Passport Office for appropriate reply." Like a good little bureaucrat, Blocker had covered all the bases and, at the same time, had accomplished exactly nothing.

On July 6, the embassy in Moscow reminded the State Department of the obvious: that the department had ruled—back on May 10—against the embassy's proposed plan to ask the Soviet Foreign Ministry to help find Oswald. Therefore, the new operations memorandum from Moscow said, "No further action has been taken on this matter by the Embassy, nor has the Embassy received any other communication in the case from the subject [Oswald] or from persons in the United States.[33] The next day, John T. White, chief of the Foreign Operations Division in the State Department's Passport Office, responded to Marguerite's question on Oswald's status as a U.S. citizen.[34] "The Department presently has no information that the Embassy at Moscow has evidence or record,'' White said after a long explanation of procedures, ''upon which to base the preparation of a certificate of loss of United States nationality in the case of your son under any section of the expatriation laws of the United States.'' It seems heartless of the State Department to send Marguerite so many letters saying that they had asked this or that of the embassy in Moscow but to repeatedly fail to tell her the results. Neither Mr. Blocker nor anyone else in the State Department told Marguerite that the embassy had found nothing in response to its latest request.

Marguerite wrote back to White on July 16, thanking him for his information.[35] Now she posed this question about Lee's U.S. passport: ''Would you possibly have information as to what date he applied for his passport and from what city and state?'' White looked into the matter simply by acquiring back copies of the memos from Moscow[36] and those from the State Department.[37] ''Your son, Lee Harvey Oswald, was issued a passport on September 10, 1959,'' White wrote to Marguerite on July 21, ''at the Passport Agency at Los Angeles, California, upon an application which he executed on September 4, 1959, before a designated officer of the Superior Court at Santa Ana, California.''[38]

There was really nothing more to ask, and this brought to an end the cheerless and unfruitful 1960 string of letters between Marguerite and the State Department on the whereabouts of Lee Harvey Oswald. In fact, all doors seemed to close at once. The marines did their part on August 17, 1960, when Oswald was given an undesirable discharge from the USMC Reserves.[39] Professor Casparis in Switzerland closed his part of the story too, sending Marguerite a letter on September 3. Casparis said they had not heard from Oswald and that they were sorry they could not refund his $25 deposit. ''We hope that by now you have heard from your son,'' Professor Casparis closed, ''for we can certainly understand your concern about him.''[40]

The impostor issue languished a little longer in the bureaucracy. The FBI's legal attaché in Paris was directed to investigate in Switzerland,[41] and the Washington field office opened a file based on the interaction with the State Department Office of Security.[42] The Washington office closed its file a month later,[43] arguing that it was sufficient that the Dallas office and the Bureau had the case fully covered. The FBI Paris legal attaché issued interim reports on September 27 and October 12,[44] and the question finally met its bureaucratic death with a final report from Paris on November 3, 1960, saying, "If any news should be received by the Albert Schweitzer College in Churwalden [Switzerland] about Lee Harvey Oswald, you will be duly informed."[45]

Upset about all that had transpired and still without word about the welfare of her son, Marguerite Oswald boarded an airplane for Washington, D.C., on January 26, 1961. There she made a personal trip to the State Department. A 1961 FBI report described the visit this way:

> She [Marguerite] advised that she had come to Washington to see what could be done to help her son, the subject. She expressed the thought that perhaps her son had gone to the Soviet Union as a "secret agent" and that the State Department was not doing enough to help him. She was advised that such was not the case and that efforts were being made to help her son.[46]

"Mrs. Oswald called at the Department," said a Department of State "instruction" airgram to the American Embassy in Moscow on February 1, 1961. "The Embassy is requested to inform the Ministry of Foreign Affairs that Mr. Oswald's mother is worried as to his personal safety, and is anxious to hear from him."[47]

It had taken Marguerite's efforts for an entire year capped by a plane trip to the nation's capital to move the State Department to ask the Soviet Foreign Ministry about Lee Harvey Oswald's whereabouts in Russia. After meetings with Gene Boster, officer in charge of Soviet Affairs, Denman Stanfield of the Office of Consular Service, and Ed Hickey, deputy director of the Passport Department, Marguerite returned to Texas emptyhanded.[48] Ironically, during this time Oswald had written to the American Embassy in December, asking to return to America, as we will establish in Chapter 10. However, the KGB intercepted that letter and Oswald wrote the embassy again on February 5, 1961, asking why there had been no response to his first letter. His second letter arrived on Richard Snyder's desk on February 13, 1961, two weeks after Marguerite's visit to Washington.

A week later, the department sent Oswald's address to his mother.

Lee had been in Minsk the entire time. He had a boring job in a radio factory but, for the most part, was having a good time falling in and out of love with Russian girls.

In Russia with Love

On January 7, 1960, the Soviet "Red Cross" greeted Lee Harvey Oswald as he arrived at the train station in Minsk,[49] the capital of Belorus, also known as White Russia. The Red Cross greeting party for Oswald in Minsk was most likely one more means of keeping a close watch on his activities. Two days earlier, the Red Cross had given Oswald 5,000 rubles, enough to retire his 2,200-ruble hotel debt in Moscow with spending money to spare.[50] At the Hotel Minsk, "Rosa and Stellina," two Intourist employees who spoke excellent English, welcomed Oswald. Stellina was in her forties and married with children, but Rosa was "twenty-three, blond, attractive," Oswald wrote in his diary, "we attract each other at once."[51] On January 8, the mayor of Minsk, a "comrade Shrapof," welcomed Oswald to his city, a recognition of special status which undoubtedly pleased the twenty-year-old boy from Texas.[52] Shrapof promised Oswald a rent-free apartment and warned him about " 'uncultured persons' who sometimes insuit foriengers [sic]."[53]

On January 11, Oswald visited the Belorussian radio and television factory, where he met Alexander Ziger, a Polish Jew from Argentina who had arrived in Russia in 1955. For many reasons, not the least of which was his job as a department head at the factory and his command of English, Ziger would become an important influence in Oswald's life. Oswald reported for work at the factory on January 13, after which Ziger and his family became good friends of the American defector.

His assignment to the factory, a major producer of electronic parts and systems with 5,000 employees, disappointed Oswald, who had hoped to continue his "education" in Russia. He was employed in the "experimental shop"[54] as a lowly "metal worker"[55] fashioning parts on a lathe.[56] On the other hand, his income allowed for a relatively luxurious lifestyle. His salary probably varied from 70 to 90 (new) rubles per month ($70–$90),[57] normal for factory workers and better than the salaries of many professionals. The Red Cross, however, again added their magic touch, by supplementing his income with an additional 70 (new) rubles per month, bringing his total income up to a level equal to that of the director of the factory.[58]

Oswald enjoyed his first months in Minsk, especially after work, when he studied Russian under the tutelage of the attractive blond Intourist guide, Rosa.[59] Oswald did not like the big picture of Lenin looking down at him at work, and was less than enthusiastic about "compulsory" physical training every morning—"shades of H. G. Wells!!" he wrote in his diary. On the other hand, there was Rosa. "At night I take Rosa to theater, movie, or operor [opera] almost every day," he wrote, "I'm living very big and am very satisfied."[60] Oswald soon had Russian friends his own age, like Pavil Golovachov,[61] and lost interest in Rosa when he noticed one of Ziger's two daughters, Anita, about whom he put this entry in his diary: "20, very gay, not so attractive, but we hit it off."[62]

Oswald's relationship with Anita Ziger did not develop because she already had a Hungarian boyfriend named Alfred, and Oswald found Anita's twenty-six-year-old sister, Leonara, "too old." During the spring and summer of 1960, however, more than Oswald's love life began to stall. After a May Day party at the Ziger's house, he wrote this in his diary: "Ziger advises me to go back to USA. Its the first voice of opposition I have heard. I respect Ziger, he has seen the world. He says many things, and relat[e]s many things I do not know about the USSR. I begin to feel uneasy inside, its true!"[63]

In June he met an attractive girl named Ella German who encouraged his interest but refused his sexual advances. Oswald obtained a hunting license in June, and in July, permission to have a 16-gauge shotgun, both privileges not usually accorded to foreigners.[64] However, his hunting hobby and his interest in Ella did little to reverse his growing pessimism about life in Russia. His diary entry for "Aug-Sept" 1960 has this note:

> As my Russian improves I become increasingly con[s]cious of just what sort of a sociaty [society] I live in. Mass gymnastics, compulsory after work meeting[s], usually political information meeting[s]. Compulsory attendance at lectures and the sending of the entire shop collective (except me) to pick potatoes on a Sunday, at a State collective farm. A "patriotic duty" to bring in the

> harvest. The opions [opinions] of the workers (unvoiced) are that its a real pain in the neck. They don't seem to be especially enthusiastic about any of the "collective" duties [—] a natural feeling.[65]

As his early enthusiasm for Russia diminished, his attention focused on Ella German. Ella was a coworker at the factory and, as the weeks rolled by, Oswald became increasingly interested in her. "I noticed her," Oswald later wrote, "and perhaps fell in love with her, the first minute I saw her."[66]

Oswald was not a bad catch—from a young Russian girl's point of view. More noteworthy than his extra income was his apartment with a balcony overlooking the river for which he paid just 60 rubles a month.[67] He describes it in his diary as "a Russian dream." Russian workers typically had to wait for several years for similar accommodations. But Oswald's relationship with Ella did not culminate in sex, as had those with other Russian girls. It is possible that this made Ella more of a challenge to Oswald, who spent New Year's Day at Ella's home with her family.

A crucial moment had arrived. After an appropriate amount of eating and drinking—to the point that Oswald says he was "drunk and happy"—Ella accompanied him back to his apartment. During the walk back Oswald proposed to Ella, but she did not respond. The following night on the way back to her home from the movies Oswald again proposed marriage, this time on Ella's front doorstep. She turned him down cold this time. She did not love him, she said, and was afraid to marry an American. Oswald was angry—"too stunned to think," he wrote later. He decided that Ella had been primarily interested in arousing the envy of other girls at her having an American as an escort. It was nevertheless a blow to Oswald's ego, and his disenchantment with Russia became linked to Ella's failure to love him.

A certain detail about the Oswald–Ella German relationship warrants our attention, for entirely different reasons. To understand its importance, we must first return to the continuing story of Oswald's files in Washington, D.C.

Chapter Ten

Journey into the Labyrinth

By the end of 1959, Marguerite Oswald was deeply concerned about the fate of her son. She had repeatedly and unsuccessfully tried to send him money. Her third—and last—such attempt, although an isolated and obscure event at the time, would eventually open a window through which we may now peer into the secret world of FBI and CIA operations. Her efforts to make sure that the money she sent reached her son set off an alarm in the FBI which, in turn, led to FBI interviews of herself and her son Robert in April 1960. These interviews culminated in a report on Oswald which the FBI sent to the CIA in May 1960.

This report, unlike the Oswald documents consumed by the "black hole" at the CIA immediately following Oswald's defection in 1959, took a lengthy and interesting ride through the Agency's Directorate of Operations. This journey through the "spook," or so-called "dark side" of the CIA included stops at several points in James Angleton's counterintelligence staff and at nearly half the branches and offices in David Murphy's Soviet Russia division.

This episode in Oswald's CIA files, however, ended just the way it had begun—in Angleton's CI/SIG unit. When the mole-hunting unit did open a 201 file on Oswald at the end of the year, it told a story about Oswald's defection in Moscow which it knew to be false. To find out why, we must first solve the riddle of the late 201 opening on Oswald.

A High-Interest Money Order[1]

On January 22, 1960, Mrs. Marguerite Oswald went to the First National Bank of Fort Worth, Texas, where she purchased a $25 money order which she posted via air mail that day to "Lee Harvey Oswald in care of Hotel Metropole, Moscow, Russia."[2] That was a Friday. "We determined on January 25, 1960," the FBI later explained to the Warren Commission, "that Mrs. Marguerite C. Oswald had transmitted the sum of $25 to 'Lee Harvey Oswald in care of the Hotel Metropole, Moscow.' "[3] How could the FBI have known by Monday what was inside the envelope Marguerite had put in the U.S. mail the previous Friday?

There is no way to avoid posing the question this way because Marguerite had tried to send money to her son only twice before: a $20 check on December 18, and a $20 bill on January 5.[4] The $25 money order nails down the sending date of her third communication to January 22, and the FBI's own record of the date they knew about it suggests the FBI had immediate access to this information. It seems reasonable to accept Marguerite's claim that the transaction was processed entirely through her bank; in a letter she wrote about it to Secretary of State Herter on March 7, 1960, she said, "I also sent a Foreign Money Transfer in the amount of $25. This draft was sent to him [Lee Oswald] thru my bank (against his receipt to be forwarded to my bank) but the receipt has not been received so I am paternally [sic] concerned about him."[5] The failure of this particular transaction led Marguerite to make high-level inquiries about her son. It would also lead the FBI to make inquiries too.

It was ten days after his defection when the FBI entered a passive collection mode on Oswald. As of that date, this is how the FBI later described its interest in him:

> A stop was placed in the files of the Identification Division of the FBI on November 10, 1959, so as to alert us in the event he [Oswald] returned to the United States under a different identity and his fingerprints were received. A file concerning Oswald was prepared and, as communications were received from other United States Government agencies, those communications were placed in his file. Our basic interest was to correlate information concern-

> ing him and to evaluate him as a security risk in the event he returned, in view of the possibility of his recruitment by the Soviet intelligence services.[6]

In other words, the FBI had opened a case file on Oswald because he presented a potential espionage threat. Notice also the FBI's statement that Oswald as a "security risk" was something to be evaluated only "in the event he returned" to the U.S., an interesting declaration to which we will return after Oswald's decision to come home. For our present purposes, however, Marguerite's January 1960 $25 money order to the U.S.S.R. hit a sensitive trip wire in the FBI which led to a new active phase in the FBI's investigation of Oswald.

The FBI has never explained exactly how it came into possession of the $25 money order information on January 25, 1960. An obvious question is this: Are there any clues about this in the documentary record? The answer is yes. The details are complicated, but they deserve our careful consideration.

Four days after the FBI learned of the funds transaction, on January 29, its New York field office sent a letter to headquarters about it and related matters. This letter and another sent by the New York field office on January 18, 1960, along with a third headquarters document (a letter dated February 2, 1960), were all referenced in a thirty-two-page New York field office memorandum sent to headquarters on February 26, 1960. Only the first and last page of this memo have been released—the other thirty pages are still classified. The last page of this memo discussed "details of receipts and disbursements set out in aforementioned bank accounts," provided to Special Agents Robert S. Barnhart and Harold F. Good by a source whose identity is still withheld. "It is noted that the above information was furnished on a strictly confidential basis," the memo said, "and cannot be made public except upon the issuance of a subpoena duces tecum."[7]

Even though the American public has been allowed to see only fragments of this lengthy February 26 memo, we do know that it was filed in a special way in both Washington and New York. At Bureau headquarters, it was not placed in Oswald's counterintelligence file, 105-82555, although it might have been placed there unofficially with an "unrecorded" notation on it.[8] The first page of the February 26 memo is almost entirely blacked out, but some of the serial numbers under which it was filed can be seen: 65-6315 for the New York field office and 65-28939 for headquarters. The FBI 65- serial is used exclusively for espionage cases. The available data is insufficient to warrant any firm conclusion, but it is extraordinary news that the FBI was filing information on Lee Harvey Oswald at this point under espionage serial numbers. (All of these documents should be shown to the JFK Assassination Records Review Board so a determination on their relevance to this case can be made independent of the FBI.)

Strange things happened to the February 26 memo in the FBI. In the New York field office it was cross-filed into a counterintelligence file for Oswald, 105-6103, presumably because it contained information about Oswald deemed to be of a counterintelligence nature. On page thirty-two of the February 26 New York field office memo, a page that discusses bank accounts, we can still see the New York field office counterintelligence file number on Oswald, 105-6103, in the upper-left-hand corner. At Bureau headquarters it was *not* placed in Oswald's counterintelligence file, the file that had been open since his defection in October 1959. Instead, someone at headquarters opened a second file on Oswald, only this time it was a domestic security file: 100-353496.[9] Today, Oswald's 105 New York file and his 100 Bureau file are not even listed in the National Archives. The information that was stored in these files was also stored in a similar file in the Dallas field office of the FBI. Today, with the exception of one document, this Dallas file is also missing.

Oswald's Missing FBI Files

When the FBI sent a list of Oswald documents—purporting to be its entire preassassination holdings—to the Warren Commission, the February 26, 1960, memo was missing. So was the entire story of what was in the FBI's 1960 Dallas field office files on Oswald. During 1960, the same Oswald information flowing into the now-missing Bureau and New York files was also filed in the FBI field office in Dallas. There, the information was placed in Oswald's Dallas counterintelligence file: 105-976. This information included the record of Fain's April 1960 interview with Marguerite, one of the most extensive preassassination reports ever written on Oswald. Yet the Fain report was not in the FBI's list to the Warren Commission.[10]

Even more intriguing is the fact this report was handed over to the Warren Commission near the end of the commission's deliberations. The Warren Commission dutifully published the Fain report, where it will stand for all time like a giant beacon, reminding us of the commission's failure to examine entire groups of FBI files containing preassassination information on the alleged assassin.

The FBI might be tempted to plead that these are special files and are not ''Oswald'' documents because the name ''Oswald'' does not appear in the subject line of the documents they contain. This argument would not look good in light of the fact that some of these documents were released by the FBI in 1978 in response to a JFK researcher's request. Until the FBI simply hands over the rest of these files, we can only look with wonder at what little they did let us see in 1978. What has not been blacked out of the few documents we have from these missing files leaves no question about the fact that they are relevant to the Oswald case.

This fact was tacitly acknowledged by the FBI when it belatedly turned over Dallas FBI Special Agent John Fain's lengthy report—the Dallas 105 file—to the Warren Commission. This document was published in the Warren Commission volumes with the Dallas 105-976 file number still visible. The current release of JFK files has done little to diminish the curiosity aroused by these separate stashes of Oswald information in the dark recesses of FBI safes. It seems reasonable to ask this question: If these documents were released as JFK documents in 1978, why are they not still JFK documents in 1994?

What are we to make of the few fragments we have seen from these missing files? A preliminary analysis of the FBI's numbers that we do find on the documents the FBI released to researcher Paul Hoch in 1978, which are still not in the National Archives, is tantalizing. Moving back in time from the February 26, 1960 memo, we find another FBI document that has the identical 65 [espionage]-series file numbers that are on the February 26 memo. This document is also from the FBI's New York field office. It is dated October 13, 1959, and is almost completely blacked out, except for the espionage file numbers, a reference to a September 11, 1959, letter from the New York office to headquarters, and one sentence: "WFO [Washington Field Office] is being furnished one copy since that office is currently conducting [an] investigation under subject caption."

While the September 11 and October 13 New York disseminations may not relate to Oswald, these dates are provocative for veteran researchers of the Oswald case. In both instances these dates fall on the days immediately following the passport and visa actions Oswald had to undergo in order to gain entry to the Soviet Union. September 11 just happens to be the day after Oswald's passport was issued in California (he had included travel plans to Russia in his application).[11] October 13 just happens to be the day after Oswald applied for a Soviet visa in Helsinki, Finland.[12]

These dates in the October 1959 memo may be a coincidence unrelated to Oswald. Yet, strangely, while this memo was sent to the CIA, the related February 26, 1960, memo—which contained the cross-referenced file numbers to Oswald—was not. Thus, the February 26 memo linking Oswald to an espionage investigation in the FBI is missing in the National Archives today and was missing from the material the FBI sent to the CIA in 1960. Wherever the tantalizing paths—if we ever will be allowed to see them—lead backward in time, there can be no doubt about where the February 26 memo leads. It takes us to a March 9, 1960, FBI document asking that Marguerite Oswald be interviewed about the money she was sending to her son.[13] "Your office is requested to identify and interview the remitters in your area," the FBI's New York field office asked the field office in Dallas, "in accordance with Bureau instructions set forth below."

"Funds Transmitted to Residents of Russia"

The February 26 New York memo was not the only item missing from the list of Oswald-related documents which the FBI sent to the Warren Commission. The March 9 request for an interview with Marguerite is missing too. These documents, along with Fain's report on the interview with Oswald's mother and brother Robert, which followed, were all absent from the list of Oswald documents that the FBI sent to the Warren Commission. Fain's interviews with

Oswald's family produced a seven-page document (not including cover sheets) on the life and times of Lee Harvey Oswald.

The March 9 FBI instructions to Dallas on how to handle the interview with Marguerite Oswald included at least six, and possibly eight, guidelines or "points." Only four were declassified in the FBI's heavily redacted version of the memo released to researcher Paul Hoch. The instructions from headquarters, which were relayed through the New York field office to the Dallas field office, were as follows:

> The Bureau has furnished the following instructions to be observed in this program:
>
> It is desired that the following points be specifically covered when conducting interviews in captioned matter.
>
> 1. Reasons for transmittal of funds.
>
> 2. Identity and relationship, if any, between the purchaser of the remittance order and the payee.
>
> [3.] [paragraph completely redacted]
>
> [4.] [paragraph completely redacted]
>
> 5. Interviews should be designed to obtain cooperation of these individuals, and the impression should not be created that the Bureau is investigating the persons being interviewed, or that their action is, in itself, derogatory as in regard to their loyalty to the US.
>
> 6. The individuals interviewed should be questioned as to whether or not they have been requested to furnish items of personal identification to their relatives abroad.
>
> [paragraph completely redacted]
>
> [paragraph completely redacted][14]

The instructions we are able to see appear to be general rules applicable to any interviews conducted pursuant to what was apparently an FBI program for siphoning information from people's bank accounts. There is no record so far released which indicates the March 9 instructions were filed at Bureau headquarters.

As the official story goes, Dallas FBI Special Agent John W. Fain located Oswald's brother, Robert, on April 27, 1960. Robert Oswald told Fain that Marguerite Oswald had attempted to send $25 to Lee Harvey Oswald in January and that she could be found at 1111 Herring Avenue, Waco, Texas. Robert Oswald told his mother the

FBI wished to interview her, whereupon she "volunteered" for an interview, presumably by phoning Fain. Fain interviewed Marguerite on April 28, during which she confirmed the story of her attempt to send the $25 money order to Lee Oswald in Russia.

Special Agent Fain put this information and much more about Lee Harvey Oswald into an FBI Dallas field office report on May 12, 1960. Fain wrote this report under the case title "Funds Transmitted to Residents of Russia," and filed it under the Bureau's domestic security serial 105, file 353496 for "Internal Security—Russia." The FBI Dallas field office chose to open their first Oswald file under the Foreign Counterintelligence Matters serial 105, file 976 for Lee Harvey Oswald. In choosing the counterintelligence serial for their file, the Dallas office was in step with the New York field office request for the interview, which came under a 105 designation.

That both the New York and Dallas field offices used a 105 serial for Oswald was to be expected, as it simply followed what the Bureau had done by opening a 105 file on Oswald. At this point, however, something strange happened. A new, separate file was opened at headquarters with the original Oswald file still open. The seven-page Fain report was put in a new domestic security file, 100-353496, instead of Oswald's counterintelligence file, 105-82555. What did this mean? Did these serials and file numbers really matter?

They mattered a great deal. The new 100 file at headquarters, like the 105 files at Dallas and New York, would never make it to the National Archives. Except, of course, for the solitary Fain report from Dallas. The opening and disappearance of these special files at the Bureau and its various field offices were part of a trend in which Oswald-related information and documents were buried in places from which they would be difficult to retrieve by investigators. In the case of the Warren Commission, such investigation was arbitrary because President Johnson put the FBI in charge of it. The Senate Select and House Select Committees, however, would not know about these special files through intuition, and so this important information from the beginning of the Oswald case never did see the light of day—that is, until now. The current JFK Assassination Records Review Board can change all of that.

Whether by accident or by design, the way information on Oswald was filed in early 1960 was misleading and inaccurate. The FBI told the Senate Select Committee on Intelligence Activities in 1979 that the FBI case on Oswald was first opened by its Dallas field office on January 13, 1961. In making this assertion, the FBI was referring not to the file that contained the May 1960 Fain report (105-976), but was referring instead to the second file opened at Dallas—a domestic security file (100-10461). This story begins to stretch under the weight of the known facts: The FBI told the Warren Commission it had "opened a file" on Oswald in October 1959, and told the Church Committee "the case on Lee Harvey Oswald was initially opened in the Dallas Field Division" in January 1961.

One hopes we would be wrong in asserting that the FBI deliberately misled the Church Committee, which could conclude from the above only that the Dallas office began tracking Oswald a year after it had, in truth, begun its investigation. Technically, since the 1960 Dallas 105-976 case was "Funds Transmitted to Residents of Russia," the FBI could say that this was not a case on "Oswald." However, the FBI had opened a counterintelligence case—105-82555—on Oswald in October 1959, which had more than a dozen documents in it by the time Dallas opened its 105 file. Moreover, the "Funds Transmitted" case (105-976) in Dallas contained the most detailed information yet about Oswald because the interviews with his family were stored there. Meanwhile, at headquarters, from the very moment the FBI intercepted the information about the transfer from Marguerite's bank account, all ensuing reports and information from this source had either been unofficially entered in Oswald's counterintelligence file as "unrecorded" or entered under a separate "Internal Security—Russia" serial and file number.

While all of these file numbers seem complicated to the untrained eye, there can be no mistake about the pattern we can now discern: Much of the early information on Oswald developed by the FBI's field investigators was deliberately withheld from Oswald's headquarters counterintelligence (105) file and was instead put into an internal security (100) file which was then suppressed. Meanwhile his Dallas (105) counterintelligence file was also suppressed and a new Dallas internal security (100) file was opened on January 13, 1961—well after the original leads generated by the funds transfer had played themselves out. The FBI provided only subsequent official government inquiries with documents from Oswald's 105 Bureau file and his 100 file from Dallas. In the case of the New York field office, two files were also used, only these were counterintelligence (105) files. The New York field office suppressed the first file, 105-6103, which contained the same information that was in the suppressed headquarters file (100-353496) and the suppressed Dallas file, 105-976.

All of these special handling procedures may have been carried out to protect the FBI's bank peeping project, but we cannot be sure until the FBI comes clean—with the complete files and an honest explanation. Whatever the reason, the result was obfuscation and secrecy, with the sensitive information stored under the 105 serial in Dallas, the 100 serial at Headquarters, and in one of the two 105 serials in New York. Fortunately for history, Fain did not identify New York as the source of the information that Marguerite had sent money to Russia, and the FBI released his report to the Warren Commission. Moreover, when the FBI inadvertently released a few documents years ago to researcher Paul Hoch, these documents provided a roadmap to the rest of the file numbers pertaining to Oswald—including the 65 serial for espionage—for both headquarters and Dallas.

An Oswald Journey Through the CIA

Sometime on Friday, May 27, 1960, the Fain report on Oswald was date-stamped into the CIA's Records Integration Division, which assigned the May 12 report a CIA number, DBF-49478. Strangely, Oswald had not yet been assigned a counterintelligence file number and so this document was filed under the number 74-500. The 74 was almost certainly the number for the U.S.S.R. The 500 was a generic number. The following Tuesday, May 31, Fain's seven-page account of Oswald was signed into the counterintelligence staff (CI/Staff) by a person with the initials "bar." From there the file moved to Joseph E. Evans in the operations section of counterintelligence (CI/OPS). Given that the mole-hunting group (CI/SIG) in the counterintelligence staff played such a central role in the November–December 1959 chapter of Oswald's CIA files, it seems strange that CI/SIG was not included among the CI elements to which this document was routed. Perhaps this omission is the reason this Oswald document, unlike the previous Oswald documents, managed to travel on to the Soviet Russia Division the following day.

On Wednesday, June 1, the Fain report rolled into the Counterespionage Branch (SR/CE) of the Soviet Russia Division. In the CE branch it was seen by the chief, Bill Bright, after which it came to rest at the desk of someone whose initials were "IEL," and whose duty section was represented by the letter P. IEL was directed to page six of the report, where the CIA copy of this Fain report has double hash marks in the left column next to these two sentences:

> Mrs. Oswald stated that she has not been requested to furnish any items of personal identification to LEE HARVEY OSWALD in Russia. She volunteered the information that LEE HARVEY OSWALD took his birth certificate with him when he left Fort Worth, Texas [underlined by CIA].

Whoever IEL was, this person apparently had the responsibility to track the birth certificate issue as a possible espionage matter—in other words, to watch for the possibility that an impostor might get hold of this document. Actually, the FBI did investigate this issue over the summer of 1960 because of a related issue centering on whether Oswald had gone to Switzerland instead of Moscow. In the end, the impostor issue, along with concern over the birth certificate, was dropped due to the lack of substantive information.

On Thursday, June 2, the Fain memo was on the move again inside the CIA, this time to SR/9, the Soviet Russia branch that provided support to CIA operations in Moscow. In 1959 there was no CIA "station" in Moscow. CIA personnel in the Moscow Embassy operated alone as "singletons." Russell Langelle had been compromised when the Soviet spy Popov had been discovered and was expelled on October 16, 1959, the very day that Oswald arrived in Moscow. This left at least one other singleton agent, George Winters. What might have been SR/9's interest in Fain's report on Oswald? In the first place, SR/9 was probably still interested in how Popov had been discovered, and was certainly interested in whether a crucial piece of intelligence Popov had provided to his CIA handlers was true.

That piece of intelligence was provocative, and suggested there might be a mole in the CIA with access to information about the supersensitive U-2 program. Popov had indicated in April 1958 that there was a leak in this top secret spy plane program. Popov's reporting indicated that a Soviet colonel, apparently during a drunken boast, had said the KGB had learned the technical details about the new high-altitude American spy plane overflying the Soviet Union. Such details had been so tightly held that the leak might have come from a highly placed mole, and the CIA could not be sure whether the Soviets knew enough about the aircraft's cruising altitude to shoot it down with a missile.[15] The navy message to Moscow after Oswald's defection mentioned Oswald's duty in "Air Control Squadrons in Japan and Taiwan," which should have been enough to raise hairs in the CIA.[16] People who were involved in the U-2 program knew that the only Marine Air Wing in that entire geographic region was at Atsugi, a CIA U-2 base. A former senior officer of the Directorate of Operations, Ed Jeunovitch, recalled this detail:

> For security during U-2 program: there was a special detachment of OS people controlled out of Tokyo. They had total responsibility for the security of the U-2 program. When I was assigned to Tokyo I initially wondered why the guy in charge of this detachment was so high in rank—a [GS] 16, while the [CIA] Station chief was only a 17 or 18. Emil Geisse was chief of the detachment during Oswald's time in Tokyo.[17]

Unfortunately, we know only that Angleton's CI/SIG unit read the navy report about Oswald's Far East Marine Air Control Squadron, and we thus cannot be sure if SR/9 had access to it. In either case, SR/9 had to be interested in Oswald's presence in Moscow simply because it occurred in the wake of the arrest of their chief asset there: Popov.

We know the Fain report circulated through the various offices of the SR Division, including some we have not yet mentioned, such as SR/4, SR/6, and SR/10. We will return to the dimmer recesses of the Soviet Russia Division in Chapters 11 and 12. For now, let us consider the bottom line of the very first report the FBI sent to the CIA about Oswald: "According to Mrs. Oswald, she was subsequently shocked to learn that he had gone to Moscow, Russia, where he is reported to have renounced his U.S. citizenship and where he sought Soviet citizenship.''

The question of whether Oswald renounced his citizenship is a fundamental one and bears directly on other issues surrounding his departure from the Soviet Union. The paper trail on the renunciation issue illustrates both the bureaucratic intrigue and lethagy that have long been the facts of life in Washington, D.C.

The ''Renunciation'' Paper Trail

On November 18, 1960, Angleton's deputy chief of CI, S. H. Horton, relayed a draft reply to a State Department query on defectors for Bissell to look at. Bissell signed it on November 21.[18] Attached to this letter was a list of defectors which, like the letter, had been assembled and drafted by Angleton's mole-hunting chief in CI/SIG, Birch D. O'Neal. The tenth name on the defector's list was Oswald, and the ''secret'' description of Oswald is noteworthy because it contains something which is not true. It said, ''He appeared at the United States Embassy in Moscow and renounced his U.S. citizenship,'' a statement which was false.[19]

The truth was that Oswald had tried but failed to renounce his citizenship. What is more, this technical distinction—between Oswald's request for the papers to renounce his U.S. citizenship and his failure to return to the embassy and actually execute the renunciation—mattered a great deal. For one thing, it was directly relevant to the ease with which Oswald could retrieve his passport and, therefore, return to America. In addition, and perhaps more important for our purposes, the fact is that the CIA was in possession of the facts concerning Oswald's failure to complete the renunciation as well as the State Department's reexamination of this very issue. CI/SIG's November 18 flat assertion that Oswald had renounced his U.S. citizenship permits us to question—at the very least—the credibility of the way in which CI was handling the Oswald file at this early date.

Lee Harvey Oswald appeared at the embassy ''to renounce [his] American citizenship,'' said Snyder's October 31, 1959, cable 1304, but added, ''we propose delay [in] execution [of] renunciation until

Soviet action known or [State] Dept advises.''[20] On November 2, Snyder wrote in dispatch 234 that ''Oswald is presently residing in non-tourist status at the Metropole Hotel in Moscow awaiting the Soviet response to his application for citizenship'' and that ''the Embassy proposes to delay action on Oswald's request to execute an oath of renunciation. . . .''[18] Both cable 1304 and dispatch 234 were sent to the CIA. A week later, November 9, 1959, Snyder sent the State Department an update, saying, ''Lee Oswald seems determined [to] carry out purpose of seeking Soviet citizenship and renouncing American citizenship, but so far as known Soviet citizenship not granted and formal renunciation not yet made at this office.''[21] This cable was not made available to the CIA until after the Kennedy assassination.

The next day, November 10, the Navy Liaison Office at the American Embassy made a mistake, inviting the chief of Naval Operations to look at embassy dispatch ''184 DTD 7 Nov X SUBJ Oswald ltr concerning renunciation of US citizenship.''[22] Dispatch 184 ''contains no mention of Oswald,'' someone wrote by hand on a copy of the Navy Liaison message from Moscow—it was about Khrushchev. The Navy Liaison message may have been referring to Snyder's November 2 dispatch. It was a harbinger of things to come that the first navy message to mention the renunciation issue would be spurious. The *Washington Post*[23] did no better on November 16, saying, ''Lee Harvey Oswald's dream of achieving Soviet citizenship in exchange for the United States citizenship he renounced appears to be unattainable.'' The fact is that Oswald failed to return to the embassy to carry out his stated intent to renounce his U.S. citizenship.

The Air Force's Office of Special Investigations (OSI), which began investigating Oswald's half brother Edward in January 1960 did somewhat better. A January 27 OSI document stated that Oswald had ''contemplated'' renunciation, ''stating his intention of renouncing his U.S. citizenship.''[24] Marguerite Oswald seemed a bit confused on March 6, when she wrote to Congressman Wright, ''According to the UPI Moscow Press, he appeared at the U.S. Embassy renouncing his U.S. citizenship.''[25] The next day, however, she summed it up nicely in her March 7, 1960, letter to Secretary of State Herter:

> All I know is what I read in the newspapers. He went to the U.S. Embassy there and wanted to turn in his U.S. citizenship and had applied for Soviet citizenship. However, the Russians refused his request but said he could remain in their country as a Resident Alien. As far as I know, he is still a U.S. citizen.[26]

It is interesting how in just twenty-four hours Marguerite's understanding progressed from a misleading use of the wording "renouncing" to the more accurate "wanted to turn in his citizenship."

If Oswald had gone through with the renunciation and signed the required papers, this would, in turn, have led to an official record of his loss of U.S. citizenship. Precisely because Oswald had not gone through with it, the State Department sent an operations memorandum to the Moscow Embassy on March 28, 1960, saying, "Unless and until the Embassy comes into possession of information or evidence upon which to base the preparation of a certificate of loss of nationality in the case of Lee Harvey Oswald, there appears to be no further action possible in this case."[27] By coincidence, the very same day, the American Embassy in Moscow sent an operations memorandum to the department, saying, "The Embassy has no evidence that Oswald has expatriated himself other than his announced intention to do so. . . ."[28]

The next episode in the renunciation story is FBI Special Agent John W. Fain's interview with Marguerite on April 28, 1960. Fain's report said Marguerite had expressed "shock" when she had learned her son "is reported to have renounced his U.S. citizenship," and again that it was "much to her surprise" that he "had renounced" his U.S. citizenship.[29] This report was sent to the CIA on May 25, whereupon a CIA file clerk wrote these words on the final page of the report: "Ex-marine, who upon his discharge from Marine Corps, Sept 59, traveled to USSR and renounced his U.S. citizenship."[30]

This false handwritten statement was placed on the Fain report for a CIA keypunch operator to type in on an IBM index card on Oswald. The clerk who typed the index card, however, was either a different individual from the person who had written "renounced" on the Fain report or had learned something new before actually typing the index card. The typed card reads, "Traveled to USSR to renounce his U.S. citizenship," which was a factual statement, the key being that Oswald had not followed through on his intent.[31]

What the CIA copy of the Fain report and the index card prepared from it show is that the CIA understood—in May 1960—that Oswald had intended to renounce his citizenship but in fact had not. It also shows that the incorrect statement—that Oswald had "renounced"—came from the FBI, and that the CIA corrected this mistake before typing the index card on Oswald.

The FBI, however, proceeded to perpetuate the myth of Oswald's renunciation, as shown by an air telegram from the New York field office to Bureau headquarters on May 23: "Interview of Mrs. Marguerite C. Oswald reveals that her son, Lee Harvey Oswald, had gone to Moscow, Russia, had renounced his citizenship and had apparently sought Soviet citizenship."[32] The New York field office was thus repeating what was in the Fain report: that, *according to Marguerite,* Oswald had renounced. The Fain report also was transmitted to the Navy's Office of Naval Intelligence (ONI) on May 26,[33] where Marguerite's misstatement influenced the Marine Board decision on her son's undesirable discharge.

It is noteworthy that neither the Fain report nor the New York air telegram contained an FBI corroboration of Marguerite's misrepresentation of the renunciation issue. In twice paraphrasing Marguerite's distortion without commenting on its correctness, these FBI reports add a strange tinge to the FBI's 1960 reporting on Oswald. Similarly, the June 3 Hoover letter to the State Department, the one containing the Oswald "impostor" thesis, contained this passage relevant to the renunciation issue:

> Reference is made to Foreign Service Dispatch Number 234 dated November 2, 1959, concerning subject's renunciation of his American citizenship at the United States Embassy, Moscow, Russia, on October 31, 1959.[34]

An interpretation of this language as Machiavellian double-speak is indicated by a close legal reading of the wording, which semantically allows for the possibility that Oswald might not have renounced and that the Hoover letter was simply "concerning" the issue. Such wording is all the more artful because the Moscow Embassy's dispatch 234 made clear that the embassy *did not act* on Oswald's request to renounce his citizenship on October 31 and, further, that the embassy was stalling him and proposed to continue stalling him to the extent the department would allow.

By June 8 Marguerite had asked Mr. Haselton of the State Department outright for a judgment of the renunciation issue,[35] and on June 22 State's deputy director of the Office of Special Consular Services, V. Harwood Blocker, responded, "With regard to your questions about your son's citizenship it will be necessary that they be answered by another office in the [State] Department. Your questions have been referred to the Passport Office for appropriate reply."[36] That judgment came from the chief of the State Department's Foreign Operations Division, John T. White, on July 7. He wrote this to Marguerite:

> The Department presently has no information that the Embassy at Moscow has evidence of record upon which to base the preparation of a certificate of loss of United States nationality in the case of your son under any section of the expatriation laws of the United States.[37]

On August 9, Verde Buckler of the State Department's Passport Office showed the file on Oswald to the FBI. Special Agent Haser of the Washington field office was the reviewer. After looking at the file, Haser wrote that Oswald had "publicly sought to renounce his American citizenship," but gone was the word "renounced" or any inference that a renunciation had taken place.[38] The same language appeared in an FBI report by Special Agent Dana Carson, also of the Washington field office, after he reviewed Oswald's passport file on September 9. Carson's September 12 report said only that Oswald "sought" to renounce his citizenship, but did not state that he had followed through on it.[39]

This brings us full circle to the State Department's October request to the CIA for data on defectors, and the Agency's response which said that Oswald had in fact renounced his citizenship at the embassy in Moscow. As we will shortly see, the special research staff of the Office of Security was not asked to look into Oswald, and this November 18 write-up was done by Birch O'Neal's CI/SIG mole-hunting branch. The only piece of paper the CIA had ever received which had the FBI replay of Marguerite's misstatement on renunciation—the Fain report—was apparently not received by CI/SIG.

The original documents from October–November 1959, which told the true story of how Oswald had tried and failed to renounce his citizenship, *were already in the possession of CI/SIG.*

When the CIA's Records Integration Division (RID) first saw the Fain report, the person preparing the words for abstraction into the data file made the mistake of repeating Marguerite's use of the word "renounced." But RID managed to straighten the problem out before typing it into the permanent card file index. Similarly, the FBI, once confronted with Oswald's official State Department passport file, dropped the term "renunciation." The same was not true for CI/SIG, however, where someone apparently wanted the Oswald script to read as if he had renounced his citizenship. Why this was so was part of the riddle of the late 201 opening on Oswald, a subject to which we must now return.

Chapter Eleven

The Riddle of Oswald's 201 File

Of all the events that occurred during the period of time that Oswald was "lost" in the Soviet Union, the most important was the late opening of his CIA 201 file in December 1960. No single page in all the quarter-million pages of Oswald-related JFK documents so far released by the CIA can compare in significance to the piece of paper that opened his 201 file. This paper reveals a wealth of important information: the document's 201 number, 201-289248; the name of the person who opened the file, Ann Egerter; the office symbol, "CI/SIG," for the Counterintelligence Special Investigation Group in which she worked; the date that the file was opened, December 9, 1960; the CIA's U.S.S.R. country code, "074"; and the wrong middle name for Oswald—"Henry" instead of Harvey. These and other integral aspects of Oswald's 201 file are dealt with throughout the chapters of this book.

This chapter deals with the basic question: Why was Oswald's 201 file opened? The apparent incongruity between the CIA's claim that the file was opened because Oswald was a defector and the reality that the file was opened a year after the CIA knew about his defection stands crooked in the landscape—like the Leaning Tower of Pisa, destined to fall down sooner or later. The public should be as "amazed" about this as was former director of Central Intelligence Richard Helms.[1]

Between 1958 and 1960, more than a dozen American defectors made their way to the Soviet Union, many of them from the U.S. military, and some of whom had been privy to classified information. The CIA ascertained that nearly half of this group were "KGB agents,"[2] some recruited well before their defections. Several of these defectors decided to return to America between 1962 and 1963. The official story has long been that Oswald's 201 file was opened after this series of defections led to questions in the Eisenhower White House and a State Department request to the CIA for information on a list of defectors. This list had Oswald's name on it. The CIA's overt story has been that this alone was the reason they opened a 201 file on Oswald.

From the CIA's files, however, comes hard evidence that more than Oswald's defector status was involved in the 201 opening—much more. In 1975, the head of the CIA's Counterintelligence Staff, George Kalaris, wrote a memo saying the file had been opened because of Oswald's "queries" about coming home.[3] This sets up a time dilemma because, when the 201 was opened on December 9, 1960, the CIA was not supposed to know where Oswald was, let alone what he might be asking about. The House Select Committee on Assassinations, which investigated the issue of the late opening, saw the Kalaris memo and dismissed this statement because, like the Warren Commission before it, the HSCA believed no one knew where Oswald was until February 13, 1963. That was the day the U.S. Embassy in Moscow found out that Oswald was in Minsk and wanted to return to America. Evidence has been accumulating, however, that Oswald's whereabouts were known to someone outside of the Soviet Union, perhaps including the CIA.

The Warren Commission's Final Report and its additional twenty-six volumes of materials, dominated by the guiding hand of former CIA director and commission member Allen Dulles, are suspiciously mute on the subject of Oswald's CIA files. The HSCA, however, did look into his Agency files, and probed the 201 issue vigorously but, in the end, unsuccessfully. One factor that contributed to this dead end in the HSCA investigation was the CIA's decision not to allow the HSCA investigators access to the Agency's internal routing sheets indicating who had handled Oswald's files on specific dates—records the HSCA was sensible enough to ask for.

The most important contributor was a flawed assumption underlying the HSCA's own analysis. By assuming that the CIA had not known where Oswald was in December 1960, the HSCA disconnected his 201 from the event which might have opened it, Oswald's request to the U.S. government to let him come home. Oswald had put this request in a letter to the embassy that was pinched by the KGB. The KGB never put the letter back in the mail to the U.S. Embassy and did not reveal its existence until 1991, after the fall of communism in the Soviet Union.

When viewed in the context of Oswald's query about returning to the U.S., the 201 opening in December 1960 invites the question: Did the CIA have access to sources in the Soviet Union that permitted them to monitor American defectors? Some useful answers can be found in the JFK files, especially those released in October 1994. According to a July 1960 CIA information report, the CIA had an informant who was a touring "clergyman" in the Soviet Union. His timely reporting provided intelligence on one of the American defectors—Joseph Dutkanicz. Clearly, the CIA was keenly interested in these defectors, so interested that some of what it learned about them sometimes came from its most sensitive and valuable sources. Protection of these sources was necessary for their continued usefulness. When significant information was not put in a 201 file but in a separate file, as was sometimes done, it was to protect the valuable sources through which it was acquired. The Agency's attempt to protect a sensitive source is the key to the riddle of Oswald's 201 opening.

In this chapter we will explore one possible hypothesis: When the CIA opened Oswald's 201 file on December 9, 1960, they *had already learned,* probably from a sensitive source, about Oswald's request to come home. In this case, the true reason for the opening of Oswald's 201 file might have been too sensitive to include in that file. Their defector-status explanation did not betray the sensitive source, possibly a KGB source, permitting the exclusion of the true trigger event from the file it brought into being.

Americans Who Might Be Called "Defectors"

"Dear Dick," Hugh Cumming began a letter to the CIA on October 25, 1960.[4] Hugh S. Cumming, Jr., was the director of the State Department's Intelligence and Research Bureau (INR), and the Dick to whom he was writing was Richard M. Bissell, Jr., Deputy Director of Plans, CIA. Cumming began his letter by noting informal yet high-level—including the White House—interest in a special kind of defectors. This is how he described them:

> Our efforts to answer recent informal inquiries, including some from the White House Staff, have revealed that, though the CIA and the FBI have detailed records concerning Americans who have been recruited as intelligence agents by [Soviet] Bloc countries, there does not appear to be a complete listing of those Americans now living in Bloc countries who might be called "defectors." . . . These persons might be described as those persons who have either been capable of providing useful intelligence to the Bloc or those whose desire to resettle in Bloc countries has been significantly exploited for communist propaganda purposes.

Cumming enclosed a list of eighteen such individuals and asked Bissell to "verify and possibly expand" it. Number eight on the list was Lee Harvey Oswald, who was described only as a "tourist."

At the CIA, Bissell turned the matter over to Angleton's Counterintelligence (CI) Staff and Sheffield Edwards's Office of Security (OS), but CI took the lead. Asked for his recollection of the OS role in the opening of Oswald's 201 file, Robert L. Bannerman said, "It would have all gone through Angleton."[5] Bannerman was in a good position to know. At the time—November 1960—Bannerman was the deputy director of the Office of Security. The 201 opening was something on which "we worked very closely with Angleton and his staff,"[6] Bannerman recalls.

Bannerman had been the OS Deputy Chief for a decade under Sheffield Edwards. Bannerman had a close working relationship with Otto Otepka of the State Department Security Office (SY). When Bissell's request for information about the defectors list came in, Bannerman made a check with SY to see what they had and told his staff to support CI. "Working directly with Bissell's people on this, sending memos back and forth, would have been too formal," Bannerman remembers, "and we didn't bother with the usual formalities in this instance. I just put our people in touch with the people at CI. That was Paul Gaynor, Bruce Solie, and Morse Allen from my staff."

Paul Gaynor was Chief of OS's Security Research Staff (SRS), and he assigned Marguerite Stevens to send information over to CI.

A Stevens memo at the time shows that Bannerman verbally requested Gaynor to assemble information on American defectors.[7] The request, as Gaynor relayed it to Stevens, however, was worded in a peculiar way, as if to dissuade her from doing research on seven people.[8] Bannerman specified that he wanted information on American defectors "*other than* Bernon F. Mitchell and William H. Martin,[9] and five other defectors regarding whom Mr. Otepka of the State Department Security Office already has information" on in his files[10] [emphasis added]. One of the "five other defectors" that Stevens was not supposed to look into was Lee Harvey Oswald. In her response, however, Stevens said a few things about him and some of the others anyway, including the fact that they already had files with numbers. We will return to those numbers, briefly introduced in Chapter Four, later in this chapter.

Someone else in the CIA, however, was putting together information on these five defectors and planning to send something on each of them back to the State Department. That person was probably working for Angleton. Among the various sketches written on this select group can be found the inscription "Prepared by CI Staff for State–Nov. 60,"[11] In addition to Oswald, the other five defectors were Army Sergeant Joseph Dutkanicz, Libero Ricciardelli, a "tourist," Army Private Vladimir Sloboda, Robert E. Webster of the Rand Development Corporation, and Bruce Davis, also U.S. Army.

"Dear Hugh," began a November 3 interim response from Bissell to Cummings, "I have your letter of 25 October 1960 requesting certain information concerning Americans living in Bloc countries who might be called 'defectors.' Our files are being searched for the information you desire, and you will be hearing further from me in a few days."[12] Fifteen days later, November 18, Angleton's Deputy Chief of CI, S. H. Horton, sent the proposed reply for State to Bissell to look at.[13] On November 21, Bissell signed this letter with the defectors list attached, both assembled and drafted by Angleton's mole-hunting chief (CI/SIG), Birch D. O'Neal. The Oswald entry, the tenth on the CIA's version of the defectors list, was classified SECRET.

This description of Oswald is noteworthy because it contains something which is not true. It said "he appeared at the United States Embassy in Moscow and renounced his U.S. citizenship," a statement which was false.[14] The truth was that Oswald had tried but failed to renounce his citizenship. As we have seen in Chapters Two and Four, the CIA was in possession of the relevant facts concerning Oswald's incomplete attempt at renunciation, including what the State Department had learned from its reexamination of this very issue.

These points draw attention to the November 18, 1960, flat assertion by CI/SIG that Oswald had renounced his U.S. citizenship. What was the point of this assertion? Was CI/SIG truly incompetent or spinning some counterintelligence yarn? The State Department had long since determined that Oswald had not renounced his citizenship. And what are we to make now of the story Ann Egerter of CI/SIG told to the HSCA about CI/SIG's opening Oswald's 201 file? She said she opened it simply because Oswald was a defector, but we know that the dark details about Oswald's defection had been familiar to Angleton's CI Staff since November 1959.

The five defectors that OS/SRS was asked not to research were in fact investigated by the "CI staff." Two of them had 201 numbers which were opened almost at the same moment: Dutkanicz was 289236 and Oswald was 289248. Egerter opened Oswald's 201 on December 9, 1960, and the proximity of Dutkanicz's 201 number to Oswald's suggests that Dutkanicz's was opened closer to the date that the CIA responded to the State Department: November 21. Dutkanicz's 201 could not have been opened much earlier, and probably not as early as the Soviet press announcement of his defection—a Tass (Soviet) blurb on July 27 or 28, 1960. The Tass report was originally held in "CI/SIG files."[15]

The CIA probably already knew about Dutkanicz's defection—from an unusual and sensitive source whose reporting ended up in a file being kept by yet another component of the CIA which was interested in this group of defectors. Their files were "set up" in a soft file by Branch 6 ("Soviet Realities") of the Soviet Russia Division. This soft file was entitled "American Defectors to the USSR."[16] Oswald's name appears to be missing from this file, but clues to its probable earlier presence remain, a subject to which we will return shortly. First we need to establish what we know about this question: When did Oswald first inquire about coming home?

The HSCA Failure to Investigate

The Warren Commission's failure to investigate Oswald's CIA files leaves an indelible blemish on its credibility. Many aspects of the HSCA investigation deserve credit, and we are indebted to it for the work it did trying to decipher the CIA's files. However, the HSCA investigation mishandled a fundamental question about the opening of Oswald's 201 file: When did Oswald first write to the U.S. Embassy about his wish to return to America? On this crucial question the HSCA failed to take seriously the most important piece of all—Oswald's December 1960 request to come home. Oswald put his request in a letter, and that letter's history was excluded from any examination of the issues surrounding Oswald's 201 file.

The Warren Commission's failure to look at Oswald's 201 file renders, by default, the HSCA's interpretation as the principal official one on this subject. It behooves us, therefore, to look at the details of the HSCA report on the subject of why Oswald's 201 file was opened and why it took a year to open it. The HSCA report connected the two in this question:

> ***Why the delay in opening Oswald's 201 file?***
> A confidential State Department telegram dated October 31, 1959, sent from Moscow to Washington and forwarded to the CIA, reported that Oswald, a recently discharged Marine, had appeared at the U.S. Embassy in Moscow to renounce his American citizenship and "has offered Soviets any information he has acquired as [an] enlisted radar operator." At least three other communications of a confidential nature that gave more detail on the Oswald case were sent to the CIA in about the same time period. Agency officials questioned by the committee testified that the substance of the October 21, 1959, cable was sufficiently important to warrant the opening of a 201 file. Oswald's file was not, however, opened until December 9, 1960.[17]

The HSCA rightfully felt that it had to know where documents about Oswald had been disseminated inside the CIA prior to the opening of his 201 file. When the HSCA asked for these records, the "Agency advised the committee that because document dissemination records of relatively low national security significance are retained for only a 5-year period, they were no longer in existence for the years 1959–63.''[18]

As previously discussed, this was not true, and these internal dissemination records were released to the public in 1993. In 1978, however, the HSCA's probe of Oswald's 201 file ground to a halt due to factual errors and faulty analysis. For example, the HSCA report contained this untrue statement about why the 201 was opened:

> An Agency memorandum, dated September 18, 1975, indicates that Oswald's file was opened on December 9, 1960, in response to the receipt of five documents: two from the FBI, two from the State Department and one from the Navy. This explanation, however, is inconsistent with the presence in Oswald's file of four State Department documents dated in 1959 and a fifth dated May 25, 1960. It is, of course, possible that the September 18, 1975, memorandum is referring to State Department documents that were received by the Directorate for Plans in October and November of 1960 and that the earlier State Department communications had been received by the CIA's Office of Security but not the Directorate for Plans.[19]

First of all, the CIA memorandum had not said the 201 had been opened ''in response to the receipt of five documents.'' Secondly, it was the HSCA—not the CIA—that offered the rationalization that perhaps the Agency's Office of Security received those documents and did not pass them on to the Directorate of Plans until December 1960. Since the 201 was opened by CI/SIG in the Directorate of Plans, this argument would explain the one-year delay. However, we now know what the HSCA did not: the same element in the DDP that opened the 201, CI/SIG, was itself in possession of most of those same Oswald files all along.

Perhaps the most significant problem for the HSCA is the way it handled the most obvious clue of all—a CIA memo that mentioned another reason Oswald's 201 file was opened. This reason was cited in the very first sentence of a September 18, 1975, memo written by Angleton's successor as Chief of Counterintelligence, George T.

Kalaris, which the HSCA even quoted it in its report. Here is what Kalaris said:

> Lee Harvey Oswald's 201 file was first opened under the name of Lee Henry Oswald on 9 December 1960 as a result of his "defection" to the USSR on 31 October 1959 and renewed interest in Oswald brought about by his queries concerning possible reentry into the United States.[20]

This is an amazing statement because no one was supposed to know where Oswald was at that time, let alone what he wanted to do. What did the HSCA make of this sentence? The answer is disappointing and cavalier. Here is the pertinent passage from the HSCA report:

> The September 18, 1975, memorandum also states that Oswald's file was opened on December 9, 1960, as a result of this "defection" to the U.S.S.R. on October 31, 1969, and renewed interest in Oswald brought about by his queries concerning possible reentry into the United States. There is no indication, however, that Oswald expressed to any U.S. Government official an intention to return to the United States until mid-February 1961.

The HSCA assumed that the "U.S. Government" did not know where Oswald was until his letter arrived on Snyder's desk on February 13, 1961. And so the committee failed to follow up on Kalaris's remark, and relied totally on the testimony of "the Agency employee who was directly responsible for initiating the opening action."

Again, that person was Ann Egerter, and she had testified that the trigger event for the opening was the State Department defector list:

> This individual explained that the CIA had received a request from the State Department for information concerning American defectors. After compiling the requested information, she responded to the inquiry and then opened a 201 file on each defector involved. Even so, this analysis only explained why a file on Oswald was finally opened; it did not explain the seemingly long delay in opening of the file.[21]

Egerter's testimony led the HSCA to review other 201 files where there were delays. However, as discussed in Chapter Four, their review was flawed because it failed to specifically address whether or not these delays persisted, as in Oswald's case, long after the defections were known to the Agency.

The HSCA was unwilling to draw a firm conclusion. In the end, they abandoned the issue, insinuating that it was because of the CIA's refusal to turn over the internal routing sheets. "In the absence of dissemination records," the HSCA noted, "the issue could not be resolved." That comment was wise; what was not wise was to glibly dismiss a memorandum by the chief of the CIA's Counterintelligence Staff. The two questions the HSCA should have asked are: Did Oswald, in December 1960, express an interest in coming home? If so, did the CIA learn of it? The answer to both questions appears to be yes.

The Missing Letter

The HSCA did have another crucial piece of evidence that fit perfectly with the Kalaris memorandum's statement that Oswald had made "queries" in 1960 about coming home. The committee failed to consider that these two pieces fit together. This second piece was not obscure: It was published in the Warren Commission volumes as Commission Exhibit number 245, the first letter American Consul Snyder received from Oswald—after more than a year of not knowing where he was. Snyder received the letter on February 13, 1961. The first sentence of this letter contains a key piece of evidence: In that sentence Oswald wrote, "Since I have not received a reply to *my letter of December 1960, I am writing again* asking that you consider my request for the return of my American passport"[22] [emphasis added].

The February 1961 letter was itself a momentous communication from Oswald to a U.S. government official. Coming at the end of a fourteen-month silence, this letter serves as the documentary turning point of Oswald's stay in Russia: It placed him in Minsk and began the eighteen-month saga of his return to America. The reference in the first sentence to an earlier letter presents historical inquiry with an interesting fork in the road, for it seems to contradict an entry in his diary. Traveling down one path, we accept the diary entry as true, which then requires us to accept that Oswald's February 1961 letter and the Kalaris 1975 memorandum are not. The other path at the fork leads us deep into the CIA labyrinth again. Kalaris's memo indicating the CIA had learned of Oswald's queries by December 9, 1960, raises the question of the source of this information. This path becomes even darker when we discover the true fate of the missing letter.

First, the Warren Commission's handling of Oswald's February 1961 letter deserves our attention. The Warren Report said Oswald "asked for the return of his passport," initially screening the other part of Oswald's sentence, which said, "I am writing again" to ask for the passport.[23] Similarly, the Warren Report went on to discuss nearly every detail of Oswald's letter, leaving the first sentence—the one explaining that he had written before—for last. "In this letter," the Warren Report added, almost as an afterthought, "Oswald referred to a previous letter which he said had gone unanswered; there is evidence that such a letter was never sent."[24]

The "evidence" that Oswald's December letter was "never sent," does not hold up well under close scrutiny. Just two pieces of evidence were offered by the Warren Commission. First, Oswald's diary entry for February 1, 1961: "Make my *first request* to American Embassy, Moscow for reconsidering my position," [emphasis added] Oswald had written. This was hardly conclusive since, by his own hand, Oswald had also informed the embassy about the request in December.

The other piece of evidence the Commission offered to show that there had been no earlier letter was Richard Snyder's testimony. The former Moscow Embassy Consul had this exchange with Allen Dulles and William Coleman:

MR. COLEMAN: Had you received a letter from Mr. Oswald at a date of December 1960, the way he mentioned in the first paragraph of this letter?

MR. SNYDER: No, sir; we did not.

MR. COLEMAN: This [February 1961 letter] is the first letter you received?

MR. SNYDER: This is the first communication since he left Moscow.

MR. DULLES: When you say he left Moscow, that was in—

MR. SNYDER: November 1959, sir.

MR. DULLES: November 1959?

MR. SNYDER: That is what we presume was the date.

MR. COLEMAN: Mr. Dulles, we have other evidence that he didn't leave until January 7, 1960.

MR. DULLES: The last the embassy heard from him was in November 1959?

MR. SNYDER: Yes, sir.[25]

The fact that Snyder had not received the letter is not hard evidence that it was not sent. Reading this part of Snyder's testimony does little to inspire confidence in the Warren Commission's analysis of this point. On the other hand, it does conjure up an image of Allen Dulles puffing on his pipe as he pondered the implications of this lengthy period where Oswald was out of touch.

During the Warren Commission's investigation of Oswald's foreign activities, William T. Coleman, Jr., and W. David Slawson wrote a report (dated March 6, 1964) about Oswald's life in Russia.[26] In a short paragraph blemished by a typographical error about the date of Oswald's second letter,[27] the report contained this solitary sentence on the missing letter: "In the letter received February 13, 1961, he [Oswald] said that he had written an earlier letter but apparently the embassy never received the earlier letter." The implied acceptance of the letter in this sentence does not fit with the final report's suggestion that it never existed in the first place.

An idea that supported the "never-existed" hypothesis was sent to the Warren Commission during its investigation but was not used in the final report. This idea came, not surprisingly, from the CIA, where it was formulated by Lee Wigren, Chief of Research and Analysis for the Counterintelligence Office in the Soviet Russia Division and put in a January 1964 report for the commission. Wigren wrote: "One possible explanation for reference to a spurious letter may be that Oswald wished to give the Embassy the impression that he had initiated correspondence regarding repatriation before having renewed his identity document on 4 January 1961."[28] Although this fit the commission's notion that the missing letter was fictitious, the final report did not use Wigren's theory or make any reference to it at all.

The State Department's own analysis of this problem after the

Kennedy assassination went only as far as to state that the letter "was never received."[29] This is a far cry from the Warren Commission's suggestion that it was "never sent." In sum, the embassy's nonreceipt of an earlier Oswald letter and the contradiction between Oswald's diary and his February letter were all the evidence the commission could muster for the proposition that Oswald had not sent an earlier letter. Ironically, just twelve lines later on the same page, the Warren Report acknowledged that "the Soviet authorities had undoubtedly intercepted and read the correspondence between Oswald and the Embassy and knew of his plans."[30] Yet the report failed to consider whether the KGB might have intercepted and held on to Oswald's first letter.

In a December 9, 1963, FBI interview, Marina said Oswald had talked with her—prior to their marriage on April 30, 1961—about his unanswered mail. The FBI special agents who interviewed her, Anatole A. Boguslav and Wallace R. Heitman, described that part of Marina's interview in their report:

> Marina said again that he had met Oswald in March and they had been married on April 30, 1961. At the time she met him and at the time she married him, she was of the impression that Oswald did not want to return to the United States. She said Oswald had prior to their marriage told her that he thought he could not return to the United States. He had told her he had written the American Embassy letters about returning to the United States, and they had not answered the letters. She said Oswald was therefore of the impression that he could not return. Marina said that if she had known of any desire on the part of Oswald to return to the United States at the time of their marriage, she probably would not have married him.[31]

At this point, Oswald wrongly suspected that it was the American Embassy, not the KGB, that was responsible for his letter's disappearance.

On February 28, 1961, the American Embassy in Moscow responded to Oswald's second letter, specifically mentioning his story about the December letter. Snyder wrote: "We have received your recent letter concerning your desire to return to the United States. *Your earlier letter of December 1960 which you mentioned in your present letter does not appear to have been received at the Embassy*'' [emphasis added].[32] This passage reflects Snyder's reaction to the story at the time, and makes it clear that Snyder had allowed for the possibility that it might have been sent.

This issue moved closer to resolution after the fall of communism in the Soviet Union. For a moment, the remnants of the former KGB apparatus opened up, a process which allowed glimpses into the KBG's *Narim* file on Oswald. ''Narim'' is a Russian word for turbot, a river fish. The event that concerns our present discussion was an American television news broadcast. ABC aired a show on November 22, 1991, entitled ''An ABC News Nightline Investigation: The KGB Oswald Files.'' During this program, hosted by Ted Koppel, the subject of Oswald's December 1960 letter to the American Embassy came up. Here is the pertinent portion of the transcript:

SAWYER: On February 13th, 1961, the U.S. embassy received a letter from Oswald that read, ''Since I have not received a reply to my letter of December 1960, I am writing again.'' What letter was he referring to? Theorists have speculated he never did write it, that he was simply unstable, or lying. *In fact, the KGB intercepted Oswald's missing first letter, and the original still exists inside the Oswald file.* In subsequent correspondence, Oswald blustered, reminding Richard Snyder of U.S. obligations to an American citizen [emphasis added].[33]

Although there is still no copy of this letter in the U.S. National Archives, ABC claims to have verified its existence with the KGB. Thus it appeared that Oswald's story was true after all, and the Warren Commission's theory that Oswald had never sent such a letter was not.

As discussed in a previous section of this chapter, the HSCA's probe into Oswald's 201 opening repeated the Warren Commission's erroneous rejection of the December letter story. In so doing, however, the HSCA had to rebut not just Oswald's statement in his second letter, but also the memorandum written by the CIA's Chief of Counterintelligence, George Kalaris. Both government investigations thus dismissed the authenticity of Oswald's original query about coming home. It is more logical to conclude that Oswald did send the letter and that it was permanently impounded by the KGB.

The next question is: Did the CIA indeed find out about Oswald's

December query? In order to answer this question, it might be useful to discuss how closely the CIA was able to monitor American defectors in Russia. We turn now to the Agency's level of interest in this unusual group of people.

American Defectors to the U.S.S.R.

For SR/6, American defectors in the Soviet Union were potentially rich repositories of information useful to the Agency's operations in the Soviet Union. From SR/6's point of view, each defector was a walking encyclopedia of his own "reality" in Russia. "Soviet Realities" was another way of referring to SR/6, because building retrievable encyclopedic descriptions of real places in Russia—down to the lampposts, buildings, mailboxes, street signs, and matchbooks—was one of its principal missions."[34]

Sometime in 1960, SR/6 set up a "soft file" on the Americans who had defected to the Soviet Union during the previous eighteen or so months. A "soft file" is an informal file that can be maintained just about anywhere, as opposed to a formal file bearing the name of the originating element, such as a Security (OS) file, which could be maintained only by the Office of Security. In 1960 SR/6 set up just such an informal file on these American defectors. In a 1966 memorandum for record, a CIA person, whose name is still classified,"[35] wrote this about the SR/6 soft file:

> The attached material was part of a soft file entitled "American Defectors to the USSR," which was set up by SR/6 (Support) around 1960 and maintained by various SR components until ca. 1963. The compilations were derived from a variety of sources, and contain both classified and overt data.[36]

"Attached material" meant the informal chronologies of each of the defectors, typed entries in chronological order with handwritten notes around them. The time period covered in this SR/6 soft file, "around" 1960 to "ca. 1963," overlaps perfectly the time between this group's defection and their return to the United States. All of this particular group of defectors redefected to the United States by

1963, except Dutkanicz, the most intriguing of the group, who died in the Soviet Union.[37]

The 1966 memo about the 1960 SR/6 defectors file has other important clues in it. For example, this paragraph:

> In the fall of 1966, the files were turned over to CIA Staff. In most instances, basic information was then extracted for the US Defector Machine Program. In all instances in which the material was unique, or represented a valuable collation effort, it has been incorporated into the appropriate 201 file, along with a copy of this memorandum.[38]

This memo indicates that there were instances where the CIA had information about these defectors between 1960 and 1963 that was not in their 201 files at the time and was not added to them until late 1966.

This filing system is an example of what is referred to in the intelligence community as "compartmentation." The whole picture is not kept in one place. Instead, pieces are kept in separate compartments because of the sensitive sources used to get those pieces of information. This presented a quandary for the CIA when the Kennedy assassination required a review of this kind of information. The 1966 memo about the SR/6 file complained about this problem in this way:

> It is suggested that any dissemination of this data should be coordinated with SB [Soviet Bloc] Division and with CI staff (CI/MRO), in view of the *frequently inadequate sourcing* and of the fact that disseminations have already been made through the US Defector Machine Program [emphasis added].[39]

This pattern of inadequate source material in the 201 files of certain defectors would also befall Oswald's 201 file from the time of its opening and beyond.

We know that Oswald was in this group at the time the soft file was set up in 1960.[40] He probably still was when the State Department passed the results of its own status check on this special group of defectors to the FBI and CIA on May 17, 1962,[41] the time at which Oswald was preparing to depart for the U.S. In Oswald's case, the probable event triggering his 201 opening—his December queries about returning home—would likely not have been included in his 201 file in order to protect the Soviet source. On the other hand, the news of Oswald's decision to return to the U.S.—as reflected in his second letter to Snyder and routinely passed to the CIA by the State Department at the CONFIDENTIAL level—was placed in his 201 file.

We have evidence that suggests the SR/6 soft file was already open by the time of the State Department's defector inquiry of October 25, 1960. It comes from the October 31, 1960, OS/SRS (Office of Security/Security Research Staff) memo on American defectors, written by Marguerite D. Stevens.[42] This was the memo in which Stevens had indicated that the Deputy Chief of Security, Bannerman, had asked SRS for information on individuals other than Webster, Oswald, Ricciardelli, Sloboda, and Dutkanicz—the very defectors who were the subjects of the SR/6 soft file. In spite of these directions, Stevens's memo did mention a few things on some of these defectors, and gave file numbers belonging to five of them: ''Robert Edward Webster, EE-18854; Lee Harvey Oswald, MS-11165; Libero Ricciardelli, MS-8295; Vladimir Sloboda, MS-10565; and Joseph Dutkanicz, MS-10724.''[43]

These file numbers are intriguing. Oswald's MS-11165 has so far appeared only on Stevens's memo. Why did four of the defectors have ''MS'' numbers and Webster have an ''EE'' number? Several former employees were unable to recall what ''MS'' or ''EE'' meant, although Ray Rocca, of Counterintelligence Research and Analysis, suggested (before he died in 1994) that MS might have been ''miscellaneous security.'' This seems redundant because Oswald already had a security file—OS-351-164. A former Soviet Russia Division employee suggested Rocca might have been wrong about this because such important defectors as Ricciardelli, Dutkanicz, Sloboda, and Oswald were hardly miscellaneous cases. Another possibility is that the MS reflected the military service status of these other four men,[44] while the EE might have reflected Webster's civilian status.[45] On the other hand, EE-29229 was a CIA file number for Gerry Patrick Hemming, an ex-Marine. The CIA should explain to the public what these file designators meant.

Several of these defectors ''have been of interest to CIA,'' Stevens said in the October 31, 1960, Security Research Staff memo, and she then listed each of them with a remark. Part of Stevens's memo is still classified, but one person on her list was Sloboda, another American serviceman who defected a month after Dutkanicz. "Sloboda is currently of interest to Security," she wrote, "in view of his assignment prior to his defection to the Soviet Union, via East Germany, on 3 August [1960]."[46] Like Dutkanicz, Sloboda had been in Army Military Intelligence (MI) at the time he defected. Sloboda's rank had been specialist five, and he had worked as a translator-interrogator and document clerk with the Army's 513th MI Group, in Frankfurt, Germany.[47]

"He had contact with at least one representative of CIA," Stevens wrote of Sloboda's Army work in her 1960 memo, "and was in a position to [have] learned the identities of CIA personnel at the EGIS Center," presumably an intelligence center associated with Sloboda's Army unit."[48] Again, like Dutkanicz, Sloboda had been recruited by the KGB prior to his defection. Here is what one CIA report said about it:

> Sloboda's prior KGB involvement was confirmed by [redacted] as reported in [redacted]. See attached memorandum of 28 March 1962 in regard to passage of this information to the Army. Further indications are the facts that Sloboda was a KGB resettlement case and that he later told an American Embassy Moscow official that he had been blackmailed and framed into going to the USSR. See Moscow Emb. tels A-572, 23 October 1962, and 851, 23 March 1962.[49]

The similarities between Dutkanicz and Sloboda were stunning. Both had been in Germany, in the Army, in Military Intelligence Branch, had defected within days of each other, and had been recruited by the KGB prior to their defections. The CIA's counterintelligence analysts even concluded that both defections were "precipitated" by the same circumstance: increased Army security measures.[50]

The Sloboda case was nastier because his true past had been concealed from the U.S. intelligence and security checks that were conducted on him. Just how serious the case was can be seen from an October 12, 1960, memorandum from Scotty Miler, a deputy to Angleton on the CI staff. Miler's memo contained this revelation:

> 1. On basis of report from Berlin [redacted] orally asked the Army for any information substantiating allegations that subject, prior to escaping to West and enlisting in the U.S. Army, had been a Staff Officer in Polish Intelligence. CI/F records were negative. A copy of the ACSI [Assistant Chief of Staff for Intelligence, U.S. Army] report concerning subject, dated 15 September 1960, was provided us through CI/Liaison but not formally transmitted to the Agency.
> 2. The attached report appears to answer the question concerning Polish Intelligence, but, of course, raises additional questions concerning Soviet Intelligence not answered in the memorandum. Specifically, there was also an interest in attempting to determine if subject could have had any knowledge of the [redacted] case and, again, except by inference in para 7 [redacted], there is no positive answer. On the larger question of general knowledge of this Agency and Agency activities we presume [redacted] will provide answers.
> 3. We do not plan an immediate follow-up inquiry to ACSI about the attached, but if you have any questions you believe might be answered by ACSI, please let us know and we can arrange to have them forwarded.[51]

When we combine the fact that Sloboda was a Polish or Soviet agent while he was working for the Army with the fact that Sloboda defected immediately after Dutkanicz, who was in the Army, it is natural to wonder whether the two cases were tied together in some sinister way. For example: Could Sloboda have been a spotter or Dutkanicz's control? How sure can we be about Sloboda's loyalties?

One of the last of the original group of defectors to return to the U.S. was Libero Ricciardelli. He came back in 1963, and was debriefed by the CIA on July 18, 1963, as this passage from a CIA Domestic Contacts Division memo makes clear:

> 1. This Division has no objection to your revealing to the FBI that Subject is a source of this Agency, provided the FBI does not disclose the source's identity outside the Bureau.
> 2. Subject, a former US citizen, who in 1958 defected to the USSR, and acquired Soviet citizenship in 1959, was interviewed by our field representative on 18 July 1963, at the house of Subject's father in Needham, Massachussetts. The results of our representative's first debriefing session with Subject are contained in the attached report, 00-A-3,269,779.[52]

It is hard not to wonder why these defectors seem to change their minds about the Soviet Union quickly and to such an extent that most were able and willing to provide the CIA with all the military and economic information they had learned while in the Communist superpower. Obviously these American defectors would be full of useful information to the CIA if they returned to the U.S.

We will later examine the possibility that Oswald might have been deliberately sent into Russia or manipulated into going there. For now, it is interesting to observe that SR/6 began files on these men at the time of their defections. Their own, even if somewhat limited, military backgrounds would facilitate observation of things military that civilian tourists might not notice. We should also observe that CI/SIG opened their 201 files later than was customary. In the intervening months, CI/OPS [Operations] displayed an interest in information on Oswald. And finally, we should note that the head of CI, James Angleton, had begun his hunt for a mole in the Soviet Russia (SR) Division before Oswald's release from the Marines in September 1959.

Before considering what the CIA might have been able to learn about Oswald in Russia during the period he was lost in Minsk, we would be well served to ask this question: Is there any hard evidence that the CIA had roving human assets in the Soviet Union at this time? Not surprisingly, the answer is yes.

The "Clergyman" In Lvov

On July 28, 1960, the Soviet news agency Tass reported that "John Joseph Dutkanicz" had requested asylum in the U.S.S.R. On August 25, 1960, U.S. military authorities in West Berlin announced that Dutkanicz had been absent without leave since July 6, 1960, and added that "the Army had no confirmation of the report that he had defected to the Soviets, or that he was in Moscow."[53] The CIA did know that Dutkanicz had defected, and they knew that he was not in Moscow, but in Lvov. This information, as well as much more about Dutkanicz and what the CIA really knew about him, was described in a memorandum responding to "questions" in late 1964, right after the publication of the Warren Report.

The subject of this memorandum, written on October 2, 1964, by

Lee Wigren, Chief of "R" [research and analysis] in the Counterintelligence Branch of the Soviet Russia Division, was "Questions Concerning Defectors Joseph J. Dutkanicz (201-289236) and Vladimir O. Sloboda (201-287527)."[54] With respect to Dutkanicz's Army assignment at time of his defection in July 1960, Wigren's memo said that although the Army Case Summary showed Dutkanicz was assigned to the 32nd Signal Battalion in Darmstadt, "his wife indicated that he had CIC [Counterintelligence Corps] connections." Mrs. Dutkanicz told State Department officials some intriguing details about her husband:

> In an interview at the American Embassy Moscow on 5 December 1961 (cited in DBA-288, 24 January 1962), she indicated that their trip behind the iron curtain "had been made possible because her husband worked for the CIC [Counterintelligence Corps] and was allowed to do things an ordinary 'GI' could not do."[55]

As previously discussed, Dutkanicz's 201 file was 201-289236, just twelve numbers away from Oswald's—201-289248.[56] The CIA personnel who had been handling Dutkanicz's 201 had left handwritten clues indicating that Mrs. Dutkanicz was right. "There are also penciled notations in the [Dutkanicz] 201 file," Wigren said, "suggesting that his Army assignment may have included intelligence functions of some kind."[57]

The CI Staff summary for the State Department in November 1960, marked "secret," said, "We are informed that Dutkanicz has had difficulties with his wife and that she reported that he had relatives in the USSR and that he admitted that he was a Communist and that he had associated with German Nationals who were Communists."[58]

As Wigren looked deeper into the files of these two U.S. Army defectors, he noticed that both men had had connections to the KGB. Again, the Army Case Summary was Wigren's source document:

> Dutkanicz himself told American Embassy officials in Moscow that he had been approached by KGB representatives in a bar near Darmstadt in 1958 and had accepted recruitment as a result of their threats and inducements. He claimed to have

> given them minimum cooperation from then until his defection, although the Army considered it probable that he had done more than he admitted. A further indication of his KGB involvement before defection is the fact that the special decree granting him Soviet citizenship was enacted three months before his arrival in the U.S.S.R.[59]

The cause of Dutkanicz's defection had been the Army's security investigations itself. He "told American Embassy Moscow officials that he had informed his KGB handler that he was under investigation for security reasons. He defected soon after, in accord with a KGB suggestion that he do so."[60]

No sooner than he had defected, however, Dutkanicz was talking with a CIA informant inside the Soviet Union. From the JFK files released by the CIA in 1994 comes the startling news that on July 10, 1960, Dutkanicz met a "clergyman" in the lobby of the Intourist Hotel in Lvov. The "clergyman" submitted this account of his encounter with Dutkanicz to the CIA that same July:

> 1. On the morning of Monday, 10 July 1960, at about 0930-1000 hours I chanced to meet one Joseph *Dutkanych,* [sic] allegedly a defected US citizen, in the lobby of the Intourist Hotel in the city of Lvov, USSR.
> 2. I was recognized and approached by Mr. Dutkanych while making my way up the hotel stairway toward my hotel room. After the customary greetings, I suggested he accompany me to my room where we remained for not more than ten minutes. Since I had arranged that morning for a private conducted tour of Lvov our conversation dealt primarily with the points of interest I was scheduled to see.[61]

The two men arranged to have dinner together that evening, but the clergyman in Lvov said, "I never saw him again as he failed to keep his appointment." Thus the CIA did have at least one interesting and capable informant in the Soviet Union whose timely reporting concerned the American defector in Lvov. Which brings us to Oswald, who was supposed to be lost in Minsk. Indeed, he was in Minsk, but was he lost?

A Clandestine Soviet Source on Oswald?

The CIA has overtly maintained that Oswald's 201 file was opened as a result of his name appearing on a list of defectors from the State Department. Yet that list was sent to the CIA on October 25, 1960, more than *six weeks before* Ann Egerter opened the 201 file on December 9. Is there a possibility that Oswald's desire to return home was known by December 1960: As we have seen, fragmentary but solid evidence has slowly accumulated over the years that suggests the Agency might have had ways of finding out about Oswald's activities in Russia.

In the present chapter we have already taken some tentative steps to explore the hypothesis that Oswald's 201 file was opened, at least in part, due to his query about coming home. When did Oswald actually begin to talk about coming home? The first signs of his disillusionment with life in Russia appeared as early as May 1960, but grew in the fall. In an entry for May 1, 1960, in his diary, Oswald wrote that he felt "uneasy inside" after his friend Ziger advised him to return to the United States.[62] In a diary entry for "August-September" 1960, Oswald wrote that he was becoming "increasingly conscious" of the "sort" of a society he lived in.[63]

After returning to the United States, Oswald often commented on life in Russia. On the positive side, he would point to the Soviet systems of public education and medical care, the fact that everyone "was trained to do something," and the system of regular wage and salary increases. His negative comments focused on the general low quality of life, the lack of freedom, and the scarcity of food products. In this regard, he was especially critical of the contrast between ordinary workers and Communist Party members.

Oswald came to view the Communist Party of the Soviet Union as corrupt. Only party members could afford luxuries, he said, while common workers could afford only food and clothing. Party members were all "opportunists," Oswald said, who "shouted the loudest" but were interested only in their own welfare. Oswald expressed similar views in a manuscript which he worked on in Russia.[64] The "spontaneous" demonstrations for Soviet holidays or distinguished visitors were "organized," he said, and elections were ''supervised'' to ensure a high turnout and continued Communist Party control.

On January 4, 1961, one year after he had been issued his ''stateless'' residence permit, Oswald was summoned to the passport office in Minsk and asked if he still wanted to become a Soviet citizen. He replied that he did not, but asked that his residence permit be extended for another year. The entry in his diary for January 4–31 reads: ''I am starting to reconsider my desire about staying. The work is drab. The money I get has nowhere to be spent. No nightclubs or bowling alleys, no places of recreation accept [sic] the trade union dances. I have had enough.''

Because the opening of Oswald's 201 file on December 9, 1960, was after his decision to return home but before the embassy knew of his whereabouts, it is reasonable to think seriously about the possibility that someone in America knew how to communicate with Oswald or to learn what the Soviets were saying about him. Is there any evidence that Oswald was in communication with someone outside of Minsk or Russia during the ''lost'' period? The answer might be yes to both. It is possible, but by no means firm, that Oswald had contact with someone in Moscow or outside of the Soviet Union.

There was a person in Moscow that Oswald could have telephoned if he had wanted to. This person slips through relatively unnoticed during the period of Oswald's defection, but it appears Oswald did try to contact him in 1961. When Oswald, accompanied this time by Marina, visited the U.S. Embassy in Moscow in July, he looked up the name of this individual in his address book. According to an FBI report by Special Agents Heitman and Griffin about their interview with Marina, that is what occurred in 1961:

> At the time of Marina's first visit to Moscow with Oswald, he referred to his address book to find the name of an individual. It was Oswald's intention to call this person on the telephone. He showed the name to Marina. This name she has identified from a photograph of one page of Oswald's address book which contains the name written in the Latin alphabet, ''Leo Setyaev.''[65]

Marina said the written name and associated writing in the address book were not hers or Oswald's. The leading candidate would appear to be Leo Setyaev himself.

Whether this handwriting in Oswald's address book was Setyaev's or someone else's, Oswald behaved as if Setyaev were a person he might call on for help. The Heitman-Griffin FBI report explains:

> Marina said Oswald tried to contact this person, but had been unsuccessful. Marina asked Oswald who this individual Leo Setyaev was. Oswald replied he was a man who had helped him make some money after his arrival in Moscow by assisting him in a broadcast for Radio Moscow. Marina asked Oswald what he had said, and he told her he had criticized the United States and said Russia was a better place in which to live. Marina asked him why he said this, and Oswald replied it was necessary to make this propaganda because at the time he had wanted to live in Russia.

This apparent connection to Setyaev was interesting indeed, as was this additional detail provided by Marina: Oswald said Setyaev had visited him at the "Hotel Metropole in Moscow." There has been a great deal of misunderstanding about the date of Setyaev's visit to Oswald, most notably, that the visit was on October 19 at the Berlin Hotel. Setyaev, however, has been interviewed and described the room in which he made the visit with Oswald. The room he describes appears to be the one described by Aline Mosby.

In the FBI interview with Heitman and Griffin, Marina recalled other relevant information about Setyaev's visit to the Hotel Metropole, including a photograph of Oswald:

> She advised further Setyaev had taken a photograph of Oswald during his visit to the latter at the Hotel Metropole. This photograph is one of the photographs of Oswald presently in possession of investigators of the assassination as Marina recalls seeing it. It is the photograph of Oswald standing in a room, in which he wears a black suit, a white shirt, and a tie. Marina said Oswald looks quite serious in the photograph. The photograph is about 5" by 7" in size. Marina said it was obvious to her Oswald was quite worried in this photograph because she noticed that a vein was standing out very noticeably on the right side of his face.

This attire sounds almost identical to what Snyder said Oswald was wearing during the October 31 defection at the Embassy, only this time the oddity was not the pair of white gloves, but a vein on his face. Heitman and Griffin just happened to have on hand for the interview with Marina ten photographs of Leo and Anita Setyaev.[66]

It appears that Setyaev was known to both the CIA and the FBI. A sensitive June 24, 1960, LINGUAL intercept, "60F24," was addressed to Leo Setyaev by Charles John Pagenhardt, and a May 1964 CIA report on LINGUAL intercepts related to the "Oswald case" explained that the Agency's interest in this letter was based on the fact that Setyaev was listed in Oswald's address book and also because Pagenhardt was known to have "contemplated defecting to the USSR."[67] The CIA document also states: "Setyaev and Pagenhardt are known to the FBI." This sidesteps, however, the issue of what the interest in Setyaev was at the time this letter was intercepted—June 24, 1960.

The Warren Commission appears not to have bothered to consider whether Setyaev had was an informant for the CIA. This was the commission's assessment:

> On October 19, Oswald was probably interviewed in his hotel room by a man named Leo Setyaev, who said that he was a reporter for Radio Moscow seeking statements from American tourists about their impressions of Moscow, but who was probably also acting for the KGB. Two years later, Oswald told officials at the American Embassy that he had made a few routine comments to Setyaev of no political significance. The interview with Setyaev may, however, have been the occasion of an attempt by the KGB, in accordance with regular practice, to assess Oswald or even to elicit compromising statements from him; the interview was apparently never broadcast.[68]

The CIA checked Setyaev's name with a KGB informant of their own, who said he had "never heard the name."[69] Setyaev claimed to have made a tape recording of the interview with Oswald in his room in the Metropole Hotel,[70] but "erased it immediately because Oswald's remarks were too political for the light tourist chatter that he needed for his show."[71]

More important is the circumstantial but credible evidence that Oswald had a contact outside the Soviet Union. It comes from his friends in Minsk, especially the girlfriend he originally wanted to marry, Ella German. During his research into Oswald's stay in

Minsk, investigative journalist Peter Wronski interviewed Oswald's first flame in Russia—Ella German. This passage is from Wronski's 1991 interview with Ella:

PETER WRONSKI: Did he tell you about his relatives?
ELLA GERMAN: No. You know . . . I was surprised. He didn't tell me he had a mother. He only used to speak about a cousin. . . .
PETER WRONSKI: Did he correspond with America?
ELLA GERMAN: He only said that he used to get some letters from his cousin. He received a package of books, he told me once. I said, "why not with things?" He said, "no, the customs duty is very expensive here. And on books there is no customs duty." . . .
PETER WRONSKI: And from whom did he get these books?
ELLA GERMAN: From his cousin.
PETER WRONSKI: Did he name him?
ELLA GERMAN: No, he didn't name him. . . . . He just said a cousin.[72]

His cousins had no idea where Oswald was and sent no packages, let alone letters, to Russia. Yet this passage suggests that Oswald was receiving mail from someone outside Russia, and that somebody might have been from the United States. Whoever it was, Oswald evidently decided to lie about it. In addition, Oswald gave his friend Titovitz a book—possibly during the "lost in Minsk" period—but then momentarily pulled back the book to razor out a dedication on the corner of the first page.[73]

Did Oswald go to the trial of Francis Powers? Dr. Lawrence Haapanen framed the case for such a visit about as incisively as it has been recently. With the understanding that the following is circumstantial and speculative, here is the "base case" for Oswald's presence at the Powers U-2 trial August 17–18, 1960. There are three pre- and one post-assassination pieces of evidence. First, that in a room full of distinguished observers from around the world, virtually all of whom are dressed in suits, we have one young man sitting, coatless, in a shirt that looks a great deal like the one Oswald was wearing when photographed in Minsk in 1961. Second, in a now-well-known letter written to his brother dated February 15, 1961, Oswald said that Francis Gary Powers "seemed to be a nice, bright American-type fellow, when I saw him in Moscow."[74] The CIA took this seriously enough to pin down the dates Powers spent in Moscow. And third, several of the words highlighted in Oswald's English-Russian dictionary could have been related to an interest in the U-2, e.g., "radar," "range," and "eject," as well as a phrase he wrote in himself, "radar locator." The U-2 carried a radar locator that could determine "the location of . . . radar installations."[75]

Finally, after the assassination, Allen Dulles sent Lee Rankin a memo and a brief article from the *Saturday Review* of May 9, 1964. Dulles's July 23, 1964, memo and associated documents became Warren Commission CD 1345. In the *SR* article, the writer (Henry Brandon) said that he talked to one of the Intourist guides who had met Oswald when he first came to Moscow in the fall of 1959. This guide said that several Intourist guides felt sorry for Oswald and, when winter came, brought him a fur cap. "But when they saw him again in Moscow several months later, he completely ignored them—didn't even speak to them." Incredibly, the WC seems to have never followed up on this.

According to the Warren Commission's findings, Oswald was in Moscow from October 1959 to early January 1960. While there is no "official" indication that Oswald was back in Moscow in August 1960, his reappearance at that time clearly could have been within the time frame mentioned in the *SR* article—"several months later"—when the Intourist guides found Oswald back in Moscow and strangely aloof. If it was Oswald, he would have had opportunities to contact someone, like Setyaev. However, there is no mention of an August 1960 visit with Setyaev, either in Oswald's accounts or Marina's.

If the hypothesis in this chapter is true, then the 1975 CIA memorandum stating that Oswald's 201 file had been opened because of his "queries" could have been considered a breach of security, revealing that the CIA had knowledge of Oswald's queries. This mistake might have resulted from Angleton's sudden firing due to public disclosure of the HT-LINGUAL mail intercept program. Indeed, there are hints in a heavily redacted part of an old register of the CIA's files of a security violation at the very moment the September 18, 1975, document was released to an official investigation.[76] Other information in this Kalaris memo is worthy of consideration as a security violation, information we will discuss in Chapter Nineteen. It is more likely that other information, concerning the Cuban Consulate, was the reason for the security violation.

Nevertheless, the possible connection of the security compromise to a Soviet source should not be overlooked.

From the above, it appears that Oswald may have had a contact outside Minsk and perhaps outside the Soviet Union, and also that the CIA had some way of knowing about Oswald's desire to come home by the time they opened his 201 file in December 1960. These observations are highly speculative and, even if true, do not, in and of themselves, indicate Oswald was a CIA agent. There are other possibilities, however, and as promised, we will now address the question: Was Oswald manipulated into going to Russia? Again, our answer here flows from the perspective that develops in his files, which may not necessarily correspond to reality or to what was inside Oswald's head. The evidence is not firm or even particularly convincing, but that is hardly surprising. Nevertheless, enough information has accumulated where a crude case can be advanced.

To begin with, those who observed him at the time of the defection reported their judgment that Oswald had obtained some sort of help, at a minimum, to prepare for the defection. This piece is convincing, only it seems impossible to take it anywhere with any certainty. In Chapter Six we explored three salient points in the unfolding mole-hunt in the Soviet Russia Division. Goleniewski's letters—which were suggestive of a mole—may not have been written soon enough to relate to an Oswald dangle in the Soviet Union, though perhaps one or two might have been early enough. The KGB's arrest of Popov—a CIA mole—occurred on the day Oswald arrived in Moscow (October 16, 1959), and thus was too late to provide a motive for dangling Oswald. Thus, the character of the mole-hunt which was in existence as Oswald prepared for and traveled to the Soviet Union was the Popov information from 1958: that the U-2 had been betrayed in some way.

From the above, we can build a rather weak case for a dangle, an operation in which the Soviets might be tested to see how much interest there was in Oswald's U-2 past. The FBI liaison to the CIA, Sam Papich, remembers "discussions of a plan to have a CIA or FBI man defect to Moscow," but he states that the plan was not implemented "to his knowledge."[77] As we will see, throughout Oswald's stay in the Soviet Union, an Agency element which appears regularly on cover sheets for Oswald documents is CI/OPS, which means "Counterintelligence Operations." If Oswald was a dangle, this might suggest that it was a counterintelligence operation run by Angleton.

Again, the evidence for this is hardly overwhelming. At the same time, however, whether or not the Agency ever considered seriously the damage that Oswald's knowledge might have had on the U-2 program if fully exploited, they could presume some level of Soviet interest. The existence of Oswald's SR/6 soft file—which had a page and a quarter worth of entries before the opening of Oswald's 201 file—confirms that Oswald was considered among a high-interest group of American military defectors to the Soviet Union.

Oswald's Communist credentials come across in the files as superficial, and his decision to return to the U.S. after just one year seems transparent, underlining all the more the superficiality of Oswald's entire Soviet sojourn. The evidence that he had a contact outside the Soviet Union is sufficient that we should, at least, take the possibility seriously, although—as in the case of the missing letter—a document or good copy of one would constitute more convincing evidence. Attention is drawn to Oswald's anomolous behavior in connection with this murky contact, especially the high probability that he was lying about who this person was, and also his action of slicing out a dedication page in a book as he gave it to Titovits. Both the credibility of these witnesses and Oswald's evasiveness establish this as a lead to be followed to its outcome. Presumably the KGB, itself a regular reader of the mails, had some answers at one time, and the present Russian government might be disposed to assist the American effort to open up all files related to the case.

Our study of Leo Setyaev, who was known to U.S. intelligence and being watched by them, is also a weak but still intriguing potential piece of the puzzle. Setyaev, by the Agency's own reasoning, was of interest to the CIA because his name appeared in Oswald's address book, but that statement does not say why they would be opening his mail in 1960. The LINGUAL documents released prove that the CIA was interested in Setyaev while Oswald was in Minsk. Setyaev would not raise suspicions by walking around corridors of hotels. After all, his job as a Radio Moscow correspondent was to seek out and interview westerners. The only question is: For whom was Setyaev really working?

The Setyaev story grows more interesting as time goes by. In his 1991 interview with Peter Wronski, Setyaev said Oswald "asked him to help write a letter to the Presidium, asking to be granted citizenship, and that he [Setyaev] refused.''[78] The June 1960 CIA HT/LINGUAL intercept on Setyaev indicated he was involved in the translation and dissemination of documents which foreigners needed to become Soviet citizens.[79] Could it have been Setyaev or someone like him who coached Oswald during his defection?

In Chapter Six, we encountered a ''Memo for the Files'' by an American Consulate official, John McVickar, which contained information on Soviet plans for Oswald for which we have no source. Peter Wronski's analysis of his interview with Setyaev contains this comment: ''Setyaev at first claimed he did not see Oswald again and that he gave Oswald his home address over the telephone when Oswald called him to tell him he was moving to *Minsk.*''[80] Setyaev did see Oswald again. And it seems that Setyaev was the person to talk to about Oswald.

All of this said, however, the process of releasing new documents is still not complete, and likely will continue through 1997 and beyond. The hypothesis advanced in the chapter is an early impression that may change radically or remain nearly the same. Time will tell.

Chapter Twelve

Turning Point

We have been watching three threads. First and foremost, we have been following the trails and intersections of Oswald's labyrinthine CIA, FBI, State Department, and ONI files. In addition, we have kept up with the general outlines of his activities in the Soviet Union, as this is the context in which these files were developed. Finally, we have observed Cuban matters in order to set the stage for the drama we know will unfold upon Oswald's return. In this regard, Oswald's preparation for his return to America took place while the Agency was planning for the Bay of Pigs invasion and the assassination of Castro. His first three months back in the U.S. would unfold against the backdrop of the Cuban Missile Crisis.

The pieces and pathways in Oswald's intelligence files become more complex in 1961 simply because they continue. While much of the meaning of these files is as arcane as the intelligence world in which they were created, at the simplest level of analysis we are struck by the sheer amount of paper the intelligence agencies created on Oswald. This quantity of documents indicates a significant level of interest in him. When viewed together, the number of intelligence offices that watched Oswald, and the degree of field-level action on him, take on a meaning not available when these events are viewed in isolation.

Stimulated by Oswald's decision to return to America, the activity among the low-level FBI, Navy, and State Department offices picked up in the first half of 1961. An act of Oswald's during this period would provide an additional stimulus to the interest in him when discovered by the intelligence community. That was his marriage to a Soviet woman, Marina Prusakova. Oswald's decision to bring a

Soviet citizen back to America led to a new level of interest in the CIA, a subject to which we will return in Chapter Thirteen.

Hiring the Mob for the Job

The Eisenhower administration's last key policy meeting on Cuba occurred in the White House on August 18, 1960. In that meeting, CIA director Dulles reported on the progress of organizing the Cuban exiles for the overthrow of Castro. President Eisenhower, present at the meeting, authorized the invasion planning to proceed. The minutes show that Dulles described the situation in this way:

> There has been developed a unified Cuban opposition outside of the country. This has been successful up to a point but the problem is that there is no real leader and 11 [sic] of the individuals are prima donnas. This unified opposition is known as the FRD [Frente Revolucionario Democratico] and has six prominent members, five of them representing groups in Cuba with the greatest potential. In response to a question from the President, Mr. Dulles said that all the names were favorably known in Cuba; that there were no Batista-ites among them and 11 of the names had been published except a recent joiner, Cardona. Their theme is to restore the revolution to its original concepts, recognizing that it is impossible to change all of the revolutionary trends.[11]

Dulles added, in response to a question from Eisenhower, that these Cuban leaders had all been identified with Castro since he assumed power. Dulles judged the CIA's work with these leaders since May as "very satisfactory."

The CIA training of the Cubans was discussed in some detail in this meeting. Dulles explained that while the FRD preferred being in the U.S., they had been persuaded to set up headquarters in Mexico. It was understood, Dulles added, "that there will be no ostensible military action directed from Mexico."[2] Eisenhower wanted to know why Mexico had been chosen. Mexico's communications and travel facilities were part of the reason, but the fact was that some of the other Latin American countries would not agree to the FRD's presence on their soil. Guatemala, however, did not present such a problem, and was already being used for training Cuban exiles.

The minutes of the White House meeting indicate that the Joint Chiefs "saw no problem" with Bissell's request for American troops to train the Cubans. Dulles said that he hoped five hundred Cubans could be finished with their training by "the beginning of November," a prediction possibly meant to fit with Nixon's election schedule. Dulles then added this:

> The FRD is acquiring some B-26s. The aircrews for these would be all Cubans. Mr. Bissell then said that it is possible that the initial para-military operations could be successful without any outside help. He pointed out that the first phase would be that of contacting local groups over a period of perhaps several months and in this period no air strikes would be undertaken. The plan would be to supply the local groups by air and also to infiltrate certain Cubans to stiffen local resistance.
>
> If local resistance is unable to accomplish the mission and the operation should expand, then there may be a requirement for air action. The plan would be to take the Isle of Pines or another small island for an ostensible base for operations of the [less than 1 line not declassified] forces. It is hoped that this may not be needed but we must be prepared for it.[3]

Bissell added that eleven groups that had potential had been identified in Cuba. "We are in the process of sending radio communications to them at this time," he said.[4] The air attacks were a significant escalation of the U.S. role. At the meeting, no one asked what the military impact of such CIA-backed air attacks would have in Cuba, and what the cost would be if this were discovered by the press.

In a historic decision remarkably like the one Kennedy would make after his inauguration, Eisenhower gave the go-ahead to proceed in Cuba, with a key condition attached. Eisenhower's decision and his reasoning are preserved in this passage of the minutes:

> The President said that he would go along so long as the Joint Chiefs, Defense, State and the CIA think we have a good chance of being successful. He wouldn't care much about this kind of cost; indeed, he said he would defend this kind of action against

> all comers and that if we could be sure of freeing the Cubans from this incubus [less than 1 line not declassified] might be a small price to pay. The President concluded the meeting by saying that he would like to urge caution with respect to the danger of making false moves, with the result of starting something before we were ready for it.[5]

There can be no argument, then, that like Kennedy later, Eisenhower would approve the invasion plan only if the top U.S. military and civilian leaders would vouch for the plan's chance of success. And so, as of August 18, 1960, the Bay of Pigs plan was set firmly into motion.

The other unspeakable part of the plan—the assassination of Castro—had taken a turn since the abortive CIA plot to arrange an accident for Castro's brother in July. Nixon, having secured the Republican nomination for president, had sent his chief lieutenant, General Robert E. Cushman, into the working levels of the CIA that were concerned with Cuban operations. It is thus likely that Nixon knew some of the details about the CIA's cooperation with the Mafia. Regarding the summer-autumn 1960 Bissell-Edwards conversation about assassinating Castro, the Church Committee report states: "Edwards recalled that Bissell asked him to locate someone who could assassinate Castro. Bissell confirmed that he requested Edwards to find someone to assassinate Castro and believed that Edwards raised the idea of contacting members of a gambling syndicate in Cuba."[6] As the Church Committee discovered, once again the Office of Security was at the center of operations, this time in the covert operations of Bissell's Cuban task force.

The Church Committee report states how the idea of using the mob to kill Castro grew from Edwards's idea of "contacting members of a gambling syndicate operating in Cuba." The report explains:

> Edwards assigned the mission to the Chief of the Operational Support Division of the Office of Security. The Support Chief [O'Connell] recalled that Edwards had said that he and Bissell were looking for someone to "eliminate" or "assassinate" Castro. Edwards and the Support Chief decided to rely on Robert A. Maheu to recruit someone "tough enough" to handle the job.[7]

At the time Maheu was a lawyer associated with billionaire Howard Hughes, and what followed was a story that mired the Agency in the swamp of organized crime. "Sometime in late August or early September 1960," the report noted, O'Connell "approached Maheu about the proposed operation." Former CIA Director William Colby testified to the Church Committee that CIA documents indicated that in August 1960, "Bissell asked Edwards to locate [an] asset to perform [a] gangster-type operation. Edwards contacted Maheu who contacted John Roselli on 9/14/60."[8]

On the issue of who had thought of Roselli first, Maheu and O'Connell pointed the finger at each other. Maheu's recollection was that O'Connell asked him to contact the underworld figure to ask if he would take part in a plan to "dispose" of Castro. O'Connell's recollection is that it was Maheu that raised the idea of using Roselli.[9] The CIA's 1967 Inspector General's Report struck this compromise: "Edwards and Maheu agreed that Maheu would approach Roselli as the representative of businessmen with interests in Cuba who saw the elimination of Castro as the first essential step to the recovery of their investments."[10]

O'Connell testified that Maheu was told to offer money, probably $150,000, for Castro's assassination.[11] What happened next found its way into a memo by FBI Director Hoover, addressed to Plans Director Bissell in the CIA—the person supervising the assassination plan. The October 18, 1960, Hoover memorandum citing "a source whose reliability has not been tested," reported this:

> [D]uring recent conversations with several friends, [Sam] Giancana stated that Fidel Castro was to be done away with very shortly. When doubt was expressed regarding this statement, Giancana reportedly assured those present that Castro's assassination would occur in November. Moreover, he allegedly indicated that he had already met with the assassin-to-be on three occasions. Giancana claimed that everything had been perfected for the killing of Castro, and that the "assassin" had arranged with a girl, not further described, to drop a "pill" in some drink or food of Castro's. Memo, Hoover to DCI (Att: DDP, 10/18/60)[12]

The Church Committee showed this Hoover memorandum, on August 22, 1975, to Sam Papich, who was the FBI liaison to the CIA in 1960. Papich said, "anyone in the Bureau would know the significance of the mention of Giancana." Papich did not further elaborate on this other than to say he would have discussed the matter with his FBI superior, Belmont, and with Edwards and Bannerman of the CIA's Office of Security.[13]

Like all of the CIA-backed schemes to assassinate Castro, the mob's poison-pill plot failed. This was right about the time Oswald changed his mind about staying in Russia. As Oswald began his eighteen-month quest to return to America, January 1961 ushered in a new twist to the CIA's assassination plans for Castro: use of the Agency's ZR/RIFLE project for a program to give the CIA an "executive action" (assassination) capability. When pressed by the Church Committee, William Harvey stated that Bissell had been pushed along on the Castro assassination plan, possibly by the Eisenhower White House.[14]

January 1961 also began in a deep freeze in U.S.–Cuban relations. Havana formally severed diplomatic relations with Washington on January 3.[15] On January 20, 1961, John F. Kennedy was inaugurated as the thirty-fifth president of the United States, and tensions immediately erupted over general Cold War strategy and ongoing planning for U.S. military intervention in Laos and Cuba, both set to occur at roughly the same time. President Kennedy found himself in a situation not unlike President Clinton's first year: a young Democratic president, after more than a decade of Repubican rule, perceived as too naive to handle the Communists.

Kennedy let stand the Cuban plan that Eisenhower had put in motion. On April 4, 1961, a major pre-invasion meeting took place in a State Department conference room. Kennedy, with his closest advisers attending, gave the go-ahead.[16] The ill-fated confrontation on the beaches of Cuba erupted on April 16–17, 1961. The American-trained and sponsored brigade of Cuban exiles were humiliated at Playa Giron, a tragically appropriate Cuban name.[17]

"The Dropping of Legal Proceedings Against Me"

As 1961 opened, Oswald was in Minsk trying to close the Russian chapter in his life.[18] The KGB had the only copy of his December 1960 query about returning to the U.S. On January 4, the Soviet passport office in Minsk "summoned" Oswald and forced the issue. Oswald was asked point-blank if he still wanted to become a Soviet citizen, and this time his answer was no. Oswald asked instead that his identity card be extended for an additional year.[19]

As discussed in Chapter Nine, on January 26, 1961, Marguerite Oswald, having failed for a year to find her son by writing letters to the U.S. government, traveled to the nation's capital and personally appeared at the State Department to demand that they do more to find him.[20] When the CIA received its copy of the department's notes of her appearance, someone placed it in Oswald's 201 file and underlined parts of these two sentences in the notes:

> She [Marguerite] also said that there was some possibility that her son had in fact gone to the Soviet Union as a US secret agent, and if this were true she wished the appropriate authorities to know that she was destitute and should receive some compensation.[21]

Whether she believed this or not, this tactic did not work, and Marguerite returned to Texas without compensation or information about Oswald's location in Russia. The State Department did send a cable to the embassy in Moscow on the "welfare-whereabouts" of Oswald on February 1, 1961. The cable told the embassy about Marguerite's visit and her concerns for her son's "personal safety," and asked that this be passed to the Soviet Ministry of Foreign Affairs.[22] As it turned out, this diplomatic maneuver would not be necessary.

Oswald finally tired of waiting for the American Embassy to respond to his first letter, and on February 5 he decided to write again. We have discussed the first sentence of this letter in Chapter Eleven. Here is the rest of the text:

> I am writing again asking that you consider my request for the return of my American passport. I desire to return to the United States, that is if we could come to some agreement concerning the dropping of any legal proceedings against me. If so, then I would be free to ask the Russian authorities to allow me to leave. If I could show them my American passport, I am of the opinion they would give me an exit visa. They have at no time insisted that I take Russian citizenship. I am living here with non-permanent type papers for a foreigner. I cannot leave Minsk without permission, therefore I am writing rather than calling in person.[23]

Oswald's insistence about an "agreement" to drop "legal proceedings" was obviously his way of asking that he not be prosecuted for espionage. It shows he fully understood the nature of the threats he had made during his October 1959 meeting with Snyder. "I hope that in recalling the responsibility I have to America," Oswald added, "that you remember yours in doing everything you can to help me since I am an American citizen.[24] This sentence seems odd because it suggests that in returning to the U.S., Oswald considered his "responsibility" to America. Moreover, his use of the verb "recall" is strange: Had Oswald suddenly remembered his duty to America or had someone recalled him?

Snyder received Oswald's second letter on February 13,[25] and responded to it on February 28. After acknowledging Oswald's request to go home and informing him that his December 1960 letter "does not appear to have been received at the Embassy," Snyder offered this advice:

> Inasmuch as the question of your present American citizenship status can be finally determined only on the basis of a personal interview, we suggest that you plan to appear at the Embassy at your convenience. The consular section of the Embassy is open from 9:00 a.m. to 6:00 p.m. The Embassy was recently informed by the Department of State that it had received an inquiry from your mother in which she said that she had not heard from you since December, 1959 and was concerned about your whereabouts and welfare.[26]

Getting Oswald to come to the embassy was obviously Snyder's objective, an idea repeated the same day in Snyder's cable to the State Department. In that cable Snyder repeated the entire text of Oswald's February 5 letter, and then added this:

> The Embassy is writing to Oswald and suggesting that he come personally to the Embassy for an interview on which to base a decision concerning the status of his American citizenship. Oswald's reference in his letter to his being unable to leave Minsk without permission may indicate that he desires to come to the Embassy, in which an invitation from the Embassy may facilitate his traveling to Moscow.[27]

Snyder said that he was prepared to give back Oswald his passport by mail, providing 1) that this was "a last resort"; 2) the State Department did not object; and 3) the embassy was "reasonably sure" that Oswald had not "committed an act" resulting in the loss of his American citizenship. Snyder also asked the department's position on "whether Oswald is subject to prosecution on any grounds should he enter the jurisdiction of the United States and, if so, whether there is any objection in communicating this to him."

Oswald received the embassy's February 28 letter by March 5, 1961, and wrote back that day.[28] "I see no reason for any preliminary inquiries," he protested, "not to be put in the form of a questionnaire and sent to me." He said he found it "inconvenient to come to Moscow for the sole purpose of an interview." He asked that the embassy mail the questionnaire to him, as it is difficult for him to travel.[29] Oswald's diary entry for this period says this: "I now live in a state of expectation about going back to the U.S. I confided with Zeger [sic] he supports my judgment but warns me not to tell any Russians about my desire to reture [sic]. I understade [sic] now why."[30] Not long after Oswald began corresponding with the embassy, his monthly payments from the "Red Cross" were cut off;[31] Snyder testified that the Soviet authorities had undoubtedly intercepted and read the correspondence between Oswald and the embassy and knew of his plans.[32]

The State Department took its time telling Oswald's mother that they had found him. A copy of the letter they sent her is no longer extant, but her March 27, 1961, response was published in the Warren Commission's twenty-six volumes, and it indicates that around the 27th she received this "most welcome news" about her son's wish to come home.[33]

As more letters between Oswald and the embassy followed,[34] the position of the embassy and the State Department remained firm: Oswald had to come to Moscow.[35] Then, on April 13 came the answer to Oswald's request for an "agreement" about dropping "legal proceedings" against him. The department refused to guarantee that Oswald would not be prosecuted.[36] If Lee Harvey Oswald wanted to come back to America, he would have to take his chances.

Lee and Marina

It was at this time that Oswald met his wife-to-be, Marina Nikolayevna Prusakova. Although accounts vary slightly on the exact date and circumstances, they evidently met at a dance in early March 1961.[37] When they first met, Oswald thought Marina was a dental technician—she was a pharmacist,[38] and Marina thought Oswald was from the Baltics (''because of his accent'').[39] Marina later explained that she and his other Russian friends called Oswald ''Alex'' because ''Lee'' was recognized as a Chinese name.[40] Marina says she had not heard of Oswald before she met him, in spite of the fact that he was the only American living in Minsk.[41]

At the dance, Oswald noticed Marina and asked Yuriy Merazhinskiy, a friend of his and Marina's, to introduce him to her. This accomplished, Oswald asked her to dance. Oswald wrote in his diary that they liked each other right away and that he got her phone number before she left the dance.[42] The two met again at another dance a week later, at which they danced together for most of the evening.[43] This time Oswald walked her home, and the two made another date, which Oswald missed due to an illness that required hospitalization.[44]

The hospital records indicate that Oswald was admitted to its ear, nose, and throat division, and stayed from March 30 until April 11, 1961, seemingly a long time to be in the hospital for an ear infection.[45] Oswald called Marina from the hospital and asked her to visit him there,[46] which she did nearly every day until his release.[47] Marina even wore her uniform in order to see him on Sundays—outside of the regular visiting hours. The first time she did this was on Easter Sunday, when she brought Oswald an Easter egg.[48]

During one of Marina's visits to the hospital, he proposed that they become engaged, which she agreed to consider,[49] and he continued to ask until she accepted his proposal on April 15.[50] Marina lived with her aunt and uncle, who knew Oswald was an American and did not disapprove of his many visits to their apartment. On April 20, 1961, Oswald and Marina applied to get married.[51] It normally took about a week for Soviet citizens to get permission to marry foreigners.[52] In this case it took ten days, and they were married on April 30 in Minsk.[53]

For her part, Marina later testified that she clearly had not married Oswald as a way of getting to the U.S. because it was her understanding that he could not return.[54] Oswald wrote in his diary that he married Marina in order to hurt Ella German, the girl who had refused his marriage proposals, but that in the end, "I find myself in love with Marina." The May 1 entry in Oswald's diary includes this passage:

> The transition of changing full love from Ella to Marina was very painful esp. as I saw Ella almost every day at the factory but as the days & weeks went by I adjusted more and more [to] my wife mentally * * * She is madly in love with me from the very start. Boat rides on Lake walks through the park evening at home or at Aunt Valia's place mark May.[55]

Oswald's attachment to Marina grew quickly. A diary entry for June reads "A continuence of May, except that; we draw closer and closer, and I think very little now of Ella."[56]

Oswald had been holding out on Marina. He had decided, probably in late 1960, and certainly no later than January 1961, to return to America, but he did not tell Marina. It was not until sometime in June that Oswald told Marina that he wanted to return home. An entry in his diary says that she was "startled" when he told her "in the last days" of June.[57] On May 16, 1961, Oswald sent notification to the U.S. Embassy (which it received on May 25) of his marriage to Marina. He explained that they both intended to go to the United States.[58] During June, the Oswalds made inquiries with the appropriate Soviet authorities about obtaining the proper exit visas.[59] On June 1, 1961, Oswald wrote to his mother about his marriage "last month."[60] Oswald's first daughter, June, was conceived in May 1961.[61]

Labyrinth II: Navy Intelligence and the FBI

When last we entered the labyrinth of the FBI and CIA files on Oswald, the FBI was bifurcating its Oswald material at the Bureau and in Dallas into two compartments at each locations. The material collected under the caption "Funds Transmitted to Russia" went into the 100 file at the Bureau and into the 105 file at Dallas; the rest of the Oswald material went into the 105 file at the Bureau and into the 100 file at Dallas. It is important to keep this detail in mind because this pattern, begun in 1960, persisted into 1961. With respect to his CIA files, 1960 witnessed the incremental involvement of the Soviet Russia Division, a trend that continued into 1961.

Stimulated by Oswald's decision to come home, his paper trail during the first half of 1961 takes us down several paths, some familiar and some new. A channel opened between the Navy Intelligence field office at Algiers, Louisiana (near New Orleans), and the Dallas FBI field office. Lateral activity picked up between the FBI field offices in Dallas and New Orleans, and after an internal struggle, the Washington, D.C., FBI field office also got involved. These connections produced more intelligence on Oswald, culminating in important FBI and CIA actions in the summer of 1961, events we will discuss in the next chapter.

The FBI's investigation of Oswald in 1959 and early 1960 had "involved the development of background information" concerning him, "and the taking of appropriate steps to insure our being advised of his return" the Bureau told the Warren Commission.[62] "Our basic interest," the FBI explained, "was to correlate information concerning him and to evaluate him as a security risk in the event he returned, in view of the possibility of his recruitment by the Soviet intelligence services." Given this, Special Agent Kenneth J. Haser appeared overly eager when he tried to open a new file on Oswald at the Washington, D.C. field office (WFO) of the FBI in August 1960.

On August 9, Haser wrote a memorandum to the special agent in charge (SAC) of the FBI WFO on the subject of "Lee Harvey Oswald, Internal Security-Russia."[63] In the memo, Haser said he had gone over to the State Department passport office that day, where he had contacted Mrs. Verde Buckler, who gave him Oswald's passport file "for appropriate review." The Bureau had asked the State Department to provide "any current information available" on Oswald, Haser said, and "it is, therefore, recommended that a case be opened for the purpose of furnishing the Bureau and office of origin a summary of information in the passport file."

The file number of the Haser memo was written by hand: "100-

16597 Sub L - 676 Newspaper Clipping.''[64] The person writing it was probably named Carson and probably filed this memo at the Bureau. Carson crossed out the ''OO - Dallas'' indicator below the subject line. In the CIA ''OO'' was a symbol for the Contacts Division, but in the FBI ''OO'' was an acronym for ''Office of Origin,'' meaning the office responsible for a particular case. On September 12, 1960, Special Agent Dana Carson, following up on Haser's August 9 memorandum on Oswald, wrote a new memorandum to the special agent in charge of the Washington, D.C., field office. Someone, probably Carson, had gone back over to the State Department passport office on September 9 and looked at Oswald's file again.

Carson's memo threw cold water on Haser's hopes of opening a file for a State Department conduit to the FBI via his desk. Carson, starting from the defection, went down the list of pertinent memos and cables and then remarked: ''From a review of this file, it would appear that the Bureau has been furnished all available information by State.''[65] Carson recommended that WFO take no further action.[66] Carson carried the day, but Haser would soon be back again asking to open a case file. Newspaper accounts and White House questions about American servicemen defecting to the Soviet Union breathed new life into FBI activity on Oswald. What happened inside the FBI became inextricably linked with the Office of Naval Intelligence (ONI).

On November 10, 1960, a week after the CIA answered a State Department request on a list of these defectors, including Oswald, someone in the Office of Naval Intelligence signed out the May 1960 FBI report by Fain on ''Funds Transmitted to Residents of Russia.''[67] On the routing slip sending the report, a person whose initials look like ''WB'' commented on the previous transmittal of the Fain report to the Defense Intelligence Officer (DIO), Ninth Naval District (9ND). It is worth adding that the Marine Corps commandant had requested that the 9ND commander ''be apprised of the intelligence documentation on Oswald on a priority basis.''[68]

When ''WB'' of 921E2 (the Programs section of the Counterintelligence Branch) signed out the Fain report on November 10, however, he had a different Naval District (ND)—the Eighth—in mind. Throughout 1960, the 9ND DIO had been involved in the Navy's handling of the Oswald case to provide support to the commander of the Marine Air Reserve Training Command, U.S. Naval Air Station, Glenview, Illinois, who processed Oswald's Undesirable Discharge. The 8ND District Intelligence Office was a long way away—in Building 255 of U.S. Naval Station, New Orleans, Louisiana. 8ND intelligence records were also kept at U.S. Naval Station, Algiers, Louisiana, which was probably also the location for one of the CIA's covert training bases near New Orleans, specifically the base referred to within the CIA as the "Old Algiers Ammo Dump."[69] On November 15, 1960, five days after "WB" checked out the Fain report, someone from that same ONI office, 921E2, sent a confidential letter to the "Officer in Charge, District Intelligence Office, Eight Naval District."[70]

ONI also sent a copy of the November 15, 921E2 letter to the 9ND, to whom these instructions in the last paragraph applied: "By copy of this letter, the District Intelligence Office of the Ninth Naval District is requested to forward the intelligence documentation concerning Oswald to the District Intelligence Office, Eighth Naval District." This information was forwarded by DIO 9ND two weeks later, comprising fourteen documents "which represent subject's intelligence file" to DIO 8ND on November 30, 1960.[71] As of that date, about one week before the CIA opened its 201 file on Oswald, the ONI changed the Navy field intelligence unit watching the case from Glenview, Illinois, to Algiers, Louisiana.

The officer in charge of the DIO 8ND was Navy captain F.O.C. Fletcher, and on January 11, 1961, he sent a letter to the Dallas field office of the FBI, opening up a potentially important lateral interagency channel on Oswald.[72] The Dallas FBI field office copy of this letter has a handwritten number after Oswald's name: 105-976—the Dallas Oswald file which ensued from Fain's "Funds Transmitted to Residents of Russia" report of May 1960. This handwritten file number also included the extension "-1, p. 17," meaning page 17 of document number one in that file.[73] This is strange because Fain's report, which was supposedly document number one, was just seven pages long. On the bottom of the letter is Fain's writing, and a new Dallas file number for Oswald: 100-10461. This 8ND letter to the Dallas FBI field office became the first document in Oswald's Dallas 100 file.

In the letter Fletcher reported that Oswald, who had been a member of the U.S. Marine Corps Reserve, had been given an undesirable discharge on August 17, 1960. Fletcher also pointed out that Oswald's last known home of record (as of July 20, 1959) was 3124 West 5th Street, Fort Worth, Texas. An information copy was sent to the director of Naval Intelligence (DNI), OP921 section D, where it was received on January 16, 1961, and to 921E (counterintelligence) on January 17.[74]

On February 27, 1961, FBI director Hoover sent a letter to the State Department Office of Security about Oswald, announcing a dead end in its search for an Oswald impostor in Europe.[75] There was no impostor there, as the FBI's sources in Switzerland found out for themselves: no one calling himself Oswald had shown up at the Albert Schweitzer College. The February 27 Hoover letter mentioned Oswald's August 17, 1960, undesirable discharge from the Marines, his old Fort Worth address, and asked "that any additional information contained in the files of the Department of State regarding subject be furnished to this Bureau."[76]

On February 28, 1961, the special agent in charge at FBI-Dallas wrote a memorandum to the special agent in charge at FBI-New Orleans on the subject of Lee Harvey Oswald, to follow up on the January 11 DIO 8ND letter from New Orleans.[77] Fain's memo discussed the largely unproductive checks he had made since Captain Fletcher's January 11 letter which had mentioned Oswald's old Fort Worth address. A February 2, 1960, check with the Retail Merchants Association netted only Marguerite C. Oswald's 1957 address at 3830 West Sixth Street, Fort Worth, along with the address of Oswald's brother, Robert, at 7300 Davenport Street, Fort Worth. There was "no record" on Oswald.[78] A February 25 check with "Dallas Confidential Informants" showed only that Oswald had never been known to be a member of the Communist Party at Fort Worth.

Fain then asked the New Orleans FBI office to review the files of 8ND District Intelligence Office of the Eighth Naval District, "for background information available on subject [Oswald] and any information available concerning CP [Communist Party] activities and attempted defection to Russia, and forward same to Dallas Office."[79] It is worth noting that while adding this as the third document in Oswald's new Dallas file, 100-10461, Fain still filed a copy of his memo in the old Dallas 105-976.

Meanwhile, on March 2, 1961, Emery J. Adams of the State Security Office (SY/E) requested several offices to "advise if the

FBI is receiving information about Harvey [Oswald] on a continuing basis. If not, please furnish this Office with the information which has not been provided the FBI so that it may be forwarded to them.''[80] Presumably, Adams meant that these offices should look at the attached February 27, 1961, FBI memo and then determine if anything was missing. On the bottom of this document is a handwritten note of March 20 from the Soviet Desk which advised that no information had been sent to date, but added, ''all future [information] will be forwarded to SY [Security Office] for transmittal.''

On March 31, 1961, Edward J. Hickey sent a memorandum to John T. White, both of the State Department's passport office. This memo addressed the question of giving back Oswald his passport, and Hickey's point was that the mails could not be trusted. He said:

> In view of the fact that this file contains information first, which indicates that mail from the mother of this boy is not being delivered to him and second, that it has been stated that there is an impostor using Oswald's identification data and that no doubt the Soviets would love to get hold of his valid passport, it is my opinion that the passport should be delivered to him only on a personal basis and after the Embassy is assured, to its complete satisfaction, that he is returning to the United States.[81]

No one had definitely said there was an Oswald impostor—it had merely been suggested because of the confusion surrounding Oswald's application to the Albert Schweitzer College in Switzerland. By the time of Hickey's memo, the impostor issue was dead. Very much alive were the surreptitious readers of Oswald's mail. ''It's hard for me to know whether you get *all* my letters,'' Oswald wrote to his brother later that year, ''they have a lot of censorship here.''[82] The KGB was not the only clandestine reader of Oswald's mail. As we will shortly see, the CIA was too.

On April 13, 1961, the State Department sent a strongly worded set of instructions to the embassy in Moscow on how to deal with Oswald.[83] The instructions boiled down to three things: Thoroughly interrogate Oswald, make no promises about legal proceedings, and report all developments promptly to Washington.[84] With respect to Oswald's demand that he receive guarantees that all ''legal proceedings'' be dropped, the State Department had this to say:

> The Department is not in a position to advise Mr. Oswald whether upon his desired return to the United States he may be amenable to prosecution for any possible offenses committed in violation of the laws of the United States [or] of the laws of any of its States. The developments in the case of Mr. Oswald should be promptly reported. In particular, a report of his travel data should be submitted when the Embassy receives confirmation of his travel plans.[85]

The seriousness of this rebuff was mitigated somewhat by the afterthought at the end of the cable. "It may be added that Mrs. Marguerite Oswald has been informed of the address given by Mr. Oswald," the State Department said. On the other hand, there was a by-now-familiar handwritten inscription on the bottom right-hand corner of the page: "U.S. Defector."

The January 11 letter from the 8th Naval District to Dallas FBI office, Hoover's February 27 request to the State Department, and new activity between the State Department and the Moscow Embassy concerning Oswald's decision to return to America were new ammunition for FBI Special Agent Haser, of the Washington, D.C. field office. His plan to open a WFO case on Oswald had been shot down the previous September by his colleague, Special Agent Carson. On April 20, 1961, Haser wrote a new memorandum to the WFO SAC, reporting his visit that day to the State Department passport office:

> This passport file of captioned subject was made available to the writer on this date by Mr. Henry Kupiec, Foreign Adjudications Division, Passport Office, Department of State, inasmuch as the file contains information subsequent to the date on which the file was last reviewed by WFO. It appears that the subject is still in the Soviet Union.
>
> It is, therefore, recommended that this case be reopened to bring up to date a review of subject's file for notification to the Bureau and interested offices. No flimsy [a sheet that enables mimeograph copies of a document to be made] is required.[86]

Within a month, Haser's recommendation was put into effect, and a channel of Oswald information between WFO and the Dallas FBI field office opened.

Meanwhile, the Dallas FBI request that the New Orleans FBI office read 8ND Navy records had borne fruit. "I had, as a result of a request of the Dallas office," New Orleans FBI Special Agent John L. Quigley recalled, "checked the Office of Naval Intelligence records at the U.S. Naval Station at Algiers."[87] Quigley had reviewed Oswald's file at Algiers on April 18, and the results were forwarded to the Dallas FBI office on April 27, 1961. On that date the special agent in charge of the New Orleans FBI office responded formally with a memorandum to the SAC in Dallas detailing SA Quigley's review of the "ONI 8th Naval District Records United States Naval Station, Algiers, Louisiana, on April 18, 1961."[88]

The Oswald Navy file at Algiers was comprehensive, covering most of the salient points of his history since his defection. For example, it included the January 27, 1960, report on Oswald's brother, John Edward Pic by Special Agent John T. Cox of the Air Force's Office of Special Investigations (OSI).[89] The New Orleans FBI memorandum, probably written by Special Agent John L. Quigley, erroneously referred to Cox's OSI report as an "ONI" report. Otherwise, Quigley was meticulous, noting such tiny details as a "Control Number 20261"—apparently assigned by ONI—for the first embassy cable from Moscow (#1304) which reported Oswald's defection and his threat to give up radar secrets.

"In reviewing this file," SA Quigley said, "it appears that much of the above material has been furnished to ONI 8th Naval District by ONI 9th Naval District." He ended the memo with a suggestion:

> Since New Orleans does not have any background information with regards to this investigation, nor is aware of what investigation is contemplated, no leads are being set forth in this communication, other than it is suggested that Dallas and Fort Worth may desire to review ONI's files at Carswell Air Force Base concerning subject.[90]

Quigley's review of the ONI's 8th Naval District file considerably broadened the database on Oswald at both the Dallas and New Orleans FBI offices. For example, these field offices now had the October 26, 1959, ONI memorandum on Robert Edward Webster who, Quigley said, "appears to have defected to the Russians at about the same time as Oswald.'' The 1959 Webster memo was assigned ONI ''Control Number 1178.''[91]

On April 28, 1961, SAC Dallas sent a memorandum to SAC New Orleans relaying the information acquired since the previous Dallas memorandum on February 28.[92] This new information came from a phone call to Special Agent Fain made by Oswald's mother. Marguerite told Fain her son wanted to come home.[93]

> On 4/10/61 [10 April], Mrs. Marguerite C. Oswald, aka Mrs. Edward Lee Oswald, telephonically contacted SA John W. Fain at the Fort Worth RA and stated that she is currently residing at 1612 Hurley Street, Fort Worth. She advised that she had returned to Fort Worth about the first of April 1961 to live . . . Mrs. Oswald also volunteered the information that she made a trip to Washington, D.C., during January 1961, for the purpose of contacting the Secretary of State's office for information concerning her son, Lee Harvey Oswald. . . . She stated that during the following month or after a lapse of about four weeks, she had learned that subject [Oswald] was at Minsk, Russia.[94]

SAC Dallas noted that when Fain had interviewed Marguerite on April 28, 1960, she had given him a photograph of Oswald with the description: ''Race: White; Sex: Male; Age: 20; Birth data: 10/18/39, New Orleans, Louisiana; Height: 5'10"; Weight: 165 lbs.; Eyes: Blue; Hair: Light brown, wavy.'' SAC Dallas asked SAC New Orleans ''to expedite [the] investigation so that this matter can be brought to a successful conclusion.'' In New Orleans, Special Agent Quigley filed this memo as the third in Oswald's file there: 100-16601.[95]

The FBI had been waiting for the day that Oswald might try to return. On May 23, 1961, the special agent in charge of the FBI Washington field office sent a memorandum to the director of the FBI, summarizing the contacts made by the Oswalds (Marguerite and Lee Harvey) to government agencies since January 1961.[96] Special Agent Vincent P. Dunn had visited the State Department passport office on May 9, where he was able to read various memoranda and cables about Marguerite's January visit, Oswald's decision to come home, and his wish ''to come to some agreement concerning the dropping of any legal proceedings against me.''

The SAC WFO said he was passing his memorandum to "the Dallas Division for information as they are the division covering the subject's permanent residence." When the memo arrived at the Bureau, someone with the initials F.L.J. wrote this on the right margin: "put cc in 100-353496."[97] That was the special file at headquarters into which Fain's 1960 handiwork on Oswald had been placed.

On May 25, 1961, Emery J. Adams of the State Department's Office of Security replied to Hoover's February 27 request for information on Lee Harvey Oswald. The State Department relayed information provided by its passport office regarding the status of his passport and his contact with the American Embassy at Moscow.[98] Adams reported this:

> The Passport Office (PPT) of the Department has advised that Mr. Oswald has been in communication with the American Embassy at Moscow, and, at this time, there is no information that he has renounced his nationality of the United States. If Mr. Oswald has not expatriated himself in any way, and when he makes satisfactory arrangements to depart from the USSR, the Embassy is prepared to furnish him with the necessary passport facilities for travel to the United States. PPT further advises that the Subject's passport file is being periodically reviewed by a representative of your Bureau.[99]

The FBI and several of its field offices were now engaged in collecting what they could on Oswald, and preparing for his return home. At this point, the paper trail on Oswald leads us back into the CIA, to which we must now turn our attention.

The details are an intelligence geography lesson. It provides the map that guides us through an intersection which is a major turning point in our story.

CHAPTER THIRTEEN

"Operational Intelligence Interest"

Along the dimly lit, mute paths that run through Oswald's CIA files we occasionally encounter surprises, like the flat statement by the Chief of SR/6, the "Soviet Realities" branch in the Soviet Russia Division, that "we showed operational intelligence interest" in Oswald. This claim stands against the official position whereby the Agency denies ever having used Oswald for any reason. In addition to the possibility, discussed in Chapter Eleven, of an Oswald dangle in the Soviet Union, we can conclude—based on other circumstances explored in Chapters Eighteen and Nineteen—that the Agency has not been forthcoming about the information it possessed on Oswald before the assassination.

By 1961 there were already two reasons for the Agency's interest in Oswald: his decision to marry a Soviet citizen and his cumulative experience in the Soviet Union. Either of these facts alone was enough to have guaranteed an operational interest in Oswald. We will revisit the CIA's sensitive mail-intercept program and the way it was used on Oswald in 1961, for it provides tantalizing clues on the issue of counterintelligence interest in Oswald.

We will cover Oswald's efforts to return to the U.S., and update developments in the Cuban exile world, through the vehicle of Gerry Hemming, a CIA informant, back in the U.S. from a stint in Castro's army, fully debriefed by the CIA, who begins infiltrating every anti-Castro exile group he can find.

Labyrinth III: Hunter and Project

"Hunter is the CIA's sensitive project involving the review of mail," said a March 10, 1961, FBI memorandum written by D. E. Moore, and the "CIA makes available to us results of their analysis to this project." Moore's memo reported important news from a meeting the day before with CIA's Counterintelligence Chief, James Angleton, concerning "illegal espionage activities":

> . . . We were advised that CIA has now established a laboratory in New York in connection with this project which can examine correspondence for secret writing, micro dots and possibly codes. He said the laboratory is fully equipped and they would be glad to make its facilities available to us if at any time we desire an examination of this nature to be made in NYC and time was of the essence and would not permit the material to be brought to our Laboratory in Washington, D. C. We expressed our appreciation for the offer and said that in the event we desired to utilize their laboratory, we would contact them.[1]

Beneath this Hoover inscribed this happy comment: "Another inroad!" Beneath his writing, still another note said optimistically that "Hunter material will increase about 20% since NY lab now established. 4/21/61."

"Hunter" was the FBI term for the CIA's HT/LINGUAL project which, as discussed in Chapter Two, was used to monitor Lee Harvey Oswald. The expansion of the HT/LINGUAL program in April 1961 came as the FBI entered a new active phase of intelligence gathering on Oswald triggered by his decision to return to America. The CIA has officially maintained that among the millions of letters it intercepted, only one directly pertained to Oswald. That letter was written by his mother in Fort Worth on July 6 and opened by the CIA in New York on July 8, 1961.

The timing was perfect: On July 3 the FBI's Dallas field office had just finished sending out the largest report it had ever compiled on Oswald. The main body of the report was ten pages, written by Special Agent Fain. According to the CIA's public statements, the secret opening of Marguerite's letter to Oswald five days later was curiously overlooked. In 1975 the Agency said the letter was ''dated 8 July 1961 but discovered only on review triggered by press publicity following the Oswalds' return to the U.S. in June 1962.''[2] On the surface, this story seems ridiculous: The only Oswald letter the CIA ever intercepted had been lost for a year and found after a newspaper drew attention to Oswald's return.

''Since Oswald was known to have sent or received more than 50 communications during his stay in the Soviet Union,'' the House Select Committee on Assassinations said in its 1978 report, ''the committee also questioned why the Agency ostensibly had just one letter in its possession directly related to Oswald.''[3] The Agency's response to the committee's question and use of the word ''ostensibly'' was defensive. ''HT/LINGUAL only operated 4 days a week,'' was the reply, ''even then, proceeded on a sampling basis.'' We will troll the CIA's files shortly for evidence contrary to this story of the one-letter LINGUAL file on Oswald. First, however, we will inspect the documents connected to the letter the CIA says it ''discovered'' a year after opening it, and then examine the documents and reports surrounding the letter in Oswald's secret files.

The word ''discovered'' in the Agency's statement was misleading. ''Rediscovered'' would have been more appropriate. A June 22, 1962, CIA memo mentioning *Washington Post* coverage of Oswald's return to the U.S. said this: ''A search of the Project [HT/LINGUAL] files revealed that the attached subject item was sent to subject by his mother on 8 July 1961.''[4] This memo does not say, let alone prove, that Marguerite's letter was discovered for the *first* time in June 1962. In view of the fact that the person using the steam iron that opened her letter was working for the CIA, their story justifiably prompts this joke: How many CIA agents does it take to read a letter? The answer: That depends on their security clearances.

There has been a startling new development in the story of Marguerite's letter since the new release of JFK documents in 1993 to 1994. A better copy of a mail intercept index card on Oswald offers, for the first time, a clear view of a handwritten note heretofore too faded to read. The note ''Delete 15/3/60'' indicates that Oswald had been deleted from HT/LINGUAL coverage on March 15, 1960.[5] This means Oswald's name was not on the Watch List when the CIA opened Marguerite's letter to him. Worse still, CI/SIG's Ann

Egerter put Oswald's name back on the list on August 7, 1961.[6] Thus, the CIA opened Oswald's mail when he was not on the list and then couldn't find the letter after putting him back on the list.

More than Marguerite's letter was missing from Oswald's CIA files. On May 25, the embassy had received a letter mailed in Minsk about ten days before, in which Oswald asked for assurances that he would not be prosecuted and divulged a new dimension to his travel plans. On May 26, Snyder sent a dispatch to the State Department containing this description of the events:

> The Embassy received on May 25, 1961, an undated letter from Lee Harvey Oswald postmarked Minsk, May 16, 1961, in which he states in part that he is asking ''full guarantees that I shall not, under any circumstances, he persecuted for any act pertaining to this case'' should he return to the United States, that if this ''condition'' cannot be met he will ''endeavor to use relatives in the United States to see about getting something done in Washington.'' According to the letter, Oswald is married to a Russian woman who would want to accompany him to the United States.[7]

The embassy sent this dispatch, Number 806, via ''air pouch'' to the State Department where, on June 3, the distribution center sent fifteen copies to the CIA.[8] On a CIA copy of this dispatch is a somewhat indistinct list of fifteen organizational elements, including parts of TSD (Technical Services Division), OO/C (Domestic Contacts Division), ORR (Office of Research in the Intelligence Directorate) and SR (Soviet Russia) division, all clearly CIA offices,[9] and constituting a peculiar combination which might be associated with the mail intercept program. For example, ORR regularly received HT/LINGUAL reports, and the laboratory at the mail intercept site was run by TSD.[10] Whether these observations are correct or not, this crude hand-drawn distribution list was unlike any that appears in all of the CIA cover sheets on Oswald. Missing from this list were any of the counterintelligence sections normally included on Oswald documents, such as CI/STAFF, CI/OPS, and CI/SIG.

The 610a CIA routing and record sheet attached to the publicly released copy of Moscow Embassy dispatch 806 only further adds to this mystery: It is from November 1961, five months after the fact. This routing sheet probably does not reflect the original internal

CIA distribution for this Foreign Service dispatch. Was there something special about it? Indeed there was: It was the first document the CIA received that revealed that Oswald was planning to bring a Soviet citizen home as his wife.

A check of the calendar suggests that the circulation of dispatch 806—with its original routing sheet—was in progress at the precise time the Agency opened but did not "discover" the letter to Oswald. Where was dispatch 806 inside the CIA at this time? Can we determine who might have seen it? The answer is yes. It probably circulated among the same CIA offices that examined the next Oswald document received at the CIA: The July 3, 1961, Fain report on Oswald. We have the original cover sheet for the Fain report, and it shows that the Fain report went to nine offices in the Soviet Russia Division and four offices in counterintelligence, including Ann Egerter in CI/SIG. The Fain report circulated among these fourteen offices between July 24 and August 14. Dispatch 806 began its rounds—probably to these same fourteen offices—on or about June 3, and on July 8, Marguerite's letter was steamed open at LaGuardia Airport in New York City.

Was there an important event which might have been connected to or have caused the July 8 secret opening of Marguerite's letter? Again, the answer is yes. An obvious place to look for clues is the Soviet Union, where, indeed, a portentous sequence of events began on July 8. Oswald suddenly surfaced in Moscow on July 8 and phoned Marina in Minsk, instructing her to proceed immediately to Moscow.[11] More important, on that date Oswald, for the first time since his defection in 1959, entered the U.S. Embassy. Inside he used the telephone.

Impatient because he had not heard anything since March about the return of his passport,[12] Oswald had taken decisive action by traveling to Moscow and showing up without warning at the American Embassy. The offices were closed,[13] prompting Oswald's use of the house telephone to reach Snyder. The two men met, talked briefly, and agreed to meet the following Monday. By this time the Oswald "Banjo" (a term the CIA used for pieces of mail they opened) was back in its envelope and on its way to Russia.

The Meaning of Freedom

When Oswald first visited the embassy on a Saturday in 1959, he declined Snyder's invitation to return the following Monday. Oswald did things differently this time. On July 10, he and Snyder initiated the application for return to America while Marina waited outside.[14] Snyder, meanwhile, asked Oswald questions about the details of his life in Russia and asked for his Soviet papers.

The American consul had to make a far-reaching determination: Had Oswald expatriated himself? Had he become a Soviet citizen? This is Snyder's account of the discussion right after it happened:

> Oswald stated that he was not a citizen of the Soviet Union and had never formally applied for citizenship, that he had never taken an oath of allegiance to the Soviet Union, and that he was not a member of the factory trade union organization. He said that he had never given Soviet officials any confidential information that he had learned in the Marines, had never been asked to give such information, and ''doubted'' that he would have done so had he been asked.[15]

The Warren Commission later rightly concluded that some of Oswald's statements during the interview were ''undoubtedly false.'' The Warren Report pointed out that Oswald ''had almost certainly applied for citizenship in the Soviet Union,''[16] and had been disappointed when he was turned down.[17] ''He possessed a membership card in the union organization,''[18] the report noted, and then declared that Oswald's ''assertion to Snyder that he had never been questioned by Soviet authorities concerning his life in the United States is simply unbelievable.''[19]

Oswald's greatest concern was whether he would be prosecuted and imprisoned after returning to the U.S., and he engaged Snyder openly about it. The most Snyder was willing to say was that although he could make no promises, he did not know of any grounds on which Oswald would be prosecuted.[20] Unlike his 1959 meeting with Snyder, Oswald did not get angry. This time he groveled before Snyder with uncharacteristic humility, pleading that he had ''learned a hard lesson a hard way" and acquired "a new appreciation of the United States and the meaning of freedom." Oswald filled out his passport renewal form[21] as an American national.[22] The "bravado and arrogance" of his 1959 defection performance were ancient history. Oswald, Snyder testified to the Warren Commission, "seemed to have matured."[23]

Time was short: Oswald's passport was due to expire on September 10, 1961,[24] and it appeared unlikely the Soviets would issue his exit papers before then. On the basis of his "written and oral statements," Snyder concluded that Oswald had not expatriated himself, and therefore gave him back his passport—stamped valid only for travel to the United States.[25] Marina joined Oswald in the embassy on the following day, July 11, to initiate the paperwork for her immigration to the United States. Both Oswalds had a routine interview with McVickar, Snyder's assistant (who had also been present during Oswald's defection in 1959).[26] Oswald signed Marina's visa application,[27] and said he had saved about two hundred rubles for the return trip and that they would try to save some more.[28]

On July 11, 1961, cables between the American Embassy in Moscow and the State Department in Washington crossed on their respective journeys. On the same day, both sent cables addressing the issue of Oswald's citizenship. The State Department was responding to the embassy's earlier cables on this and other passport and immigration issues, and the department now authorized the embassy to use its own discretion within the narrow realm of whether Oswald was "entitled to the protection of the United States should an emergency situation arise." If there was no emergency, the embassy was expected to ask Washington before making a final decision on granting Oswald documentation of United States citizenship.[29] The embassy cable the same day reiterated its view that Oswald had not committed any expatriating acts, and that his American passport should be returned so that he could begin the application process for a Soviet exit visa. The embassy also asked the department to "approve or disapprove" Oswald's renewal application.[30]

On July 14, Lee and Marina returned to Minsk,[31] and Oswald chose that day to reopen contact with his brother Robert, telling him he had his passport back and describing what a "test" he had endured to get it. "I could write a book," Oswald said, "about how many feelings have come and gone since that day." The letter was unusually affectionate toward his family.[32] "The letter's tone of firm purpose to return to the United States in the face of heavy odds," the Warren Commission observed, "reflected Oswald's attitude thereafter."[33] In spite of these odds, Lee and Marina began the procedures with local authorities to acquire permission to leave the Soviet Union.[34]

On July 15, 1961, Oswald reported their progress to the embassy, and offered to keep them informed "as to the overall picture." Marina was having difficulties at work because of her decision to go to the United States with her husband, Oswald said, but added that such "tactics" were "quite useless" and that Marina had "stood up well, without getting into trouble."[35] For August 21 through September 1, Oswald's diary has this entry: "I make repeated trips to the passport & visa office, also to Ministry of For. Affairs in Minsk, also Min. of Internal Affairs, all of which have a say in the granting of a visa. I extracted promises of quick attention to us.[36] For September through October 18, Oswald wrote, "No word from Min. ('They'll call us.')."[37]

For a time, events seemed to be moving more quickly than they actually were. On July 17, Oswald guaranteed to support Marina if she was allowed to enter the U.S.,[38] and the next day Marina filled out Oswald's application for a Soviet exit permit.[39] On July 24, the embassy wrote to Oswald asking him to send copies of his marriage certificate,[40] which he managed to send, along with Marina's birth certificate, to the embassy in August.[41] By August 8 Oswald was already planning the trip itself. He wrote to the embassy to ask if they could travel by train through Poland and then catch a military hop from Berlin.[42] On August 21, Marina put in a request for her own Soviet exit visa,[43] and had it and her Soviet passport in hand by December 1, 1961.[44]

Oswald's decision to bring Marina to America presented a different sort of problem for the CIA. One of the Soviet Russia Division elements in SR/6, the section handling biographic research work—SR/6/BIO—had been included in the internal routing of the July 3 Fain report. The chief of SR/6 at the time, known only by the initials T.B.C., described the problem in this way:

> I was becoming increasingly interested in watching develop a pattern that we had discovered in the course of our bio and research work in [SR/]6: the number of Soviet women marrying foreigners,

> being permitted to leave the USSR, then eventually divorcing their spouses and settling down abroad without returning ''home.'' The [redacted] case was among the first of these, and we eventually turned up something like two dozen similar cases. We established links between these women and the KGB. [redacted] became interested in the developing trend we had come across. It was partly out of curiosity to learn if Oswald's wife would actually accompany him to our country, partly out of interest in Oswald's own experiences in the USSR, that we showed *operational intelligence interest* in the Harvey [Oswald] story[45] [emphasis added].

''Per your request for any info on Oswald,'' said a September 28, 1961, internal CIA memo, ''pls[please] note: Marina . . . has apparently applied for a visa to the U.S., as reflected in Dept. of State, Visa Office notice received in CIA, which is dated 9/21/61.''[46] The memo added that this notation ''is being placed in Oswald['s] 201.''

On October 4, 1961, Oswald wrote to the embassy asking for help in securing Soviet exit visas,[47] and on October 9 Marina's petition to the U.S. Immigration and Naturalization Service was filed. On October 13, the embassy sent dispatch number 317 to the State Department, stating that ''Oswald is having difficulty in obtaining exit visas for himself and his wife, and they are subject to increasing harassment in Minsk.''[48] The records office noted on the attached CIA routing sheet that this dispatch ''has not been integrated into the CS [clandestine services] Record System.'' The only person who signed for it outside of the records office was CI/SIG's Ann Egerter. On December 1, 1961, the Soviets notified the embassy that Marina had her Russian passport and exit visa, which would be good until December 1, 1962.[49] Marina said she was surprised to get an exit visa.[50] So was U.S. Ambassador Thompson in Moscow. He testified to the Warren Commission that it was ''unusual'' for Marina to have been given her exit visa so quickly.[51]

It was also unusual, as the HSCA noted, that out of all the mail to and from Oswald in Russia, the CIA intercepted just one letter. From a 1962–1963 LINGUAL ''Progress Report'' dated April 1964, located in an obscure box of CIA records in the National Archives, however, comes this suggestive comment:

> The [HT/LINGUAL] Project has produced many items over the years concerning defectors and repatriates from the United States

> now living in the USSR. Among these have been numerous re-defectors who have returned to the United States, the most interesting among whom, during the past year, has been Lee Harvey Oswald. The Project's files contain several items to and from Oswald and his wife, and these were the source of the information that Oswald's pseudonym was used in the USSR as well as when he ordered the murder weapon from the gun store in Chicago.[52]

This was written by John Mertz, who should have known what was most interesting in Oswald's HT/LINGUAL file because he was the chief of the program at the time. His comment about "several" letters to and from Oswald and Marina leaves open the possibility that the Agency saw more of Oswald's mail than it has publicly acknowledged. We will return to the pseudonym and the rifle mail order later. Now, however, we return to the story of Gerry Patrick Hemming.

Hemming II: 1961

"After a period of weeks with no orders from the CIA," Hemming later wrote of his time in Los Angeles after his debriefing sessions of October 1960, "I decided to drop my cover and proceed to the Miami area to aid former Cuban associates that needed instructors for their personnel." Hemming had become impatient for more action, and Miami was where the Cuban action was. Naturally, it was also the location of the CIA's JMWAVE station, from which much of its Cuban operations were run. "After arrival in Miami [March 1961]," he said, "I then helped organize a group of volunteer U.S. and foreign Guerrilla Warfare Instructors.[53] He named the group "Intercontinental Penetration Forces," or "Interpen" for short. A 1976 CIA memo states Hemming was a "long-time cohort" of Frank Anthony Sturgis, of Watergate fame, and who organized a group of mercenaries for Caribbean and Central American activities which he named the International Anti-Communist Brigade.[54] This memo said that the "backers of Sturgis' group have never been fully established," and added that a reported "sub-unit" of this brigade was Hemming's Interpen.

Hemming's planned move to Miami was the cause of considerable security activity at the CIA as early as January 1961. On January 3 the chief of CI/Operational Approval and Support Division initiated a CIA Form 693 on Hemming. This form was used to get approval for contact with informants like Hemming and, in this case, listed the "Use of Subject" as "Contact and Assessment."[55] The previous day, an internal CIA memo asking for National Agency Checks (NACs) on Hemming said he was "now engaged in revolutionary activities in Nicaragua." The memo added that Hemming "will be debriefed with OCI requirements requesting all possible information concerning current military, economic and political developments in various Latin American countries."[56]

The CIA assessment of Hemming continued into March 1961. On the final day of March, a CIA report on "[EE-]29229, Subject: Gerald P. Hemming, Jr., Moves to Miami to Engage in Anti-Castro Operations" was submitted internally, along with a list of numbered reports based on "several debriefing sessions" with him. The purpose of this unsigned but highly significant CIA document was to "give a better idea of whether or not Hemming might prove useful." According to the report, Hemming revealed his new plans to CIA Los Angeles Field Office Agent Hendrickson, who reported that Hemming had said he was "moving to Miami" to train Cubans, and planned to arrive on Monday, March 20, 1961.[57] The March 31 CIA report provided these details:

> Hemming stated that he was going to contact Jimmy Gentry, 953 SW Penn St., Apt. 8, Miami, Florida (Telephone: Franklin 4-3265) and that these two men were then going to proceed with a plan of action aimed at organizing a small group of "professionals" (experienced revolutionaries) who would attempt to conduct certain reconnaissance operations on the mainland of Cuba via parachute drops and either light plane or water pick-ups. Hemming also stated that he wanted to do what he could in Miami to attempt to unite the anti-Castro forces there and also to lessen the influence of a number of "mercenaries" who had joined various of these movements and were doing it more harm than good while bleeding off much of the available money.[58]

The CIA report added that Hemming had been honing his parachuting skills "during his recent stay in Los Angeles (September

1960–March 1961), and claimed to have jumped at least once a month with one of the local parachute and skydiving clubs.''

Hemming's future plans made it necessary, in the view of the anonymous author of the March 31 CIA report, to evaluate him, a feasible task given the large body of recent debriefing material in his files. The report predicted ''it appears likely that the Agency may wish either (1) to make certain that no amateur reconnaissance operations directed at Cuba are undertaken, or (2) in one way or another to guide such activities to maximize their usefulness.'' Hendrickson, the report concluded, ''is inclined to believe that Hemming is both sincere and serious in his desire to assist the U.S. government, provided that this can be accomplished through his continuing to act as a soldier of fortune.[59]

These CIA documents, then, set the dates for Hemming's stay in Los Angles as September 1960 through the end of March 1961, and the date of his time of arrival in Florida as sometime soon after that. Some of the CIA's checking into Hemming involved odd places like Dallas where, on May 10, 1961, the special agent in charge of the CIA field office in Dallas, Texas, sent a cable to the ''Chief Invest Div.'' This was possibly the investigations branch chief of the Security Support Division (SSD) of the CIA's Security Office. From the ''Open Desk'' at SSD, the check was passed to the ''Clearance Branch, PSD,'' probably the Personnel Support Division.[60]

The content of the cable is vague but fascinating. The first line was ''SUBJ G P H JR EE 29229,'' undoubtedly meaning ''Subject: Gerald P. Hemming Jr., EE-29229.'' The second line, ''Agency Results,'' is unclear, and could have been meant a Dallas request for information from the Agency, or the results of an Agency check in Dallas. The third line was ''FBI NIC,'' possibly meaning Federal Bureau of Investigation: nothing of intelligence concern.'' The last line was revealing: ''5 others NR,'' meaning ''no records on the other five people.'' Apparently, the CIA already had information that connected Hemming to five other people.[61]

By July 25, 1961, the CIA investigation had run its course. On that date, M. D. Stevens of the Security Office's Security Research Staff (SRS) wrote a memorandum for the file on Hemming, wrapping up the year's events with this remark: ''Hemming prefers to use the name Jerry Patrick when commanding Interpen. He was approved as a CIA contact on 6 March 1961 and as of 2 June 1961 a security check turned up no derogatory information.''[62] By this time the FBI and the Office of Naval Intelligence (ONI) began asking questions about Hemming. On May 25, ONI section 921E2 called in a ''Status Check'' to the ''ABN'' section of the Marine Corps Commandant's Office on Hemming, ''Alleged ex-Marine.''[63] The next day, Navy YN1 Pierce, of the same ONI section, prepared an ONI cross-reference sheet for information from a May 19 FBI report. The subject of the FBI report was ''Anti-Communist Legionnaires and Neutrality Matters,'' and it contained information on Gerald Patrick Hemming, Robert Wills aka Robert Willis, and Dick Watley.[64] A May 23 Miami FBI report, also on anti-Communist legionnaires, was used by a person with the initials ''mlb'' to prepare another ONI cross-reference sheet. On this sheet, dated June 16, 1961, ''mlb'' typed the following data:

> MM T-1, who has been connected with Cuban revolutionary activities for the past three years, and who has furnished reliable information in the past, on May 12, 1961, advised that between 30 and 40 Americans arrived in Miami from Texas on May 11, 1961. They were recruited by Allen Lushane, who temporarily resides at the Cuban Hotel, 35 Northwest 17th Court, Miami, Fla., and who previously made a trip to Texas to recruit Americans for some future military action against the Government of Cuba. The first training camp was established by Gerald Patrick Hemming with Dick Watley and Ed Colby running the camp.[65]

MM T-1 was a Miami FBI source whom Hemming believes might have been Justin Joseph ''Steve'' Wilson. ''He had been an agent for Batista and Papa Doc,''[6] Hemming states, reporting ''through Clode in the Intelligence Division of the Dade County Sheriff's Department (now it is Metro Dade Police).''[67] This source, whoever it was, would continue to provide informative reports on Hemming for years.

''Jesse Smith and Joe Murphy, owners of the Congress Inn Hotel, Lejeune Road, Miami, Fla., have donated three rooms in the hotel for the use of Henning [Hemming]'s group,'' the May 23 report continued, ''and stated they will try to get political and financial backing for this group.'' The next day the same informant offered this additional note:

> On May 13, 1961, MM T-1 advised that C. F. Riker, 2610 MacGregor #2, Houston, Texas, phone number RI 7-6666, was in Miami and claimed to represent a group of assassins that operate exclusively against Communists. Riker is described as being well educated, and claims to have attended a number of Government schools having to do with arms, demolitions and languages. Riker claims he lived in Mexico during his youth, and speaks Spanish.[68]

The ''Riker'' story underlined the perilous nature of the Cuban exile community in Miami that Hemming was mixed up in. It also illustrated the usefulness of the FBI's Miami sources in keeping track of Cuban exile activities.

Meanwhile, documentation of Hemming's activities continued to build in the ONI's offices in the Pentagon and the Marine Corps G-2 [intelligence] offices in the Arlington Annex in Washington, D.C. on July 5, 1961, the ONI asked USMC Headquarters for information on Hemming,[69] and on July 6 ''ajd'' in ONI's 921E office asked the FBI for information on Hemming.[70] After a minor clarification sent on September 19, 1961 that they had nothing on ''Hemming.''[71] the Marine Corps came up with Hemming's old Los Angeles address, which ''cn'' of 921E then passed along to the FBI on October 23. ''Any information which may become available concerning Hemming,'' ONI said, ''will be of interest to this office in view of his membership in the U.S. Marine Corps Reserve.''[72] The analysts at ONI were beginning to have doubts about the Hemming's Marine Corps association. The same day, ONI wrote a letter to the Officer in Charge, District Intelligence Office (DIO), Sixth Naval District (6ND), asking for information on Hemming, ''who allegedly has had U.S. Marine Corps status.'' This time the ONI had Hemming's ''latest'' address—the Blue Bay Motel in Miami Beach, Florida.[73]

On November 3, 1961, DIO 6ND broadened its Hemming coverage by writing to the Director, Sixth Marine Corps Reserve and Recruitment District, in Atlanta, Georgia,[74] and on December 5 sent these intriguing remarks to the DIO 11ND:

> 2. The Director SIXTH Marine Corps Reserve and Recruitment District upon being informed of the foregoing advised DIO-6ND

> as follows: ''There is no record of the subject named man having been nor is he now carried on the rolls of this District.''
> 3. Obvious sources in Miami, Florida area were checked with negative results as to the Subject's present whereabouts.
> 4. In view of the above facts, no further action is contemplated in regard to reference (a), unless future developments warrant it.[75]

This was extraordinary news: The Marine Corps could not find any information on Hemming's reserve status. This only fueled ONI interest in Hemming's activities.

Hemming's old contacts in the Los Angeles field office of the CIA had no problem keeping informed about his Miami activities. Hemming took care of that by writing letters to an informant of that Agency field office. Analysts at the Office of Naval Intelligence spent their time preparing FBI reports for Navy files on Hemming. On August 8, 1961, a person named Carter in the 921E office of ONI prepared a July 12, 1961, FBI report, ''Cuban Rebel Activities in Cuba,'' for eventual filing in M5 files. In filling out the accompanying Cross-Reference Sheet, Carter mentioned a few details in the ''identifying data'' space:

> Damon also stated that one Jerry [Gerry] Patrick Hemming is now in Cuba and has as his mission the demolition of generator stations. Patrick at the present time is setting off about a pound of TNT nightly to create terror and confusion. When Patrick's mission is completed, he will receive $10,000.[76]

On August 10, 1961, the person with the initials ''mlb'' processed another FBI report for filing in ''M-5 FF'' (Finished Files), this providing the details of parachute jumps from a Cessna and Piper Colt by Hemming and three friends: Dick Watley, Frank Little, and Orlando Garcia.[77]

On August 25, 1961, a person by the name of Pierce in 921E processed a July 31, 1961, FBI report but his comment, ''see report for details,'' was not as thoughtful as Carter and ''mlb'' had been on previous reports. This was unfortunate, for the subject of this FBI report was Gerald Hemming and his Interpen organization.[78] Just what Interpen was up to became apparent from a few clues Hemming put in a letter he sent to a CIA Los Angeles field office

(LAFO) source, Dave Burt, who turned the letter over to the LAFO on October 4. Hemming said he needed parachutes and that his group was "really overworked with the Cuban problem." He said that "CBS and NBC have been bothering the hell out of us to go along" on their runs, but he could not allow this in order to "comply with security."[79]

"Did you get my letter last week?" Hemming wrote in a follow-up letter to Burt which was passed to the Agency LAFO on October 16. This time Hemming gave a lot more of the picture:

> At present "InterPen" boys are working their fingers to the bone. We are working as the military coordinators for Major Evelio Duque (Escambray mountains), Major Eloy Menoya (Escambray), Major Nino Diam (Oriente & Camagney Provinces), and other Captains that were leaders of guerrilla units in the mountains in Cuba up to about a month ago. As you probably read, there are three guerrilla units operating in the Escambray right now, they are being commanded by Majors Thorndyke, Ramires, and Campito.[80]

Hemming added that he might travel to the West Coast in the "near future," and enclosed a brochure published by the "Beachhead Brigade."

The fall of 1961 saw more interesting Hemming material. On September 5, 1961, MM T-1, who had been involved in Cuban revolutionary activities during the past four years and who had furnished reliable information in the past, advised that Saul Sage, an American, had been seen frequenting the hangouts of Cuban revolutionists in Miami. MM T-1 said that Sage belonged to the would-be organization of Gerald Patrick Hemming, an American soldier of fortune who was previously a member of the Cuban Revolutionary Air Force.[80]

"This Individual Looks Odd"

During the year following Oswald's decision to return home, some of the trails we have been following since his defection suddenly take peculiar turns. Oswald "the file" becomes a supplicatory pro-American character who has "matured." As discussed in Chapter Eleven, Oswald offered a revealing explanation for his earlier anti-American remarks: ''it was necessary to make this propaganda because at the time he had wanted to live in Russia.''[81] He had begged the American Consulate in Moscow to let him out of the Soviet Union. In much the same way he would later beg the Soviet Consulate in Mexico City to let him back in.

We encounter another curve in the Agency's disingenuous discourse about how Oswald's HT/LINGUAL file was insignificant. The record, as released, presents a puzzle: They did not open any of his letters when he was on the Watch List but did open one after he had been taken off it. Two clues suggest an answer. One comes from the memo mentioned in the introduction to this chapter in which the Soviet Realities Branch Chief explained that the pattern that existed of Russian women entering America through marriage and then working for the KGB was one of the reasons for operational interest in Oswald. To that piece we add this one: The date the single letter was opened in New York was July 8, 1961. Earlier that same day in Moscow, Oswald surfaced out of the blue, entered the embassy, and called Snyder on the house phone and then used a public phone to call Marina in Minsk with instructions to join him. The events in Moscow may well have triggered the intercept in New York.

''I remember that Oswald's unusual behavior in the U.S.S.R. had struck me from the moment I had read the first State dispatch on him,'' wrote a CIA employee whose initials were T.B.C. on November 25, 1963. T.B.C.'s full name is still classified, even though the Agency has released his initials.[82] The fact that he remembered the first Snyder dispatch and its shocking impact is significant. Oswald ''the file'' as he looked to the author of this memo, was summed up with this phrase: ''this individual looks odd.''

Chapter Fourteen

Oswald Returns

While Oswald prepared to return to the U.S., distant groups were at work in the CIA and in New Orleans shaping the context of the forces that would engulf and eventually destroy him. In New Orleans, currents shifted among the anti-Castro Cuban exiles. This movement provides a useful contextual background against which we watch Oswald extricate himself, and his family, from the Soviet Union. That backdrop also brings to our story key characters whose paths would cross and double-cross Oswald's, including the irrepressible Gerald Hemming.

Meanwhile, CIA security and propaganda elements were at work. Oswald was destined to collide with CIA operations against Cuba, especially those against the Fair Play for Cuba Committee (FPCC) which produced a long and tantalizing Agency security-propaganda thread involving two important CIA officers: James McCord and David Phillips. This thread begins when McCord and Phillips launched a domestic operation against the FPCC—outside the Agency's jurisdiction. At the other end of this thread—in fall 1963—we find Phillips again, this time running the CIA's anti-Cuban operations in Mexico. Mexico City is a subject to which we will return in the final chapters. Now we will turn our attention to the events that unfolded during Oswald's return from the Soviet Union.

McCord, Phillips, and CIA-FBI Operations Against the FPCC, 1961

The Fair Play for Cuba Committee (FPCC) emerged at the same time that the Agency began serious operations against Castro. A

July 15, 1960, Hoover memo to the State Department Office of Security tied—with the help of a fertile imagination—the pamphleting activities of the FPCC at the Los Angeles Sports Arena to a Cuban government radio broadcast that "announced that Mexico should join Cuba in a revolution and reclaim Texas and New Mexico which rightfully belonged to Mexico."[1] CIA interest in the FPCC and the chief of its New York chapter, Richard Gibson, was underscored by Gibson's active involvement with Patrice Lumumba, the premier of newly independent Congo. Lumumba was "viewed with alarm by United States policymakers because of what they perceived as his magnetic public appeal and his leanings toward the Soviet Union."[2] Gibson's support of Castro and Lumumba put him in a special category at the CIA: Both of these leaders had been targeted for assassination.[3]

Gibson spoke to June Cobb about the work "his group" was doing for Lumumba, according to the notes she wrote the morning after their conversation. The previous evening, Gibson had paid a visit to Cobb's hotel room for a chat. Before long, he had consumed half a bottle of scotch, and their dialogue reflected it. Cobb's notes contain this entry:

> At every possible opportunity he sought to turn the conversation to sex, particularly involving sex between Negroes and whites, for example: that Swedish girls are not kept satisfied by Swedish men since Swedish men are so often homosexual and that therefore there is a colony of Negroes and Italian[s] in Sweden to satisfy the erotic craving of the Swedish girls.[4]

But Gibson talked about more than Swedish cravings. He spoke about FPCC leaders, such as Bob Taber, and about the FPCC's relationship with American Communists. Presumably, Gibson did not know that June Cobb's hotel room was part of a carefully prepared CIA surveillance operation, with CIA technicians in the next room, eavesdropping. Cobb's notes of this encounter, preserved in her CIA 201 file, undoubtedly were not the only material produced, and must have supplemented tapes, transcripts, and surveillance logs filled out by the surveillance team.

The CIA's analysis of these materials is often entertaining reading, but for the individuals involved—Gibson, Cobb, and the surveillance technician on the other side of the wall—these were serious moments. Cuba had become part of the Cold War. A great deal was at stake. It was in the wake of Castro's and Lumumba's sudden emergence that Vice President Nixon had declared a crisis. It is not surprising that the CIA was interested in the FPCC and Richard Gibson. Ironically, their connection was destined to change: a few years after the Kennedy assassination, Gibson became an informant for the CIA. In 1960 and 1961, however, the CIA had its eyes on Gibson. Take, for example, this passage from a CIA report:

> On the 27th [October 1960], Richard Gibson of the Fair Play for Cuba Committee (FPCC), spent the evening with Cobb (drank half bottle of scotch), and talked rather freely about the [FPCC] Committee. Said they "want to destroy the world." In the beginning they received $15,000 from the Cuban government. Their expenses amounted to about $1500 per month—always feast or famine—trying to get money from Cuba. Once had to sit down with Dorticos and Fidel Castro to get $5000 the Committee needed. Gibson works closely with Raul Roa and little Raul—wanted Gibson to be Public Relations Officer for the Cuban Mission to the UN.[5]

Cobb was a valuable asset to the CIA because of her extensive knowledge about Latin American affairs and her personal relationships with many of the players and leaders. In this case, Gibson, already an intelligence target, seemed personally interested in Cobb, a weakness that had been turned to the advantage of the Agency. "As far as I'm concerned," Gibson said to Cobb on the telephone the day after his visit, "I'm always awkward around pretty girls." Cobb filed this remark on October 26, 1960.

Through Gibson, the CIA learned important details of the policy, personnel, and Cuban financial backing of the FPCC. The CIA had carefully evaluated his background and his activities, as this extract from an Agency report demonstrates:

> Gibson apparently received a Columbia University fellowship from Columbia Broadcasting Company before he was ousted. Now they will not take it away from him because it would cause a scandal—he uses it as a cover for his work. *FPCC* is working in Africa and particularly with the Lamumba faction. Roa wants to

> send Gibson to Africa since money from Cuba promotes "the thing" in Africa. FPCC is also involved in the Algerian situation. Gibson and his French wife were in Paris after the war and also in Algeria. He has been to Russia and to Ghana. Robert F. Williams is also apparently instrumental in stirring up trouble (in the US over racial issues?). Gibson has no love in his heart for the US. The FPCC is stirring up the Negroes in the South—says their plans have lots of loopholes and they expect to be arrested but they intend to carry on war against the US.[6]

Remarkably, the CIA saw the FPCC and Gibson as the instruments for a Castro-financed effort to foment insurrection in America. This was as menacing a thought as Hoover's July 15, 1960, allusion to a Cuban-inspired Mexican attack on Texas. While these threats were obviously exaggerated, knowledge about the FPCC and its activities was a matter of some urgency in the CIA in view of ongoing assassination planning for Lamumba and Castro. A counterintelligence officer in Phillips' WH/4 Branch wrote this in a memo to Jane Roman (liaison for Angleton's counterintelligence staff): "As you know, the FBI has expressed an interest in such information that Subject [Cobb] can provide concerning the Fair Play Committee [sic]."[7]

Not everybody at the CIA was happy about June Cobb's association with the Agency. In particular, Birch O'Neal of Angleton's mole-hunting unit, CI/SIG, did some sniping with his pen. On November 22, 1960, O'Neal wrote a memorandum critical of the "liberal press" in general and of June Cobb in particular for promoting an English-language edition of an old Castro speech "to show that Castro is not a Communist." O'Neal's memo said:

> The first edition was paid for by Miss Cobb and the second edition was paid for by the Cuban Consulate in New York. As far as we know, Miss Cobb is a rather flighty character. She comes in and out and we have not been able to find out where she lives or where she is now. Perhaps she is tied up with the so-called Fair Play for Cuba Committee.[8]

The innuendo radiating from this last sentence illuminates O'Neal's hostility toward Cobb, a view that may have had other adherents within the Agency's counterintelligence staff. From their perspective, Cobb's connections seemed to carry with them as many potential risks as awards.

In any event, the combination of Agency elements most closely associated with the "take" from Cobb at that time was O'Neal's CI/SIG, CI/OPS/WH (Counterintelligence/Operations/Western Hemisphere), and WH/4/CI. As CI/Liaison, Jane Roman also had access to the results of the Cobb debriefs and surveillance operations.[9]

In early 1961, eleven weeks before the Bay of Pigs invasion, the CIA seized an opportunity to become more actively involved in running operations against the FPCC. CIA Security Office and Western Hemisphere elements had identified an Agency employee who knew Court Wood, an American student just returned from Cuba under the sponsorship of the FPCC. This opportunity to surveil Court Wood, which developed at the end of January, was irresistible in the judgment of the person in the CIA's Security Research Service (SRS) of the Security Office who conceived and authorized the operation. That person was James McCord, the same James McCord who would later become embroiled in the scandal during the Nixon Presidency.

On February 1, 1961, McCord met with people from Western Hemisphere Division to discuss the "case" of an Agency employee who happened to be Court Wood's neighbor and former high school classmate. At issue was whether to use this employee operationally to extract intelligence information from Wood. The employee, conveniently, worked in WH/4, the very branch that McCord wanted to run the illegal domestic operation he had in mind. The memo of record for this meeting states the following:

> 1. On this date Subject's case was coordinated with Mr. McCord of SRS in connection with Subject's operational use within the US by WH/4/Propaganda. The implications of a CI operation with[in] the US by this Agency and the possibility Subject might come to the attention of the FBI through association with Court Wood were discussed.
> 2. Mr. McCord expressed the opinion that it was not necessary to advise the FBI of the operation at this time. However, he wishes to review the case in a month. The file of the Subject, along with that of the WH man who is supervising the operation (David Atlee Phillips #40695) will be pended [suspended] for the attention of Mr. McCord on 1 March 1961.[10]

It is fitting that one of the Agency's legendary disinformation artists, David Atlee Phillips, should have been in charge of the CIA's CI and propaganda effort against the FPCC. Phillips would reappear in Mexico City at the time Oswald visited there, taking over the anti-Cuban operations of the CIA station in Mexico during the very days that CIA headquarters and the CIA Mexico City station exchanged cables on Oswald's visit to the Mexican capital.

"At the request of Mr. Dave Phillips, C/WH/4/Propaganda," wrote the fortunate CIA employee picked to spy on his neighbor, "I spent the evening of January 6 with Court Wood, a student who has recently returned from a three-week stay in Cuba under the sponsorship of the Fair Play for Cuba Committee." The employee said that Court and his father both were pro-Castro and "extremely critical" of American foreign policy. "I've been advised by Mr. Phillips," the employee wrote, "to continue my relationship with Mr. Wood and I will keep your office informed of each subsequent visit."[11]

Indeed, the employee did keep Jack Kennedy, Chief of Security for Western Hemisphere Branch 4 (C/WH/4/Security), apprised. The next occasion occurred on March 3, 1961, after which the employee had new information, as reported March 8:

> Several months ago I wrote you a letter concerning the pro-Castro sentiments of Court Wood, son of Foster Wood, a local attorney. Since that time I've seen Court only once, on March 3, 1961, and he appears to be actively engaged in the organization of a local chapter of the Fair Play for Cuba Committee.

Little did Court Wood know that he was organizing his new chapter under the watchful eye of the CIA.

Our budding spy was beginning to blossom in his new assignment for David Phillips. Wood's neighbor also had this to say in his March 8 report:

> Complete with beard, Court has been meeting with "interested groups" and lecturing to students in several eastern cities. He specifically mentioned Baltimore, Philadelphia, and New York. Apparently there are a number of students envolved [sic] in this activity; I met David Lactterman from George Mason High School

> in Falls Church, Va. and Walt MacDonwald, a fellow student of Court's, and both are obviously active. What action, if any, should I take in regard to my relationship with Court and his father?[12]

It seems comical, that a group of high school students, led by a college student who had grown a beard to emulate Castro's appearance were the subjects of such CIA reporting. But it is actually sad.

Our spy now wanted more time to get additional intelligence. "Court Wood seems to be extremely naive about my position with the Agency," said the neighbor's next bulletin. Dated March 18, 1961, and, again, addressed to Mr. Jack Kennedy, the memo boasted that Wood "is very open and frank with me in all areas." Phillip's spy had spent "hours" with Court Wood and was sure his naiveté could be further exploited. "I am certain that if given enough time," the spy wrote, "I can obtain a great deal of information on the backgrounds and activities of many of his associates." The report also contained this passage:

> While visiting his apartment I observed that both Court and hisfather are interested in a large number of Communist publications. These included "USSR," "The Worker," and many prop. pamphlets that were obviously published in England. Court is an extreme Leftist in his political views and he believes fanatically in Castro's Cuba.
>
> Mr. Wood mentioned to me that he and several of his friends are making plans to enter Cuba in June; illegally if necessary. He apparently wants to become a teacher for the Castro government and to make his permanent home there. Members of the "26th of July Movement" are in close contact with Court and they are involved in this proposed move to Cuba. Court does have some money and he seems to be very serious about this thing. Within the next few days I have to be able to get some names and specific facts concerning their plans.[13]

Not a bad bit of work for three weeks, especially considering that this kind of assignment was not in the fellow's job description.

Ironically, just when our fledgling spy was about to acquire more intelligence, the matter came to the attention of the FBI, and his mission came to an abrupt end. In an October 7, 1961, memo to

FBI Liaison Sam J. Papich, CIA Acting Director of Security, R. F. Bannerman wrote this about the case of Court Wood:

> Reference is made to a 25 March 1961 and a 6 July 1961 investigative report on captioned Subject which have previously been furnished to this Agency.
>
> [redacted] who is a current Agency employee, has recently been interviewed concerning his knowledge of Court Foster Wood whom [redacted] had known since mutual attendance in high school. Attached is a detailed report of the information furnished by [redacted] concerning his knowledge of Wood.
>
> Since [redacted] personally has sufficient reason to question the activities of Wood and the activities of the associates of Wood, [redacted] has been advised to discontinue any further contact with Wood.
>
> It would be appreciated if your Bureau would furnish this Agency any additional information brought to your attention concerning Court Foster Wood and of particular interest would be any information received by your Bureau concerning past association of Court Foster Wood with N-[redacted].[14]

Thus it would appear that the FBI had learned of Court Wood's activities in March and again in July 1961, and had reported them to the Agency. The CIA then pulled its employee out of David Phillips's CI operation against the FPCC.

What the operation tells us is that the Agency was sufficiently interested in countering the FPCC to engage in an illegal domestic operation. The fact that controversy would follow the two men in charge, McCord in connection with Watergate and Phillips in connection with the Kennedy assassination, causes this page in the Agency's anti-Cuban operations to stand out in hindsight.

While the Court Wood operation was grinding to a halt at the CIA, the FBI was gearing up for its own operation against the FPCC. Fragments of an FBI document released by the Church Committee suggest that Cartha DeLoach, assistant director of the FBI, was in charge of a Bureau operation to compile "adverse" data on FPCC leaders. A handwritten note at the bottom of the FBI headquarters copy of the document includes this detail: "During May 1961, a field survey was completed wherein available public source data of adverse nature regarding officers and leaders of FPCC was compiled and furnished Mr. DeLoach for use in contacting his sources.''[15]

The fact that an assistant director of the FBI was collecting dirt on FPCC leaders underlines the extent of the Bureau's interest. The ''adverse'' data in the FPCC files kept by DeLoach probably grew considerably as a result of another CIA operation in October 1961. As we have seen, this operation netted significant intelligence on the FPCC from the Gibson material collected in June Cobb's room. This material included certain derogatory statements by Gibson which appear to be the sort of ''data'' DeLoach was looking for.

In December 1961, the FBI launched another operation, using the incendiary tactic of planting disinformation. The handwritten note discussed above contains this account:

> We have in the past utilized techniques with respect to countering activities of mentioned [FPCC] organization in the U.S. During December 1961, New York prepared an anonymous leaflet which was mailed to selected FPCC members throughout the country for the purpose of disrupting FPCC and causing split between FPCC and Socialist Workers Party (SWP) supporters, which technique was very effective.[16]

These tactics dramatize the lengths to which the FBI was willing to go to discredit the FPCC, whose chapters in Chicago, Newark, and Miami were infiltrated early on by the Bureau. As we will see in Chapter Sixteen, during Oswald's tenure with the FPCC, FBI break-ins to their offices were a regular occurrence.

Oddly, the day Patrice Lumumba's death was announced, February 13, 1961, was the same day Snyder received Oswald's letter about returning to America. As the FBI and CIA became engaged in a campaign to discredit the FPCC, Oswald was nearing his goal of having obtained all the necessary authorizations to return with his family.

Oswald Returns

Oswald wrote to his mother on January 2, 1962, telling her that he and Marina would arrive in the United States sometime around

March and asking her to have the local Red Cross request that the International Rescue Committee (IRC) assist them.[17] It would take longer than Oswald anticipated. Letters from Oswald[18] and the American Embassy,[19] both dated January 5, crossed in the mail. Oswald's letter was a request that the U.S. government pay for his and Marina's return to America, while the embassy's letter said that because of "difficulties" in obtaining an American visa for Marina, he might want to leave by himself and bring his wife later. The replies also crossed in the mail. Oswald insisted (on January 16) that he would not leave alone,[20] while the embassy (January 15) noted that Marina had no American visa, and suggested that a relative file an affidavit of support for her.[21]

Both responses were interesting. Oswald's January 16 letter revealed more than he may have intended, "Since I signed and paid for an immigration petition for my wife in July 1961," Oswald said with exasperation, "I think it is about time to get it approved or refused." The most intriguing aspect of the letter was this declaration: "I certainly will not consider going to the U.S. alone for any reason, particularly since it appears my passport will be confiscated upon my arrival in the United States."[22] It is difficult to know his precise thinking; perhaps he was afraid he'd never see her again, or perhaps he viewed Marina as some form of protection when he returned to the U.S.[23]

On January 23, 1962, Oswald responded with characteristic dualism to the embassy suggestion. He complained about their January 15, 1962, request for a support affidavit for Marina,[24] arguing that his two-year absence from the U.S. made this difficult. On the same day Oswald wrote to his mother asking that she file such an affidavit with the Immigration and Naturalization Service.[25]

The letter suggesting that Oswald leave without Marina had another noteworthy feature: It appeared to use Oswald's request for a loan as a lure to get him to the embassy. "The question which you raise of a loan to defray part of your travel expenses to the United States," the letter said, "can be discussed when you come to the Embassy." By February 6, however, the embassy had a change of heart. On this day, American Consul Joseph B. Norbury sent Oswald a letter saying, "We are prepared to take your application for a loan." Norbury instructed Oswald to provide twelve items of information, in triplicate copy.[26]

On February 1, 1962, Oswald again wrote to his mother.[27] The State Department had notified her that it would need $900 to make the travel arrangements for Lee and Marina.[28] Oswald dismissed his mother's suggestion that she raise money by telling his sad financial story to the newspapers.[29] In his February 9 letter to his mother,[30] he reminded her to file the affidavit for Marina and to send him clippings from the Fort Worth newspapers about his defection to Russia. Oswald gave the same assignment to his brother Robert.[31] Oswald told his mother that he wanted these clippings so that he could be "forewarned."[32] His January 30 letter to Robert included this passage: "You once said that you asked around about whether or not the U.S. government had any charges against me, you said at that time 'no.' Maybe you should check around again, its possible now that the government knows I'm coming they'll have something waiting."[33]

On the morning of February 15, 1962, Oswald took Marina to the hospital in Minsk, where she gave birth to their first daughter, June Lee, at ten A.M.[34] That same day, Oswald wrote to his mother,[35] and to his brother.[36] On February 23, the Oswalds brought their baby home from the hospital.[37] After the birth of June Lee, the health of the mother and baby obviated any sense of urgency over the date of departure for the U.S.[38] Oswald wrote to his mother on February 24[39] and his brother on February 27[40] that he did not expect to arrive for several months.[41] His return was just over three months away.

There were a few setbacks, however. Oswald did not get as much money as he asked for. On February 24, 1962, he wrote to the U.S. Embassy in Moscow asking for his loan.[42] The embassy received his letter on March 3. Oswald wanted $800.[43] The embassy wrote back that they would lend him only $500.[44] On February 26, Senator John Tower received an undated letter from Oswald asking for help in returning to the U.S.[45] The same day, Senator Tower forwarded Oswald's letter to the State Department.[46] What happened there is hard to explain. In spite of the confusion that existed in the State Department in early 1961 over the legal question of whether Oswald had renounced his citizenship, it was no longer an issue by early 1962. Oswald had never signed the papers, a fact duly noted by U.S. officials in Moscow and Washington. Now, in February 1962, the U.S. State Department decided that Oswald had never attained

Russian citizenship.[47] Therefore the State Department might have some difficulty explaining why a November 25, 1963, *New York Times* story reported that the department had told Senator John Tower (in February 1962) that Oswald had renounced his citizenship. According to the article, Senator Tower then closed his Oswald file.[48]

Oswald's correspondence with Texas picked up noticeably as he prepared for his return to America. On January 20, 1962, Oswald had written to his mother,[49] and three days later wrote to her again.[50] Marguerite responded, and it was from this correspondence that Oswald learned that the Marines had given him a dishonorable[51] discharge from the reserves.[52] This again provoked fears of prosecution, prompting Oswald to write his brother Robert asking for more information.[53] On that day, Oswald also wrote to former Secretary of the navy John Connally[54] to protest his undesirable discharge from the U.S. Marine Corps Reserves. "I ask that you look into this case," Oswald's letter said, and then added presumptuously, "and take the necessary steps to repair the damage done to me and my family."[55] Connally referred the letter to the Department of the Navy, and on February 23, 1962, Connally politely wrote to Oswald that his letter of January 30, 1962, had been turned over to the secretary of the navy, Fred Korth.[56] The Navy sent Oswald a letter stating that the Navy decided "that no change, correction or modification is warranted in your discharge."[57]

In a March 3, 1962, cable, four days before the Marine Corps mailed Oswald his undesirable discharge, the 921E2 section of the Office of Naval Intelligence sent a strongly worded message to the Navy Liaison officer in Moscow. Written by LTJG P. C. LeSourde (who also helped manage the Gerry Patrick Hemming case at this ONI office), the cable recalled Oswald's acts during his defection, including his offer to share his military knowledge with the Soviets. The cable's ominous tone was indicative of what was to follow: On March 7, 1962, the USMC sent Oswald his certificate of undesirable discharge.[58] Oswald was incensed, and on March 22, 1962, he wrote back protesting their decision and insisting that his discharge be given a full review.[59] The department promptly replied that it had no authority to hear and review petitions of this sort and referred Oswald to the Navy Discharge Review Board.[60] Oswald filled out an enclosed application for review while in Minsk but did not mail it until he returned to the United States.[61] More letters were exchanged—on April 2 from the USMC[62] to Oswald and on April 28 from Oswald to the USMC[63]—but nothing was accomplished.

Then Oswald's situation improved. By February 28, the San Antonio office of the Immigration and Naturalization Service sent word to him that Marina's visa petition had been approved.[64] By March 28, he had received an affidavit of support on Marina's behalf from his mother's employer, Byron Phillips (a Texas landowner from Vernon, Texas),[65] which Oswald filed even though it was no longer necessary to do so.[66] In March 1962, Phillips had agreed to sponsor Marina as a U.S. immigrant.[67] There followed several communications to Texas: letters to Marguerite on March 28[68] and April 21,[69] a card to Mrs. Robert Oswald on April 10,[70] and a letter to Robert on April 12,[71] in which Oswald wrote that only "the American side" was holding up their departure. Oswald added, however, that since the winter was over, he didn't "really want to leave until the beginning of fall, since the spring and summer [in Russia] are so nice."[72]

In fact, Oswald had nothing to complain about. From the available documents, a strong case could have been made—and Oswald knew and feared it—to prosecute him under military or civilian espionage laws. As things stood in the spring of 1962, he was lucky to be coming home without facing the consequences of his actions, and to have had all the U.S. bureaucratic obstacles removed, possibly too easily, so that he could be accompanied by his wife and child. Discussions with the embassy to complete financial and travel arrangements continued in April and May,[73] and finally, on May 10, the embassy wrote to Oswald saying that everything was in order, inviting him to bring his family to the embassy to sign the official paperwork.[74]

At his request,[75] Oswald was discharged from his job at the radio factory on or about May 18,[76] an event he recorded in his workbook.[77] The final resolution of his trip plans led to a new round of mail. On May 21, Oswald wrote to his brother again,[78] telling Robert that he and his family would leave for Moscow on May 22 and depart for England ten to fourteen days later, then cross the Atlantic by ship. Repeating a point he had made in an earlier letter to his mother, Oswald said that he knew from the newspaper clippings what Robert had said about his defection to Russia, and suggested that Robert had talked too much. Oswald now asked him not to offer comments to the newspapers.[79]

The Oswalds spent their last night in Minsk with Pavel Golovachev.[80] A "Minsk" exit visa was stamped in Oswald's passport on May 22, 1962.[81] His clearance procedures for departure included an interview with an official of the MVD.[82] On May 24, 1962, the embassy in Moscow renewed Oswald's U.S. passport, amending it to reflect June Lee's birth.[83] All three arrived in Moscow on May 24[84] and, after filling out various documents at the embassy, Marina was given her American visa.[85] The rest was up to the Soviets. On May 26, Marina's passport was stamped in Moscow,[86] and on May 30, Oswald wrote to his mother from Moscow, "We shall leave Holland for the USA on June 4."[87]

On June 1, 1962, Oswald borrowed $435.71 from the U.S. State Department for his return trip,[88] and on June 2 the Oswalds boarded a train for Holland,[89] which passed through Minsk that night,[90] crossed the Russian border at Brest,[91] and transited Poland and Germany.[92] On June 3, Oswald's passport was stamped at the Oldenzaal Station, in the Netherlands.[93] Marina recalled having spent two or three days in Amsterdam.[94] On June 4, 1962, the Oswalds' steamship tickets were delivered to them in Rotterdam. On June 6, they departed on the *Maasdam,* a Holland-American Line ship,[95] bound for New York.[96] On board the ship, the Oswalds stayed by themselves; Marina later testified that she did not often go on deck because she was poorly dressed and her husband was ashamed of her.[97] On the *Maasdam,* Oswald wrote some notes on ship stationery that appear to be a summary of what he thought he had learned by living under both the capitalist and Communist systems.[98]

On June 5, 1962, the New York Department of Health, Education and Welfare notified the New York Travelers Aid Society that the Oswalds were coming.[99] The *Maasdam* landed at Hoboken, N.J., at one P.M. on June 13.[100] The Oswalds were met by Spas T. Raikin, a representative of the Travelers Aid Society, which had also been contacted by the Department of State. Raikin said he had to chase Oswald, who tried to "dodge" him. Raikin had the definite impression that Oswald wanted to "avoid meeting anyone."[101] When they talked, Oswald told Raikin that he had only $63 and no plans for that night or for travel to Fort Worth. Oswald, says Raikin, accepted the society's help "with confidence and appreciation."[102] They passed through customs and immigration, with Raikin's help,[103] without incident.[104]

The Travelers Aid Society handed the Oswalds over to the New York City Department of Welfare, which found the family a room at the Times Square Hotel.[105] In one of the many different versions of his Soviet story, Oswald told both Raikin and the welfare department representatives that he had been a marine stationed at the American Embassy in Moscow, had married a Russian girl, renounced his citizenship, and worked in Minsk; soon he found out, he said, that Russian propaganda was inaccurate, but he had been unable to obtain an exit visa for Marina for more than two years. He also said that he had paid the travel expense himself.[106] Of course, Oswald had not been a marine stationed at the embassy, had not renounced his citizenship, had not worked for two-plus years on Marina's visa, and had not paid for his or their travel himself. Oswald's motives for telling these needless lies are obscure.

When the New York City Welfare Department called Robert Oswald's home in Fort Worth, his wife answered and offered to help. She contacted her husband, who sent $200 immediately.[107] At first Oswald refused to accept the money. He insisted that the welfare department should pay his family's fare to Texas, and threatened, apparently thinking the welfare department would suffer from the publicity, that they would go as far as they could on his $63 and then rely on "local authorities" to get them to Fort Worth. The welfare department was not intimidated by such tactics and Oswald had no choice but to accept his brother's money.[108] On the afternoon of June 14, the Oswalds flew from New York to Fort Worth.[109]

Meanwhile, across the Mississippi River in Louisiana, events were unfolding in the underworld of Cuban exiles and CIA Cuban operations, the focal point of which was the port city of New Orleans. Oswald's entanglement with this world was just months away. Eleven days after Oswald stepped off the plane in Fort Worth, an anti-Castro group from the Florida Everglades, including Gerry Hemming, came to New Orleans with the help of Frank Bartes, the AMBUD delegate there. AMBUD was the Agency cryptonym for the Cuban Revolutionary Council (CRC), a CIA-funded and controlled organization that had extensive operations in New Orleans. It is to Gerald Hemming's story that we now turn.

Hemming III: The Los Angeles Gun Incident

On January 30, 1962, an event took place that created a new batch of paperwork on Hemming, and something even more interesting. The trigger event occurred in Los Angeles, where the Sheriff's Office reported picking up a .45-caliber U.S. government pistol, serial number 1504981-SA, at 0200 A.M. Based on an anonymous tip, the police located and removed the pistol from a parked car.[110] Thirty minutes later, Hemming walked into the police station. The resulting police report described the event this way:

> At 2:30 AM, 1-30-62, a Gerald P. Hemming Jr. of 3843 East Blanche St., Pasadena entered Temple Station and informed us that the .45 automatic was his. Mr. Hemming stated the automatic was issued to him by the US Government Central Intelligence Agency in Miami, Florida approximately nine months ago and that he, Mr. Hemming, has been in training for a free-lance organization regarding Cuban invasion. Mr. Hemming stated he was a friend of Dodd's and that he had left the pistol at Dodd's Barber Shop and that it had disappeared from there. This detail contacted Central Intelligence Agency, a Mr. DeVanon, who said he could neither confirm nor deny the issuance of this pistol to Mr. Hemming; that he would appreciate no publicity be given the incident and that he would contact Lt. Wilber of this detail tomorrow morning with further information.[111]

Shortly thereafter, the Agency field office in Los Angeles notified CIA headquarters of the Sheriff's Office report containing Hemming's claim that he was a "CIA agent," and that he "was training people in Florida for another invasion."

This Los Angeles CIA cable drew attention to the remark by Hemming that the pistol had been "issued" to him by the CIA in Miami. The cable provided headquarters with this, possibly related, detail:

> Meanwhile, Sixth Army-CID got in Act, but CIC got them out again. However, if weapon is not property of some other agency they want to recover on presumption it is Army property. We have

> prevailed on sheriff's office to keep it off blotter and away from press, denying all the time that we ever heard of a Hemming. Hemming called this office later in day to report pistol stolen but recovered by sheriff's office. Did not mention having previously claimed association with the agency.[112]

The Army's stake in the matter was noted in the February 7 CIA headquarters response to the Los Angeles field office. "You were also informed that the local Army CID office had expressed an interest in the case on the presumption that said weapon may be Army property."[113] What was missing from the headquarters response was this question: For what reason and under whose authority did Army Counterintelligence get the 6th Army's Criminal Investigation Division to back out of the case?

An internal CIA Headquarters memo of February 2, 1962, indicated that the culprit claiming the pistol was probably Hemming, "identical with the Subject of Security File # EE-29229," but that he was not and had not been in the past of interest to Western Hemisphere Division, which maintained "information" on Hemming anyway.[114] This internal memo, however, contained a slightly different variation of the incident. Written in the Operational Support Division of the Security Office, the memo contained this paragraph:

> The sheriff's office contacted the OO/C [Domestic Contacts] Los Angeles office who, in turn, requested the sheriff's office to attempt to keep the matter out of the newspapers and that they would attempt to trace the identity of the individual. The local CID office of the U.S. Army also became interested in this matter; however, they also were requested to suspend any active investigation of this matter.[115]

Putting this together with information from the Los Angeles field office, we now have this picture: The Army Counterintelligence Corps requested the 6th Army Criminal Investigation Division to suspend any active investigation into the Hemming gun incident. Was the U.S. Army issuing, in Miami or elsewhere, sidearms to Cuban training groups subordinate to or associated with the Cuban Revolutionary Council? We know the Army was involved in training

Cuban rebels. Was Hemming's Interpen connected to the Army or to an Agency project to which the Army provided support?

The CIA response to the Los Angeles field office also mentioned Hemming's statement "that he was a GOLIATH agent who was on a training mission in connection with an assignment aimed at Cuba. . . . Subsequently, this matter was brought to the attention of the overt GOLIATH field office in your area."[116] GOLIATH* was another way of referring to the CIA. GOLIATH headquarters, however, forgot to ask GOLIATH Los Angeles how Hemming got to the police station so fast. There is no record of the police having traced the gun's serial number or having called Hemming. Who was the "anonymous" caller? Could the call and Hemming's appearance shortly thereafter to lay claim to his weapon be connected? Did Hemming make that call?

Ernst Liebacher was chief of Operations at the CIA Los Angeles field office (LAFO) at the time, and he interviewed Hemming after the gun incident in Hemming's office on 403 West 8th Street. Liebacher submitted his report of the details on February 15. In the report, Liebacher explained that Hemming had been known to the LAFO "since approximately October 1960 when he voluntarily contacted the office and furnished certain information concerning activities in Cuba." The report added that, "from time to time," Hemming had "furnished additional information which has been forwarded to Washington, DC in the form of reports of interest to the agency."

Liebacher's report also revealed who in the CIA LAFO had been Hemming's point of contact. Liebacher said that for a long time it had been Paul R. Hendrickson, who "had many contacts," and later, after Hendrickson was transferred to the Seattle office, Sergeant W. D. Pangburn had been "designated for contact." Liebacher's February 15 memo added this note:

> Within the past two weeks, Subject furnished Pangburn with a large envelope marked "Cubana Revolucion," or some such legend on it, and it contained all sorts of plans for training Cuban guerrillas. Subject claimed to have been working with the Office of Naval Intelligence and said that he had also been in contact with the Federal Bureau of Investigation in Miami, Florida.[117]

---

*Another cryptonyn for the CIA was "KUBARK."

According to Liebacher, Hemming never claimed to have worked for the Central Intelligence Agency. This is correct. Hemming claimed only to be an informant, "a snitch," as he said, for the Agency, and sometimes as a "singleton" for Angleton. The point here, however, is that the gun story led to other trails, to Cuban exiles and the counterrevolution against Castro.

We know that the gun incident illuminates only a portion of Hemming's CIA activity which went back well before his October 1960 debriefing by the LAFO. What concerns us now are his corresponding ONI files in the first half of 1962. It is from those files that we catch a glimpse of Hemming's associates and of who was processing his files in ONI. The above CIA documents and the ONI documents below are most valuable when viewed together, a combination that provides insights into otherwise shadowy parts of the Cuban exile underworld. From the time of the L.A. handgun incident in January 1962 to Hemming's trip to New Orleans in June 1962, his ONI and FBI files cross-reference into an interesting tangle of names: Menoyo, Quesada, Seymour, Sosa, Bartes, and Wesley.

Three of these names, Seymour, Bartes, and, possibly Wesley too, would become involved with the Oswald story in important ways.

Hemming IV: A Trail of Names

The CIA February 15 summary of events discussed above also noted the Pangburn interview of Hemming on February 6, 1962. Pangburn had obtained the following information from Hemming:

> Subject claimed that he was issued the .45-caliber automatic pistol about 1½ months ago by a Cuban named Captain Sosa, who had obtained permission from one Arturo Gonzales Gonzales. Sosa was reported to have been with the "30th of November group" and to have spent considerable time in the mountains. It was Subject's understanding that Sosa was known to the Central Intelligence Agency.
>
> Two (or possibly three) guns were issued to Subject and his cohorts, one of them a former OSS-type, named Davis, who was also said to be connected with the "30th of November group." Subject stated that these weapons had been issued to them because other underground Cuban groups in Miami had been "giving them

> trouble'' by putting sugar in gas tanks and tossing small grenades in their quarters.[118]

The Office of Naval Intelligence (ONI) file contained intelligence on the members and leaders of the 30th of November Group. Some, possibly much, of this intelligence was gained through an FBI informant in Hemming's circle. The FBI, in turn, shared this information with ONI.

On April 24, 1962, P. Carter, an ONI clerk working in Op-921E (Security, Espionage, and Counterintelligence Branch), prepared, as an enclosure to a cross-reference sheet, information on Hemming.[119] This report contains a tiny detail on the final destination of the Robert James Dwyer file which seems worth making a note of—the appearance of the organizational designator ''F5''—a detail we will return to when it crops up again. The other information entered into Hemming's ONI files on June 11 said that, as of April 19, the 30th of November Group had ''about'' twenty-seven members, and its leaders included such former prominent Cubans as Jesus Fernandez, formerly Havana Province financial coordinator; Orlando Rodriguez, ''who had no position in the movement in Cuba''; Guido De La Vega, transportation coordinator and known to Rodriguez as ''anti-U.S.''; Joaquin Torres, formerly Matanzas Province coordinator; Osvaldo Betancourt, formerly Havana Province general coordinator; Manuel Cruz, Havana Province financial coordinator (succeeded Jesus Fernandez); and Horiberto Sanchez, brother-in-law to the founder of the 30th of November Group, David Salvidor. The leader at the time was named Carlos Rodriguez Quesada.

This information, placed on Hemming's cross-reference sheet on June 11 by ''jgr'' in ONI's 921E office, had apparently been picked up from Quesada by an FBI informant on April 19. The cross-reference sheet contains this useful passage:

> Carlos Rodriquez Quesada, head of group, advised 4/10/62 he just returned from Washington, DC where he was gratified to find that a number of military leaders and some Senators disagreed with State Department policy with regard to Cuba, and that aid for Cuban exiles may be forthcoming. [Informant] MM T-2 advised a part of the 30th of November under Jesus Fernandez is still connected to CRC. . . . On March 26, 1962 [informant] MM T-1, an

> individual who has been active in revolutionary activity in the Miami area for the past 4 years, advised that 5 men from the 30th of November Movement went into the Everglades west of Miami on the previous weekend, where they practiced shooting M-1 carbines. An American adventurer named Jerry Hemming accompanied this group.[120]

As we will see, heat from summer fires would soon force Hemming and his friends out of the Everglades. For now it is important to note that Quesada led the 30th November Group when it joined other factions in the spring of 1963 to form a Cuban government-in-exile.[121]

Another anti-Castro leader we meet in Hemming's early 1962 ONI files is Eloy Gutierrez Menoyo. A cross-reference sheet prepared on January 16, 1962, by P. Carter, the same clerk in the Programs section of the Espionage and Counterintelligence (SEC) branch of ONI (OP921E2), had the following story typed under the optional space on the form ''Identifying Data'':

> On 10/30/61, Eloy Gutierrez Menoyo said that 2 of his men made a trip to Cuba in a small boat and an American went along. On 11/13/61, Roger Redondo Gonzalez said that in the middle of 8/61, he, Gerald Patrick Hemming, and others, went to Cay Guillermo, Cuba, on a fishing boat. The boat captain contacted an underground member and delivered a message. On 11/13/61, Rafael Huget Del Valle said that in the middle of 8/61, he, Hemming, and others left in a fishing boat for Cuba, and arrived five days later in Cay Guillermo, Cuba. They remained there for 3 days and then returned to Miami. Redondo said Hemming previously claimed to know the location of an arms cache located in British Bahama Islands, but when they were at sea, Hemming said he did not know where the arms were.[122]

This material was derived from an FBI report, the subject of which was Hemming's Interpen.

On September 10, 1962, another interesting Hemming cross-reference sheet was prepared by the clerk ''jgr'', in which we encounter William Seymour and Jose Rodriguez Sosa. The cross-reference sheet contains this story:

> [Informant] MM T-1, who has been actively engaged in Cuban revolutionary activities for the past four years and who has furnished reliable information in the past, on June 11, 1962, advised that Larry J. Laborde called Miami, Florida the previous evening and said he expected the 67-foot schooner ''Elsie Reichart'' to arrive in Miami on or about July 14, 1962, Laborde said the boat would have four Americans and three Cubans aboard as crewmen.
>
> [Informant] MM T-1 advised that the schooner ''The Mariner'' is still located in Ft. Myers, Florida, needs an anchor and other repairs. Both of these boats are reportedly being operated by their owners and crews without monetary remuneration from Laborde.
>
> Bill Seymour, an American citizen who had previously been trained as a mechanic while serving in the United States Navy, has been residing in Miami and is closely connected with Gerald Patrick Hemming, an American soldier of fortune who is closely associated with persons in Cuban revolutionary activities in the Miami, Florida area. Hemming, who is a close friend and associate of Laborde, planned to send Seymour to St. Petersburg to work on the boat's engine.
>
> Captain Jose Rodriguez Sosa, a Cuban national residing in Miami and a member of the Directorio Revolucionario Estudiantil, a Cuban revolutionary organization, has been in close contact with Laborde and plans on sending another Cuban from Miami to join the ''Elsie Reichart'' which recently sprung a leak in the hull, and whose engine is still inoperative.[123]

Here, Hemming is connected to the DRE in Miami through Sosa. As we will see, Hemming was about to make his way to New Orleans. William Seymour is of special interest because his name later turns up in a bogus FBI story swallowed hook, line, and sinker by the Warren Commission. That story had Seymour as one of the three men who visited Silvia Odio on September 25, 1963,[124] two days before Oswald arrived in Mexico City. These are subjects we will cover in Chapters Seventeen and Eighteen.

It is remarkable how many threads of information eventually weave themselves into a part of the Oswald story. The FBI had an informant in Hemming's Interpen group, and much of his reporting was naturally cross-filed into Hemming's ONI files. An example of this was the obscure but engaging piece of filing information we set aside earlier in this chapter—that an April 24, 1962, FBI report on Robert James Dwyer in Hemming's file showed that the final ONI destination for this document was "F5."[125] Perhaps this was routine in the Navy, but it rarely appears elsewhere in the JFK collection.

This office might have been in 923F, the Personnel Branch of ONI's Administrative Division (923), but if so, it was not listed in the documents consulted for this study.[126] It was probably an F5 branch in the same general part of ONI—Administration and Security (921)—that was handling the job of excerpting the Hemming material for final filing. This would make the full designation "921F5," which is worth mentioning because the only other document in the JFK files from 921F5 has an intriguing person's name on it. The document makes a brief reference to a discussion by "M. Wesley" of a "complete file" and "case history" on Interpen.[127] Even though it may be only a coincidence, it is an intriguing fact that there is a mysterious person by the name of "Wesley" who shows up in Mexico City after (or perhaps during) Oswald's visit there and makes his way into Oswald's FBI file.

Hemming and Bartes in New Orleans

In June 1962, Hemming connected with another anti-Castro Cuban leader: Frank Bartes. According to a July 2, 1962, CIA memorandum from the Agency's New Orleans office of the Domestic Contacts Division, Frank Bartes provided the CIA with this information:

> On 25 June 1962 Laurence Joseph Laborde and two other men had called on him [Bartes]. He had met Laborde earlier in Miami. The men said that they wanted to train Cuban refugees as guerrilla fighters and demolition experts who would then go to Cuba. The other men were Gerald P. Hemming, Jr. and Howard Kenneth Davis.[128]

Bartes added that Laborde was "anti-CIA," which the New Orleans office said it had "confirmed." Bartes reported that he had "reached an agreement" with Laborde. Possibly related to such an agreement were documents that Laborde gave to Bartes, one of them a letter of recommendation from 30th of November leader Carlos Rodriguez Quesada.[129]

There is further documentary corroboration of the assistance Bartes provided in getting Hemming, Laborde, and Davis into a training camp near New Orleans. According to a CIA "internal component" (presumably Task Force W or Branch 3 or 4 of the Western Hemisphere Division), a proposal had been made to a New Orleans "Cuban refugee group," probably the Cuban Revolutionary Council (CRC), for military training of another Cuban refugee group, possibly the 30th of November Group. This the Agency learned on June 28, 1962, when Bartes, "one of our sources among the Cuban refugees," the CIA memo said, "asked for an appointment so that he could give us some interesting information."

Bartes explained how it was that his activities in New Orleans became known to Laborde. Bartes and the other "Cuban refugee from New Orleans" had been in Miami "a month or so ago" and met Laborde. At that time Laborde had told them of his interest in working with the Cuban refugees. Laborde lamented that "he had previously been connected with a training camp in the Everglades in Florida, but that that camp had to be abandoned because of fires in the Everglades." The CIA memo explains what happened then:

> When Bartes returned to New Orleans, according to him, he contacted the local office of the Federal Bureau of Investigation and asked them if they could, in his words, "clear" Laric Laborde. The Bureau told him that while they could not give him an official clearance, they would look into the situation and would contact Bartes and Mr. Ravel, who is the nominal head of the Cuban refugee movement in New Orleans.
>
> Bartes says that sometime later the Federal Bureau of Investigation did contact Ravel and told him that as far as Laborde was concerned it was "hands off." Curiously enough, both "source" [Bartes] and Ravel took this to mean that this was a clearance of Laborde by the FBI, so that when Laborde and the other two US citizens contacted Ravel and Bartes in New Orleans they had no hesitancy in dealing with them.[130]

The CIA memo said that the Agency Domestic Contacts office in New Orleans had told Bartes that "all of this" was out of their jurisdiction, that the CIA "had absolutely nothing to do with such matters,'' and that they ''could not give him any advice'' about what ''he seemed to be seeking.''

Bartes countered with the remark that the reason he was providing the CIA with this information was that ''these three men hate CIA and they said that CIA is doing nothing and is preventing other people from doing anything and they are anxious to do something to help the Cubans without the help of CIA.'' Bartes added, defensively, that since he had furnished the CIA information in the past, ''he thought that we should know about the present situation.''

The documents that Hemming, Laborde, and Hall gave to Bartes were turned over to the CIA by the latter. They were a ''clipping'' from the June 3 *Denver Post* castigating the CIA and CRC leader Miro Cardona, and an undated document. The second (undated) document was signed by Luis del Nodal Vega, ''who styles himself Military Coordinator'' of the 30th of November Group, and Hemming and Davis, both instructors for Interpen. The document was ''approved'' by Quesada. Hemming told Bartes that this document ''had been presented to CIA in Miami last year but that nothing had come of it.'' When Bartes passed this on to the Agency, they said they would be glad to ''have copies of any of the documents which he had,'' but reiterated that they ''could not and would not advise him in any manner, shape, or form in connection with any such operation.''

''He seemed to understand that we could not help him,'' the CIA memo said of Bartes, ''and when he left he said that he thought he would tell the three men, Laborde, Hemming, and Davis, that he could not go along with them.'' The CIA memo went on to disclose that they had learned from another source who was a ''close friend'' of Bartes's, that he had seen Bartes with Hemming, Laborde, and Davis and that ''they looked like a bunch of thugs.'' The friend also said that Bartes had said, ''confidentially,'' that he was dealing with the three men ''as a representative of the New Orleans Cuban Refugee Organization,'' meaning the CIA-backed CRC. Bartes added, said the friend, ''that these three men were armed and therefore potentially dangerous.''[131]

CIA files on Bartes show that on January 4, 1961, the Operational Approval and Support Division asked the Security Office for a check on Bartes for use in a ''contact and assessment'' role in the area ''WH [Western Hemisphere] Cuba.''[132] By September 1965, Bartes was working for the CIA's Special Operations Division.[133] In between, he had a date on television with Oswald. That event, however, would not transpire until August 1963, and will be discussed in Chapter Seventeen. Before his Cuban escapades in New Orleans, however, Oswald spent almost ten months in Dallas. It is to that part of the story that we now turn.

CHAPTER FIFTEEN

The Unworthy Oswald

The outward appearance of the documentary record covering Oswald's ten months in Fort Worth and Dallas, from June 1962 to April 1963, is dominated by a gaping hole. The story that goes with that record is about how the FBI closed its file on Oswald in October 1962, became interested in him again six months later because he wrote a letter to a communist newspaper, and then lost track of him in April 1963 only a month after reopening his file.

There are several problems with this activity, especially at the points when the Oswald FBI file is opened and closed. First of all, why was it that the FBI, which had been primed for Oswald's return from Russia, calmly closed the book on him in spite of his uncooperative and obstreperous attitude, refusal to take a lie detector test, and immediate mail activities with just about any communist or left wing organizations he could think of. For his performance, Oswald was deemed "unworthy" of further attention, so unworthy that when, on a Dallas spring day in 1963, when someone from the FBI went looking for Oswald and found he had gone, nobody cared. Oswald was just routine.

As we will see, the first intercepted FPCC letter to land in Oswald's file was discounted by the FBI agent in charge of the file. Dallas Special Agent James Hosty claims he did not believe Oswald's remark that he had handed out FPCC literature in Dallas. Perhaps, but the inconsistency is the FBI's claim that Oswald's file was reopened in March because of a letter to the *Worker*. The file had been closed in October 1962, just after learning—on 28 September—of a similar letter to the *Worker*.[7] The circumstances surrounding the closure of Oswald's file directly contradict the stated rationale for its reopening.

During the documentary dark zone covered in this chapter, Oswald wrote to—and received mail from—the Soviet Embassy, the American Communist Party, the Socialist Workers Party, and an assortment of other far left periodicals and organizations. FBI Director Kelley's book admits that the FBI knew about this all along. The story the FBI told the Warren Commission about its interest in Oswald was, at best, fictionalized to cover sensitive programs such as the opening of mail to and from the Soviet Embassy in Washington D.C. As we will see, this problem persisted and was related to Oswald's move to New Orleans.

New Orleans is the subject of Chapters Sixteen and Seventeen. They begin a new phase in Oswald's about-to-be-shortened life: his venture into the shadowy world of the Cuban exiles there, handing out leaflets on the streets, and appearing in courtroom scenes and debates covered by radio and television. Oswald's transition into his Cuban role begins in Dallas, just before the end of the period to which we now turn.

Labyrinth V: Closing the Oswald File

"You should be alert for subject's [Oswald] return to the United States," FBI headquarters directed the Dallas FBI office on May 31, 1962, "and immediately upon his arrival you should thoroughly interview him to determine whether he was recruited by Soviet intelligence or made any deals with Soviets in order to obtain permission to return to the United States." The Bureau memorandum further directed the following:

> In your interview with subject, you should attempt to ascertain exactly what information he furnished to the Soviets. If any doubt exists as to subject's truthfulness during such interview, you should consider requesting his consent to a polygraph examination and, thereafter, obtain Bureau authority for such an examination. Results of interview with subject should be submitted in form suitable for dissemination.[1]

By the end of May 1962, the Bureau had already decided it wanted Oswald grilled. On June 14, FBI headquarters sent an air telegram to the New York FBI office relaying to them that "Bureau liaison was informed by ONI [Office of Naval Intelligence] on 6/14/62 that ONI is aware of subject's [Oswald's] scheduled arrival in US but has no confirmation of his actual arrival.'' The air telegram also indicated that ONI contemplated taking no action against Oswald but ''requested to be advised of results of our interview.''

The point of adding the ONI's expressed interest in this telegram to New York was to underline the importance of monitoring Oswald's movements when he returned so that he could be immediately interviewed. The telegram then repeated all the instructions previously sent to Dallas about ''thoroughly interviewing'' Oswald, and added these additional orders: ''New York should contact INS to verify subject's arrival, determine his destination in US, and advise Bureau, Dallas, and WFO.''[2] The New York FBI office verified Oswald's June 13 arrival and, as ordered, furnished Oswald's destination: Fort Worth, Texas.[3]

It was perhaps fitting that on the day the FBI interviewed Oswald, June 26, 1962, he walked into the Commercial Employment Agency and applied for a job saying he had been in Moscow working for the State Department.[4] The unsuspecting clerk probably failed to see the comedy in this. The FBI did not fare much better when Special Agent John Fain interviewed him in Fort Worth, Texas at one P.M. on June 26.[5] Oswald reportedly went with Fain to the FBI office but refused to take a lie detector test.[6] But according to former FBI Director Kelley, the interview did not exactly begin this way. Kelley says Fain was trying to schedule a ''fact-finding meeting'' with Oswald when he burst into the Dallas FBI office unannounced, and said, ''Here I am, what do you want me to talk about?''[7]

Before discussing the interview with Oswald, it is useful to know that, amazingly, the CIA was not furnished with a report of this interview. The moment that the FBI, ONI, INS, and the State Department had all been waiting for arrived the handwritten dissemination list neglected to add CIA,[8] and there is no surviving routing sheet from 1962 associated with the report. The State Department, INS, and the ONI all got their copies.

What did the CIA miss? Quite a show, from what the FBI says. Oswald was arrogant, intemperate, and impatient, often declining to answer questions. The agents' standing instructions when meeting such resistance were to request the subject to submit to a polygraph. They asked and he refused. Oswald said he had borrowed $435 from the American Embassy with which to come home, but then refused to answer Fain's question as to why he had gone to the Soviet Union in the first place. Oswald then made an angry "show of temper" stating that he did not want to "relive the past."[9] Oswald reportedly shouted this last remark at Fain, after which "Fain and Oswald nearly squared off right there in Fain's office."[10]

"From the very beginning," said Director Kelley in his 1987 autobiography, "dealing with Lee Harvey Oswald was no picnic for the FBI." It was certainly no picnic for John Fain. This recollection includes this passage:

> During most of the interview, Oswald exhibited an impatient and arrogant attitude. Oswald finally stated that Soviet officials had asked him upon his arrival why he had come to Russia. Oswald stated that he told them, "I came because I wanted to." Oswald added that he went to Russia to "see the country."
>
> Oswald advised that newspaper reports which have appeared in the public press from time to time are highly exaggerated and untrue. He stated that the newspaper reports had pictured him as out of sympathy with the United States and had made him look attractive to the Russians. Oswald stated that by reason of such newspaper reports he had received better treatment by the Soviets than he otherwise would have received.

Oswald might have thought his remarks were clever, but Fain obviously did not. In addition, the interview highlighted Oswald's deep dislike for journalism.

Significantly, the interview did explore what Oswald had done in the Soviet Union, how he had had spent his time as a metal worker in a "television factory" [wrong, it was a radio factory], and had been permitted to live in Minsk as a "resident alien." Oswald said he had learned Russian by "self instruction" while in the Marines, but denied ever having been in the American Communist Party. According to Fain's recapitulation:

> He denied that he went to Russia because of his lack of sympathy for the institutions of the United States or because of an admiration for the Russian system. He admitted that he had read books by Karl Marx while a resident of New Orleans, Louisiana, but he stated that he was merely interested in the economic theories.

> Oswald declined to explain what he meant when he wrote his mother while en route to Russia that his "values" and those of his mother and brother were different.
>
> Oswald stated he does not know where his birth certificate is and he denied that he took same to Russia with him.

On April 10, 1961, Marguerite Oswald said that Oswald took his birth certificate with him when he left Fort Worth.[11] In the interview, Oswald denies knowledge of the location of his birth certificate. Yet, as soon as September 17, Oswald presented his birth certificate in New Orleans to get a Mexican tourist card.[12] On November 22, 1963, a negative of Oswald's birth certificate was found and became Exhibit 800 in the Warren Report.[13]

Oswald was evidently willing to alter any truth that suited his advantage in the conversation. Here is a portion of the interview with a point-by-point critical analysis:

1. "Oswald denied that he had renounced his United States citizenship and stated that he did not seek Soviet citizenship while in Russia." False. He had sought Soviet citizenship while in the Soviet Union.

2. "Oswald stated that he was never approached by the Soviet officials in an attempt to pull information from him concerning his experiences while a member of the US Marine Corps." Possibly true, but it is likely that the circle around him in Minsk was used for such a purpose. It would not be surprising if he had been approached for his information. After all, he had offered it, with KGB ears listening, inside the American Embassy in Moscow.

3. "Oswald also stated that he was not recruited at any time while in Russia by the Soviet intelligence." Probably true.

4. "He stated that he made no deal with the Soviets in order to obtain permission to return to the United States." Possibly true, but it would not be surprising if the reverse were true.

5. "He stated that the Soviets made it very difficult for him to obtain permission for his wife to leave Russia, and that the process of obtaining permission for her to leave was a long difficult course requiring much paper work." Mostly accurate.

6. "He stated that no attempt was made by the Soviets at any time to "brainwash" him." Possibly true, but it is difficult to be certain.

7. "Oswald stated that he never at any time gave the Soviets any information which would be used in a detrimental way against the United States." This is doubtful. It certainly appeared to be his intention to do so. A pat denial afterward is difficult to accept in the face of his earlier eagerness.

8. "He stated that the Soviets never sought any such information from him. Oswald denied that he at any time while in Russia had offered to reveal to the Soviets any information he had acquired as a radar operator in the US marines." False. He made precisely such an offer in front of American officials.

Oswald provided Marina's Soviet passport number, Ky37790, and explained she was required to keep the Soviet Embassy in Washington, D.C. informed of her address and her periodic "whereabouts" while she was in the United States. Oswald mentioned that he was thinking of contacting the Soviet Embassy in "a few days" to tell them what Marina's current address was. But Oswald went a little further than that. Soon, in July, according to FBI director Kelley,[14] the FBI found out that Oswald "had sought information from the Soviet Embassy in Washington, D.C., about Russian newspapers and periodicals." Of course, Fain's report included this passage:

> Oswald stated that in the event he is contacted by Soviet Intelligence under suspicious circumstances or otherwise, he will promptly communicate with the FBI. He stated that he holds no brief for the Russians or the Russian system.[15]

Oswald neglected to say that he would tell the FBI if he contacted the "Russians or the Russian system." He did not have to tell them. Oswald's mail was a kaleidoscope of communist literature and organizations, and, as we will see, the FBI knew it.

On July 16, 1962, Oswald went to work as a metal worker for $1.25 per hour at Leslie Welding Company.[16] Oswald then rented a house, 2703 Mercedes, Fort Worth, for $59.50 a month from Chester Allen Riggs, Jr.[17] On August 17, Oswald filed a change of address notice from 7313 Davenport to 2703 Mercedes, Fort Worth.[18] At this time, Oswald started bugging the Navy yet again: On August 1 he wrote, using his 2703 Mercedes address, complaining about his undesirable discharge.[19] On August 6, the U.S. Navy Review Board responded.[20] He lost his job at Leslie Welding on October 9, which is not surprising, as it seems Oswald's primary interest was his pursuit of communist literature and organizations. Chester Riggs knew that something about Oswald's mail was out of the ordinary. Riggs told the Secret Service after the assassination that the U.S. Postal Inspection Service had investigated Oswald for receiving subversive mail while he was living at 2703 Mercedes.[21]

Oswald lived at the Mercedes address between August 17 and October 7, 1962.[22] The mail to and from that address during this period was so unusual for Texas that Oswald was probably watched closely. He began with a two-dollar subscription to the *Worker* on August 5,[23] and an August 12 inquiry to the Socialist Workers Party,[24] both using 2703 Mercedes as the return address. The Socialist Workers Party was, of course, on the list of subversive organizations,[25] and FBI agent Hosty later testified he considered it a "Trotskyite" type of political party.[26] On August 23, 1962, the Socialist Workers Party answered Oswald's inquiry,[27] and Oswald was at it again on August 26, sending $.25 for material on Trotsky.[28] On September 29, Pioneer Publishers wrote to Oswald telling him that the Trotsky pamphlet he had ordered was not available.[29] In September, Oswald sent another $2.20 for a one-year subscription to the Russian periodical *Krokodil.*[30]

Meanwhile, Fain admitted the first interview had been a failure. "Agent Fain reported to the special agent-in-charge of the Dallas office," says Director Kelley, "that the interview had been most unsatisfactory, that he was less than trusting of Oswald's answers, and that he would attempt another interview with Oswald." On August 14, 1962, FBI agent Fain called Robert Oswald to find out where his brother was working.[31] Fain got his opportunity on August 16, 1962, when he and Agent Arnold Brown pulled up in front of Oswald's house on Mercedes. All three sat in the FBI agents' car during the interview.

Because in this, the second interview, Fain claimed relative success, we must carefully compare it to the first interview to see where he makes progress. Unlike the June 26 interview, the FBI report on this interview was sent to the CIA. We will return to that point shortly. For convenience we will reconstruct the second interview, beginning with what was similar to the first one.

Oswald repeated the requirement to keep the Soviet Embassy informed about Marina's address,[32] lied about his attempt to renounce his U.S. citizenship and affirm allegiance to the Soviet Union,[33] lied about his offer of military information to the Soviets,[34] complained about his travails in returning home with his family,[35] refused to answer why he had gone to the Soviet Union in the first place, and then added:

> He stated he considers it ''nobody's business'' why he wanted to go to the Soviet Union. Oswald finally stated he went over to Russia for his ''own personal reasons.'' He said it was a ''personal matter'' to him. He said, ''I went, and I came back!'' He also said ''it was something that I did.''

This hostile rhetoric added little new to the equation. But this had a crucial bearing on several other questions that Oswald glibly dismissed, such as the question of possible KGB recruitment or attempted recruitment. He acknowledged but did not answer the question about having different values from those of his mother,[36] still declined to give names of relatives in the U.S.S.R., still denied making any ''deals,'' discounted the idea of Soviet intelligence interest in his activities,[37] and said no one ever attempted to recruit him or elicit any secret information.

After complaining about the Marine Corps and a few comments about his new address and job, along with assurances that no Soviet intelligence agents were in contact with him, Oswald said this:

> Oswald advised when he first arrived in the Soviet Union, and also when he started to leave, he was interviewed by representatives of the MVD, which he characterized as being the secret police, who, for the most part handle criminal matters among the population generally. He stated their operation is widespread.

In addition, Oswald stated he might have to return to the Soviet Union in about five years in order to take his wife back home to see her relatives. No definite plans had been made. A useful piece of news was Oswald's clarification that he had not taken his birth certificate to the Soviet Union; he said he thought it had been ''packed in a trunk at his mother's home.''

Director Kelley described the second interview with Oswald this way: ''Oswald, though much more placid this time, still evaded as many questions as he could.''[38] But, strangely, the Dallas office decided to close Oswald's file. Kelley's account picks up the story:

> Agent Fain and officials at FBI headquarters, however, were apparently satisfied that Oswald was not a security risk, that he was not violent, and that, as a sheet metal worker in Fort Worth, he was not working in a sensitive industry in this country. They, therefore, recommended that his file be placed in an inactive status, a decision routinely made by officials within the FBI's Soviet espionage section.[39]

The inactive status lasted from late August through October. In that later month John Fain retired and Oswald's file was officially closed instead of being reassigned to Hosty. We will return to this closing shortly.

Why did the FBI send only the second Oswald interview to the CIA? Of the two, the first would have been more interesting to the Agency. That interview contained more information about Oswald's activities in the Soviet Union and therefore would have been more useful from a ''Soviet Realities'' SR/6 perspective. Obviously, the FBI should have sent them both, just as both were sent to the State Department. Therefore, we should not overlook the possibility that the FBI did send a copy to the CIA, and that it is the Agency that is responsible for the missing document. Whatever the explanation, the incident is worth noting, because it appears to be part of a pattern in Oswald's CIA and FBI files, a pattern that continued through 1963.

Unworthy of Any Further Consideration

When Oswald left his job at Leslie Welding, his time card for that day is marked with the word ''quit.''[40] Oswald asked Leslie Welding to forward his pay to P. O. Box 2915, Dallas.[41] He had rented that post office box that same day for $4.50 at the main post office, where he received two keys.[42] This post office box would be used to order the alleged murder weapon of President Kennedy. Then there was the baby baptism flap.[43] Mrs. Elena Hall brought Marina to St. Seraphim Eastern Orthodox Church, Dallas, where Father Dimitri Royster baptized June Lee Oswald. Mrs. Hall was named as the godparent.[44] Marina claimed Oswald knew about the baptism.[45] But on October 19, Oswald asked Marina's friend, Mrs. Taylor, why Marina had not told him about it.[46]

Oswald and Marina had been having marital difficulties, but Oswald tried to put on a good performance at a Thanksgiving gathering at Robert Oswald's house. On November 17, Oswald had written to Robert accepting the invitation to come,[47] and on November 22, Thanksgiving Day, the Oswalds went by bus to Fort Worth, where brothers John Pic and Robert met them. Marguerite, oddly, was not invited. The families enjoyed a pleasant day. John Pic reportedly said Oswald could not get a driver's license with his undesirable discharge, and Oswald spoke about getting his discharge changed.[48] Later, at the bus station, the Oswalds bought a recording of the theme music from *Exodus* and had snapshots made.[49]

The Thanksgiving Day event obscures what the baby baptism flap demonstrated: that Oswald was often in his own sphere, unconnected to ordinary events. Oswald was far from idle, however, at least where the U.S. mail was concerned. His mail was so radically left wing that he could have expected to be the subject of FBI scrutiny. The date September 28 is a benchmark, for on that day the FBI learned that Oswald subscribed to the *Worker*.[50] Oswald now looked like a Communist. An FBI source in New York, NY 2354-S*, had turned over photographs that included Oswald's subscription sent on August 5.[51] This led to a memorandum from New York to Dallas, on October 17,[52] with an enclosed photograph of Oswald's name and address—taken from a subscriber list for the *Worker,* obtained from inside the newspaper's premises.

Strangely, these new additions to Oswald's FBI files did not find a receptive audience. Stranger still is what the FBI says it did with Oswald's file at this point: They closed it down. Kelley acknowledges that the FBI knew in July 1962 that Oswald had sought information about Russian newspapers and periodicals from the Soviet Embassy in Washington, D.C., and knew in October that Oswald had "renewed his subscription to the *Worker,* the U.S. Communist Party newspaper."[53] Then the FBI closed its file on Oswald in October 1962, when Fain retired. Kelley says that at that time the Oswald case "was regarded as merely routine, unworthy of any further consideration."[54]

As odious and deplorable as the tracking of private American citizens is, we know that many people with a far more benign history than Oswald were closely watched. Oswald was a known redefector married to a Soviet citizen. Headquarters had ordered Oswald thoroughly interviewed, but Oswald proved contentious as well as untruthful, and the FBI agents did not believe his story. The second interview was at best inconclusive, and Fain's reasons for not considering Oswald a threat—as described by FBI director Kelley—took no account of what the FBI had already learned about his mail activities. These activities had taken place since the first interview, and Oswald had hidden them from the FBI during the second interview. At this point, Fain could just as easily have argued for aggressively pursuing the case. Oswald's behavior was not "routine," even if closing his file was.

To add a twist of irony, in October 1962, according to Kelley, "Agent Hosty was given the assignment of reopening Marina Oswald's file. His instructions were to interview her in six months, which meant the FBI agent was to contact her in March of 1963."[55] So it was against the backdrop of Marina's open case and Oswald's closed case that the following sequence of left wing mail activity took place: on October 27, Oswald notified the Washington Book Store, through which he ordered Soviet magazines from Washington, D.C., of his change of address to Box 2915, Dallas[56]; on October 30, Oswald applied for membership in the Socialist Workers Party[57]; on November 5, 1962, the Socialist Workers Party responded that "as there is no Dallas chapter there can be no memberships in this area"[58]; on November 10, Oswald sent $.25 with a self-addressed envelope to *New York Labor News*[59]; on December 6 Oswald sent examples of his photographic work to the Socialist Workers Party[60] and they answered him on December 9[61]; in early December, Oswald sent examples of his photographic work to the Hall-Davis Defense Committee, a communist front, in New York[62]; on December 13, the Hall-Davis Committee answered[63]; on December 15, Oswald sent one dollar for a subscription to the *Militant*[64]; on December 19, Louis Weinstock of the *Worker* wrote to Oswald[65]; on January 1, 1963, Oswald contacted Pioneer Press for speeches by Castro[66]; in January, Oswald wrote to the Washington Book Store, which was probably recommended to him by the Soviet Embassy, and enclosed $13.20 for a subscription to *Ogonek, The Agitator*, and *Krokodil,* or *Sovetakaya Belorussia,*[67] and also requested that these subscriptions end in December 1963[68]; in September 1962, Oswald sent two dollars for a subscription to *Krokodil*[69]; on January 2, 1963, Oswald sent $.35 for some communist literature, including the English words for the "Internationale." In this various correspondence, Oswald used Box 2915, Dallas, as his address.[70]

The above was not all of Oswald's mail activity. But it led to actions by the post office which Oswald protested. He had to execute a post office Form 2153-X, instructing them to "always" deliver foreign propaganda mailings. He added this comment to the form: "I protest this intimidation."[71] Oswald had more than paper delivered to his P.O. box. In January 1963, the February issue of *American Rifleman* had a coupon that Oswald used to order the alleged assassination rifle.[72] He filled it out using the name of "A.J. Hidell," and Post Office Box 2915, Dallas.[73] He also ordered the pistol that was allegedly used to murder Dallas policeman J. D. Tippit. He originally indicated he wanted to order a holster and ammunition, but he scratched out this part before mailing the coupon.[74]

By March it was time for Hosty's first talk with Marina. Hosty had only just learned on March 4 of Oswald's apartment at 602 Elsbeth, Dallas.[75] On March 10, Hosty visited Mrs. M. F. Tobias, the apartment manager.[76] Oswald had moved to 214 West Neeley Street on March 3, Tobias told the FBI. This was only a week after Oswald had made the move, so Hosty had not wasted time finding out they had moved. Hosty then recommended that Oswald's case be reopened, which it was on March 26.[77] The reason for reopening the file was because "of Oswald's newly opened subscription to the Communist newspaper," the *Worker*.[78]

On the previous occasion that the Dallas FBI office had learned of Oswald's subscription to the *Worker* (October 1962), they had closed his file. Now the same event was the stated reason for opening it again. This makes little sense. In fact, this reopening had a caveat. "Agent Hosty, deciding that the apparently tense Oswald domestic situation would not be conducive to a proper interview," Kelley explained, "jotted a note in his file to come back in forty-five to sixty days."[79] By that time, Oswald had skipped town.

A Castro Placard Around Oswald's Neck

In the first three months of 1963, Oswald's mail activity remained steady and his particular diet of literature resembled that of the previous fall. Oswald received the January 21, 1963, issue of *The Militant* by January 24,.[80] Oswald received the March 11 issue of *The Militant* by March 14.[81] On March 27 or 28, 1963, Oswald received the March 24 issue of *The Daily Worker*.[82] On February 20, 1963, Oswald wrote to the Communist Party headquarters, New York, requesting information and asking to subscribe to two newspapers, the *Worker* and *The Militant*.[83]

On March 24, 1963, Oswald wrote to the Socialist Workers Party. Their copy of the letter and an enclosed newspaper clipping Oswald sent have been lost.[84] On March 27, 1963, the Socialist Workers Party wrote back to Oswald, at his P.O. Box 2915 address. The Socialist Workers Party cannot find this correspondence either.[85] According to the FBI, by this time the FBI Dallas office had finally decided to look into Oswald again, reopening his file on March 26. It was too late, however, as Oswald had less than a month left in Dallas. On March 31, 1963, Marina took photographs of Oswald in their backyard. He was holding a copy of *The Militant*[86] and the *Worker* in one hand,[87] and the rifle alleged to have later killed the president in the other.[88]

Meanwhile, Oswald had one more important composition to mail, one that was destined to become a catalyst in Oswald's CIA files. On April 18, 1963, Oswald wrote to the Fair Play for Cuba Committee New York office. At the end of the summer, the contents of this letter would finally land in Oswald's CIA files. In the April 18 letter, Oswald said that he had passed out FPCC literature on the street the day before, and he asked for more copies. The fact that Oswald used his Dallas address raises the possibility he may not have made final plans to move to New Orleans until the end: he left on April 24.[89] On April 19, 1963, the Fair Play for Cuba Committee New York office sent Oswald more literature.[90]

Like the CIA, the FBI had a mail-reading capability of its own, and Oswald's correspondence would shortly generate a flurry of reporting on his activities by the New York office of the FBI. On

April 6, 1963, Oswald lost his job at Jaggers-Chiles-Stoval because he could not do the work or get along with his coworkers. It is difficult to judge when Oswald began planning to move to New Orleans.[91] Three days before his departure, the FBI intercepted Oswald's letter to the FPCC describing his public FPCC activities.[92] The letter, which Oswald sent via air mail, was postmarked April 18.[93] According to FBI records, on April 21, 1963, Dallas confidential informant "T-2" reported this letter to the FPCC, in which Oswald said he had passed out FPCC pamphlets in Dallas with a placard around his neck reading HANDS OFF CUBA, VIVA FIDEL.[94] Actually, this Dallas T-2 source on Oswald was really a New York FBI source—NY-3245-S—as can be seen from newly released JFK files.[95] Similarly, an earlier Dallas T-1 source who had spied on Oswald's letters to the *Worker* also turned out to be a New York source, NY-2354-S.[96]

The Warren Commission questioned the FBI about the April letter and its contents, asking, "Is this information correct as the date indicated and does it describe activities before Oswald's move to New Orleans?" The FBI's answer was vague, slippery, and paltry: "Our informant did not know Oswald personally and could furnish no further information. Our investigation had not disclosed such activity on Oswald's part prior to this type of activity in New Orleans."[97]

Special Agent Hosty, who barely expanded on this in his testimony to the commission on the Oswald placard-around-his-neck letter, added his disbelief of the story. Hosty explained: "We had received no information to the effect that anyone had been in the downtown streets of Dallas or anywhere in Dallas with a sign around their neck saying 'hands off Cuba, viva Fidel.' " Thus Hosty links his belief to negative intelligence, i.e., no reports had come to their attention on Oswald, and Hosty was confident that the Dallas FBI had adequate surveillance and reporting mechanisms tight enough to catch any activity as flagrant and provocative as this. "It appeared highly unlikely to me," Hosty testified, "that such an occurrence could have happened in Dallas without having been brought to our attention."[98]

Hosty's argument suggests that Oswald made a false claim—apparently to impress the FPCC—that failed to fool the Dallas office of the FBI. If Hosty is correct, we should be impressed, not only with the

Dallas FBI office's knowledge of what Oswald was doing, but also with their ability to figure out what he was not doing. As we have already seen, however, the performance of the Dallas FBI office was lackluster at best, where keeping track of Oswald was concerned.

Whether Oswald had stood on a street corner or not, important undercover FBI assets in New York were in motion against the FPCC during the time or shortly after Oswald wrote the letter. As we already know, the Fair Play for Cuba Committee was the subject for intense FBI and CIA interest and counterintelligence operations. A major FBI Chicago office investigation of the FPCC appeared on March 8, four days before Oswald ordered the rifle from Chicago. This study was transmitted to the CIA.[90] By picking such an organization to correspond with and carrying out actions on its behalf, Oswald—by default or by design—had insinuated himself into the gray world of the watchers and the watched.

George deMohrenschildt and the CIA

In any discussion of Oswald in Dallas the name George deMohrenschildt arises because of the help he gave the Oswald family and his likely contacts with the CIA. DeMohrenschildt, to whose Dallas home the Oswalds made many visits,[100] was a petroleum geologist. His travels overseas made him knowledgeable about the affairs of countries in which the CIA was interested. When introduced to Oswald in the fall of 1962 by a friend,[101] deMohrenschildt asked, "Do you think it is safe for us to help Oswald?" DeMohrenschildt told the Warren Commission he worried that "Oswald could be anything" because he had been to the Soviet Union, and that another Dallas resident had refused to meet the Oswalds.[102] After checking with FBI contacts,[103] deMohrenschildt says he concluded, "Well, this guy seems to be OK."[104]

One of the people deMohrenschildt checked with was J. Walton Moore. Moore was not in the FBI. He was the Dallas CIA Domestic Contacts Service chief at the time. In his testimony to the Warren Commission, deMohrenschildt described Moore in these words:

> Walter [sic] Moore is the man who interviewed me on behalf of the Government after I came back from Yugoslavia. . . . He is

> a Government man—either FBI or Central Intelligence. A very nice fellow, exceedingly intelligent who is, as far as I know—was some sort of an FBI man in Dallas. Many people consider him the head of the FBI in Dallas. Now, I don't know. Who does—you see. But he is a government man in some capacity. He interviewed me and took my deposition on my stay in Yugoslavia, what I thought about the political situation there. And we became quite friendly after that. We saw each other from time to time, had lunch. There was a mutual interest there, because I think he was born in China and my wife was born in China. They had been to our house once or twice. I just found him a very interesting person.[105]

J. Gordon Shanklin was the head of the Dallas FBI office, and it is likely that deMohrenschildt knew that Moore was CIA. The point is that the Agency's Domestic Contacts person in Dallas was in frequent contact with deMohrenschildt during the period that he was helping Oswald.

Could deMohrenschildt have been a CIA "control" for Oswald, with Moore as the reporting channel? Almost certainly not in the traditional sense, unless Moore worked in more than the Domestic Contacts division, whose mission was routine contacts and debriefings. For his part, deMohrenschildt explicitly denied that Oswald would have been suited for intelligence work. "I never would believe that any government would be stupid enough to trust Lee with anything important," deMohrenschildt testified, "even the government of Ghana would not give him any job of any type."[106] Of course this judgment would be untrustworthy if Moore and deMohrenschildt were pawns in a plot to murder the president, a highly circumstantial and speculative possibility at best.

Most of the deMohrenschildt's contact with Oswald took place during the six-month period when the FBI closed its books on him—from October 1962 through March 1963. Wading through the morass of Oswald's personal relationships in Dallas in search of the deMohrenschildt story is outside the scope of this work. Several new works on Oswald presumably will add much to what we already know about this story. As previously stated, ours is a study focused not on Oswald "the person" but on Oswald "the file"—especially his CIA files. In that regard, looking for an operational CIA channel for deMohrenschildt is clearly in order. Before moving on, therefore, we must pose this question: Did deMohrenschildt have other contacts with the CIA?

"Yes, I knew George," says Nicholas M. Anikeeff. "From young manhood before World War II, back in the 30s, we were close friends." In a recent interview, Mr. Anikeeff acknowledged not only his close and continuous friendship with deMohrenschildt, but also his former employment with the CIA. Anikeeff, however, stubbornly refused to disclose what part of the Agency he had worked for, even when told it is publicly known. His reticence may be explainable by the traditional Agency intransigeance to reveal anything about its internal structure. But such resistence today simply raises our antennae.

"Yes, I believe I saw him," Anikeeff says of deMohrenschildt, "in the spring of 1963." That would have been during deMohrenschildt's travel to Washington, D.C., a stopover on his way to relocation in Haiti, where prospective business deals awaited him. Researchers have often wondered if deMohrenschildt called on someone from the Agency during this visit to Washington, and now we know that he did. Anikeeff, however, maintains that Oswald's name did not come up in the discussions. "I don't recall any specific instance of speaking with deMohrenschildt about Oswald prior to the assassination," Anikeeff insists. "Yes, I talked with deMohrenschildt," he concedes, "and may have spoken with him about Oswald." However, Anikeeff is adamant that he "never had said anything to the Agency" about these discussions.

Who was Nicholas Anikeeff? During the early 1950s, when the CIA dispatched two groups of Lithuanian infiltrators into Poland, Anikeeff was intimately involved. Tom Bower's study of the KGB and British intelligence, *The Red Web,* contains this interesting detail:

> In preparing both operations, the CIA case officer Mike Anikeeff had liased in detail with the Reinhard Gehlen group which would become West Germany's foreign intelligence service and was sure that security was perfect. Yet the landings ended in swift disaster.[107]

Similarly, David Wise's *Invisible Government* names the chain of command for a CIA employee, John Torpats, who had become embroiled in a controversy after being fired by Allen Dulles. From the top down: Frank Wisner (the DDP), Richard Helms (the A/DDP), John Maury (chief of the Soviet Russia Division), and "N. M. Anikeeff." It would appear that Anikeeff was a branch chief in the Soviet Russia Division.

That deMohrenschildt had a close contact in the Soviet Russia Division of 1962–1963 is newsworthy. It does not, however, prove that Oswald or deMohrenschildt worked for the Agency or that deMohrenschildt was reporting to Anikeeff about Oswald's activities. For the time being, we will add this to the already large and growing pile of interesting coincidences in this case.

The Duran-Lechuga Affair

In the fall of 1962, a scandalous affair took place in Mexico City that bears on Oswald's visit there in September–October 1963. That visit, including the allegation that Oswald had sex with a married Mexican woman, is the subject of Chapter Eighteen. For now we consider what happened after the Cuban ambassador's wife decided not to return to Cuba in 1962. Intelligence acquired through very sensitive channels suggests that the Cuban Embassy in Mexico City resorted to an unusual measure to keep the ambassador "on the revolutionary path." The embassy used the sexual services of two young women to turn the ambassador against his wife. One of these women, Silvia Duran, is the same woman Oswald was later alleged to have had an affair with.

The documentary trail began on February 18, 1963, when a sensitive CIA source reported on the volatile marriage and extramarital affairs of Carlos Lechuga, the Cuban ambassador to the U.N., who had previously served as the Cuban ambassador to Mexico. According to the CIA information report, classified "Secret No Foreign DISSEM," this is what their Cuban source said:

> In late December 1962, Carlos Lechuga Hevia, described as an ambitious, evasive, and not overly intelligent man, was unhappy in New York, as Cuban Ambassador to the UN, because neither the United States nor the USSR paid any attention to him. In spite of being in love with his wife, Lechuga had denounced her to

> Raul Roa and Osvaldo Dorticos Torrado, President of Cuba, as being a passive enemy of the revolution.[108]

The Cuban source to which this less-than-flattering portrait of Lechuga was attributed was described in the CIA report's subject line as "a Former Cuban Government Official." Whoever it was knew a lot about what was happening inside the Cuban missions in New York and Mexico City.

How Lechuga's denunciation of his wife had come about was an interesting story. According to the CIA information report, the "former Cuban official described it this way:

> The denunciation was allegedly made under pressure by certain members of the Cuban Embassy in Mexico, who, in their attempts to persuade Lechuga, had employed the influences of Ana Maria Blanco, then First Secretary at the Embassy, and Silvia Duran, a Mexican married woman employed at the Cuban-Mexican Cultural Institute. Lechuga had offered to marry Duran after divorcing his wife, since she was ready to accompany him to Cuba, and Lechuga considered this a requisite indispensable to his revolutionary spirit. In addition, at that time his wife was emphatically refusing to return to Cuba so long as the Castro regime continued in power, and especially after learning that she had been denounced.[109]

The Cuban source pointed out that when Lechuga and his wife had arrived in Mexico City in May 1962, he had promised her that he would renounce his job as soon as he could find an opportunity, because he was "not a Communist" and did not want to lose her. "Far from doing that," the Cuban source lamented, "as of late December 1962, Lechuga seemed to have surrendered more and more to the revolution."[110]

The next piece to this story occurred on November 24, 1963, two days after the Kennedy assassination, in a memo on Oswald prepared for FBI Counterintelligence chief W. C. Sullivan.[111] The memo mentioned CIA information from the "Liaison Agent,"[112] possibly Sam Papich, about the arrest of Silvia Duran in Mexico City and "that she had allegedly been in contact" with Oswald. The CIA told the FBI liaison that they were following the story and would report any developments of significance. The memo then mentioned this:

> Bureau files indicate that Duran may be identical with Silvia T. DeDuran, who was described by CIA on November 30, 1962, as a Mexican national who had been the mistress of Carlos Lechuga, former Cuban Ambassador to Mexico and now his country's Ambassador to the United Nations. CIA further indicated that the aforementioned woman had served as a director of the Mexican-Cuban Cultural Institute and that her husband was Horacio Duran, a well-known Mexican decorator (105-77113-57). Raichhardt stated that this information was also being furnished to our Legal Attaché, Mexico City. Legal Attaché will be kept apprised of information coming to the attention of CIA in Mexico City.[113]

If accurate, this would indicate that at least one more CIA document on the Duran-Lechuga affair exists, and bears the date November 30, 1962. By the end of 1962, the information on Duran in CIA and FBI files was substantial and growing.

Up to now, Duran's alleged affairs in Mexico City have been shrouded in controversy. In an interview conducted for this book by British journalist Anthony Summers, Mrs. Duran admitted to the affair with Lechuga. Here is the pertinent passage from the interview transcript:

SUMMERS: [After explaining to Duran there are new documents released mentioning she supposedly had an affair with Carlos Lechuga.] Is this true?

DURAN: Yes, but it's—that's top secret.

SUMMERS: It is all over the documents, clearly the Americans knew about it in '62. Is it possible that you were being used by anyone, or was it entirely a spontaneous thing? Or were you perhaps pointed in Lechuga's direction?

DURAN: No. No. It was completely accidental, I mean it was not . . . No, I don't think so. Because, no, no. I had problems in my marriage, and you know what happens in these things, no? And I didn't divorce because my husband didn't let my child come to Cuba. So that's why I didn't divorce. I divorced later, but not in that moment.

SUMMERS: Was the Lechuga affair over by '63? The time of the assassination?

DURAN: Yes.

SUMMERS: You see no connection?

DURAN: No. This is the first time I've talked about that. But no, of course not. He even went to New York, so I could get a divorce and—he was named Ambassador at the United Nations. He asked Fidel for that, so we can get married. But, no, we couldn't. It was impossible. Very complicated. It was going to mean problems. People were going to use that for, oh, you know . . . [114]

For whom was this affair "top secret"? Probably the Cubans, but Duran's insistence that it was "accidental" seems problematical, for the story intercepted by the CIA explained the affair as a device to separate Lechuga from his wife and keep him on the revolutionary path.

Whether or not the affair was orchestrated by the Cuban Embassy, it made the rounds of both the CIA and FBI in the U.S., and therefore became relevant two years later when the story of an affair between Oswald and Duran surfaced. That is a subject to which we will return in Chapter Nineteen. For now, we turn out attention to events taking place in the anti-Castro segments of the Cuban underworld in Miami and New Orleans.

Hemming IV: WQAM Radio Show, Miami

Oswald's participation in a live debate on WDSU Radio in New Orleans in August 1963 is covered in Chapter Seventeen. There was a lesser-known call to a local radio show, the *Alan Courtney Show,* on WQAM, Miami. We do not know the precise date of the program, but surviving FBI records suggest it was in November 1962. A November 27, 1963, FBI report by Miami Special Agent Vincent K. Antle summarized an interview on that date with Alan Courtney, including this segment:

> Approximately one year ago, Alan Courtney had Jerry Patrick and three other individuals on his night program on WQAM Radio. These individuals were involved with the training of anti-Castro troops. At the conclusion of the program, Courtney received a telephone call from an individual who had a very young voice. This young man said he would like to talk to one of the persons

> that had been on the show. He explained that he was from New Orleans and a former Marine and that he wanted to volunteer his services to be of assistance to them.[115]

The person who called in, according to Courtney, "gave the name of Lee Oswald or something like that, such as Harvey Lee or Oswald Harvey or Oswald Lee." Courtney said he gave the phone to one of the guests named "Davey." A December 2, 1963, FBI report by Special Agent James Dwyer identified the man as Howard Kenneth Davis, who, in his own words, was "associated with American mercenaries involved in Cuban revolutionary activities for the past six years."[116]

Once again, Hemming's path crosses Oswald's—providing that the caller was Oswald. Antle's report continues:

> Courtney could not recall his last name nor did he recall the names of any of the other individuals except Jerry Patrick whom he described as 6'4" in height. Courtney said that Davey and Oswald did talk on the phone but he does not know if they agreed to an appointment date subsequently. Courtney said he knew that the caller said he stayed up to hear the program so that he could call and attempt an appointment with the participants on the radio show.[117]

While it is not impossible for this caller to have been Oswald, we need harder evidence that he was in Miami in November 1962. The FBI report also states that John Martino alleged that "during the last year" Oswald had been in a "fracas in Bayfront Park" in Miami. After the Kennedy assassination, Martino reportedly claimed advance knowledge of plans for the assassination.[118]

More Oswald Banjos: Alex in Minsk and Chicago

The most sensitive part of Oswald's mail was to and from the Soviet Embassy in Washington, D.C. and to and from the Soviet Union. The Soviet Embassy "take" was handled by the Washington field office of the FBI, and the amount was not insubstantial, as the last five months of 1962 indicate: On August 5, 1962, Marina wrote to the Soviet Embassy regarding the return of her passport[119]; on July

20 Oswald wrote to the Soviet Embassy,[120] asking for information on how to subscribe to Russian periodicals[121]; the embassy may have told Oswald of the Washington Book Store, Washington, D.C., where Oswald does place an order[122]; on August 17, Oswald filed a change-of-address notice (from 7313 Davenport to 2703 Mercedes, Fort Worth[123]; on September 6, 1962 Marina's passport is returned by the Soviet Embassy, Washington[124]; and on December 31, Marina wrote New Year's greetings to the Soviet Embassy.[125] The FBI opened all mail going into and out of the Soviet Embassy. The above demonstrates that the FBI had a very good handle on Oswald's whereabouts.

In the first half of 1963, the CIA's HT/LINGUAL project produced fascinating material on Oswald. The postassassination context of the intercepted material is the link between Oswald and the alleged murder weapon. This was relevant to one of the most important aspects of the case. The HT/LINGUAL "take" on the Oswalds, however, contains several anomalies. For example, it was a distinction to be put on the CIA's illegal mail intercept program once, let alone twice, like Oswald had been. But then, Oswald's mail was opened even after he was taken off the list.

Just as anomolous was having mail opened before one is even on the list. This is what happened to Marina. According to the records released by the CIA, Marina was not listed until four days after the assassination, November 26, 1963. But two letters to Marina from the Soviet Union were opened by the CIA in January and May 1963. They prove that the CIA's HT/LINGUAL program did produce important evidence that bears directly upon fundamental aspects of the case and links the disparate ends of Oswald's official files.

Unfortunately, over the years the CIA has made misleading statements about the Oswald letters they opened. Take, for example, this CIA memo—prepared during the Warren Commission investigation—about the 1961 opening of a Marguerite letter: "The letter contains no information of real significance."[126] How strange then, that a SECRET EYES ONLY, June 22, 1962, CIA memorandum from the deputy chief of the mail intercept program to the deputy chief of Counterintelligence said this about the same missive: "This item will be of interest to Mrs. Egerter, CI/SIG, and also to the FBI." Years later, in a response to an FOIA request by researcher

Paul Hoch, the CIA stated that "a copy of the document [Marguerite's letter] was forwarded to the FBI immediately upon discovery." Why would the CIA and the FBI be interested in items of no significance?

We don't know whether the CIA told the Warren Commission about Marguerite's letter. The timing of the comment about the letter's insignificance leaves a bad taste, especially because we know the deputy chief of the mail intercept program at the Agency thought it was significant before the assassination. We know more about what the CIA told the HSCA, which probed this intercept program. The HSCA report contains this revealing comment:

> Although the Agency had only one Oswald letter in its possession, the HT/LINGUAL files were combed after the assassination for additional materials potentially related to him. Approximately 30 pieces of correspondence that were considered potentially related to the investigation of Oswald's case (even though not necessarily directly to Oswald) were discovered. None of these was ultimately judged by the CIA to be of any significance. These materials, however, were stored in a separate Oswald HT/LINGUAL file.[127]

We know that this story is not true. The CIA's claim that they judged none of these materials to be of "any significance" appears to be a cover story. Any other explanation requires an unbelievable level of incompetence.

From the newly released files, we have begun to learn much more about the value the CIA attached to the Oswald HT/LINGUAL file. During the course of Oswald's return from Russia, this program was expanding. "During 1962 the number of disseminations stemming from project HT/LINGUAL increased," said an April 1964 internal CIA assessment, "as it has each year since the inception of the project. The total number of disseminations in 1963 was 10,999 as compared to the total in 1962 of 8,391." As preciously discussed in Chapter Thirteen, the mail intercept chief, John Mertz, concluded in early 1964 that some of "the most interesting" items intercepted from "ie-defectors" were the "several items" to and from Oswald and Marina.

Mertz singled out one of those particular "banjos" (intercepted pieces of mail) that showed that Oswald's Russian nickname, "Alik," was similar to the "Alex Hidell" pseudonym.[128] Mertz, however, did not indicate when the CIA came into possession of these banjos. From the available record, it would appear the CIA did not show the Mertz memo to the Warren Commission. They should have. Presumably, the Warren Commission would have been interested in this.

Still more clues to what the senior Agency leadership felt about the Oswald HT/LINGUAL materials can be found in the newly released files, including this comment to FBI director Hoover by CIA Counterintelligence chief James Angleton, four days after the assassination:

> Your representatives in Mexico advised our representative there that it had not been determined whether Hidell is a person, or an alias used by Oswald. In this connection we refer you to the attached HUNTER items—63 E 22 U and 63 A 24 W. These items indicate that Oswald was known to his wife's friends as "Alik" (also spelled "Alick"). While we have no items in which the name Hidell (or Hydell) appears, it is believed that the fact Oswald was known to his Russian friends as "Alik" may be significant."[129]

The importance that the head of CIA Counterintelligence attached to these two letters was lost when the Agency told the HSCA none of the HT/LINGUAL items was "of any significance." Although Angleton apparently did not know it, Oswald also went by the name Alex while he was in the Soviet Union.[130]

This Angleton memo is also helpful to researchers because it specifies the HT/LINGUAL numbers for two letters in which Oswald's Russian name "Alik" appears. A simple analysis of 63 A 24 W and 63 E 22 U indicates that these must mean letters of January 24, 1963 (item "W" for that day), and May 22, 1963 respectively. Thus these letters in Oswald's HT/LINGUAL file which connect to the alias spanned both the March 4 rifle order and Oswald's April 24 move to New Orleans. The two 1963 "Alik" letters, both to Marina, were listed in the 1964 summary of the Oswald LINGUAL file, but the descriptions for both of them lacked the insight that the Counterintelligence chief had passed on to Hoover in the wake of the assassination.

When Oswald ordered the weapon he used an alias that was similar to a nickname already in his HT/LINGUAL file.[131] The CIA claims it intercepted no Oswald mail of importance.[132] This obviously false claim raises the suspicion that another claim—that Oswald was not the subject of the mail program after May 1962—is also dubious. We know for a fact that three letters, one to Oswald and two to Marina, were opened when neither was on the Watch List. Maybe someone else with a steam iron had a different list.

Until the early 1990s release of documents, the public had no idea that a continuity between Oswald's Russian sojourn and the alleged murder weapon existed—or that the Agency's Counterintelligence chief would write about it, and that the project officer would use it as a showcase example. The Hidell alias story is fraught with problems. One such problem surfaced on the day of the assassination, when the U.S. Army knew, apparently too early, about an identification card in Oswald's possession with the infamous alias on it. We will return to the Hidell problem later.

Chapter Sixteen

Undercover in New Orleans

Up to April 1963, the FBI had little trouble tracking Oswald's footsteps. His return to Texas in June 1962 had made things easier because the Dallas FBI office had begun investigating him soon after his defection in 1959. After Oswald's return, FBI field activity on him had been conducted by several offices, but principally by those in Dallas and New York, the former in whose district he lived and the latter where the FBI office spied on his mail to the Communist Party, the *Worker,* and the Fair Play for Cuba Committee (FPCC). Then something strange happened: The FBI lost track of Oswald for two months, from April 24, through June 26. These dates cover Oswald's move to New Orleans and his first month of FPCC activity there. The FBI maintains it did not discover that Oswald was in New Orleans until June 26. Moreover, the Bureau left the Warren Commission with the impression that Oswald's place of residence in New Orleans had not been "verified" until August 5. Five days later, from a cell in the jail of the First District Police Department of New Orleans, Oswald asked to speak with someone from the FBI.[1]

Oswald's August 9 arrest on Canal Street and the events that followed are the subject of Chapter Seventeen. The present chapter is a study of the period between his move to New Orleans and the time the FBI says that it confirmed his residence on Magazine Street. We open with an obvious question: Why couldn't the FBI find Oswald? As we will see, the FBI should have known about the move and the Magazine Street address by mid-May, not June 26 and August 5 respectively, as they assert. This prompts the question: What was Oswald doing during the period that the FBI files went blind? The answer is intriguing: He was organizing a chapter of the Fair Play for Cuba Committee in New Orleans.

Using his real name, Oswald wrote often about his plans and activities to FPCC national director Vincent Lee, who encouraged him to undertake organizational work in New Orleans. Lee advised Oswald not to open an office, advice that Oswald ignored. Lee lost interest in Oswald when he violated the bylaws of the FPCC by claiming charter status for his New Orleans "branch." While the FBI remained in the dark and Vincent Lee's interest in Oswald waned, curiosity about FPCC developments in New Orleans was growing in Army counterintelligence, whose agents began following the paper trail in New Orleans left by "A. J. Hidell." Unlike his letters to Vincent Lee, Oswald did not use his real name in the initial—undercover—stage of his FPCC activities in New Orleans. Oswald disappeared from the sights of the FBI Dallas office as A. J. Hidell entered the cross-hairs of Army surveillance, using a false New Orleans post office box and the address of 544 Camp Street.

The 544 Camp Street address deepens the mystery, for this was the location where Guy Banister and the Cuban Revolutionary Council (CRC) maintained their offices. The CRC was the successor to the Frente Revolutionario Democratico (FRD), set up by the CIA in Mexico during the last year of the Eisenhower administration to overthrow Castro by military force. As discussed in Chapter Eight, most of the FRD's military forces—Brigade 2506—had been trained by the U.S. Army at sites in southern Guatemala. In the early months of the Kennedy administration, the CRC was formed to coordinate FRD activities for the U.S. government. The Bay of Pigs fiasco resulted in centrifugal tendencies in the Cuban exile community, but the CRC remained the stable core among the various exile factions. Kennedy's support for the CRC was drastically reduced in the wake of the Cuban missile crisis, and all government funding for the CRC was terminated on May 1, 1963.

Born in a Louisiana log cabin in 1901, Guy Banister had done work with Navy intelligence in World War II, and had developed deep associations within the FBI. He worked for the FBI for twenty years, rising to the position of special agent in charge of the Bureau's Chicago office. In 1955 he moved to New Orleans, where he left the FBI to serve as assistant superintendent of the New Orleans Police Department. His mission was to investigate police corruption, but Banister was forced into retirement in 1957 after threatening a waiter with a pistol in the Old Absinthe House. He then formed his own detective agency, Guy Banister Associates, which he threw into a crusade to root out Communists in New Orleans. In 1961 Banister played a role in the CRC activities associated with the Bay of Pigs Invasion, and he helped organize the Friends of Democratic Cuba, a fund-raising organ for the New Orleans branch of the CRC under Sergio Arcacha Smith. Banister continued to work for the CRC—or "AMBUD" as it was known in the Agency. He ran background investigations of local Cuban students who wanted to join Smith's group, in order to weed out potential pro-Castro sympathizers who might be infiltrators. It was Banister who arranged for the CRC's office space at 544 Camp Street. While hard evidence is lacking, Oswald's undercover pro-Castro activities may have been—whether Oswald was witting or not—associated with a CRC recruiting operation in New Orleans.

Oswald chose a propitious moment to enter the dark world of Guy Banister and the Cuban underground. The day—June 5—that Oswald picked up the FPCC application forms he would distribute in New Orleans, President Kennedy's trip to Dallas was announced in the newspapers.

"How and When Did the FBI Learn of Oswald's Move to New Orleans?"

A hefty slice of the FBI—including headquarters, and the Dallas, New Orleans, Chicago, Miami, and Washington field offices—had been watching Oswald. Add to this a wide array of the CIA's clandestine services, including the Soviet Russia Division, the Security Office, and the counterintelligence staff, then mix in the State Department's intelligence, security, passport, and Russian components, and then top it off with Navy intelligence, Marine Corps intelligence, Air Force intelligence, and possibly even Army intelligence. Given this level of watchfulness, one would be tempted to think that the FBI, which was actively investigating Oswald, would have known when he moved. This is reasonable because, immediately upon finding his place at Magazine Street, Oswald sent written notification to the Communist Party, the FPCC, the Soviet Embassy, and, most important, the Dallas post office. Much of Oswald's mail to these same organizations was being read surreptitiously by the FBI.

One thing readers of FBI documents quickly encounter is the Bureau's commendable precision about names, dates, and places—especially the "hows" and "whens" with respect to the information it collects and reports. This precision vanishes on a crucial subject: the FBI's knowledge of Oswald's move to New Orleans. The lingering mystery surrounding the Bureau's ignorance of Oswald's move, as well as his early activities there, stands out as one of the Bureau's great failures—if their tale of neglect can be believed. This problem became apparent early during the Warren Commission inquest, when the FBI was asked to clarify the record. On April 6, 1964, the FBI responded to a series of questions concerning its investigation of Oswald. Question Number 9 on this list was answered as follows:

QUESTION: How and when did the FBI learn of Oswald's move to New Orleans?

ANSWER: A confidential source advised our New York Office on June 26, 1963, that one Lee H. Oswald, Post Office Box 30061, New Orleans, Louisiana, had directed a letter to "The Worker," New York City. Our New Orleans Office checked this post office box and determined it was rented to L. H. Oswald on June 3, 1963, residence 657 French Street, New Orleans. This was an incorrect address and further inquiries showed Oswald was residing at 4905 Magazine Street, New Orleans. Oswald's residence in New Orleans was verified on August 5, 1963, by Mrs. Jesse James Garner, 4909 Magazine Street, New Orleans. On the same date his employment at the William B. Reilly Coffee Company, 640 Magazine Street, New Orleans, was determined.[2]

This answer is not satisfactory. It does not explain *when* the New Orleans FBI office "determined" that on June 3 Oswald had rented P.O. Box 30061. Similarly, it fails to explain *when* the "further inquiries" were made that came up with 4909 Magazine, a wrong address. Most important, it fails to disclose the truth known to the FBI at the time of this response to the Warren Commission.

A broad view of FBI operations suggests that the FBI learned that Oswald had moved to Magazine Street no later than a few days after the move took place. The Washington and New York field offices played key roles not accounted for in the FBI response to the Warren Commission. On July 5, 1963, SAC (Special Agent in Charge) New York sent SAC New Orleans a copy of Oswald's June 10, letter to the *Worker,* along with the envelope bearing Oswald's P.O. address in New Orleans.[3] Three days later the New York office discovered something better: Oswald was on 4907 Magazine Street in New Orleans. New York source "48 S" had intercepted a change-of-address card Oswald mailed to the *Worker,* revising his mailing address from Magazine Street to P.O. Box 30061.[4]

It seems likely that New York informed the Bureau soon after, but an administrative glitch[5] prevents an authoritative statement about the date this card was placed in Oswald's headquarters file. At the same time, it is likely that the FBI's Washington field office had already reported Oswald's Magazine Street address to headquarters, probably May 17-18, after intercepting Oswald's May 16 change-of-address card to the Soviet Embassy.[6] We will return to this card and the Washington field office intercept program shortly. There are no FBI interoffice memoranda showing that the New York office or headquarters told the New Orleans or Dallas offices about the change-of-address card intercepted on July 8 in New York. The record shows that not until July 17 did New York share this card with New Orleans. Could New Orleans already have known?

A missing piece from New Orleans was provided in an October 31, 1963 New Orleans FBI report that disclosed that when Oswald sent his July 8 change-of-address card to the *Worker,* New Orleans informant T-1 reported it. The surviving New Orleans documents are missing the paperwork for this claim, but it likely was informant T-1 in the New Orleans post office. If true, this would mean that Oswald's Magazine Street address was known on or shortly after July 8 in the New Orleans, New York, and Washington field offices, and at FBI headquarters, and that none of them informed Dallas. Perhaps Dallas was informed by telephone, but there is no record of Oswald's Magazine Street address being shared with Dallas. The record looks odd: It shows it was not until July 17 that New Orleans informed Dallas of Oswald's new post office box.[7]

The foregoing makes it appear that much of the FBI system was derelict for not reporting Oswald's locations to the agent responsible for keeping track of him, James P. Hosty. Could it be that they presumed Hosty knew of Oswald's various addresses in New Orleans? Since Oswald had sent change-of-address cards to virtually everyone else, New York and Washington might have assumed that he had obtained the address from the Dallas post office. The July 17 New Orleans memo to Dallas exudes a hint of exasperation with the state of affairs. After pointing out an obsolete letter concerning Oswald, the memo continued:

> By letter dated 7/5/63 the New York Office furnished information to the effect that one Lee H. Oswald has an address of P.O. Box 30061, New Orleans, Louisiana.
>
> It is believed possible this person is identical with Lee Harvey Oswald, subject in captioned case.
>
> Since New Orleans has received no information subsequent to referenced letter, Dallas is requested to advise New Orleans of the status of Dallas case captioned above.
>
> New Orleans is instituting inquiries to determine residence address of holder of P.O. Box 30061, New Orleans, Louisiana.[8]

If we accept the October 31 FBI claim that New Orleans knew of the change-of-address card on July 8, then the above July 17 memo is evidence that New Orleans withheld Oswald's Magazine Street address from Dallas.

While New Orleans was passing Oswald's post office box number to Dallas, the New York office was discussing Oswald's Magazine Street address in a letter to the New Orleans office.[9] It appears that New Orleans received a copy of the card from New York on July 20,[10] and that Dallas was not informed at the time. The knowledge levels of the various FBI offices are important to compare. New York appeared to be in possession of all the pieces except the May 16 Oswald letter to the Soviet Embassy. On July 1 New York sent Dallas an Oswald letter with the Dallas post office box address; on July 5 New York sent New Orleans the letter to the *Worker* with the New Orleans post office box address[11]; and on July 8 New Orleans and New York learned of Oswald's Magazine Street residence and said nothing about it to the Dallas office. Dallas appears to have been fast asleep, and was startled on July 17 by the news from New Orleans that Oswald had a post office box there.[12] Still sluggish, it took Dallas twelve days just to say the case on Oswald and Marina was "pending," that Dallas was looking for them, and that the last residence they knew about was the Neely Street address which the Oswalds "left, giving no forwarding address."[13]

Hosty Checks the "Postmaster"

The vagaries in the FBI's story of how and when it learned of Oswald's move to Magazine Street beckon us to look again at this central subject. Is it possible that after three months Dallas had still not learned of Oswald's forwarding address? What is the documentary evidence for the FBI's claim to the Warren Commission that it did not know about Oswald's move to New Orleans until two months after his arrival there? There are just two FBI documents—both from Dallas—that buttress this proposition. One was a July 29, 1963, Dallas office memo stating that Oswald had left Neely Street without leaving a forwarding address.[14] This was based on an earlier, May 28, internal memo from Special Agent Hosty to SAC Shanklin.[15] Thus, the evidence boils down to one sentence in a memo written by Hosty: He said a "check with the Postmaster" showed that Oswald had moved without leaving a forwarding address.

As discussed in Chapter Fifteen, the Dallas FBI office had closed the Oswald case in October 1962 and reopened it in March 1963. A file on Marina had been opened in the interim, but no attempt to interview her had been made until March 11, 1963, when Hosty had learned from the apartment manager for Oswald's 602 Elsbeth apartment, Mrs. M. F. Tobias, that the Oswald family had moved on March 3. What did Hosty do to find out where Oswald had gone? He had a dependable source: the U.S. post office. Hosty wasted no time, and contacted an FBI informant there, Mrs. Dorthea Myers. She told Hosty that the Oswalds had moved into 214 West Neely in Dallas.[16] That was the address at which Oswald remained until he moved to New Orleans on April 24. The question is: When did Hosty find out Oswald was no longer on Neely Street?

On May 27, 1963, someone from the Dallas office of the FBI (probably Hosty) attempted to interview Oswald and Marina "under pretext.'' A pretext interview is a subterfuge in which the true purpose and often the true identity of the interviewer are disguised. The FBI person doing the checking discovered the Oswalds were gone, and the next day, May 28, Hosty wrote this memo to Shanklin, the special agent in charge in Dallas:

> On 5/27/63 an attempt to interview subjects at 214 Neely, Dallas under pretext reflected that they had moved from their residence. A check with the Postmaster reflects that the subjects have moved and left no forwarding address.
>
> The owner of subjects['] former residence at 214 Neely Dallas, M.W. George TA 3 9729 and LA6 7268 will be interviewed for information re subjects as will subject[']s Brother in Fort Worth.[17]

This memo deserves our close attention. FBI director Clarence Kelly's account—much of it perhaps written by Hosty—claims that Hosty actually discovered the Oswalds had vacated the Neely Street apartment twelve days earlier, on May 15.[18] Researchers have been unable to see this contradiction because the first paragraph of the above Hosty memo remained classified until 1994.

The release of the full memo in 1994 exposes more than the conflict between dates (May 15 and 27) for the attempted pretext interview at Neely Street. The unredacted version of this memo points to some glaring deficiencies in Hosty's account to Shanklin and the FBI's account to the Warren Commission. The second sentence contains three claims: 1) Hosty or a colleague checked with ''the Postmaster,'' 2) this check showed that the Oswalds had moved, and 3) this check showed that the Oswalds ''left no forwarding address.'' It was strange that Hosty, normally so precise in the ''who what when where, and how'' department, neglected to give the name of the ''Postmaster.'' The standard operating procedure for these internal memos was to name the informant and specify ''(protect identity)'' if the name was considered sensitive. For external memos an informant number was always used (such as ''T-1'' or ''NO-6'') and the names supplied in a detachable administrative cover sheet. The second point, that the ''Postmaster'' check showed the Oswalds had moved, is suspicious because it is logically incongruous with the third point, namely, that they had left no forwarding address. If the Oswalds had not provided a forwarding address, how did this "Postmaster" know that they had moved? Would Oswald have contacted the "Postmaster" just to say "we're moving"?

The third point—that Oswald had left no forwarding address—is the most startling error. Oswald did leave a forwarding address. Tucked away in the twenty-six volumes of Warren Commission materials is Commission Exhibit 793, which is a change-of-address card that Oswald sent to the Dallas post office after his arrival in New Orleans.[19] Oswald listed May 12 as the effective date, which is probably the date he mailed it. The card is stamped "May 14, 1963," indicating this was the date when the post office received it, which is either one day or thirteen days before Hosty checked with the "Postmaster," depending on which version of his story we are dealing with. The FBI's top handwriting expert, James C. Cadigan, who had more than twenty-three years of experience, testified that the handwriting was Oswald's.[20] Cadigan's handiwork—a marked-up copy of the card—can be found in another location of the Warren Commission's published materials.[21]

Within hours of the Kennedy assassination, the Dallas office of the FBI sent an "urgent" cable to Bureau headquarters and the New Orleans FBI office. That cable included this information:

> Inspector Harry Holmes, US Post Office, Dallas, advised tonight [a] check of postal records at Dallas rep(f)lects following info.
>
> On May ten last [10 May 1963], USPO, main branch, Dallas, received forwarding order for any mail for Mrs. Lee H. Oswald to be forwarded from box two nine one five, located main PO, Dallas, to two five one five West Fifth St., Irving, Texas. On May fourteen last [14 May 1963], PO received forwarding order again for mail in box two nine one five, Dallas, for Mr. Lee H. Oswald to be forwarded to four nine zero seven Magazine, New Orleans, La. Post Office subsequently had forwarding order from Mrs. Lee H. Oswald, date unknown, to forward all mail for Mrs. Lee H. Oswald to box three zero zero six one New Orleans.[22]

Hosty's claim to have queried the "Postmaster" was dubious. Hosty's claim that such a check showed the Oswalds had moved without leaving a forwarding address is baseless. Hosty's claims provide the only documentary evidence buttressing the FBI's story that it did not learn of Oswald's move to New Orleans until June 26. This story is headed for a new conclusion.

More Than the Postmaster Knew

The idea that the FBI did not know where Oswald lived from April 24 until June 26 is incredulous, especially so in view of all the sources to whom Oswald had immediately mailed his Magazine Street address. This is the key point: For thirty years the first paragraph of Hosty's May 28 memo to Shanklin has been classified. Underneath that redaction has been the solitary sentence that is the documentary basis for the FBI's response to the Warren Commission on when and how the FBI learned of Oswald's move to New Orleans. The withholding of this evidence, which turned out to be false, did significant damage to the public's ability to understand the facts.

The list of problems that surround Hosty's suspicious May 28 story about a "check with the Postmaster" underlines the need to examine the facts to which the FBI had access indicating that on May 10, 1963, Oswald had moved into an apartment at 4907 Magazine Street.[23] From the documents available, there were *at least seven* occasions when the FBI might have learned about Oswald's Magazine Street address prior to June 26—the date it claimed it learned of Oswald's post office box in New Orleans. Four of these opportunities occurred *before* Hosty's May 28 note to Shanklin, and all were well before June 26.

The first communication containing Oswald's Magazine Street address was the change-of-address card he sent on May 9, 1963, effective May 12, and received at the Dallas post office on May 14.[24] Presumably the Irving change-of-address card that Marina sent to the Dallas post office on May 10 would have been available with Oswald's card. The second opportune communication with the Magazine Street address was the notice Oswald mailed to the Dallas post office on May 12, 1963, asking them to close his old box, 2915.[25] Given the close cooperation between the Dallas post office and the FBI on Oswald's mail activities, the Bureau should have learned about this address card and the box closure soon after these events occurred.

The third communication that should have tipped off the FBI happened on May 14, 1963, when Oswald sent a change-of-address card—with the new 4907 Magazine Street address—to the FPCC.[26] Given that the FBI gained access to Oswald's letters to the FPCC through an informant for the New York FBI office, the Bureau should have learned about this letter sometime in May. Skipping out of order, the fifth and sixth communications occurred on May 22, when FPCC national director V. T. Lee wrote to Oswald at 4907 Magazine,[27] and on May 29, when the FPCC sent Oswald a membership card[28] and told him it was all right to form a New Orleans chapter.[29] Because access to FPCC offices probably required a break-in, we cannot be sure the FBI had access to these three letters.

The fourth and seventh events that should have enabled the FBI to learn of Oswald's whereabouts are more intriguing. They were the May 17 change-of-address card Oswald sent to the Soviet Embassy in Washington, D.C., alerting them to his new Magazine Street address,[30] and a June 4 letter to Marina—mailed to 4907 Magazine Street—from the embassy, asking her why she wished to return to the Soviet Union.[31] The early 1960s were tense years in the U.S.–Soviet Cold War, and the Soviet Embassy in Washington was enemy territory as far as the FBI and CIA were concerned. That embassy would have been among the highest priority targets of the American intelligence community, and the embassy's mail would have been carefully watched—especially mail to and from Soviet citizens in America.

We know from FBI files that "the highly confidential mail coverage of the Embassy" was handled by agents from the FBI's Washington field office.[32] The day after the Kennedy assassination, FBI director Hoover, in a telephone conversation with President Johnson, explained:

> Now, of course, that letter information, we process all mail that goes to the Soviet Embassy—it's a very secret operation. No mail is delivered to the Embassy without being examined and opened by us, so that we know what they receive.[33]

Based on this statement, it is reasonable to believe that at least the May 17 Oswald change-of-address card and the June 4 embassy letter to Marina were known to the FBI.

We can now return to the FBI's incredible claim that it did not know about Oswald's move to New Orleans until June 26, and recall that it was on this date that a New York informant mentioned seeing P.O. Box 30061 on Oswald's June 10 letter from New Orleans to the *Worker*.[34] Since New York was being credited as the source for this story, the purpose of feigning ignorance of any of the above seven events could not have been to hide the Bureau's sources in New York—as sensitive and valuable as those sources were. No, the purpose would more likely have been to cover something even more sensitive. Perhaps it was to cover the FBI's interception of the letter to the Soviet Embassy, or perhaps even to cover the CIA's interception, on May 22, of the Titovitz letter to Marina by its super-secret HT/LINGUAL program (this letter opening was discussed in Chapter Fifteen). On the other hand, there does not appear to have been enough time for Marina to have notified Titovitz of the Magazine Street address and receive his reply between May 10 and 22.

The FBI's operation to open the Soviet Embassy's mail might have required a false cover story to hide it, but this would still not explain why Hosty would not have learned from any of Oswald's three communications to the Dallas post office about his relocation to Magazine Street in New Orleans. Furthermore, Special Agent Hosty's May 28 memo said that Oswald's brother and the owner of Oswald's old West Neely address would be "interviewed for information re subjects [Oswald and Marina]." There is no indication that Hosty followed up anytime soon. If Hosty really wanted to find out, all he had to do was go to the post office, just as he had done when he had learned of Oswald's previous move, from Elsbeth to Neely Street.

It is possible but unlikely that the FBI did not intercept mail between Oswald and the FPCC on May 14, 22, and 29, and June 5. We do know that the FBI had access to Oswald's mail to the FPCC. In addition, we also know that the FBI had productive sources in the FPCC.

TABLE A: FBI Sources on the FPCC and Oswald-FPCC Correspondence: May 14–June 5, 1963

Date	Coverage	Activity or Event
May 14	No report:	Oswald change-of-address card to the FPCC.[35]
May 16	Report:	FBI FPCC source on Communist Party (CP) power struggle with Social Workers Party (SWP) over influence in the FPCC.[36]
May 20	Report:	FBI FPCC source on FPCC relations with CP and SWP: Hosty report September 10, 1963.[37]
May 22	No Report:	FPCC director V. T. Lee, letter to Oswald.[38]
May 28	Memorandum:	SA Hosty somehow knows Oswald has moved
May 29	No Report:	FPCC issues card to Oswald and authorizes him to start FPCC New Orleans chapter
June 5	No Report:	Oswald letter to FPCC re: his New Orleans activities

Information exists that was inserted in Oswald's FBI and CIA files in August and September 1963, the source of which was informants reporting on the FPCC to the FBI's Chicago office. An appendix prepared by the Chicago office contains this passage:

> On May 16, 1963, a source advised that during the first two years of the FPCC's existence there was a struggle between Communist Party (CP) and Socialist Workers Party (SWP) elements to exert their power within the FPCC and thereby influence FPCC policy. However, during the past year this source observed there has been a successful effort by FPCC leadership to minimize the role of these and other organizations in the FPCC so that today their influence is negligible.
>
> On May 20, 1963, a second source advised that the National

TOP: American Embassy Complex, Moscow 1959.
(*Courtesy of Richard Snyder*)

LEFT MIDDLE: Marina Oswald, Minsk 1961.

RIGHT MIDDLE: Lee and Marina Oswald departing Soviet Union, June 1962.

BOTTOM: John McVickar (left) and Richard Snyder (right), Moscow 1959.
(*Courtesy of Richard Snyder*)

TOP LEFT: CIA Files on Oswald, National Archives.

TOP RIGHT: FBI Files on Oswald, National Archives.

BOTTOM RIGHT: CIA Routing and Record Sheet for Fain Report, 12 May 1960.

BOTTOM LEFT: CIA Routing and Record Sheet for DeBrueys Report, 25 October 1963.

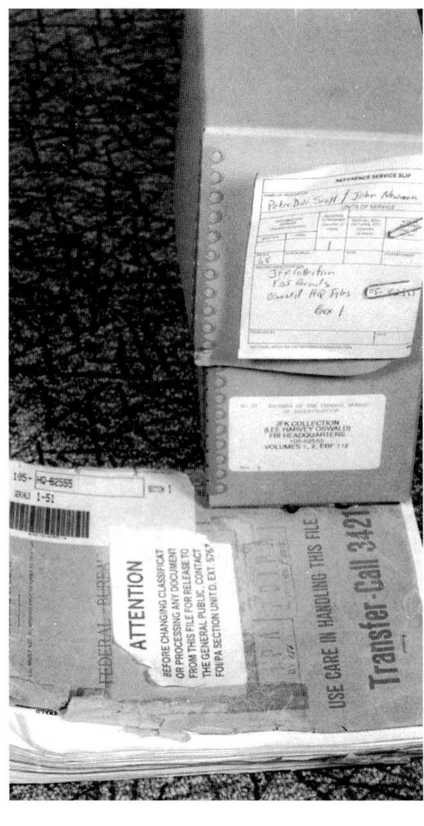

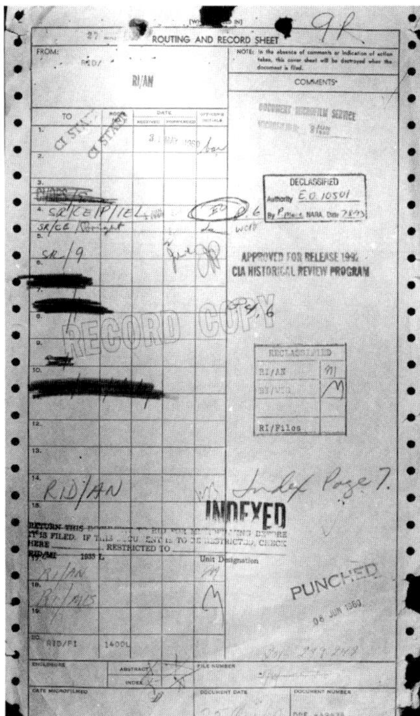

ROUTING AND RECORD SHEET

FROM: RI/AN

NOTE: In the absence of comments or indication of action taken, this cover sheet will be destroyed when the document is filed.

COMMENTS

DECLASSIFIED Authority E.O. 10501

APPROVED FOR RELEASE 1993 CIA HISTORICAL REVIEW PROGRAM

RECORD COPY

INDEXED

RID/AN

PUNCHED 08 JUN 1960

RID/FI

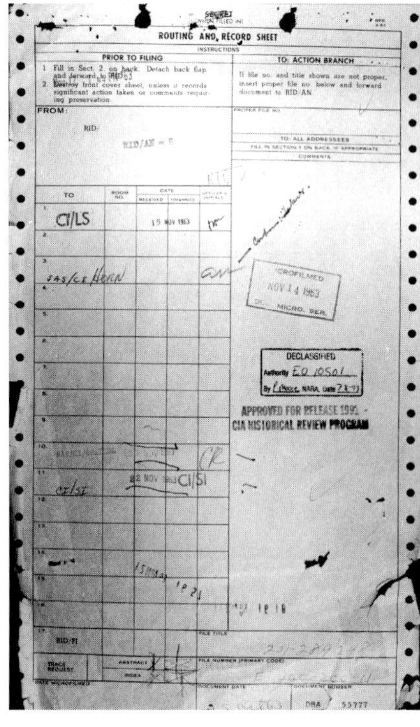

ROUTING AND RECORD SHEET

INSTRUCTIONS

PRIOR TO FILING

TO: ACTION BRANCH

FROM: RID/AN

CI/LS 15 NOV 1963

DECLASSIFIED Authority E.O. 10501

APPROVED FOR RELEASE 1993 CIA HISTORICAL REVIEW PROGRAM

RID/FI

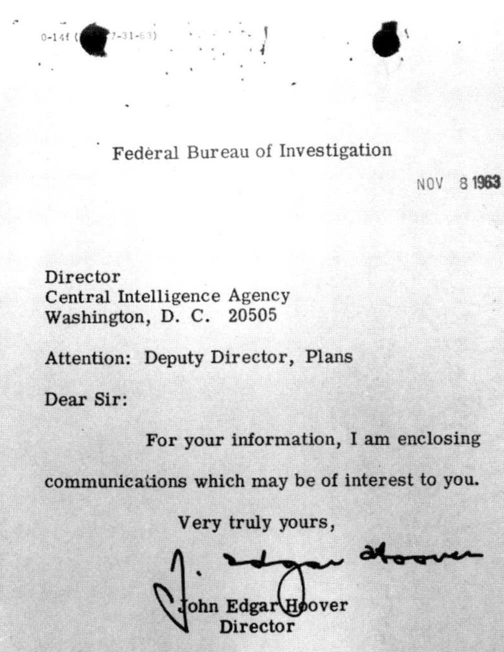

0-14f (7-31-63)

Federal Bureau of Investigation

NOV 8 1963

Director
Central Intelligence Agency
Washington, D. C. 20505

Attention: Deputy Director, Plans

Dear Sir:

For your information, I am enclosing communications which may be of interest to you.

Very truly yours,

J. Edgar Hoover

John Edgar Hoover
Director

Enc.

(Upon removal of classified enclosures, if any, this transmittal form becomes UNCLASSIFIED.)

RELEASED PER P.L. 102-526 (JFK ACT)
NARA KSW DATE 9/17/93

RIGHT: FBI cover letter to Letterhead Memorandum, 24 September 1963.

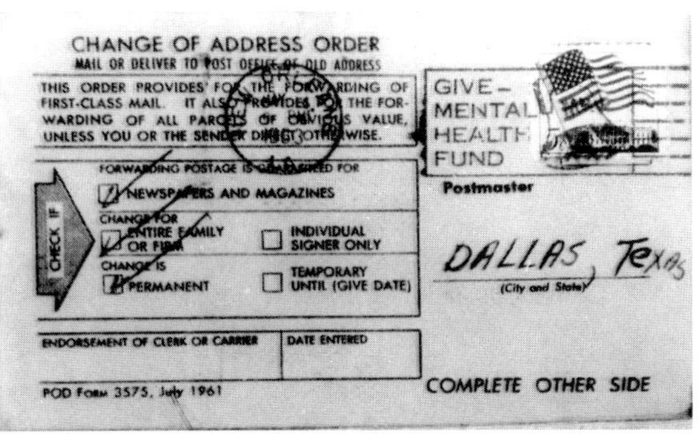

CHANGE OF ADDRESS ORDER
MAIL OR DELIVER TO POST OFFICE OF OLD ADDRESS

THIS ORDER PROVIDES FOR THE FORWARDING OF FIRST-CLASS MAIL. IT ALSO PROVIDES FOR THE FORWARDING OF ALL PARCELS OF OBVIOUS VALUE, UNLESS YOU OR THE SENDER DIRECT OTHERWISE.

CHECK IF

FORWARDING POSTAGE IS GUARANTEED FOR
☒ NEWSPAPERS AND MAGAZINES

CHANGE FOR
☒ ENTIRE FAMILY OR FIRM
☐ INDIVIDUAL SIGNER ONLY

CHANGE IS
☒ PERMANENT
☐ TEMPORARY UNTIL (GIVE DATE)

ENDORSEMENT OF CLERK OR CARRIER | DATE ENTERED

POD Form 3575, July 1961

GIVE — MENTAL HEALTH FUND

Postmaster

DALLAS, Texas
(City and State)

COMPLETE OTHER SIDE

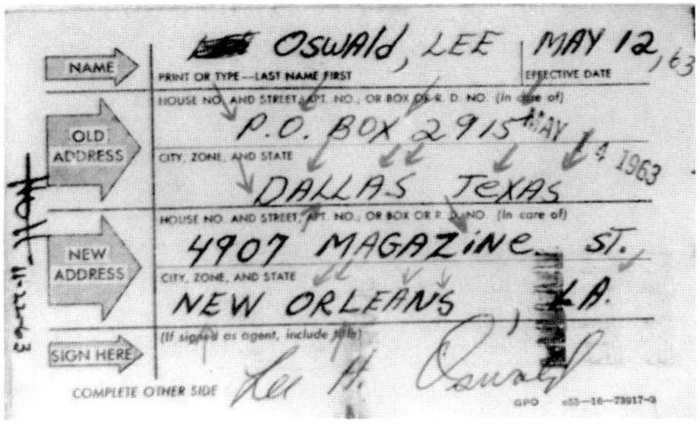

NAME: OSWALD, LEE — PRINT OR TYPE—LAST NAME FIRST

EFFECTIVE DATE: MAY 12, 63

OLD ADDRESS:
HOUSE NO. AND STREET, APT. NO., OR BOX OR R. D. NO. (In care of): P.O. BOX 2915
CITY, ZONE, AND STATE: DALLAS TEXAS

MAY 14 1963

NEW ADDRESS:
HOUSE NO. AND STREET, APT. NO., OR BOX OR R. D. NO. (In care of): 4907 MAGAZINE ST.
CITY, ZONE, AND STATE: NEW ORLEANS, LA.

SIGN HERE (If signed as agent, include title): Lee H. Oswald

COMPLETE OTHER SIDE

GPO

LEFT: Oswald change of address card, 12 May 1963. Arrows placed on exhibit by FBI handwriting experts.

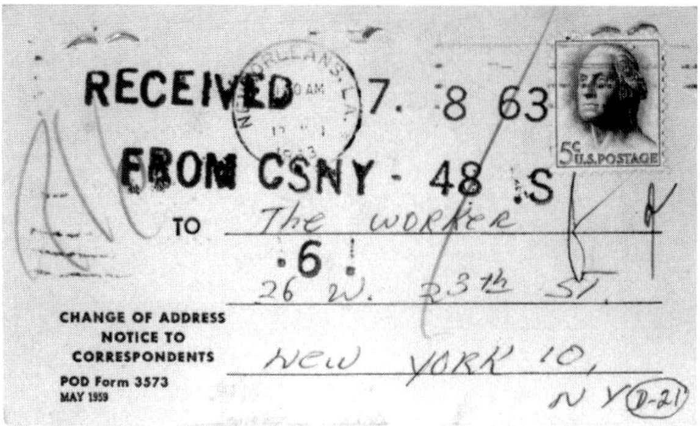

RECEIVED 7. 8 63
FROM CSNY - 48 S
TO The worker
6
26 W. 23th ST.
CHANGE OF ADDRESS NOTICE TO CORRESPONDENTS
NEW YORK 10,
POD Form 3573
MAY 1959
N Y (D-21)

LEFT: Oswald change of address card to the *Worker,* July 1963.

OSWALD DISTRIBUTING FAIR PLAY FOR CUBA HANDBILLS IN NEW ORLEANS, AUGUST 16, 1963 -- INSETS SHOW SAMPLES OF HIS HANDBILLS ON WHICH HE HAD STAMPED HIS NAME AND THE NAME OF "A J HIDELL"

COMMISSION EXHIBIT 2966 B

HANDS OFF CUBA!
Join the Fair Play for Cuba Committee
NEW ORLEANS CHARTER MEMBER BRANCH
Free Literature, Lectures
LOCATION:
A J HIDELL
P. O. BOX 30016
NEW ORLEANS, LA.
EVERYONE WELCOME!

COMMISSION EXHIBIT 2966 A

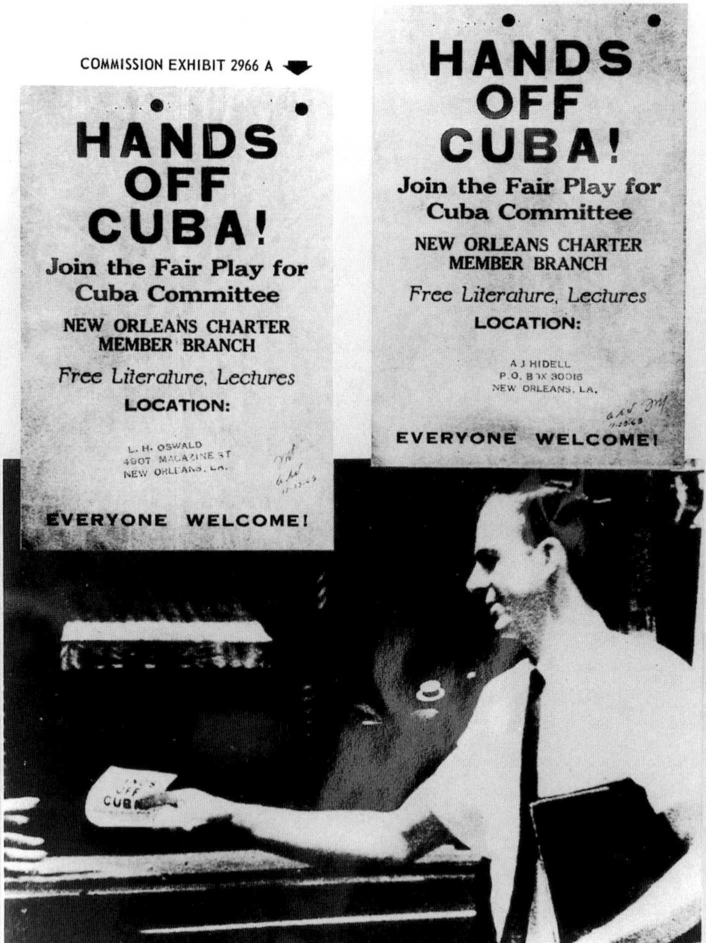

HANDS OFF CUBA!
Join the Fair Play for Cuba Committee
NEW ORLEANS CHARTER MEMBER BRANCH
Free Literature, Lectures
LOCATION:
L. H. OSWALD
4907 MAGAZINE ST
NEW ORLEANS, LA.
EVERYONE WELCOME!

GARNER DEPOSITION EXHIBIT 1

HANDS OFF CUBA!
Join the Fair Play for Cuba Committee
NEW ORLEANS CHARTER MEMBER BRANCH
Free Literature, Lectures
LOCATION:
EVERYONE WELCOME!
5

J-730-200 B1538
139½ strip page
816

HANDS OFF CUBA!
Join the Fair Play for Cuba Committee
NEW ORLEANS CHARTER MEMBER BRANCH
Free Literature, Lectures
LOCATION:
EVERYONE WELCOME!
5

COMMISSION EXHIBIT No. 1412—Continued

Commission Exhibit 1412

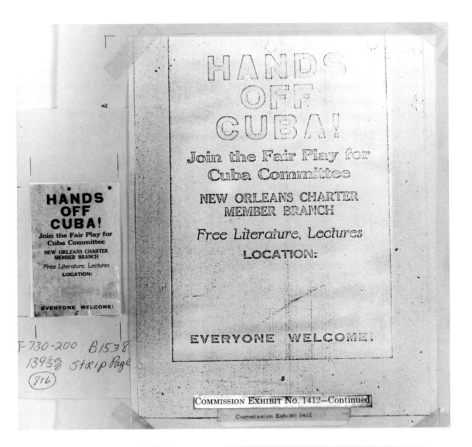

ABOVE: Contact sheet and falsified handbill from USS *Wasp*, CE 1412.

RIGHT: False handbill enlarged, CE 1412.

HANDS
OFF
CUBA!

Join the Fair Play for
Cuba Committee

NEW ORLEANS CHARTER
MEMBER BRANCH

Free Literature, Lectures

LOCATION:

F P C C-A J HIDELL
P.O. BOX 30016
NEW ORLEANS, LA.

EVERYONE WELCOME!

LEFT: Handbill, FBI Exhibit D-25. Oswald probably handed out at USS *Wasp*.

HANDS
OFF
CUBA!

Join the Fair Play for
Cuba Committee

NEW ORLEANS CHARTER
MEMBER BRANCH

Free Literature, Lectures

LOCATION:

F P C C-A J HIDELL
P.O. BOX 30016
NEW ORLEANS, LA.

EVERYONE WELCOME!

RIGHT: Handbill from NASA handed out at USS *Wasp*.

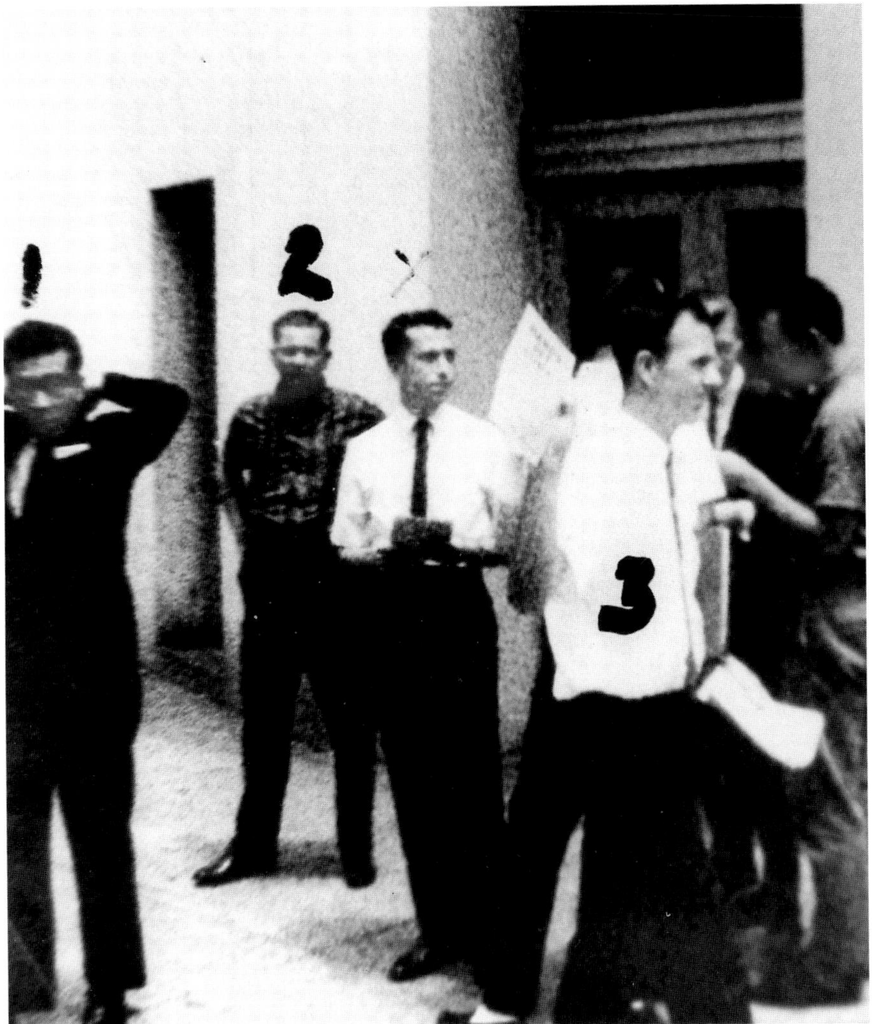

ABOVE: Oswald handing out handbills at International Trademart, 16 August 1963.

BELOW: FPCC application form, FBI Exhibit D-31.

A J HIDELL
P.O. BOX 30016
NEW ORLEAN

To: The Fair Play for Cuba Committee
New Orleans, La.

☐ I wish to join the Committee. Enclosed is my Initiation Fee of $1.00 and dues are $1.00 a month.

☐ I cannot participate as an active member of the Committee, but wish to become a subscriber to mailings. Enclosed find $5.00 for one year.

☐ I would like to have a more active part in supporting the cause of FPCC. Enclosed is my contribution for . . . . ______

Name______________________

Address ____________________

City _______________ Zone ___ State __________

D-31

TOP: Frank Bartez (center, white shirt, tie and sunglasses), October 1959.

BOTTOM RIGHT AND LEFT: The "Mystery Man," photographed by the CIA in Mexico City, early October 1959.

> Headquarters of the FPCC is located in Room 329 at 799 Broadway, New York City. According to this source, the position of National Office Director was created in the Fall of 1962 and was filled by Vincent "Ted" Lee, who now formulates FPCC policy. This source, observed Lee, has followed a course of entertaining and accepting the cooperation of many other organizations including the CP and SWP when he has felt it would be to his personal benefit as well as the FPCC's. However, Lee has indicated to this source he has no intention of permitting FPCC policy to be determined by any other organization. Lee feels the FPCC should advocate resumption of diplomatic relations between Cuba and the United States and support the right of Cubans to manage their revolution without interference from other nationals, but not support the Cuban revolution per se.[39]

The FBI had effective sources inside the FPCC, obviously in Chicago, but probably in New York as well, where the CIA acquired intelligence on the head of the FPCC chapter there, Richard Gibson. As previously discussed, the Agency had tape-recorded him in June Cobb's hotel room in 1960,[40] a time when Gibson was actively supporting Castro and Lumumba, both targets of ongoing assassination planning in the CIA.[41]

Over the course of 1961, Richard Gibson wrote many letters to June Cobb, letters that ended up in the hands of the CIA. His letters revealed much about FPCC policies, personnel and financial matters, and, of course, friends and lovers. It is not clear when Gibson learned of Cobb's intelligence connections, but if the apparent tapering off of his letters after 1961 reflects what happened, it seems that the media-fueled speculation about Cobb (discussed in Chapter Seven) put a damper on Gibson's flame.[42] During interrogation after the Kennedy assassination Gibson signaled interest in cooperation, and later provided some services for the CIA.

A short update on Cobb's activities are an appropriate digression here. Since last we visited her in 1960–1961, her first round of work with the CIA had ended. She traveled to Guatemala and managed to get expelled with much media fanfare. She became the subject of an article, "She's a Soldier of Fortune," by Jack Anderson in the *Washington Post Parade,* on August 12, 1962, a copy of which went straight into her CIA 201 file, 201-27884.[43] Today we can also read the lengthier original essay, written by Cobb herself, which

Anderson used for his *Post* story and which was also read by the propaganda section of the CIA's Task Force W, which handled Cuban matters.[44]

In June 1963, June Cobb was reapproved by security for her new role "as an informant" for "WH/3-Mexico, D.F." The previous October, a CIA security memo to chief of Counterintelligence/Operational Approvals (CI/OA) had warned:

> As we advised on 1 October 1962 a search of our Indices on Subject disclosed note-worthy and derogatory information which is available for review by your office. . . . In view of the note-worthy and questionable information reflected above, it is recommended that no contact beyond assessment be permitted at this time. In view of the voluminous information available on the Subject and Subject's controversial background, this office will not conduct any additional investigation on the Subject until the available note-worthy and derogatory information has been reviewed thoroughly.[45]

By June 17, 1963, however, it is clear that CI/OA had certified the use of Cobb to Security, which went along, reluctantly, and "only for the proposed assignment."[46]

While the CIA was securing approval to keep Cobb on assignment as an informant for WH/3/Mexico, the Dallas office of the FBI was in the process of "losing" Oswald. In his 1964 testimony to the Warren Commission, Hosty said he checked on Oswald in mid-May, but did not say why he chose that date.[47] This would corroborate the statement in FBI director Kelly's book, discussed previously, that Hosty had checked the Neely Street apartment on May 15 and found that Oswald had left.[48] This means that by the time Hosty wrote his May 28 memo to Shanklin about the "check with the Postmaster," he had two full weeks to discover Oswald's New Orleans Magazine Street address. This seeming incompetence may well have been purposeful, to create plausible deniability for what Oswald was up to in New Orleans before June 26.

We will shortly discuss Oswald's activities—especially those of "A.J. Hidell" at the aircraft carrier *Wasp* on June 16—and wonder at how strange it is that the very next day, according to Special Agent Hosty's testimony to the Warren Commission, "New Orleans contacted our office, and advised that they had information that the Oswalds were in New Orleans.''[49] There is no written record of this contact. It appears Hosty confused June 17 and July 17, when New Orleans in fact sent word to Dallas that the Oswalds were in New Orleans. Again, the seeming incompetence of Hosty becomes an issue. In his defense, the Bureau's policy was not to let agents review documents before they testified. Perhaps the further release of documents will better illuminate motives and distinguish plans from accidents. In the meantime, it is reasonable to suspect there was something crucial about this strange period between April 24 and June 26. What did Oswald do during the time he was ''lost'' in New Orleans?

Oswald's New Orleans ''Branch'' of the FPCC

A good deal of Oswald's energy in May, June, and July centered on the FPCC. On April 19, 1963, just five days before he left Dallas, Oswald wrote to FPCC national headquarters in New York. We have elsewhere mentioned this letter, quoted here in full:

> Dear Sirs, I do not like to ask for something for nothing but I am unemployed. Since I am unemployed, I stood yesterday for the first time in my life, with a placard around my neck, passing out fair play for Cuba pamplets, etc. [sic] I only had fifteen or so. In 40 minutes they were all gone. I was cursed as well as praised by some. My home-made placard said: HANDS OFF CUBA! VIVA FIDEL! I now ask for 40 or 50 more of the fine [five?], basic pamplets [sic]. Sincerely, Lee H. Oswald.[50]

As stated previously, this letter was intercepted by the FBI. It was postmarked April 21, and a photograph of it provided by source ''3245-S*'' was in the hands of the FBI's New York office that same day. It took the New York office until June 27, over two months, to mail the photographs to the Dallas FBI office. The negatives were retained in New York.[51]

A possible explanation for the delay in transmitting the images of the letter to Dallas might have been that the FBI broke into FPCC headquarters, photographed a large number of documents, and took several weeks to develop the negatives, so that a print of Oswald's letter became available only in late June. If this explanation is true, the FBI would have coincidentally broken into the FPCC nearly on the day that Oswald's letter arrived in New York. This is so because the negatives were in hand by April 21. Hosty, however, claimed that the source "advised" of the letter's existence *on April 21,* which means Oswald's letter had to have been among the very first film to be developed, and even opens the possibility that the break-in was done to get Oswald's letter. This would have required knowing when the letter was sent, information that might have been acquired from someone besides Oswald. For example, someone in the Dallas post office might have spotted the letter on its way out and, based on this tip, the FBI's New York office broke in to retrieve the letter.

According to Hoover biographers Dr. Anthan G. Theoaris and John Stuart Cox, the New York office's "Surreptitious Entries" file indicates that "no radical or left-liberal organizations escaped the Director's surveillance interest, and when it came to the American left, the bureau's illegal break-ins were not used with restraint."[52] According to these sensitive files, maintained "informally" in the special agent in charge's "personal" folder, the FBI did break into the FPCC offices during April 1963. As previously discussed, FBI informant reports on May 16 and 20, 1963 indicate that the FBI also had access to the FPCC by means other than breaking in.

By May 26, Oswald had been in New Orleans more than a month. On that date he sent another letter to the FPCC, requesting "formal membership" in the organization.[53] Oswald said he had received their pamphlets, some of which he paid for. "Now that I live in New Orleans," Oswald wrote, "I have been thinking about renting a small office at my own expense for the purpose of forming a F.P.C.C. branch here in New Orleans." Then Oswald asked, "Could you grant me a charter?" Oswald also requested more information about buying large quantities of pamphlets, blank FPCC application forms, and added presumptiously, "also a picture of Fidel suitable for framing would be a welcome touch." Oswald confessed he could not "supervise the office" all of the time but that he could get volunteers to man it. "I am not saying this project would be a roaring success," he cautioned, "but I am willing to try." Oswald said that providing he had "a steady flow of literature," he would gladly pay for the office rent, which would be $30 a month.

FPCC national director Vincent Lee responded to Oswald on May 29, enclosing Oswald's FPCC membership card.[54] Lee encouraged Oswald's plan to form a chapter in New Orleans but suggested, "It would be hard to conceive of a chapter with as few members as seem to exist in the New Orleans area." Lee said he was not "adverse" to a small chapter, providing Oswald could get twice the number of members needed to convene a "legal" executive board. Lee advised against renting an office in New Orleans:

> I definitely would not recommend an office, at least not one that will be easily identifyable[sic] to the lunatic fringe in your community. Certainly, I would not recommend that you engage in one at the very beginning but wait and see how you can operate in the community through several public experiences.[55]

A post office box was a "must," Lee added. The FPCC national director might have been concerned, however, if he had known that while he was composing this go-ahead letter in New York, Oswald was taking matters into his own hands in New Orleans.

On May 29, Oswald went to the Jones Printing Company at 422 Girod Street, where he ordered 1000 FPCC handbills, using the name "Osborne."[56] This printing company was opposite the Reily Coffee Company, where Oswald worked as a machinist. Myra Silver, the secretary at Jones Printing, told him the handbills would be ready on June 4. On June 1 Oswald dropped off a down payment of $4.00.[57] On June 3, Oswald entered the offices of Mailers Service Company, where he "ordered 500 offset printed copies of an application form" from John I. Anderson. Anderson later told the FBI that the name he wrote on the bill was "Lee Osborne."[58] Oswald picked up his FPCC application forms "within a couple of days" from Mailers Service.

On June 3, Oswald opened a post office box—30061—in the Lafayette Square Station, located on the first floor of the Federal Building at 600 South Street.[59] According to New Orleans postal inspector J. J. Zarza, "the persons designated by Oswald [besides himself] to receive mail in this Post Office box were: A. J. Hidell and Marina Oswald." On or about June 12, Oswald notified both

The Militant and the *Worker* to use this post office box. However, the only box number that appeared on any of Oswald's FPCC and socialist literature was a false variant of Oswald's, 30016. This creates another Oswald riddle: Why did he always—without mistake—put 30061 on his letters and his change-of-address cards and, at the same time, always—and therefore without mistake—use 30016 on his FPCC handbills? He bought a stamp kit that permitted the user to manipulate the letters and numbers, meaning Oswald could easily have corrected the stamp to 30061 if he had wanted to do so. We will return to the post office box riddle shortly.

On June 4 Oswald returned to Jones Printing, where he paid off the balance of $5.89 and picked up his FPCC handbills.[60] The handbills contained the words "New Orleans Charter Member Branch," something Oswald had not been authorized to print, as he found out when he received Lee's May 29 letter. After picking up the handbills from Jones Printing, Oswald wrote this to Lee:

> I see from the circular [handbill] I had jumped the gun on that charter business but I don't think its [sic] too important, you may think the circular is too provocative, but I want it too [sic] attract attention, even if its [sic] the attention of the lunatic fringe. I had 2000 of them run off.[61]

Oswald wrote this letter between June 5 and 14.[62] His exaggeration of the number of handbills he ordered—the true number was 1000—seems less noteworthy than the fact that he had proclaimed the existence of a "charter" FPCC branch in New Orleans.

Two other details in Oswald's early June letter to Vincent Lee merit our close attention. "As per your advice," Oswald told Lee, he had rented New Orleans P.O. Box 30061.

> Against your advice, I have decided to take an office from the very beginning. . . . In any event I will keep you posted, even if the office stays open for only 1 month more people will find out about the F.P.C.C. than if there had never been any office at all, don't you agree?[63]

Lee did not agree. It was the end of the line for Oswald from Vincent Lee's point of view. He testified to the Warren Commission that he had considered Oswald's act a fundamental transgression of the FPCC bylaws and procedures. (Lee had taken the trouble to send these rules to Oswald.)

On June 8, 1963, Oswald was trying out his new stamp kit.[64] It was a ninety-eight-cent Warrior Rubber Stamping Kit, a picture of which was published in volume XVI of the Warren Commission exhibits.[65] This exhibit includes a piece of paper on which Oswald practiced stamping. Neither the Hidell alias nor the false (30016) post office box appears on this document.

On June 10, Oswald showed off his new wares—by sending an FPCC handbill and application card—to the *Worker*. ''I ask that you give me as much literature as you judge possible,'' Oswald said, ''since I think it would be very nice to have your literature among the 'Fair Play' leaflets (like the one enclosed) and phamplets [sic] in my office.''[66] On these materials Oswald did not use his stamp kit. On June 12, Oswald sent letters to the FPCC and the U.S. Navy. He sent a change-of-address card to the FPCC newspaper *The Militant,* changing from 4907 Magazine Street to P. O. Box 30061.[67] He also sent a change-of-address card to the Naval Discharge Review Board, changing his address from 2703 Mercedes, Fort Worth (Oswald had moved from there on October 8, 1962), to New Orleans P. O. Box 30061.[68] On none of this correspondence, and on none of his letters to Vincent Lee, did Oswald ever use the name Hidell.

From the available evidence, including evidence that was deliberately falsified at the Government Printing Office during the publication of the Warren Commission exhibits, there are two stamp configurations on the early handbills and pamphlets. Leaving aside the New Orleans and Louisiana part of the stamp, these two variants were ''FPCC-A J Hidell P. O. Box 30016'' and ''FPCC 544 Camp Street.'' These stamps—while not conclusive—are nevertheless documentary evidence suggestive that Oswald had or pretended to have had an office for the FPCC at 544 Camp Street. What other evidence is there for this possibility?

In early June, Oswald had written to the FPCC saying that he had, against Vincent Lee's advice, rented an office in New Orleans.[69] The building numbered 544 Camp Street is also numbered 531 Lafayette around the corner.[70] On the second floor were the offices of W. Guy Banister. Sam Newman, the owner of the ''Newman Building'' at the corner of Lafayette and Camp streets, remembers that a white male, aged thirty-seven to thirty-eight, 5 feet 11 inches tall, with a medium build, light olive complexion, dark eyes, and dark brown hair rented one of his offices at 544 Camp Street for thirty dollars. This man said he wanted to use the office as a night school classroom for students of Spanish. The description rules out Oswald, unless this person was working with Oswald. Newman recalls, however, that this happened in July or August, much too late to correspond to Oswald's June letter to Vincent Lee. If this event was connected to Oswald and an office at 544 Camp Street, Newman would have to be wrong about the time. Thus, the statements of the building owner, Sam Newman, do not resolve the issue one way or the other. What about others who worked in and around 544 Camp Street?

Witnesses interviewed by the HSCA, such as Banister's brother, Ross, said that Banister had become "aware" of Oswald before the assassination. The HSCA found no proof that Banister had an Oswald file and could not find "credible witnesses" who had seen Oswald and Banister together. The HSCA observed, however, "that Banister at least knew of Oswald's leafletting activities and probably maintained a file on him." A search of Banister's files after his death by the Louisiana State Police indicated "Oswald's name was included among the main subjects of the file on the Fair Play for Cuba Committee." A partial index of Banister's file compiled by New Orleans district attorney Jim Garrison's investigators did not include Oswald or the FPCC.[71]

The HSCA's comment that it could not find credible witnesses to a Banister-Oswald contact is troubling. Presumably, this comment refers to the committee's inability to verify Delphine Roberts's claims that Oswald had come into the building looking for a job and had, on one occasion, brought Marina with him. Roberts was Banister's longtime friend and secretary. She also told the HSCA that Banister "had become angry" with building owner Newman for Oswald's use of the 544 Camp Street stamp on his handbills. There were, however, other witnesses who were deemed credible. Ross Banister said he did not know of a direct association between his brother and Oswald, but "did confirm Guy's interest in the assassination and Oswald," and said his brother "had mentioned seeing Oswald hand out Fair Play for Cuba literature on one occasion."[72]

Moreover, there was William George Gaudet, a CIA asset in New Orleans of many years, who testified to the HSCA that he knew about Oswald's distribution of literature before the assassination and that "on one occasion, he observed Oswald on a street corner speaking with Guy Banister."[73] Gaudet's file with the Agency's Domestic Contacts Division (DCD) shows he was a "casual contact" for the New Orleans office from 1956 through 1961. At one point Gaudet claimed he "had once been employed by the CIA." Gaudet went to Mexico at the same time in the fall of 1963 that Oswald did, a subject to which we will return in Chapter Seventeen.[74] This information appears in the HSCA's final report but, strangely, not in its 544 Camp Street analysis, which appears in Volume X of the committee's work. There, the Gaudet piece is missing.

There was also Ivan E. Nitschke, who had served in the FBI with Banister and had "for a short time worked for Banister in the office [of] the Newman Building." Nitschke told the HSCA that Oswald's distribution of handbills had led to Banister's interest in him during the summer of 1963. Nitschke's HSCA deposition claimed that "Banister had some of these handbills in his office or made reference to them. From the context of the conversation, however, he [Banister] was not pleased."[75]

What might Banister have used Oswald for? Banister and the extreme right wing in New Orleans had targeted leftwing professors at Tulane like La Violette and Reissman and organizations like the New Orleans Council on Peaceful Alternatives (NOCPA), of which Professor Reissman was a member. Members of the NOCPA reportedly met at Tulane University.[76] After the Kennedy assassination someone else "had a dim recollection that sometime in 1962, date not recalled, some Fair Play for Cuba literature had been found in the street in the 1200 or 1300 block of Pine Street in New Orleans."[77] The person with this "dim recollection" was J. D. Vinson, a private eye from the Isaac Detective Agency, hired by Jack N. Rogers, the legal counsel for the Joint Legislative Committee on Un-American Activities for the State of Louisiana. It is possible that Banister was using Oswald to smoke out pro-Castro Cuban students in local universities and to discredit local leftwing or communist academics.

The above evidence of an Oswald-Banister association is far from conclusive, but it is enough to take this possibility seriously. Another tantalizing piece of evidence comes from the newly released files. Not long after the assassination, New Orleans FBI special agent in charge Harry Maynor drafted a message that was changed before it was sent to the Bureau. Two pieces of information, apparently in Maynor's handwriting, for insertion into the text of the message were scratched out, but the handwriting is still visible. The first deletion concerned the fact that Bartes had been a reliable FBI informant "whose identity must be protected." The other deletion were these words: "*Several Fair Play for Cuba pamphlets contained address 544 Camp Street*" [emphasis added].[78]

"FPCC-A J Hidell"

"About May" 1963, Hugh T. Murray, a graduate student at Tulane, noticed a pile of handbills lying in the foyer of the university library. Murray picked one up and saw that it was captioned "Hands off Cuba," and that the handbill was "under the sponsorship" of the FPCC. Murray recalled that the handbill had a name and post office box stamped on it, but he could remember neither the address nor the name.[79] If these handbills were Oswald's, the earliest they could have been at Tulane would have been about June 10. Oswald had not picked up the handbills until June 4, and did not purchase the stamp kit until June 9.

We know what name was stamped on the handbill from another graduate student at Tulane University, Harold Gordon Alderman. Murray mentioned the handbill to Alderman, who wanted to see it. Murray, "shortly thereafter," gave it to him.[80] Alderman had collected FPCC literature from the FPCC office in New York at the time of the Bay of Pigs and during the same period had participated in an FPCC picket of the CIA in Washington, D.C. Later, he joined another FPCC action directed at President Kennedy in Seattle, Washington. In October 1962 Alderman debated anti-Castro writer and adventurer Alexander Rorke at Tulane University.

Alderman recalled that Murray handed over the Tulane FPCC handbill "in the summer of 1963, possibly in July, 1963." Alderman tacked the handbill on a door in his apartment on Delord Street, and there it stayed until President Kennedy was assassinated in November. As Alderman read the local newspaper accounts of the assassination, he learned that the alleged murderer had used an alias—A. J. Hidell. Alderman knew this name because it was on the handbill in his apartment. He called the New Orleans office of the FBI and offered to turn over his "Tulane" handbill to them. Whoever he spoke with "advised that the FBI Office already had this handbill and did not want his copy."[81] This was strange, especially in view of the fact that collecting these FPCC handbills was an important part of the FBI's investigation of Oswald's activities.[82]

More than students at Tulane picked up these FPCC handbills. Four days after the assassination, U.S. Army Major Robert H. Erdrich of the 112th Intelligence Corps Group in New Orleans walked into the New Orleans office of the FBI. Major Erdrich said he had heard they "were interested in the Fair Play for Cuba Committee in connection with the investigation of this [Kennedy assassination] case," and offered some interesting information. The resulting New Orleans FBI report contains this passage:

> He [Major Erdrich] advised that one of the 112th Agents sometime during the last week in May or the first week in June, 1963, picked up a handbill of the Fair Play for Cuba Committee which was attached to a wall on the campus of Tulane University. This handbill was approximately 8" × 11" and was faded green in color.[83]

The stamp on the handbill read, "FPCC - A.J. Hidell P.O. Box 30016 New Orleans, Louisiana." Erdrich delivered two copies of the handbill to the New Orleans FBI office later that same afternoon.

Erdrich also told the FBI that the Army had found copies of this handbill at other locations. One was "laying on the grounds of the Port of Embarkation, New Orleans." Major Erdrich returned later the same November afternoon with copies of the handbill. The stamp read, "FPCC-A J Hidell P.O. Box 30016."[84] The subsequent FBI investigation gathered more information about what had happened at the port. On July 14, 1964, ONI received a request from a Mr. Morrissey of the FBI, asking if ONI records could substantiate a story about Oswald's activities during June 1963 in New Orleans: "Oswald distributed Fair Play for Cuba Committee leaflets to sailors on street; aircraft carrier was in port. Oswald apparently impressed with number of officers in Navy who appeared sympathetic to his leaflets."[85]

We know where Morrissey got some of this story. On August 1, 1963, Oswald had written this to FPCC national director Vincent Lee: ''We also managed to picket the fleet when it came in and I was surprised at the number of officers who were interested in our literature.''[86] Oswald's letter had not mentioned an aircraft carrier or ''sailors on street,'' details which Morrissey had to have learned elsewhere in the summer of 1964. Indeed there had been an aircraft carrier, the USS *Wasp,* in port from June 13 to June 20, 1963, berthed at the Dumaine Street wharf. Moreover, Patrolman Girod Ray of the harbor police had written a memorandum on June 16, 1963, entitled ''Distribution of Propaganda Literature'' describing a man passing out pamphlets. According to his memo, Patrolman Ray had apprehended and ejected the man from the wharf on June 15 or 16, 1963.[87] The man was Oswald.

In June 1963, the harbor police did not—as far as can be determined from the available records—notify the New Orleans Police or the FBI about this incident. The Army counterintelligence unit, which had scarfed up copies of the handbills from the ground, apparently did not notify the Navy, the New Orleans Police, or the FBI. We know from Major Erdrich's report, however, that the New Orleans 112th INCT did send a copy of the handbill to ''headquarters at Washington D.C.,'' meaning the national headquarters of military intelligence for the U.S. Army. According to Major Erdrich, they sent the handbill to Washington on June 18, 1963.[88]

A copy of Patrolman Ray's June 16, 1963, report surfaced in the Church Committee files a decade later with two pieces of paper attached to it: a handbill and a flyer under the headline ''The Truth About Cuba Is in Cuba!''[89] The address stamped on this handbill is different from the one Army counterintelligence recovered from the wharf. The Church Committee handbill associated with Ray's report bears the stamp ''A J Hidell P.O. Box 30016,'' while the FBI described the Army handbill as bearing the stamp ''FPCC - A. J. Hidell P.O. Box 30016.'' The periods after the letters ''A'' and ''J'' may have been inattentiveness on the part of Major Erdrich or the FBI, but the addition of ''FPCC'' to the Army handbill appears to be a more substantive conflict.

Frustrating our efforts to reconcile this conflict is an act that the U.S. Army should publicly admit was a serious mistake: the ''routine'' destruction of Oswald's Army files. If it is true, as the Army claims, that they destroyed the files of the alleged assassin of President Kennedy, we will never be sure what stamp was on the *Wasp* handbill the 112th INCT sent to Washington on June 18, 1963. Most mysterious is the fact that by the time the Warren Commission published its version of the handbill from the Domaine Street wharf, the stamp had disappeared entirely! We need to retrace the path traveled by this magical handbill from the time it left Oswald's hands—if indeed it was Oswald—to its final official destination on page 807 of Warren Commission volume XXII. Something is fishy about the handbills from the wharf.

The Great Handbill Caper

On a Sunday afternoon, June 16, 1963, harbor police Patrolman Girod Ray was between the Toulouse and Domaine Street wharves when an "enlisted man" approached and said that "the Officer of the Deck of the 'USS *Wasp*' desired Patrolman Ray seek out an individual who was passing out leaflets regarding Cuba and to request this individual to stop passing out these leaflets."[90] Ray went immediately to the Domaine Street wharf, where he found a man handing out white and yellow-colored leaflets. (As previously discussed, Major Erdrich described a faded green handbill as well.) According to Ray, the man was a white male in his late twenties who was 5 feet 9 inches tall, weighed 150 pounds, and had a slender build. This description is consistent with the appearance of Oswald.

The man at the wharf was distributing leaflets to "Navy personnel" and also to "civilians" who were leaving the *Wasp.* Patrolman Ray asked the man if he had permission from the Dock Board to issue these leaflets, to which the man responded "that he thought as an American citizen he did not need anyone's permission."[91] Ray told the man that the wharfs and buildings along the Mississippi River encompassing the Port of New Orleans were operated by the Board of Commissioners and that if they gave their permission, he could hand out the leaflets. The man "kept insisting that he did not see why he would need anyone's permission," whereupon Ray told him that "if he did not leave the Domaine Street wharf, Patrolman Ray would arrest him." The man left. In a 1964 interview with the FBI, Patrolman Ray identified the man handing out the leaflets as Oswald.[92]

The same day that Patrolman Ray ejected the man from the wharf, he wrote a memo to harbor police chief L. Deutchman, and enclosed the "pamphlets" that had been distributed. Those copies remained unnoticed in the harbor police files for a year. They were not the only copies preserved from that day. As previously discussed, U.S. Army counterintelligence agents were at the wharf too, where they picked up copies "laying on the ground," sending one to Washington on June 17, 1963, and providing the New Orleans FBI office with two copies on November 26, 1963. Yet another agency of the U.S. government obtained a copy of the *Wasp* handbills that June summer—the National Aeronautics and Space Administration (NASA) security office in Houston.

An employee of Lockheed Aircraft Corporation on special assignment at the NASA Houston Manned Spacecraft Center, Martin Samuel Abelow, was vacationing in New Orleans in the summer of 1963 and just happened to be walking along side the aircraft carrier *Wasp* on that particular Sunday. There Abelow saw "a young man" handing out FPCC leaflets.[93] An FBI "confidential source"—apparently a coworker of Abelow's—told the FBI that Abelow had "several items" of FPCC literature he had obtained from his visit to the wharf. According to the FBI informant, Abelow had said "he should probably furnish these items to the Federal Bureau of Investigation."[94] Abelow decided, however, to turn them over to the security office of the Space Center, which he did on June 21, 1963. The stamp on the FPCC handbill was "FPCC-A J Hidell P.O. Box 30016," the same as the stamp on the handbill sent to Army intelligence in Washington, D.C., on June 18, 1963, and provided to the FBI on November 26, 1963.

On November 25, 1963, the day before Major Erdrich dropped off the Army copies of the *Wasp* handbills, a matching handbill—stamped "FPCC-A J. Hidell P.O. Box 30016"—turned up in the New Orleans office of the FBI. There it was mixed up with handbills from Oswald's August 8 Canal Street activity (stamped "A J Hidell P.O. Box 30016"), and August 16 Trade Mart activity (stamped "L.H. Oswald 4907 Magazine St"), events we will discuss in the next chapter. Together these three handbills formed FBI Exhibit D-25, furnished to the Warren Commission. There is no indication where the "FPCC A J Hidell P.O. Box 30016" handbill came from, but if this three-handbill set was to give an example from each leafleting event, then this handbill would have been from the *Wasp* event. The next episode, which occurred on February 4, 1964, seems to corroborate this possibility. In response to a Warren Commission routine request for information from all government agencies, Lloyd W. Blankenbaker, director of security, NASA, sent the Commission a copy of the Abelow handbill from the *Wasp* incident. The stamp read, "FPCC-A J Hidell P.O. Box 30016."

The next episodes in the unfolding mystery of the *Wasp* handbills were the May 25, 1964, FBI interview with the NASA FBI informant and the May 28, 1964, FBI interview with Martin "Marty" Abelow, both discussed previously. Neither interview added any new information about the stamp on the handbills. Next was a July 14, 1964, request from the FBI agent Morrissey to the ONI about the *Wasp* leafleting, also discussed previously.[95] The same day Wilbur Sartwell, ONI, Potomac River Naval Command, informed the FBI that his office had no record of the *Wasp* leafleting incident and added that "any such record would be at Headquarters, ONI." The next day, July 15, Don Gorham, acting chief of NCISC (Naval Counter Intelligence Support Center)-3, "made available to a representative of the FBI, the Headquarters, ONI files pertaining to the subject." No information has been found in these files either.[96]

On July 21, 1964, two leaflets "were obtained from Lieutenant Roy Alleman of the New Orleans Harbor Police." It is at this point that trouble begins in the official record. The Church Committee records contain a copy of the June 16, 1963, Patrolman Ray report with the attached handbill and "Truth about Cuba" flyer, presumably the ones enclosed by Ray. The handbill bears the stamp, "AJ Hidell P.O. Box 30016."[97] The two documents turned over to the FBI by Alleman—presumably from the harbor police files—were likewise a handbill and a "Truth about Cuba" flyer, the former designated FBI exhibit D-234, and the latter D-235. These exhibits are in the National Archives today. The handbill has no stamp on it at all. This seems odd: What would be the purpose of enticing people to join the FPCC with a handbill with no address? FBI exhibits D-234 and D-235 were tested for fingerprints on July 21, 1964. Two latent fingerprints were found, neither of which belonged to Oswald.

The Church Committee's copy of the Ray report has handwriting on it: "Sunday - 1 pm - 4 pm. 5'6" × 5'7"." This writing does not appear on the version printed in CE 1412 of Warren Commission volume XXII. This contradiction is only the tip of the iceberg. An August 4, 1964, Hoover memo to the commission, with attached FBI memos of July 16 and 22, 1964, and Patrolman Ray's June 16, 1963, report with the attached handbill and "Truth about Cuba" flyer, were combined as an eleven-page document, Commission Document 1370. At this stage, the stampless handbill has developed a faint diagonal line in the area where the address stamp would normally have appeared. This handbill was attached, using Scotch tape, to the contact sheet in preparation for the publication of the Warren Commission's twenty-six volumes. (The contact sheets were large blank sheets of paper upon which each prospective page was placed before final publication.)

At this point, while the contact sheet was still in the Government Printing Office and nearing publication, someone took a photograph of CE 2966A, a handbill that Oswald handed out on August 8, 1963, on Canal Street. This handbill had the stamp "L.H. Oswald 4907 Magazine St," next to which were the initials "JLF" (presumably Special Agent Joseph L. Flemming, New Orleans FBI office), another illegible notation, and a date, November 23, 1963. After the photograph of CE 2966A was developed, a white paste was applied to the stamp and the adjacent handwritten notations. The doctored picture of 2966A was then enlarged and printed as if it were the handbill in CD 1370!

If the "great handbill caper" tells us anything, it is that someone in the Government Printing Office was willing to take a considerable risk in connection with the *Wasp* handbills. This brings us back to the question asked at the beginning of this chapter, namely, what was Oswald up to during the period that the FBI claims to have lost track of him. Our suspicions are justifiably aroused by the skullduggery in the published Warren Commission materials connected to a crucial event during this period, which lasted from April 24 to June 26.

Two other events stand out toward the end of this "lost" period in New Orleans: On June 24 Oswald applied for a passport, and on July 1 Marina, reportedly at Oswald's request, wrote to the Soviet Embassy asking to return to the Soviet Union. Marina testified that Oswald "planned to go to Cuba,"[98] but on his passport application form Oswald indicated his desire to travel to England, France, Germany, Holland, U.S.S.R., Finland, Italy, and Poland.[99] Cuba was missing. Moreover, on June 25, when he received his passport, it was stamped with a warning that a person traveling to Cuba would be liable for prosecution.[100] Accompanying Marina's request to the Soviet Embassy was a letter by Oswald requesting that Marina's visa be approved on a rush basis. ''As for my return entrance visa,'' he wrote, ''please consider it separately''[101] [underline in original]. Thus, while engaging in an undercover game of Alex Hidell, FPCC New Orleans branch chief, Oswald was making plans to travel to the Soviet Union, Cuba, or both.

Although the FBI claims to have discovered Oswald's presence in New Orleans on June 26, the Bureau, as previously discussed, claims it still was not aware of Oswald's street address. On July 29, 1963, the Dallas FBI office had asked the New Orleans FBI office to ''verify'' both Lee and Marina's presence in New Orleans:

> For the information of New Orleans, the case on both subjects is in a pending status. The Dallas Office is attempting to locate the subjects. Their last known place of residence was 214 Neely Street, Dallas, Texas, and they left giving no forwarding address. New Orleans is requested to verify the presence of the two subjects in New Orleans and advise the Dallas Office.[102]

Finally, on August 5, the FBI says it ''verified'' where Oswald was living in New Orleans. On that date Jessie James Garner, a neighbor of Oswald's, told the New Orleans FBI office that Oswald was living in an apartment at 4905 Magazine Street, New Orleans, and had been living there since 'about'' June.[103]

It was fitting that the FBI ''found'' Oswald on August 5. That same day Oswald broke cover and contacted some Cuban exiles, using his real name. In other words, the FBI's alleged blind period covers—to the day—the precise period of Oswald's undercover activity in New Orleans. Again, while the evidence is circumstantial and speculative, his activity may have served, whether he realized it or not, the local CRC recruiting program by flushing pro-Castro students out into the open, where Banister could identify them. Presumably, Banister's background checks were designed to insulate the local CRC from obvious infiltrators. Oswald, moreover, was preparing to launch an infiltration game of his own.

Chapter Seventeen

Oswald and AMSPELL

By the end of July 1963, there was no longer any ambiguity about Oswald's address: The FBI knew he was living at 4907 Magazine, New Orleans. He had been working at the Reily Coffee Company, also on Magazine, until he was fired on July 19.[1] The records indicate that at about this time, Oswald decided to stamp his real name and address, "L. H. Oswald 4907 Magazine St," on his FPCC handbills. At the earlier Tulane and *Wasp* leafleting events the stamp read: "A J Hidell P.O. Box 30016." As discussed in the previous chapter, during the first half of his sojourn in New Orleans Oswald apparently played an undercover pro-Castro role, possibly associated with a Cuban Revolutionary Council (CRC) recruiting operation.

Beginning with his August 5 visit to Carlos Bringuier, Oswald's role changed to that of an apparent double agent. This period lasted for the rest of his stay in New Orleans and included Oswald's September 25 meeting with Silvia Odio. In contacting both Bringuier and Odio, Oswald feigned anti-Castro sympathies. In between these Odio-Bringuier bookends, Oswald played out his pro-Castro FPCC role overtly, using his real name on radio, television, and streets corners—and even from inside a jail cell. At all of the salient points of his pro-Castro performance, he became involved with the Cuban Student Directorate (DRE). Unlike the CRC which, as of April, had lost its CIA funding, the DRE was still partially funded by the CIA. AMBUD was the CIA cryptonym for the CRC, and AMSPELL was the cryptonym for the DRE. The CIA AMSPELL mission during the summer of 1963 was for propaganda, instead of military, operations. Oswald's activities in New Orleans proved to be a bonanza for AMSPELL's mission.

The Oswald we watch through the eyes of the FBI agents who

tracked him down—and through the eyes of the CIA personnel who read the FBI reports—looks like a would-be double agent caught in a web of intrigue far stickier than he had anticipated. Again, whether Oswald's actions were his own or the result of direction or manipulation, by carrying out both pro-Castro and anti-Castro activities in New Orleans, Oswald was playing a dangerous game. During this spectacle Oswald actually insisted on seeing an FBI agent while in jail, to supply him, Oswald said, with information on his FPCC activities. It was a strange place to play the part of informant, an oddity underlined by a strange FBI act: They withheld the fact—for quite some time—that Special Agent Quigley had interviewed Oswald in jail.

When the FBI reported Oswald's FPCC activities to the CIA in September, the Quigley interview was missing. At that point, incoming material on Oswald was no longer placed in Oswald's 201 file, but in a new, active file—a subject we will deal with in Chapter Nineteen. For now we will focus on Oswald's virtuoso August performance in New Orleans. This performance appeared designed to maximize media and FBI coverage. It culminated in his "exposure" as a Marxist defector to the Soviet Union, which, in the short run, left a stain on the FPCC. In the long run it was the kiss of death.

Bust at Lake Ponchartrain, Louisiana

"The Lake Ponchartrain activity," said a February 1, 1977, CIA Security Office (OS) memo, "was run by Gerald Patrick Hemming as part of his Intercontinental Penetration Force (Interpen)."[2] A CIA training camp had been located near the Algiers Naval Station, but the OS memo explained that this camp "should not be confused with the infamous training activity" at Lake Ponchartrain. "Frank Sturgis (aka Frank Fiorini) of Watergate fame," said the memo, "was also connected with the activities of Interpen." In the present chapter we are concerned with the Ponchartrain camp, not the Algiers camp. The CIA knew about Hemming's activities at Ponchartrain from the moment he arrived in June 1962, because the person who helped Hemming was an informant for the CIA office in New Orleans. As discussed in Chapter Fourteen, that informant was Frank Bartes. On June 20, 1963, the FBI sent a report concerning Bartes[3]—

which has not been publicly released—and on July 31 the FBI raided a house where arms were kept for the group that was training at the Ponchartrain camp.

On July 30, the day before the raid, the FBI had received a tip from Elise Cerniglia, an informant in the Catholic Cuban Center in New Orleans.[4] Mrs. Cerniglia told the FBI that "approximately ten Cuban refugees arrived in New Orleans from Miami on the night of 7/24/63 for the purpose of attending a training camp some two hours from New Orleans after which they were to be transferred to a training camp in Guatemala." As the FBI later learned, nineteen Cubans had been sent to the Ponchartrain camp by Laureano Batista, a Cuban leader of the Movimento Democratica Cristiano (MDC) in Miami. This camp was not two hours from New Orleans, but was instead just ten to fifteen miles away. The FBI learned later that the house where these Cubans had been staying "was located in St. Tammany Parish in Lacombe, La. about a mile from Highway 190 West on a secondary road." Lacombe was the location for the Ponchartrain training camp.

The Cuban Student Directorate (DRE) was probably active at the Ponchartrain camp in July 1963. At least John Koch, a member of the DRE Military Section,[5] was among those arrested during the arms raid. Although the CIA denied any connection to this camp, the DRE was linked to the Agency, as was another person locked up during the July bust. His name was John Noon, and he had been a CIA asset in Project JMATE—an anti-Castro program—in 1960 to 1961. A CIA request for operational use of Noon specified that he was to be used for "across the board training" by PA/PROP (Paramilitary and Propaganda).[6]

A CIA report apparently written during the Garrison investigation (Jim Garrison was the district attorney for New Orleans Parish who tried—unsuccessfully—a local business leader and CIA informant, Clay Shaw, for conspiring to assassinate Kennedy) in 1967 contains this fragment about the Ponchartrain site from a July 1963 report:

> . . . The camp was located about 15 miles from New Orleans, right after crossing very long bridge right at entrance of state of Louisiana. Source of Report did not know name of ranch which belonged to some American millionaires who were defraying expenses for maintenance of men in training and providing equip-

ment. Approx 30 men were in training there. Source also stated that on 24 July 63 two automobiles left for Louisiana with Commandante Diego. (Note Diego is [also known as] Victor Manuel (Paneque) Batistia. . . .[7]

Victor Batista was an assistant to Laureano Batista, military coordinator of MDC.

On August 3, 1963, Victor Batista was interviewed by the FBI. He said that a man named Fernando Fernandez had tried to ingratiate himself with the MDC Miami office in June. Apparently he tried too hard, and the MDC assigned Henry Ledea the task of gaining Fernandez's confidence to determine the reasons for Fernandez's "unusual interest" in the MDC. Ledea succeeded in this task, and Fernandez entrusted Ledea to mail some letters. Ledea promptly opened the letters, which exposed Fernandez as an infiltrator. In one letter, written on August 1 to the Cuban ambassador in Mexico, Fernandez said that he had "had infiltrated a commando group who was preparing to engage in an operation in Cuba." Fernandez stated he had "detailed reports" about this operation and asked for diplomatic asylum so that he could return to Cuba "in order to serve the revolution" under Castro. Not surprisingly, Ledea did not mail the letter.[8]

In spite of the fact that at least one person at the Ponchartrain camp was a member of the DRE, the New Orleans DRE delegate, Carlos Bringuier, professed only slight awareness of the camp. When the Church Committee interviewed him in 1976, Bringuier said he "was vaguely familiar with anti-Castro training camps on the north side of Lake Ponchartrain. He remembered that one Cuban named Fernando Fernandez Barcena (the same Fernandez mentioned above) was identified as a Castro agent."[9] In 1963, Bringuier was anxious about the FBI's surveillance of DRE activities, a concern that had roots back into 1962. In April 1964 Bringuier told this to the Warren Commission:

And you see, in August 24, 1962, my organization, the Cuban Student Directorate, carry on a shelling of Havana, and a few days later when person from the FBI contacted me here in New Orleans—his name was Warren C. de Brueys. Mr. de Brueys was

> talking to me in the Thompson Cafeteria. At that moment I was the only one from the Cuban Student Directorate here in the city, and he was asking me about my activities here in the city, and when I told him that I was the only one, he didn't believe that, and he advised me—and I quote, "We could infiltrate your organization and find out what you are doing here." My answer to him was, "Well, you will have to infiltrate myself, because I am the only one."[10]

After that conversation with de Brueys, Bringuier explained, "I always was waiting that maybe someone will come to infiltrate my organization from the FBI, because I already was told by one of the FBI agent that they will try to infiltrate my organization."

On August 2, 1963, a series of events unfolded that aroused Bringuier's concern. On that day two Cubans showed up in his haberdashery, saying they had deserted the "training camp that was across Lake Ponchartrain here in New Orleans." This was the first he had heard of the camp. The two Cubans said the camp was a branch of the MDC and told Bringuier that they feared "there was a Castro agent inside that training camp."[11] A few days earlier, Bringuier recalled, the New Orleans police had found "a lot of ammunition and weapons" a mile from the camp.

Oswald and Bringuier

In the same breath that Bringuier told the Warren Commission about the arms bust at Ponchartrain, he added, "And when Oswald came to me on August 5 I had inside myself the feeling, well, maybe this is from the FBI, or maybe this is a Communist, because the FBI already had told me that maybe they will infiltrate my organization. . . .[12] Bringuier also testified that just "4 days later I was convinced that Oswald was not an FBI agent and that he was a Pro-Castro agent." This noteworthy testimony cuts to the heart of the double-agent role Oswald was apparently undertaking during August and September 1963.

Bringuier's disparate impressions of Oswald deserve close scrutiny. As previously discussed, Bringuier was the local delegate for the DRE, one of whose members had been caught in the FBI arms bust near Lake Ponchartrain. Bringuier had good reason to be guarded when, five days after the raid, Oswald sauntered into the Casa Roca, Bringuier's retail clothing store at 107 Decatur Street, and began talking about guerrilla warfare.[13] According to Bringuier's testimony, this is what happened:

> Now that day, on August 5, I was talking in the store with one young American—the name of him is Philip Geraci—and 5 minutes later Mr. Oswald came inside the store. He start to look around, several articles, and he show interest in my conversation with Geraci. I was explaining to Geraci that our fight is a fight of Cubans and that he was too young, that if he want to distribute literature against Castro, I would give him the literature but not admit him to the fight.
>
> At that moment also he start to agree with I, Oswald start to agree with my point of view and he show real interest in the fight against Castro. He told me that he was against Castro and that he was against communism. He told me—he asked me first for some English literature against Castro, and I gave him some copies of the Cuban report printed by the Cuban Student Directorate.
>
> After that, Oswald told me that he had been in the Marine Corps and that he had training in guerrilla warfare and that he was willing to train Cubans to fight against Castro. Even more, he told me that he was willing to go himself to fight Castro. That was on August 5.[14]

Bringuier says he "turned down" Oswald's offer, explaining that his duties were propaganda and information, not military activities. "Oswald insisted," Bringuier says, "and he told me that he will bring to me next day one book as a present, as a gift to me, to train Cubans to fight against Castro."

Oswald was not finished. He offered money to Bringuier too, whose recollection led to this exchange with Warren Commission lawyer Wesley Liebler:

MR. BRINGUIER: . . . Before he left the store, he put his hand in the pocket and he offered me money.

MR. LIEBELER: Oswald did?

MR. BRINGUIER: Yes.

MR. LIEBELER: How much did he offer you?

MR. BRINGUIER: Well, I don't know. As soon as he put the hand in the pocket and he told me, "Well, at least let me contribute to your group with some money," at that moment I didn't have the permit from the city hall here in New Orleans to collect money in the city, and I told him that I could not accept his money, and I told him that if he want to contribute to our group, he could send the money directly to the headquarters in Miami, because they had the authorization over there in Miami, and I gave him the number of the post office box of the organization in Miami.

Oswald gave Bringuier his correct name and Magazine Street address.[15] Bringuier then left the store to go to the bank. Oswald remained talking to Rolando Pelaez, Bringuier's brother-in-law, for about a half an hour.

When Bringuier returned to the Casa Roca, Pelaez told Bringuier that Oswald "looked like really a smart person and really interested in the fight against communism," but Bringuier claims he warned his brother-in-law that he did not trust Oswald, "because—I didn't know what was inside of me, but I had some feeling that I could not trust him. I told that to my brother that day."[16] For the Oswald who had written the FPCC in April that he had stood in Dallas with a pro-Castro sign around his neck, this visit to the Casa Roca was a remarkable twist. It was all the more interesting because Oswald would shortly hand out his pro-Castro literature not far from the store. What Oswald was getting ready to spring on Bringuier was a deliberate provocation.

It is curious how the Warren Commission Report finessed the two-faced role demonstrated by Oswald's approach to Bringuier:

> On August 5, he visited a store managed by Carlos Bringuier, a Cuban refugee and avid opponent of Castro and the New Orleans delegate of the Cuban Student Directorate. Oswald indicated an interest in joining the struggle against Castro. He told Bringuier that he had been a Marine and was trained in guerrilla warfare, and that he was willing not only to fight Castro but also to join the fight himself. The next day Oswald returned and left his "Guidebook for Marines" for Bringuier."[17]

The Warren Report then leaps right into Oswald's pro-Castro leafleting, which angers Bringuier and causes a scene, without attempting to explain Oswald's contradictory behavior. The Warren Report also neglected to mention that Bringuier's organization had for years been covertly funded by the CIA. Did Commission member and former CIA director Allen Dulles realize that Bringuier might have been involved in a CIA program at the time of Oswald's visit?

A June 1, 1967, CIA memorandum by Counterintelligence Research and Analysis (CI/R&A) said Bringuier had no "direct association with the Agency. But see enclosure one in respect to the Student Revolutionary Directorate (DRE), the New Orleans branch of which was once headed by Bringuier. The DRE was conceived, created, and funded by CIA."[18] Whether or not Allen Dulles knew about AMSPELL and Bringuier's connection to this program, important Agency memoranda describing this connection have emerged over the years. A memo written for the record by CI/R&A, dated April 3, 1967, pointed out that Bringuier considered Oswald "either an FBI informant or a Communist penetration agent" and for this reason rejected his offer to train anti-Castro Cubans. The memorandum also said this:

> The Student Revolutionary Directorate (DRE) was undoubtedly the group to which the Warren Commission referred. It was funded covertly by CIA. It was penetrated by the DGI [Cuban intelligence] and, in the fall of 1962, rolled up. We continued nominal support until September 1966 and terminated the relationship on 1 January 1967.[19]

This language avoids the ticklish question of what Bringuier's "indirect" association with the CIA in 1963 might have been. The same goes for Bringuier's associates Bartes, Quiroga, and Butler, all of whom had "indirect" links to the CIA and, together with Bringuier, were about to enter a three-week propaganda extravaganza with Oswald, which would be covered by local radio, television, and newspapers.

The same April memo complained about how writer-attorney Mark Lane was "trying to use" New Orleans district attorney Jim Garrison's investigation to implicate anti-Castro Cubans in a "rightist plot" to assassinate Kennedy. The memo then contains this illuminating passage:

> Bringuier is a leader of a New Orleans anti-Castro group. He was summoned to Garrison's office [date not reported] and asked to take a polygraph test. He agreed. During the test he was asked whether he had been contacted by the CIA. He said no and feels that deception reactions did not result because it was the other way around; *he contacted CIA*[20] [emphasis added].

The questioner failed to ask the right question and Bringuier's answer did not give away his links to the Agency.

A similar failure marks the end of the FBI's inadequate answer to the Warren Commission on how it established Oswald's whereabouts and activities in New Orleans. It was August 5 that the FBI checked with the William B. Reily Coffee Company about when Oswald began employment there. By this time the FBI should have asked if Oswald was still working there, but they neglected to ask about his termination.[21] "Mrs. Mary Berttucci, personal Secretary, William Reily Coffee Company, 640 Magazine St., advised on 8/5/63," said the FBI, "that Lee Harvey Oswald has been employed as a maintenance man since 5/15/63. His address at the time of his employment was 757 French St." Someone should have added that Oswald had been fired back on July 19. A New Orleans FBI cable to Dallas on August 13 said, "Mr. Jesse James Garner, 4909 Magazine St., New Orleans, advised on 8/5/63 that the subjects [Oswalds] have occupied the apartment at 4905 Magazine St. since about 6/63." As we have shown, however, the FBI had probably known since mid-May that Oswald had been residing on Magazine Street.

On August 6, 1963, Oswald returned to the Casa Roca and, as he had promised the previous day, left his U.S. Marine Corps manual.[22] He had underlined something on page 189: "Sight setting: 1 minute of angle or approximately 1 inch on target for each 100 yards." Bringuier recalled Oswald's second visit to the Casa Roca in this way:

> Next day, on August 6, Oswald came back to the store, but I was not in the store at that moment, and he left with my brother-in-law a Guidebook for Marines. I was looking in the Guidebook for marines. I found interest in it and I keep it, and later—I forgot about that just for 3 days more—on August 9 I was coming back to the store at 2 o'clock in the afternoon, and one friend of mine

> with the name of Celso Hernandez came to me and told me that in Canal Street there was a young man carrying a sign telling "Viva Fidel" in Spanish, and some other thing about Cuba, but my friend don't speak nothing in English, and the only thing that he understood was the "Viva Fidel" in Spanish. He told me that he was blaming the person in Spanish, but that the person maybe didn't understood what he was telling to him and he came to me to let me know what was going on over there.[23]

Bringuier's account of the second Oswald visit is corroborated by a secret service report written after the assassination by New Orleans Special Agent in Charge John Rice.[24] On November 27, 1963, Rice called special agent in charge Robert I. Bouck to tell him Bringuier had turned over the "Guidebook for Marines" given to him by Oswald. "At the time Oswald pretended to be against Castro," Rice said, "and told Bringuier that he would be willing to assist in training Cubans with a view to overthrowing Castro."[25]

It seems appropriate to review the two-sided role that Oswald had begun to play. The timing, flow, and changes of direction were not aimless. They seem intelligently related to the larger structure of Oswald's life and possibly to a great deal more. The Oswald character who emerges in FBI files and from there into CIA files begins in New Orleans by doing two things: infiltrating the FPCC as "Lee Harvey Oswald" while simultaneously forging an undercover identity. In this undercover role, his character, "A.J. Hidell," a pro-Castro activist, hands out FPCC literature under a false organizational title, "Fair Play for Cuba Committee, New Orleans Charter Member Branch," with a false post office box (30016), and a false office address (544 Camp Street).

Those roles lasted throughout June and July. In August, Oswald switched to an overt pro-Castro role, but not before cashing in on his false identity. This he did by deliberately baiting Carlos Bringuier on August 5 and 6. Why Bringuier? Oswald had managed to pick the Cuban with the best connections to the CIA in New Orleans. When Bringuier rushed to interfere with Oswald's pro-Castro leaflet operation, Oswald was waiting for him.

The Canal Street Caper, August 9

Around one P.M. on a Friday afternoon, Oswald casually walked to the 700 block of Canal Street, not far from Bringuier's store, and began distributing FPCC literature.[26] Upon receiving this news, Bringuier and two associates, Celso Macario Hernandez and Miguel Mariano Cruz, moved quickly to the scene. There was an argument and some shouting, and an altercation ensued. Bringuier prepared to punch Oswald when the latter, as if expecting this, dropped his hands and invited "Carlos" to throw the punch. The Cubans then decided to trash Oswald's leaflets, scattering them over the ground. A few moments later, the police arrived and all four men were arrested.[27]

The above brief sketch is comprehensive compared to the three-sentence treatment of the Canal Street episode by the Warren Report: "On August 9, Bringuier saw Oswald passing out Fair Play for Cuba leaflets. Bringuier and his companions became angry and a dispute resulted. Oswald and the three Cuban exiles were arrested for disturbing the peace."[28] The Warren Commission was happy to let the American public fill in the details, and to ask obvious questions such as, why did Oswald want an altercation? and why did he pick Bringuier to have it with? The Warren Report did not think it useful to point out to readers that there was a pertinent sentence from New Orleans police lieutenant Frances Martello's testimony about the clash. Martello had said that Oswald "seemed to have set them up, so to speak, to create an incident, but when the incident occurred he remained absolutely peaceful and gentle."[29]

Martello's incisive account had little impression on the Warren Commission. The same was true for an even more extraordinary event that occurred in the police station—which earned a grand total of nine words in the Warren Report: "At Oswald's request, an FBI agent also interviewed him."[30] We will return to that shortly. On the day of the Canal Street caper, a New Orleans FBI report written by Special Agent Stephen M. Callender reported the arrest of Oswald and the three Cubans at 4:20 P.M. by Lieutenant William Galliot.[31] Callender's brief description of the four men,[32] based upon Galliot's report and information provided by an informant[33] who witnessed the leafleting incident did little to explain the nature of the disturbance. Another person who saw Oswald passing out his handbills was New Orleans attorney Dean Andrews, who recalled that Oswald told him he was being "paid $25.00 per day for the job."[34]

Habana Bar owner Orestes Pena posted bond for Carlos Bringuier's release.[35] One or two days before Oswald's clash with Bringuier on August 9, Oswald and another man reportedly met at the Habana Bar, 117 Decatur, just a few doors from Bringuier's store (at 107 Decatur).[36] Pena was present.[37] He recalled that Oswald's companion was a Cuban.[38] Previously, Pena overheard two Cubans in his bar, posing as Mexicans, making anti-American remarks. He reported them to the FBI. Bringuier claimed he was told that one of these men was not only Oswald's companion but also a Mexican Communist wanted by the FBI.[39] Another Cuban exile, a waiter at the Habana Bar by the name of Evaristo Gilberto Rodriguez, also recalls seeing Oswald and a Latino male in the bar around the second week of August.[40]

After spending the night in jail, Oswald found himself speaking with Lieutenant Martello. Martello had previously been assigned to the department's intelligence unit. After he found out that Oswald had been handing out FPCC literature, Martello said he decided to interrogate him to see if this would produce "any information which would be of value and to ascertain if all interested parties had been notified."[41] Martello directed that Oswald be brought into the interview room. Martello introduced himself and asked Oswald for identification papers. Oswald pulled out his wallet and gave Martello a social security card and a selective service card, both in the name of Lee Harvey Oswald, and two FPCC membership cards in the name Lee Harvey Oswald, one signed by V. T. Lee, and one signed by "A. J. Hidell, Chapter President, issued June 6, 1963."

Oswald had told the arresting officers that he was born in Cuba,[42] a lie which he did not repeat to Lieutenant Martello. Oswald told him he had been born in New Orleans, which was the truth, but then Oswald immediately lied about his date of birth, which he claimed was October 18, 1938. Oswald said that he had served three years in the Marine Corps and that he was discharged on July 17, 1959, at El Toro. In fact, Oswald had been discharged on September 11, 1959. Oswald said he had lived at 4907 Magazine for four months, but he had lived there for three months to the day. Several other pieces of information Oswald furnished were inaccurate or outright lies.[43]

Martello's contemporaneous account of this important interview is preserved only in his handwriting, which he set down at three A.M. on the morning after the Kennedy assassination. That day, the Secret Service took his original report and associated papers and documents from his office. His account described their considerable discussion of the FPCC. This is how this part of the interview started:

> When questioned about the Fair Play for Cuba Committee, Oswald stated that he had been a member for three months. I asked how he had become affiliated with the Fair Play for Cuba Committee and he stated he became interested in that Committee in Los Angeles, California in 1958 while in the U. S. Marines Corps. The facts as to just how he first became interested in the Fair Play for Cuba Committee while in the Marine Corps are vague, however I recall that he said he had obtained some Fair Play for Cuba Committee literature and had gotten into some difficulty in the Marine Corps for having this literature.[44]

This tale was completely false. The Fair Play for Cuba Committee did not exist until seven months after Oswald left the Marines, by which time Oswald was deep in the Soviet Union. Oswald probably did not receive his first FPCC material until the spring of 1963.

Martello wanted to know how many members there were in the New Orleans chapter. Oswald lied again when he said there were thirty-five. Martello's handwritten account, entered into his Warren Commission testimony, describes how he then proceeded to grill Oswald on the FPCC:

> I asked him to identify the members of the Fair Play for Cuba Committee in New Orleans and he refused to give names of the members or any identifying data regarding them. Oswald was asked why he refused and he said that this was a minority group holding unpopular views at this time and it would not be beneficial to them if he gave their names. Oswald was asked approximately how many people attended meetings of the New Orleans Chapter of the Fair Play for Cuba Committee and he said approximately five attended the meetings, which were held once a month. He

> was asked where and he said at various places in the city. He was asked specifically at what addresses or locations were the meetings held and stated that the meetings were held on Pine Street. He was asked at whose residence the meetings were held and he refused to give any further information.[45]

Perhaps Martello thought he had reached what Oswald was hiding. At this point Martello digresses, explaining how a "prior investigation" that he conducted while a member of the intelligence unit had discovered FPCC literature in the 1000 block of Pine Street, "near" the residence of Dr. Leonard Reissman, who, as discussed in Chapter Sixteen, was a leftwing professor at Tulane University.

Martello was looking for a connection between Oswald and Reissman, who probably never met. Martello's report went on about how Dr. Reissman was a "reported" member of the New Orleans Council of Peaceful Alternatives (NOCPA), which Martello described as a "ban the bomb" group. This group had conducted meetings and demonstrations in New Orleans. He is less than convincing, however, when it comes to explaining their relevance to Oswald:

> Knowing that Dr. Reissman was reportedly a member of the New Orleans Council of Peaceful Alternatives I thought there might be a tie between this organization and the Fair Play for Cuba Committee. When Oswald stated that meetings of the Fair Play for Cuba Committee had been held on Pine Street, the name of Dr. Reissman came to mind. I asked Oswald if he knew Dr. Reissman or if he held meetings at Dr. Reissman's house. Oswald did not give me a direct answer to this question, however I gathered from the expression on his face and what appeared to be an immediate nervous reaction that there was possibly a connection between Dr. Reissman and Oswald; this, however, is purely an assumption on my own part and I have nothing on which to base this.[46]

One cannot help but wonder what "expression" Oswald made that permitted such an interpretation. Martello seemed to have obtained a small victory, i.e., that Reissman and Oswald were connected, even though Oswald had actually said nothing. What Martello apparently did not know was that Ruth Kloebfer, a New Orleans resident who was on the NOCPA mailing list, had been recommended to Oswald by a relative in Dallas, Ruth Paine. Also, Carlos Bringuier knew "a Bruce Walthzer who was somehow associated with Kloepfer and Reissman." Presumably, if he had known of Oswald's tie-in to Kloepfer, Martello would have made much ado about it too.[47]

In any event, Martello evidently felt he had enough on Reissman, and was ready to move to his next target, another leftwing political figure that was dimly connected to the FPCC in Martello's mind: Dr. Forrest E. La Violette, also, as previously discussed, a professor at Tulane University. Martello asked Oswald about La Violette "because I remembered that La Violette allegedly had possession of Fair Play for Cuba literature during the year 1962."

> I cannot remember any further details about this or do I have any information that he is or was connected with the Fair Play for Cuba Committee in New Orleans. Oswald became very evasive in his answers and would not divulge any information concerning the Fair Play for Cuba Committee, where the group met, or the identities of the members. . . . I asked him again about the members of the Fair Play for Cuba Committee in New Orleans and why the information was such a big secret; that if [he] had nothing to hide, he would give me the information. Oswald said one of the members of the Fair Play for Cuba Committee in New Orleans was named "John" and that this individual went to Tulane University. He refused to give any more information concerning the Fair Play for Cuba Committee in New Orleans.[48]

"John" might have existed, but he probably did not. Oswald was treading on dangerous ground—if indeed he was a genuine pro-Castro activist. He had engaged a rabid anti-Castro organization and their CIA masters.

In one sense, it does not matter whether Oswald himself picked the DRE or whether he was steered to them. From their perspective, Oswald was a propitious propaganda opportunity. After the assassination, this was all the more true. Then, the Joint Legislative Committee on Un-American Activities for the State of Louisiana hired J. D. Vinson of the Isaac Detective Agency to research Oswald. FBI special agent Quigley interviewed Vinson on November 27, 1963, who said he had checked on Forrest E. La Violette and Leonard Reissman, since "he had a dim recollection that sometime in

1962,'' FPCC literature had been found in the 1200 or 1300 block of Pine Street.[49] It is striking how similar were Martello's and Vinson's ''dim'' memories of FPCC literature near the 1200 block of Pine Street in 1962.

When arrested, Oswald had the booklet ''The Crime Against Cuba,'' stamped with the address ''FPCC 544 Camp Street, New Orleans, La.''[50] By this time, however, the 544 Camp Street address was an anachronism: Oswald had begun stamping his real name and 4907 Magazine Street on his FPCC handbills. As we have seen, from the moment he walked into Bringuier's store on August 5, Oswald had entered the overt phase of his FPCC activities in New Orleans. The Camp Street address was not the only anachronism among Oswald's possessions when he was arrested. When Lieutenant Martello turned over his file on Oswald to Agent A. G. Vial from Secret Service at three A.M. on November 23, 1963, Martello noticed ''a small white piece of paper containing handwritten notes.'' In response to the Warren Commission's question on how this piece of paper was ''taken from Oswald,'' Martello answered that ''it wasn't actually taken from him . . . it was left—it was inadvertently picked up with the [FPCC] literature, and I put it in a file folder and it remained there.''[51] Martello's testimony to the Warren Commission included this remark:

> This piece of paper, which was folded over twice and was about 2" by 3" in size, contained some English writing and some writing which appeared to me to be in a foreign language which I could not identify. Before I gave this paper to Mr. Vial, I made a copy of the information. . . .[52]

On one side of this piece of paper were street addresses for relatives in Dallas and New Orleans, but on the reverse side was handwriting in Russian, including the name ''Leo Setyaev.''[53] Setyaev, of course, was the Radio Moscow man who had interviewed Oswald at the time of his defection. Oswald had also tried—on at least one occasion—to contact Setyaev during his stay in the Soviet Union.

Why Oswald would have a name from his Russian past, let alone Setyaev's on a piece of paper in his pocket in the summer of 1963 is a mystery. So was his request to be interviewed in jail by the FBI. The FBI man who did the interview knew about Oswald's

Russian past, because it was the same man who looked over the ONI file on Oswald at the Algiers station in 1961.[54]

The Quigley Jailhouse Interview

On August 10, 1963, Lieutenant Martello notified the New Orleans FBI that Oswald had been picked up the day before and charged with disturbing the peace. Martello told them that Oswald had been handing out FPCC literature in the 700 block of Canal Street. But Martello had a special reason for contacting the FBI that day. According to Agent John Quigley, Martello "said that Oswald was desirous of seeing an Agent and supplying to him information with regard to his activities with the 'Fair Play for Cuba Committee' in New Orleans."[55]

Oswald had been evasive about the FPCC with Martello, so asking to be interviewed by the FBI appears stranger still, unless, as in the Canal Street caper, Oswald wanted to attract attention to himself. As if on cue, Quigley quietly slipped into the First District jail to interview Oswald. The interview was "at his request," Quigley wrote in his recapitulation of the August 10 encounter.[56] Quigley reported that Oswald did not answer all the questions put to him.[57] Moreover, Quigley's report was suppressed until after Oswald's trip to Mexico City in October.

When going over his background, Oswald told Quigley that "about four months ago he and his wife, Marina Oswald nee Prossa, whom he met and married in Fort Worth, moved to New Orleans." Oswald must have known the FBI was knowledgeable about his marriage to Marina, and so this fabrication seems pointless. Quigley's August memo on the interview recalls the following:

> After coming to New Orleans he said he began reading various pieces of literature distributed by the "Fair Play for Cuba Committee", and it was his understanding from reading this material that the main goal and theme of the committee is to prevent the United States from invading or attacking Cuba or interfering in the political affairs of that country. . . . Oswald said that inquiry in New Orleans developed the fact that there apparently was a chapter of the "Fair Play for Cuba Committee" in New Orleans, but he did not know any of the members or where their offices were located.[58]

Oswald was lying when he suggested there was an existing New Orleans FPCC chapter. Oswald had, of course, been corresponding with the FPCC while in Dallas,[59] and now was attempting to give Quigley the impression that it was his reading of FPCC materials in New Orleans that had stimulated his interest in joining the organization.

Oswald told Quigley he had sent a letter to the FPCC in New York City, asking if he could join the committee, and added that in "the latter part of May" 1963 he had received a membership card dated May 28, 1963, made out in the name of "Lee H. Oswald" and signed by "V. L. Lee." All of this was true, but the same cannot be said for what Oswald said next:

> A short time thereafter he said he received in the mail a white card which showed that he was made a member of the New Orleans Chapter of Fair Play for Cuba Committee. This card was dated June 6, 1963. It was signed by A.J. Hidell, and it bore in the lower right hand corner the number 33 which he said indicated membership number. Oswald had in his possession both cards and exhibited both of them.

Marina later testified that she signed the name "A. J. Hidell" on this FPCC card.[60] Oswald's alias, of course, would assume a terrible significance after the assassination: The alleged murder weapon in the Kennedy assassination, a Manlicher-Carcano rifle, had been ordered in February from Klein's in Chicago under the name Hidell.

The Hidell story continued to grow, as can be seen from this passage in Quigley's jailhouse interview:

> Since receiving his membership card in the New Orleans chapter of the committee he said that he had spoken with Hidell on the telephone on several occasions. On these occasions, Hidell would discuss general matters of mutual interest in connection with committee business, and on other occasions he would inform him of a scheduled meeting. He said he has never personally met Hidell, and Hidell did have a telephone, but it has now been discontinued. He claimed that he could not recall what the number was.[61]

Oswald said the committee held meetings in residences of "various members, and at each meeting there were "about five different individuals'' who ''were different'' at each of these meetings. Not that any of this mattered, because Oswald said he had not been introduced to them by their last names and he could not recall any of their first names.

After more fairy tales, Oswald got around to the events on Canal Street:

> Last Wednesday, August 7, 1963, Oswald said he received a note through the mail from Hidell. The note asked him if he had time would he mind distributing some Fair Play literature in the downtown area of New Orleans. He said Hidell knew that he was not working and probably had time. Hidell also knew that he had considerable literature on the committee which had been furnished to him by the national committee in New York. Since he did not have anything to do, Oswald said he decided he would go down to Canal Street and distribute some literature. He denied that he was being paid for his services, but that he was doing it as a patriotic duty.[62]

Oswald said that about one P.M. on August 9, 1963, he went to Canal Street by himself and began distributing literature, including FPCC handbills. Quigley saw a handbill with the stamp ''A J Hidell, P.O. Box 30016.'' In addition, Oswald said he had FPCC membership applications and several copies of a thirty-nine-page pamphlet entitled ''The Crime Against Cuba'' by Corliss Lamont, ''which he carried with him as it contained all of the information regarding the committee, and he would be in a position to refer to it for proper answers in the event someone questioned him regarding the aims and purposes of the committee.'' Oswald gave a handbill, an application form, and a pamphlet to Quigley.

At no point did Quigley indicate he knew the details of Oswald's Russian past, details that had been in Oswald's ONI records at nearby Algiers Naval Station and, thanks to Quigley's 1961 report, also in Oswald's FBI file in New Orleans. Whether or not Quigley remembered these details, his questioning during the interview did not show any awareness of where Oswald's story strayed from the facts.

Toward the end of the interview, Oswald said he understood that on August 12 he was to be taken into court and charged with disturbing the peace. When he showed up, the Cuban exiles, and the television cameras, were waiting.

Bartes, Quiroga, and Oswald on Television

The courtroom fracas on August 12 was well attended by local television and newspaper reporters. Presiding at the hearing was second municipal court judge Edwin A. Babylon.[63] Alongside Carlos Bringuier was Frank Bartes who, although not a member of Bringuier's DRE group, "respected" Bringuier and came to the hearing as a "show of support."[64] According to the clerk's office, Oswald entered a plea of guilty to the charge of disturbing the peace.[65] Oswald was sentenced to pay a fine of ten dollars or serve ten days in jail. He elected to pay the fine.[66]

Bringuier and the Cubans pleaded innocent.[67] The charges against them for disturbing the peace "were dropped by the court."[68] Bartes, however, was not yet finished. After the hearing, when the news media surrounded Oswald for a statement, Bartes said he "got into an argument with the media and Oswald because the Cubans were not being given an opportunity to present their views."[69]

Bartes also said that he spoke to an FBI agent that day, warning that Oswald was a dangerous man.[70] Bartes made this statement to the HSCA, but he refused to reveal the agent's name. Bartes would say only that he had frequent contact with this agent. Corroborative evidence comes from the FBI's files. We know from an early draft of a New Orleans FBI document that Bartes was an informant for the FBI, and that his identity was considered sensitive.[71] Bartes told the HSCA that after the court scene he had no further contact with Oswald.[72]

There is irony in how this court scene unleashed the sequence of events that followed. Bartes's argument with Oswald and warning to the FBI about him occurred at the very sentencing that led to the *Times-Picayune* article which, in turn, led the Bureau to direct an inquiry by the New Orleans FBI office during which Bartes denied knowing Oswald. Thus, during this sequence, which lasted less than a month, Bartes did a flipflop on Oswald: from warning the FBI about Oswald in August to telling the FBI in September "that Oswald was unknown to him."[73]

Oswald's arrest and sentencing caused a fresh review of events taking place in New Orleans that would be disseminated from that city's FBI office to the CIA. On August 21 Hoover sent a directive to New Orleans and Dallas, reminding Dallas that they had been on the hook since March to find out what Oswald's job was and to determine whether or not to interview Marina. Hoover pointed out to the New Orleans office that the man arrested there had an FBI identification record number—327-925-D—the record containing Oswald's fingerprints.

The Hoover directive repeated every detail of the arrest and sentencing from the *Times-Picayune,*[74] and then told Dallas to "promptly" get its information in order. For New Orleans, Hoover had these instructions:

> New Orleans ascertain facts concerning subject's distribution of above-mentioned pamphlet including nature of pamphlet following which contact should be made with established sources familiar with Cuban activities in the New Orleans area to determine whether subject involved in activities inimical to the internal security of the U.S. Submit results in letterhead memorandum form suitable for dissemination with appropriate recommendation as to further action.[75]

The resulting letterhead memorandum was dynamite when it landed in Oswald's CIA files in early October. Oswald's activities from the time of his arrest on August 9 until the release of the letterhead memorandum on September 24 would be encapsulated in this FBI report. The fate of this report at the CIA will be covered in Chapter Nineteen.

On August 16, 1963, at about 12:30 P.M., Oswald and a companion, a white male (about nineteen to twenty years old and approximately six feet tall, with a slender build, dark hair, and olive complexion) arrived at the International Trade Mart at Camp and Gravier streets (124 Camp).[76] Oswald hired three or four additional men at two dollars apiece to help distribute his FPCC literature.[77] The leaflets were stamped with Oswald's real name and his 4907 Magazine Street address. Oswald told one of the men helping him, Charles Steele, that Tulane University was sponsoring the leaflet distribution.[78] A local television station, WDSU-TV, filmed the event.[79]

Bringuier went to the Trade Mart in an attempt to find Oswald but was not successful. Afterward, Quiroga showed Bringuier one of the leaflets. Bringuier recalls that these leaflets were different from those Oswald handed out on Canal Street. When asked by the Warren Commission to explain the difference, Bringuier gave this answer:

> The leaflet he was handing out on Canal Street August 9 didn't have his name of Oswald, at least the ones that I saw. They have the name A.J. Hidell, and one post office box here in New Orleans and the address, and the leaflets that he was handing out on August 16 have the name L.H. Oswald, 4907 Magazine Street. . . . My friend asked to me if I think that it would be good that he will go to Oswald's house posing as a pro-Castro and try to get as much information as possible from Oswald. I told him yes; and that night he went to Oswald's house with the leaflets. . . . My friend went to Oswald's house and he was talking to Oswald for about 1 hour inside his house, in the porch of the house, and there was when we found that Oswald had some connection with Russia, or something like that, because the daughter came to the porch and Oswald spoke to her in Russian, and my friend heard that language and he asked Oswald if that was Russian, and Oswald told him yes, that he was attending Tulane University and that he was studying language, that that was the reason why he speak Russian. He give to my friend an application to become a member of the New Orleans Chapter of the Fair Play for Cuba Committee.[80]

Quite aside from the leafleting event at the Trade Mart, August 16 was a busy day for Oswald. Around two P.M., he went to both New Orleans newspapers in hope of getting pro-Castro material printed.[81] He also claims to have applied for a job at the *Times-Picayune* and the *States-Item,* though both papers maintain he did not.[82] By late in the afternoon he was back home on 4907 Magazine, when a stranger knocked at the door.

''Well, there was that Cuban- or Spanish-looking guy one time rang my bell in the late afternoon,'' Mrs. Garner, Oswald's landlady, told the Warren Commission, ''kind of short, very dark black curly hair, and he had a stack of these same pamphlets in his hand he was spreading out on Canal Street there on the porch,'' she recalled, assuming that her visitor had been passing out FPCC leaflets. That assumption was wrong. Mrs. Garner was outspoken, as she explained to the commission:

> . . . And he had a stack of them in his hand and he asked me about Oswald, and I said he was living around on that side where the screen porch is, and I saw those things in his hand and I said, ''You are not going to spread those things on my porch,'' and that was all, and I closed the door and went on about my business. I don't know, but I guess he went over there.[83]

Commission lawyer Liebeler asked Garner, ''How many pamphlets did this man have in his hand?'' Mrs. Garner groped for words and said, ''a stack about that high.'' ''About five to six inches?'' asked Liebeler. ''About that high,'' Garner replied. ''About the width of your hand?'' Liebeler persisted. ''Yes,'' Mrs. Garner agreed. And what did Mrs. Garner remember of the date for the stranger's visit with the fistful of handbills? ''That I don't remember,'' she says, but adds, ''I know it was around that time, just right after he was picked up on Canal Street for disturbing them. It was a few days after that.''

On November 30, 1963, Quiroga told the Secret Service that after Oswald's arrest, Carlos Bringuier ordered him ''to infiltrate Oswald's organization if he could.''[84] It therefore seems certain that the individual Mrs. Garner saw was Quiroga.[85] The December 3 Secret Service report preserves Quiroga's recollection of his encounter with Oswald:

> He said he went to Oswald's home at 4907 Magazine St. . . . He said he spent about an hour talking to Oswald who told him he learned to speak Russian at Tulane University, New Orleans. . . . He said Oswald had not mentioned to him that he had defected to Russia. He said Oswald asked him to join the Fair Play for Cuba group and had given him an application form. Oswald told him he could join for $1. He said that during the conversation, Oswald stated that if the United States should invade Cuba, he, Oswald, would fight on the side of the Castro Government. He said Oswald never did mention any of the names of the mem-

> bers of the Fair Play for Cuba group. He did say that meetings were held at various private homes in New Orleans.
>
> Carlos said he had been willing to join the Fair Play for Cuba group provided it was done with the backing of the FBI or the local police force. He said he had made this known to Lt. Martello, NOPD, who apparently forgot about it. He said he did not contact the FBI for the reason on a previous occasion he had notified their office that Oswald was handing out what he assumed to be pro-communist literature in front of the International Trade Mart, New Orleans, and the FBI had given him the cold shoulder.[86]

According to the December 3 Secret Service report, Quiroga had been associated with Arcacha Smith, former head of the CRC in New Orleans. Another CRC member, a Mr. Rodriguez, Sr., told the Secret Service agents that Quiroga ''knew Arcacha well and was with him frequently (very close connection) at 544 Camp Street.''

Although Quiroga has been viewed as a CRC member or an ''associate'' of DRE delegate Bringuier, the newly released files show that he was an intriguing fellow in his own right. He had come to the attention of the CIA for his previous pro-Castro leanings (he was now anti-Castro), which resulted in his consideration for operational use in a dangerous role. According to a 1967 CIA memorandum, Quiroga had been designated for recruitment into an important project while he had been attending classes at Louisiana State University. Quiroga, stated the report, was ''a candidate for the CIA Student Recruitment Program, designed to recruit Cuban students to return to Cuba as agents in place.''[87] Quiroga had the perfect pedigree: Until mid-1961 he had been pegged as ''an ardent Castro supporter'' who made anti-U.S. statements.

Quiroga had been attractive to the CIA as someone who might be enticed to take advantage of his pro-Castro pedigree to spy in Cuba. None of this meant, as the Counterintelligence/Research and Analysis report was quick to point out, that Quiroga had been ''employed'' by the Agency. Quiroga, however, had vices: ''He reportedly had homosexual tendencies,'' the report added, ''and low morals.'' These tendencies may have made him more vulnerable as a target for recruitment.

Quiroga's visit was not the end of Oswald's contacts with individuals who were associated with the AMSPELL propaganda being wrapped around Oswald. Oswald was about to meet Ed Butler.

Butler, Oswald, and the WDSU Radio Debate

''Dear General,'' an old friend of U.S. Air Force Major General Edward Lansdale wrote on August 1, 1963, ''here is the letter I mentioned to you concerning the anti-communist student operation in the Dominican Republic, where Father Barrenechea operates, though his mail address is Miami.'' Lansdale had served as the operations officer for Kennedy's anti-Cuban operations in 1962, and Lansdale's friend happened to be a respected editor for the *Reader's Digest,* Gene Methvin. Methvin told Lansdale this about the letter:

> This is the first ''nuts-and-bolts how to do it'' approach I've seen to organizational warfare. The author, Ed Butler, has an organization going in New Orleans called ''The Information Council of the Americas'' (INCA), which is sending ''Truth Tapes,'' dramatic interviews with Cuban refugees and other anti-Communist programs, to more than 100 radio stations in 16 Latin countries.[88]

Lansdale read Methvin's letter and knew just what to do. He wrote a note on August 2 to his assistant, Colonel Jackson: ''Discuss this with Frank Hand. Is this something for us to help, to stay away from, what? The Methvin article attracts me. The letter to the padre says whoa, caution. There is tricky background, which is where Frank Hand comes in.'' Tricky background about Ed Butler's letter? What did Lansdale mean by this? Frank Hand was detailed to Lansdale's office from the CIA. Lansdale must have been referring to Butler's connections to the Agency when he said ''where Frank Hand comes in.'' On August 6, Colonel Jackson wrote back to Lansdale, ''Based on comments by Frank Hand recommend the Orlando Group be left alone.''

That was probably just as well for Lansdale, given the level of post-assassination interest that developed in Oswald's activities over the summer and fall of 1963. Lansdale already knew some of the background story on Butler, and deftly dodged entanglement with his operations. In all the interviews with Lansdale during the seventies and eighties, no one asked him for his views on Butler's debate with Oswald, an event that took place within days of Lansdale's decision to steer clear of Butler. This point may seem obscure, but its value may become apparent as we learn more about Lansdale. The general impression gleaned—after two separate investigations by two different research teams—from the voluminous Lansdale papers at the Hoover Institution is that Lansdale would ordinarily have been interested in the sort of propaganda opportunities Butler was working to open up for the Agency. Lansdale was one of the creators of modern psychological warfare, and he patronized the efforts of many people like Butler. Who was Ed Butler? The answer to that question became apparent during the last week of August 1963, when he and a radio host in New Orleans managed to get Oswald into a live radio debate.

At ten A.M. on August 21, 1963, the phone rang in the New Orleans office of the FBI, and SAC Harry Maynor took the call.[89] The caller said he was with the"Ross Agency," an advertising business, but added he also had a Latin American program on WDSU radio, a local station in New Orleans. His name was "Bill" Stuckey. He had a thirty-two-minute tape of an interview with Oswald made the previous evening in Oswald's home. Stuckey said he had spoken with Oswald because of Oswald's claim to be an officer of the local Fair Play for Cuba Committee, and had been arrested by the NOPD.

Was the FPCC cited as a "subversive" organization? Stuckey asked. Maynor replied he was not authorized to comment, and advised Stuckey to call the U.S. Department of Justice. Before hanging up, Stuckey mentioned that at 6:05 P.M. that evening Oswald and Edward Butler would debate for thirty minutes on his radio program, *Carte Blanche.* Stuckey suggested to Maynor, "that I might like to hear this program." Stuckey also offered him the thirty-two-minute tape. Maynor passed all of this on to SA Milton Kaack, to whom the Oswald case had been assigned. The New Orleans office did get a copy of the taped interview, but not from Stuckey. Kaack got it from Butler on August 26, and returned it to Butler—presumably after making a duplicate—on August 30.[90]

When Oswald showed up for the debate, Stuckey and his co-host, Slatter, as well as Butler and Bringuier, were already there. The program began, and after some sparring back and forth, Stuckey dropped this bomb on Oswald:

STUCKEY: Mr. Oswald, if I may break in now a moment, I believe it was mentioned that you at one time asked to renounce your American citizenship and become a Soviet citizen, is that correct?

OSWALD: Well, I don't think that has particular import to this discussion. We are discussing Cuban-American relations.

STUCKEY: Well, I think it has a bearing to this extent. Mr. Oswald, you say apparently that Cuba is not dominated by Russia and yet you apparently, by your own past actions, have shown that you have an affinity for Russia and perhaps communism, although I don't know that you admit that you either are a Communist or have been, could you straighten out that part? Are you or have you been a Communist?

OSWALD: Well, I answered that prior to this program, on another radio program.

STUCKEY: Are you a Marxist?

OSWALD: Yes, I am a Marxist.

Oswald was suddenly on the defensive, and his hesitation suggests that he wanted to hide his connections to the Soviet Union.

If Oswald had set up Bringuier for the Canal Street caper, Oswald was the target on this evening. Back on the air from a commercial break, host Slatter said, "Mr. Oswald, as you might have imagined, is on the hot seat tonight." With that, Slatter gave the floor to Stuckey, who continued skewering Oswald. The transcript has this passage:

STUCKEY: Mr. Oswald . . . so you are the face of the Fair Play for Cuba Committee in New Orleans. Therefore anybody who might be interested in this organization ought to know more about you. For this reason I'm curious to know just how you supported yourself during the three years that you lived in the Soviet Union. Did you have a government subsidsy [subsidy]?

OSWALD: Well, as I er, well—I will answer that question directly then as you will not rest until you get your answer. I worked in Russia. I was not under the protection of the—that is to say, I was not under protection of the American government, but as I was at all times considered an American citizen I did not lose my American citizenship.

SLATTER: Did you say that you wanted to at one time though? What happened?

OSWALD: Well, it's a long-drawn-out situation in which permission to live in the Soviet Union being granted to a foreign resident is rarely given. This calls for a certain amount of technicality, technical papers and so forth. At no time, as I say, did I renounce my citizenship or attempt to renounce my citizenship, and no time was I out of contact with the American Embassy.

Here Oswald, caught off guard by his opponents' knowledge of his Soviet background, lost control of the debate. To his credit, he maintained his composure, but this attack by Stuckey and Butler clearly directed the discussion.

Butler pressed his advantage, further drawing out Oswald on the sticky subject of whether he had renounced his U.S. citizenship. The argument was not a useful subject from Oswald's point of view:

OSWALD: As I have already stated, of course, this whole conversation, and we don't have too much time left, is getting away from the Cuban-American problem. However, I am quite willing to discuss myself for the remainder of this program. As I stated, it is very difficult for a resident alien, for a foreigner, to get permission to reside in the Soviet Union. During those two weeks and during the dates you mentioned I was of course with the knowledge of the American Embassy, getting this permission.

BUTLER: Were you ever at a building at 11 Kuznyetskoya St. in Moscow?

OSWALD: Kuznyetskoya? Kuznyetskoya is—well, that would probably be in the Foreign Ministry, I assume. No, I was never in that place, although I know Moscow, having lived there.

SLATTER: Excuse me. Let me interrupt here. I think Mr. Oswald is right to this extent. We shouldn't get to lose sight of the organization of which he is the head in New Orleans, the Fair Play for Cuba.

The damage was done, however, and Oswald appeared compromised as a closet Communist and suspect tool of Moscow. His usefulness for any purpose in New Orleans, including pro-Castro leafleting, was finished.

"Our opponents could use my background of residence in the U.S.S.R. against any case which I join," Oswald lamented in a letter to the American Communist Party a week later.[91] Oswald said that "by association, they could say the organization of which I am a member, is Russian controled, ect [sic]. I am sure you see my point."

The WDSU radio debate brought to an end Oswald's odyssey into the world of AMSPELL in New Orleans. Did AMSPELL report these contacts with Oswald to the CIA at the time? The answer is yes, according to this passage from the HSCA:

> Isidor "Chilo" Borja, another leader of the DRE, was interviewed by the committee on February 21, 1978. Borja said he knew Clare Booth Luce was supportive of the DRE, but said he did not know the extent of her financial involvement. He also recalled Bringuier's contact with Oswald and *the fact that the DRE relayed that information to the CIA at the time*[92] [emphasis added].

Who in the CIA learned of these events in August 1963? That answer remains elusive. Most likely the information was passed from Bringuier to the AMSPELL control in the CIA's JMWAVE station in Miami, which managed much of the Agency's anti-Cuban operations. We can be less certain, however, if this information was passed to headquarters. The FBI did pass the story to the Agency in September, a subject to which we will return in the remaining chapters. Now we address another vital episode in Oswald's saga: his preparations to travel to Mexico City.

The Man in the Mexican Tourist Line

On September 17, Oswald went to the New Orleans Mexican Consulate[93] where he obtained a fifteen-day tourist permit, number 24085.[94] The three-dollar permit was valid for ninety days but only for fifteen days inside Mexico.[95] After the assassination, the FBI laboratory typed an erroneous number—24084—for Oswald's tourist card, and then scratched it out and replaced it with the right number, 24085.[96] In October 1976 the CIA released a document which was an English translation of a Mexican government study of Oswald's tourist permit.[97] The numbers 24082, 24083, 24085, 24086, and 24087 were accounted for, but, strangely, there was no mention of 24084. Why all the mystery about permit 24084?

That number belonged to the man in front of Oswald in line at the Mexican Consulate.[98] Not surprisingly, that person was someone with lengthy connections to the CIA. It happened to be William

Gaudet, who, as discussed in Chapter Sixteen, testified that he had seen Oswald speaking with Banister on a street corner. Again, Gaudet's CIA files indicated he had been a "contact" for the New Orleans office, while Gaudet himself preferred to boast that he had "once been employed by the CIA."[99]

According to the HSCA, "Gaudet said he could not recall whether his trip to Mexico and other Latin American countries in 1963 involved any intelligence-related activity."[100] Gaudet testified that he had never met Oswald and had not seen him on the trip to Mexico. Gaudet did, however, testify that he knew about Oswald in the summer of 1963 because of his leafleting activity near Gaudet's office in the Trade Mart. Gaudet also testified that he had seen Oswald speaking with Banister on a street corner.

A study of the United Fruit Company, headquartered in New Orleans, contained this passage about Gaudet:

> The company founded newspapers for employees in Guatemala, Panama, Costa Rica and Honduras. A weekly "Latin American Report" for journalists and businessmen was spun off, written by William Gaudet, who was one of several actors in the unfolding Guatemalan drama said to have had simultaneous connections with both United Fruit and the Central Intelligence Agency.[101]

"Mr. William G. Gaudet publishes the 'Latin American Reports,' " said an internal CIA request to fund his activities. "His reports have been made available to OO [Domestic Contacts Division]," said the description of the project, "and *he has supplied other information of value.* OO believes that specific requirements of ORE (Office of Research) can be met by requesting Mr. Gaudet to get special reports from his correspondents" [emphasis added].

Now that we know about Gaudet, the question arises: What was he doing standing in line in front of Oswald? Was this one more of the incredible coincidences that pepper this story? Gaudet stated that he was unaware his Mexican tourist card immediately preceded Oswald's, and he could not recall having seen Oswald on that day.[102] However, Gaudet's presence reinforces the question: Why did Oswald come into contact with so many people with CIA connections in August and September 1963? Besides Gaudet, the list included Bartes, Bringuier, Butler, and Quiroga.

Oswald's Escalating CIA Profile

On September 10, 1963, Special Agent Hosty sent a report on Oswald to the Bureau and to New Orleans. It was the first FBI document to make it into Oswald's CIA files since the Fain report of August 30, 1962. Hosty began by acknowledging Oswald's Magazine Street address, an address everyone else in the FBI had known about for a month. Hosty then said Oswald had been working at the William Reily Coffee Company on August 5. He apparently did not know that Oswald had been fired from his job at Reily Coffee on July 19.[103] Hosty did mention the April 21 Oswald letter to the FPCC from Dallas. It would appear, however, that he did not know about Oswald's arrest in New Orleans or chose for some reason not to say anything about it. Hosty did not know about the Quigley jailhouse interview.

On Monday, September 23, the employees at CIA headquarters were still catching up on the weekend's traffic when Hosty's report arrived under FBI director Hoover's signature. It was 1:24 in the afternoon when someone named Annette in the CIA's Records Integration Division attached a CIA routing and record sheet to the report and sent it along to the liaison office of the counterintelligence staff, where Jane Roman was still working. As discussed in Chapter Two, Roman received the first phone call from the FBI about Oswald on November 2, 1959.

When Jane Roman got the Hosty report, she signed for it and, presumably after having read it, determined the next CIA organizational element to whom it should be sent. The office she chose was Counterintelligence Operations, CI/OPS. The telltale "P" of William ("Will") Potocci, who worked in Counterintelligence Operations, appears next to the CI/OPS entry, along with the date that Roman passed the report on to him—September 25. Potocci presumably worked in this office, although something on the routing sheet—probably Potocci's name or some activity indicator in CI/OPS—is still being withheld by the CIA.

CIA readers of the Hosty report were treated to the outlines of the story we have followed in this and the previous three chapters: how Oswald had returned from Russia to Fort Worth, Texas, where he subscribed to the communist newspaper the *Worker,* and then moved to New Orleans, where he took a job in the Reily Coffee Company; most important, the CIA learned that on April 21 Oswald, having moved from Fort Worth to Dallas, contacted the Fair Play for Cuba Committee in New York City. The report also recounted Oswald's claim to have stood on a Dallas street with a placard around his neck that read ''Hands Off Cuba-Viva Fidel.''

The CIA did not put this report into Oswald's 201 file, but instead into a new file with a different number: 100-300-11. We will return to that file in Chapter Nineteen. Even as the Hosty report made its way from Jane Roman to Will Potocci, an FBI agent in New Orleans was preparing yet another report on Oswald that would arrive at the CIA on October 2. This, as we will see, was the very day that Oswald, having spent five nights in Mexico City, departed from the Mexican capital.

On his way from New Orleans to Mexico City, Oswald is reported to have visited the home of Silia Odio in Dallas. The Odio ''incident,'' as it has become known with the passage of time, was labeled by researcher Sylvia Meagher as the ''proof of the plot,'' because the Warren Commission accepted that Odio was visited by three men—one of whom was ''Oswald.'' Meagher's point was that whether it was an impostor or Oswald himself, as Odio believes, the group that visited her apartment and phoned her afterward, and their preassassination discussion of killing Kennedy, is awkward, if not antithetical, for the lone-nut hypothesis. The Warren Commission accepted that the event occurred, but dismissed Odio's version of it. First, the commission found that a September 26 or 27 visit was not possible given Oswald's time requirements for arriving in Mexico City at ten A.M. on September 27. Second, the Warren Commission believed it had identified the three men who visited Odio: Loran Eugene Hall, Larry Howard, and William Seymour, who was ''similar in appearance to Lee Harvey Oswald.'' All three were soldiers of fortune involved with the Cuban exiles. Hall was a self-described gun runner.[104] As discussed in Chapter Fourteen, Seymour was an associate of Hemming's.

Both of these Warren Commission contributions damaged the public's understanding of the facts in the case and the public's confidence in the integrity and objectivity of the Commission's work. The Hall-Howard-Seymour story, supplied by the FBI just in time to save the Warren Report—on its way to press—the embarrassment of not having discredited Odio's version of the incident, later turned out to be wholy fraudulent. No official connected to the Warren Report has ever apologized to the public or Silvia Odio for their shabby treatment of her and their acceptance of a concocted story, an egregious error given what was at stake.

In spite of this, strong feelings about the Odio incident remain. Silvia Odio is "full of hot air," FBI special agent Hosty said in a recent interview. Hosty did not elaborate further about the meaning of this remark, but he offered an interesting variation of the Hall and Seymour part of the story: "Hall told us [the FBI] that it was he who had been by Odio's. When the police arrested Hall they talked to Heitman." Special Agent Heitman, Hosty says, was the FBI agent "who worked among the Cubans. I was working the right wing extremists, like General [Edwin] Walker, etc." After Hall told the authorities he had visited Odio, Hosty claims, "Seymour threatened him and so he changed his story."[105] Hosty's account also raises the possibility that William Pawley might have been involved.

"I knew of him," Hosty said of William Pawley in a recent interview.[106] As discussed in Chapter Seven, Pawley was working for the CIA in Miami, reporting on the Cuban situation through an extensive network of contacts. Hosty told researcher Dr. Larry Haapanan in 1983 that he thought the men who visited Odio might have been agents working for Pawley.[107] In 1995 Hosty contacted the author, and in a follow-up interview he said,

> It could be Pawley. H. L. Hunt was backing Pawley's people, and they were also getting support from Henry Luce. It could be that Pawley's guys spying on JURE [Junta Revolucionaria Cubana, led by Amador Odio]. They could have been working for Pawley or one of the other splinter groups.[108]

The possibility that on September 25, Pawley and his right wing anti-Castro allies were using Oswald and his cohorts to collect information on the left wing JURE faction led by Silvia's father (then in one of Castro's prisons) is intriguing. It only further magnifies what the Warren Commission feared about the rest of the Odio story: It fits into the lone-nut hypothesis like a two-by-four in a Cuisinart.

We need to discuss one more document before turning our attention to Oswald's trip to Mexico City. On September 16, 1963, the CIA "informed" the FBI that the "Agency is giving some consideration to countering the activities of [the FPCC] in foreign countries."[109] In one of the many suspicious coincidences of this case, the next day Oswald was standing in a line to get his Mexican tourist visa. He would take his FPCC literature and news clippings of his FPCC activities with him. In the CIA's memo to the FBI, they said they were interested in "planting deceptive information which might embarrass the [FPCC] Committee in areas where it does have some support." A week later Oswald boarded a bus for Mexico City, where he would represent himself as an officer of the FPCC and use his FPCC card as identification in an attempt to obtain a visa to get to Cuba. This raises the possibility that Oswald's trip was part of a CIA operation or an FBI operation linked to the CIA's request. We will return to that subject in Chapter Nineteen, after a detailed analysis of Oswald in the Mexican capital.

Chapter Eighteen

Mexican Maze

Mexico City, during Oswald's visit there in September to October 1963, was one of the most intensely surveilled spots on the planet. After the Kennedy assassination, the events that took place during that visit became the subject of close examination by several government investigations and numerous researchers. Yet, in spite of all the surveillance data and cumulative man-years of scrutiny, what really happened during Oswald's trip to Mexico City has, for more than thirty years, remained an unsolved mystery. There have been too many pieces to fit into the puzzle. In this chapter we will examine the possibility that there are two puzzles into which these pieces fit.

The 1964 investigation into the Mexican maze by the Warren Commission produced a story along these general lines: First, although Oswald visited both the Cuban and Soviet consulates and said he wanted to travel to the Soviet Union via Cuba, "the evidence makes it more likely he intended to remain in Cuba"; second, Oswald was informed he could not get a Cuban visa without a Soviet visa and that getting a Soviet visa would take four months; third, Oswald pestered the Cubans, resulting in "a sharp argument" with the consul, Eusebio Azcue, and "failed to obtain visas at both Embassies"; and, fourth, until his departure "Oswald spent considerable time making his travel arrangements, sightseeing and checking again with the Soviet Embassy to learn whether anything had happened on his visa application."[1] As we will see, the problem with this story is that once he learned of the four-month wait, Oswald gave up and *never made an application for a Soviet visa,* a fact apparently not known by the Warren Commission. At a minimum, this raises the question, why Oswald would check on a visa application he did not make?

The Mexican mystery deepened as a result of the 1978 congressional investigation into the Kennedy assassination. The HSCA inquiry presented the startling possibility that someone might have impersonated Oswald in the Mexican capital. However, the HSCA determined that there was not sufficient evidence to "firmly" conclude that such a deception took place. The report added, however, that "the evidence is of such a nature that the possibility cannot be dismissed."[2] This grim uncertainty looms large in what has become known as the *Lopez Report,* the HSCA's long-secret study* of "Oswald, the CIA, and Mexico City." Parts of the *Lopez Report,* a few of them large and several of them small, are still classified. During the three decades that have come and gone since Oswald's visit to Mexico, suspicions have grown among the American public about possible CIA involvement in the assassination. The JFK Records Act mandated that the government's files be opened. Yet, the CIA continues to resist, just as they resisted Eddie Lopez and Dan Hardaway, all attempts to find the whole truth about Oswald's trip to Mexico City.

The possibility of an impostor has drastic consequences for how we view Oswald, and therefore is relevant to the investigation of the president's murder in Dallas. We will return to these consequences in the next two chapters. For now, we must focus first on what we know happened in Mexico. We have new information with which to test the *Lopez Report*'s suggestion about an Oswald impostor. Namely, a major Russian contribution: the published recollections of Paval Yatskov, Valery Kostikov, and Oleg Nechiporenko in the latter's 1993 work, *Passport to Assassination.*[3] Yatskov was the head of the Soviet consular office in Mexico City and, with Vice Consul Nechiporenko, worked for the foreign counterintelligence subdivision of the KGB. Kostikov was part of the KGB's notorious Department Thirteen, which handled assassinations.

We also have a great many new documents released since the passage of the JFK Records Act in 1992. Among these are transcripts of telephone conversations between J. Edgar Hoover and President Johnson, including this exchange:

*released with redactions in 1993

JOHNSON: Have you established any more about the [Oswald] visit to the Soviet Embassy in Mexico in September?

HOOVER: No, that's one angle that's very confusing for this reason. We have up here the tape and the photograph of the man who was at the Soviet Embassy, using Oswald's name. That picture and the tape do not correspond to this man's voice, nor to his appearance. In other words, *it appears that there is a second person who was at the Soviet Embassy* [emphasis added].[4]

Hoover indicated an interest in identifying "this man." Unfortunately, the tape Hoover mentioned has since disappeared. The issue of an Oswald impostor, however, remains.

Oswald in Mexico City

The Soviet Embassy, which also housed the Soviet Consulate, is just two blocks from the Cuban Consulate and Cuban Embassy which, although in different buildings, are inside the same compound. Thus, it would have taken Oswald more time to leave one consulate, find a phone, and call the other consulate than it would have to simply walk there. As we will see, this detail is crucial in sorting out which of the six or seven visits and as many phone calls were Oswald's and which were not. Oswald's bus arrived in Mexico City at 10 A.M. Friday, September 27, 1963,[5] and departed for Texas at 8:30 the following Wednesday morning, October 3.[6] This establishes the time available for his visits and calls.

The first three telephone calls reportedly occurred shortly after Oswald's arrival on September 27. These calls, initially thought to have been made by Oswald, "may have been by an impostor," according to *Lopez.*[7] These calls were placed at 10:30 A.M. [see table X, below],[8] 10:37 A.M., and 1:25 P.M., all to the Soviet military attachè or the Soviet Consulate. This is the CIA transcript of the 10:37, or second, call:

CALLER: May I speak to the Counsel?

SOVIET: He is not in.

CALLER: I need some visas in order to go to Odessa. [A city in southern Ukraine on the shore of the Black Sea]

SOVIET: Please call at 11:30.

CALLER: Until when?
SOVIET: [hangs up the phone.][9]

This call was recorded by the CIA's Mexico City station. A week or two later they identified it having been from Oswald. It was in Spanish, which poses a serious problem. The transcriber did not indicate the speaker was less than fluent, whereas in later calls, where Oswald supposedly spoke in Russian, the transcriber characterized the usage as "terrible" and "hardly recognizable."

Oswald's Marine friend Nelson Delgado claimed to have taught him a modicum of Spanish in 1959, but there is no evidence Oswald could have handled the above script without an accent. In 1978, *Lopez* concluded that "either the above detailed calls were not made by Oswald or Oswald could speak Spanish."[10] It seems odd that his Spanish would have been better than his Russian. Thirty years later came the Russian addition to the story. Valery Kostikov met and spoke with Oswald in the Soviet Consulate. "When I asked him if he spoke Spanish," Kostikov recalled, "he shook his head no."[11]

The first and third calls were not even included in copies of Oswald's "conversations" passed from the Mexico City CIA station to the U.S. Embassy legal attaché four days after the assassination.[12] The HSCA stated it had "not been able to determine why the 9/27 10:30 and 9/27 1:25 calls were not included in this memorandum." The *Lopez Report* was probably right to question whether Oswald had made these three calls. In addition to the impostor explanation is the possibility that they were not connected to either Oswald or an Oswald impostor. Oswald's name was never used in them, and the third call, made to the Soviet Consulate, may have been made when Oswald was already inside the building. After the publication of the *Lopez Report,* an internal CIA analysis rejected these three calls as having had any connection to Oswald.[13]

For our purposes, it does not matter whether these first three calls were from Oswald or not. If it was Oswald, there is no real problem, because Oswald's focus was on the Cuban instead of the Soviet Consulate. On the other hand, if these calls were not made by Oswald, it does not necessarily mean the caller had to be an impostor. The most prudent interpretation is, therefore, that these calls were not made by Oswald or an impostor.

TABLE B: Sequence of Mexico City Oswald-Related Events

Friday, September 27
[LE1] 10:30 A.M. (Spanish-speaking male caller to Soviet Consulate)
[LE2] 10:37 A.M. (Spanish-speaking male caller to Soviet Consulate)
[DE1] 11:00 A.M. (Oswald visit to Cuban Consulate)
[DE2] 1:00 P.M. "approximately" (12:15 Oswald visit to Cuban Consulate)
[NE1] 12:30 to 1:20–1:30 P.M. (Oswald visit to Soviet Consulate)[14]
[LE3] 1:25 P.M. (Spanish-speaking male caller to Soviet Consulate)
[DE3] late afternoon (Oswald third visit to Cuban Consulate)
[LE4] 4:05 P.M. (Duran call to Soviet Consulate)
[LE5] 4:26 P.M. (Soviet Consulate call to Duran)
[NE2] evening (Nechiporenko and Kostikov discuss LE5)
Saturday, September 28
[NE3] 9:00 A.M. to 10:15–10:30 A.M. (Oswald visit to Soviet Consulate)[15]
[LE6] 11:51 A.M. (woman and man call the Soviet Consulate)[16]
Monday, September 30
[LE*] The missing Mrs. T transcript
Tuesday, 1 October
[LE7] 10:31 A.M. (man, in poor Russian, calls Soviet Consulate)
[LE8] 10:45 A.M. (man, in poor Russian, using name Oswald, calls Soviet Consulate)

Legend: LE expands to Lopez Event, events based on CIA transcripts (see *Lopez Report,* p. 117); DE expands to Duran Event—Duran was the secretary working in the Cuban Consulate at the time of Oswald's visit to Mexico City, and these events are based on her various testimonies and interviews; NE expands to Nechiporenko Event, and these events are based on the accounts of Yatskov, Nechiporenko, and Kostokov, the consul and two vice consuls working in the Soviet Consulate at the time of Oswald's visit to Mexico City. The above table combines all three lenses: the Cuban Consulate, Soviet Consulate, and CIA surveillance.

Oswald's first in-person contact was with the Cuban Consulate [DE1], which he entered at around 11 A.M.,[17] requesting an in-transit visa for travel through Cuba to the Soviet Union. Oswald reportedly showed Silvia Duran several documents, but apparently had no passport-style pictures of himself necessary for the visa. He left and returned [DE2], not at one P.M., as Duran recalls, but probably earlier—around 12:15 P.M., this time with the photos.[18] This conclusion—that Duran's time was off by forty-five minutes—is necessary in order not to violate the logical sequence of events. Once Oswald gave Duran the photos, she filled out duplicate visa application forms for him and then explained he would have to get his Soviet visa before she could issue his Cuban visa. Thereupon Oswald went immediately to the Soviet Consulate [NE1], where he arrived at 12:30.

When Duran filled out Oswald's application, which he signed in her presence, he showed, among other things, his FPCC membership card for identification. Duran, however, was suspicious because Oswald had not been sent by the American Communist Party, which had a deal with the Cuban Communist Party allowing approved Americans to get visas immediately. Oswald's first visit to the Soviet Consulate lasted for about one hour, raising a time conflict with the third call to the Soviet Embassy [LE3] at 1:25 P.M., in which a "Man calls Soviet Consulate asks for the consul."[19] Clearly Oswald could not be outside calling in to the consulate if he was already inside talking to Vice Consul Nechiporenko. As previously discussed, this call, like the first two, raises the issue of Oswald's Spanish-speaking abilities.[20]

At 12:30 P.M. Oswald rang the buzzer at the Soviet Embassy [NE1].[21] The sentry alerted Kostikov, who met Oswald inside, spoke with him, and then turned him over to Nechiporenko. According to Nechiporenko, this is what happened next:

> Even though I had seen the letter to our embassy in the United States, I nevertheless asked him if he had appealed to the Soviet embassy in Washington. Oswald said he had already sent a letter there and had been turned down. He later mentioned his fear that the FBI would arrest him for establishing contact with our Washington embassy. So as not to give the FBI additional cause to seize him, he decided to come to Mexico to follow through on his plan. I explained to Oswald that, in accordance with our rules, all matters dealing with travel to the USSR were handled by the embassies or consulates in the country in which a person lived. As far as his case was concerned, we could make an exception and give him the necessary papers to fill out, which we would

> then send on to Moscow, but the answer would still be sent to his permanent residence, and it would take, at the very least, four months.[22]

Oswald, upset at this response, shouted, "This won't do for me! This is not my case! For me, it's all going to end in tragedy." Nechiporenko decided to end the meeting. He led Oswald out of the compound and told the sentry to tell Kostikov "that I had not promised our visitor anything."

Rejected by the Soviets, Oswald returned to the Cuban Consulate again between four P.M. and five P.M. [DE3], during which the fourth and fifth telephone calls occurred. Duran recalled that Oswald came between five P.M. and six P.M., but, again, this was too late by about an hour. This conclusion is supported by the corresponding Duran phone transcript of this event and Nechiporenko's account, which corroborates the Duran call. Normal working hours had ended at two P.M., so the guard had to call Duran. The guard then escorted Oswald into Duran's office, where Oswald proceeded to lie to her, claiming that the Soviets had said there were no problems with his visa application. Suspicious, Duran called the Soviet Consulate at 4:05 P.M. [LE4] for confirmation. The CIA transcript of the intercepted call has this:

> There is an American here who has requested an in-transit visa because he is going to Russia. I sent him to you thinking if he got a Russian visa that I could then issue him a Cuban visa without any more processing. Who did he speak to? He claims he was told there were no more problems.[23]

The unidentified Soviet asked Duran to wait and then could be heard in the background explaining to someone that Silvia Duran was calling about an American who said he had been to the Soviet Embassy. "Please leave the name and number," the voice from the Soviet Embassy instructed, "and we will call you back."[24] As requested, Duran left her name and phone number.

At 4:26 P.M. [LE5], the Soviet Consulate called back. Kostikov came on the line and told Duran that Oswald's visa had not been approved. The CIA transcript has this exchange:

RUSSIAN EMBASSY: Has the American been there?

SILVIA DURAN: Yes, he is here now.

RUSSIAN EMBASSY: According to the letter that he showed from the Consulate in Washington, he wants to go to Russia to stay for a long time with his wife who is Russian. But we have received no answer from Washington, and it will probably take four to five months. We cannot give a visa here without asking Washington. He says he belongs to a pro-Cuban organization and the Cubans cannot give him a visa without his first getting a Russian visa. I do not know what to do with him. I have to wait for an answer from Washington.

SILVIA DURAN: We have to wait too, because he knows no one in Cuba and therefore it's difficult to give him a visa. He says he knew it would take a long time to process the Soviet visa but hoped to await that in Cuba.

RUSSIAN EMBASSY: The thing is that if his wife [Marina was actually in Texas] is now in Washington she will receive the visa for return to Russia. She will receive it and then can send it any place but right now she does not have it.

SILVIA DURAN: Naturally, and we can't give him a visa here because we do not know if his Russian visa will be approved.

RUSSIAN EMBASSY: We can issue a visa only according to instructions.

SILVIA DURAN: That is what I will put in my plans.

RUSSIAN EMBASSY: We can't give him a letter of recommendation either, because we do not know him. Please pardon the bother.

SILVIA DURAN: No bother. Thank you very much.[25]

The CIA Spanish transcript[26] is appended with an English note stating the man in the Soviet Embassy was "unidentified." More important, the transcriber wrote that "the person answering the phone *is* Silvia Duran.[27] [emphasis added]" As we will shortly see, this notation was important, as was the fact that Duran had verified that Oswald had been in the Soviet Consulate that same day. Also noteworthy is how well this transcript fits with the recollections of the people in both consulates involved in the conversation. Finally, it is noteworthy that neither Duran nor Kostikov mentioned Oswald's name, a fact whose crucial importance will shortly become apparent.

Duran's check with Kostikov exposed Oswald's ploy. He became "excited" and quarreled with the Cuban consul, Eusebio Azcue.[28] Oswald never went back to or contacted the Cuban Consulate again. However, he may have had further contact with Duran and other

Cubans outside the consulate, a subject to which we will return later in this chapter. Duran, a Mexican citizen, was in the section known as the Mexican-Cuban Institute of Cultural Affairs, headed by Augustin Canovas. Duran worked closely with Luisa Calderon and Luis Alberu, the cultural attachés in the embassy. Alberu had been recruited as an agent of the CIA.[29] Duran was an attractive twenty-six-year-old woman, married with a daughter, who since 1962 had been the object of rumors of extramarital sexual liaisons, rumors that would come to include Oswald.

The 4:26 P.M, transcript suggests that a phone call was made or a cable was sent from the Soviet Embassy in Mexico City to the Soviet Embassy in Washington. Oswald's presence had lit up Soviet and Cuban intelligence channels in all three national capitals. The Cubans sent a cable to Havana on September 27,[30] and the Soviets sent a cable to Moscow on September 28.[31] The response from Havana came on October 15, nearly two weeks after Oswald's departure.[32] We can only wonder how the contents of the cable to Moscow mixed with what was already in Oswald's files in the Soviet Union.[33]

That Friday evening Kostikov joined Nechiporenko for a mug of beer [NE2] in a noisy cantina that was a ''favorite spot among the local blue-collar crowd,'' and the day's events were discussed. According to Nechiporenko, Kostikov reported this to him:

> As soon as I came back from lunch and the sentry passed on your message to me, I got a call from the Cubans. It was Sylvia Duran from the consulate. It turns out that our ''friend'' had been to see them after us and supposedly told them that we had promised him a visa, so she decided to call and double check. She asked specifically for me because this guy had given her a name that sounded like mine. I'd shown him my ID when he doubted I was a Soviet. I told her we hadn't promised him anything and that even if we did begin processing his visa, it would take at least four months. She thanked me and that's it.[34]

We should be careful to note that in this conversation, Kostikov had confirmed for Duran the fact that Oswald had been inside the Soviet Consulate.

When Kostikov arrived at the Soviet Consulate at 9:30 A.M. on Saturday morning to meet his colleagues for their regular volleyball game, Oswald was already sitting with Soviet consul Pavel Yatskov [NE3].[35] Oswald tried again to convince the Soviets to grant him a visa. Again they refused. Kostikov's account (as it appears in Nechiporenko's book) of the discussion includes this:

> Throughout his story, Oswald was extremely agitated and clearly nervous, especially whenever he mentioned the FBI, but he suddenly became hysterical, began to sob, and through his tears cried, ''I am afraid . . . they'll kill me. Let me in.'' Repeating over and over that he was being persecuted and that he was being followed even here in Mexico, he stuck his right hand into the left pocket of his jacket and pulled out a revolver, saying, ''See? This is what I must now carry to protect my life,'' and placed the revolver on the desk where we were sitting opposite one another.[36]

Nechiporenko then ''flew into the room'' with his gym bag for the volleyball game at ''a little after ten o'clock,'' as Yatskov was unloading the revolver. Eventually, Oswald ''calmed down, evidently after having understood and reconciled himself to the fact that he was not about to get a quick visa.''

Most important, Kostikov states that Oswald ''did not take the [visa application] forms we offered him.''[37] Nechiporenko escorted Oswald from the premises and they never heard from him again. As Oswald left the compound, he pulled his coat over his head to conceal his face from photographic coverage. Yatskov, Kostikov, and Nechiporenko then conferred, and decided that Yatskov and Kostikov immediately report the Oswald events in a coded cable to Moscow [KGB] Center. As a result, their team lost the volleyball game. At the time this might have seemed a high price to pay for the nutty performance they had just witnessed, but after the Kennedy assassination, they would come to refer to this telegram as their ''life preserver.''

This was the end of the line for Oswald's attempts to get a visa in Mexico City. He had not even bothered to fill out the application forms offered by the Soviet Consulate. None of the Mexican, Cuban, or Soviet officials again saw Oswald enter any of the consulates or embassies. Nor did they receive or hear about any calls made by him.[38] Oswald's name did not appear in any of the CIA transcripts of calls intercepted from the time of his arrival Friday morning through the time that he left the Soviet Consulate at 10:30 A.M. on Saturday. That was about to change. The next set of transcripts bears no resemblance to the reality recalled by those who experienced the events firsthand. Something amazing was about to happen to "reality" in Mexico City. We will return to Duran's testimony on this subject in Chapter Nineteen when we deal with cover stories created after the assassination.

Mexican Realities

Eldon Hensen was a cattleman from Athens, Texas. On July 19, he tried—for the second time in a week—to make contact with the Cuban Embassy in Mexico City. He spoke by telephone with Maria Luisa Calderon, but did not state his business and refused to go to the Cuban Embassy because of the possibility that an "American spy might see him." At 6 feet 4 inches and over 200 pounds with a "powerful build" and a "Bob Hope ski nose," he probably had a point. Hensen did state that he was staying in Room 1402 at the Alameda Hotel and was leaving for Dallas the next morning on American Airlines.[39]

Hensen was in luck—or so it seemed. Miraculously, that same afternoon Hensen received a telephone call from a man who identified himself as a Cuban Embassy officer who suggested a meeting in a restaurant. Happy to have avoided American intelligence, Hensen agreed. When the two met, Hensen gave his Athens, Texas, phone number as OR-5-4787, and offered to "help" the Castro government "in the U.S.," traveling, providing "good contacts," and moving "things from one place to another." Hensen said he wanted money in exchange for his cooperation and said that he was under "financial pressure." The Cuban "played cagey," made no commitments, told Hensen he would check him out, said that some delay was inevitable, and warned Hensen "never again" to phone the Cuban Embassy because it was "too dangerous."

The reason it was too dangerous was that the CIA was always listening in, as they had been to Hensen's calls. Unfortunately for Hensen, the Cuban, while possibly from the Cuban Embassy, was not representing the Cubans at all. His loyalties were to the CIA, and he was probably a defector in place or double agent. Hensen walked straight into a web of deceit. The station's cable to headquarters afterward explained how they had pulled off this sleight of hand:

> At Station request [redacted] posing as Cubemb [Cuban Embassy] officer made contact on house phone afternoon 19 July, alluded to call to Embassy, lured Subj [Hensen] to Hotel restaurant. . . . Subj [Hensen] family not aware of his trip to Mexi. Said this his second trip Mexi specifically to establish contact with Cubemb. Agreed accept phone call with key word "Laredo" as call from [redacted] contact. . . . [Redacted] believes [Hensen] had been drinking. [Redacted] witnessed meeting from nearby table. . . . [Redacted] (probably ODENVY, i.e., the FBI) informed 20 July, will pick up hotel registration card and handle stateside investigation.

The Mexico City CIA station said that the Cuban was available for further contact with Hensen in Mexico City if headquarters wanted the game to continue.

What the CIA station in Mexico City did to Eldon Hensen in July 1963 was to "step into" his reality and direct it a way designed to achieve the Agency's objectives—in this instance, to see what he was up to. This CIA capability, to enter surreptitiously into someone's life to control or manipulate it, was made possible in this case by the telephone taps. In other cases it might have been photo surveillance, bugs, or agents and informants who provided the data necessary to play the game. The Hensen case makes it clear that this capability existed and was used in Mexico City in July 1963. It would be used again in September and October of that fateful year.

At approximately 10:30 to 10:45 A.M., Oswald, his revolver back in his pocket, left the Soviet Consulate. Kostikov and Yatskov, instead of going to the volleyball game, stayed to write the cable to KGB Central in Moscow. An hour later, 11:51 A.M., the CIA intercepted a telephone call [LE6] purporting to be from the Cuban Consulate. This was strange: The Cuban Consulate was always closed on Saturdays. Moreover, the woman doing the calling was not identifiable to the transcriber of the tape made from the call. It was not until "later" that she was identified as "Silvia Duran," although just how much later is not revealed.[40] Stranger still is the CIA transcript, which the *Lopez Report* describes as "incoherent."[41]

Here is the full CIA transcript of the September 28, 11:51 A.M., telephone call:

SILVIA DURAN: There is an American here who says he has been to the Russian consulate.
RUSSIAN CONSULATE: Wait a minute.
Silvia Duran is then heard to speak in English to someone apparently sitting at her side. This conversation goes as follows:
DURAN: He said wait. Do you speak Russian?
[OSWALD]: Yes.
DURAN: Why don't you speak with him then?
[OSWALD]: I don't know. . . .
The person who was at the side of Silvia Duran and who admitted to speaking some Russian then gets on the line and speaks what is described as "terrible, hardly recognizable Russian." This person is later identified as Lee Harvey Oswald.
OSWALD: I was in your Embassy and spoke to your Consul.
RUSSIAN EMBASSY: What else do you want?
OSWALD: I was just now at your Embassy and they took my address.
RUSSIAN EMBASSY: I know that.
OSWALD: I did not know it then. I went to the Cuban Embassy to ask them for my address, because they have it.
RUSSIAN EMBASSY: Why don't you come by and leave it then, we're not far.
OSWALD: Well, I'll be there right away.[42]

Prior to proceeding with an analysis, it should be pointed out that Mr."T"[43] (for 'transcriber"), who transcribed this intercept, claims the male speaker is identical with the man who would, in a telephone call three days later, state, "My name is Oswald."

We know from the Hensen story that the CIA station routinely and successfully impersonated people. The September 28 transcript should therefore be examined from two possible perspectives. From the first perspective, the call *was* both Oswald and Duran calling the Soviet Consulate. In this scenario, the Soviets were incorrect in their earlier conclusion that Oswald had "reconciled himself to the fact that he was not about to get a quick visa."[44] Between the time of Oswald's visit to the Soviet Consulate and Duran's call an hour later, he had regained hope and had managed to get the Cubans to call in Silvia Duran on her day off and admit him into the consular offices, and then persuaded her to call the Soviet Consulate with whom she had, just eighteen hours earlier, reached the mutual conclusion that Oswald could not receive a visa inside of four months. From the second perspective, the speakers were *not* Oswald and Duran, but two impostors who had stepped into Oswald's "reality" and were trying to acquire intelligence information.

Let us examine the first sentence spoken by the Duran character: "There is an American here who says he has been to the Russian consulate." Less than twenty-four hours previously Duran had sent Oswald to the Soviet Consulate to get a Soviet visa and, when he had returned with his phony claim that it had been approved, Duran had telephoned the Soviets. Kostikov had confirmed Oswald's visit there. Why would the real Duran state the following day that Oswald "says he has been" if she already knew it to be a fact? On the other hand, if this "Duran" character had not yet seen any transcripts or listened to tapes of the previous day, she might not know that the real Duran had already verified Oswald's September 27 visit.

Upon closer analysis, the possibility emerges that her exact words were carefully chosen to reflect only what was known—possibly from direct observation. The Duran impostor would have known that Oswald had been in the Soviet Consulate but not necessarily whether the real Duran knew this. Thus, the wording suggests that this call was not made by the real Duran because she would have chosen words that were consistent with her information (from Kostikov) that Oswald had made the visit. We will set aside the problem of who actually received this telephone call,[45] and emphasize that, of the two perspectives we are examining, Duran's opening line is more consistent with an impostor than with the real Silvia Duran.

After the Soviet said "Wait a minute," the Duran character put the Oswald character on the line. He said, "I was in your Embassy and spoke to your Consul." This was true, Oswald had just spent over an hour with the consul, Yatskov. Since Yatskov had, in all likelihood, entered the consulate overtly, an impostor could have had this information. This sentence, along with the Soviet reply, "What else do you want?" is consistent with what either the real Oswald or an impostor knew. Since Oswald's business was finished and because he had not even bothered to fill out the paperwork for a visa, it made no sense for Oswald to call back. But in a wrap-around operation, the impostor would have had no way of knowing that Oswald had decided against submitting the application forms. Certainly, Oswald would not drag the Cubans in to work on a Saturday just to phone the Soviet Consulate and tell them that he had been there a few minutes earlier.

When the Soviet asked the Oswald character "what else" he wanted, his answer was not responsive. He said, "I was just now at your Embassy and they took my address." The first part of this sentence adds little except that the words "just now" identify the visit referred to as the Saturday morning session. The second part, that the Soviets had taken his address, seems too trivial to warrant the Cubans working on their day off. No wonder the Soviet reply was, "I know that." It is pertinent to point out that neither part of this sentence by the Oswald character is consistent with the fact that Oswald had not filled out a visa application form.[46] They are, however, consistent with the perspective that the male voice belonged to an imposter who, with limited information, was winging his way, trying to keep the conversation going for some unknown (to us) purpose. It should also be pointed out that an impostor might well have assumed that the real Oswald had given an address, as would the Soviet speaker because he, too, presumably, had no personal knowledge of what Oswald and Yatskov had done. Apparently, the impostor presumed that it was safe to say that the Soviets had taken an address for Oswald. It was an educated guess that was wrong.

The Soviet's acknowledgment was perfunctory. At this point the Oswald character had to come up with something more substantive to justify his apparent presence in the Cuban Consulate and this telephone call. Here is what the Oswald character devised: "I did not know it then. I went to the Cuban Embassy to ask them for my address, because they have it." This is possibly what the *Lopez Report* was referring to with the remark that this transcript was "incoherent." How had the Soviet Consul managed to take Oswald's address without him knowing it? This is not consistent with what we might anticipate from Oswald, who should have been asking the Soviets to reconsider their refusal. It does, however, make sense if we think of the male voice as that of an impostor trying to keep the conversation going.

The Oswald character's tap dance was beginning to falter since Oswald could not have forgotten his addresses in the U.S., and would not have succeeded in getting the Cubans into the consulate on their day off just to ascertain his address at the Commercial Hotel and then call the Soviet Consulate to tell them that they had it. This line makes no sense at all from the real Oswald's perspective. "Why don't you come by and leave it then," said the Soviet, "we're not far." The Soviet must have hoped this would put an end to this seemingly aimless and pointless conversation. Indeed, the Oswald character was out of things to say, except, "Well, I'll be there right away."

The CIA later paraphrased the end of this call in a misleading manner: "The American then acceded to the Soviet official's invitation to come by and give the address."[47] There is no evidence that Oswald or an impostor returned to the Soviet Consulate that day. Obviously the real Oswald had no reason to take an address to the Soviet Consulate if he was not going to fill out the visa application forms. To its credit, the HSCA probed further. According to the *Lopez Report,* another employee at the station had this to say about that call:

> When [redacted] was asked why she had stated that it had been "determined" that Oswald had been in contact with the Soviet Embassy on 28 September she said that it must have been because she had rechecked the [telephone] transcripts by this time as otherwise she would not have used such certain language. When asked why the memo said that there was no clarifying information on Oswald's "request" when it was known by this time that he was seeking a visa, [redacted] said that "They [the HSCA investigators] had no need to know all those other details."[48]

How presumptuous it seems now that this CIA employee felt she had the power to decide what Congress had a need to know. This attitude and these tactics no longer serve the public interest. Hopefully, the recent passage of a law by Congress mandating the release of all information relevant to the case can overcome this kind of institutional arrogance and obstructionism.

Clearly, these "other details" are relevant to whether or not an impostor was doing the talking, and the impostor issue is fundamental to the larger question of whether the Agency ever used Oswald—with or without his knowledge. An impostor might not have known for sure at the time of this call that Oswald was seeking a visa.

Duran remains adamant to this day that this Oswald visit, and, therefore, this call, did not take place.[49] Nechiporenko specifically denies that this call took place, and claims that call could not have gone through because the switchboard was closed.[50] We could subject the remarks of the man who is supposed to be talking in the Soviet Consulate to a similar analysis, and suggest that he was also an impostor. Why didn't he ask for the address over the phone? Here, however, an already bizarre story becomes more so: The entire conversation becomes false and the deception target becomes the CIA station. While this is possible, it seems improbable.

The *Lopez Report,* written in 1978, was not constructed with the benefit of the third corner of the triangle: the Soviet angle. There is no question but that their records and recollections of details such as times and places are invaluable. Now we have the recollections of Yatskov, Kostikov, and Nechiporenko. Moreover, what they say buttresses Silvia Duran's testimony that neither she nor Oswald made this call. The man in this conversation later uses Oswald's name after Oswald has departed Mexico City. Therefore the man in this September 28 call cannot be Oswald. It is also interesting to ask this question: Was the Silvia Duran in this phone call real or an impostor?

On this question we find the CIA transcriber's notes useful. The transcriber of the Saturday phone call did not identify the woman speaking as Duran at the time of the transcription. The female speaker was described as "someone at the Cuban Consulate later identified as Sylvia Duran," which contrasts sharply with the September 27 transcript in which Silvia Duran is definitely and immediately identified. Again, the ostensible subject—an address—about which the person claiming to be Oswald was calling was not a legitimate issue with the embassy. The idea that the staffs of both consulates were engaged with Oswald and each other over an address on their off-duty time seems ridiculous. As previously stated, we will return in Chapter Nineteen to Duran's insistence that Oswald did not return on Saturday. For now we will note that it appears that as of Saturday morning, the impostors were proceeding without knowing what had happened to Oswald while he was inside the Soviet Embassy.

The CIA has not officially acknowledged any calls on Monday, September 30. Does the lack of activity on Monday make sense?

The answer is yes if Oswald had—as the Soviets maintain he had—accepted the fact that he would not get a visa. The answer is no if he changed his mind and decided that it was still worth pursuing a visa in Mexico City. The answer is also no if the impostors still had their own reasons for keeping the Oswald reality in play. Monday would have provided an opportunity to keep the game going. It was a business day. Is there evidence of additional intercepted phone calls? Not surprisingly, there is, and it comes from credible CIA sources.

Mrs. T's Missing Transcript

There is substantial anecdotal evidence that other Oswald-related telephone calls were intercepted and transcribed by the CIA in Mexico City. Consider, for example, Winston Scott's manuscript, *Foul Foe,* which claims that Oswald contacted the Soviet Embassy four times. Win Scott was the longtime chief of the CIA Mexico City station, and close friend of CIA counterintelligence chief James Angleton. After Scott's death in April, 1971, Angleton flew to Mexico City, removed the contents of Scott's safe, and demanded that the family turn over Scott's papers to him. Angleton returned to Washington with, among other things, a manuscript. The manuscript, which has never been published, contains this passage:

> Oswald told a high-ranking officer of the Soviet Embassy that that officer should have had word from the Soviet Embassy in Washington about his visit and its purpose, after he had spelled out his full name, slowly and carefully, for this Soviet. He further told this Soviet that he should know that Oswald, his wife and child wanted to go to the Crimea, urgently, and that he (Oswald) had learned that he would have to go by way of Cuba. Oswald was then directed to the Cuban Embassy by the Soviet, who told Oswald that he would need a Cuban transit visa.[51]

This became important, says Scott, after the Warren Commission Report was published, because, "on page 777 of that report the erroneous statement was made that it was not known that Oswald had visited the Cuban Embassy until after the assassination!"[52] We will return to that statement and its true origin in Chapter Nineteen.

What Scott is describing, however, appears to be a conversation not in any of the extant transcripts. In none of them does Oswald spell his name, let alone enunciate it slowly. Moreover, the name Oswald does not appear in any of the transcripts until the October 1, 10:45 A.M. call. HSCA investigator Eddie Lopez noticed Scott's remark about Oswald spelling "his name very slowly and carefully," and remarked that "although the transcripts available do not bear out Scott's recollections, there are interesting parallels with the testimony of [redacted] and David Phillips.[53]

We will shortly return to Phillips's offerings on this subject, but there was more in Win Scott's manuscript suggestive of other intercepted phone calls. Take, for example, this passage:

> Lee Harvey Oswald, having just arrived in Mexico City, made his first contact with the Soviet Embassy in Mexico, giving them his name very slowly and carefully, and saying that the Soviet Embassy in Mexico should have received word from the Soviet Embassy in Washington that he (Oswald) would contact them about a visa for himself, his wife, who he said was a Soviet citizen, and their child.[54]

This is the same missing call on Friday, only here Scott provides the additional detail that word was expected from the Soviet Embassy in Washington. A question about a telegram from Washington was asked in the October 1 call at 10:45 A.M. Finally, Scott's manuscript also states that while Oswald was in Duran's office, Oswald "decided to ask the help of a Soviet Embassy official in convincing the Cubans that they should give Oswald the transit visa through Cuba, even before he had his Soviet visa. This, he did."[5] While this appears similar to the (probably fictitious) Saturday morning (11:51 A.M.) call, the Oswald character said nothing about visas in the transcript that survives.

More than Win Scott's manuscript suggests there were other calls. Convincing evidence comes from a person who actually remembers typing a transcript that bears no resemblance to those that exist today. The *Lopez Report* probed the possibility that additional phone calls were intercepted by the surveillance team, and discovered credible evidence that this had been the case. Mrs. T, who assisted her husband, Mr. T, in transcribing tapes from the Soviet Embassy, testified before the HSCA on April 12, 1978. Mrs. T recognized as her husband's work the transcripts from the conversations intercepted on 9/28/63, at 11:51 A.M.; on 10/1/63, at 10:31 A.M. and 10:45 A.M.; and on 10/3/63.[56] Her recognition of these transcripts as her husband's was based on "the style of his writing or typing and the use of slash marks."

In addition to her husband's work, Mrs. T testified that she, too, transcribed tapes, at least one [LE*] of which "involved" Oswald. According to the *Lopez Report,* this is what she said:

> According to my recollection, I myself, have made a transcript, an English transcript, of Lee Oswald talking to the Russian Consulate or whoever he was at that time, asking for financial aid. Now, that particular transcript does not appear here and whatever happened to it, I do not know, but it was a lengthy transcript and I personally did that transcript. It was a lengthy conversation between him and someone at the Russian Embassy.

This transcript was "approximately two pages long," Mrs. T testified, and *"the caller identified himself as Lee Oswald"* [emphasis added]. To test her claim, the HSCA tried to see if she was actually referring to the 10/1/63 call, but her story appears unshakable.

Mr. T testified that he recognized the 10/1/63 conversation as his work because the name Lee Oswald was underlined. Mr. T then added this important detail:

> We got a request from the station to see if we can pick up the name of this person because sometimes we had a so-called "defector" from the United States that wanted to go to Russia and we had to keep an eye on them. Not I—the Station. Consequently they were very hot about the whole thing. They said, "If you can get the name because I put them in capitals. In this case I did because it was so important to them."[57]

Mr. T said he had no idea how "Oswald had come to the Station's attention prior to this conversation or what led to the request to get his name." In his testimony, he "speculated that it was possible that *Oswald first came to the Station's attention through Oswald's contacts with the Cuban Embassy*[58] [emphasis added].

Could she have confused her call with the 10/1/63, 10:45 A.M.

conversation? the HSCA asked. Mrs. T stuck to her guns and then added a crucial detail:

> This would not be the conversation that I would be recalling for the simple reason that this is my husband's work and at that time probably the name didn't mean much of anything. But this particular piece of work that I am talking about is something that came in and *it was marked as urgent*[59] [emphasis added].

Mrs. T explained the procedure for ''urgent tapes'' and the HSCA confirmed this procedure through its own review of the files. She said a piece of paper would be enclosed with the reel indicating the footage number locating the conversation that had been requested for ''priority handling over the other conversations on the reel.'' After transcription, the translators would ''immediately notify their contact and then turn the transcript over to him on the same day that it had been delivered.''

If Mrs. T is telling the truth, there is a missing transcript. If it was the only one marked urgent, then the missing transcript was probably the most important call of the lot. Naturally, the HSCA wanted to know what was on the transcript:

> [Mrs. T] was questioned about the details of the conversation which she remembered. She stated that Oswald definitely identified himself and that he was seeking financial aid from the Russians. (H)e was persistent in asking for financial aid in order to leave the country. They were not about to give him any financial aid whatsoever. He had also mentioned that he tried the Cuban Embassy and they had also refused financial aid.

Oswald spoke only English, Mrs. T explained, and the 10/1/63, 10:45 A.M. conversation could not be the call that she remembered for four reasons. First, because that transcript indicates that Oswald spoke in broken Russian; second, because that transcript is shorter than the one she remembers; third, that transcript is in her husband's style as opposed to her own; and fourth, there is no mention of Oswald's finances in the transcript.

It is also possible that the missing transcript was from a call made on Tuesday. The CIA transcripts indicate two more calls [LE7 and

LE8] were made on Tuesday, October 1, but neither transcript resembles Mrs. T's description of the offer of information for money. The two calls acknowledged by the CIA transcripts were made by the same man and, in the second of these calls, he said, "My name is Oswald."[60] The caller asked the Soviets to check on the status of the telegram to the Soviet Embassy in Washington. This request raises the same problem as the Saturday morning call: It does not logically follow from the events as known from other source material. If Oswald had been eager to learn about a response from the Soviet Embassy in Washington, he would have done so on Monday. Moreover, what sense does it make for the real Oswald to be checking on his visa application after he had decided not to fill out the application? This request for a check with Washington adds up only in this scenario: The impostors knew that Oswald was seeking a visa and that the Soviet Consulate had sent a telegram to Washington, but they did not know that Oswald had, inside the Soviet Consulate on Saturday, declined to fill out the application.

Of the eight calls attributed to or involving Oswald, his name appeared in only one of them: the last call at 10:45 A.M. on Tuesday.[61] This too seems odd. There must be something more going on here. It seems likely that the impostors who made the Saturday call knew of an American's presence in the consulates but did not yet know his name. In order to make sense of this, we need to know when the transcripts from the Friday (legitimate) and Saturday (impostor) calls circulated inside the CIA station. Not surprisingly, here too we face a dubious account. The CIA station personnel told the HSCA that the Saturday transcripts was available on Monday and that the Friday transcripts were available on Tuesday.[62] Is this credible? Why would the Saturday transcript take forty-eight hours to show up in the CIA station and the Friday transcripts take ninety-six hours?

The key question is, why did it take so long for the Friday Duran-Kostikov conversation to become available? According to the *Lopez Report,* "Ms. Goodpasture brought these transcripts into the Station on that [Tuesday] morning and put them on [redacted] desk."[63] Now the importance of Mrs. T's claim that Oswald identified himself in the missing transcript becomes apparent. If our impostor scenario is correct, it means the impostors had discovered Oswald's name by the time of that call: If the missing transcript was from Monday, then Oswald's name was known as of Monday; if the transcript was from Tuesday, then Oswald's name was not known until then. This leads us to the most important question of all: How did the impostors learn of Oswald's name in the first place?

In this connection we are drawn back to Mr. T's speculation, mentioned above, that Oswald's name first came to the station's attention through his contacts with the Cuban Embassy. If he is right, then the CIA's knowledge of what happened inside the Cuban Consulate is the key to the puzzle. Did the CIA station learn Oswald's name through an informant inside the Cuban Consulate? From a bug in the wall? From photographic coverage of the entrance? For thirty years the CIA has claimed they did not know that Oswald was inside the consulate until after the Kennedy assassination. In the next chapter we will demonstrate that this is a lie—a cover story to protect CIA sources inside. For now it is sufficient to stay focused on the fact that it was Goodpasture who walked into the CIA station with the Cuban Consulate transcripts in her hands on Tuesday.

Who in the CIA station figured out that Oswald had visited the Cuban Consulate? At the end of Goodpasture's career, David Phillips, not Win Scott, wrote up her retirement award in 1973. It contained this passage: "She was the case officer who was responsible for the identification of Lee Harvey Oswald in his dealings with the Cuban Embassy in Mexico."[64] Besides her role "in support of the successful coup against the communist government in Guatemala in 1954," her identification of Oswald in the Cuban Consulate was the only specific action in her entire career singled out by Phillips in her award.

There is something strange about Ann Goodpasture's role in the CIA Mexico City station. She may have been functioning in a special capacity outside the control of the station chief, Win Scott, her nominal supervisor there. A key clue is this: Scott gave her a lukewarm fitness report for 1963, whereas Phillips singled out this same performance as the jewel in her tiara. From the fitness report and award recommendation we know something else about Goodpasture: She was connected to a super-secret element at headquarters: Staff D.[65] According to David Martin's CIA study *Wilderness of Mirrors,* Staff D "was a small Agency component responsible for communications intercepts."[66] In addition, within Staff D was hidden the ZR/

RIFLE project, the Agency's program to develop a capability for assassination. According to the 1967 CIA inspector general's report, it was the Staff D "workshop" that throughout the night of November 20, 1963, fashioned the poison-pen device with which AM/LASH (Rolando Cuebela) was to murder Castro.[67] "D was the perfect cranny," according to Martin, "in which to tuck a particularly nasty piece of of business" like ZR/RIFLE.

Thus there is no doubt that it was Goodpasture who pinned the tail on the donkey in Mexico City. The question is: When did she manage the feat for which she was regaled ten years later? Is it possible that it was her identification of Oswald that permitted the impostors to use his name in Mrs. T's missing transcript and the Tuesday call to the Soviet Consulate asking about the telegram to Washington?

Phillips's Recollections: Evidence of an Oswald "Dangle"?

Mrs. T's claim that Oswald offered information for money to the Soviet Consulate raises the question, was Oswald part of a dangle to the Soviets in Mexico City? Is there other evidence relevant to this question? Indeed there is, and it comes from David Phillips. However, the problem with Phillips' story about this is that it changed—in the space of twenty-four hours. It was a story which, in one place, was about an "information offer" and in another place was about an "assistance request." In the second instance Phillips was testifying under oath to the HSCA.

In November 1976, David Phillips, who had been chief of Cuban Operations in the CIA Mexico City station in 1963, told the *Washington Post* that Oswald offered "information" to the Soviet Embassy in exchange for money. If true, this might have been a "counter-intelligence dangle" similar to the Sigler dangle operation in 1966, when an apparently disgruntled U.S. Army sergeant entered the Soviet Embassy in Mexico City and offered them information in exchange for money, and proceeded to feed disinformation to the Soviets for ten years. Sigler's success led to an award from CIA director William Colby at the same time he was being promoted to the rank of colonel in the KGB by Leonid Brezhnev. Sigler died under mysterious circumstances in 1976.[68]

Is it possible that Oswald was an integral part of—or had stumbled into—a plan to deceive the KGB and the Cuban DGI? The Phillips story about information for money has some complications—which is typical Phillips. According to the *Lopez Report,* Phillips testified to the HSCA that "Oswald indicated in his discussions with the Soviet Embassy that he hoped to receive assistance with the expenses of his trip." This account, however, misses the Oswald half of the story.

Phillips told the *Washington Post* that Oswald had been overheard saying words "to the effect, 'I have information you would be interested in, and I know you can pay my way [to Russia].' " Ron Kessler, the *Post* reporter, wrote that Phillips's claim was corroborated by other CIA sources, such as the "translator" and "typist" of the intercepted call. " 'He said he had some information to tell them,' the 'typist' said in an interview in Mexico. 'His main concern was in getting to one of the two countries [Russia or Cuba] and he wanted them to pay for it.' "[69]

Phillips failed to tell the *Post* the version of this story that would appear in his book *Night Watch* written the same year. There, Phillips categorically stated that "I know of no evidence to suggest that . . . any aspect of the Mexico City trip was any more ominous than reported by the Warren Commission."[70] Phillips's book is also at odds with his accounts elsewhere about Oswald's Mexican adventure. For example, his book identifies the authors of the October 8 cable on Oswald, discussed below, as the husband-and-wife team headed by " 'Craig,' the case officer in charge of Soviet operations." In his HSCA testimony Phillips claimed that the cable "did come to me, also to sign off, because it spoke about Cuban matters." Phillips was not even in Mexico when the cable was sent![71] He was on a trip to Washington and Miami, and did not return until October 9.

Underlining the contradiction between Phillips's remarks to the *Washington Post* and his testimony to the HSCA is the short amount of time between the two versions. The *Washington Post* story appeared on November 26, 1976. The very next day, when testifying under oath to the HSCA, Phillips again stated that Oswald had asked for money, but this time he did not mention the offer of information. On Phillips's key allegation that Oswald offered information for money, FBI director Kelley confirms this happened, and was known, not just from the wiretaps, and cameras, but also from informants and other types of foreign intelligence techniques.''[72]

The HSCA later found out that the story of Oswald's request for assistance had also been told by Win Scott (after his retirement) in a 1970 letter:

> . . . his activities from the moment he arrived in Mexico, his contacts by telephone and his visits to both the Soviet and Cuban Embassies and his requests for assistance from these two Embassies in trying to get to the Crimea with his wife and baby [emphasis added]. During his conversations he cited a promise from the Soviet Embassy in Washington that they would notify their Embassy in Mexico of Oswald's plan to ask them for assistance.[73]

This letter, along with Scott's manuscript, was one of the items James Angleton removed from Scott's personal safe immediately after his death.

June Cobb, Elena Garro De Paz, and the Oswald-Duran ''Affair''

By 1978, when the HSCA conducted its investigation into the Kennedy assassination, startling information had come to light concerning Oswald's social activities in Mexico City. ''The Committee believes that there is a possibility,'' states the *Lopez report,* that ''a U.S. Government agency requested the Mexican government to refrain from aiding the Committee with this aspect of its work.''[74] This was especially so when the HSCA tried to dig into the sources of the persistent story about an Oswald affair with Silvia Duran. The relevance of this story is clear: American intelligence contained reports that Duran's sexual services had already been used by the Cuban government. Sexual entrapment was then a commonly employed and highly successful espionage technique. Thus, on the surface the story implicates the Castro regime in the Kennedy assassination.

The story began, after the assassination, at a twist (i.e. dance) party at the home of Silvia's brother, Ruben Duran. The source of the story was Elena Garro de Paz, a popular playwright and wife of famed Mexican poet Octavio Paz. Two years later the source was the same but the story had grown to include Elena's allegation of an affair between Oswald and Duran. It was the CIA's spy in the Cuban Embassy, Luis Alberu, who finally convinced the station chief Win Scott that the affair was a fact. The documentary trail on the twist party, however, began with a June Cobb memo. She had been working as an informant for the CIA in Mexico City since 1961.

"June Cobb is promiscuous and sleeps with a large number of men," wrote Scott in 1964, and "sometimes spends several nights (consecutively) with a man in his apartment."[75] Actually, Win Scott was passing this along from the legal attaché, Clark Anderson, and neither was in a position to know about Cobb's love life which, as rich and tragic as it had been, did not include sleeping with "a large number of men." The name of the asset who passed this information to Anderson is still protected, but the choice of words—"promiscuous," "large number of men," and "several nights consecutively," were not only excessive, but border on character assassination. June was both an attractive and highly knowledgeable young woman, and was discriminating in her relationships.

We applaud full disclosure, but a comment seems in order here. Since the CIA has seen fit to release scurrilous, unsubstantiated allegations about their former informants while they are alive, the continued withholding of other documents such as their own memo to the FBI (just before Oswald's visit) on running an operation against the FPCC in Mexico, seems unconscionable.

The CIA claims that it did not learn of the stories about the twist party and the affair until after the publication of the Warren Report. The FBI, according to a 1979 CIA report, had conducted an investigation in Mexico after the assassination and had concluded that the Garro allegations were "without substantiation."[76] This investigation, however, was a little late. "On October 5, 1964, eleven days after the publication of the Warren Commission Report," the *Lopez Report* observed, "Elena Garro de Paz's story alleging Lee Harvey Oswald's presence at a party in Mexico City attended by Cuban government personnel came to the attention of the Central Intelligence Agency."

The allegations of Duran-Oswald social contacts outside the Cuban Consulate have relevance to other issues, such as possible Cuban government involvement in the assassination and whether or not Duran had Cuban, Mexican, or American intelligence ties. The *Lopez Report* identified the author of the October 5 report as June Cobb:

> The source of the memo was [several lines redacted] whom the Committee identified as June Cobb Sharp while reviewing the [redacted] file. According to Elena, Ms. Cobb was sent to her house shortly after the assassination for a few days, by a mutual friend, a Costa Rican writer named Eunice Odio. Ms. Garro asserted that while at her house, Ms. Cobb expressed interest in the Kennedy assassination. One night, Elena's sister Deva, who was visiting, got drunk and told the whole story.[77]

The words ''whole story'' are vague, but probably refer only to the twist party at Ruben Duran's. Eddie Lopez and Dan Hardaway tried and were unable to locate a number of witnesses, including June Cobb. ''The committee attempted to obtain an interview with Ms. Cobb,'' said the *Lopez Report,* ''but was once again frustrated.'' If they had located Cobb, they doubtless would have realized that Elena's recollection as to the date of Cobb's visit was a mistake.

First, if Elena's dates were right, then Cobb would have learned about the twist party in the first days after the assassination and not reported it for an entire year. This would have been strange had it happened, but it did not. Elena had been whisked away to a safe house in the wake of the assassination, supposedly because of her knowledge of Oswald's extracurricular activities in Mexico City, but Cobb did not visit Elena at the Hotel Vermont safe house. Cobb moved into Elena's real home ten months later.[78]

The question is this: Did Elena really tell Cobb ''the whole story'' as described in the *Lopez Report*? Or was it an early scalded-down version of a story that would later grow in imaginative ways? As we shall see, what eventually unfolded was a tale better suited for James Bond than Lee Oswald. So far, the *Lopez Report* attributes coverage of the twist party only to June Cobb's still-classified October 5 memo. Elena and her sister were first cousins to the Duran brothers, Horatio, who was married to the Silvia Duran from the Cuban Consulate, and Ruben, who held the twist party at his home in the fall of 1963. The interesting, if fragmentary, recapitulation of Cobb's memo in the *Lopez Report* contains this segment:

> Lee Harvey Oswald was alleged to have been at this party in the company of "two other beatnik-looking boys." The Americans remained together the entire evening and did not dance. When Elena [her daughter] tried to speak with the Americans, she was "shifted" to another room by one of her cousins. The [Cobb] memo does not state whether Elena had mentioned which cousin had not allowed her to speak to the Americans. One of Elena's cousins told her at that time that (he or she) did not know who the Americans were except that Silvia Duran . . . had brought them to the party.[79]

Not much else of significance about Cobb's memo is described in the *Lopez Report,* except for Elena's claim that the day after the party she and her sister saw Oswald and his two companions on the Avenida Insurgentes, one of the main avenues in the Mexican capital, and that they recognized Oswald's photograph after the assassination. Silvia Duran's arrest after the Kennedy assassination "underlined the Garros' certainty" that the man at the twist party had been Lee Harvey Oswald.

June Cobb remembers Elena telling her story, but the description of Cobb's handling of this story in the *Lopez Report* seems unfamiliar to her today. From a recent interview, here is Cobb's recollection of Elena's story as told in September 1964:

> A quick social gathering had been slapped together for a purpose. When Elena and her sister got to this unlikely party there were these American guys there. And after the assassination they recognized Oswald as one of them. Elena had concluded that the Cubans were in on the assassination, and that the party must have been set up by those Cuban individuals involved, and some of their Mexican friends, so that they could provide an underground for Oswald after the assassination, in which there would be people available who would recognize him and assist in his escape.[80]

It seems prudent to be sceptical of Elena's story, which, if true, would raise suspicions of Cuban government involvement in the assassination. Elena was not entirely objective. While a champion of the peasant cause in Mexico, Elena detested Communists, and thus Cobb's comment about the Garros going to an "unlikely" gathering of communist sympathizers. Elena had concluded that she and her sister were asked to the party as a sort of "camouflage to alter the appearance of the meeting."[81] That is the way Cobb remembers hearing and reporting the story in 1964. In March 1995 she initiated inquiries with the CIA for the release of this document.

Cobb had been living with Elena for only about a month when the story of the twist party came up. Cobb does not recall, however, the actions attributed to her in the *Lopez Report*:

> Claiming to be a CIA agent, Cobb suggested that Elena and Deba go to Texas to tell their story. Elena stated that when Cobb's suggestion was rejected, Cobb stated that she would arrange a meeting with the Chief of the CIA in Mexico. The meeting did not occur because Ms. Cobb was asked to leave the Garro house evidently because she kicked Elena's cat. A notation on the memo says that [redacted, but possibly LI/COOKY-1, Cobb's cryptonym] never regained contact with Elena Garro de Paz.[82]

The trail of evidence on this report by Cobb is as intriguing as this—probably false—story itself. The memo was apparently "lost" in the files, perhaps because it had not been placed in either the Elena Garro or Oswald "P" (personality) files at the CIA Mexico City station. Instead, it was put into a "local leftist and Cuban project file." The HSCA found out about it from another source—a chronological history of the Oswald case designated Wx-7241, prepared by Raymond Rocca for the CIA in 1967. According to Rocca, the Cobb memo was first found in December 1965 by an employee whose name is still withheld. A marginal notation on the Wx-7241 history asked, "Why was this not sent to headquarters?" That is a good question. The HSCA admitted they did not have the answer.

Cobb does remember how the story with Elena turned out. It all ended abruptly one night in late September or early October 1964, when Bobby Kennedy arrived in Mexico City, possibly in connection with his own investigation of his brother's murder.

> Robert Kennedy came to Mexico that night. And the Garros had a crush on Kennedy, and so they went out to the airport to see him arrive. The word got around that he was coming, but I was sick and did not go to the airport. I stayed home in my bed

with my humidifier, but they went to the airport. They had some yellow roses they wanted to give to Kennedy.[83]

This trip to Mexico City by Bobby Kennedy is not widely known, but there is documentary evidence that supports Cobb's recollection. On November 25, 1964, CIA station chief Win Scott wrote under his pseudonym Willard C. Curtis a "memo for the files."[84] "Paz tried to talk to Robert Kennedy when he was here," Scott wrote, and added, "She wanted to tell him she had personally met Lee Harvey Oswald when he was here in Mexico City. She said she met him and two friends (Cubans) at the home of Horacio (and Silvia) Duran."

In a recent interview, Dallas FBI agent Hosty recalled that the CIA assistant deputy director for Plans, Thomas Karamessines, went down to Mexico City to "call off the investigation," and that Ambassador Mann obliged by halting it. "When the CIA agents in Mexico City heard that Bobby Kennedy wanted the probe to stop," says Hosty, "they in fact stopped it."[85] If Hosty is correct, it is possible that Bobby Kennedy's trip may have been an attempt to lay the matter to rest. If so, he did not succeed.

"Suddenly Elena and her daughter came home from the airport," Cobb remembers, "and soon there was a lot of raised voices about her cat and what had happened to it." Cobb could not understand how harm had come to the poor cat. "They stayed up all night long," Cobb says, "and decided I had broken the cat's legs. By the time I woke up it was over. I moved out to a hotel the next day."[86] By the time this story made it into Win Scott's memo, Cobb had also "smashed the ribs" of the cat.[87] Another memo or two and the cat would not have had any bones left to break.

After Cobb's infamous but still secret report, the next piece in this documentary trail is an October 12, 1964, CIA memo for the record from the Mexico City station's chief of covert action Jim Flannery.[88] The Flannery memo states that Elena had told her story to Eunice Odio; the HSCA investigation was unable "to determine if Elena Garro told Ms. Odio the story personally or if Ms. Cobb related the story to Ms. Odio who relayed it to [redacted.]"[89] Cobb says that Elena probably told her own story to Eunice.[90] According to the *Lopez Report,* the next piece of the story came on November 24, 1964, when a CIA agent reported information derived from an ''asset.'' This was the slanderous memo about Cobb, previously discussed. The agent erroneously characterized Cobb as a ''American Communist'' who had rented a room from Garro, and that Garro had also told her story to a U.S. Embassy official ''who claimed to represent the Warren Commission.''[91] June Cobb was not a Communist.

Charles Thomas's first discussion with Elena Garro de Paz about Oswald occurred on December 10, 1965, more than two years after the assassination. Charles Thomas, a career Foreign Service officer, was the political officer at the American Embassy at the time. There was something odd about him which we will return to at the end of this chapter. He wrote a memorandum about his conversation with Elena that, according to the *Lopez Report*, had ''more details'' than the story as told to Cobb more than a year earlier. Elena repeated the story of the twist party, but according to Thomas's memo, one of the new ''details'' was Elena's charge that Silvia Duran ''was Oswald's mistress while he was there.''[92] According to the *Lopez Report,* this Thomas memo was also filed in the Oswald chronological file Wx-7241:

> A note by this entry in Wx-7241 says, ''How did Elena Garro know about Silvia being the mistress of Oswald? This is 1965.'' The Mexico City Station did not hear about the Oswald-Duran ''affair'' until July 1967 when a CIA asset, [redacted] reported it.[93]

This almost certainly indicates that the October 5 Cobb report did not contain the story of the Oswald-Duran affair. It would also mean that Charles Thomas did not pass this information to the CIA station in Mexico City when he learned it in 1965. However, the *Lopez Report* also notes that Thomas circulated his memorandum in the embassy and the CIA's Mexico City station.

Clearly, these claims cannot all be true: If the CIA ''asset'' did not bring the story to the station's attention until 1967, Charles Thomas could not have circulated the story in 1965. This issue is resolved by Win Scott's marginalia on the Thomas memo:

> The COS wrote a note on the memo: ''What an imagination she [Elena] has!?! Should we send to Headquarters?'' The Officer replied, on the memo, ''Suggest sending. There have been stories

> around town about all this, and Thomas is not the only person she has talked to . . . If memory serves me, didn't [redacted] refer to Oswald and the local leftists and Cubans in one of her Squibs?''[94]

The name behind the redaction is probably Cobb. The CIA station cabled the information in Thomas's memo to CIA headquarters, and Win Scott wrote on the cable, ''Please ask Charles Thomas if he'll 'follow up.' Get questions from Ann G[oodpasture]. Please let's discuss. Thanks.'' Scott called a meeting with Thomas and asked him ''to get a more detailed account of Ms. Garro's story.''

Thomas obliged, and met again with Garro on December 25, 1965, after which he wrote a new memo about the Garro allegations. This time Elena's story about the twist party was ''much more detailed,'' and she explained that she had earlier held back part of her story because ''the Embassy officers did not give much credence to anything she and Elenita said.'' According to Thomas's December 25, 1965, memo,

> Elena stated that it was ''common knowledge'' that Silvia had been Oswald's mistress. When asked who could verify the allegation, she could only remember one person who had told her this. Elena claimed that person was Victor Rica Galan, a ''pro-Castro journalist.''[95]

Clearly, Elena wasn't holding back any longer. Thomas gave his memo to the CIA station ''to aid in its investigation'' of the assassination. On the first page of the memo Scott wrote: ''Shouldn't we send to Headquarters?'' Someone responded: ''Of course.'' The Mexico City station did send a cable to headquarters on December 12, 1965, reporting that it was ''following up'' the story and would send the results in another cable.

On December 27, 1965, the embassy legal attaché, Nathan Ferris, wrote a memo to the ambassador reporting the results of his interviews on November 17 and 24 with Elena and her daughter. According to Ferris, Elena told substantially the same story as she had to Thomas. The Ferris memo further stated this:

> . . . Inquiries conducted at that time (November 1964), however, failed to substantiate the allegations made by Mrs. Garro de Paz

> and her daughter. In view of the fact that Mrs. Garro de Paz' allegations have been previously checked out without substantiation, no further action is being taken concerning her recent repetition of those allegations.[96]

Ferris, obviously not interested in Elena's allegations, sent a copy of the memorandum to the CIA station. Goodpasture summarized the interview, including Ferris's "failure to substantiate Elena's story," in a cable to headquarters on December 29.

> The cable promised to keep Headquarters advised if any further information was to [be] developed. . . . A note stapled to this cable by [redacted] stated, "I don't know what FBI did in November 1964, but the Garros have been talking about this for a long time and she is said to be extremely bright." Anne Goodpasture wrote that the FBI had found Elena's allegations unsubstantiated but that "we will try to confirm or refute Ms. Garro de Paz' information and follow up." Win Scott wrote, "She is also nuts."[97]

In the Duran interview with Summers for this work she again adamantly denied having had a sexual relationship with Oswald: "No, no, no. Of course not. I had a relation with someone in the embassy, but not with Oswald . . . he was somebody you couldn't pay attention to."[98] As we saw in Chapter Fourteen, Duran admitted having had the affair with Lechuga, and was willing to discuss these important, if embarrassing, contacts. While her candor about Lechuga and "someone in the embassy" does not make her denial about Oswald true, it does add to her credibility.

On June 18, 1967, the CIA station in Mexico City sent a dispatch to the chief, Western Hemisphere Division, J. C. King. It included this passage:

> Headquarters attention is called to paragraphs 3 through 5 of [redacted] report dated 26 May. The fact that Silvia Duran had sexual intercourse with Lee Harvey Oswald on several occasions when the latter was in Mexico City is probably new, but adds little to the Oswald case. The Mexican police did not report the extent of the Duran-Oswald relationship to this Station.[99]

Duran owed her job in the Cultural Institute to the Cuban cultural attaché, Teresa Proenza. The above report was from an agent familiar with Silvia Duran and Teresa Proenza, a telltale sign that it was the handiwork of Luis Alberu, whose name fits perfectly in the corresponding redacted space in the *Lopez Report* which also describes the contents of the May 26, 1967, report.[100] The news from Alberu represented, for the first time, independent corroboration of Elena's 1965 version of the story to Charles Thomas, in which the Oswald-Duran affair had been added to what had been a twist party in her earlier version to Cobb.[101]

For the CIA station chief Win Scott, Alberu's report had established the Oswald-Duran affair as a "fact." HSCA investigator Ed Lopez agreed that the Alberu report "confirmed" Elena Garro's story that "Silvia Duran had been Oswald's mistress while he was in Mexico City."[102] According to the May 26 report, Alberu had explained to his case officer that "he was doing his best to keep active certain contacts he had had in the past that were on the periphery of the official Cuban circle." This suggests that Alberu had been away from Mexico, perhaps for as long as three years, and had recently returned to the embassy in Mexico City. Alberu's case officer explained:

> He [Alberu] mentioned specifically the case of Silvia and Horacio Duran that then explained the background of the relationship with them. He related that Silvia Duran worked as a receptionist at the Consulate in 1959–64 and was on duty when Lee Harvey Oswald applied for a visa. She had been recommended to the Cubans by Teresa Proenza, the Press Attaché from 1959 until 1962. [Redacted] described Teresa Proenza as a Cuban woman aged about 52, a lesbian, and a member of the Communist Party of Cuba, who was currently in jail in Cuba as a result of a conviction for espionage on behalf of CIA.[103]

The CIA station in Mexico City knew the real reason that Proenza had been jailed. Proenza had been used in a pernicious and successful CIA "political action" deception of which she and her longtime friend, the Cuban vice minister of defense, were the targets.

We need to briefly summarize this story of Proenza's arrest because it illuminates the nature and success of the Agency's anti-

Cuban operations that were connected with the Cuban Consulate in Mexico City. This helps us to understand how sensitive the Oswald Mexico City story is, and the Agency's dogged resistance to our efforts to find out more.

The CIA saw to it that false papers had been planted on Proenza, documents that made the vice minister of defense look like a CIA agent who had betrayed the Soviet missile buildup in Cuba to the Americans. Actually, this official was a highly placed and extreme pro-Moscow Communist—and was probably the KGB's chief agent in the Cuban government. The CIA hoped that Moscow would jump to the vice minister's defense and that a collision would result between Moscow and Havana. The Proenza deception was associated with the Agency's AMTRUNK and AMROD anti-Cuban operations, part of a general CIA strategy to "split the Castro regime" and sour relations between Moscow and Havana. Proenza, the vice minister, the vice minister's wife, and a subordinate of the vice minister were all arrested, tried for treason, and jailed for various terms. They were all innocent.

The CIA refused to turn over the Proenza file to the House Select Committee on Assassinations, arguing that

> The story would make dramatic headlines if it became publicly known, especially in the present moralistic environment. The fact that several persons were deprived of their freedom as a result of the operation would attract further attention. Furthermore, this operation laid the basis for other operations of a similar nature that were successfully mounted against Cuban and other hostile targets. In short, this file is a Pandora's box the opening of which would not only expose the cryptonyms of other operations of this type but would attract unfavorable publicity for the Agency in certain quarters and would expose hitherto secret techniques and assets.

From the records so far released we cannot determine whether Alberu knew the full truth behind Proenza's fate. He did tell his case officer that while in Havana the person from whom he had learned the story of her arrest also told Alberu that "in the event he was asked, he deny that he had known Teresa Proenza or had had anything to do with her."[104]

As previously discussed, Alberu was the key to the Oswald-Duran sex story. Elena Garro was anti-Communist and had an ax to grind with her cousin's wife, Silvia Duran. These factors reduce her credibility, while Alberu's position inside the Cuban Embassy presumably makes his account more authoritative. After his return to Mexico City in 1967, Alberu reestablished his relationship with Silvia Duran. Some of what he learned from or about Duran is still classified, including one-third of a page in the May 26 report written by his case officer. The Agency has decided, however, that this passage from that report may now be revealed:

> [Alberu] continued that Silvia Duran [redacted] had first met Oswald when he applied for a visa and had gone out with him several times since she liked him from the start. She admitted that she had sexual relations with him but insisted that she had no idea of his plans. When the news of the assassination broke she stated that she was immediately taken into custody by the Mexican police and interrogated thoroughly and beaten until she admitted that she had had an affair with Oswald.[105]

Setting aside the torture tactics, it was no wonder, given Alberu's apparent trustworthiness, that the CIA station chief Win Scott believed him and sent a message the following day saying the affair was "fact." Unless Alberu or his source was lying, it had to be a fact because Duran herself had "admitted" it. We will return to Duran's treatment later.

Because of the large redeaction preceding this part of the May 26 report, we do not know whether Duran was talking to a third person or to Alberu, and, if she was talking to Alberu, whether she knew he was a CIA agent. The FBI special agent sent to Mexico City in the wake of the assassination, Larry Keenan, reports that he heard from the FBI legal attaché, Clark Anderson, that "Silvia Duran was possibly a source of information for Agency or the Bureau."[106] The HSCA learned that the CIA had at least considered recruiting Duran. HSCA investigator Edwin Lopez recalls: "We saw an interesting file on Duran. It said that the CIA was considering using her affair with Carlos Lechuga [Cuban Ambassador to the U.N.] to recruit her."[107] Nevertheless, the *Lopez Report* was inconclusive on the subject of Duran's alleged intelligence ties.

Mexico City station chief Winston Scott wrote about the Lechuga-Duran affair in the manuscript that CIA counterintelligence chief Angleton scarfed up after Scott's death.[108] Strangely, the CIA has redacted Lechuga's name from the spot in the *Lopez Report* that discusses this, even though the Agency released Proenza's statement that the Cubans had "employed" Duran's sexual services to entrap Lechuga (discussed in Chapter Fourteen).[109] It is unclear what the CIA is hiding under this redaction. When this hidden text was shown to David Phillips, he professed surprise and added, "No one let me in on this operation."[110]

Besides Charles Thomas and Luis Alberu, Phillips provides another intriguing episode in the Oswald-Duran sex story. During his interview with the HSCA, Phillips at first claimed ignorance with respect to any CIA interest in Duran. After being surprised by the "operation," Phillips still said he doubted that the station would have "pitched" [tried to recruit] Duran "because the Station could not identify her weaknesses." The *Lopez Report* then indicates this occurred:

> The Committee staff members then told Mr. Phillips about the reporting on file concerning Ms. Duran from one of the Station's [1 entire line redacted]. At one point [name redacted] had reported to his case officer that all that would have to be done to recruit Ms. Duran was to get a blonde, blue-eyed American in bed with her. With this, Mr. Phillips said that it did indeed sound as if the Station had targeted Ms. Duran for recruitment, that the Station's interest had been substantial, and that the weaknesses and means had been identified.[111]

This sequence of denial, professed ignorance, surprise, and then agreement appears contrived. Phillips had served as chief of Cuban operations at the CIA Mexico City station right after Oswald's visit. It strains credibility to think that Phillips would have been unaware of any operation involving Duran or the Cuban Consulate.

The CIA station's chief of Cuban operations, the Agency's ace spy inside the Cuban Embassy, and the embassy's political officer is nevertheless a powerful combination for any story, let alone this one. Alberu's report also included other contextual—and apparently supporting—details. He reported that Duran declared she had cut off all contact with the Cubans since her arrest and interrogation, and that she suspected her phone was tapped by the Mexican police or the CIA. Then something odd occurred at the end of the May 26 report:

> [Redacted] counseled [Alberu] against any further contact with the Durans on the grounds that it might put him under some sort of suspicion either in the eyes of the Mexican police or the Cubans. He pointed out that little or nothing was to be gained from such a contact.[112]

If Alberu had not understood that the truth about Oswald's affair with Duran was not something the CIA wished to hear more about, this directive from Alberu's case officer made that point. But why not look into this matter further?

The HSCA had been given just enough material to suggest that the affair was real. Again, the fact that Duran was working for the Cuban Consulate, when combined with the intelligence reporting that alleged that her sexual services had been used for the Cuban government on a previous occasion, was dynamite. It made it look as if the Cuban government might have been involved in the assassination. In the next chapter we will add to this the story that Oswald threatened to kill Kennedy when he visited the consulate. For now we need to finish placing the pieces we have discussed in this chapter.

In view of the above, the HSCA naturally wanted to look closely at Duran's personality file in the Mexico City station. "This Committee has asked the CIA to make Mrs. Duran's Mexican "P" (personality) file available for review," the *Lopez Report* explained. "The CIA informed the Committee," the report stated, "that there was no "P" file available on Mrs. Duran."[113] This might have been a lie, if the newly released CIA documents are genuine. On one of the documents associated with Charles Thomas is a "P" file number that appears to belong to Silvia Duran.[114]

Finally, we return to Charles Thomas, who upon retiring from the State Department in 1969, again stirred up the Oswald-Duran sex story, this time with Secretary of State William Rogers. "I believe the story merits your attention," Thomas wrote to the secretary. "Since I was the Embassy officer in Mexico who acquired this intelligence information,'' Thomas wrote, ''I feel a responsibility for seeing it through to its final evaluation.''[115] Were Thomas's motives pure? Perhaps. But from the newly released CIA files a new twist has emerged in his story. This particular career Foreign Service officer had been working for the CIA all along—for Branch 4 of the Covert Action Staff.[116]

The anomalies in the story about Oswald's activities in Mexico City that proliferated in CIA channels do seem to fall into a pattern suggesting an extraordinary possibility: The story was invented after the Warren Commission investigation to falsely implicate the Cuban government in the Kennedy assassination. In this regard, the ease with which Lopez convinced Phillips about the sex story now stands out like a beacon. But who was the spider and who was the fly.

And what about Charles Thomas? His previous assignment had been to Haiti, from January 8, 1961 until the ''summer'' of 1963. DeMohrenschildt arrived there on June 2, 1963, and it seems likely that both men were there at the same time. In another interesting coincidence, in the fall of 1969, Thomas became involved in deMohrenschildt's business deals with the Haitian government. This involvement continued after Thomas's retirement. ''I would . . . be interested in knowing,'' Thomas's lawyer wrote in 1970, ''whether you have found a solution to the problem of helping Mr. deMohrenschildt.''[117]

In Mexico City in 1965, however, Charles Thomas was a CIA covert action operative, and a key player in the development of the Oswald-Duran sex story. That story gained credibility in CIA channels in a way that leaves open an unsavory possibility: the story may have been invented after the Warren Commission investigation to falsely implicate the Cuban government in the Kennedy assassination.

Chapter Nineteen

The Smoking File

Within the labyrinth of Oswald's intelligence files at CIA headquarters is a set of papers which, together, demonstrate that the Agency had a keen operational interest in Oswald's activities during the eight weeks before the murder of President Kennedy. The story contained in these documents comes from sources in two different locations: FBI sources in New Orleans and CIA sources in Mexico City. These documents include cable traffic between the CIA and its Mexico City station concerning Oswald's visit there, Agency copies of FBI reports on Oswald received in the fall of 1963, and the CIA's reports to the FBI, State, and Navy.

The extent of interest in Oswald during those fateful final two months was inextricably intertwined with details about Oswald known to the Agency and its Mexico City station at the time. The CIA has doggedly withheld some of these details from public view. A few documents released years ago were suggestive, such as the Kalaris memo discussed in Chapter Eleven. It had mentioned—possibly in violation of this security blanket—October 1963 cables about Oswald's activities in the Cuban Consulate. The Agency has long claimed, falsely, that it did not know of his visits there until after the assassination. As we will see, this story was concocted as a cover to protect the Agency's sources in Mexico City. In addition, newly released documents prove that the CIA was spinning a false yarn about Oswald before the assassination. The Oswald deception cooked up at CIA headquarters began on October, 10, 1963, the day after the CIA station reported his presence in Mexico City.

The interlocking cables, cover sheets, and reports on Oswald that collectively formed his CIA file—from late September to late November 1963—revealed a remarkable change in Oswald's internal record. As Oswald made his way to Mexico, a new data stream collided with his 201 file. That information was the FBI's reporting on Oswald's FPCC activities, a story we dealt with in detail in Chapters Sixteen and Seventeen. It "collided" in the sense that it did not merge with his 201. Instead, the FPCC material effectively knocked aside the 201 file in favor of a new, operational file.

A week after Oswald's departure from Mexico, another data stream on Oswald surfaced in the CIA, this one from the Agency's own surveillance net in Mexico City. Strangely devoid of anything about Cuba or the FPCC, this information *was* merged with Oswald's 201 file. Thus, the two streams were kept in separate compartments—the 201 and 100-300-11 files—and not permitted to touch until the assassination of the president. It is the thesis of this chapter that the connection between these two compartments was known before the assassination, a connection closely held on a "need-to-know" basis. Together they formed the real Oswald file, a set of records that might appropriately be referred to as a "smoking file." On November 22 this file was smoldering in the safes at headquarters: The accused assassin of the president had been involved in very sensitive CIA operations.

The Hidden Compartments in Oswald's CIA Files

Prior to Oswald's trip to Mexico City, information on his activities reached the CIA via FBI, State, and Navy reports.[1] Again, the "routing and record" sheets attached to these reports tell us who read them and when they read them. They show how the collision between Oswald's 201 and his FPCC story altered the destination of incoming FBI reports to a new file with the number 100-300-11.

What did this new number signify? On August 24, 1978, the CIA responded to an HSCA inquiry about Oswald's various CIA file numbers. That response contained this paragraph:

> The file 100-300-011 is entitled "Fair Play for Cuba Committee." It consists of 987 documents dated from 1958 through 1973. All but approximately 20 are third agency (FBI, State, etc.) documents.[2]

(Note: FPCC portion of the above quote classified until 1995).

CIA documents lists show that Hosty's September 10, 1963, report—the first piece of paper associating Oswald with the FPCC—was the catalyst for the diversion of the FBI data stream into 100-300-11.[3] The routing and record sheet attached to this report shows this redirection occurred on the afternoon of September 23. The documents lists show that Hosty's report was also filed in Oswald's CI/SIG soft file and in his security file, OS 351-164, a point to which we will return momentarily.

By traveling to Mexico City and contacting both the Soviet and Cuban consulates there, Oswald inserted himself into the middle of an elaborate complex of espionage and counterespionage. This resulted in message traffic from the Mexico City station that was entered into his 201 file. The bifurcation of the New Orleans and Mexico City data streams into separate locations is fascinating. This is all the more so because the mechanism for this separation, the 100-300-11 file, was set into motion in the hours before Oswald departed for Mexico City, when Hosty's report from Dallas arrived. That seminal report contained the opening move of Oswald's FPCC game, but the routing and record sheet is strangely devoid of any indication that a Cuban affairs (SAS) office read it.[4] The document was read primarily by counterintelligence elements. After this report, three major FBI reports on Oswald, all of them from the New Orleans office, were placed in the 100-300-11 file. After the Kennedy assassination, all four FBI reports reverted into Oswald's 201 file.

What was the purpose behind the separation of the New Orleans and Mexico City data streams? It might have been sloppy CIA accounting. But it might have been more: Could Oswald's trip have been part of a CIA effort at countering the FPCC in foreign countries and "planting deceptive information which might embarrass" the FPCC?[5] The still-classified September 16 CIA memo to the FBI discussing such efforts is the beginning of a suggestive sequence of events.[6] Was it just a coincidence that the next day Oswald and a CIA informant stood next to each other in a line to get Mexican tourist cards? Was the compartmentation of the FBI reporting on Oswald's FPCC activities—which began six days later—related? Were these all random events or were they connected:

TABLE C: Selected Chronology of Events

September 10:	Hosty report [Oswald letter to FPCC]
September 16:	CIA to FBI re ''countering'' FPCC in ''foreign countries''
September 17:	Oswald gets tourist card
September 23:	Hosty report arrives, placed in CIA 100-300-11
September 24:	New Orleans FBI memo [Oswald's FPCC activities]
September 25:	Oswald at Odio's
September 26:	FBI HDQS to New York office re CIA request on FPCC
September 27–October 3:	Oswald in Mexico City
October 2:	The September 24 FBI memo arrives at CIA
October 4:	New York FBI office airtel on upcoming 10/27 ''contact''
October 9:	Mexico City station cable
October 10:	2 headquarters cables

If Oswald's trip was related to an operation, what was the role of the Oswald impostor in Mexico? Was he part of a headquarters operation or part of an unconnected local operation against the Cuban and Soviet consulates? Answers to these questions await the full release of the pertinent documents. In their absence, we can still reconstruct some of this intricate puzzle. In assembling the pieces, it is crucial to properly place the cables between the CIA and its station in Mexico City and the Agency's reporting to the FBI, State, and Navy.

Where were the cables between headquarters and the Mexico City station filed before the assassination? During the 1975 Church Committee investigation, investigators Dan Dwyer and Ed Greissing visited the CIA on November 3 and examined Oswald's 201 file. Their report contained this passage on the comments of Mr. Wall, a member of the CIA's counterintelligence staff:

> Mr. Wall explained that some of the documents now filed in the Oswald 201 were not filed there at the time of the President's

> assassination. Some were located in file 200 (miscellaneous international file); others in file 100 (miscellaneous domestic file); others in the *WH Division files (those generated by the Mexico City station);* and, others in the files reserved for documents with sensitivity indicators[7] [emphasis added].

According to the documents lists, the cables to and from the CIA station in Mexico City, as well as the CIA reports to the FBI and other governmental departments, were also placed in Oswald's 201 file.[8]

From the above, it is apparent that Oswald documents were going to several different locations. Was there anyone who had access to all of them? Again, the 100-300-11 location seems to be the latchkey. Besides those directly involved in Cuban operations, such as the SAS and the Mexico City desk, other CIA elements had been involved with FPCC operations. As previously discussed, Birch O'Neal had written reports about the FPCC for CI/SIG, and in the Security Office James McCord had been connected to counterintelligence operations against the FPCC since at least early 1961.[9] Were either of these offices associated with the special handling of the New Orleans FBI reporting on Oswald?

The answer is yes. One of the two documents lists contains an interesting note in the "Formerly Filed" column for the September 10 Hosty report. It states, "Copy CI/SIG [351 164] 100-300-11."[10] The other documents list has a column with the heading "Location of Original," that has this entry: "CI/SI File 100-300-11."[11] CI/SI was short for CI/SIG, and it appears that the mole-hunting unit was again connected with a key change in Oswald's CIA file designators.[12] Moreover, the association of Oswald's security number (351-164) with the 100-300-11 file denotes a security office tie-in. They had been tracking Oswald all along and now had access to this file too. Thus it appears that it was Angleton's CI/SIG which, in conjunction with the Security Office, had all the pieces to the Oswald puzzle.

Piecing together the story of the government's operations against the FPCC is a puzzle in its own right. The considerable CIA-FBI cooperation at the time of Oswald's trip is noteworthy. On October 2, while Oswald was in Mexico City, FBI agents were searching for him in New Orleans.[13] Six days earlier, FBI headquarters had informed its New York office of the CIA's request for the FPCC's mailing list and "other documents," and directed that office to find out if these materials were "obtainable." Remarkably, on October 4, the New York office responded that an "informant" might be able to provide "both of the above-mentioned items" on October 27. This means that while Oswald was in Mexico City, the FBI—on behalf of the CIA—was planning another break-in into the FPCC offices in New York.

The CIA has not been forthcoming about these operations over the years. The Agency knew about Oswald's FPCC activities before his trip to Mexico and the exchange of information with their station there, yet the Agency blocked an attempt by the Church Committee in 1975 to find out if and to whom such information had been circulated. At the urging of researcher Paul Hoch, the committee asked the CIA whether any information about the FPCC "other than" an October 25, 1963, report (which we will shortly discuss) had been disseminated to "any CIA employees or informants." The Agency's response was misleading at best. "Prior to the assassination," stated the reply, "CIA had no information concerning Oswald's activities in New Orleans beyond this report." This was not true. Perhaps this was another Agency attempt at a technically accurate but tricky and evasive response. If so, the CIA outwitted itself and became vulnerable to the charge of misleading Congress. Earlier New Orleans FBI reports on Oswald's FPCC activities did constitute other information. The record and routing sheets attached to these earlier reports show that they were examined by a variety of CIA counterintelligence, Soviet, and Cuban operations offices.

As we have seen, the real CIA paper trail on Oswald and the FPCC began with the arrival of Hosty's report on September 23. The next report, written on September 24, arrived on October 2, five days before the Mexico City station notified headquarters of Oswald's visit.[14] This FBI report contained the details of most of Oswald's New Orleans FPCC activities—minus the Quigley jailhouse interview. It was in the hands of the SAS counterintelligence office during the crucial exchange of cables between the station and headquarters on October 9–10. It is to those cables that we now turn.

Smoke I: The Six-Foot Balding Oswald

When the Mexico City station did finally decide to inform headquarters about Oswald's presence, it referred to the transcript of an intercepted telephone call. As discussed in Chapter Eighteen, this September 28 call was probably made by an impostor. This is the full text of the Mexico City station cable 6453, sent on October 9:

> 1. Acc [redacted] 1 Oct 63, American Male who spoke broken Russian said his name Lee Oswald (phonetic), stated he at Sovemb on 28 Sept when spoke with consul whom he believed be Valeriy Vladimirovich Kostikov. Subj asked Sov Guard Ivan Obyedkov who answered, if there anything new re telegram to Washington. Obyedkov upon checking said nothing received yet, but request had been sent. 2. Have photos male appears be American entering Sovemb 1216 hours, leaving 1222 on 1 Oct. apparent age 35, athletic build, circa 6 feet, receding hairline, balding top. Wore khakis and sport shirt. Source [redacted]. 3. No local dissem.[15]

The station's description of this man was based on photographic surveillance of his entry and exit from the embassy. He has earned the appellative "mystery man" because his true identity has never been established. Obviously this physical description did not fit Oswald. Most important, the station did not state that the man in the photograph was the man who used Oswald's name. The cable reports only two facts: A man used Oswald's name on the phone, and a six-foot balding man entered the building 12:15 P.M.

It is reasonable to assume that the station thought the photograph might have been of the man using Oswald's name, but the cable deserves credit for not making this connection explicit and for reporting only the facts. The station could not be expected to know whether Oswald was thirty-five, six feet tall, and balding. At headquarters, however, they knew better.

The following day, October 10, at 5:12 P.M., the CIA did something strange. They sent a cable to the FBI, State, and Navy, which *did* connect the call to the photograph:

> On 1 October 1963 a reliable and sensitive source in Mexico reported that an American male, who identified himself as Lee Oswald, contacted the Soviet embassy in Mexico City inquiring

> whether the embassy had received any news concerning a telegram which had been sent to Washington. The American *was described* as approximately 35 years old, with an athletic build, about six feet tall, with receding hairline[16] [emphasis added].

Moreover, the CIA went on to state that it "believed that Oswald may be identical to Lee Henry Oswald," a statement which suggests that the drafter had Oswald's 201 opening sheet close by. On that 1960 document Oswald's name was incorrectly given as "Lee Henry Oswald."

"As I recall," a CIA employee later wrote in the margin of the cable, "this description was of the individual in Helms's affidavit of 7 Aug [1964]. Not Oswald! *WRONG!*" [emphasis on original]. Indeed. But this headquarters cable is more than just wrong. They knew it was wrong when they sent it at 5:12 P.M. The evidence that it was deliberate is rock solid. Just two hours later (7:29 P.M.) the Agency said this in a cable to the station in Mexico: "Oswald is five feet ten inches, one hundred sixty-five pounds, light brown wavy hair, [and] blue eyes."[17] This description proves that the CIA knew Oswald's true physical characteristics and therefore that the cable to the FBI, State, and Navy was deliberately misleading.

It is noteworthy that the headquarters cable to the FBI, State, and Navy slightly edited the bogus Oswald description. It dropped the station's description "balding," but was nevertheless content to report to official Washington that a six-foot man believed to be Lee Henry Oswald had been walking around the Soviet Embassy. Who was responsible for this?

The CIA isn't telling. The drafter's name is still classified.[18] So is the name of the "authenticating officer," who is identified only as CH/WH/R, possibly meaning Chief, Western Hemisphere, Research. The names of the two people with whom it was coordinated are also redacted, but their offices, CI/SIG and SR/CI, along with the fact that their names have been released as coordinators for the associated cable to Mexico, permits us to identify them as Ann Egerter and Stephan Roll respectively. The only CIA name the Agency let remain on the cable was that belonging to the "releasing officer," Jane Roman. We will return to her comments about these cables.

"She took the routine steps of requesting a name trace," the

Lopez Report says of the Mexico City desk person to whom the station's cable was assigned after its arrival in headquarters.[19] Indeed, she considered the cable itself to be "routine." But not for long. The name trace led her to Oswald's 201 file, and the fact that it was restricted to Ann Egerter in Angleton's mole-hunting unit, CI/SIG. Egerter acceded to a request by our nameless Mexico City desk "person" for access to the 201 file. CI/SIG lent the Oswald 201 to the Mexico City desk (WH/3/Mexico) until the Kennedy assassination. So we know that this desk had the 201 files and the cables. What is not clear is whether they had access to the 100-300-11 file.

After examining the 201 file, the nameless woman at the Mexico City desk concluded that the station cable was "very significant." When asked by the HSCA why she changed her mind, this is what she said:

> Any American who had tried to renounce his U.S. citizenship in the Soviet Union now having again a relationship with the Soviet Embassy would lead one to wonder why he had tried to renounce his citizenship in the first place, and why he was still in contact with the Soviets, whether there was a possibility he really was working for the Soviets or what.[20]

Egerter recalled the station cable "caused a lot of excitement" because of "the contact with Kostikov." The CIA denies that they figured out Kostikov's connection to Department 13—which handled assassination for the KGB—until after Kennedy's murder. Perhaps. But at the very least the Agency knew he was KGB. When asked what significance the Agency attached to Kostikov at the time the cable arrived, she responded, "I think we considered him a KGB man." Was there any other reason, the HSCA asked? "He had to be up to something bad," Egerter replied, "to be so anxious to go back to the Soviet Union. At least that is the way I felt."[21]

According to the *Lopez Report,* the "six-foot Oswald" cable to the FBI, State, and Navy and the "five-foot-ten-inch Oswald" cable to Mexico were drafted at the same time. The excitement over the cable from Mexico and the idea that Oswald was up to something bad and in contact with the KGB makes implausible any explanation that this contradiction was inadvertent or trivial. It is reasonable to conclude that the false description of Oswald was a deliberate act. The HSCA wanted to know why. The answers they got were less than convincing.[22] One was the so-called third agency rule, under which the Agency could not disseminate any information obtained from a third agency of the government. However, this did not square with the instruction in the cable to Mexico to disseminate the true description of Oswald to the Navy and FBI. Clearly, if the third agency rule applied to headquarters disseminations to the FBI and State, it also applied to Mexico Station disseminations to the FBI and State.

Another CIA employee tried this: "they had not been sure" that the Oswald reported by Mexico was the same Oswald "on whom they [headquarters] had a file." If so, then why state in the cable that he "probably" was the same Oswald? The person most knowledgeable about Oswald's CIA file, Ann Egerter, signed off on both cables for accuracy. When she was asked to explain the contradiction, Egerter would say only that "she could not say why the description discrepancies occurred." We will return to this issue after examining the cable to Mexico City.

Smoke II: The "Latest HDQS Info" on Oswald

More than Oswald's physical description was different in the two cables. Other distinctions included the content and coordination process. For the cable to the FBI, State, and Navy, Jane Roman was the releasing officer, while for the cable to the station in Mexico, Thomas Karamessines was the releasing officer. Roman worked for the liaison section of Angleton's counterintelligence staff, while Karamessines was the assistant deputy director for Plans (A/DDP), the man next in line after the DDP himself, Richard Helms. Why these differences?

A clue lies in the larger number of organizations that were involved in the coordination of the cable to Mexico. In the space reserved for the authenticating officer, William Hood (a WH division deputy) signed in place of J. C. King, chief of Western Hemisphere Division. Three people were involved in the draft coordination process: Stephan Roll for SR/CI/A (Analysis, Counterintelligence, Soviet Russia Division); Jane Roman for CI Liaison, and Ann Egerter.[23] After their names, John Scelso (possibly a pseudonym), Chief/WH/3, signed on the line at the bottom of the cable.

From the above it is obvious that the coordination process was more extensive for the cable to Mexico than the cable to the FBI, State, and Navy. Why was it necessary to go so high for the releasing authority? The HSCA interviewed several of those involved, and in the *Lopez Report* reported that the "request for further investigation and dissemination" was the reason the Mexico cable was sent to the A/DDP for release. The HSCA based this conclusion on a report written a month after the Kennedy assassination from John Scelso to James Angleton.[24] But during the HSCA's interview with Scelso, he said that the directive to the station to report "follow-up" evidence on an American citizen was the reason for high-level coordination. On the other hand, Scelso also said this to the HSCA: "We could just as well have sent this cable out without Mr. Karamessines releasing it. I do not know why we did it."

Scelso was the first line supervisor above the Mexico City desk responsible for both the cables. He might even have been the drafter. His confusion about the reasons and the necessity (or lack of it) for such high-level coordination strikes one as implausible. According to the *Lopez Report,* the nameless person from the Mexico City desk (referred to above) recalled an entirely different reason for the Karamessines signoff. She said it was sent to the A/DDP because Oswald was important enough to "merit" the A/DDP's attention:

> I can only surmise now that I might have thought or what several of us might have thought at the time, [was] that since it involved somebody of this nature who had tried to renounce his citizenship, who was in the Soviet Union, married to a Soviet, got out with a Soviet wife presumably, which is very strange, and now the contact with the Soviets, we could have a security, a major security problem. This was one way of informing him and getting attention at the higher level.[25]

This woman agreed, however, with Scelso about one thing: It was not necessary to bring the cable to Karamessines's attention in the first place.

To recapitulate, we have heard four possible answers as to why the A/DDP had to sign off on the cable: 1) because of the third agency rule on dissemination, 2) because Oswald was an American citizen, 3) because Oswald presented a major security problem, and 4) it actually was not necessary. Of these four possibilities, the potential security risk posed by Oswald seems the most plausible for going as high as Helms's assistant.

There was an even greater discrepancy between the two October 10 cables. The cable to Mexico City gave a cut-off date for the latest information on Oswald held at headquarters. No such cut-off date was furnished in the cable to the FBI, State, and Navy two hours earlier. The cable to Mexico stated that the "latest HDQS info" was a State Department report dated May 1962. This statement was false. Why was it made?

"CIA Headquarters sent a lengthy cable summary to the Mexico City Station," the Agency reported to the Warren Commission, "of the background information held in the Headquarters' file on Oswald"[26] That statement, too, was false. The cable did not contain a "summary" of the information held at headquarters; rather, it was a summary of information for the thirty-one months leading up to May 1962. No information was included for the eighteen-month period since Oswald's return to America. This period, including FBI interrogations in 1962, Oswald's life in Dallas, and correspondence with the Soviet Embassy and various communist organizations, his move to New Orleans, attempts to found a New Orleans chapter of the FPCC, his altercation with the DRE, his arrest, jailing, and sentencing, were all spelled out in FBI reports that were held in the headquarters file. Yet none of this information was included in the "summary."

From our perspective, there are two problems here. First, it is reasonable to expect that current information should have been included in any summary on Oswald, especially because this cable ordered the station to "keep HDQS advised on any further contacts or positive identification of Oswald." How was the station supposed to investigate further with intelligence a year and a half out of date? The second problem, of course, is that headquarters were all aware of the eighteen months of Oswald's activities since his return.[27]

As previously discussed, Egerter admitted she felt Oswald was up to something "bad" and that she knew he was in contact with a KGB officer in the embassy in Mexico. The reports held at headquarters since Oswald's return to America showed he had been in contact with communist organizations, information that would have been both relevant and useful to any follow-up investigation by the station. Moreover, one of the reports at headquarters concerned Oswald's "contact with the Soviet Embassy since [his] return."[28] Thus there is no question but that the post–May 1962 reports at headquarters contained new and important information that should have accompanied the order to conduct further investigation. Thus the transmission to Mexico stating that the latest information at headquarters was a May 1962 State cable remains a mystery.[29]

In February 1995, *Washington Post* editor Jefferson Morley sent a letter to the CIA in which he asked this question:

> Does the Agency know why Mr. Karamessines told the Mexico City station on October 10, 1963 that the CIA had no information on Oswald since May 1962 when the Agency's records show that it had received three FBI reports on Oswald between May 1962 and October 1963?[30]

The letter notified the CIA that their answer would be used in an article and added that the *Post* wanted to give the CIA "the opportunity to comment on these records." The CIA Public Affairs Office replied the following day:

> The cable referred to in your letter appears to focus only on the status of Oswald's citizenship. As such, it draws on information available from the State Department that bears on the question of citizenship. The cable is not regarded as an attempt to summarize all the information in CIA files on Oswald at the time.[31]

This response seems fatuous in view of the Agency's explanation to the Warren Commission: "a lengthy cable summary . . . of the background information held in the headquarters' file on Oswald."[32]

The Agency's 1995 response to the *Post* is troubling. Such cavalier retorts further undermine public trust and confidence. Of course the cable did not summarize all the information held at headquarters. That was the reason for asking the question in the first place. The Agency's explanation is tricky, legalistic, and evasive. It failed to answer the question asked: Why did headquarters state its latest information was a May 1962 report?

An analogy is useful here. There would be little sense in asking a biologist to write an update on the human fossil record while giving him data only on Homo erectus fossils and leaving out fossils of Homo sapiens. Furthermore, imagine that knowing we had several specimens from the last 100,000 years, we told our biologist that the youngest specimen in our laboratory was over two million years old.

On October 4, Jane Roman read the latest FBI report on Oswald's FPCC activities in New Orleans, an event that was impossible if the October 10 cable to Mexico City—which she coordinated on behalf of CI/Liaison—was true. When recently shown both the cable and the FBI report with her initials, Roman said this: "I'm signing off on something that I know isn't true."[33] Roman's straightforward answer is as noteworthy as the fact that the CIA has released her name on these reports while redacting the names of others. One explanation might be that she was not in on the operation and therefore not in a position to question why the two cables were being drafted with such ridiculous sentences. "The only interpretation I could put on this," Roman says now, "would be that this SAS group would have held all the information on Oswald under their tight control, so if you did a routine check, it wouldn't show up in his 201 file."[34] Roman made this incisive comment without being shown the documents lists that demonstrate that she was right. "I wasn't in on any particular goings-on or hanky-panky as far as the Cuban situation," Roman states. Asked about the significance of the untrue sentence on the "latest headquarters" information, Roman replied: "Well, to me, it's indicative of a keen interest in Oswald, held very closely on a need-to-know basis."

Smoke III: Duran's Damaging Testimony

On December 11, 1963, John Scelso, chief of Western Hemisphere Branch 3,[35] wrote an alarming memo to Richard Helms, deputy director of Plans. In bold handwriting at the top of the memo are the words "not sent." Below this is written "Questions put orally to Mr. Helms. 11 Nov. 63." In smaller handwriting under this are the words "Dec. presumably," reflecting the obvious fact that the Helms oral briefing was December 11, not November 11. Scelso wasted no time in throwing this stone into the pond:

> It looks like the FBI report may even be released to the public. This would compromise our [13 spaces redacted] operations in Mexico, because the Soviets would see that the FBI had advance information on the reason for Oswald's visit to the Soviet Embassy.[36]

How could the FBI have known Oswald's reason in advance? Next to this piece of text was a handwritten clue: "Mr. Helms phoned Mr. Angleton this warning." Perhaps "this morning" was meant, but in either case this may mean that CIA counterintelligence operations were involved.

It is intriguing that anyone in U.S. intelligence would have had advance notice of Oswald's visit to the Soviet Embassy. Evidently the FBI report that was mentioned was worded so that its readers might conclude that the FBI had been the source of information, but from Scelso's report, it is not hard to guess that it was the CIA's operations in Mexico that had yielded "advance information on the reason for Oswald's visit to the Soviet Embassy." But just what exactly does this phrase mean?

Oswald had told the Soviet Consulate in Mexico City that he corresponded with the Soviet Embassy in Washington about returning to the U.S.S.R. As previously discussed, the FBI would have learned of the contents of this correspondence. But this would not have compromised CIA operations in Mexico City. The CIA station monthly operational report for October 1963 did mention Oswald's visit to the Soviet Consulate, and did so under the subtitle "Exploitation of [7 letters redacted] Information." The same seven-letter cryptonym is redacted in the line beneath this subtitle, but the last letter is partially visible, enough to see that it is the letter *Y*. In another CIA document from the Mexico City station the cryptonym LIENVOY has been left in the clear, and it was apparently used for the photo surveillance operation against the Soviet Embassy and Consulate.[37] If this is true, the point of the Scelso memo above might have been this: Publication of the October 9–10 cables would show the telephone intercept had been linked to the photo surveillance, and that since the phone call came first, the cable showed the Agency had advance knowledge of the reason for Oswald's (the impostor) visit to the Soviet Consulate.

It appears that the CIA had advance knowledge about more than

Oswald's October 1 visit to the Soviet Embassy. There is circumstantial evidence that the CIA Mexico City station might have been watching Oswald since his arrival on September 27. This evidence, according to the *Lopez Report,* was the Agency's decision to investigate the transcripts back to September 27, before they had learned of that date through post-assassination investigation:

> This Committee has not been able to determine how the CIA Headquarters knew, on 23 November 1963, that a review of the [redacted] material should begin with the production from 27 September, the day Oswald first appeared at the Soviet *and Cuban Embassies*[38] [emphasis added].

This was an incisive point. So was the direction in which the *Lopez Report* then headed: what headquarters knew about Oswald's visits to the Cuban Consulate.

The CIA had more to worry about than the LIENVOY operation if the October 9–10 cables were published. These cables discussed a transcript from October 1. As we saw in Chapter Eighteen, the Oswald in this conversation was probably an impostor. The real Oswald had decided to abandon his visa request on Saturday and had no reason to call about a response to his request from Washington. As previously discussed, the impostors were apparently unaware of the fact that Oswald had declined to fill out the Soviet visa application. By November 24 the real Oswald was dead and therefore not able to debunk the false transcript. But this transcript was linked to the Saturday transcript by the transcriber himself (Mr. T). That transcript included not only an Oswald impostor but also a Duran impostor. The problem was that Duran was very much alive.

The day after the assassination, the CIA's station in Mexico City sent a note to the Mexican government containing the addresses of Duran, her mother, and her brother, her phone number, place of work, and license plate number, and a request that she be "arrested as soon as possible by Mexican authorities and held incommunicado until she can be questioned on the matter."[39] The Cuban government protested that Duran was "physically mistreated."[40] According to the transcript of the interrogation, Duran told the story about Oswald's visits on Friday, September 27, and stated flatly, "he never called again."[41] Her statement undermined the Saturday transcript wherein she and Oswald were supposed to have placed a call to the Soviet Consulate. Her statement was not repeated in the Warren Report, which stated that after the Friday altercation, ''Oswald contacted the Russian and Cuban Embassies again during his stay in Mexico.''[42] The evidence given for this false statement in the Warren Report is ''confidential information.''[43]

Where did the Warren Commission get this idea? Was it from the September 28 transcript, or was there more? The answer is: The CIA and the Mexican government were the source of this bogus story. The Agency told the Warren Commission that ''we deduce'' that Oswald visited the Cuban Consulate on September 28, but added, ''we cannot be certain of this conclusion.''[44] Moreover, among the exhibits of the Warren Commission twenty-six volumes is a report from the Mexican government. It stated that Duran ''could not recall whether or not Oswald later telephoned her'' at the Consulate.[45]

The contradiction between what Duran actually said—that Oswald never called back—and the above CIA–Mexican government explanation is striking. The Warren Commission did have access to both pieces of information but followed the CIA's ''deduction'' about the events on Saturday. Again we encounter another example of the Warren Commission missing basic pieces, in this case the FBI's record. That version was reflected in a December 3, 1963, FBI memo to A. H. Belmont from W. C. Sullivan. That memo contains this extraordinary passage:

> Duran stated that Oswald returned to the Cuban Consulate at approximately 11:30 a.m. on 9/28/63 [Saturday] and again inquired about obtaining a Cuban transit visa to Russia. Again, Duran stated, Oswald was advised that the issuance of Cuban transit visa to him was contingent upon his first acquiring a Soviet visa. She stated she again on behalf of Oswald telephoned the Soviet establishment, at which time Oswald was requested to present himself in person at the Soviet establishment.[46]

This is a whole-cloth fabrication. Either the FBI crafted it or the Mexicans did. The latter is the more likely of the two, possibly at U.S. insistence. The key evidence, as previously discussed, is the original transcript of the November 23 Duran interrogation.

The very existence of the December 3 FBI document is damaging. Like the Warren Commission, the FBI had access to the real story. The evidence for this is an FBI report from it own representative in Mexico City on the ''Activities of Oswald in Mexico City.''[47] It is undated, but we can guess the time span because it displays awareness of only the first interrogation. Thus this intricate fabrication dates between November 23 and November 27, when Duran was rearrested and interrogated a second time. FBI records reflect that Belmont sent a memo to Deputy Director Tolson the day of the second arrest. That memo said this:

> Assistant Director Sullivan called to advise that CIA has informed us that Mexican authorities have arrested Sylvia [sic] Duran, just as she was about to leave for Cuba. CIA wanted to know if we objected to Mexican authorities interrogating Duran vigorously and exhaustively. We agreed to this interrogation. They will give us the results of the interrogation promptly.[48]

Besides this brutal passage, the memo also repeated the elaborate fabrication made of Duran's first interrogation, in which she talked in detail about Oswald visits after Friday. This sequence of events raises the possibility that this was a cover story, created between the two interrogations, to cover up the penetration operation in Mexico City. The Mexicans had no reason to make up stories about Duran's interrogation. The same was not true for the CIA, whose ''Oswald'' transcripts were threatened by what she was saying.

Duran's testimony to the HSCA was devastating to the authenticity of the Saturday telephone call. (Duran's full name was Silvia Tirado de Duran, and she was addressed as Tirado by the committee.) This is the pertinent part:

CORNWELL: Let's just talk hypothetically for a moment. Is there any chance that he was at the Consulate on more than one day?

TIRADO [Duran]: No. I read yesterday, an article in the *Reader's Digest,* and they say he was at the Consulate on three occasions. He was in Friday, Saturday, and Monday . . . That's not true, that's false.

CORNWELL: All right. Let's try a different hypothetical. If the one in the *Reader's Digest* is definitely wrong, is it possible that he first came in like a Thursday, and then came back on a Friday?

TIRADO: No, because I am positively sure about it. That he came in the same day.[49]

An interesting aspect of Duran's account is how well it does fit with the September 27 calls between the Cuban and Soviet consulates. As discussed in Chapter Eighteen, these two transcripts appear authentic given the recollections of the Soviets, so Duran's statement to the HSCA provides further corroboration for these transcripts.

During the HSCA questioning of Duran by Gary Cornwall, the following exchange took place:

CORNWELL: Is it possible that, in addition to his visits on Friday, he also came back the following day on Saturday morning?

TIRADO [Duran]: No.

CORNWELL: How can you be sure of that?

TIRADO: Because, uh, I told you before, that it was easy to remember, because not all the Americans that came there were married with a Russian woman, they have lived(d) in Russian and uh, we didn't used to fight with those people because of you, they came for going to Cuba, so apparently they were friends, no? So we were nice to them with this man we fight, I mean we had a hard discussion so we didn't want to have anything to do with him.

CORNWELL: Okay. I understand that but I don't understand how that really answers the question. In other words, the question is, what is it about the events that makes you sure that he did not come back on Saturday, and have another conversation with you?

TIRADO: Because I remember the fight. So if he (come) back, I would have remembered.

CORNWELL: Did Azcue work on Saturdays?

TIRADO: Yes, we used to work in the office, but not for public.

CORNWELL: Was there a guard, was there a guard out here at the corner near number seven on your diagram on Saturdays?

TIRADO: Excuse me?

CORNWELL: Was there a doorman out near the area that you marked as number seven, on the diagram?

TIRADO: Yes, but on Saturday he never let people . . .

CORNWELL: Never let people in.

TIRADO: No.

CORNWELL: Not even if they came up to the doorman and didn't speak Spanish? And were very insistent?

TIRADO: No, because they could answer or something. They could ask me for instance, no? by the inter-phone.

CORNWELL: They could do that on a Friday, though.

TIRADO: But what I remember is that Oswald has my telephone number and my name and perhaps he show to the doorman (Spanish).

CORNWELL: When did you give him the telephone number and name?

TIRADO: In the second visit, perhaps.

CORNWELL: Okay.

TIRADO: I used to do that to all the people, so they don't have to come and to bother me. So I used to give the telephone number and my name and say "give me a call next week to see if your visa arrived."

CORNWELL: Well. Are you saying that based on your memory the guard was allowed to bring people in during the five till eight o'clock at night uh, sessions during the week but not on Saturdays?

TIRADO: No.

CORNWELL: Is that correct?

TIRADO: Yes.

CORNWELL: Do you have a distinct recollection with respect to telephone calls to the Russian Consulate, was it just one call or was it more than one call?

TIRADO: Only one.

CORNWELL: Just one.[50]

This was very powerful testimony, which confirmed the story in the September 27 transcripts and raises fatal complications for the September 28 call. As discussed earlier in this chapter, the Warren Commission would say only that it had "confidential information" to back up the extra calls and visits, and published Commission Exhibit 2021, the false version of Duran's Mexican interrogation provided by the Mexican government.

It is noteworthy how such important information known to Duran was apparently not known to the Warren Commission. The CIA did, however, inform the Warren Commission of Duran's claim that Oswald never called back. The Warren Commission chose to ignore it. The HSCA did notice, and Cornwell surfaced the issue for yet a third time with Duran. This is what happened:

CORNWELL: Did you ever see him again, after the argument with Azcue?

TIRADO: No.

CORNWELL: Did you ever talk to him again?

TIRADO: No.
CORNWELL: Not in person nor by telephone.
TIRADO: No, he never call. He could have called when I wasn't there, but I used to get the message, if somebody answer, I used to get a message.[51]

It is difficult not to observe the irony in how an interrogation arranged by the CIA helped blow the cover off one of its operations. In retrospect, Duran's arrest does not appear to have been a smart move.

Not everybody in the CIA thought it was a good idea to arrest Duran. A CIA memo for the record the day after the Kennedy assassination reflects the panic that ensued at headquarters upon Duran's arrest, Written by John Scelso, it states this:

> After receipt of MEXI 7029 at about 1715 on 23 Nov 1963, saying that Mexi was having the Mexicans arrest Silvia Duran, Mr. Karamessines, A/DDP ordered us to phone Mexi and tell them not to do it. We phoned as ordered, against my wishes, and also wrote a FLASH cable which we did not then send. [Win Scott] answered and said it was too late to call off the arrest. He emphasized that the Mexicans had known of the Oswald involvement with Silvia Duran through the same information. He agreed with our request that the arrest be kept secret and that no information be leaked.[52]

According to the *Lopez Report,* after his conversation with Scelso, Scott asked the Mexicans to pass all information from Duran to the Mexico City station and not to inform "any leftist groups." The draft flash cable ordered by Karamessines stated, "Arrest of Silvia Duran is extremely serious matter which could prejudice U.S. freedom of action on entire question of Cuban responsibility."[53]

After Duran's rearrest on November 27 and the Agency's request that Duran be "vigorously and exhaustively" interrogated, the following day headquarters sent a "clarification" to the Mexico City station, "seeking to insure that neither Silvia Duran nor the Cubans would have any basis for believing that the Americans were behind her rearrest. The cable stated: 'We want the Mexican authorities to take the responsibility for the whole affair.' "[54]

There were other changes made to Duran's original interrogation besides the addition of visits after Friday. Her description of Oswald as blond and short was mysteriously ignored by the Warren Report.[55] Likewise for Duran's statement that "the only aid she could give Oswald was advising that he see the Soviet Consul."[56] Perhaps this was changed because it alluded to Oswald asking for some type of aid, a possibility raised by David Phillips discussed in Chapter Eighteen. Had Duran's real statements been included, the *Lopez Report* concludes, "the Warren Commission's conclusions would not have seemed as strong."

Smoke IV: CIA Knowledge of Oswald's Cuban Consulate Visit

Where Oswald's contacts with the Cuban Consulate are concerned, we encounter still more suspect explanations. One of the most interesting details is when the Agency discovered these contacts. "After the assassination of President Kennedy and the arrest of Lee Harvey Oswald, an intensive review of all available sources was undertaken in Mexico City," said the CIA in January 1964, "to determine the purpose of Oswald's visit." It was during this review, the Agency claims, that "it was learned that Oswald had visited the Cuban Consulate in Mexico City" and had spoken with Duran.[57] The documentary underpinning for this claim is the Mexico City cable on October 9 and the October 10 headquarters response. Neither cable mentions an Oswald visit to the Cuban Consulate.

Because the September 27 and 28 calls all involved the Cuban Consulate, the above explanation requires a surprising condition: Headquarters could not have had knowledge of those calls until after the assassination. Ann Goodpasture told the HSCA that Mexico City did not inform headquarters about this visit. The *Lopez Report,* however, contains an interview with yet another "unidentified" CIA person from the CIA Mexico City station. In this case it was a woman, and this is what took place in her question and answer session with the HSCA:

A: I did not send another cable but I know another cable was sent. I didn't send it.

Q: Another cable concerning Oswald was sent?

A: I think so. Where is the whole file? Wasn't there a cable saying he was in touch with the Cuban Embassy?
Q: We have not seen one.
A: I am pretty such [sure] there was.
Q: Did you send that cable?
A: No, I did not send the cable. When I found out about it I remember this, I said how come?
Q: Who did? Do you know?
A: I don't know who sent it. I think Ann (Goodpasture) might have. She might have sent a follow-up one with this information.[58]

If Goodpasture did send such a cable, her statement to Lopez would have had to have been false. Still, the anecdotal evidence is mixed: Some people remembered that headquarters was notified of the Cuban Consulate angle and others remembered that it was not.

Outwardly the Agency has doggedly stuck to its story, staunchly denying any preassassination knowledge of Oswald's visit to the Cuban Consulate. There is a convincing and growing body of evidence that suggests this is a false denial to protect the Agency's sources in Mexico City. We will comment in the final chapter about what is at stake in this strategy. For now we look at the documentary evidence, which is impressive. The Agency personnel with whom these documents are associated are authoritative with respect to the issue at hand: the CIA deputy director for Plans (DDP), the CIA counterintelligence chief, and the CIA Mexico City station chief.

Let us begin with Richard Helms, who was the DDP when he and his subordinates met formally with Lee Rankin and other Warren Commission attorneys on March 12, 1964. The SECRET EYES ONLY Memorandum for the Record of the meeting contains this telltale passage:

> Mr. Helms pointed out that the information on Oswald's visit to the Cuban and Soviet embassies in Mexico City came from [three lines redacted]. Such information is routinely passed to other agencies and entered in CIA files. [two lines redacted]. Thus the information on Oswald was similar to that provided on the other American citizens who might have made contacts of this type. In Oswald's case, it was the combination of visits to both Cuban and Soviet Embassies which caused the Mexico City Station to report this to Headquarters and Oswald's record of defection to the Soviet Union which prompted the Headquarters dissemination.[59]

In Helms's view, it was Oswald's presence in both consulates that caused the event to be reported. Moreover, Helms did not make this statement lightly. He warned Rankin that this information "was extremely sensitive" and the very existence of these [2 to 3 words redacted] had to be very carefully protected.

New documentary evidence emerged on September 18, 1975, when George T. Kalaris, who had replaced Angleton as chief of Counterintelligence, wrote a memo to the executive assistant to the deputy director of Operations (DDO) [formerly DDP] of the CIA, describing the contents of Oswald's 201 file. This is the same memo discussed in Chapter Eleven, in which Kalaris claimed that Oswald's 201 file had been opened, in part, by the Agency's "renewed interest in Oswald brought about by his queries concerning possible reentry into the United States." Kalaris's memo also had this:

> There is also a memorandum dated 16 October 1963 from [redacted, but likely "Win Scott"] COS Mexico City to the United States Ambassador there concerning Oswald's visit to Mexico City and to the Soviet Embassy there in late September–early October 1963. Subsequently there were several Mexico City cables in October 1963 also concerned with Oswald's visit to Mexico City, as well as his visits to the Soviet and Cuban Embassies.[60]

In this case the significance of the Kalaris memo is that it disclosed the existence of preassassination knowledge of Oswald's activities in the Cuban Consulate, and that this had been put into cables in October 1963.[61]

Win Scott's unpublished manuscript backs up the Kalaris memo on Oswald and the Cuban Consulate—and then some. Scott wrote this passage:

> In fact, Lee Harvey Oswald became a person of great interest to us during this 27 September to 2 October, 1963 period. He contacted the Soviet Embassy on at least four occasions, and once went directly from the office of Sra. Sylvia Tirado de Duran, a Mexican employee of the Cuban Consulate, to his friends, the Soviets. During the conversation with the Soviet official, he said, "I was in the Cuban Embassy—and they will not give me a transit visa through Cuba until after I have my Soviet visa."[62]

Literally taken, this would have to be from a transcript the Agency has never released, from an informant inside the Soviet Consulate, or bogus. Scott may have been referring to the Saturday, September 28 call in which the Duran character puts the Oswald character on the line. However, Scott has added the remark about the Cuban visa refusal, whereas the transcript recently released to the public has the memorable discussion about an address.

On the larger issue of when the Agency knew Oswald had been in the Cuban Consulate, Scott's manuscript, *Foul Foe,* contained this indictment of the Warren Commission:

> This contact became important after the Warren Commission Report on the assassination of President Kennedy was published; for on page 777 of that report the erroneous statement was made that it was not known that Oswald had visited the Cuban Embassy until after the assassination!
>
> Every piece of information concerning Lee Harvey Oswald was reported immediately after it was received to: U.S. Ambassador Thomas C. Mann, by memorandum; the FBI Chief in Mexico, by memorandum; and to my headquarters by cable; and included in each and every one of these reports was the conversation Oswald had, so far as it was known. These reports were made on all his contacts with both the Cuban Consulate and with the Soviets.[63]

While Scott pokes fun at the Warren Commission's error, he fails to address whether the CIA withheld this information from the commission. Moreover, neither the Church Committee nor the HSCA was able to get to the bottom of this issue.

For example, the *Lopez Report* turned up data that was suggestive but was unable to use it. Critical of the Mexico City station for rechecking the transcripts and discovering the substantive ones that concerned Oswald and reporting them "in a misleading manner," the *Lopez Report* concluded that Oswald's visit to the Cuban Consulate had been recognized by the Mexico City station shortly after they received the headquarters cable on October 11.[64] Nevertheless, Goodpasture's contention that it was not passed on to headquarters remained a problem:

Q: In fact, headquarters did not know that he had also been to the Cuban Embassy?

A: At that point, no.
Q: At least, according to your recollection, it was not until after the assassination that Headquarters was informed of that fact?
A: That is probably right.[65]

Why was this information not passed along? The answer remains elusive.[66]

''If the cable was sent,'' Lopez concluded, ''it is not in the files made available to the HSCA by the CIA.'' Still, Lopez did not take this to mean that headquarters did not have other means of learning this information. His report contained this thought:

> There is no record that Headquarters had been informed of the 9/27 visits prior to this cable having been sent. It is possible, as some witnesses have suggested, that his information was provided to CIA Headquarters by the FBI in Washington. If that is the case then it merely shifts the question. *This may indicate that CIA Headquarters was aware of the 9/27 visits prior to the assassination*[67] [emphasis added].

However, as discussed above, there are indications that there was another cable from the Mexico City station, probably more than one, which discussed the Cuban Consulate visit.

When shown all of these documents today, former CIA officials are reluctant to defend the old story of no preassassination knowledge of Oswald in the Cuban Consulate. When pressed on this point in a recent interview, former director of Central Intelligence Helms had this to say: [shows Helms the minutes of meeting with Rankin and the Kalaris memo]

NEWMAN: You make the statement in Oswald's case that it was the combination of visits to both places, the Cuban and Soviet Embassy, that caused the station to report it in the first place to headquarters. So the point of asking you to look at both of these documents together is to make clear that there is no mistake here, that they reported this in October because he was in both the Soviet and Cuban places and there were several cables about it afterwards. This is what I would conclude from this.
HELMS: Yes.
NEWMAN: Would you say that's a fair characterization?

HELMS: Sure.

NEWMAN: Again, this is a problem.

HELMS: I don't quite understand. What is your problem?

NEWMAN: The problem is that the Agency never admitted to knowing that he was in the Cuban Consulate until *after* the assassination, *after* 22 November. That is the problem, sir.

HELMS: I think probably the answer is that they didn't want to blow their source.

NEWMAN: Well, that may be and I appreciate candor in this matter.

HELMS: Sure.[68]

Clearly we have a deepening chasm under the Agency's denial that it knew of Oswald's visit to the Cuban Consulate. Denials of preassassination knowledge about Oswald fit the general pattern of missing pieces in the CIA October 9 and 10 cables. There have been some disturbing reports about the lengths to which the Agency went in order to pretend it did not know this information until after the assassination.

"CIA Withheld Data on Oswald, Assassination Panel Report," said a *Los Angeles Times* headline over a story by reporter Norman Kempster. The article contained this passage:

> Chief Counsel Richard A. Sprague said that the committee staff had learned that a CIA message describing Oswald's activities in Mexico to federal agencies such as the FBI had been rewritten to eliminate any mention of his request for Cuban and Soviet visas. The message was sent in October, more than a month before the assassination.[69]

Sprague added, in a press conference, that "it was impossible without more information to know why the CIA had censored its own message." The name of the internal CIA component that drafted this cable to the State, FBI and Navy is still classified.

If Sprague's claims are right, there is no telling how many more levels there are in the story of Oswald and the CIA. This alteration of the cable, if it occurred, would be just one more example to add to those we have already discussed, of how the Cuban details about Oswald's escapades were deliberately excised from key places in the CIA cables while being simultaneously entered into the Agency's "smoking file" on Oswald: 100-300-11. The CIA has released to the public a list of documents from their 100-300-11 file. It has been stripped clean of the Oswald reports that were maintained in it during the eight weeks before the president's murder.

As previously mentioned, one other thing the CIA denies knowing about before the assassination was that Kostikov was KGB department thirteen (assassination). It would be an incredible travesty if the CIA knew that Oswald had been linked to a KGB assassination officer and had failed to inform the FBI, which had been sending the Agency reports on Oswald since 1960. But the fact is that the CIA was withholding its anti-Cuban operations in Mexico City from the FBI.[70] Had the CIA shared all it knew about Oswald in Mexico City with the FBI, John Kennedy might be alive today. That, tragically, was part of the smoke rising from the Oswald files on November 22, 1963.

CHAPTER TWENTY

Conclusion: Beginning

The JFK murder case cannot be truly closed before it has been genuinely opened. It was a tribute to the insanity that has surrounded this subject when, in the fall of 1993, the American national media leveled inordinate praise on a book whose author was attempting to close the case just as the government's files were being opened. That opening was created by the passage of the JFK Records Act in 1992, a law that mandates that the American government must make available all its information on this case.

Three years and two million pages later, there is much that remains closed. Like a huge oil spill, a glut of black "redactions" is still strewn across the pages that have been released. The real opening of this case is in its early stages. But we have finally arrived at the beginning.

For more than three decades the rules for how the case has been presented in the national media were these: The government has the facts, citizens who do not believe the official version of events guess and make mistakes, and the apologists for the official version poke fun at the people who venture their guesses. That game is finished. The rules have changed. The law is now on the side of our right to know as much of the truth about this case as does the government. The only guessing-game left is how much damage to the national psyche has been inflicted in the futile attempt to keep the truth hidden.

The threat to the Constitution posed by the post–World War II evolution of the unbridled power and sometimes lawless conduct of the intelligence agencies is grave. The level of public confidence in American government is now at a crisis stage. The moment that the JFK Records Act was passed in 1992, the Kennedy case became a test for American democracy. It is no longer a matter of whether American institutions were subverted in 1963 and 1964, but whether they can function today.

For this reason, adherents on both sides of the Kennedy assassination debate would do well to keep their eyes on the work of the intelligence agencies and the Review Board. If excuses begin to build, and the exceptions game begins anew, a golden opportunity to reverse this country's slide into cynicism will be lost. The interests of neither side in the debate are served by that outcome. No intelligence source or method can be weighed on the same scale as the trust of the people in their institutions. That this state of distrust has persisted and has been allowed to fester is as tragic as the assassination. It is an unhealed wound on the American body politic.

The purpose of this book is to carry out an examination of the internal records on Oswald in light of the newly released materials. The attempts to resolve the continuing riddles and mysteries of the Oswald files offered here are first impressions. They may change as new information comes to light. It is safe to state now, however, that American intelligence agencies were far more interested in Oswald than the public has been led to believe. Let us review the broad outlines that emerge from our journey through the labyrinth of Oswald's files.

Oswald's Defection to the Soviet Union

Our story has a strange beginning: Oswald's defection, which may have been rehearsed with the help of "unknown" parties, included an explicit threat to give up radar data to the Soviet Union. The dogs did not bark, however, in the United States. Especially at the CIA, where a personality file at headquarters—called a "201" file—should have been opened as a counterintelligence measure, but was not. Fourteen months later, when a 201 was finally opened on Oswald, the Agency's explicit reason for doing so was that he was a defector, a condition that had been explicit from the beginning. Oswald's 1959 defection tripped, not the 201, but the HT/LINGUAL alarm. The CIA's mole-hunters placed Oswald on the supersensitive Lingual Watch List of three hundred persons whose mail was to be secretly opened. Thus the evidence proves that Oswald was of ''particular interest'' to the CIA a year before his 201 file was opened, rendering the concomitant absence of a 201 file a deliberate act, and not an oversight.

This combination of being on the Watch List without a 201 file makes Oswald special. Perhaps not unique, but certainly peculiar. It was as if someone wanted Oswald watched quietly. The Agency component most likely to have an interest in Oswald, the Soviet Russia Division, was not shown any of the State Department, Navy, or other documents pertaining to Oswald in the first half year after his defection. The incoming material went to either Oswald's soft file at CI/SIG, the mole-hunting unit, or into his file 351-164 in the Security Office. The backdrop for this configuration of Oswald's files was the hunt that had been launched as a result of Popov's 1958 tip that the U-2 program had been betrayed by a mole. Popov's subsequent betrayal, and his arrest—ironically, on the day that Oswald arrived in Moscow—was taken as an indication that the mole was inside the Soviet Russia Division.

Even without knowing what we now do about the chronology of Angleton's mole-hunt, the anomalies surrounding Oswald's early CIA files encourage speculation about whether or not U.S. intelligence had a hand in Oswald's defection. In the Lingual files we encounter evidence that a Soviet man in contact with Oswald at the time of his defection, Leo Setyaev, was translating forms concerning defection to the Soviet Union. At the very least, the way in which Oswald-related information was handled was part of an operation to search out the suspect mole. There is limited evidence that suggests that an Agency counterintelligence operation made use of Oswald's defection.

In the FBI, where a conscious decision was made to open a counterintelligence file, something equally strange happened. Oswald's mother tried to wire Oswald money, tripping a ''funds transmitted to Russia'' buzzer in the New York FBI office which triggered an FBI investigation into Oswald in Dallas. Yet the information developed by this probe was not filed in Oswald's counterintelligence file at FBI headquarters, but put into a separate location under a domestic security file. This file cross-references into some earlier espionage files at headquarters, at the Washington field office, and at the New York FBI office.

The ''funds transmitted'' file that produced a major report by

Special Agent Fain in May 1960 was to become the first external document circulated within the Soviet Russia Division at the CIA. This event may have triggered the opening of the Oswald soft file which was maintained in the Soviet Realities section of the Soviet Russia Division. The FBI belatedly turned over the Fain report to the Warren Commission, which published it with the Dallas file number still visible. The current release of FBI files on Oswald thus arouses our curiosity. The 105-976 (Dallas), 100-353496 and 65-28939 (Bureau), 105-6103 and 65-6315 (New York), and 65-1762 (Washington field office) files have not been released to the public. This is not satisfactory. Again, if these documents were released (in almost completely redacted form) as JFK documents in 1978, why are they not still JFK documents in 1994? All of the pertinent sections of these files must be opened. Without them we do not have the full FBI story on Oswald.

Coming Home

If we have learned nothing else about the files on Oswald maintained by the FBI and CIA in the year after his defection, it is how scattered the pieces were. The bifurcation of early Oswald material within the FBI continued into 1961, and there are hints of it up to the spring of 1963. A 201 file at the CIA from the beginning would have united many of the disparate threads on Oswald. Within the Agency, 1960 witnessed the incremental involvement of the Soviet Russia Division, a trend that continued into 1961 and 1962.

Oswald's decision to come home stimulated the paper trail on his activities during the first half of 1961. This trail takes us down several paths at once—some familiar and some new. A channel opened between the Navy Intelligence field office at Algiers, Louisiana, and the Dallas FBI field office. Lateral activity picked up between the FBI field offices in Dallas and New Orleans, and, after an internal struggle, the Washington field office as well.

During the eighteen-month lag between Oswald's decision to return home and his arrival in June 1962, the most sensitive CIA program used to collect information on Oswald, the HT/LINGUAL program, produced the most enigmatic results. The new release of JFK documents in 1993 and 1994 has turned up a better copy of

HT/LINGUAL index card that offers, for the first time, a clear view of a handwritten note that reads: "Delete 15/3/60." This means Oswald was deleted from HT/LINGUAL coverage on March 15, 1960. Oswald's name was thus not on the Watch List when his mother's letter to him was opened by the CIA in July 1961. Stranger still are these two facts: 1) CI/SIG's Ann Egerter put Oswald's name back on the list on August 7, 1961, and 2) the Agency claims it did not discover the July 1961 mail intercept for another year. Putting these pieces together, we have a situation in which the CIA opened Oswald's mail when he was not on the list and then couldn't find the letter after they put him back on the list.

All these apparent anomalies leave one wondering about the competence of the CIA. But more important, we have to start asking where the incompetence factor is a cover to protect sensitive sources.

The FBI was prepared to grill Oswald upon his return to the United States. FBI headquarters directed the Dallas office to "thoroughly" interview Oswald "immediately upon his arrival," to find out if he had been recruited by the KGB or had made any deals with the Soviets in order to obtain their permission to return to the U.S. with his wife and child. Amazingly, the report of the FBI interview with Oswald, after it occurred on June 26, 1962, was not sent to the CIA. This was the moment that the FBI, the Office of Naval Intelligence (ONI), the Immigration and Naturalization Service (INS), and the State Department had all been waiting for, and all got their copies of the interview by special agents Tom Carter and John Fain. The handwritten dissemination list neglected to add CIA.

The CIA missed an important interview. Oswald was arrogant, intemperate, and impatient, and declined to answer many of the questions. The FBI's standing instructions to the interviewing agents covered this possibility: They were to request that Oswald submit to a polygraph, which they did. Oswald refused. Oswald was particularly evasive about his reasons for having defected to the Soviet Union in the first place. In the FBI accounts of the interview he made an angry "show of temper" and engaged in a shouting match with Special Agent Fain, at which point "Fain and Oswald nearly squared off right there in Fain's office."

A second interview in August 1962, Fain claimed, was relatively successful. Significantly, unlike the first interview, this one was sent to the CIA. In the second interview, Oswald lied about his attempt to renounce his U.S. citizenship and affirm allegiance to the Soviet Union, lied about his offer of military information to the Soviets, complained about his travails in returning home with his family, refused to answer why he had gone to the Soviet Union in the first place. He said it was "nobody's business" and that it was for his "own personal reasons." He said, "I went, and I came back!" Thus Oswald provided little new to enable the FBI to determine his motives. He acknowledged but did not answer the question about having different values from those of his mother, still declined to give names of relatives in the U.S.S.R., still denied making any "deals," discounted the idea of Soviet intelligence interest in his activities, and said no one ever attempted to recruit him or elicit any secret information.

Oswald did admit to having been interviewed by the Ministry of Internal Affairs, but nothing in the FBI report of this interview could be considered sufficient to rule out his potential recruitment by the KGB. If we are to believe that the FBI was then or is now satisfied that this interview produced enough data to obviate a possible hostile intelligence connection, the appropriate committees on Capitol Hill may want to ask a few questions. In light of the Aldrich Ames spy case, the CIA might have some friendly advice for the FBI.

FBI director Kelley said this of the second interview: "Oswald, though much more placid this time, still evaded as many questions as he could." But, strangely, Agent Fain and "officials at FBI headquarters" were satisfied that Oswald was not a security risk and, therefore, "recommended that his file be placed in an inactive status." The inactive status lasted from late August through October, when Special Agent John Fain retired and Oswald's file was officially closed, even though information on Oswald's communist mail activities had already begun flowing into it. Strangely, these new additions to Oswald's FBI files did not find a receptive audience, and the FBI simply closed the file. Kelley acknowledges that the FBI knew in July 1962 that Oswald had sought information about Russian newspapers and periodicals from the Soviet Embassy in Washington, D.C., and knew in October that Oswald had "renewed his subscription to the *Worker,* the U.S. Communist Party newspaper." The Oswald case as of October 1962, Kelley says, "was regarded as merely routine, unworthy of any further consideration."

Oswald, a known redefector married to a Soviet citizen, proved contentious and untruthful in a "thorough" interview ordered by FBI headquarters. The FBI agents who conducted the interviews did not believe Oswald's story. The second interview was, at best, inconclusive, and Fain's reasons for not considering Oswald a threat—as described by FBI Director Kelley—took no account of what the FBI had already learned about his mail activities. Moreover, these activities were new, and had taken place since the first interview. Oswald had hidden them during the second interview. At this point Fain could more easily have argued for aggressively pursuing the case. Oswald's performance during the interviews and in the U.S. mail were not "routine." Neither was closing his file.

In October 1962 Hosty was given the assignment of reopening Marina Oswald's file, but his instructions did not allow him to interview her for six months, which meant he was not to contact her until March 1963. So, with Marina's case open and Oswald's case closed, Oswald corresponded with a cavalcade of left wing and communist organizations, while Marina stayed in the house. March 1963 arrived and it was time for Hosty's talk. He had just learned of Oswald's address, but when he arrived, the apartment manager said that the wife-beating Oswald had moved. Hosty now recommended that Oswald's case be reopened. It was, on March 26.

The reason Hosty gave for reopening the file was that Oswald subscribed to a communist newspaper. This is extremely odd. When the Dallas FBI office had previously learned of Oswald's subscription to the same paper, they had closed his file. Moreover, in an act that was beginning to look like a pattern, Hosty decided that the violent Oswald might have caused a situation not conducive to an interview. Therefore, Hosty, "jotted a note in his file to come back in forty-five to sixty days." As we know, by that time Oswald had skipped town to embark upon the perilous journey that would end in his murder as well as the president's seven months later.

Oswald's Cuban Escapades

It was Oswald's Fair Play for Cuba Committee that led to the "smoking file" described in Chapter Nineteen. His FPCC activities set off alarm bells at the FBI and its field offices in Washington, New York, New Orleans, and Dallas, and at the CIA. Both organizations had long been actively involved in operations against the FPCC. Just as the Soviet Realities Branch at the CIA had earlier developed an operational interest in Oswald. It is difficult to proceed with certainty because the public record contains cover stories. All we can say for sure is that the Special Affairs Staff, the location for anti-Cuban operations, was discussing (with the FBI) an operation to discredit the FPCC in a foreign country at the time of Oswald's visit to Mexico, and that the CIA has been denying what it knew about Oswald's Cuban activities ever since.

The record of Oswald's stay in New Orleans, May to September 1963, is replete with mistakes, coincidences, and other anomalies. As Oswald engaged in pro-Castro and anti-Castro activities, the FBI says they lost track of him. The Army was monitoring his activities and says it destroyed their reports. The record of his propaganda operations in New Orleans published by the Warren Commission turned out to have been deliberately falsified. A surprising number the characters in Oswald's New Orleans episode turned out to be informants or contract agents of the CIA. The FBI jailhouse interview with Oswald, which focused on the FPCC, was suppressed until after Oswald returned from Mexico.

The story after Oswald's return from Mexico becomes even murkier. The CIA claims it did not know Oswald had visited the Cuban Consulate in Mexico City until after the assassination. Something else they also claim not to have known until after the assassination was the fact that Kostikov, a Soviet official with whom Oswald spoke during his visit, worked for the KGB assassination department. In pursuing the Cuban Consulate and Kostikov questions, the Review Board may consider using its powers, including its power to subpoena records and witnesses and, if necessary, to grant them immunity (section 7-J of the Records Act). If the CIA did know Kostikov's connection to assassination before November 22, the public needs to know the details. All of them.

What about the Cuban Consulate cover story? Why was it considered so sensitive if the CIA knew, before November 22, that Oswald had visited the consulate in Mexico City? We noted Helms's explanation that it was to cover the Agency's sources there. Was it erected to cover something more troubling that the CIA knew about Oswald? There have long been rumors in the media that during his Cuban Consulate visit Oswald had threatened to kill Kennedy. FBI director Hoover informed the Warren Commission that Castro told this privately to the Bureau's "Solo" source, but this was withheld from the public. Solo's file was released in early 1995 by the National Archives, and there are enough clues in the release to suggest what the research community has long suspected: The Solo source was probably Morris Childs.

The files show that Childs repeated Castro's statement about the Oswald threat to the FBI. Hoover's replacement as FBI director, Clarence Kelley, believed that Oswald made such a threat. In 1987, Kelley wrote about it in his book, in effect declassifying the substance of the Hoover letter. Cuban Consulate employees such as Azcue and Duran claim they heard no such threat, and so it remains a mystery. The question is this: Did the CIA know of an Oswald threat against Kennedy? Castro told Childs that he had received the story from "our diplomats." When was this? Which diplomats? How was it communicated to Havana?

The answers to these questions would help us to find out if, before the assassination, the CIA learned of a threat to the president made by Oswald which it did not pass on to the FBI. This point has to be resolved. It is too important to put off for ten or twenty more years to protect sources and methods. It is also the kind of question that in order for the answers to be believable requires all the documents and all the details. Without exception.

Consider the following claim made by FBI director Kelley:

> It was known at the time by members of the United States intelligence community, including the Central Intelligence Agency headquarters, and the FBI's Soviet espionage section—but not by the Dallas or New Orleans field offices (thus not by Agent Hosty)—that Oswald spoke with Valery Vladimirovitch Kostikov at the Russian Embassy in Mexico City.
>
> The importance of Kostikov cannot be overstated. As Jim Hosty wrote later: "Kostikov was the officer-in-charge for Western Hemisphere terrorist activities—including and especially assassination. In military ranking he would have been a one-star general. As the Russians would say, he was their Line

V man—the most dangerous KGB terrorist assigned to this hemisphere!''[1]

And yet, due to ''the tangle of red tape,'' says Kelley, Hosty did not learn about the Oswald-Kostikov contact until the end of October. Even then Kostikov was identified only as a vice-consul. ''No mention was made of Oswald's visit to the Cuban Embassy. Worse yet, no identification of Kostikov as a high-ranking assassination specialist was given to New Orleans. Or to Agent Hosty.''

Kelley is convinced that during his visit to the Cuban Consulate, Oswald ''definitely offered to kill President Kennedy.'' Although he does not say it explicitly, Kelley seems to be hinting that the CIA knew this and did not inform the FBI. He said the ''Solo'' source on Castro ''verified that Oswald had offered to kill the American President,'' language that suggests that there was another source before Castro's comments. It is time to remove the ambiguity from this discussion. The question is: Did the CIA learn in October 1963 and fail to share with the FBI information indicating that Oswald had met with a KGB assassination specialist and may have threatened to assassinate Kennedy?

That question needs to be answered. We know that when the Protective Research Section of the Secret Service put together their list of dangerous persons in the Dallas–Fort Worth area, Oswald's name was not on it.[2] We need a fuller discussion of why it was not, but such a discussion seems pointless without first putting all the facts on the table. The potential magnitude of the problem and the possible corrective measures that may be indicated are too important to put off until the next century.

The foregoing is only a first look at the internal record of Oswald since the government began releasing files in accordance with the JFK Assassination Records Act. Of the many riddles we have attempted to solve in this book, the Dealey Plaza puzzle is not among them. The author lacks the requisite skills in ballistics, forensic pathology, photo and imagery interpretation, and criminal psychology, to name but a few. We need fewer studies that claim to have all the answers and more that focus on specific areas and are built on firm robust evidentiary foundations. The fact that the public has made several inaccurate guesses does not mean that their suspicions about the Warren Commission conclusions are not justified.

What Does This Do for the Case?

The CIA was far more interested in Oswald than they have ever admitted to publicly. At some time before the Kennedy assassination, the Cuban affairs offices at the CIA developed a keen operational interest in him. Oswald's visit to Mexico City may have had some connection to the CIA or FBI. It appears that the Mexico City station wrapped its own operation around Oswald's consular visits there. Whether or not Oswald understood what was going on is less clear than the probability that something operational was happening in conjunction with his visit.

While we are unclear on the precise reasons for the CIA's pre-assassination withholding of information on Oswald, we have yet to find documentary evidence for an institutional plot in the CIA to murder the president. The facts do not compel such a conclusion. If there had been such a plot, many of the documents we are reading—such as the CIA cables to Mexico City, the FBI, State, and Navy—would never have been created. However, the facts may well fit into other scenarios, such as the "renegade faction" hypothesis. Oswald appears—from the perspective of a potential conspirator with access—to have been a tempting target for involvement because of the sensitivity of his files. It is prudent to remember when speculating about where the argument goes from here that the government and the Review Board have yet to deliver what the Records Act promised: full disclosure.

On the other hand, we can finally say with some authority that the CIA was spawning a web of deception about Oswald weeks before the president's murder, a fact that may have directly contributed to the outcome in Dallas. Is it possible that when Oswald turned up with a rifle on the president's motorcade route, the CIA found itself living in an unthinkable nightmare of its own making?

What Price Secrecy?

It is a shame that protecting sources and methods may have contributed to the president's murder. Each day these secrets are kept from the public only does more harm. Cover stories, deceptions, and penetrations are the kinds of secrets the CIA and FBI will fight hardest to protect. Yet they are clearly the kinds of secrets whose release would signal that the promise of full disclosure has been kept.

We are reading documents that were inappropriately denied to the House of Representative investigation in 1978. Congress created the CIA, and congressional oversight is not possible without access. It is especially wrong for the CIA to withhold information when it is being investigated by Congress.

The issues raised by the past conduct of our intelligence organizations must be discussed openly. Practical, effective solutions must be found. Tangible measures must be devised and implemented that will build reasonable constraints into the system and the public's confidence with them. For example, no federal agency should ever be allowed to obstruct the course of justice in order to protect a source. This issue should not be politicized. It does not belong to the right or the left. It is one of the fundamental ethical issues of the late twentieth century. Do we have any practical means of enforcing compliance with this principle? In fact we do, and it need not cost the taxpayer a penny. We need only to add one question to the polygraph exam.* If we can rationalize using these devices in order to protect intelligence, we can use them to protect the interests of the people.

The story in these pages is a story about how a redefector from the Soviet Union became increasingly embroiled with targets of the CIA and FBI, about how he was used in New Orleans and in Mexico City, and about how, after the Kennedy assassination, history was altered to obscure these links with the president's accused murderer. It raises fundamental constitutional issues. What legal term should we use to describe the action of a government agency when it lies to a presidentially appointed investigation? Obstruction of justice? Can institutions be held accountable if the people who work for them lie to a formal congressional investigation? Is this "perjury"

---

*The polygraph—or lie detector test—is used routinely throughout the intelligence community. Employees are tested regularly (usually every five years) and on an aperiodic (surprise) basis. In addition to questions on counterintelligence, employees should also be asked if they have knowledge of illegal operations or actions which contravene the Constitution.

or "misleading Congress"? These may sound like questions for lawyers, but they are also issues for citizens. What do we do when we discover lies by a government agency thirty or forty years after the act?

The secrecy in which intelligence agencies conduct their operations has the unfavorable effect of insulating abuses from detection. So much time elapses before the facts are declassified that there is little interest left in reforming the aspects of the system that led to the abuse. As early as 1976 Henry Commager observed:

> The fact is that the primary function of governmental secrecy in our time has not been to protect the nation against external enemies, but to deny the American people information essential to the functioning of democracy, to the Congress information essential to the functioning of the legislative branch, and—at times—to the president himself information which he should have to conduct his office.[3]

A different criterion for secrecy—from the perspective of the people's need to function effectively at the ballot box—is needed. That might suggest, for example, that the basic period of classification be reduced to four or eight years, to coincide with the presidential rhythm of the national security apparatus.

Many of the political and social issues that have emerged from the history of the Kennedy assassination as a conspiracy "case" will find their resolution in years to come, when less will be at stake and American academe can discuss them safely. In the short term, there are compelling realities that must be faced. The moment the JFK Records Act was passed, we passed the point of no return. Not releasing the government's files now does more harm than good.

As diverse a people are we Americans are, we are unified by the democratic concepts we share: that ultimate power belongs with the people, and that the government cannot govern without the consent of the governed. For thirty years we have watched aghast as one lie begot another and as one half-baked solution gave way to the next, and our confidence in our institutions slowly dissipated. At the heart of this situation is a relatively new development in American history: the emergence of enormously powerful national intelligence agencies. As Commager so eloquently observed twenty years ago:

> The emergence of intelligence over the past quarter-century as an almost independent branch of the executive, largely immune from either political limitations or legal controls, poses constitutional questions graver than any since the Civil War and Reconstruction. The challenges of that era threatened the integrity and survival of the Union; the challenges of the present crisis threaten the integrity of the Constitution.[4]

The unsavory truth confronting American citizens, just as it confronts the citizens of Russia and China, is this: Unbridled power cannot reform itself. The reform of the intelligence system is something the people, not the intelligence agencies, must control.

Because the Kennedy assassination is but one instance of hiding the truth, the passage of the JFK Records Act and how honestly it works have implications for the government's records in all cases where its acts are questionable in the eyes of the people. The stakes are high, and include nothing less than the credibility of our institutions today. The present generation has the responsibility to hold the government accountable.

Documents

This work is based primarily on documents released since 1992. Some of the documents referred to in the approximately 1,500 footnotes have been included here for convenience. Most are new. Those that are not new are less redacted versions of what was previously in the public record. All are available in the National Archives.

The documents published in this annex are generally arranged in chronological order. Some, however, have been grouped according to a particular subject. There are five such subject categories: American defectors, HT/LINGUAL materials, Fair Play for Cuba Committee handbills and associated literature, CIA Routing and Record sheets, and documents associated with Oswald's September-October 1963 trip to Mexico City.

For more information on documents, photographs, and documentary working aids, write to John Newman, P.O. Box 592, Odenton, Maryland, 21113.

PASSPORT APPLICATION
(See Information for Passport Applicants on page 4)

PASSPORT ISSUED SEP 10 '59 LOS ANGELES PASSPORT AGENCY

PART I—TO BE COMPLETED BY ALL APPLICANTS

(First name) LEE (Middle name) HARVEY (Last name) OSWALD, A CITIZEN OF THE UNITED STATES DO HEREBY APPLY TO THE DEPARTMENT OF STATE FOR A PASSPORT.

DESCRIPTION OF APPLICANT

Height: 5 ft. 11 in. Hair: BROWN Eyes: GREY

Approximate date of departure: 21 SEPT, 1959

Visible distinguishing marks: None

Place of birth: NEW ORLEANS, LA. Date of birth: OCT. 18, 1939

Occupation: SHIPPING EXPORT AGENT

Permanent residence: 3124 WEST 5th ST. FORT WORTH, TEXAS

MAIL PASSPORT TO: MR. LEE H. OSWALD, 3124 WEST 5th ST., FORT WORTH, TEXAS

OSWALD, (Last name) LEE (First name) HARVEY (Middle name) — TO BE PRINTED IN FULL

($11.00 ENCLOSED—FOR PASSPORT AND CLEARANCE FEE)

PERSONS TO BE INCLUDED IN PASSPORT

THIS SECTION TO BE COMPLETED IF WIFE OR HUSBAND IS TO BE INCLUDED IN APPLICANT'S PASSPORT (INCLUDE PHOTOGRAPHIC LIKENESSES IN GROUP PHOTO)

(WIFE'S) (HUSBAND'S) FULL LEGAL NAME

(WIFE'S) (HUSBAND'S) LAST U. S. PASSPORT WAS OBTAINED FROM

LOCATION OF ISSUING OFFICE / DATE OF ISSUANCE / Number: ☐ Submitted herewith ☐ Other disposition (State)

9/9/59

THIS SECTION TO BE COMPLETED IF CHILDREN ARE TO BE INCLUDED IN APPLICANT'S PASSPORT (INCLUDE PHOTOGRAPHIC LIKENESSES IN GROUP PHOTO)

NAME IN FULL / PLACE OF BIRTH (CITY, STATE) / DATE OF BIRTH / RESIDED IN THE U. S. FROM TO

MY LAST PASSPORT WAS OBTAINED FROM: (NOTE: IF INCLUDED IN ANOTHER'S PASSPORT, STATE NAME OF BEARER)

LOCATION OF ISSUING OFFICE / DATE OF ISSUANCE

Number: ☐ Submitted for cancellation ☐ Other disposition (State)

(DO NOT USE THIS SPACE)

Lee H. Oswald

SEP-9-59 000009 LT.ACCTPT

SEP-9-59 000009 LT.ACCTEL

FEE 9 EXEC. ___ TWX 2 POST postal M.O.

COMMISSION EXHIBIT NO. 1114

Father's name: ROBERT E. LEE OSWALD — NEW ORLEANS, LA. ☐ Not U.S. Citizen

Father's date of birth: DEC. 8, 1908 ☑ Father deceased ☐ Father residing at: — Father resided in U.S. From 1908 To DEATH

Mother's name: MARGUERITE C. OSWALD — Mother's place of birth: NEW ORLEANS, LA. ☑ U.S. Citizen ☐ Not U.S. Citizen

Mother's date of birth: JULY 3, 1909 ☐ Mother deceased ☑ Mother residing at: 3124 W 5th FORT WORTH, TEXAS — Mother resided in U.S. From 1909 To THIS DAY

☑ I was never married ☐ I was last married on — DATE OF MARRIAGE — PRESENT FULL LEGAL NAME OF HUSBAND OR WIFE

HUSBAND'S OR WIFE'S PLACE OF BIRTH — HUSBAND'S OR WIFE'S DATE OF BIRTH

☐ Husband or Wife is U. S. Citizen ☐ Husband or Wife is NOT U. S. Citizen ☐ Marriage not terminated ☐ Marriage terminated by (death) (divorce) on — HUSBAND OR WIFE NOW RESIDING AT — DATE.

I HAVE BEEN ABSENT FROM THE U. S. DURING THE PAST 5 YEARS AT THE FOLLOWING PLACES FOR THE PERIODS STATED. (LIST ABSENCES OF MORE THAN 2 MONTHS' DURATION). (IF ADDITIONAL SPACE IS NEEDED A SUPPLEMENTAL SHEET SHOULD BE USED AND ATTACHED.)

PLACE: MILITARY DUTY ONLY — FROM — TO

PROPOSED TRAVEL PLANS

Traveling by organized tour? ☐ Yes ☑ No

Port of departure: NEW ORLEANS — Approximate date of departure: SEPT 21, 1959

Name of ship or airline: GRACE LINES — Number of previous trips abroad within last 12 months: none

Means of transportation: Departure: Ship ☒ Air ☐ Other ☐; Return: Ship ☒ Air ☐ Other ☐

Would you please indicate whether you expect to take another trip abroad in the next: ☑ 1 Year ☐ 2 Years ☐ 4 Years

Purpose of trip: TO ATTEND THE COLLEGE OF A. SCHWEITZER CHUR SWITZERLAND, AND THE UNI. OF TURKU, TURKU FINLAND. TO VISIT ALL OTHER COUNTRIES AS A TOURIST

Proposed length of stay: 4 months

List each country to be visited: CUBA, DOMINICAN REPUBLIC, ENGLAND, FRANCE, SWITZERLAND, GERMANY, FINLAND, RUSSIA

I have not (~~and my wife~~/~~husband~~/~~my children have not~~), since acquiring United States citizenship, been naturalized as a citizen or as citizens of a foreign state; taken an oath or made an affirmation or other formal declaration of allegiance to a foreign state; entered or served in the armed services of a foreign state; accepted or performed the duties of any office, post, or employment under the government of a foreign state or political subdivision thereof; voted in a political election in a foreign state or participated in an election or plebiscite to determine the sovereignty over foreign territory; made a formal renunciation of nationality either in the United States or before a diplomatic or consular officer of the United States in a foreign state; ever sought or claimed the benefits of the nationality of any foreign state; been convicted by a court of competent jurisdiction of committing or of conspiring to commit any act of treason against, or of attempting by force to overthrow, or of bearing arms against the United States; or departed from or remained outside of the jurisdiction of the United States for the purpose of evading or avoiding training and service in the armed services of the United States.

[If any of the above-mentioned acts or conditions have been performed by or apply to the applicant, or to his wife or his children (when included in this application), the portion which applies should be struck out, and a supplementary explanatory statement under oath by the person to whom the portion is applicable should be attached and made a part hereof.]

I solemnly swear that the statements made on all the pages of this application are true and that the photograph attached is a likeness of me and of those people to be included in my passport.

OATH OF ALLEGIANCE

Further, I do solemnly swear that I will support and defend the Constitution of the United States against all enemies, foreign and domestic; that I will bear true faith and allegiance to the same; and that I take this obligation freely, without any mental reservations, or purpose of evasion: So help me God.

Lee H. Oswald
(TO BE SIGNED BY APPLICANT IN PRESENCE OF A CLERK OF COURT OR PASSPORT AGENT)
LEE H. OSWALD

Subscribed and sworn to before me this 4th day of September, 1959.

MCR/Inactive I. D. Card
#N4,271,617 SUBMITTED

L. B. WALLACE
Clerk of the Superior Court
at Santa Ana, California

(SEAL OF COURT) Clerk of the ___ Court at ___

Passport Agent, Department of State, at ___ Deputy.

COMMISSION EXHIBIT NO. 1114—Continued

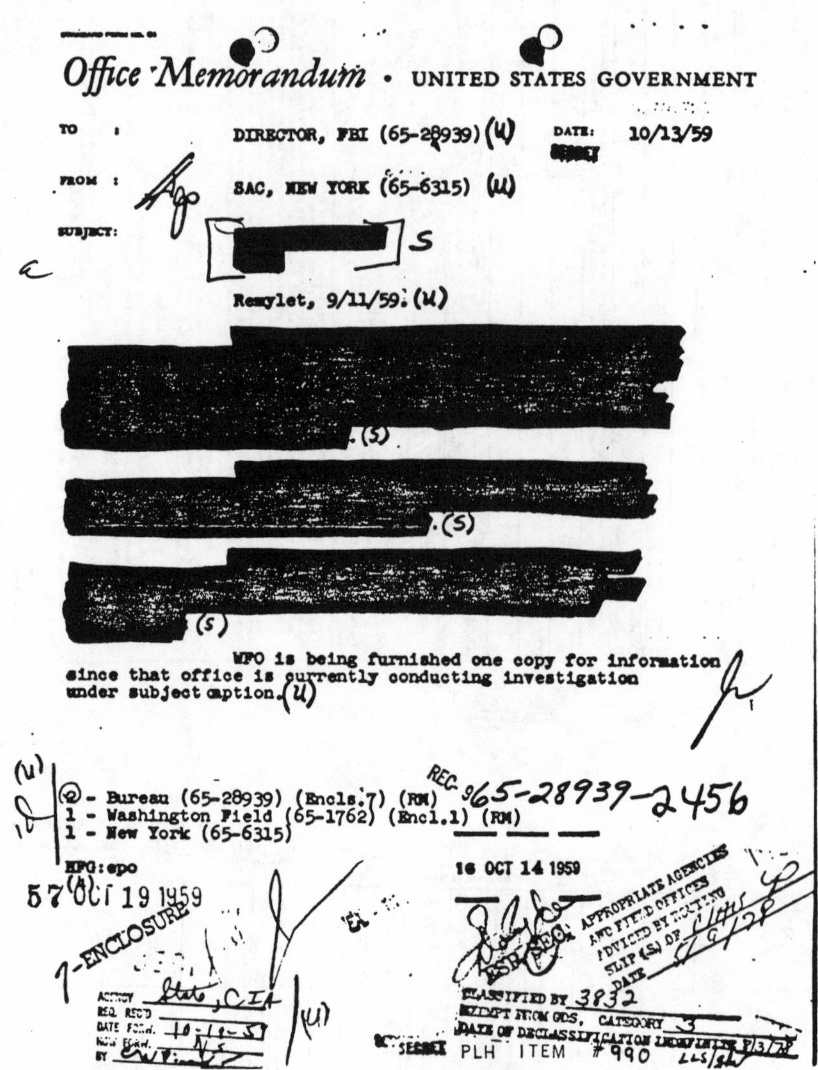

Office Memorandum • UNITED STATES GOVERNMENT

TO : DIRECTOR, FBI (65-28939) (U) DATE: 10/13/59

SECRET

FROM : SAC, NEW YORK (65-6315) (U)

SUBJECT: [redacted] S

Remylet, 9/11/59. (U)

[redacted] .(S)

[redacted] .(S)

[redacted] (S)

WFO is being furnished one copy for information since that office is currently conducting investigation under subject caption. (U)

(U)
2 - Bureau (65-28939) (Encls. 7) (RM)
1 - Washington Field (65-1762) (Encl. 1) (RM)
1 - New York (65-6315)

REC- 9 65-28939-2456

HFG:epo

16 OCT 14 1959

57 OCT 19 1959

7-ENCLOSURE

AGENCY State, CIA
REQ. REC'D
DATE FORW. 10-19-59
HOW FORW. N.S.
BY

APPROPRIATE AGENCIES AND FIELD OFFICES ADVISED BY ROUTING SLIP(S) OF

CLASSIFIED BY 3832
EXEMPT FROM GDS, CATEGORY 3
DATE OF DECLASSIFICATION INDEFINITE

SECRET PLH ITEM #990

The above information was obtained on a highly confidential basis. It is requested that it not be disseminated outside the agencies receiving same without prior reference to this Bureau. (U)

INCOMING TELEGRAM **Department of State** 1 15

35

[classification marking]

Action
PPT
Info
L
H
INR
EUR
P
CU
SEWC
USIA
SCS
SY
DCL
IRC
CIA
OSD
NAVY

Control: 20261
Rec'd: OCTOBER 31, 1959
7:59 A.M.

FROM: MOSCOW

TO: Secretary of State

NO: 1304, OCTOBER 31, 1 P.M.

FOR PO

LEE HARVEY OSWALD, UNMARRIED AGE 20 PP 1733242 ISSUED SEPT 10, 1959 APPEARED AT EMB TODAY TO RENOUNCE AMERICAN CITIZENSHIP, STATED APPLIED IN MOSCOW FOR SOVIET CITIZENSHIP FOLLOWING ENTRY USSR FROM HELSINKI OCT 15. MOTHER'S ADDRESS AND HIS LAST ADDRESS US 4936 COLLINWOOD ST., FORT WORTH TEXAS. SAYS ACTION CONTEMPLATED LAST TWO YEARS. MAIN REASON "I AM MARXIST". ATTITUDE ARROGANT AGGRESSIVE. RECENTLY DISCHARGED MARINE CORPS. SAYS HAS OFFERED SOVIETS ANY INFORMATION HE HAS ACQUIRED AS ENLISTED RADAR OPERATOR.

IN VIEW PETRULLI CASE WE PROPOSE DELAY EXECUTING RENUNCIATION UNTIL SOVIET ACTION KNOWN OR DEPT ADVISES. DESPATCH FOLLOWS. PRESS INFORMED.

FREERS

JR

CIA COPY

CONFIDENTIAL

CD 692 Wash. Post
11-1-59

Ex-Marine Asks Soviet Citizenship

MOSCOW, Oct. 31 (UPI) NR Lee Harvey Oswald, 20, a recently discharged United States Marine from Fort Worth, Tex., disclosed today that he had taken steps to renounce his American citizenship and become a Soviet citizen. He said the reasons for his move were "purely political."

"I will never return to the United States for any reason," Oswald told a reporter in his room at Moscow's Hotel Metropole.

The young Texan declined to give any details on his background or the reasons for his decision. But a U. S. Embassy official said Oswald had told him he arrived in Moscow on Oct. 15 immediately after his discharge from the Marine Corps and had no regular job in the United States.

Oswald was the third American to have sought to renounce his American citizenship and stay in Russia in recent months.

The first, sheetmetal worker Nichols Petrulli, of Valley Stream, N. Y., changed his mind after applying for Soviet citizenship and returned home to Long Island.

The other is Robert Edward Webster, a plastic technician of Cleveland, Ohio, who came to the Soviet Union in connection with the U. S. fair in Moscow this summer.

"I cannot make any statement until after I receive my Soviet citizenship," Oswald said. "It might jeopardize my position—I mean the Soviet authorities might not want me to say anything."

The U. S. Embassy official said that he had advised Oswald to wait for the Soviet reply to his application for citizenship before giving up his American passport. He said Oswald would retain his full U. S. citizenship until he formally signed a document of renunciation and before he officially accepted Soviet citizenship.

[Oswald's mother, who lives in Forth Worth, could not be reached for comment, the Associated Press said.

[His sister-in-law in Fort Worth said: "He said he wanted to travel a lot and talked about going to Cuba."

[An acquaintance said Oswald was a youth who would rather stay in his room than make friends. She said Oswald seemed to be intelligent but showed little inclination for attending high school.]

Document Number 591-252A

for FOIA Review on JUN 1976

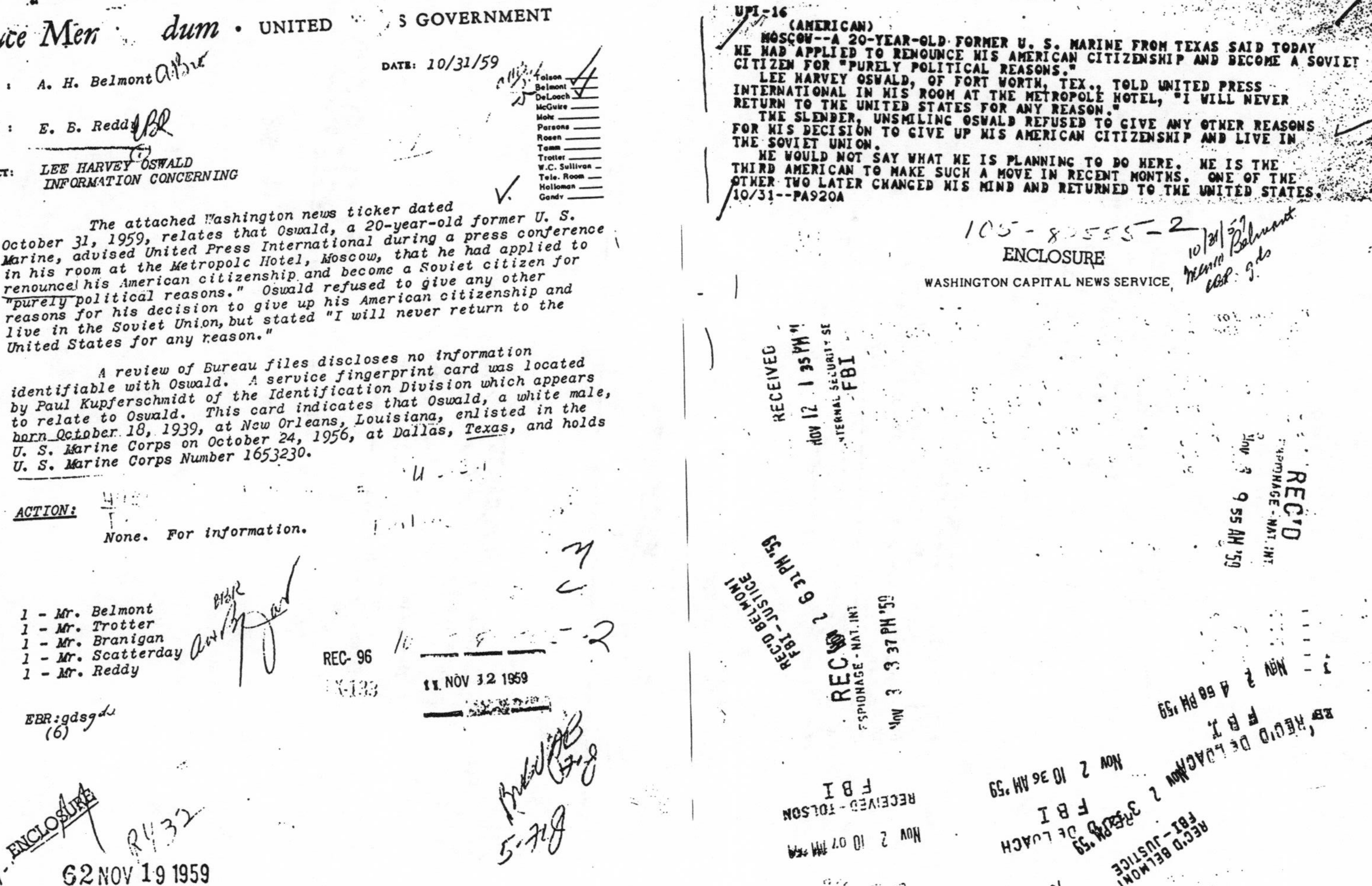

...ice Memorandum • UNITED STATES GOVERNMENT

TO : A. H. Belmont

FROM : E. B. Reddy

SUBJECT: LEE HARVEY OSWALD
INFORMATION CONCERNING

DATE: 10/31/59

Tolson
Belmont
DeLoach
McGuire
Mohr
Parsons
Rosen
Tamm
Trotter
W.C. Sullivan
Tele. Room
Holloman
Gandy

The attached Washington news ticker dated October 31, 1959, relates that Oswald, a 20-year-old former U. S. Marine, advised United Press International during a press conference in his room at the Metropolc Hotel, Moscow, that he had applied to renounce his American citizenship and become a Soviet citizen for "purely political reasons." Oswald refused to give any other reasons for his decision to give up his American citizenship and live in the Soviet Union, but stated "I will never return to the United States for any reason."

A review of Bureau files discloses no information identifiable with Oswald. A service fingerprint card was located by Paul Kupferschmidt of the Identification Division which appears to relate to Oswald. This card indicates that Oswald, a white male, born October 18, 1939, at New Orleans, Louisiana, enlisted in the U. S. Marine Corps on October 24, 1956, at Dallas, Texas, and holds U. S. Marine Corps Number 1653230.

ACTION:

None. For information.

1 - Mr. Belmont
1 - Mr. Trotter
1 - Mr. Branigan
1 - Mr. Scatterday
1 - Mr. Reddy

EBR:gds
(6)

REC- 96

11 NOV 12 1959

ENCLOSURE

62 NOV 19 1959

UPI-16

(AMERICAN)

MOSCOW--A 20-YEAR-OLD FORMER U. S. MARINE FROM TEXAS SAID TODAY HE HAD APPLIED TO RENOUNCE HIS AMERICAN CITIZENSHIP AND BECOME A SOVIET CITIZEN FOR "PURELY POLITICAL REASONS."

LEE HARVEY OSWALD, OF FORT WORTH, TEX., TOLD UNITED PRESS INTERNATIONAL IN HIS ROOM AT THE METROPOLE HOTEL, "I WILL NEVER RETURN TO THE UNITED STATES FOR ANY REASON."

THE SLENDER, UNSMILING OSWALD REFUSED TO GIVE ANY OTHER REASONS FOR HIS DECISION TO GIVE UP HIS AMERICAN CITIZENSHIP AND LIVE IN THE SOVIET UNION.

HE WOULD NOT SAY WHAT HE IS PLANNING TO DO HERE. HE IS THE THIRD AMERICAN TO MAKE SUCH A MOVE IN RECENT MONTHS. ONE OF THE OTHER TWO LATER CHANGED HIS MIND AND RETURNED TO THE UNITED STATES.

10/31--PA920A

105-82555-2

ENCLOSURE

WASHINGTON CAPITAL NEWS SERVICE

RECEIVED
NOV 12 1 35 PM '59
INTERNAL SECURITY SE
FBI

REC'D
ESPIONAGE - NAT. INT.
NOV 3 9 55 AM '59

REC'D BELMONT
FBI - JUSTICE
NOV 2 6 31 PM '59

REC'D
ESPIONAGE - NAT. INT.
NOV 3 3 37 PM '59

REC'D DE LOACH
FBI
NOV 2 4 50 PM '59

RECEIVED - TOLSON
FBI
NOV 2 10 07 PM '59

NOV 2 10 36 AM '59

REC'D DE LOACH
FBI
NOV 2 3 ... PM '59

REC'D BELMONT
FBI - JUSTICE

This document has been approved for release through the HISTORICAL REVIEW PROGRAM of the Central Intelligence Agency.

Date 8 MAY 92

HRP 92-5

OSWALD, Lee Harvey

Mr. Papich would like to know what we know about this ex-Marine who recently defected in the USSR. 2 Nov. 1959

Mr. Papich was advised that we had no info on subject. 4 Nov. 59

CLASSIFICATION CANCELED
By authority of: C. . ., 12/22/72

Name and title of person making the change

Date 1/11/73

Document Number 592-252 B

for FOIA Review on JUN 1976

'94

Goodbye

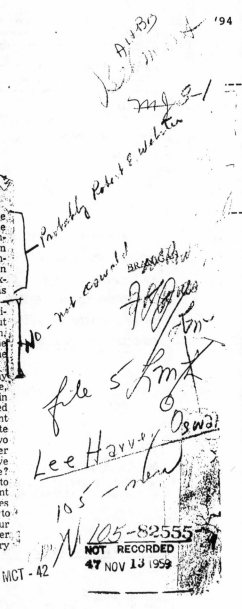

Another American citizen has gone over to the Soviet Union—this time hook line and sinker. He was employed at the American exhibit in Moscow, fell in love with the country—or at least one pretty citizen thereof, according to one of his ex-co-workers—and applied for and was granted Soviet citizenship.

In another similar case, an American applied for Soviet citizenship but before action could be taken, recanted his renunciation of the U. S. and was premitted to come home and be a good boy again.

As far as we are concerned any American citizen, male or female, who renounces his citizenship in favor of the Soviet Union, is entitled to the protection of this government in two particulars only. The State Department should ask him two questions: Was he drunk or sober when he did it? Did he seem to have all his marbles with him at the time?

Having settled these questions to its own satisfaction, the government and people of the United States should wave him goodbye and see to it that his name is wiped off our national books forever, and he never be allowed to set foot in this country again, dead or alive.

Probably Robert E. Webster

NO - not coward

file

Lee Harvey Oswald

105 -

105-82555

NOT RECORDED
47 NOV 13 1959

MCT - 42

THE CORPUS CHRISTI TIMES
10/23/59
Corpus Christi, Texas
ROBERT M. JACKSON, Editor
HOUSTON DIVISION

NOV 17 1959

NAVAL MESSAGE — NAVY DEPARTMENT

RELEASED BY	DRAFTED BY	EXT NR	COPY NR.

DATE	TOR	ROUTED BY	CHECKED BY
3 NOVEMBER 59	1704Z/3 NOV 59	HAMNER	RE/HEDIGER

2090 — NO

031215Z NOVEMBER 59 (DATE/TIME GROUP (GCT))

Sov files

FROM: ALUSNA MOSCOW

TO: CNO

W & W

INFO:

PRECEDENCE (ACT) (INFO): FLASH, EMERGENCY, OPERATIONAL IMMEDIATE, PRIORITY, ROUTINE RRR, DEFERRED

ATTENTION INVITED TO AMEMB MOSCOW DISPATCHES 234 DTD 2 NOVEMBER AND 224 DTD 26 OCTOBER CONCERNING THE RENUNCIATION OF US CITIZENSHIP AND REQUEST FOR SOVIET CITIZENSHIP BY LEE HARVEY OSWALD FORMER MARINE AND ROBERT EDWARD WEBSTER 7917938 FORMER NAVY. OSWALD STATED HE WAS RADAR OPERATOR IN MARCORPS AND HAS OFFERED TO FURNISH SOVIETS INFO HE POSSESSES ON US RADAR.

CIA COPY

THE C.I.A. HAS NO OBJECTION TO THE DECLASSIFICATION OF THIS DOCUMENT.

92....ACT

06..60..61..63..IP..BFR..FLAGPLOT..

ADD:FBI..STATE..CIA..CMC..Ø9M..IMMIGRATION NATURALIZATION SERVICE
PER:92 11/Ø4/59/EW/

Declassified
Authority: Ltr of President to AG 11/23/64 (29 FR 15893)
By MMJ NARS 7/28/78

REPRODUCTION OF THIS DOCUMENT IN WHOLE OR IN PART IS PROHIBITED EXCEPT WITH PERMISSION OF THE ISSUING OFFICE.

~~CONFIDENTIAL~~
(When filled in)

OPNAV FORM-2110-4
(REV. 1-58)
DEPT. USE ONLY

031215Z NOVEMBER — DTG — PAGE 1 OF 1

A — Paraphrase not required except prior to Category "B" encryption. Physically remove all internal references by date-time group prior to declassification.

ENCL 92 to DST 11705 — 201-289248

Office Memorandum • UNITED STATES GOVERNMENT

TO : A. H. Belmont

FROM : W. A. Branigan

DATE: November 4, 1959

SUBJECT: LEE HARVEY OSWALD
IS - R

Tolson ___ Belmont ___ DeLoach ___ McGuire ___ Mohr ___ Parsons ___ Rosen ___ Tamm ___ Trotter ___ W.C. Sullivan ___ Tele. Room ___ Holloman ___ Gandy ___

The "Washington Capital News Service" dated 10/31/59, announced that subject, a 20-year-old former United States Marine, advised the United Press International during a press conference in his room, Metropole Hotel, Moscow, that he had applied to renounce his American citizenship and become a Soviet citizen for "purely political reasons." He refused to give any other reasons for his decision but stated "I will never return to the United States for any reason."

State Department telegram from Moscow dated 10/31/59, advised that subject is age 20, unmarried, who was issued U. S. passport on 9/10/59, appeared at the American Embassy that date to renounce his U. S. citizenship, stating he applied in Moscow for Soviet citizenship following his entry into Russia from Finland on 10/15/59. Subject advised the Embassy that he contemplated taking this action for the last two years; that the main reason for his action was "I am a Marxist." His attitude was described as arrogant and aggressive. Subject was described as having recently been discharged from the U. S. Marine Corps, and he has said that he has offered the Soviets any information he has acquired as enlisted radar operator. Subject's mother's address and his last home address in the U. S. was given as 4936 Collinwood Street, Fort Worth, Texas. The American Embassy in Moscow proposes delaying executing subject's renunciation of his U. S. citizenship until Soviet action is known or until advice is received from the State Department.

Bureau files contain no information identifiable with subject. Service fingerprint card in the Identification Division which appears to relate to subject shows that he is a white male born 10/18/39, at New Orleans, Louisiana, and he enlisted in the U. S. Marine Corps on 10/24/56, at Dallas, Texas, and that he holds U. S. Marine Corps number 1653230.

105-82555-3

FLJ:mst:njc
(5)
1 - Belmont
1 - Branigan
1 - De Loach
1 - Jones

REC-96 EX-133

11 NOV 12 1959

62 NOV 19 1959

53 NOV 30 1959

ONI COPY

3(8)

Memorandum Branigan to Belmont
Re: LEE HARVEY OSWALD

On 11/2/59, it was determined through Liaison with the Navy Department that the files of ONI contained no record of subject. However, subject's record at the headquarters with the U. S. Marine Corps shows the following: He was born 10/18/39, at New Orleans, Louisiana, and entered the U. S. Marine Corps at Dallas, Texas, on 10/24/56, to serve for three years. He was released to inactive duty at El Toro, California on 9/11/59, and has obligated service until 12/8/62. He speaks, reads, and writes Russian very poorly. While in the service of the U. S. Marine Corps he attended the Aviation Fundamental School and completed the Aircraft Control and Warning Operators' Course. He was released from active duty because his mother depended upon him for support. Serial #1653230.

Undesirable discharge from Marines. See serial 17. FLJ

ONI advised that they contemplated taking no action in this matter. No derogatory information was found in the files of the U. S. Marine Corps concerning subject, and there is no indication of any Soviet contacts involving subject.

RECOMMENDATION:

Since subject's defection is known to Department of the Navy, and since subject apparently has no knowledge of any strategic information which would be of benefit to the Soviets, it does not appear that any action is warranted by the Bureau in this matter.

It is recommended however, that this memo be referred to the Identification Division so subject's service fingerprints can be placed in the criminal files and that a stop be placed against the prints to prevent subject's entering the U. S. under any name. Espionage Section should be advised if subject again enters the U. S.

FLJ

- 2 -

3(8)

1124

NAVAL MESSAGE — **NAVY DEPARTMENT**

RELEASED BY	DRAFTED BY	EXT NR	COPY NR.
CAPT F. R. KLAVENESS, USN	LT D. E. SIGSWORTH, USN Op-921E	75711	5
DATE	**TOR**	**ROUTED BY**	**CHECKED BY**
4 November 1959	04/1550Z NOV 59	Drafter	M/HEDIGER

22257

041529Z NOV 59
(DATE/TIME GROUP (GCT))

SOV file

W & R Webster

PRECEDENCE (ACT) (INFO): FLASH; EMERGENCY; OPERATIONAL IMMEDIATE; PRIORITY; RRRRRRRRRR; DEFERRED

FROM: CNO

TO: ALUSNA MOSCOW

INFO:

Your 031215Z. WEBSTER discharged from USN in 1951 and has no present naval status. OSWALD is PFC Inactive Marine Corps Reserve with obligated service until 8 December 1962. OSWALD attended Aircraft Control and Warning Operator Course in 1957. Served with Marine Air Control Squadrons in Japan and Taiwan with duties involving ground control intercept. Job description code indicates he is aviation electronics operator. No record of clearance at HQ, Marine Corps but possibility exists he may have had access to CONFIDENTIAL info. OSWALDS service number 1653230, DOB 18 October 1939 at New Orleans, released to inactive duty 11 September 1959, home of record 4936 Collinwood Street, Fort Worth, Texas. Has brother, John Edward PIC, 11313239 on active duty in USAF. Request significant developments in view of continuing interest of HQ, Marine Corps and U. S. intelligence agencies.

"INTELLIGENCE MATTER"

CIA COPY

Drafter: Op-92 (921E)

Dist: 06...60...61...63...09...09M...IP...BFR..
FBI...CIA...I&NS...OSI/USAF...ACSI/ARMY

~~CONFIDENTIAL~~
(When filled in)

OPNAV FORM-2110-4
(REV. 1-58)
DEPT. USE ONLY

041529Z NOV 59 — Page 1 of 1
DTG

A — Paraphrase not required except prior to Category "B" encryption. Physically remove all internal references by date-time group prior to declassification.

ENCL 98 to DST 1120... CS COPY 201-289248

ROUTING

TO:	NAME AND ADDRESS	DATE	INITIALS
1	Scott Breckenridge, OLC		
2	6D15, Hqs.		
3			
4			

ACTION	DIRECT REPLY	PREPARE REPLY
APPROVAL	DISPATCH	RECOMMENDATION
COMMENT	FILE	RETURN
CONCURRENCE	INFORMATION	SIGNATURE

REMARKS:

FROM: NAME, ADDRESS, AND PHONE NO.	DATE
AEO/DDS&T, 6E60, Hqs., x6561	

Top Secret

(Security Classification)

CONTROL NO. SC-01836-78
Copy 1

Handle Via

COMINT

Channels

Access to this document will be restricted to those approved for the following specific activities:

Warning Notice

Sensitive Intelligence Sources and Methods Involved

NATIONAL SECURITY INFORMATION

Unauthorized Disclosure Subject to Criminal Sanctions

Top Secret

(Security Classification)
E2 IMPDET

Attachment To:
SC-01836-78

SUBJECT: DDS&T Interim Reply to HSCA Request, 8 May 78, OLC 78-1573

General Background: Detachment C advance party of security and communication personnel departed the U.S. for Atsugi, Japan, on 20 February 1957, the second echelon of administrative personnel departed 4 March, and the main body of the detachment with two U-2 aircraft and equipment began deployment on 15 March. On 29 March Headquarters was notified that all personnel and equipment were on base. Operational readiness was forecast for the week of 8 April. Operating procedures and liaison had been accomplished with the following major U.S. components:

Far East Air Force
Far East Command and Theater Commander
Agency's [ ] and local support unit
54th Weather Reconnaissance Squadron
Atsugi Naval Air Station

Details or specific operating agreements or procedures with the above components have not been located.

[ ] Attached are copies of the Soviet Aide Memoires of 5 March and 21 April 1958 (Tab A).

The Detachment continued to perform [ ] and all personnel and other equipment cleared the base and turned the facilities back to the Navy on 19 August 1960.

TOP SECRET [ ]

TOP SECRET -

During the deployment of

1. Any and all information pertaining to the take-offs and landings of the U-2 at Atsugi, Japan, limited to the years 1959 through 1962.

We have been unable to locate files which would contain logs of all take-offs and landings of the U-2 aircraft

2. Any and all information concerning the radar procedures, facilities, and staff involved with the U-2 flights at Atsugi, Japan, limited to the years 1959 through 1962.

As stated in the General Background above we have not located details or specific operating procedures or agreements with the local Navy base at Atsugi.

3. Any and all information pertaining to contact between Marine Air Control Squadron #1, Air Group II, 1st Marine Wing, and U-2 personnel at Atsugi, Japan, including but not limited to housing, recreational, and eating facilities - limited to the years 1959 through 1962.

We have not identified any relationship between Detachment C and Marine Air Control Squadron #1. On the subject of housing, we have noted that late in 1957 families were permitted at Detachment C and as a result housing was provided in the compound assigned to the Agency Support Unit and ten houses were rented on the local market.

4. Any and all information pertaining to defectors with knowledge of the U-2 program.

The DDS&T has not located any information pertaining to defectors. We defer this request to the DDO.

- 2 -

TOP SECRET -

TOP SECRET - EIDER - CHESS

5. Any and all information within the U-2 program file pertaining to defectors with knowledge of the U-2 program.

See above.

6. Any and all information concerning Soviet knowledge of the U-2 program previous to May 1, 1960.

Attached is an extract from a report dated 3 March 1958

Also attached is a copy of the Soviet protest note of 10 July 1956 concerning Mission 2013

- 3 -

IX - 11

Commission Exhibit No. 942

NOTE FOR OSWALD FILE

Nov. 9, 1959

I took a typed copy of the message from Pic down to the Metropole Hotel today to deliver to Oswald. I went directly to the room (233) and knocked several times, but no one answered. The cleaning lady told me that he was in the room and only came out to go to the toilet. She suggested that I ask the dojornay in charge of the floor. The latter told me that he was not in his room. I decided not to leave the message, but to have it sent by registered mail. On the way out I phoned from downstairs, but no answer.

McV

WC Vol XVIII: p-156

OFFI CIAL USE ONLY

MEMO FOR THE FILES

Nov. 17, 1959

Pricilla Johnson of NANA aksed me today about Oswald. I gave her a general run down of the outlines of the case as I knew they were known to the public, suggesting that she also check with Korengold for any factual details I might have omitted and which were already generally known.

She told me that on Sunday, May 15, she had spent several hours talking with Oswald and that she had left it with him that she was available if he wanted somebody to talk to again.

Her general impression of Oswald was the same as ours has been. His naiévete about what he can expect here is balanced by a rather carefully worked out set of answers and a careful reserve about saying things he feels he shouldn't. He made one interesting comment to her to the effect that he had never in all his life talked to anyone so long about himself. (2+ hours) She remarked that although he used long words and seemed in some ways well read, he often used wrods incorrectly, as though he had learned them from a dictionary. He told her that his Soviet citizenship was still under consideration, but that the Soviets had already assured him that he could stay here as a resident alien if he so desired. They are also looking into the possibility of getting him into a school. He said that in any case he would never return to the United States. He also said that he had had a dependency discharge fbom the Marines to care for his mother, but had come right here instead. He said that his reason for taking this step was that he had seen imperialism in action against minority groups; to wit, Communists, negros, and workers. Miss Johnson asked him whether it had occured to him

Encl 5 DST 11705 CS COPY 201-289248

to desert from the Marines, since he had apparently intenzded so extreme a step as this anyway. He said that he did not wish to do anything "illegal". It was herx opinion that he might have been consciously or not trying to leave a loophole for himslef. Along this line zhe had also told her that he did not yet intend to come back to the Embassy, He seemed very much annoyed at the Embassy for having prevented him from formally giving up his citizenship.

Miss Johnson was particularly interested in picking me up on what she called a discrepancy in his statement: at different times he had said that the Embassy had not allowed him to give up his citizenship because it had been too busy and again on another occasion because we could not do it until he had heard from the Soviets about their decision. I explained that the law required that we not withhold the right to give up citizenship, but that the regulations and common sense also required that we taxxx be sure that someone was not going to take any such serious step without due consideration and understanding of what he was about. I said that we had duly informed Oswald that he had a right to come in and give up his citizenship.

I also pointed out to Miss Johnson that there was a thin line somewhere between her duty as a correspondent and as an American. I mantioned Mr. Korengold as a man who seemed to have known this difference pretty well. I said that if someone could persuade Oswald at least to delay before taking the final plunge on his American citizenship, or for that matter Soviet citship, they would be doing him a favor and doubtless xxyxx the USA as well. She seemed to understand this point. I beleive that she is going to try and write a story on what prompts a mazn to do such a thing.

OFFICIAL USE ONLY

PS (11/19/59) Priscilla J. told me since:that O. has been told he will be leavir the hotel at the end of this week;that he will be trained in electronics; that she has asked him to keep in touch with her; that he has showed some slight signs of disillusionment with the SU, but that his "hate" for the US remains XXXX strong although she cannot fathom the reason.

McV

CS COPY

CF: 17 M 719

SPEEDLETTER

USE FOR URGENT LETTERS ONLY

DO NOT CLEAR THROUGH COMMUNICATION OFFICE

(One box must be checked)

☐ ORDINARY MAIL ☐ SPECIAL DELIVERY ☐ AIR MAIL ☐ REGISTERED MAIL

CLASSIFICATION: ~~FOR OFFICIAL USE ONLY~~

IN REPLY REFER TO: DK-MPV

DATE: 8 MARCH 1960

TO: COMMANDER
MARINE AIR RESERVE TRAINING COMMAND
NAVAL AIR STATION
GLENVIEW, ILLINOIS

(Fold)

NAVAL SPEEDLETTER
Permits dispatch or informal language.
May be sent (1) with enclosures, (2) in a window envelope (size 8¾" x 3⅞"), if contents are not classified as confidential or higher, (3) to both naval and nonnaval activities.
Is packaged 500 sheets of white or of one color: yellow, pink, or green.

ARRANGEMENTS BEING MADE WITH A FEDERAL INVEST AGENCY TO FURNISH YOU WITH RPT WHICH RELATES TO PFC LEE HARVEY OSWALD 1653230 USMCR INACT CMM A MEMBER OF YOUR COMD X UPON RECEIPT CMM YOU ARE DIRECTED TO PROCESS PFC OSWALD FOR DISCH IAW PARA 10277.2.f MARCORMAN X

A. LARSON
By direction

COPY TO

ok

ADDRESS: COMMANDANT OF THE MARINE CORPS
HEADQUARTERS, U. S. MARINE CORPS
WASHINGTON 25, D. C.

← SENDER'S MAILING ADDRESS
Address reply as shown at left or reply hereon and return in window envelope (size 8¾" x 3⅞"), if not classified as confidential or higher.

CLASSIFICATION: ~~FOR OFFICIAL USE ONLY~~

I can't use this check, of course — Put the $20 bill in an envelope and send it to me. I'm also short of cash and need the rest.

Love
Lee

FORT WORTH, TEXAS, Dec 18 1959 NO.

THE FIRST NATIONAL BANK
OF FORT WORTH
37-1/1113

PAY TO THE ORDER OF Mr. Lee H. Oswald $20.00
KNOW YOUR ENDORSER - REQUIRE IDENTIFICATION
Twenty dollars exactly DOLLARS

Marguerite C Oswald
1013 5th Av.

Commission Exhibit No. 202

МЕЖДУНАРОДНОЕ
ГЛЯЦИОЛОГИЯ
МОСКВА ПОЧТАМТ 28 12 59 22
AIR MAIL

MRS. M. OSWALD
~~1013 5th Av.~~
FORT WORTH, 1605 8 Ave
TEXAS, U.S.A.

COMMISSION EXHIBIT 202

VOL 16: p. 583

CONFIDENTIAL

OFFICE MEMORANDUM UNITED STATES GOVERNMENT

TO: DIRECTOR, FBI (65-28939) DATE: 2/26/60

FROM: SAC, NEW YORK (65-6315)

SUBJECT:

CONFIDENTIAL

Classified by 3832
Exempt from GDS, Category 3
Date of Declassification Indefinite 7/22/78

Rebulet 2/2/60, and NY letters to Bureau 1/18/60, and 1/29/60.

APPROPRIATE AGENCIES AND FIELD OFFICES ADVISED BY ROUTING SLIP (S) OF Classification DATE 7-28-78 GAT/TLB

UNRECORDED COPY FILED IN 100-3-34196

4-Bureau (65-28939)
(2-100-353496) (RM)
1-Boston (65-1639) (INFO) (RM)
1-San Francisco (100-20316) (INFO) (RM)
1-Washington Field (65-1762) (INFO) (RM)
42-New York (65-6315)
(40-105-6103)

HFG:moh
(49)

REC-48

EX-133

65-28939-2503

16 FEB 29 1960

PLH ITEM #991

CONFIDENTIAL

NY 105-6103

The identity of [redacted] who has furnished reliable information in the past, should be concealed when the above information is used in a report. This information was furnished to SAAS ROBERT S. BARNHART and HAROLD F. GOOD on 2/15/60.

Copies of this letter have been designated for the information of the Boston, San Francisco, and Washington Field Offices, inasmuch as they are conducting investigations under this program.

The sources supplying the details of receipts and disbursements set out in aforementioned bank accounts have been previously identified.

It is noted that the above information was furnished on a strictly confidential basis and cannot be made public except upon the issuance of a subpoena duces tecum. -P-

- 33 -

CONFIDENTIAL

PLH ITEM #991

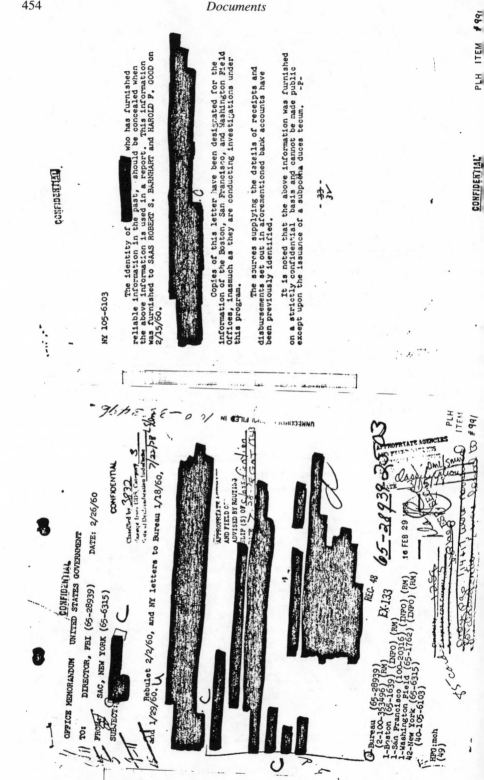

SECRET

OFFICE MEMORANDUM UNITED STATES GOVERNMENT

TO: SAC, DALLAS Date: 3/9/60

FROM: SAC, NEW YORK (105-6103)

SUBJECT: (S)

(S)

Your office is requested to identify and interview the remittors located in your area in accordance with Bureau instructions set forth below. The items to be covered by your office are: 12. (u)

The Bureau has furnished the following instructions to be observed in this program: (u)

It is desired that the following points be specifically covered when conducting interviews in captioned matter. (u)

1. Reasons for transmittal of funds. (u)

2. Identity and relationship, if any, between the purchaser of the remittance order and the payee. (u)

2 - Dallas (Encl.2)(RM)
1 - New York (105-6103)

HFG:mts
(3)

Classified by 1308 on 8-1-78
Exempt from GDS, Category 1+2
Date of Declassification Indefinite

SECRET 105-6103-854 PLH ITEM #992

NY 105-6103

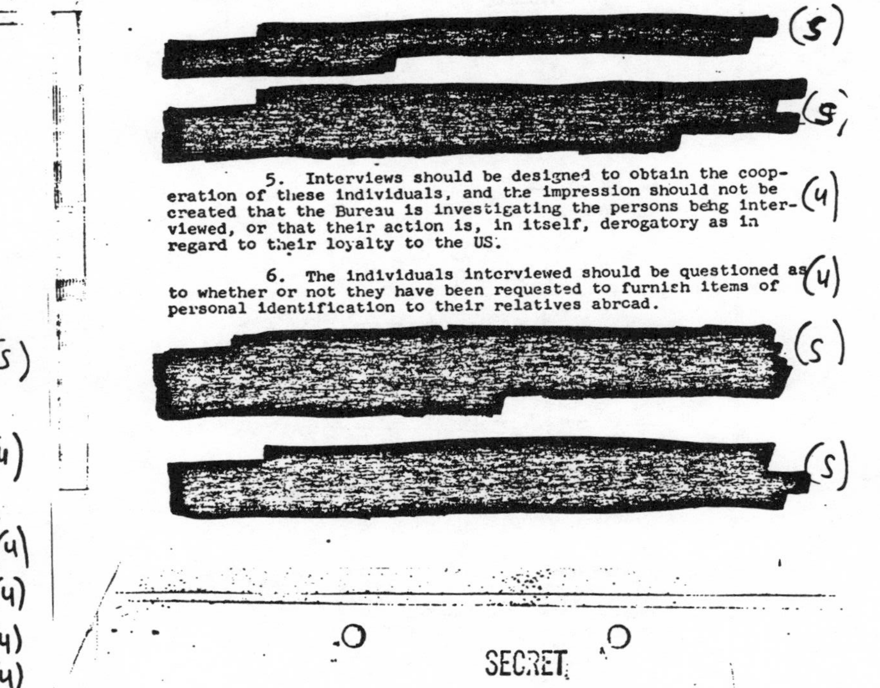

(S)

(S)

5. Interviews should be designed to obtain the cooperation of these individuals, and the impression should not be created that the Bureau is investigating the persons being interviewed, or that their action is, in itself, derogatory as in regard to their loyalty to the US. (u)

6. The individuals interviewed should be questioned as to whether or not they have been requested to furnish items of personal identification to their relatives abroad. (u)

(S)

(S)

SECRET

NY 105-6103

(S)

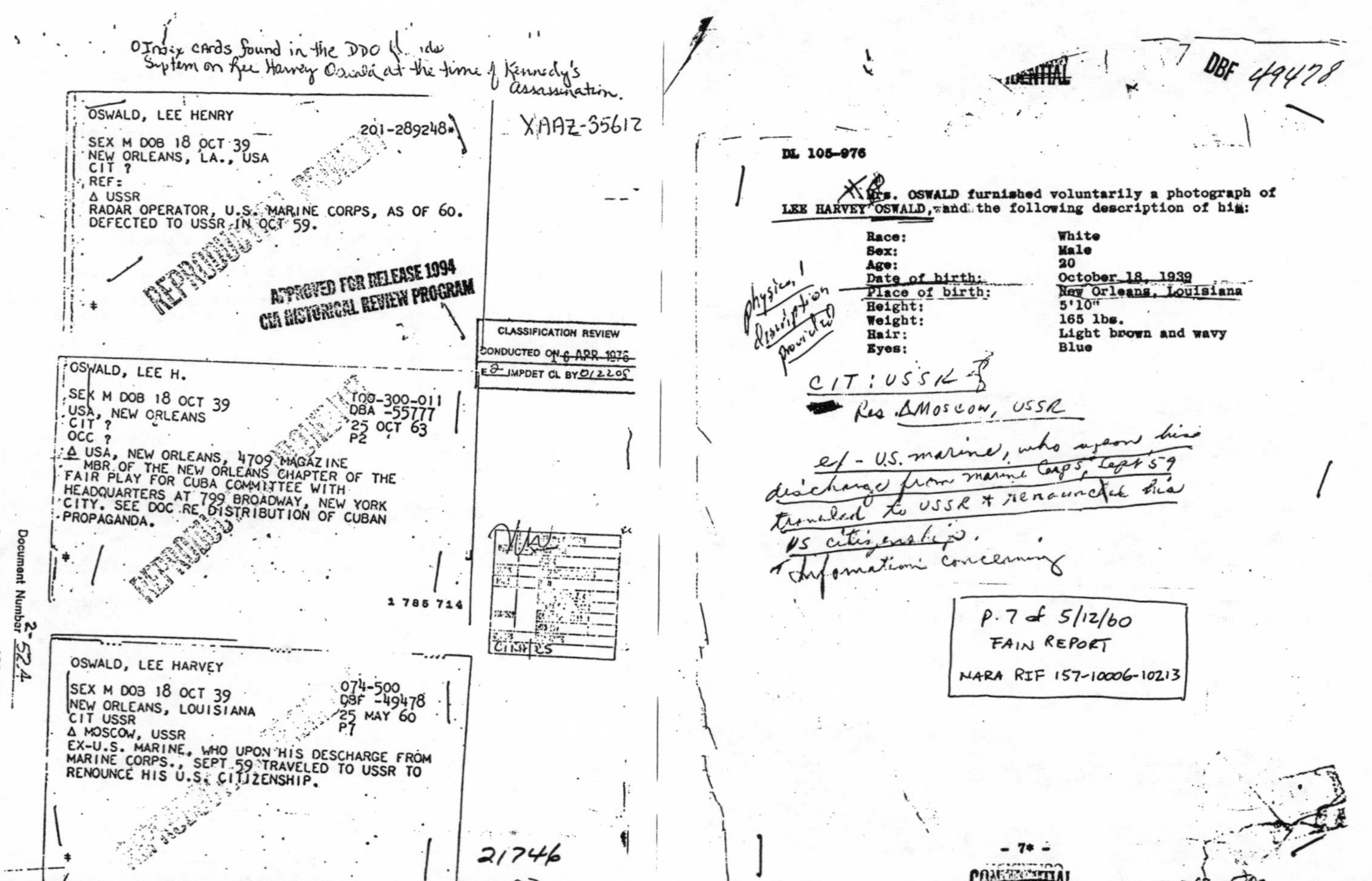

O Index cards found in the DDO [illegible] System on Lee Harvey Oswald at the time of Kennedy's Assassination.

XAAZ-35612

OSWALD, LEE HENRY
201-289248*
SEX M DOB 18 OCT 39
NEW ORLEANS, LA., USA
CIT ?
REF:
Δ USSR
RADAR OPERATOR, U.S. MARINE CORPS, AS OF 60.
DEFECTED TO USSR IN OCT 59.

REPRODUCED [illegible]

APPROVED FOR RELEASE 1994
CIA HISTORICAL REVIEW PROGRAM

CLASSIFICATION REVIEW
CONDUCTED ON 6 APR 1976
E2 IMPDET CL BY 012205

OSWALD, LEE H.
SEX M DOB 18 OCT 39
USA, NEW ORLEANS
CIT ?
OCC ?
100-300-011
DBA -55777
25 OCT 63
P2
Δ USA, NEW ORLEANS, 4709 MAGAZINE
MBR OF THE NEW ORLEANS CHAPTER OF THE FAIR PLAY FOR CUBA COMMITTEE WITH HEADQUARTERS AT 799 BROADWAY, NEW YORK CITY. SEE DOC RE DISTRIBUTION OF CUBAN PROPAGANDA.
1 785 714

OSWALD, LEE HARVEY
SEX M DOB 18 OCT 39
NEW ORLEANS, LOUISIANA
CIT USSR
Δ MOSCOW, USSR
074-500
DBF -49478
25 MAY 60
P7
EX-U.S. MARINE, WHO UPON HIS DESCHARGE FROM MARINE CORPS., SEPT 59 TRAVELED TO USSR TO RENOUNCE HIS U.S. CITIZENSHIP.

21746

Document Number 2-524
for FOIA Review on APR 1976

[illegible]IDENTIAL

DBF 49478

DL 105-976

Mrs. OSWALD furnished voluntarily a photograph of LEE HARVEY OSWALD, and the following description of him:

Race:	White
Sex:	Male
Age:	20
Date of birth:	October 18, 1939
Place of birth:	New Orleans, Louisiana
Height:	5'10"
Weight:	165 lbs.
Hair:	Light brown and wavy
Eyes:	Blue

physical description provided

CIT: USSR

Res Δ MOSCOW, USSR

ex - U.S. marine, who upon his discharge from marine Corps, Sept 59 traveled to USSR & renounced his US citizenship.

Information concerning

P. 7 of 5/12/60
FAIN REPORT
NARA RIF 157-10006-10213

- 7* -

CONFIDENTIAL

5/23/60

AIRTEL

TO: DIRECTOR, FBI (100-353496)

FROM: SAC, NEW YORK (105-6103)

SUBJECT: FUNDS TRANSMITTED TO RESIDENTS OF RUSSIA IS-R

Re report of SA JOHN W. FAIN, Dallas, 5/12/60.

Interview of Mrs. MARGUERITE C. OSWALD reveals that her son, LEE HARVEY OSWALD had gone to Moscow, Russia, had renounced his US citizenship and had apparently sought Soviet citizenship. She recently received a letter addressed to her son from the Albert Schweitzer College in Switzerland indicating that LEE OSWALD was expected at the college on 4/20/60. She stated that LEE OSWALD had taken his birth certificate with him when he left home. The fact that she had sent three letters to her son in Moscow since 1/22/60, which were returned undelivered, has caused her to fear for his safety.

There appears to be a possibility of locating LEE OSWALD outside the USSR at the Albert Schweitzer College in Switzerland. Furthermore, since OSWALD had his birth certificate in his possession, another individual may have assumed his identity.

The info furnished by Mrs. OSWALD may be of interest to the US State Department and it is suggested for the consideration of the Bureau, that a copy of her interview be furnished to the State Department for any action they deem appropriate.

3- Bureau (100-353496) (RM)
1- Dallas (105-976) (RM)
1- New York (105-6103)

HFG:jr
(6)

105-82555-UNREC
NOT RECORDED
148 JUN 6 1960

F258

59 JUN 10 1960

ORIGINAL COPY FILED IN

DD/P 6-5678

DEPARTMENT OF STATE
THE DIRECTOR OF INTELLIGENCE AND RESEARCH
WASHINGTON

SECRET

OCT 25 1960

Dear Dick:

Our efforts to answer recent informal inquiries, including some from the White House Staff, have revealed that, though CIA and the FBI have detailed records concerning Americans who have been recruited as intelligence agents by Bloc countries, there does not appear to be a complete listing of those Americans now living in Bloc countries who might be called "defectors". Using the definitions of DCID 4/2, these persons might be described as those who have either been capable of providing useful intelligence to the Bloc or those whose desire to resettle in Bloc countries has been significantly exploited for communist propaganda purposes. This would mean that no attention need be paid to Americans whose resettlement within the Bloc had no counter-intelligence implications or had attracted no particular attention; for instance, this definition would not cover individual US citizens of East European or Chinese origin who returned to the "homeland" because they had never been completely assimilated into the American society.

There is attached a list of such persons, covering the last 18 months, and it would be appreciated if the Agency could verify and possibly expand this list for the use of interested Bureaus of the Department.

Sincerely yours,

Hugh S. Cumming, Jr.

Attachment:

List of American "Defectors" from May 1959 - October 1960.

Mr. Richard M. Bissell, Jr.
Deputy Director, Plans,
Central Intelligence Agency.

This document has been approved for release through the HISTORICAL REVIEW PROGRAM of the Central Intelligence Agency.

Date 8 MAY 92

92-5

CONFIDENTIAL

LIST OF AMERICAN "DEFECTORS"

1.) Morris and Mollie BLOCK, living in the USSR, and possibly Communist China, since the fall of 1959.

2.) David DuBOIS (aka DUPEBOY), living in Peiping since May 1960, but may have returned to the U.S.

3.) Sgt. Joseph DUTKANICZ, U.S. Army, defected to East German Forces about the spring of 1960.

4.) Sgt. Ernie F. FLETCHER, U.S. Army, defected to East German Forces in June 1959 and stated that he wished to remain in East Germany at a confrontation held on August 5, 1959 (CINCUSAREUR telegram SX 5307 of 061744 2 August).

5.) Sgt. (fnu) JONES, U.S. Air Force, defected in mid May 1960 to East German Forces (Air Intelligence Information Report number 1430223 of August 9, 1960.)

6.) William MARTIN, NSA employee.

7.) Bernon MITCHELL, NSA employee.

8.) Lee Harvey OSWALD, tourist.

9.) Libero RICCIARDELLI, tourist.

10.) Pvt. Vladimir SLOBODA, U.S. Army, defected to East German Forces in the spring of 1960.

11.) Robert Edward WEBSTER, tourist, (see New York Times article of October 20, 1959).

12.) Bruce Frederick DAVIS, U.S. Army, defected to East German Forces, August 19, 1960 (Embassy Moscow telegram 1032 of October 22, 1960).

31 October 1960

MEMORANDUM FOR: Chief, Security Research Staff

FROM : M. D. Stevens

SUBJECT : American Defectors

Reference is made to a verbal request to you from the DC/OS for information regarding any American citizens who have defected to the USSR, Red China, or other Satellite countries during the past eighteen months—other than Bernon F. MITCHELL and William H. MARTIN, and five other defectors regarding whom Mr. OTEPKA of the State Department Security Office already has information (i.e. Robert Edward WEBSTER, EE-18854; Lee Harvey OSWALD, MS-11165; Libero RICCIARDELLI, MS-8295; Vladimir SLOBODA, MS-10565; and Joseph DUTKANICZ, MS-10724).

Security files reflect that the subjects of the attached memoranda are additional American citizens who have defected to the Soviets or their Satellites during the past eighteen months.

Several of the above referred to defectors have been of interest to CIA:

Herbert Lee NORTHRUP, 68923, was a staff employee of this Agency from May 1951 to May 1958. A more detailed summary than that included in the attached group has been prepared on him.

Robert Edward WEBSTER, EE-18852, and Nicholas PETRULLI, EE-19439, were subject of OO/C requests on 29 May 1959 and 15 June 1959, respectively, with a view to their being debriefed upon their returns from visits to Russia. Neither was interviewed by CIA, either before or after their visits.

With reference to Nicholas PETRULLI, [

] in May 1953 [

] PETRULLI was employed as a sheet metal worker in Valley Stream,

p. 460

...e left the U. S. for Russia in 1959, and his five brothers live on Long

...imir SLOBODA is currently of interest to Security in view of his assignment prior to his defection to the Soviet Union, via East Germany, on 3 August to the 513th Military Intelligence Group in Frankfurt, Germany, (EGIS Center). ...he had contact with at least one representative of CIA and was in a position to ...learned the identities of CIA personnel at the EGIS Center.

...illiam A. MORGAN has been of interest to Security in that on 27 March 1959, ...A requested a check on him [ ]

...dward NIXON, on 6 September 1960, approached a [ ] in Freddy's Bar in ...uene and engaged him in conversation, following which [ ] found himself ...r surveillance. The surveillance continued for two days, after which [ ] ...approached in Freddy's Bar by an unknown G-2 officer who asked him about ...ON; and thereafter the surveillance ceased. (The owner of Freddy's Bar had ...rted NIXON to G-2, as he said he was ruining his business.)

...hile defectors to Cuba and the UAR may not technically be defectors to Soviet ...llite countries, it seems a close thing, and the names of such known defectors ...e past eighteen months have been included in this memorandum.

M. D. Stevens

SBS:MDS:djc

OSWALD, Lee Henry
Defected October 1959

The following information is SECRET:

Born 18 October 1939 in New Orleans, Louisiana, Lee Henry OSWALD joined the United States Marines at the age of seventeen because he did not want to be a "burden" to his mother who was widowed prior to his birth. While in the Marines, OSWALD, a Private First Class, became a radar operator and had fourteen months service in Japan and the Philippines. About a year before his discharge from the Marines OSWALD began to teach himself to read and speak Russian. After receiving an honorable discharge from the Marines on 3 September 1959 OSWALD visited his mother in Waco, Texas for about three days and then departed. A note written to his mother from New Orleans stated that he had booked passage to Europe and that he was doing something he felt he must do. Shortly thereafter he appeared at the United States Embassy in Moscow and renounced his U. S. citizenship, giving as his reason the plight of the American Negro and U. S. "imperialism" abroad. OSWALD acknowledged mail addressed to him at the Hotel Metropole in Moscow in 1959; however, he has failed to do so in 1960. OSWALD is reported to have stated that regardless of any material shortcomings he sees in the USSR, he will never return to the United States.

FROM CIA RESPONSE TO STATE
ATTACHMENT TO BISSELL MEMO
TO CUMMINGS 21 NOV 1960

CIA DOCUMENT NUMBER
596-252F

CONFIDENTIAL

CI 315-75

18 SEP 1975

EX-10931

MEMORANDUM FOR: Executive Assistant to the DDO

FROM : Chief, CI Staff

SUBJECT : Lee Harvey Oswald

1. Lee Harvey Oswald's 201 file was first opened under the name of Lee Henry Oswald on 9 December 1960 as a result of his "defection" to the USSR on 31 October 1959 and renewed interest in Oswald brought about by his queries concerning possible reentry into the United States.

2. The file contains two Federal Bureau of Investigation reports, dated 25 May 1960 and 3 July 1961, respectively, which contain interviews of Oswald's mother and brother concerning the possible return to the United States of Oswald and of his loyalty. The American Embassy in Moscow also sent two telegrams in May and October 1961 conveying Oswald's wish to return to the United States and five of Oswald's letters asking for compliance with his request. The file also contains an Oswald letter sent to the Marine Corps disputing the Marine Corps discharge classification of him as undesirable. It is believed that the above documents were also circulated among the FBI, State Department, Immigration and Naturalization Service as well as Naval Intelligence.

3. There is also a memorandum dated 16 October 1963 from[ ] COS Mexico City to the United States Ambassador there concerning Oswald's visit to Mexico City and to the Soviet Embassy there in late September-early October 1963. Subsequently there were several Mexico City cables in October 1963 also concerned with Oswald's visit to Mexico City, as well as his visits to the Soviet and Cuban Embassies. These cables were passed on to the FBI, State Department and Naval Intelligence while Mexico City Station was told to pass the information on to

Document Number 1187-436

for FOIA Review on NOV 1976

CONFIDENTIAL

RECORD COPY

18 Sep 1975

201 - 289248

CONFIDENTIAL

the FBI, Immigration and Naturalization Service and Embassy in Mexico City.

4. There are several other FBI reports dated October 1963 concerning Oswald's activities in the Fair Play for Cuba Committee and his eventual arrest for disturbing the peace in New Orleans in August 1963. These were passed on to the Immigration and Naturalization Service. There are no other substantive documents in our files prior to the assassination date.

George T. Kalaris

George T. Kalaris
Chief
Counterintelligence Staff

DDO/CI/R&A/O/[ ]po (18 Sept 75)

Distribution:
Orig & 1 - Addee
1 - C/CI
2 - CI/R&A/O (1 - Oswald 201; chrono

CONFIDENTIAL

201-289248

SECRET
(When Filled In)

PERSONALITY (201) FILE REQUEST

TO - HEADQUARTERS, RI

DATE 9 December 1960

FROM CI/SIG - Ann EGERTER 1408 J (X2621)

ACTION: OPEN | AMEND | CLOSE

INSTRUCTIONS: Form must be typed or printed in block letters.

SECTION I: All known aliases and variants (including maiden name, if applicable) must be listed. If the identifying data varies with the alias used, a separate form must be used. Write UNKNOWN for items you are unable to complete.

SECTION II: Cryptonym or pseudonym will be entered in Headquarters.

SECTION III: To be completed in all cases.

SECTION I

SENSITIVE / NON-SENSITIVE

201 NO. 289248

1. SOURCE DOCUMENT, CI/SIG

NAME (Last) OSWALD, (First) LEE (Middle) HENRY (Title)

SEX M

NAME VARIANT

TYPE NAME 2. (Last) (First) (Middle) (Title)

CLASSIFICATION REVIEW
CONDUCTED ON 16 APR 1976
E2 IMPDET CL BY 012208

NB: HARVEY!

[illegible] 30/4/75

PHOTO 4. YES ✓ NO

BIRTH DATE 5. D 18 M 10 Y 39

COUNTRY OF BIRTH 6. USA

CITY OR TOWN OF BIRTH 7. New Orleans, La.

OTHER IDENTIFICATION 1. AG 2. 3.

OCCUPATION/POSITION Radar operator, U.S. Marine Corps, orig 1960 NAVY

OCC/POS. CODE D

SECTION II

CRYPTONYM

PSEUDONYM

SECTION III

COUNTRY OF RESIDENCE USSR - [ ]

11. ACTION DESK CI/SIG [ ]

12. 2ND COUNTRY INTEREST SR

3RD COUNTRY INTEREST

COMMENTS: cit; P.

Defected to the USSR in October 1959

Document Number 1-1B

for FOIA Review on APR 1976

CS Copy

201- 289248

PERMANENT CHARGE YES ✓ NO

RESTRICTED FILE YES ✓ NO

SIGNATURE Ann Egerter

FORM 10-57 831a

SECRET

RECORD COPY

[illegible]

Civil Action Number

U.S. CENTRAL INTELLIGENCE AGENCY, :

Defendant :

DOCUMENT DISPOSITION INDEX

Document No.	Date	No. of Pages
1187 - 436	18 September 19755	2

Disposition - This document was released with portions deleted. The deleted portions contain information identifying Agency staff employees, Agency components, information identifying an Agency station in a specific city abroad and Agency internal filing instructions. The deletions were made under the authority of exemptions (b)(1), (b)(2) and (b)(3).

Document No.	Date	No. of Pages
1188 - 1000	18 September 1975	6

Disposition - This document was released with portions deleted. The deleted portions contain information identifying Agency components and Agenc staff employees, as well as Agency internal filing instructions. Also deleted was information confirming the existence of an Agency station in a specific city abroad. The deletions were made under the authority of exemptions (b)(1 (b)(2) and (b)(3).

Document No.	Date	No. of Pages
1189 - 1001	22 September 1975	2

Disposition - This document was denied. The document discusses the compromise of some classified intelligence information and the possible consequences in terms of damage to foreign intelligence sources and methods. The release of this document would provide public confirmation of the validity of the information leaked and would make certain the damage which at this point is only problematical. The document is therefore properly classified and denied. In addition, this document contains information confirming the existence of an Agency station in a specific city abroad, information identifying Agency components and Agency internal filing instructions. The document is therefore denied under the authority of exemptions (b)(1), (b)(2) and (b)(3).

Document No.	Date	No. of Pages
1190 - 1002	22 September 1975	1

Disposition - This document was denied. The document contains a continuation of the discussion of the compromise of the classified information stated in the document listed immediately above. The same consequences would be entailed should this document be released. It is therefore properly classified and denied. The document was denied under the authority of exemptions (b)(1), (b)(2) and (b)(3).

Commission Exhibit No. 245

EMBASSY OF THE UNITED STATES OF AMERICA
Feb. 13, 1961
MOSCOW

Dear Sirs;

Since I have not received a reply to my letter of December 1960, I am writing again asking that you consider my request for the return of my american passport.

I desire to return to the United States, that is if we could come to some agreement concerning the dropping of any legal proceedings against me. If so, then I would be free to ask the Russian authorities to allow me to leave. If I could show them my American passport, I am of the opinion they would give me an exit visa.

They have at no time insisted that I take Russian citizenship. I am living here with non-permanent type papers for a foreigner.

I cannot leave Minsk without permission, therefore I am writing rather than calling in person.

I hope that in recalling the responsibility I have to america that you remember your's in doing everything you can to help me since I am an american citizen.

Sincerely
Lee Harvey Oswald

Минск
ул. Калинина
Дом 4, кв. 24
А. Л. Освальд

CE 245 VOL XVI P 685

CE 245 VOL XVI P 686

EX - 786
5 December 1966

MEMORANDUM FOR THE RECORD

SUBJECT: "American Defectors to the USSR"

1. The attached material was part of a soft file entitled "American Defectors to the USSR", which was set up by SR/6 (Support) around 1960 and maintained by various SR components until ca. 1963. The compilations were derived from a variety of sources, and contain both classified and overt data.

2. In the fall of 1966, the files were turned over to CI Staff. In most instances, basic information was then abstracted for the US Defector Machine Program. In all instances in which the material was unique, or represented a valuable collation effort, it has been incorporated into the appropriate 201 file, along with a copy of this memorandum.

3. It is suggested that any dissemination of this data should be coordinated with SB Division and with CI Staff (CI/MRO), in view of the frequently inadequate sourcing and of the fact that disseminations have already been made through the US Defector Machine Program.

Orig - CI/MRO
1 - RID/FI
1 - SB/RMO
1 - CI/R&A/[redacted]
1 - CI/R&A/chrono

to US Defector
chine Program

SECRET

SECRET

PP

WASH STAR
30/11/64

2 U.S. Army Defectors Linked to Soviet Police

By the Associated Press

Two European-born U.S. soldiers who defected to the Soviet Union more than four years ago were disclosed today to have had prior connections with the Soviet secret police.

The two, both World War II displaced persons, were stationed in West Germany with U.S. Army units when they crossed over to the Russians separately in the summer of 1960. Their defection and identities were disclosed then, but not their prior connection with the Soviet secret police.

One was Vladimir Sloboda, a native of the Ukraine, who is now 37. The other was Joseph Dutkanicz, a native of Poland who died a year ago today at the age of 37.

Their defection was mentioned two months ago in the Warren Commission report on the assassination of President John F. Kennedy.

Fled on Security Check

In discussing Soviet defection procedures — Lee Harvey Oswald, Kennedy's assassin, had defected to the Soviet Union after leaving the U.S. Marine Corps — the commission report quoted the Central Intelligence Agency:

"Two defectors from U.S. Army intelligence units in West Germany appeared to have been given citizenship immediately, but both had prior KGB (Russian secret police) connections and fled as a result of Army security checks."

The CIA did not identify the two defectors in the Warren report.

The Associated Press asked the Army for their names and records. Now, two months later, the Army — after consulting with the CIA — reports the defectors referred to by the CIA and the two who crossed over in the summer of 1960 are the same.

There were indications the CIA was reluctant to elaborate on the Warren Commission reference.

Second Now Dead

Sloboda has made broadcasts denouncing the United States and "has also written articles for the Soviet press which follow the Soviet propaganda line," the Army said. He now lives in Lvov, a former Polish city now part of the Soviet Union.

Dutkanicz worked in a television factory before he died in Lvov, the Army said.

After the defection, the Russians quoted Sloboda and Dutkanicz as saying they acted partly out of revulsion against U2 plane flights over the Soviet Union. This was shortly after Francis Gary Powers was shot down over the Soviet Union while on a U2 flight.

The Army supplied no details on how, where or when the two men had had connections with the Soviet secret police.

Basic in U. S.

Its summary said Sloboda was born in Podkamion in the Ukraine and during World War II was sent to Germany as a forced laborer.

After the war, he spent time in a displaced persons camp in Germany, emigrated to England, and then returned to Germany where he enlisted in the U. S. Army in 1953.

After basic training in the United States, Sloboda was assigned in August 1958 to an Army military intelligence group in Europe. Two years later he defected.

The Army summary said Dutkanicz was a native of Gorlice Bartne in Poland, entered the United States December 1951 and was inducted into the Army in February 1951.

After nearly six years of service in the United States, Dutkanicz was sent to Germany in 1957.

A# 13545

A# 13551

201-287537

201-284736

SECRET

DUTKANICZ Joseph John, 201-289236 — file — A# 13551

9 June 1926, Gorlice, Poland

Sergeant, USA. Darmstadt, address in US - Tujunga, Calif; some kind of intell and/or signal assignment

1940's and 50's. Left-wing though not actual CP activities in U.S., where had some as D.'s U.S. residence all or part of time in Tujunga. American wife Mary. (Emd despatch 851, 27 March 62, in OO file)

1958. He later told the Moscow Embassy (as reported in a USAREUR case summary) that he had been approached by the KGB in a bar near Darmstadt. Threats and inducements got his promise of cooperation at first meeting. He claimed that from then on he never gave them anything but a few negative imminence reports. (201)

1958-1960. He had some kind of difficulty with his wife. She later said that she knew he had relatives in the USSR, and that he had admitted he was a communist and had associates among German national who were communists. (CI/SIO). During this period she suspected what was going on and reported to the CIC - who investigated and cleared him, just as he had been cleared for an intelligence unit despite his left-wing activities in the 40's and 50's. (Embtel 851, 27 Mar 62 in OO files)

March 1960. This is the date of Supreme Soviet decree No. 135/3. "This decree, enacted three months prior to D's arrival in the SU but after he began cooperating with Soviet agents in West Germany, apparently was something akin to a private bill bestowing citizenship on him." (Embtel 851 in OO files)

May 1960. He told his KGB handlers that he was being investigated by the Army in connection with a security drive. KGB advised him to apply for leave and then defect. He later told all of this to the American Embassy in Moscow, when his wife was processing to leave the USSR. (201)

Early July 1960. He and his wife went on leave with their three children, driving in the family car. She later claimed no knowledge of his intention to defect. They drove to Czechoslovakia on lure of seeing his father in Bratislava; father of course not there, so on to USSR. (201)

24 July 1960. [illegible] said he [illegible], almost [illegible] *

27 or 28 July 1960. Tass announced that the family had sought asylum in the USSR. (CI/SIO files)

29 July 1960. Translation of article in Rome communist daily L'Unita which published Izvestiya story with 27 July dateline; autobiographical statement by D, giving his history and motivation in the usual anti-American terms. (ID-2148307 in CI/SIO files)

9 August 1960. See attached FBIS report.

25 August 1960. USA in Heidelberg announced that he had been AWOL since 6 July 1960 but that there was no confirmation he had defected. (CI/SIO)

201 - 289236

24 September 1960. Date of his Soviet internal passport, based on decree of March 1960 (see entry above). It was also delivered to him in September. "He was told by his police contacts, who were constantly in touch with him (he was required to i.e. KGB, phone them daily since arrival in the SU) that Soviet citizenship had been obtained for him, but somehow he found a way to insist on behalf of his wife that at least she be documented as a foreigner. He was told he had to take a Soviet passport in order to get

* ing, denied being Polish, [illegible] friends. According to [illegible], he had great interest in world politics — vs. US position in Hong Kong — admitted [illegible] [illegible] superiority [illegible] (SRS file, Overseas [illegible])

SECRET

SECRET

A13597

DAVIS Bruce Frederick, 201-289235
Circa 1936, Rome, N.Y.
Enlisted man USA, West Germany; previous tour in USMC and unsuccessful try at college

All entries through 7 Aug 67 come from his 201 and/or CI/SIG files.

18-19 August 1960. He deserted his unit, left his car and belongings on the Bavarian-East German border, and crossed over, intending defect to Sovs. Claimed motive was racial prejudice in U.S., doubts U.S. Government genuinely ~~pursuing~~ pursuing peaceful policy, and feeling U.S. leaders not working for peace as they should. However, he was an unstable and insecure drifter type who, though likeable, couldn't get ahead. For instance, he was denied his chance to go to OCS because he was caught in forbidden pranks involving fire-works. He was taken to East Berlin. US residence listed at time of defection: Los Angeles.

Circa 22 September 1960. ~~After five weeks~~ After about five weeks in East Berlin he was allowed to enter the USSR and settle in Kiev as a student at the university there. He did not denounce U.S. citizenship and did not legally expatriate himself; was officially documented by the Soviets as a stateless resident -"which is normal for a non-Soviet citizen not in possession of a valid national passport". (As a CI he would probably not have had one.)

October 1960. As of this month he was settled as a student at the Kiev Institute of National Economy with a free dormitory room and a stipend of 900 old rubles per month: three times what Soviet students got but normal for a non-Bloc student. He was also given an outright grant of 10,000 old rubles, a fantastically high sum;(perhaps it should read 1000) this according to a letter he wrote a buddy from his former unit in West Germany.

21 October 1960. Statement in Isvestiya attributing his defection to disillusionment with U.S. foreign and military policy.

22 October 1960. Similar statement in Pravda. This was presumably the 22.10.60 article in which, acc. to the US Emb, he stated desire to repudiate US citizenship and hope of

February 1961. Authorized trip to Khar'kov with student group. OVER

1 May 1961. Made unauthorized air trip to Moscow. Claimed air cheaper than railroad: only 15.35 rubles one way. Stayed three days. Not caught or bothered by police. As a result of this trip or one of his other unauthorized trips to Moscow, he was reprimanded by the Deputy Chief of the Institute for leaving the city without permission. This was probably the cause of the delay in his receiving the promised free apartment. He never did get it, although he could have had one at ~~$~~ 25 rubles for "66 square meters for three rooms".

June-July 1961. He started out unauthorized to hitchhike to the Crimea but was naturally caught by the police, who returned him to Kiev for a reprimand by the Institute Chief.

February 1962. Unauthorized eight-day trip to Yalta. Not caught.

April 1962. Unauthorized week-end bus trip to Zhitomir.

~~Summer~~ May 1962. He approached an American girl guide at the U.S. medical exhibition (March-July 1962) when it was in Kiev. She and another girl guide reported that he was studying at a Soviet school, was disillusioned, but was

201-289235

SECRET

147

OSWALD, Lee Harvey

Date of Birth: 18 October 1939. New Orleans, Louisiana

Date of Defection: October 1959

Education: High school. Always a studious type, read boc [illegible] considered "deep".

Military Service:

Joined the Marines at 17. Says he did this because he d[illegible] want to be a burden on his mother. Became a PFC, radar operator. 14 months service Japan and the Philippines. Honorable discharge on 3 September 1959 (dependency discharge). [illegible]

Background:

Father, an insurance salesman, died before Lee was born. Ha[illegible] a brother who is a salesman at Acme Brick Company, Fort Worth, Te[illegible], and a half brother John Edward Pic age 28, a US Air Force Staff Sergeant stationed in Japan. Mother is currently employed as a supply [illegible] at the Methodist Orphans Home, Waco, Texas.

According to newspaper article, reasons for his defection w[illegible] nation of family poverty, what he considers the plight of US n[illegible], the US Marines or American imperialism abroad. At 15 or s[illegible] "Das Kapital" and agreed with its theories. A year before [illegible] he began to prepare for life in the Soviet Union by using [illegible] grammar to teach himself how to read and write Russian. N[illegible] did he consider deserting the Marine Corps.

After discharge from the Marines, Lee visited his mother in [illegible] Wo[illegible] for about 3 days, then left for New Orleans where he planned to [illegible] employment with an export-import company for which he had work[illegible] to enlisting in the Marines. Shortly after he arrived in New [illegible] he sent his mother a note saying that he had booked passage [illegible] that he was doing something he felt he must do. His arriv[illegible] came as a shock to the family. Travel money probably cam[illegible] saved while in the Marines. He had never expressed any s[illegible] the Soviet Union or Communism. He had been interested in [illegible] America and his family would have expected him to go there. [illegible] Mail sent to him since his defection has been addressed to [illegible] Metropole, Moscow. He acknowledged receipt of his mail in [illegible] letters sent in 1960 have been returned to the senders.

In November 1959 the Soviets were investigating the possibili[illegible] sending Lee to a Soviet higher technical institute. (Wash [illegible] May 1960 Mrs. Oswald received a letter from the Albert Sch[illegible]

- 2 -

in Switzerland, and which was addressed to Lee, which said in effect that this college was expecting Lee Oswald on 20 April 1960. After receipt of the letter, Mrs. Oswald planned to write to the college to learn if her son was in actual attendance there.

The Soviets neither encouraged nor discouraged Oswald's desire to become a Soviet citizen. The American Embassy wanted him to think it over before hearing his oath renouncing American citizenship. As a result, Oswald is bitter towards the consul there. He has stated that regardless of any material shortcomings he sees while in the USSR, he will never go back to the USA.

Residing Minsk. Desires return USA under certain conditions (drop legal proceedings. Cannot leave Minsk w/o permission.

Married Marina Nicholaevna Prusakova, born July 1941, Moletovsk, Archangelsk Obl. Laboratory assist. Sept 61 applied visa come USA with Oswald.

Unless so noted, info is from the Washington Evening Star, 26 Nov. 1959.

Accused assassin of President John F. Kennedy 22 November 1963 in Dallas, Texas

Shot + killed by Jack Ruby on 25 November 1963. while being moved from Dallas Jail.

INFORMATION REPORT INFORMATION REPORT

CENTRAL INTELLIGENCE AGENCY

This material contains information affecting the National Defense of the United States within the meaning of the Espionage Laws, Title 18, U.S.C. Secs. 793 and 794, the transmission or revelation of which in any manner to an unauthorized person is prohibited by law.

~~C-O-N-F-I-D-E-N-T-I-A-L~~

COUNTRY	USSR	REPORT NO.	CO-A-3169910
SUBJECT	US Defector in Lvov Dutkanych.	DATE DISTR.	5-4 October 1960
		NO. PAGES	1
		REFERENCES	AH 13551
DATE OF INFO.	July 1960		CD/OO Guide 325
PLACE & DATE ACQ.	Lvov, USSR July 1960		

THIS IS UNEVALUATED INFORMATION

SOURCE: [ ]

[ ]

1. On the morning of Monday, 10 July 1960, at about 0930-1000 hours I chanced to meet one Joseph Dutkanych, allegedly a defected US citizen, in the lobby of the Intourist Hotel in the city of Lvov, USSR.

2. I was recognized and approached by Mr. Dutkanych while making my way up the hotel stairway toward my hotel room. After the customary greetings, I suggested he accompany me to my room where we remained for not more than ten minutes. Since I had arranged that morning for a private conducted tour of Lvov our conversation dealt primarily with the points of interest I was scheduled to see.

3. Dutkanych seemed to be quite familiar with the city and knowing I was a clergyman, suggested I visit a well known Russian Orthodox church, just up the street. Looking out the window I called his attention to a billboard advertising the latest movie, "Moscow Souvenir". He suggested, however, that I take in another movie that was playing around the corner from the hotel. That afternoon I saw the recommended movie. It was an old war film, depicting the heroism of a young soldier defending his native village from the invading German armies.

4. We had arranged to have dinner that evening, but I never saw him again as he failed to keep his appointment.

- END -

AH-6688

The attached CO-A-3169910 will not receive further dissemination.

~~C-O-N-F-I-D-E-N-T-I-A-L~~

201-289236

STATE		ARMY		NAVY		AIR		FBI		AEC				

INFORMATION REPORT INFORMATION REPORT

NO DISSEM ABROAD

NOFORN LIMITED: Dissemination limited to full time employees of CIA, AEC and FBI, and, within State and Defense, the offices producing NIS elements, and higher echelons with their immediate supporting staffs. Not to be disseminated to reserve personnel on active duty (excepting individuals who are normally full time employees) without permission of the originating office ...

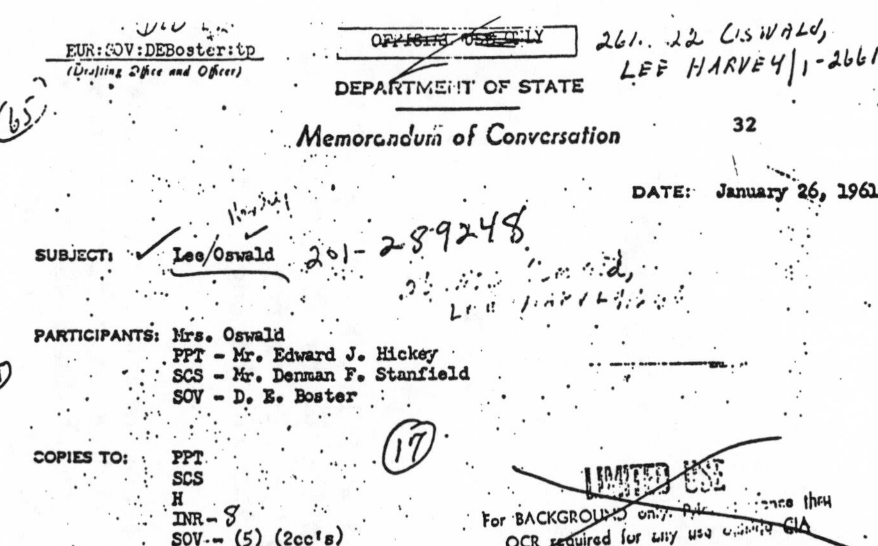

EUR:SOV:DEBoster:tp
(Drafting Office and Officer)

~~OFFICIAL USE ONLY~~

261. 22 OSWALD, LEE HARVEY 1-2661

DEPARTMENT OF STATE

Memorandum of Conversation

32

DATE: January 26, 1961

SUBJECT: Lee Oswald 201-289248

PARTICIPANTS: Mrs. Oswald
PPT - Mr. Edward J. Hickey
SCS - Mr. Denman F. Stanfield
SOV - D. E. Boster

COPIES TO: PPT
SCS
H
INR - 8
SOV - (5) (2cc's)
Amembassy Moscow

~~LIMITED USE~~
For BACKGROUND only. ... thru OCR required for any use ... CIA

Mrs. Oswald came in to discuss the situation with regard to her son, Lee Oswald, who had gone to the Soviet Union and attempted to renounce his citizenship in a visit to the Embassy on October 31, 1959. Mrs. Oswald said she had come to Washington to see what further could be done to help her son, indicating that she did not feel that the Department had done as much as it should in his case. She also said she thought there was some possibility that her son had in fact gone to the Soviet Union as a US secret agent, and if this were true she wished the appropriate authorities to know that she was destitute and should receive some compensation.

Mrs. Oswald was assured that there was no evidence to suggest that her son had gone to the Soviet Union as an "agent", and that she should dismiss any such idea. With respect to her son's citizenship status, Mr. Hickey explained that he had not yet taken the necessary steps in order legally to renounce his citizenship. At the same time, we did not know whether he had taken any action which would deprive him of his American citizenship under our laws. Mrs. Oswald conceded that there was a good possibility that her son was acting in full knowledge of what he was doing and preferred the Soviet way of life. If this were the case, she would respect his right to do so.

It was agreed that the Department would send a new instruction to the Embassy at Moscow asking that the Soviet Foreign Ministry be informed that Mrs. Oswald had not heard from her son in several months and was very anxious to have word from him.

Mrs. Oswald said that her address at the present time was Box 305, Boyd, Texas.

~~OFFICIAL USE ONLY~~

This document has been approved for release through the HISTORICAL REVIEW PROGRAM of the Central Intelligence Agency.

Date 8 MAY 92

HRP 92-5

201-289248

~~SECRET~~

FOR THE RECORD 1 Feb. 1961

FROM: Kammer

SUBJECT: [redacted]
#188074

1. On this date Subject's case was coordinated with Mr. McCORD of SRS in connection with Subject's operational use within the US by WH/4/Propaganda. The implications of a CI operation with the States by this Agency and the possibility Subject might come to the attention of the FBI through association with Court WOO[redacted] were discussed.

2. Mr. McCORD expressed the opinion that it is not necessary to advise the FBI of the operation at this time. However, he wishes to review the case in a month. The file of Subject, along with that of the WH man who is supervising the operation (David Atlee PHILLIPS # 40695) will be pended for the attention of Mr. McCORD on 1 March 1961.

C O P Y 33

DEPARTMENT OF STATE INSTRUCTION

A-273, April 13, 1961

CITIZENSHIP AND PASSPORTS: Lee Harvey Oswald

The American Embassy MOSCOW

The Embassy's Dispatch No. 585 of February 26, 1961, concerning Lee Harvey Oswald has been studied with particular reference to the last two paragraphs thereof. Dispatch No. 659 of March 24, 1961 concerning him has also been noted.

If and when Mr. Oswald appears at the Embassy, he should be thoroughly questioned regarding the circumstances of his residence in the Soviet Union and his possible commitment of an act or acts of expatriation and, as contemplated by the Embassy, his statements should be taken under oath. If the Embassy is fully satisfied that he has not expatriated himself in any manner and if he presents evidence that he has arranged to depart from the Soviet Union to travel to the United States, his passport may be delivered to him on a personal basis only, after being rendered valid for direct return to the United States. For security reasons, the Department does not consider that it would be prudent for the Embassy to forward Oswald's passport to him by mail.

The Department is not in a position to advise Mr. Oswald whether upon his desired return to the United States he may be amenable to prosecution for any possible offenses committed in violation of the laws of the United States or the laws of any of its States.

The developments in the case of Mr. Oswald should be promptly reported. In particular, a report of his travel data should be submitted when the Embassy receives confirmation of his travel plans.

It may be added that Mrs. Marguerite Oswald has been informed of the address given by Mr. Oswald in his recent undated communication referred to in dispatch No. 585 and of his desire to return to the United States. She has also been appropriately informed in the light of Dispatch No. 659.

RUSK

This document has been approved for release through the HISTORICAL REVIEW PROGRAM of the Central Intelligence Agency.

Date 8 MAY 92

HRP 92-5

U.S. Defecto

CLASSIFICATION CANCELED
By authority of: C.D.A. ..., 12/22/72
Name and title of person making the change
MMG
Date 1/11/73

28 Sept 61

Per your request for any info on OSWALD, pls note:

Marina Nicholaevna OSWALD, nee PRUSAKOVA, born Jul 41, Maletovsk (Archangelski Oblast), address: Moscow, now residing in Minsk, occupation: laboratory assistant in Kliminchoskaya, Minsk (hospital), has apparently applied for a visa to the U.S., as reflected in Dept. of State, Visa Office notice received in CIA, which is dated 9/12/61.

(Above info was transmitted to the writer by 

Notation of the above is being placed in OSWALD 201.

Document Number 598-252 H
for FOIA Review on JUN 1976

This document has been approved for release through the HISTORICAL REVIEW PROGRAM of the Central Intelligence Agency.

Date 8MAY92
HRP 92-5

CONFIDENTIAL DST 8863

MICROFILMED MAY 25 1962 DOC. MICRO. SER.

y refer to

TO: The Honorable
J. Edgar Hoover,
Director,
Federal Bureau of Investigation,
Washington 25, D. C.

MAY 17 1962

FROM: John Keenan, Chief,
Records and Services Branch,
For the Director,
Office of Security.

SUBJECT: AMERICAN DEFECTORS: STATUS OF IN THE U. S. S. R.

There is attached a copy of report entitled "Status of American Defectors in the Soviet Union" which was prepared and sent by the Security Officer at the American Embassy in Moscow, April 23, 1962. The memorandum covers:

BLOCK, Marris and Mollie

DUTKANICZ, Joseph

OSWALD, Lee

SLOBODA, Vladimir

WEBSTER, Robert

The Security Officer has commented that Bernon Martin and William Mitchell are omitted due to their absence from the local scene. If and when they make an appearance, it will be reported.

Copies of the despatches on Dutkanicz and Sloboda were furnished your Bureau and CIA via liaison. If additonal information is desired on any of the individuals, please advise, and we will endeavor to obtain it.

THE C.I.A. HAS NO OBJECTION TO THE DECLASSIFICATION OF THIS DOCUMENT.

CONFIDENTIAL

SS COPY

ATTACH H/W

200-5-1

CONFIDENTIAL

Status of American Defectors in the Soviet Union

1. JOSEPH DUTKANICZ (see Embassy Despatch 851, dated March 27, 1962): Subsequent to the information which has already been reported on , his wife departed for the United States, and he is making every effort to bring about his own release. He was awarded Soviet citizenship by a special decree of the Supreme Soviet, apparently for his espionage activities on behalf of the Soviets while he was still a member of the U.S. Army in Germany, but his present citizenship status with respect to his American citizenship is unclear. For the time being, at least, is residing in Lvov with his three children (all of whom are American citizens), trying to figure out how he can get back to the U.S.A. He called the Embassy as recently as the 17th or 18th of April in an effort to determine what he should next undertake in his efforts to get back to the U.S.A., and was merely told that he will require a Soviet exit visa before he can leave. In his call, he also mentioned that he had received a severe grilling from the Soviet authorities for having visited the American Embassy in Moscow, and indicated that they were more than a bit displeased with his conduct on that occasion. Since he has received an "Undesirable Discharge" from the U.S. Army and was granted Soviet citizenship by special decree, his American citizenship is in doubt at the moment, and even were it to be established, it is at best problematical if the Soviets will issue him an exit visa and permit him to leave the country.

2. VLADIMIR SLOBODA, (see: Embassy Despatch 841, dated March 23, 1962): Although is equally anxious to leave the Soviet Union, his case at the moment appears rather hopeless; his wife has returned to England, but he remains with his three children in Lvov, although his wife plans to initiate measures from England to secure the release of the three children to her. A letter has recently been sent to by the Embassy requesting him to come in to arrange for the renewal of his child's passport, since one of the children, Victor Edwin, is an American citizen by birth, although his passport has expired.

3. Robert WEBSTER: After a considerable period of delay, Webster has now received an exit permit from the Soviet authorities, but the Embassy is awaiting Departmental advisory approval before issuing an American passport for his return to the U.S.A.

4. Lee OSWALD: It has been determined that Oswald, the ex-Marine, is still an American citizen; both he and his Soviet wife now have exit permits, and the Department has given approval for their travel with their infant child to the U.S.A. There is a problem with his wife, however, in that SOV in the Department is trying to get a waiver of 243G, which requires that Oswald's wife pick up her visa for entry into the U.S.A. in Western Europe. As soon as this question has been settled, they will be free to travel.

Transmitted by SO/Moscow ltr of 4/23/62

CONFIDENTIAL

SIFIED ☐ ☐ CONF. TIAL ☐ SEC

ROUTING

25 November 1963

SUBJECT: Mr. Lee Harvey Oswald

TO : ▇▇▇▇▇▇▇▇

1. It makes little difference now, but ▇▇▇▇ had at one time an OI interest in Oswald. As soon as I had heard Oswald's name, I recalled that as Chief of the 6 Branch I had discussed -- sometime in Summer 1960 -- with the then Chief and Deputy Chief of the 6 Research Section the laying on of interview(s) through ▇▇▇▇ or other suitable channels. At the moment I don't recall if this was discussed while Oswald and his family were en route to our country of if it was after their arrival.

2. I remember that Oswald's unusual behavior in the USSR had struck me from the moment I had read the first State dispatch on him, and I told my subordinates something amounting to "Don't push too hard to get the information we need, because this individual looks odd." We were particularly interested in the OI Oswald might provide on the Minsk factory in which he had been employed, on certain sections of the city itself, and of course we sought the usual BI that might help develop target personality dossiers.

3. I was phasing into my ▇▇▇▇ assignment, ▇▇▇▇▇▇ at tho time. Thus, I would have left our country shortly after Oswald's arrival. I do not know what action developed thereafter.

T ▇▇▇▇▇▇▇▇

Addendum

4. As an afterthought, I recall also that at the time I was becoming increasingly interested in watching develop a pattern that we had discovered in the course of our bio and research work in 6: the number of Soviet women marrying foreigners, being permitted to leave the USSR, then eventually divorcing their spouses and settling down abroad without returning "home". The ▇▇▇▇ case was among the first of these, and we eventually turned up something like two dozen similar cases. We established links between some of these women and the KGB. ▇▇▇▇ became interested in the developing trend we had come across. It was partly out of curiosity to learn if Oswald's wife would actually accompany him to our country, partly out of interest in Oswald's own experienced in the U SSR, that we showed operational intelligence interest in the Harvey story.

T.B.C.

Document Number 1622-1125-B

for FOIA Review on FEB 1978

OSWALD, Lee Harvey
USSR

CI-Project/RE
9 November 1959
7-305
MR-R1
20 NOV. 59

Recent defector to the USSR. Former Marine.

Delete 15/3/60

CIA puts Oswald on Watch List HT/LINGUAL

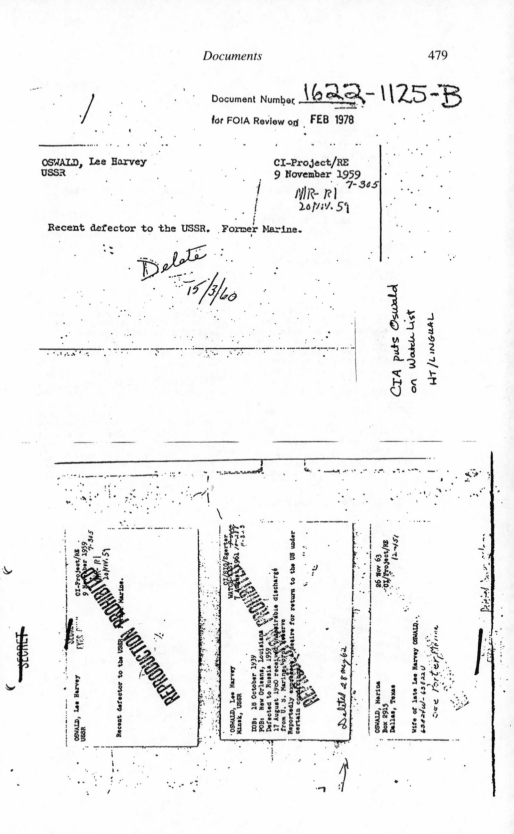

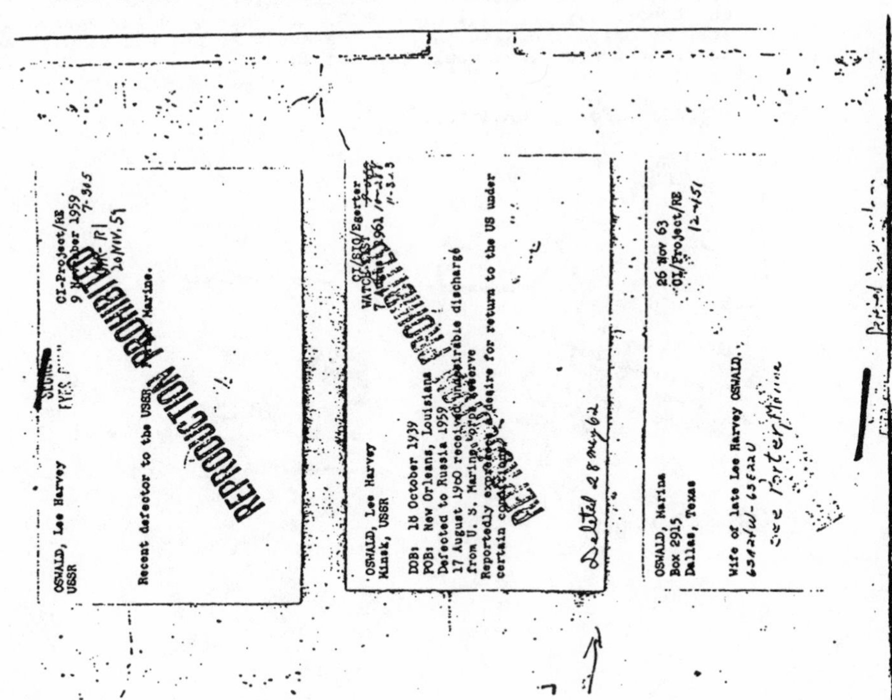

SECRET

OSWALD, Lee Harvey
USSR

CI-Project/RE
9 November 1959
7-305

Recent defector to the USSR. Former Marine.

REPRODUCTION PROHIBITED

OSWALD, Lee Harvey
Minsk, USSR

CI/SIG/Egerter
WATCH LIST
7 August 1961

DOB: 18 October 1939
POB: New Orleans, Louisiana
Defected to Russia 1959
17 August 1960 received undesirable discharge from U. S. Marine Corps Reserve
Reportedly expressed a desire for return to the US under certain conditions.

Deleted 28 May 62

OSWALD, Marina
Box 2915
Dallas, Texas

26 Nov 63
CI/Project/RE
12-451

Wife of late Lee Harvey OSWALD.

See Porter, Marina

page 244

EXHIBIT 22

OPTIONAL FORM NO. 10

UNITED STATES GOVERNMENT

Memorandum

HTLINGUAL

TO : MR. A. H. BELMONT DATE: March 10, 1961

FROM : MR. D. E. MOORE

SUBJECT: HUNTER
ESPIONAGE - R

Hunter is CIA's sensitive project involving the review of mail going to the CIA makes available to us results of their analysis relative to this project.

On 3-9-61 during a conference on illegal espionage activities between Special Agents and and Messrs. Angleton, of CIA, we were advised that C IA has now established a laboratory in New York in connection with this project which can examine correspondence for secret writing, micro dots and possibly codes. He said the laboratory is fully equipped and they would be glad to make its facilities available to us if at any time we desire an examination of this nature to be made in NYC and time was of the essence and would not permit the material to be brought to our Laboratory in Washington, D.C. We expressed our appreciation for the offer and said that in the event we desired to utilize their laboratory, we would contact them.

ACTION: For information.

(7)

another mood!

SA advised 4/19/61 that Hunter material will increase about 20% since NY lab now established. 4/21/61

Classified by

Exempt from GDS, Category

Date of Declassification Indefinite

EX-114

REC- 22

MAR 23

83 MAR 28 1961

HTLINGUAL
SOFT FILE

Deputy Chief, CI 22 June 1962

Deputy Chief, CI/Project

HTLINGUAL - 61G10AK
Correspondence of a US Defector Who Recently Left the USSR Homebound

1. As may be seen from the attached news item, which appeared in the WASHINGTON POST, 9 June 1962, a former Marine Sgt. of Fort Worth, Texas, who defected to the USSR three years ago, left Moscow recently, together with his infant child and Russian-born wife bound for the United States. A search of the Project files revealed that the attached subject item was sent to subject by his mother on 8 July 1961. In this item writer discusses sending a parcel and requests him to write more frequently.

2. This item will be of interest to Mrs. Egerter, CI/SIG, and also to the FBI.

Attachment

JUL 10 1961

61G10AK Eglal

HTLINGUAL

26 November 1963

SPECIAL HANDLING

MEMORANDUM FOR: Director
Federal Bureau of Investigation
Attention: Mr. S. J. Papich

SUBJECT: HUNTER Report # 10815

1. Reference is made to your report of 25 October 1963, Subject: Fair Play for Cuba Committee - New Orleans Division, prepared by Special Agent Warren C. De BRUEYS at New Orleans, your file No. 97-4196-33. This report contains information on Lee Harvey OSWALD, who was suspected of having assassinated President John F. KENNEDY. According to your report OSWALD had in his possession a membership card for the New Orleans Chapter of the Fair Play for Cuba Committee. The card was issued on 6 June 1963, and it was signed by A. J. HIDELL. Your report also indicates that when OSWALD was arrested in New Orleans on 9 August 1963, he was distributing throwaways for the Fair Play for Cuba Committee bearing the name, A. J. HIDELL, P. O. Box 30016, New Orleans, Louisana.

2. We are informed that OSWALD ordered a rifle of the same type used in the assassination of President KENNEDY from Kleins, a mail order house in Chicago, Illinois. The rifle reportedly was ordered in the name of Alek HIDELL, but it was mailed to OSWALD at a P. O. box registered in OSWALD's name. Although your report referenced above indicates that OSWALD said that he had talked to a person by the name of HIDELL by telephone several times, your Bureau had not established that a person by the name of HIDELL resided in New Orleans, at the time the report was prepared.

3. Your representative in Mexico advised our representative there that it had not been determined whether HIDELL is a person, or an alias used by OSWALD. In this connection we refer you to the attached HUNTER items - 63 E 22 U and 63 A 24 W. These items indicate that OSWALD was known to his wife's friends in Russia as "Alik" (also spelled "Alick"). While we have no items in which the name HIDELL (or HYDELL) appears, it is believed that the fact that OSWALD was known to his Russian friends as "Alik" may be significant.

pat dep -f
1519-1094

SECRET

HTLINGUAL

4. Your attention is also drawn to items 62 L 11 A 0607 and 62 L 11 A 0606, copies of which are attached. It will be noted that these items are from M. OSWALD (presumably Marina OSWALD) 602 Elsbeth Street, Dallas, Texas, and that they contain the name of the following company:

Texas Import Export Co.
P. O. Box 7
Ft. Worth, Texas.

5. For your information, copies of the following item were delivered by hand to Mr. S. J. Papich of your Bureau on 23 November 1963:

62 L 11 A 0606
62 L 11 A 0607
62 C 05 A 3109
63 E 22 U
63 A 24 W
61 G 10 AK

FOR THE DEPUTY DIRECTOR (PLANS):

James Angleton

Attachments: 63 E 22 U
63 A 24 W
62 L 11 A 0606
62 L 11 A0 607

- 2 -

SECRET

HTLINGUAL

1 May 1964

MEMORANDUM

SUBJECT: HTLINGUAL Items Relating to the OSWALD Case

Material from this operation is handled on a need-to-know basis within this Agency and such of the material that is given to the FBI receives special handling and limited distribution within that Bureau.

A. Item 53J18AT - This item was written by one Irina Aleksayevna MIKHAYLOVICH of Kharkov, USSR, to Captain Donald L. BURT and his wife, Lydia BURT. The latter appears to be the daughter of Irina MIKHAYLOVICH, who mentions seeing one Marina. As Marina OSWALD is known to have an aunt in Kharkov named Poline MIKHAYLOVICH, it is considered possible that Irina MIKHAYLOVICH and Lydia BURT may be related to Marina OSWALD.

B. Item 61G1GAK - This item was written by Mrs. Marguerite OSWALD to her son, Lee Harvey OSWALD, when the latter was in the USSR. The letter contains no information of real significance.

C. Item 62C05A3109 - This item is addressed to Miss June Marina OSWALD, Lee Harvey OSWALD's daughter, by Mrs. Marguerite OSWALD. This item is only a cover and its contents were not examined. Presumably this item was written shortly after the birth of June OSWALD.

D. Item 62L11A0606 - This is an item addressed to one Pavel SOLOVASTEV in Minsk, USSR, by Marina OSWALD. CI/SIG cards on the OSWALD case do not reveal any other reference to a Pavel SOLOVASTEV, and it is not known whether Marina OSWALD has mentioned this individual. It is noted that one "Pavel," last name not given, is mentioned in a document, FBI Item 127-55.

E. Item 62L11A0607 - This item is addressed to Tamara Aleksandrovna SAHKOVSKAYA and Sophiya VASILEVSKAYA, both residing in Minsk, USSR, by Marina OSWALD. CI/SIG files do not indicate that the names of these two individuals appear in any other documents.

Document Number 1619-1122-Y
for FOIA Review on FEB 1978

~~SECRET~~ ~~EYES ONLY~~

HTLINGUAL

F. Item 63A24W - This item was written to Marina OSWALD by one Galina KHOMTULEVA, one of Marina OSWALD's close friends. FBI Item 350 is a photograph of a letter from KHOMTULEVA to Marina OSWALD, therefore, KHOMTULEVA is known to the FBI.

G. Item 63E22 - This item is from Erick TITOVIETS (TITOVETS) to Marina OSWALD. This appears to be the "Erick" frequently mentioned by OSWALD in his "Historic Diary." One Ernst TITOVET is also mentioned in an FBI report, [illegible], 31 December 1963, page 24.

H. Item 56M05K and 59D09BX - These two items, written in the Hungarian language, were addressed to one John RUBY, 4539 West Congress Street, Chicago, Illinois. As no one is available to translate HTLINGUAL items in Hungarian, the full contents of these items are unknown. The items were forwarded to the FBI as being of possible interest in connection with the Bureau's investigation of Jack RUBY. The items are not believed to be pertinent to the OSWALD case.

I. Items 58J22A5, 59K1C30107, 59J23A2114, 59J23A2115, 59K09R1320, [illegible], [illegible], [illegible], [illegible], [illegible], 59K030, [illegible], [illegible], 62313V, [illegible], [illegible] - These items relate to a Solomon GOLDIN who was hospitalized in 1956 in the Botkinskaya Hospital in Moscow, which is the hospital to which OSWALD was reportedly taken after he attempted to commit suicide. These items have no real bearing on the OSWALD case, although it was hoped that they might lead to the identification of the "elderly American" referred to by OSWALD in his "Historic Diary."

J. Item 60F24 - This item addressed to Lev SETYAEV by one Charles John PAGENHARDT is of interest as Lev SETYAEV was listed in OSWALD's address book and PAGENHARDT is known to have contemplated defecting to the USSR. SETYAEV and PAGENHARDT are known to the FBI.

~~SECRET~~

~~EYES ONLY~~

ATTACHMENT TO JOHN HERTZ MEMO ON LINGUA PROGRAM APRIL, 1964

SECRET
EYES ONLY

the Division. There were three blind memos issued on 11 December 1963, concerning . all of which stemmed from one banjo item.

4. The Project has produced many items over the years concerning defectors and repatriates from the United States now living in the USSR. Among these have been numerous re-defectors who have returned to the United States, the most interesting among whom, during the past year, has been Lee Harvey OSWALD. The Project's files contain several items to and from OSWALD and his wife, and these were the source of the information that OSWALD's pseudonym was used in the USSR as well as when he ordered the murder weapon from the gun store in Chicago. A recent listing of Americans or former Americans, living for extended periods in the USSR, who have been recognized as defectors or repatriates from banjo items, totals 113.

5. The Project frequently reports on items to and from foreign students in the USSR. The majority of such students noted are from Latin America and Africa. Frequently items to or from these students will be transitting the United States and not addressed to or from this country. In such cases dissemination is made, using SR Division's project . In this manner the item can be disseminated under a secret classification and thus can go directly to the area desk concerned, which in turn, can have it indexed in RI, send it to the field or take whatever action they may wish without having to further disguise the source. When items to or from these foreign students originate in or are addressed to the United States, the "Eyes Only" classification must be applied and they then can only be disseminated to persons cleared and briefed on the Project. During the latter part of 1963, a system was devised whereby foreign student's names, their home countries and the date they were known to be in the USSR have been listed in memoranda over the signature of of CI/OG/SS. These memoranda are addressed to RID with the request that the students be indexed. So far there have been only 54 students included in such memoranda, but if RI agrees to index them, it is planned to extract many more such names from the Project's fanfold for indexing.

SECRET

OPTIONAL FORM NO. 10
5010-104

UNITED STATES GOVERNMENT

Memorandum

TO : SAC, NEW ORLEANS (89-69) DATE: 11/26/63

FROM : Supvr. LEON M. GASKILL

SUBJECT: ASSASSINATION OF PRESIDENT JOHN F. KENNEDY, 11/22/63, DALLAS, TEXAS Re: HANDBILL OF FAIR PLAY FOR CUBA COMMITTEE

On 11/26/63 Major ROBERT H. ERDRICH, 112th Intelligence Corps Group, New Orleans, personally came to this office and advised he understood we were interested in the Fair Play for Cuba Committee in connection with the investigation of this case and for this reason wanted to furnish the following information:

He advised that one of the 112th Agents sometime during the last week in May or the first week in June, 1963, picked up a handbill of the Fair Play for Cuba Committee which was attached to a wall on the campus of Tulane University. This handbill was approximately 8" x 11" and was faded green in color. The 112th Intelligence Corps Group subsequently found additional copies of this handbill laying on Canal Street and others laying on the grounds of the Port of Embarkation, New Orleans. Some of the bills found by the 112th were faded green and some were faded orange.

On 6/18/63 Major ERDRICH's office sent one of these bills to their headquarters at Washington, D. C., and maintained a photograph of one of the bills in the files of the 112th. Major ERDRICH advised he would obtain photographic copies of this photograph and would furnish them to the New Orleans FBI Office.

The handbills in question read as follows:

"HANDS OFF CUBA!
JOIN THE FAIR PLAY FOR CUBA COMMITTEE.
NEW ORLEANS CHARTER MEMBER BRANCH
FREE LITERATURE, LECTURES
LOCATION:
FPCC - A. J. HIDELL
P. O. Box 30016
NEW ORLEANS, LOUISIANA
EVERYONE WELCOME!"

89-69-166

SEARCHED .... INDEXED ....
SERIALIZED .... FILED ....
NOV 26 1963
FBI — NEW ORLEANS

LMG:lil
(2)

NO 89-69

Major ERDRICH indicated he understood that OSWALD had used the name of A. J. HIDELL in the past.

ADDENDUM:

On the afternoon of 11/26/63, Major ERDRICH furnished the attached two copies of the Fair Play for Cuba Committee handbill.

Commission Exhibit 115

HANDS OFF CUBA!

Join the Fair Play for Cuba Committee

NEW ORLEANS CHARTER MEMBER BRANCH

Free Literature, Lectures

LOCATION:

EVERYONE WELCOME!

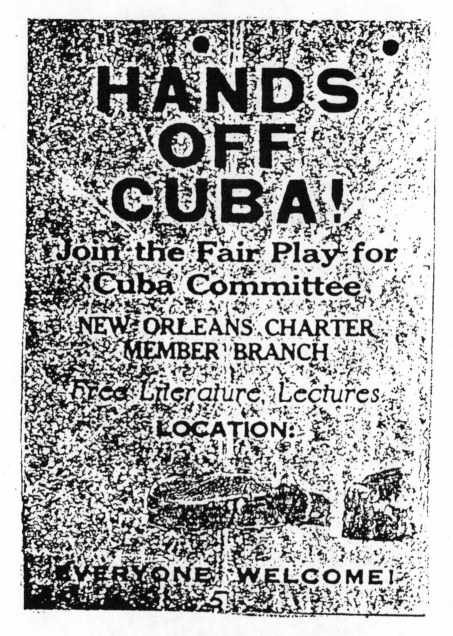

1370

HANDS OFF CUBA!

Join the Fair Play for Cuba Committee

NEW ORLEANS CHARTER MEMBER BRANCH

Free Literature, Lectures

LOCATION:

EVERYONE WELCOME!

5

5

CD 1370

CD 1370

HANDS OFF CUBA!

Join the Fair Play for Cuba Committee

NEW ORLEANS CHARTER MEMBER BRANCH

Free Literature, Lectures

LOCATION:

FPCC-A J HIDELL
P.O. BOX 30016
NEW ORLEANS, LA.

EVERYONE WELCOME!

ON BACK:

MARTIN ABELOW HANDBILL

BOARD OF COMMISSIONERS OF THE PORT OF NEW ORLEANS
(AN AGENCY OF THE STATE OF LOUISIANA)
INTER-OFFICE COMMUNICATION

DATE: June 16, 1963

TO: Chief L. Deutschman C.C.

FROM: Patrolman Girod Ray

SUBJECT: Distribution of Propaganda Literature

While working a special assigament at Dumain St. Wharf I was approached by a U.S.S. Navy Officer from the U.S.S. Wasp, who stated that he saw a white male adult subject handing out the enclosed pamphlets to persons visiting the Wasp, berthed at Dumaine St. Wharf.

I immediately looked for this subject and found him distrubuting these pamphlets and asked him if he had received permission from the Dock Board to issue these papers. He stated that he thought as an American citizen he did not need anyones permission. I ordered this man off of our property and told him he would have to refrain from issuing anything on Dock Board Property without their express consent.

Ptn. Girod Ray

Sunday - Between 1Pm - 4 P.m.

5'6"-5'7"

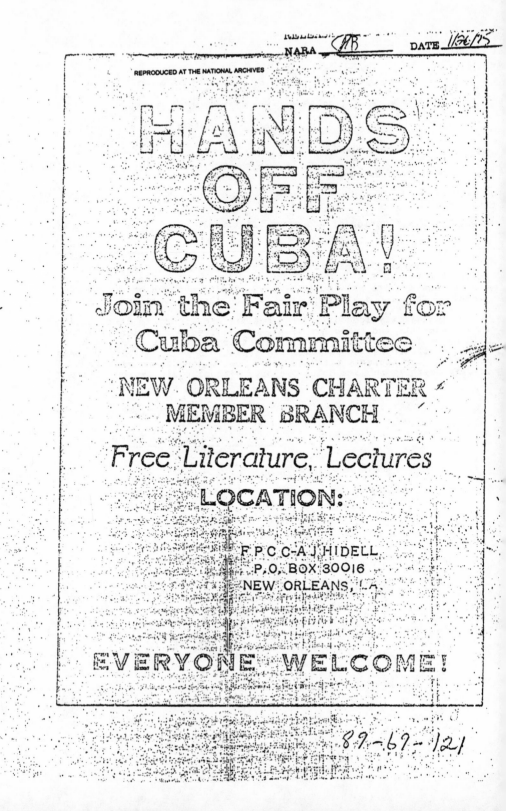

HANDS OFF CUBA!

Join the Fair Play for Cuba Committee

NEW ORLEANS CHARTER MEMBER BRANCH

Free Literature, Lectures

LOCATION:

F P C C-A J HIDELL
P.O. BOX 30016
NEW ORLEANS, LA.

EVERYONE WELCOME!

9 l

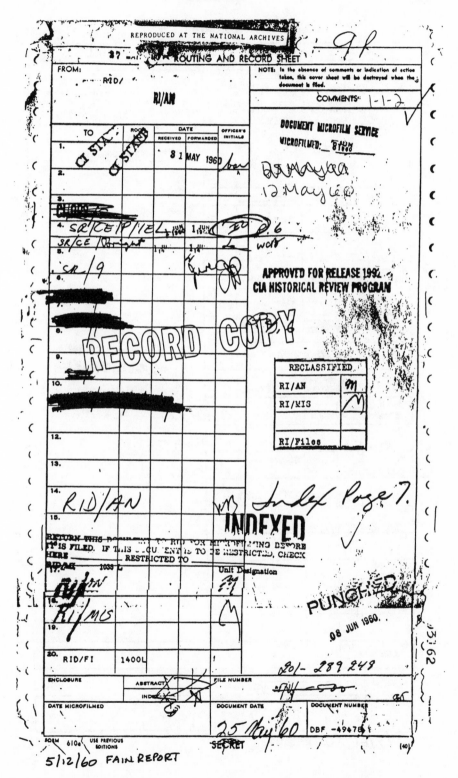

ROUTING AND RECORD SHEET

FROM: RID/

RI/AN

NOTE: In the absence of comments or indication of action taken, this cover sheet will be destroyed when the document is filed.

COMMENTS: 1-1-2

DOCUMENT MICROFILM SERVICE
MICROFILMED: 8 JUN 1960

TO	ROOM	DATE RECEIVED	DATE FORWARDED	OFFICER'S INITIALS
1. CI STAFF	CI STAFF		31 MAY 1960	
2.				
3. [redacted]				
4. SR/CE/P/IEL		1 JUN 1960	1 JUN 1960	
5. SR/CE/Bright		1 JUN	1 JUN	
6. SR/9				
7. [redacted]				
8. [redacted]				
9.				
10.				
11. [redacted]				
12.				
13.				
14. RID/AN				
15.				
16.				
17. RID/AN	1033 L			
18. RI/MIS				
19.				
20. RID/FI	1400L			

12 May 60

APPROVED FOR RELEASE 1992
CIA HISTORICAL REVIEW PROGRAM

RECORD COPY

RECLASSIFIED	
RI/AN	
RI/MIS	
RI/Files	

Index Page 7.

INDEXED

RETURN THIS DOCUMENT TO RID FOR MICROFILMING BEFORE IT IS FILED. IF THIS DOCUMENT IS TO BE RESTRICTED, CHECK HERE ______ RESTRICTED TO ______
Unit Designation

PUNCHED
08 JUN 1960

201- 289 248

ENCLOSURE	ABSTRACT / INDEX	FILE NUMBER

DATE MICROFILMED	DOCUMENT DATE	DOCUMENT NUMBER
	25 May 60	DBF -49478

FORM 610a USE PREVIOUS EDITIONS SECRET (40)

5/12/60 FAIN REPORT

SECRET (WHEN FILLED IN)

FEB. 60

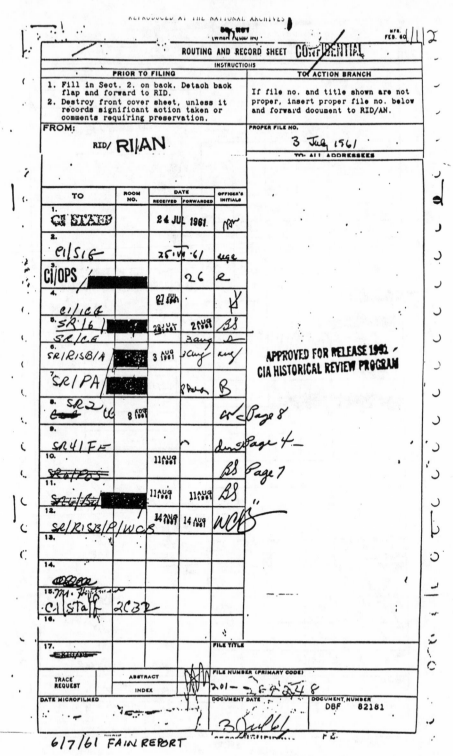

ROUTING AND RECORD SHEET CONFIDENTIAL

INSTRUCTIONS

PRIOR TO FILING	TO ACTION BRANCH
1. Fill in Sect. 2. on back. Detach back flap and forward to RID. 2. Destroy front cover sheet, unless it records significant action taken or comments requiring preservation.	If file no. and title shown are not proper, insert proper file no. below and forward document to RID/AN.

FROM: RID/ RI/AN

PROPER FILE NO.: 3 July 1961

TO: ALL ADDRESSEES

TO	ROOM NO.	DATE RECEIVED	DATE FORWARDED	OFFICER'S INITIALS
1. CI STAFF		24 JUL 1961		[illegible]
2. CI/SIG		25 VII 61		[illegible]
3. CI/OPS / [redacted]			26	[illegible]
4. CI/ICG		27 [illegible]		[illegible]
5. SR/6 / [redacted] SR/CG		28 JUL 1961	2 AUG 1961 3 aug	BS
6. SR/RISB/A [redacted]		3 AUG 1961	3 aug	[illegible]
7. SR/PA [redacted]			[illegible]	B
8. SR2 CI		8 AUG 1961		[illegible] Page 8
9. SR4/FE				[illegible] Page 4
10. [illegible]		11 AUG 1961		BS Page 7
11. [illegible] [redacted]		11 AUG 1961	11 AUG 1961	BS
12. SR/RISB/P/WCB		14 AUG 1961	14 AUG 1961	WCB
13.				
14. [illegible]				
15. M. [illegible] CI Staff	2C32			
16.				
17. [illegible]				

APPROVED FOR RELEASE 1992 CIA HISTORICAL REVIEW PROGRAM

FILE TITLE

TRACE REQUEST	ABSTRACT / INDEX	FILE NUMBER (PRIMARY CODE): 201-264248

DATE MICROFILMED	DOCUMENT DATE: 3 Jul 61	DOCUMENT NUMBER: DBF 82181

6/7/61 FAIN REPORT

☐ UNCLASSIFIED ☐ INTERNAL USE ONLY ☐ CONFIDENTIAL ☐ SECRET

ROUTING AND RECORD SHEET

SUBJECT: (Optional)
OSWALD, Lee Harvey

9544
XAAZ 9644

FROM:
SR/CI/P/dl

NO.
AMemb Moscow Desp. #806

DATE
May 26, 61

TO: (Officer designation, room number, and building)	DATE RECEIVED	DATE FORWARDED	OFFICER'S INITIALS	COMMENTS (Number each comment to show from whom to whom. Draw a line across column after each comment.)
1. C/SR/CI/P				FYI. (WP had originally asked me to pull together all refs on this man.) Since then it has been determined that [redacted] is interested & either holds the 201-289248 or has it restricted to her.
2.				
3.				
4. CI/SIG/[redacted]	1. XI. 61			For 201– 289248
5. RI/AN	16 NOV 1961			
6. RID/IP/FS				
7.				
8. RI/FI				
9.				
10.				
11.				
12.				
13.				
14.				
15.				

201-289248
ABSTRACT X INDEX
DATE 26 MAY 61

APPROVED FOR RELEASE 1993
CIA HISTORICAL REVIEW PROGRAM

FORM 1 DEC 56 610 USE PREVIOUS EDITIONS ☐ SECRET ☐ CONFIDENTIAL ☐ INTERNAL USE ONLY ☐ UNCLASSIFIED

5/26/61 FOREIGN SERVICE DISPATCH 806

3

☐ UNCLASSIFIED ☐ INTERNAL USE ONLY ☐ CO[illegible]FIDENTIAL ☐ ~~SECRET~~

ROUTING AND RECORD SHEET

SUBJECT: (Optional)

FROM:	NO. XAAZ 9645
RID/ANALYSIS	DATE 30 OCT 1961 13 Oct 61

TO: (Officer designation, room number, and building)	DATE RECEIVED	DATE FORWARDED	OFFICER'S INITIALS	COMMENTS (Number each comment to show from whom to whom. Draw a line across column after each comment.)
1. CI/Staff/				RETAIN ~~OR DESTROY~~
2. Sig	slub			THIS DOCUMENT HAS BEEN REVIEWED BY RID/AN
3.				It has not been integrated into the CS Record System.
4.				If further processing is desired, please so indicate and return to RID/AN.
5. RI/AN	16 NOV 1961		MK	
6.				
7. RI/MIS				
8.				
9.				201-289248 ABSTRACT ☒ INDEX
10.				DATE ~~26 May 61~~ 13 Oct 61
11. RI/FI				
12.				
13.				
14.				APPROVED FOR RELEASE 1992 CIA HISTORICAL REVIEW PROGRAM
15.				

FORM 1 DEC 56 610 USE PREVIOUS EDITIONS OP-58 4-61 ☐ SECRET ☐ CONFIDENTIAL ☐ INTERNAL USE ONLY ☐ UNCLASSIFIED

11/13/61 MOSCOW AIR POUCH

4

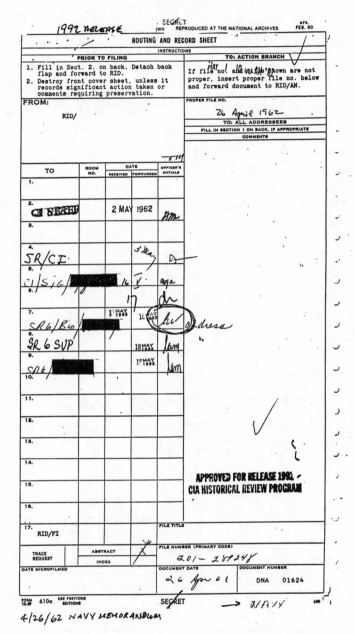

1992 RELEASE SECRET (WH MFR. FEB. 60

ROUTING AND RECORD SHEET

INSTRUCTIONS

PRIOR TO FILING	TO: ACTION BRANCH
1. Fill in Sect. 2. on back. Detach back flap and forward to RID. 2. Destroy front cover sheet, unless it records significant action taken or comments requiring preservation.	If file no. and title shown are not proper, insert proper file no. below and forward document to RID/AN.

FROM: RID/

PROPER FILE NO.: 26 April 1962

TO: ALL ADDRESSEES

FILL IN SECTION 1 ON BACK, IF APPROPRIATE

COMMENTS

TO	ROOM NO.	DATE RECEIVED	DATE FORWARDED	OFFICER'S INITIALS
1.				
2. CI STAFF		2 MAY	1962	
3.				
4. SR/CI			3 May	
5. CI/SIG/ [redacted]			16 V	
6.			17	
7. SR6/Bio/ [redacted]		1? MAY 1962	18 MAY 1962	
8. SR 6 SUP			18 MAY 1962	
9. SR6/ [redacted]			1? MAY 1962	
10.				
11.				
12.				
13.				
14.				
15.				
16.				
17. RID/FI				

address

TRACE REQUEST	ABSTRACT / INDEX	FILE TITLE / FILE NUMBER (PRIMARY CODE)
		201-289248

DATE MICROFILMED	DOCUMENT DATE	DOCUMENT NUMBER
	26 Apr 62	DNA 01624

FORM 12-59 610a USE PREVIOUS EDITIONS SECRET → NAVY

4/26/62 NAVY MEMORANDUM

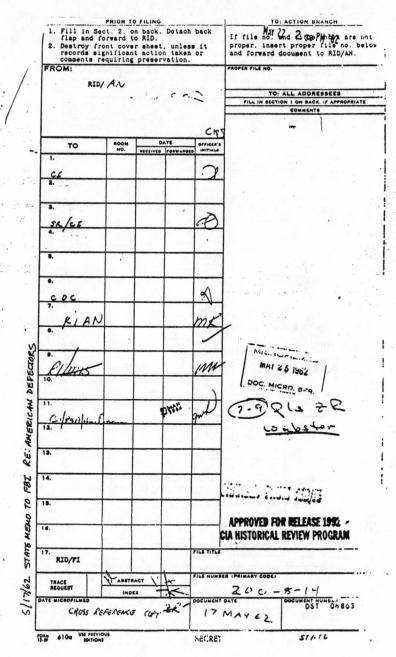

PRIOR TO FILING	TO: ACTION BRANCH
1. Fill in Sect. 2. on back. Detach back flap and forward to RID. 2. Destroy front cover sheet, unless it records significant action taken or comments requiring preservation.	MAY 22 2 PM '62 If file no. and [illegible] are not proper, insert proper file no. below and forward document to RID/AN.
FROM: RID/AN	PROPER FILE NO.
	TO: ALL ADDRESSEES FILL IN SECTION 1 ON BACK, IF APPROPRIATE
	COMMENTS

TO	ROOM NO.	DATE RECEIVED	DATE FORWARDED	OFFICER'S INITIALS
1. CE				[initials]
2.				
3. SR/CE				[initials]
4.				
5.				
6. CDC				[initials]
7. RIAN				mK
8.				
9. [illegible]				[initials]
10.				
11. C/[illegible]			[stamp]	[initials]
12.				
13.				
14.				
15.				
16.				
17. RID/FI				

MICROFILMED
MAY 25 1962
DOC. MICRO. SER.

(7-9) [illegible] ZR
webster

APPROVED FOR RELEASE 1992
CIA HISTORICAL REVIEW PROGRAM

5/17/62 STATE MEMO TO FBI RE: AMERICAN DEFECTORS

TRACE REQUEST	ABSTRACT / INDEX	FILE TITLE FILE NUMBER (PRIMARY CODE) 200-5-14	
DATE MICROFILMED CROSS REFERENCE COPY		DOCUMENT DATE 17 MAY 62	DOCUMENT NUMBER DST 04863

FORM 610a USE PREVIOUS EDITIONS SECRET STATE

6

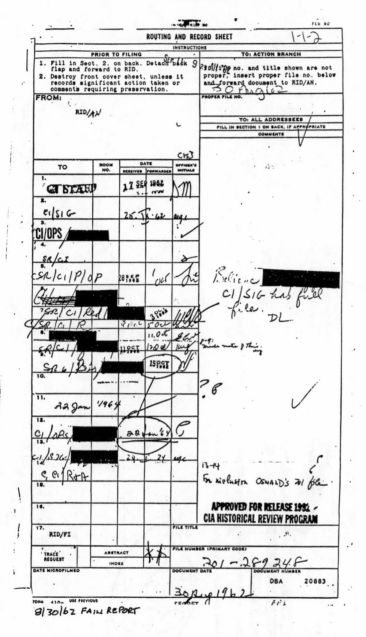

ROUTING AND RECORD SHEET 1-1-2

INSTRUCTIONS

PRIOR TO FILING

1. Fill in Sect. 2. on back. Detach back flap and forward to RID.
2. Destroy front cover sheet, unless it records significant action taken or comments requiring preservation.

TO: ACTION BRANCH

If file no. and title shown are not proper, insert proper file no. below and forward document to RID/AN.

30 Aug 62

FROM: RID/AN

PROPER FILE NO.

TO: ALL ADDRESSEES

FILL IN SECTION 1 ON BACK, IF APPROPRIATE

COMMENTS

TO	ROOM NO.	DATE RECEIVED	DATE FORWARDED	OFFICER'S INITIALS
1. CI STAFF		17 SEP 1962		DM
2. CI/SIG		25. IX. 62		
3. CI/OPS/				
4. SR/CI				
5. CSR/CI/P/OP		28 SEP 1962	1 Oct	
6.				
7. SR/CI/Red			3 Oct 1962	
C/SR/CI/R		4 Oct	5 Oct	
8.			11 Oct	
SR/CI/		11 OCT 1962	12 Oct	
9. SR 6/B		15 OCT 1962		
10.				
11. 22 Jan 1964				
12. CI/OPS/		22 Jan '64		
13. CI/SIG		24. I. 24		
14. C, CI/R&A				
15.				
16.				
17. RID/FI				

Believe CI/SIG has full file. DL

make note of this

? B

13-14 For inclusion OSWALD's 201 file

APPROVED FOR RELEASE 1993
CIA HISTORICAL REVIEW PROGRAM

FILE TITLE

TRACE REQUEST | ABSTRACT | INDEX

FILE NUMBER (PRIMARY CODE) 201-289248

DATE MICROFILMED

DOCUMENT DATE 30 Aug 1962

DOCUMENT NUMBER DBA 20883

FORM 610 USE PREVIOUS

SECRET

8/30/62 FAIN REPORT

UNITED STATES GO[illegible]MENT

Memorandum

TO : SAC DALLAS (100-10461)
(105-1435)

DATE: 5/28/63

FROM : SA JAMES P HOSTY JR

SUBJECT: LEE HARVEY OSWALD
IS-R
100-10461
MARINA NIKOLAEVNA OSWALD AKA
IS-R
105-1435

The owner of sub jects former residence at 214 Neely Dallas, [redacted] and [redacted] will be interviewed for information re subjects as will subjects Brother in Fort Worth.

Post

2- 100-10461
1- 105-1435

100-10,461-35
SEARCHED ___ INDEXED ___
SERIALIZED ___ FILED ___
MAY 2 8 1963
FBI — DALLAS

verified to Bur 12/18/63 #

PLH ITEM # 984

Memorandum

TO : SAC DALLAS (100-10461)
(105-1435)

DATE: 5/23/63

FROM : SA JAMES P HOSTY JR

SUBJECT: LEE HARVEY OSWALD
IS-R
100-10461
MARINA NIKOLAEVNA OSWALD AKA
IS-R
105-1435

On 5/27/63 an attempt to interview subjects at 214 Neely, Dallas under pretext reflected that they had moved from their residence . A check with the Postmaster reflects that the subjects have moved and left no forwrding address.

The owner of sub jects former residence at 214 Neely Dallas, M.W. GEORGE TA 3 9729 and LAC 7268 will be interviewed for information re subjects as will subjects Brother in Fort Worth.

Post

1- 100-10461
1- 105-1435

100-10,461-35
SEARCHED ___ INDEXED ___
SERIALIZED ___ FILED ___
MAY 2 8 1963
FBI — DALLAS

verified to Bur 12/18/63 #

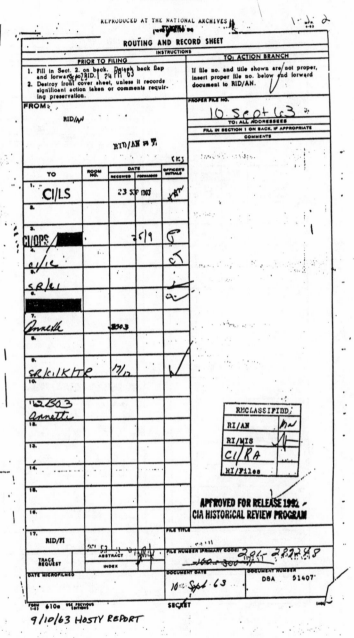

ROUTING AND RECORD SHEET

INSTRUCTIONS

PRIOR TO FILING	TO: ACTION BRANCH
1. Fill in Sect. 2. on back. Detach back flap and forward to RID. 2. Destroy front cover sheet, unless it records significant action taken or comments requiring preservation.	If file no. and title shown are not proper, insert proper file no. below and forward document to RID/AN.

SEP 23 RID. 24 PM '63

FROM: RID/AN

RID/AN

PROPER FILE NO. 10 Sept 63

TO: ALL ADDRESSEES

FILL IN SECTION 1 ON BACK, IF APPROPRIATE

COMMENTS

TO	ROOM NO.	DATE RECEIVED	DATE FORWARDED	OFFICER'S INITIALS
1. CI/LS		23 SEP 1963		
2.				
3. CI/OPS/[redacted]			25/9	
4. CI/IC				CT
5. SR/CI				
6. [redacted]				
7. Annette		2B03		
8.				
9. SR/CI/K/TR		17/12		
10. 2B03 Annette				
12.				
13.				
14.				
15.				
16.				
17. RID/FI				

RECLASSIFIED	
RI/AN	
RI/MIS	
CI/RA	
RI/Files	

APPROVED FOR RELEASE 1992
CIA HISTORICAL REVIEW PROGRAM

TRACE REQUEST | ABSTRACT | INDEX

FILE TITLE

FILE NUMBER (PRIMARY CODE) 201-282288 (~~100-300-11~~)

DATE MICROFILMED

DOCUMENT DATE 10 Sept 63

DOCUMENT NUMBER DBA 51407

FORM 1-63 610a USE PREVIOUS EDITIONS

SECRET

9/10/63 HOSTY REPORT

1-1-2

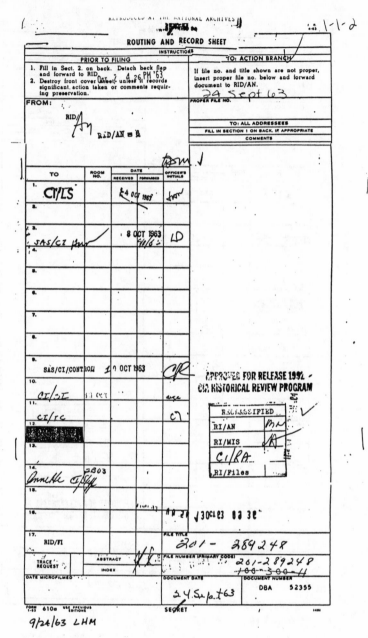

ROUTING AND RECORD SHEET

INSTRUCTIONS

PRIOR TO FILING	TO: ACTION BRANCH
1. Fill in Sect. 2. on back. Detach back flap and forward to RID. Oct 7 4 26 PM '63 2. Destroy front cover sheet, unless it records significant action taken or comments requiring preservation.	If file no. and title shown are not proper, insert proper file no. below and forward document to RID/AN. 24 Sept 63
FROM: RID/AN RID/AN = R	PROPER FILE NO.
	TO: ALL ADDRESSEES — FILL IN SECTION 1 ON BACK, IF APPROPRIATE
	COMMENTS

TO	ROOM NO.	DATE RECEIVED	DATE FORWARDED	OFFICER'S INITIALS
1. CI/LS		4 OCT 1963		
2.				
3. SAS/CI		8 OCT 1963		LD
4.				
5.				
6.				
7.				
8.				
9. SAS/CI/CONTROL		10 OCT 1963		CR
10. CI/SI		11 OCT		
11. CI/IC				CJ
12. [redacted]				
13.				
14. Annette CI/Staff	2B03			
15.				
16.				
17. RID/FI				

APPROVED FOR RELEASE 1992
CIA HISTORICAL REVIEW PROGRAM

RECLASSIFIED	
RI/AN	
RI/MIS	
CI/RA	
RI/Files	

30 Oct 63 08 38

TRACE REQUEST	ABSTRACT / INDEX	FILE TITLE: 201-289248
		FILE NUMBER (PRIMARY CODE): 201-289248 ~~100-300-11~~
DATE MICROFILMED	DOCUMENT DATE: 24 Sept 63	DOCUMENT NUMBER: DBA 52355

FORM 1-63 610a USE PREVIOUS EDITIONS SECRET

9/24/63 LHM

Federal Bureau of Investigation CD 692

NOV 8 1963

DBA-52355

Director
Central Intelligence Agency
Washington, D. C. 20505

Attention: Deputy Director, Plans

Dear Sir:

For your information, I am enclosing communications which may be of interest to you.

Very truly yours,

J. Edgar Hoover

John Edgar Hoover
Director

Enc.

(Upon removal of classified enclosures, if any, this transmittal form becomes UNCLASSIFIED.)

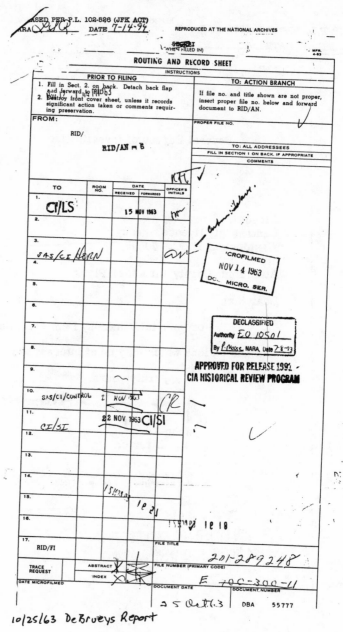

[RELE]ASED PER P.L. 102-526 (JFK ACT)
[N]ARA [initials] DATE 7-14-94

~~SECRET~~
(WHEN FILLED IN)

MFR. 4-63

ROUTING AND RECORD SHEET

INSTRUCTIONS

PRIOR TO FILING

1. Fill in Sect. 2. on back. Detach back flap and forward to RID.
2. Destroy front cover sheet, unless it records significant action taken or comments requiring preservation.

TO: ACTION BRANCH

If file no. and title shown are not proper, insert proper file no. below and forward document to RID/AN.

FROM:

RID/

RID/AN – B

PROPER FILE NO.

TO: ALL ADDRESSEES
FILL IN SECTION 1 ON BACK. IF APPROPRIATE

COMMENTS

TO	ROOM NO.	DATE RECEIVED	DATE FORWARDED	OFFICER'S INITIALS
1. CI/LS			15 NOV 1963	
2.				
3. SAS/CI HORN				
4.				
5.				
6.				
7.				
8.				
9.				
10. SAS/CI/CONTROL		2[?] NOV 1963		CR
11. CI/SI		22 NOV 1963	CI/SI	
12.				
13.				
14.				
15.				
16.				
17. RID/FI				

'CROFILMED
NOV 14 1963
DOC. MICRO. SER.

DECLASSIFIED
Authority EO 10501
By P. Moore NARA, Date 7-8-93

APPROVED FOR RELEASE 1992
CIA HISTORICAL REVIEW PROGRAM

TRACE REQUEST

ABSTRACT X

INDEX X

DATE MICROFILMED

FILE TITLE

FILE NUMBER (PRIMARY CODE) 201-289248

E 100-300-11

DOCUMENT DATE 25 Oct. 63

DOCUMENT NUMBER DBA 55777

10/25/63 DeBrueys Report

1992 RELEASE

SECRET

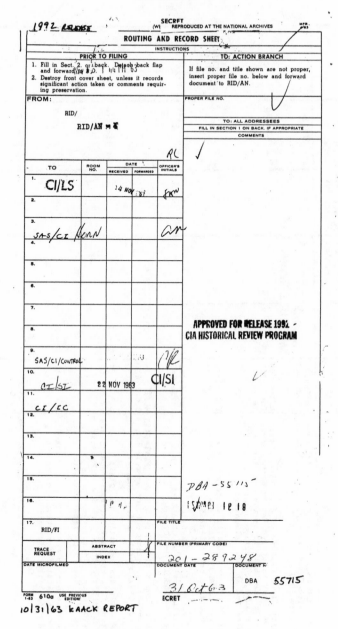

ROUTING AND RECORD SHEET

INSTRUCTIONS

PRIOR TO FILING	TO: ACTION BRANCH
1. Fill in Sect. 2. on back. Detach back flap and forward to RID. 14 NOV 63 2. Destroy front cover sheet, unless it records significant action taken or comments requiring preservation.	If file no. and title shown are not proper, insert proper file no. below and forward document to RID/AN.

FROM:

RID/

RID/AN

PROPER FILE NO.

TO: ALL ADDRESSEES

FILL IN SECTION 1 ON BACK. IF APPROPRIATE

COMMENTS

RC

TO	ROOM NO.	DATE RECEIVED	DATE FORWARDED	OFFICER'S INITIALS
1. CI/LS		14 NOV 63		[illegible]
2.				
3. SAS/CI Horn				[illegible]
4.				
5.				
6.				
7.				
8.				
9. SAS/CI/CONTROL				CR
10. CI/SI	22 NOV 1963			CI/SI
11. CI/CC				
12.				
13.				
14.				
15.				
16.				
17. RID/FI				

DBA - 55715

15 NOV 63 12 18

FILE TITLE

TRACE REQUEST | ABSTRACT | INDEX X

FILE NUMBER (PRIMARY CODE) 201 - 289248

DATE MICROFILMED

DOCUMENT DATE 31 Oct 63

DOCUMENT NO. DBA 55715

FORM 1-63 610a USE PREVIOUS EDITION

SECRET

10/31/63 KAACK REPORT

Page 26

Date	Description of document and subject	Doc. No. (CIA)	FOIA No.	In file before 22 November '63	In file before 20 February '64	CS Copy Location	Formerly Filed
20 Jul 63	Eldon HENSEN, attempts to establish contact with Cuban Embassy, Mexico City, on 19 July 1963.	MEXI-05448 20 Jul 63		*	*	201-0289248	
25 Jul 63	Letter from Captain D. W. BOWMAN, President, Navy Discharge Review Board, advising OSWALD that "it is the decision that no change, correction or modification is warrented in your discharge."	DST 11705 Encl. 15 26.11.63			*	201-0289248	
[illegible]9 Sep 63	FBI report from Dallas concerning Lee Harvey OSWALD; Dallas file no. 100-10461 Bureau file no. 105-82555.	DBA 51407 10 Sep 63		*	*	201-0289248	Copy CI/SIG [351 164] 100-300-011
[illegible]4 Sep 63	FBI report from New Orleans, Louisiana, relating arrest of OSWALD et al on 9 August 1963 in New Orleans.	DBA 52355 24 Sep 63		*	*	201-0289248	100-300-011
[illegible] Oct 63	Cable from Mexico City Station [MEXI-6453 IN 36017] reporting contact by telephone by Lee OSWALD with Soviet Embassy.	MEXI 6453 9 Oct 63	5 - 1A	*	*	201-0289248	
10 Oct 63	CIA cable dissemination no. 74673, to State, FBI, and Navy informing addressees of OSWALD's contact with Soviet Embassy in Mexico City. Includes erroneous description of OSWALD's physical characteristics.	DIR-74673 10 Oct 63	6 - 3	*	*	201-0289248	
10 Oct 63	Hqs response to MEXI 6453; gives OSWALD's true physical description - paragraph 1, and biographic information.	DIR-74830 10 Oct 63	7 - 2	*	*	201-0289248	
15 Oct 63	Mexico City Station requests a photograph of Lee Harvey OSWALD.	MEXI-6543 15 Oct 63	8 - 4	*	*	201-0289248	
16 Oct 63	Chief of Station, Mexico City, to Ambassador; Lee OSWALD contact with Soviet Embassy.	TX-01913 16 Oct 63	9 - 5				P 8593 [Mexico City file] 25 Feb 70

CIA DOCUMENTS LIST → HSCA

CLASSIFIED MESSAGE

SECRET

TO : DIRECTOR
FROM : [redacted] Mexico City
ACTION: C/WH 5
INFO : DDP, ADDP, C/CI, C/FI 2, C/SAS 5, RF 2

SECRET 201826Z

20 Jul 63 IN 83858

DIR CITE [redacted] 0548

APPROVED FOR RELEASE 1993
CIA HISTORICAL REVIEW PROGRAM

1. HITHERTO UNIDENTIFIED AMERICAN PHONED CUBEMB 19 JULY TRYING FOR SECOND TIME IN WEEK TO ESTABLISH CONTACT, SPOKE IN ENGLISH WITH MARIA LUISA CALDERON, SAID LEAVING FOR DALLAS ON AMERICAN AIRLINES MORNING 20 JULY, STAYING AT ROOM 1402 ALAMEDA HOTEL, REFUSED GO CUBEMB BECAUSE POSSIBILITY AMERICAN SPY MIGHT SEE HIM.

2. AT STATION REQUEST [redacted] POSING AS CUBEMB OFFICER MADE CONTACT ON HOUSE PHONE AFTERNOON 19 JULY, ALLUDED TO CALL TO EMBASSY, LURED SUBJ TO HOTEL RESTAURANT. SUBJ IDENTIFIED SELF AS ELDON HENSEN, CATTLEMAN, ATHENS, TEXAS, PHONE OR-54787. SAID WILLING HELP CASTRO GOVERNMENT IN US, WILLING TRAVEL, HAS MANY GOOD CONTACTS IN STATES, CAN "MOVE THINGS FROM ONE PLACE TO ANOTHER". [redacted] SAID WOULD HAVE TO CHECK OUT SUBJ FIRST, SOME DELAY INEVITABLE. WARNED SUBJ NEVER AGAIN PHONE CUBEMB, TOO DANGEROUS. SUBJ SAID WANTS MONEY FOR COOPERATION, IS NOW UNDER FINANCIAL PRESSURE. SUGGESTED [redacted] OR REPRESENTATIVE CONTACT HIM IN STATES BY PHONE, NOT VISIT. SUBJ FAMILY NOT AWARE HIS TRIP TO MEXI. SAID THIS HIS SECOND TRIP MEXI SPECIFICALLY TO ESTABLISH CONTACT WITH CUBEMB. AGREED ACCEPT PHONE CALL WITH KEY WORD "LAREDO" AS CALL FROM [redacted] CONTACT.

GROUP 1
SECRET
EXCLUDED FROM AUTOMATIC DOWNGRADING AND DECLASSIFICATION.

REPRODUCTION BY OTHER THAN THE ISSUING OFFICE IS PROHIBITED. Copy No.

266

OSWBX1 F2

CLASSIFIED MESSAGE

SECRET

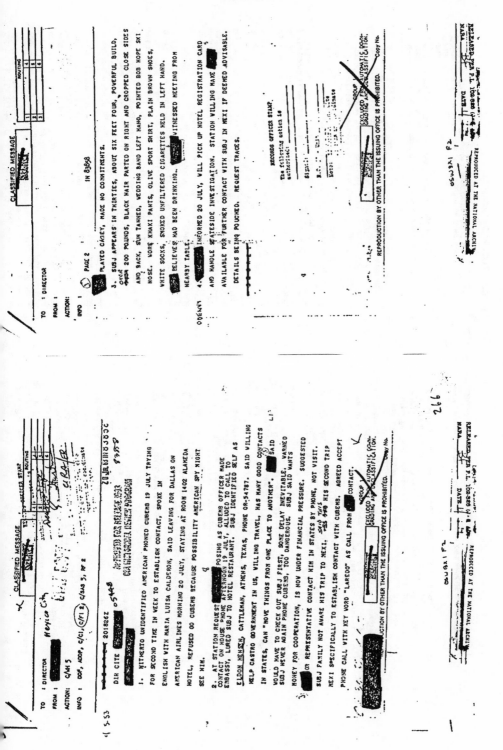

TO : DIRECTOR
FROM :
ACTION:
INFO :

PAGE 2 IN 83858

[redacted] PLAYED CAGEY, MADE NO COMMITMENTS.

3. SUBJ APPEARS IN THIRTIES, ABOUT SIX FEET FOUR, POWERFUL BUILD, OVER 200 POUNDS, BLACK HAIR PARTED ON RIGHT AND CROPPED CLOSE SIDES AND BACK, SUN TANNED, WEDDING BAND LEFT HAND, POINTED BOB HOPE SKI NOSE. WORE KHAKI PANTS, OLIVE SPORT SHIRT, PLAIN BROWN SHOES, WHITE SOCKS, SMOKED UNFILTERED CIGARETTES HELD IN LEFT HAND. [redacted] BELIEVES HAD BEEN DRINKING. [redacted] WITNESSED MEETING FROM NEARBY TABLE.

4. [redacted] INFORMED 20 JULY, WILL PICK UP HOTEL REGISTRATION CARD AND HANDLE STATESIDE INVESTIGATION. STATION WILLING MAKE [redacted] AVAILABLE FOR FURTHER CONTACT WITH SUBJ IN MEXI IF DEEMED ADVISABLE. DETAILS BEING POUCHED. REQUEST TRACES.

SECRET

RECORDS OFFICER STAMP

The following action is authorized:

Signed:

R.O. #

Note:

GROUP 1
SECRET
EXCLUDED FROM AUTOMATIC DOWNGRADING AND DECLASSIFICATION.

REPRODUCTION BY OTHER THAN THE ISSUING OFFICE IS PROHIBITED. Copy No.

OSWBX1 F2

determine. The Warren Commission might have asked the Army and the CIA to use their sources in these groups to obtain additional information on the groups' activities. More importantly, such information might have given the Warren Commission a better understanding of the background of the individuals it was investigating. For example, one Cuban in the Dallas area was investigated by the FBI at the request of the Warren Commission, because he was alleged to be an agent of the Cuban government.[103] The FBI agent who interviewed the individual was apparently unaware that this Cuban exile was an approved, though unused, source of Army intelligence in 1963 in an operation centered in the Miami area and that he had been used as a source in 1962 in Miami.[104]

The FBI reports on Alpha 66 furnished the Commission did note that Alpha 66 was responsible for an attack on a Soviet vessel in March 1963,[105] but did not detail the fact that it had continued planning paramilitary operations against Cuba.[106] These reports did not include information, scattered through several other FBI reports, that Alpha 66 had held discussions with other anti-Castro groups in an attempt to unite their efforts.[107] The FBI reports did not include the fact that the Alpha 66's leaders in September 1963 had been negotiating for the use of aircraft with which to conduct raids against Cuba, with those involved in a New Orleans anti-Castro training camp.[108]

Although the FBI informed the Warren Commission that the CIA and the Army had "pertinent information" on some of these groups, the Select Committee has been unable to find any evidence to indicate that the FBI itself contacted these other agencies. The Select Committee has been unable to find evidence that either the CIA or the Army independently contacted their sources in these groups to determine what they might be able to contribute to the investigation.

The CIA also took an interest in the Fair Play for Cuba Committee with which Oswald was associated. According to the FBI documents, on September 16, 1963, the CIA advised the FBI that the "Agency is giving some consideration to countering the activities of [the FPCC] in foreign countries."[109] The memorandum continued:

> CIA is also giving some thought to planting deceptive information which might embarrass the Committee in areas where it does have some support.
>
> Pursuant to a discussion with the Liaison Agent, [a middle level CIA official working on anti-Castro propaganda] advised that his Agency will not take action without first consulting with the Bureau, bearing in mind that we wish to make certain the CIA activity will not jeopardize any Bureau investigation.[110]

[103] Memorandum from Dallas Field Office to FBI Headquarters, 6/14/63.
[104] Army Intelligence Dossier.
[105] Memorandum from Miami Field Office to FBI Headquarters, 6/3/64.
[106] *Ibid.*
[107] *Ibid.*
[108] *Ibid.*
[109] Memorandum from FBI liaison to Liaison Section Chief, 9/18/63.
[110] Memorandum from FBI liaison to Liaison Section Chief, 9/18/63.

CHURCH COMMITTE VOL V

The CIA specifically wanted the FPCC's foreign mailing list and other documents.[111] On September 26, 1963, FBI Headquarters wrote its New York office about the proposed CIA operation, concluding:

> New York should promptly advise whether the material requested by CIA is available or obtainable, bearing in mind the confidential nature and purpose of CIA's request. If available, it should be furnished by cover letter with enclosures suitable for dissemination to CIA by liaison.[112]

At the bottom of the Headquarters copy of this directive is the note:

> We have in the past utilized techniques with respect to countering activities of mentioned organization in the U.S. During December 1961, New York prepared an anonymous leaflet which was mailed to selected FPCC members throughout the country for purpose of disrupting FPCC and causing split between FPCC and its Socialist Workers Party (SWP) supporters, which technique was very effective. Also during May 1961, a field survey was completed wherein available public source data of adverse nature reagrding officers and leaders of FPCC was compiled and furnished Mr. DeLoach for use in contacting his sources.
>
> It is noted, with respect to present status of FPCC during July and August, 1963, several New York sources reported FPCC was "on the ropes for lack of funds" and in danger of being taken over by Progressive Labor members.[113]

By Airtel of October 4, 1963, the New York office responded to the Headquarters directive saying: "The NYO plans to contact an (informant) on about 10/27/63 and it is believed possible that this source will be able to furnish both of the above mentioned items."[114]

By Airtel of October 28, 1963, the New York Office reported to Headquarters:

> "On 10/27/63, [the informant] was contacted by agents of the New York office. This source furnished approximately 100 photographs of data pertaining to the current finances and general activities of the FPCC. In addition, the source furnished other documents and information regarding the FPCC mailing list. After processing the photographs, prompt dissemination will be affected and the material of interest to CIA per referenced Bureau letter will be immediately forwarded to the Bureau."

The FBI documents indicate processing of the 100 photographs was not completed before the assassination. The New York office began an expedited review of the material so obtained on the afternoon of the assassination to determine whether it contained anything about Oswald. This was mentioned in a November 23 memorandum to William Sullivan.

[111] *Ibid.*
[112] Memorandum from FBI Headquarters to New York Field Office, 9/26/63.
[113] *Ibid.*
[114] Memorandum from New York Field Office to FBI Headquarters, 10/4/63.

CHURCH COMMITTEE VOLUME 5

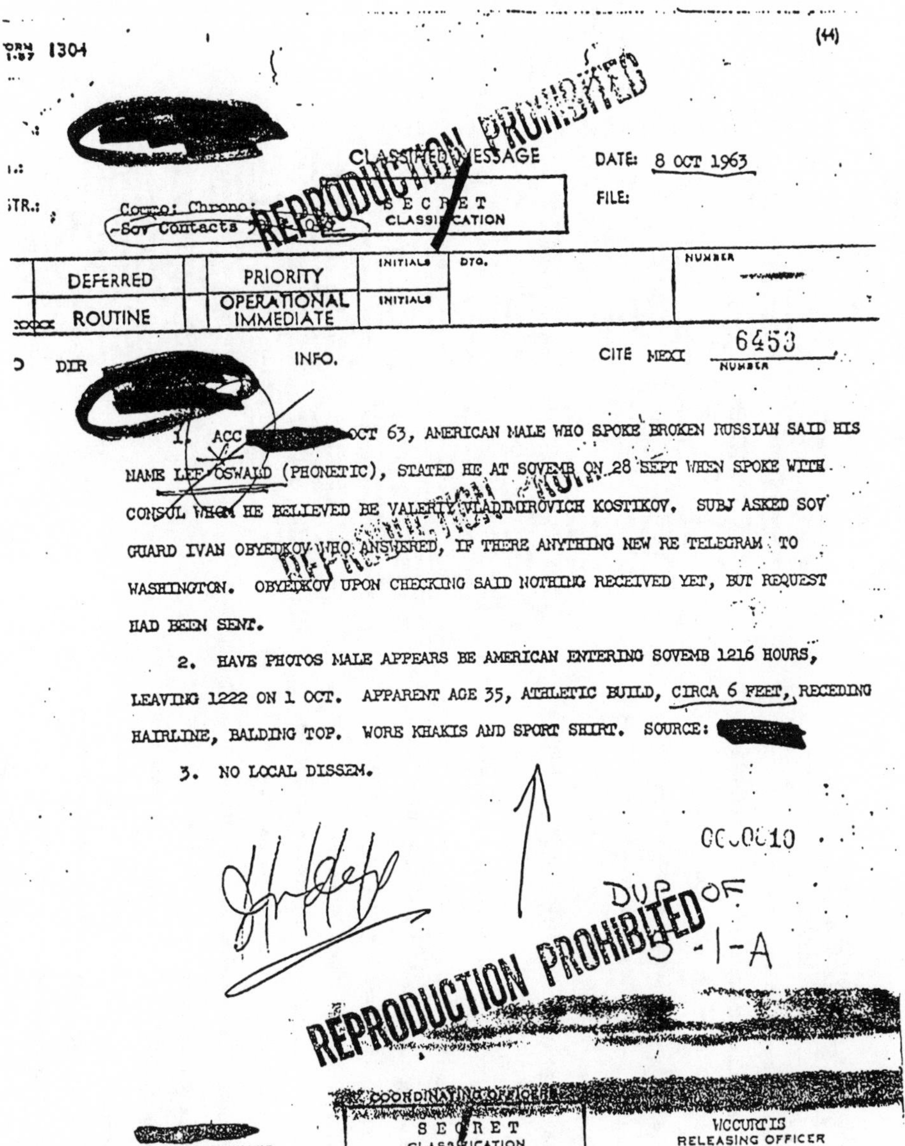

FORM 1304

(44)

CLASSIFIED MESSAGE

SECRET
CLASSIFICATION

DATE: 8 OCT 1963

FILE:

Compo: Chrono:
Sov Contacts

	DEFERRED		PRIORITY	INITIALS	DTG.	NUMBER
xxxx	ROUTINE		OPERATIONAL IMMEDIATE	INITIALS		

TO DIR INFO. CITE MEXI 6453

1. ACC [redacted] OCT 63, AMERICAN MALE WHO SPOKE BROKEN RUSSIAN SAID HIS NAME LEE OSWALD (PHONETIC), STATED HE AT SOVEMB ON 28 SEPT WHEN SPOKE WITH CONSUL WHOM HE BELIEVED BE VALERIY VLADIMIROVICH KOSTIKOV. SUBJ ASKED SOV GUARD IVAN OBYEDKOV WHO ANSWERED, IF THERE ANYTHING NEW RE TELEGRAM TO WASHINGTON. OBYEDKOV UPON CHECKING SAID NOTHING RECEIVED YET, BUT REQUEST HAD BEEN SENT.

2. HAVE PHOTOS MALE APPEARS BE AMERICAN ENTERING SOVEMB 1216 HOURS, LEAVING 1222 ON 1 OCT. APPARENT AGE 35, ATHLETIC BUILD, CIRCA 6 FEET, RECEDING HAIRLINE, BALDING TOP. WORE KHAKIS AND SPORT SHIRT. SOURCE: [redacted]

3. NO LOCAL DISSEM.

000010

DUP OF 5-1-A

COORDINATING OFFICERS

AUTHENTICATING OFFICER

SECRET
CLASSIFICATION

WCCURTIS
RELEASING OFFICER

1992 RELEASE

31 January 1964

CD6

Information Developed by CIA on the Activity of
Lee Harvey OSWALD in Mexico City
28 September - 3 October 1963

Natura... [illegible] ...port noting the likelihood that the subject, Lee OSWALD, was probably identical with the former Marine who had defected to the Soviet Union in 1959. (The report disseminated by CIA in Washington on 10 October also included a physical description of an individual who was believed to have been the OSWALD who had contacted the Soviets in Mexico City. It was subsequently established by investigation that the description did not pertain to OSWALD.)

4. On the same day, 10 October 1963, CIA Headquarters sent a lengthy cable summary to the Mexico City Station of the background information held in the Headquarters' file on OSWALD. An instruction was included for the Mexico City Station to pass the substance of its 9 October report to the local representatives of the same Federal departments and agencies that had been given the information in Washington. This instruction was immediately carried out. In this manner the information on OSWALD's contact with the Soviets on 1 October was passed in Mexico City to the Embassy, the FBI representative, the Naval Attache, and to the office of the Immigration and Naturalization Service. There were no requests from recipients of the report for further information or for follow-up investigation.

-3-

WARNING NOTICE
SENSITIVE SOURCES AND [illegible]

CIA Withheld Data on Oswald

Assassinations Panel Issues Report to House

BY NORMAN KEMPSTER
Times Staff Writer

WASHINGTON—The CIA withheld from the FBI for almost two months in 1963 information that Lee Harvey Oswald had talked with Cuban and Soviet officials about his desire to visit those countries, a House committee reported Friday.

The Select Committee on Assassinations indicated in a report to the full House that its investigation of the murder of President John F. Kennedy would focus early in 1977 on a trip Oswald had made to Mexico City in October, 1963.

Chief Counsel Richard A. Sprague said that the committee staff had learned that a CIA message describing Oswald's activities in Mexico to federal agencies such as the FBI had been rewritten to eliminate any mention of his request for Cuban and Soviet visas. The message was sent in October, more than a month before the Nov. 22, 1963, assassination.

The CIA discovered Oswald's presence at the embassies through its routine surveillance of those facilities. Because Oswald had once defected to the Soviet Union, the CIA and FBI had been interested in his activities even before the Kennedy assassination.

The CIA's decision to withhold information was reversed shortly after Kennedy was killed. The agency reported Oswald's efforts to visit Cuba and the Soviet Union both to the FBI

Please Turn to Page 18, Col. 1

CIA Withheld Data on Oswald, Assassination Panel Reports

Continued from First Page
nd to the Warren Commission, which concluded that Oswald was the assassin and ad acted alone.

Sprague told a press conference that it was impossible without more information to know why the CIA had censored its own message.

But he said the incident raised two interesting questions: what might the other agencies have done differently if they had been more fully informed and why did the CIA decide to remove "information that was considered pertinent enough to be put in an initial draft of the message?"

There were no firm conclusions in the report, which the 12-member committee prepared after the first three months of its investigation into the murders of Kennedy and civil rights leader Dr. Martin Luther King.

Technically, the committee goes out of business Tuesday with the end of the session of Congress in which it was formed. The purpose of the year-end report was to urge the new Congress to reestablish the committee and to give it $6.5 million to pay for the first year of what could be a two-year investigation.

"In the three months since its establishment, the committee has initiated preliminary investigations into new and previously unpursued leads in both assassinations," the report said.

The committee said its staff investigators had recently questioned a former CIA agent who had "personal knowledge" of Oswald's visits to the Soviet and Cuban embassies in Mexico. As a result of that interview, the report said, staff members were sent to Mexico, where they found and questioned additional witnesses.

"These witnesses had never been sought out before by any investigative body, notwithstanding the fact that they had important information concerning statements by Lee Harvey Oswald in Mexico within 60 days of the assassination of President Kennedy," the report said.

The report said also that the committee staff had interviewed a person who asserted that he had discussed the King murder with James Earl Ray, who pleaded guilty to the crime. The unidentified witness said that Ray had told him about contacting an associate in Europe to receive further instructions. The story, which was told to reporters by a committee member several weeks ago, has not been verified.

In a letter to New York Times columnist Anthony Lewis, Ray offered this week to testify under oath at a committee hearing. But Sprague and Walter F. Fauntroy, the District of Columbia's congressional delegate and the chairman of the King subcommittee' said that no decision had been made on accepting Ray's offer.

However, Sprague indicated that it probably would be accepted.

"Any and all people who have relevant information will be interrogated," Sprague said.

In a personal statement issued in conjunction with the report, Rep. Henry B. Gonzalez (D-Tex.), who is to become committee chairman in the new year, said a thorough investigation was needed to answer hundreds of pressing questions.

Gonzalez said that the committee hoped to discover whether former FBI Director J. Edgar Hoover's now well-known animosity toward King had affected the FBI's investigation of the assassination.

However, Gonzalez said, the committee's work could go well beyond the killings of Kennedy and King.

"The committee can shed light on the larger issue of political murder and violence," Gonzalez said. "We should not forget that President Ford had his own narrow escapes; no member of the House should forget that the Capitol Building was bombed. . . ."

He said the committee's ultimate task was "to find out not just what happened but why."

L.A. TIMES
1/1/77 P. 1

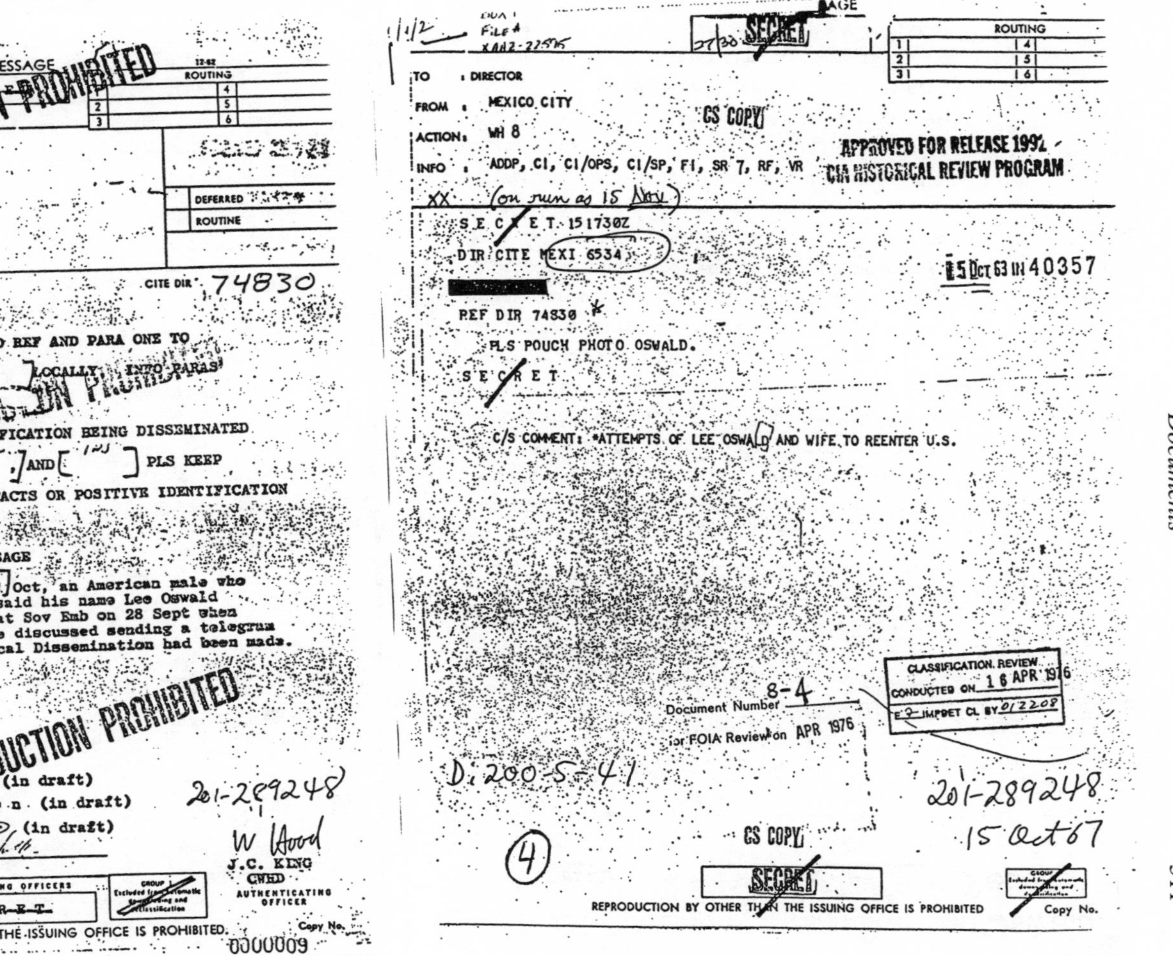

CLASSIFIED MESSAGE

SECRET

REPRODUCTION PROHIBITED

☐ INDEX
☐ NO INDEX
☐ FILE IN CS

ROUTING 1 2 3 4 5 6

TO:
FROM: DIRECTOR
CONF:
INFO:

DEFERRED
ROUTINE

PAGE THREE

TO: INFO: CITE DIR 74830

4. STATION SHOULD PASS INFO REF AND PARA ONE TO [ ] [ ] [ ] AND [ ] LOCALLY. INFO PARAS TWO AND THREE ORIGINATES WITH

5. REF AND POSSIBLE IDENTIFICATION BEING DISSEMINATED TO HDQS OF [ ] [ ] [ ] AND [ ] PLS KEEP HDQS ADVISED ON ANY FURTHER CONTACTS OR POSITIVE IDENTIFICATION OF OSWALD.

END OF MESSAGE

WH CMT: *According to [ ] Oct, an American male who spoke broken Russian said his name Lee Oswald (phonetic) stated he at Sov Emb on 28 Sept when spoke with Consul. He discussed sending a telegram to Washington. No local Dissemination had been made.

REPRODUCTION PROHIBITED

SR/C (in draft)
CI/Liaison (in draft)
CI/SPG/Egerter (in draft)
C/WH/3
WH/COPS

201-289248

T. KARAMESSINES
ADDP
RELEASING OFFICER

COORDINATING OFFICERS

SECRET

GROUP 1 Excluded from automatic downgrading and declassification

W Wood
J.C. KING
C/WHD
AUTHENTICATING OFFICER

REPRODUCTION BY OTHER THAN THE ISSUING OFFICE IS PROHIBITED. Copy No.

0000009

File # XAAZ-22595

SECRET

PAGE

ROUTING 1 2 3 4 5 6

TO : DIRECTOR
FROM : MEXICO CITY
ACTION: WH 8
INFO : ADDP, CI, CI/OPS, CI/SP, FI, SR 7, RF, VR

CS COPY

APPROVED FOR RELEASE 1992
CIA HISTORICAL REVIEW PROGRAM

XX (on run as 15 Nov)

SECRET 151730Z

DIR CITE MEXI 6534

15 Oct 63 IN 40357

REF DIR 74830 *

PLS POUCH PHOTO OSWALD.

SECRET

C/S COMMENT: *ATTEMPTS OF LEE OSWALD AND WIFE TO REENTER U.S.

CLASSIFICATION REVIEW CONDUCTED ON 16 APR 1976 E2 IMPDET CL BY 012208

Document Number 8-4 for FOIA Review on APR 1976

D. 200-5-41

201-289248
15 Oct 67

4

CS COPY

SECRET

GROUP 1 Excluded from automatic downgrading and declassification

REPRODUCTION BY OTHER THAN THE ISSUING OFFICE IS PROHIBITED Copy No.

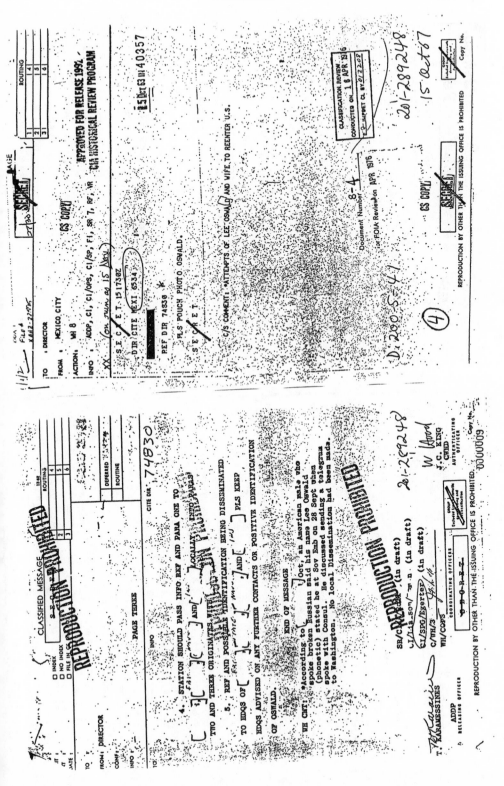

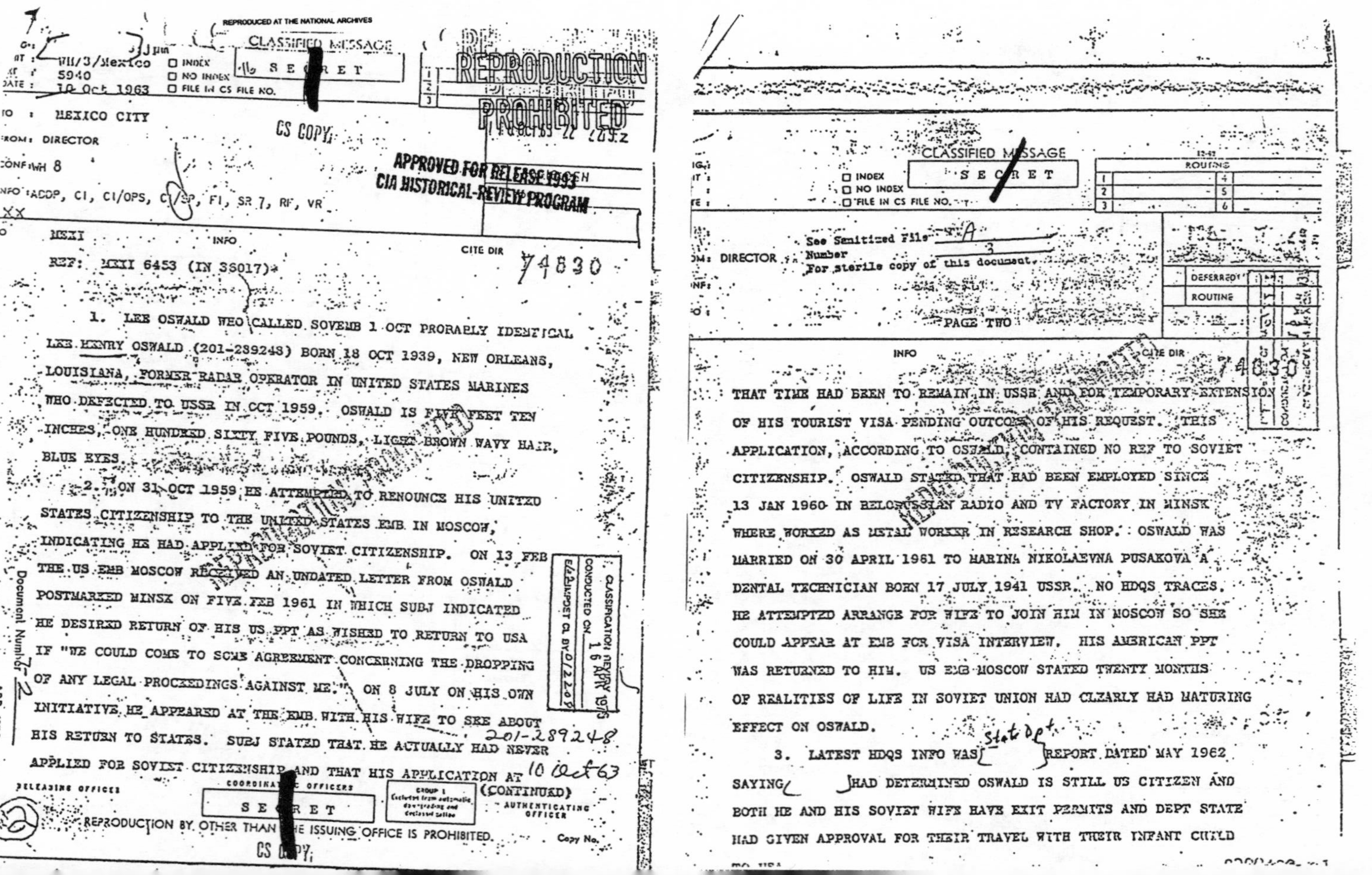

REPRODUCED AT THE NATIONAL ARCHIVES

CLASSIFIED MESSAGE

SECRET

WH/3/Mexico
5940
10 Oct 1963

☐ INDEX
☐ NO INDEX
☐ FILE IN CS FILE NO.

REPRODUCTION PROHIBITED

TO : MEXICO CITY

FROM: DIRECTOR

CONF: WH 8

INFO: ADDP, CI, CI/OPS, CI/SP, FI, SR 7, RF, VR

CS COPY

APPROVED FOR RELEASE 1993
CIA HISTORICAL-REVIEW PROGRAM

MEXI INFO CITE DIR 74830

REF: MEXI 6453 (IN 36017)*

1. LEE OSWALD WHO CALLED SOVEMB 1 OCT PROBABLY IDENTICAL LEE HENRY OSWALD (201-289248) BORN 18 OCT 1939, NEW ORLEANS, LOUISIANA, FORMER RADAR OPERATOR IN UNITED STATES MARINES WHO DEFECTED TO USSR IN OCT 1959. OSWALD IS FIVE FEET TEN INCHES, ONE HUNDRED SIXTY FIVE POUNDS, LIGHT BROWN WAVY HAIR, BLUE EYES.

2. ON 31 OCT 1959 HE ATTEMPTED TO RENOUNCE HIS UNITED STATES CITIZENSHIP TO THE UNITED STATES EMB IN MOSCOW, INDICATING HE HAD APPLIED FOR SOVIET CITIZENSHIP. ON 13 FEB THE US EMB MOSCOW RECEIVED AN UNDATED LETTER FROM OSWALD POSTMARKED MINSK ON FIVE FEB 1961 IN WHICH SUBJ INDICATED HE DESIRED RETURN OF HIS US PPT AS WISHED TO RETURN TO USA IF "WE COULD COME TO SOME AGREEMENT CONCERNING THE DROPPING OF ANY LEGAL PROCEEDINGS AGAINST ME." ON 8 JULY ON HIS OWN INITIATIVE HE APPEARED AT THE EMB WITH HIS WIFE TO SEE ABOUT HIS RETURN TO STATES. SUBJ STATED THAT HE ACTUALLY HAD NEVER APPLIED FOR SOVIET CITIZENSHIP AND THAT HIS APPLICATION AT

(CONTINUED)

201-289248

10 Oct 63

CLASSIFICATION REVIEW CONDUCTED ON 16 APR 1976
E2 IMPDET CL BY 012209

Document Number 7-2
for FOIA Review on APR 1976

RELEASING OFFICER — COORDINATING OFFICERS — SECRET — GROUP 1 Excluded from automatic downgrading and declassification — AUTHENTICATING OFFICER

REPRODUCTION BY OTHER THAN THE ISSUING OFFICE IS PROHIBITED. Copy No.

CS COPY

CLASSIFIED MESSAGE

SECRET

☐ INDEX
☐ NO INDEX
☐ FILE IN CS FILE NO.

ROUTING 1 2 3 4 5 6

FROM: DIRECTOR

See Sanitized File A
Number 3
For sterile copy of this document.

DEFERRED
ROUTING

PAGE TWO

INFO CITE DIR 74830

THAT TIME HAD BEEN TO REMAIN IN USSR AND FOR TEMPORARY EXTENSION OF HIS TOURIST VISA PENDING OUTCOME OF HIS REQUEST. THIS APPLICATION, ACCORDING TO OSWALD, CONTAINED NO REF TO SOVIET CITIZENSHIP. OSWALD STATED THAT HAD BEEN EMPLOYED SINCE 13 JAN 1960 IN BELORUSSIAN RADIO AND TV FACTORY IN MINSK WHERE WORKED AS METAL WORKER IN RESEARCH SHOP. OSWALD WAS MARRIED ON 30 APRIL 1961 TO MARINA NIKOLAEVNA PUSAKOVA A DENTAL TECHNICIAN BORN 17 JULY 1941 USSR. NO HDQS TRACES. HE ATTEMPTED ARRANGE FOR WIFE TO JOIN HIM IN MOSCOW SO SHE COULD APPEAR AT EMB FOR VISA INTERVIEW. HIS AMERICAN PPT WAS RETURNED TO HIM. US EMB MOSCOW STATED TWENTY MONTHS OF REALITIES OF LIFE IN SOVIET UNION HAD CLEARLY HAD MATURING EFFECT ON OSWALD.

3. LATEST HDQS INFO WAS [State Dept] REPORT DATED MAY 1962 SAYING [ ] HAD DETERMINED OSWALD IS STILL US CITIZEN AND BOTH HE AND HIS SOVIET WIFE HAVE EXIT PERMITS AND DEPT STATE HAD GIVEN APPROVAL FOR THEIR TRAVEL WITH THEIR INFANT CHILD TO USA

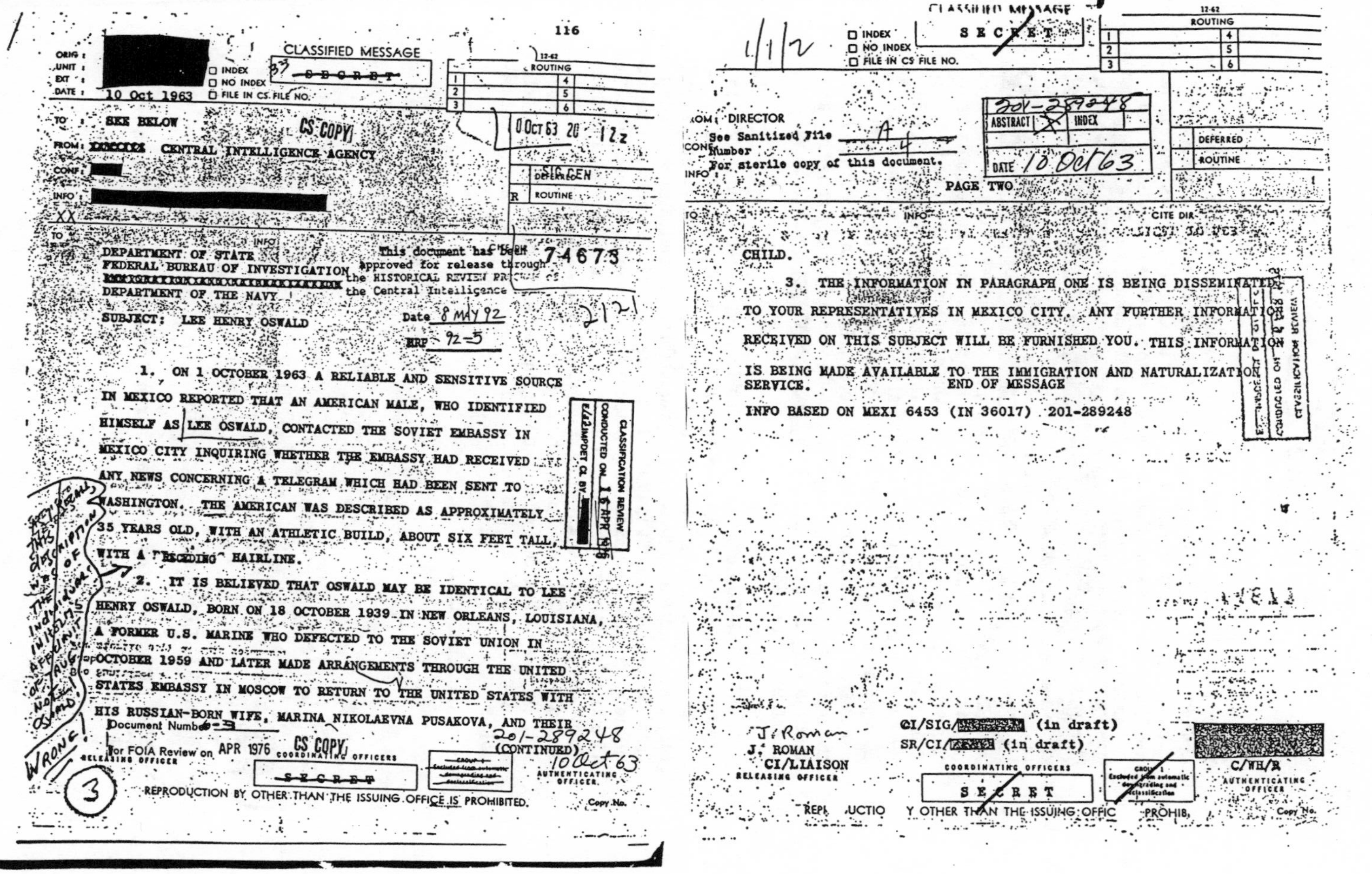

116

CLASSIFIED MESSAGE

~~SECRET~~

ORIG: [redacted]
UNIT:
EXT:
DATE: 10 Oct 1963

☐ INDEX
☐ NO INDEX
☐ FILE IN CS FILE NO.

ROUTING: 1, 2, 3, 4, 5, 6

10 Oct 63 20 12z

TO: SEE BELOW

CS COPY

FROM: CENTRAL INTELLIGENCE AGENCY

CONF: [redacted]

INFO: [redacted]

SIG CEN

ROUTINE

TO: DEPARTMENT OF STATE
FEDERAL BUREAU OF INVESTIGATION
DEPARTMENT OF THE NAVY

This document has been approved for release through the HISTORICAL REVIEW PROGRAM of the Central Intelligence Agency.

74673

2121

SUBJECT: LEE HENRY OSWALD

Date 8 MAY 92

HRP 92-5

1. ON 1 OCTOBER 1963 A RELIABLE AND SENSITIVE SOURCE IN MEXICO REPORTED THAT AN AMERICAN MALE, WHO IDENTIFIED HIMSELF AS LEE OSWALD, CONTACTED THE SOVIET EMBASSY IN MEXICO CITY INQUIRING WHETHER THE EMBASSY HAD RECEIVED ANY NEWS CONCERNING A TELEGRAM WHICH HAD BEEN SENT TO WASHINGTON. THE AMERICAN WAS DESCRIBED AS APPROXIMATELY 35 YEARS OLD, WITH AN ATHLETIC BUILD, ABOUT SIX FEET TALL, WITH A RECEDING HAIRLINE.

CLASSIFICATION REVIEW
CONDUCTED ON 16 APR 1976
E2 IMPDET CL BY [redacted]

2. IT IS BELIEVED THAT OSWALD MAY BE IDENTICAL TO LEE HENRY OSWALD, BORN ON 18 OCTOBER 1939 IN NEW ORLEANS, LOUISIANA, A FORMER U.S. MARINE WHO DEFECTED TO THE SOVIET UNION IN OCTOBER 1959 AND LATER MADE ARRANGEMENTS THROUGH THE UNITED STATES EMBASSY IN MOSCOW TO RETURN TO THE UNITED STATES WITH HIS RUSSIAN-BORN WIFE, MARINA NIKOLAEVNA PUSAKOVA, AND THEIR

(CONTINUED)

Document Number 3
for FOIA Review on APR 1976

CS COPY

201-289248
10 Oct 63

WRONG!

3

RELEASING OFFICER — COORDINATING OFFICERS — ~~SECRET~~ — GROUP 1 Excluded from automatic downgrading and declassification — AUTHENTICATING OFFICER

REPRODUCTION BY OTHER THAN THE ISSUING OFFICE IS PROHIBITED. Copy No.

1/1/2

CLASSIFIED MESSAGE

~~SECRET~~

☐ INDEX
☐ NO INDEX
☐ FILE IN CS FILE NO.

ROUTING: 1, 2, 3, 4, 5, 6

FROM: DIRECTOR

See Sanitized File Number A 4 For sterile copy of this document.

201-289248
ABSTRACT ☒ INDEX
DATE 10 Oct 63

DEFERRED
ROUTINE

PAGE TWO

TO — INFO — CITE DIR

CHILD.

3. THE INFORMATION IN PARAGRAPH ONE IS BEING DISSEMINATED TO YOUR REPRESENTATIVES IN MEXICO CITY. ANY FURTHER INFORMATION RECEIVED ON THIS SUBJECT WILL BE FURNISHED YOU. THIS INFORMATION IS BEING MADE AVAILABLE TO THE IMMIGRATION AND NATURALIZATION SERVICE.

END OF MESSAGE

INFO BASED ON MEXI 6453 (IN 36017) 201-289248

CLASSIFICATION REVIEW
CONDUCTED ON

J. Roman
J. ROMAN
CI/LIAISON
RELEASING OFFICER

CI/SIG/[redacted] (in draft)
SR/CI/[redacted] (in draft)

COORDINATING OFFICERS

~~SECRET~~

GROUP 1 Excluded from automatic downgrading and declassification

C/WH/R
AUTHENTICATING OFFICER

REPRODUCTION BY OTHER THAN THE ISSUING OFFICE IS PROHIBITED. Copy No.

~~SECRET~~
~~EYES ONLY~~

-4-

believe that the information on Oswald was unusual enough to have caused recipients to take special measures which might conceivably have led to a closer scrutiny of Lee Harvey Oswald and his movements. Mr. Helms pointed out that the information on Oswald's visit to the Cuban and Soviet embassies in Mexico City came from [redacted] Such information is routinely passed to other agencies and entered in CIA files. [redacted] Thus the information on Oswald was similar to that provided on other American citizens who might have made contacts of this type. In Oswald's case, it was the combination of visits to both Cuban and Soviet Embassies which caused the Mexico City Station to report this to Headquarters and Oswald's record of defection to the Soviet Union which prompted the Headquarters dissemination. At the conclusion of his remarks on this subject, Mr. Helms specified that the information he had given Mr. Rankin was extremely sensitive and that the very existence of these [redacted] had to be very carefully protected.

10. The Commission, Mr. Rankin said, would be interested in any information held by CIA on Jack Ruby. Mr. Rankin said the Commission staff had prepared a roundup on Ruby, a copy of which he handed Mr. Helms. He said he would appreciate any file reflections or commen that CIA analysts might make on this material. Mr. Rankin and member of his staff then discussed Ruby's confirmed trip to Havana in 1959. The Commission has received information from an unspecified source that Ruby was in Havana again in 1963 under a Czech passport. Mr. Rankin asked whether CIA could provide any assistance in verifying this story. Mr. Helms replied that CIA would be limited in its possibility of assisting, to air manifest checks in Mexico. These would be carried out he said.

~~SECRET~~
~~EYES ONLY~~

O Memo for Record on 12 March meeting of RANKIN, WILLEMS, HELMS, MURPHY, ROCCA, et al on CIA contribution to COMMISSION.

XAAZ-27168

12 March 1964

MEMORANDUM FOR THE RECORD

SUBJECT: Meeting with the Warren Commission on 12 March 1964 on that morning.

In fact, Lee Harvey Oswald became a person of great interest to us during this 27 September to 2 October, 1963 period. He contacted the Soviet Embassy on at least four occasions, and once went directly from the office of Sra. Sylvia Tirado de Durán, a Mexican employee of the Cuban Consulate, to his friends, the Soviets. During the conversation with the Soviet official, he said, "I was in the Cuban Embassy --- and they will not give me a transit visa through Cuba until after I have my Soviet visa." This contact became important after the Warren Commission Report on the assassination of President Kennedy was published; for on page 777 of that report the erroneous statement was made that it was not known that Oswald had visited the Cuban Embassy until after the assassination!

Every piece of information concerning Lee Harvey Oswald was reported immediately after it was received to: U.S. Ambassador Thomas C. Mann, by memorandum; the FBI Chief in Mexico, by memorandum; and to my headquarters by cable; and included in each and every one of these

WIN SCOTT MANUSCRIPT
FOUL FOE

reports was the conversation Oswald had, so far as it was known. These reports were made on all his contacts with both the Cuban Consulate and with the Soviets.

Because we thought at first that Lee Harvey Oswald might be a dangerous potential defector from the U.S.A. to the Soviet Union, he was of great interest to us, so we kept a special watch on him and his activities. He was observed on all his visits to each of the two communist embassies; and his conversations with personnel of these embassies were studied in detail, so far as we could get them.

Soon after his arrival and first talk with the Soviets, we received a brief sketch on Lee Harvey Oswald from headquarters, in answer to our request for information on him. We learned then that he had spent some two and one-half years in the USSR, had married a daughter of a Soviet, who worked for a Soviet intelligence/security service. Oswald and his Soviet wife had one child. Further, we learned that he, his wife and child were given permission to leave the Soviet Union for the U.S.A. --- an unusual fact and on the face of it suspicious, when it is known that the USSR builds walls and that they

WIN SCOTT MANUSCRIPT
FOUL FOE

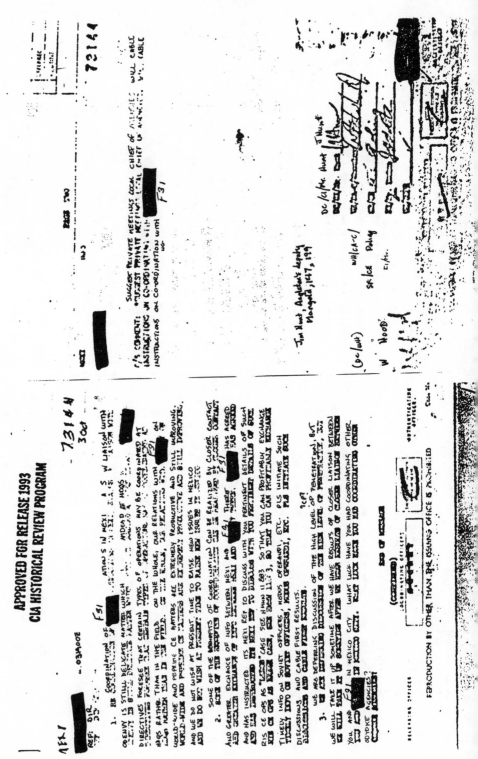

APPROVED FOR RELEASE 1993
CIA HISTORICAL REVIEW PROGRAM

MEXI

[redacted] 031900Z

73144
30 Oct

REF: DIR [illegible]

1. RE COORDINATION OF F31 [redacted] ATIONS IN MEXI AS W LIAISON WITH ODENVY IS STILL DELICATE MATTER WHICH [illegible] MIDEAD AT HQS [illegible] [redacted] DIRECTIVES FORESEE THAT CERTAIN TYPES OF OPERATIONS MAY BE COORDINATED AT HQS RATHER THAN IN THE FIELD. ON THE WHOLE, OUR RELATIONS WITH F31 [redacted] ON WORLD-WIDE AND PEPRIME CE MATTERS ARE EXTREMELY PRODUCTIVE AND STILL IMPROVING. AND WE DO NOT WISH AT PRESENT TIME TO RAISE NEW ISSUES IN MEXICO.

2. SOME OF THE BENEFITS OF COORDINATION CAN BE REALIZED BY CLOSER CONTACT AND GREATER EXCHANGE OF INFO BETWEEN MEXI AND F31 [redacted] THERE. F31 [redacted] HAS AGREED AND HAS INSTRUCTED ITS MEXI REP TO DISCUSS WITH YOU PERTINENT DETAILS OF SUCH RIS CE OPS AS "LCCB" CASE SEE HMMW 11883, SO THAT YOU CAN PROFITABLY EXCHANGE TIMELY INFO ON SOVIET OFFICERS, MODUS OPERANDI, ETC. PLS INITIATE SUCH DISCUSSIONS AND CABLE FIRST RESULTS.

3. WE ARE DEFERRING DISCUSSION OF THE HIGH LEVEL OF PENETRATION (CP?), BUT WE WILL TAKE IT UP SOMETIME AFTER WE HAVE RESULTS OF CLOSER LIAISON BETWEEN YOU AND F31 [redacted] IN MEXICO CITY. WHAT LUCK HAVE YOU HAD COORDINATING OTHER ODYOKE AGENCIES?

END OF MESSAGE

(CONTINUED)

RELEASING OFFICER — COORDINATING OFFICERS — SECRET — AUTHENTICATING OFFICER

REPRODUCTION BY OTHER THAN THE ISSUING OFFICE IS PROHIBITED

PAGE TWO

MEXI — INFO — 73144

C/S COMMENT: SUGGEST PRIVATE MEETINGS LOCAL CHIEF OF AGENCIES. WILL CABLE INSTRUCTIONS ON CO-ORDINATION WITH [redacted] F31 NG

Jim Hunt, Angleton's deputy
Maingold, 147, 199

DC/CI/Mr. Hunt — J Hunt

(DC/WH) — WH/CA-C/

W. HOOD — SR/CE — Poling

EI/Mr.

SECRET

TX 1884

11 December 1963

Not sent. Questions put orally to Mr. Helms. 11 Nov. 63

MEMORANDUM FOR: Deputy Director (Plans)

SUBJECT: Plans for the [redacted] OSWALD Investigation

1. Here are several recommendations for the further handling of the [redacted] OSWALD case:

a. It looks like the FBI report may even be released to the public. This would compromise our [redacted] operations in Mexico, because the Soviets would see that the FBI had advance information on the reason for Oswald's visit to the Soviet Embassy. Our clearing the FBI report was not for its publication, but only for its passage to the Warren Commission. I recommend that you call this to the attention of the Director and ask that page 39 and part of page 40 be revised before release.

b. CIA should get four copies of the report right away, to be used as follows:

1. DCI and DDCI
2. DDP and then CI Staff
3. SR
4. WH Branch 3

Copying an FBI original would be costly and the exhibits, which are vitally important, could hardly be read in some cases. I think the DCI should ask for these copies.

c. SR should assign someone to concentrate on processing, tracing, and analyzing the information on Oswald's activities in the Soviet Union. This person could work under me, or under the CI Staff, as you choose.

d. If you wish we can write up for the Warren Commission a summary of all the information we have produced on the case to date, with [redacted]

CLASSIFICATION REVIEW CONDUCTED ON 25 MAY 1976 E IMPDET CL BY 012308

Document Number 377-731 for FOIA Review on MAY 1976

RECORD COPY

SECRET APPROVED FOR RELEASE 1992 CIA HISTORICAL REVIEW PROGRAM

11 DEC 63

201-289248

SECRET

-2-

attachments. I can do this myself, but I will need a permanent assistant. I will nominate one as soon as I find someone suitable.

e. I am presuming that you want me to stay with this project. If I do, I will have to ask relief from my present job as Chief, WH/3. I cannot handle [redacted] and at the same time run my Branch which has about [redacted]

2. If you will just indicate your decisions on this page, I will take those actions which are in my province.

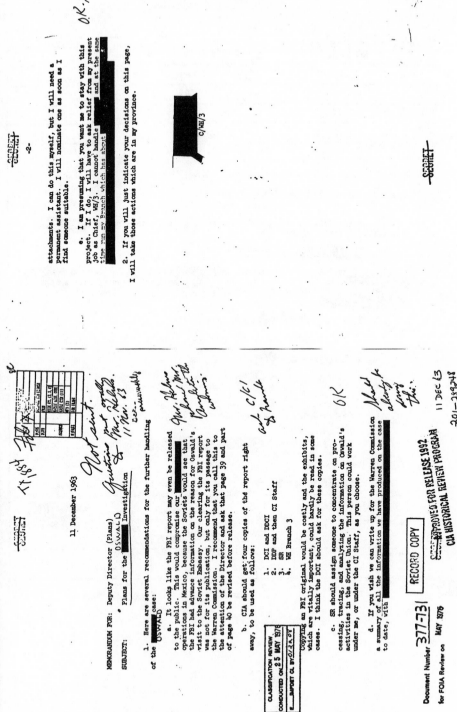

C/WH/3

SECRET

DISPATCH

CLASSIFICATION

PROCESSING ACTION

TO Chief, WH Division

INFO.

FROM Chief of Station, Mexico City

SUBJECT Monthly Operational Report for Project [redacted]

ACTION REQUIRED - REFERENCES

Action: None. For Headquarters' information.

Ref : HMMA-22257 dated 8 October 1963

1. There follows the monthly operational report for Project [redacted] activities during October 1963.

2. [redacted] - October 1963

There was only one change [redacted] during October. [redacted] on 30 October to provide [redacted] for use against a [redacted] The number and identity [redacted] will be provided when the new [redacted]

3. Processing of [redacted] Information

There was no change in the processing during this reporting period.

4. Exploitation of [redacted] Information

During this period [redacted] provided operational data of interest in connection with the visit to Mexico of President Tito of Yugoslavia.

MEXI-6453 reported a contact by an English-speaking man with the Soviet Embassy in Mexico City. This was forwarded to Headquarters for further dissemination.

MEXI-6591 reported [redacted] Herb PROVOST from Las Vegas who claimed to be a student working with the Cuban Embassy in Mexico. Further dissemination was left to Headquarters.

MEXI-6615 reported contact between New York Times writer, Herbert MATTHEWS and the Cuban Embassy in Mexico. No investigative action was taken by the Mexico Station.

Distribution:

Removed from Project [redacted]
CS Classification: [redacted]
JOB # 73 ...
Box: 29 Fold: 6

CROSS REFERENCE TO	DISPATCH SYMBOL AND NUMBER	DATE
	HMMA-22432	7 November 1963
	CLASSIFICATION	HQS FILE NUMBER

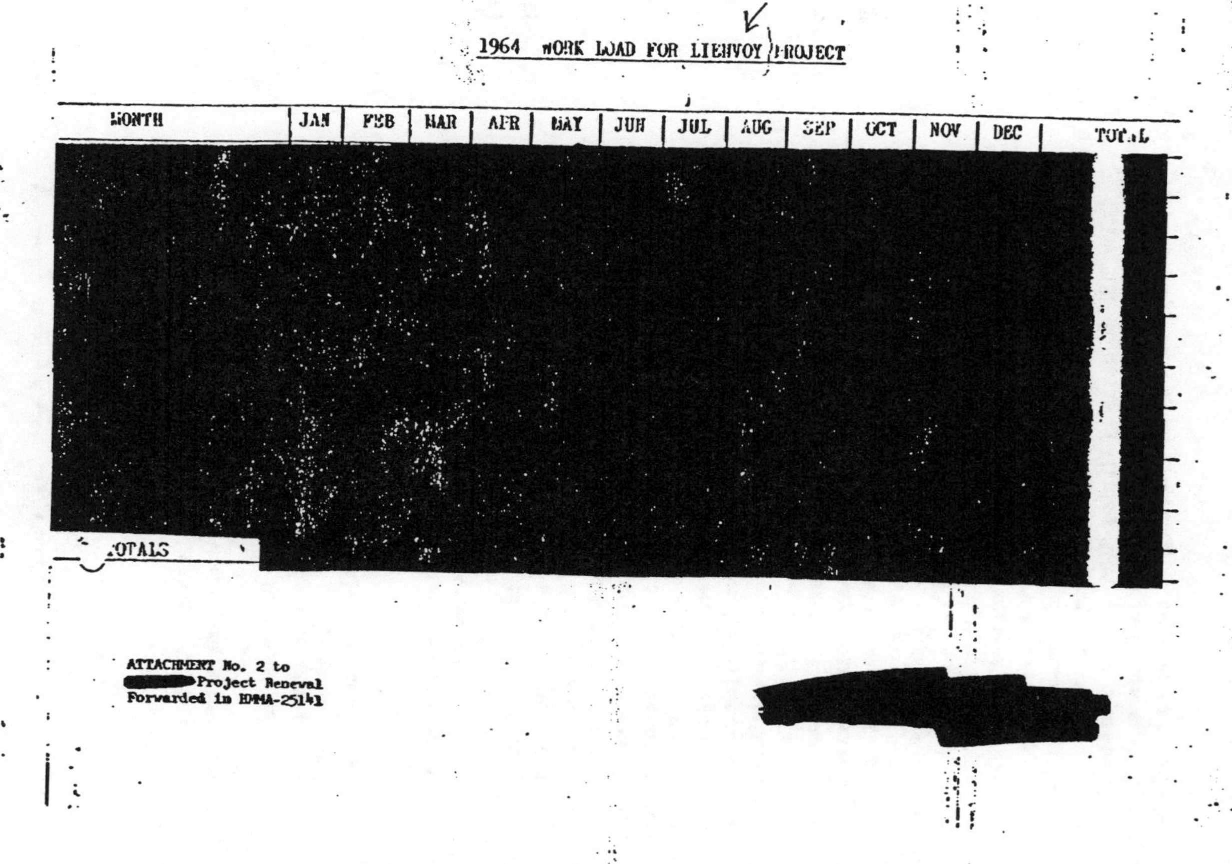

1964 WORK LOAD FOR LIENVOY PROJECT

MONTH	JAN	FEB	MAR	APR	MAY	JUN	JUL	AUG	SEP	OCT	NOV	DEC	TOTAL
TOTALS													

ATTACHMENT No. 2 to
Project Renewal
Forwarded in HMMA-25141

000787

TELEPHONE CONVERSATION BETWEEN THE PRESIDENT ... 11-23-63

-2-

jeh (cont.) accommodation will be made of that. He did carry some kind of a package down there, which could have been the gun yesterday morning in the car. None of us can swear to that. But the important thing at the time is that the location of the purchase of the gun by a money order apparently to the Klein Gun Company in Chicago, we were able to establish that last night.

lbj Have you established any more about the visit to the Soviet Embassy in Mexico in September?

jeh No, that's one angle that's very confusing for this reason. We have up here the tape and the photograph of the man who was at the Soviet Embassy, using Oswald's name. That picture and the tape do not correspond to this man's voice, nor to his appearance. In other words, it appears that there is a second person who was at the Soviet Embassy down there. We do have a copy of a letter which was written by Oswald to the Soviet Embassy here in Washington inquiring as well as complaining about the harrassment of his wife and the questioning of his wife by the FBI. Now, of course, that letter information, we process all mail that goes to the Soviet Embassy -- it's a very secret operation. No mail is delivered to the Embassy without being examined and opened by us, so that we know what they receive. Such a letter was sent to the Embassy by this fellow Oswald, making a complaint about his wife being harrassed and being questioned. The case as it stands now isn't strong enough to be able to get a conviction. Then there is gun angle... I think we have a very, very close plan. Now if we can identify this man who is at the Mexican Embassy at -- the Soviet Embassy in Mexico City, the Embassy in Mexico City, -- this man Oswald has still denied everything. He doesn't know anything about anything but the gun thing, of course, is a definite trend.

lbj It definitely established that he -- the same gun killed the policeman?

jeh That is an entirely different gun. We also have that gun. That was a revolver.

HOOVER AND LBJ, 23 NOVEMBER 1963

REQUEST FOR INVESTIGATION AND (OR) NAME CHECK

DATE: 27 July 62 cjb

PROJECT: [redacted]

TO : Deputy Director of Security

FROM : Chief, CI/Operational Approval and Support Division

SUBJECT : C 101331 NO.

1. TYPE OF REQUEST: POA | OA | SPEC. INQ. | CHC

2. FBI CHECK REQUESTED BY (Date)

APPROVED FOR RELEASE 1993
CIA HISTORICAL REVIEW PROGRAM

3. INDICES RESULTS REQUESTED BY: 8 Aug 62

4. AREA OF SUBJECT'S ASSIGNMENT: [redacted]

5. USE OF SUBJECT: agent

6. INVESTIGATION AND COVER

	YES	NO
A. U.S. GOVERNMENT INTEREST MAY BE SHOWN DURING INVESTIGATION	X	
B. C.I.A. INTEREST MAY BE SHOWN DURING INVESTIGATION		X
C. SUBJECT AWARE OF U.S. GOVERNMENT INTEREST IN HIM	X	
D. SUBJECT AWARE OF C.I.A. INTEREST IN HIM		X

E. LIMITATIONS ON COVERAGE IN THE INVESTIGATION OF SUBJECT: None

F. SUGGESTED "COVER PRETEXT" TO BE USED IN CONDUCTING PERSONAL INVESTIGATION OF SUBJECT

G. REASON FOR NO INVESTIGATION OUTSIDE OF CIA (Explain fully)

7. RI TRACES: NDI

8. DIVISION TRACES: NDI

9. FIELD TRACES: see attached

10. GREEN LIST INITIATED: X YES | NO

11. ATTACHMENTS: PRO PART I | X PARTIAL BIO. | OTHER:

12. REMARKS

JUL 30 9 30 AM '62

CI/OA Advised [initials] Date 7/31/62

/s/ Thomas Carroll, Jr.

INITIALS [initials]

FORM 4-61 693 USE PREVIOUS EDITIONS. SECRET (9)

SECRET

30 AUG 1962

Chief, CI/OA

Deputy Director of Security (IOS)

APPROVED FOR RELEASE 1993
CIA HISTORICAL REVIEW PROGRAM

C-101331
#279 089

1. Reference is made to your memorandum dated 27 July 1962 wherein [redacted] interest, only, was indicated for possible use of Subject [redacted] TF[redacted]

2. On 31 July 1962 your office was advised telephonically that Office of Security indices contained no record of the Subject.

3. On 17 August 1962 you were advised that the FBI has not conducted an investigation on the Subject, However, the FBI made reference to data re "Foreign Political Matters-Cuba" which was sent to this Agency on 28 December 1961. The date of said report is not given, however, it is known that the FBI has provided this Agency with numerous reports so captioned, on a continuous basis. Office of Security indices were searched for the above referenced report received on 28 December 1962, with negative results, Therefore, it is assumed it is available in RID, TFW or WH Division files.

4. No further action is contemplated in this case unless otherwise requested by your office.

FOR THE DIRECTOR OF SECURITY:

Victor R. White

CLOSED
TOBIAS[...]/vsf
29 August 1962

SECRET

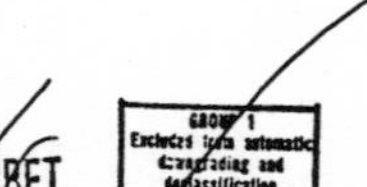
GROUP 1
Excluded from automatic downgrading and declassification

SECRET

REQUEST FOR INVESTIGATION AND/OR NAME CHECK

DATE: 27 April 1967 jep

TO: Deputy Director Security, IOS
FROM: Chief, CI/Operational Approval and Support Division

PROJECT AND AREA OF ASSIGNMENT: WH/1/X Mexico

APPROVED FOR RELEASE 1993
CIA HISTORICAL REVIEW PROGRAM

SUBJECT: 201 - 329609 — SO# 279089

TYPE OF REQUEST: X

OS INDICES RESULTS BY (Date) 2 May 1967

FBI CHECK RESULTS BY (Date)

[...] OF SUBJECT: [...]I informant

[...]IAL INSTRUCTIONS (Limitations on investigation, cover pretext, etc.)

[...]ACE RESULTS: RI: DEROG. INFO IN CI/OA | DIVISION: DEROG. INFO IN CI/OA | FIELD: DEROG. INFO IN CI/OA

GREEN LIST INITIATED — ATTACHMENTS: PRQ - PART I; X PARTIAL BIO; Other

[...]KS

CHIEF, CI/OA

ENDORSEMENT

TO: Chief, CI/OA
FROM: Deputy Director Security, IOS

DATE 5 JUN 1967

☑ 1. OS Indices results: ~~no data since~~ see remarks

☑ 2. Checks were conducted at the indicated Agencies with negative results:

FBI	ONI	ACSI	STATE	PP	CSC	HCUA	OSI	I & N		
☐	☒	☒	☐	☐	☐	☐	☒	☒	☐	☐

☐ 3. Checks were conducted at the following Agency(ies) with positive results, reports attached FBI

☐ 4. Domestic Field Investigation has been completed, _______ reports attached.

☐ 5. Domestic Field Investigation favorable, reports will follow within 60 days.

[REMAR]KS: nothing subsequent to July 1963 except cable dated 29 Oct 1963 in #49286

[C]LOSED

DEPUTY DIRECTOR SECURITY, IOS

693 SECRET 2

PERSONAL RECORD QUESTIONNAIRE
PART I - BIOGRAPHICAL INFORMATION

PRQ NO.

DISPATCH NO. HMMA-33863

INSTRUCTIONS: 1. Write clearly. 2. Answer all questions. If question is not applicable, write "NA." 3. Attach blank pages, if additional space is needed.

SECTION I GENERAL PERSONAL AND PHYSICAL DATA

NAME (First) Luis (Middle) (Last) ABREU Souto (Sex)

NAME IN NATIVE LANGUAGE OR SCRIPT: NA | 3. NAME AT BIRTH (If different than Item 1.): NA

ALIASES, NICKNAMES, TELECODES, LEGAL CHANGE IN NAME (State time, reason for and place of use): NA

APPROVED FOR RELEASE 1993
CIA HISTORICAL REVIEW PROGRAM

DATE OF BIRTH: Circa 1915 | 4. PLACE OF BIRTH: Oviedo, Spain

PERSONAL HABITS (Liquor, drugs, gambling, paramours): No known immoderate vices

COURT RECORD (Court, date, arrests, charges, punishments, sentences, acquittals): Not known

DESCRIPTION (Use American standards of measurements, if possible)

SEX	b. AGE	c. APPARENT AGE	d. HEIGHT	e. WEIGHT	f. COMPLEXION	g. FACE (Shape)
	53	53		170		Round

COLOR OF HAIR	i. COLOR OF EYES	j. TEETH	k. BUILD	l. POSTURE
Black				

SCARS AND MARKS OR OTHER DISTINGUISHING FEATURES: [illegible] marks on face

GENERAL APPEARANCE

PROMINENT FEATURES

OTHER IDENTIFYING FEATURES

ATTACH SAMPLES OF SIGNATURE AND HANDWRITING; ALSO DATED PHOTOGRAPH AND FINGERPRINTS, IF OBTAINABLE

1050 USE PREVIOUS EDITIONS. 1 (4-20)

1304 (44)

CLASSIFIED MESSAGE

DATE: 28 NOV 1963

Commo; Dummy Chrono;
P-8593; P-6079

SECRET
CLASSIFICATION

FILE:

DEFERRED	XXXX	PRIORITY	INITIALS	DTG.	NUMBER
ROUTINE		OPERATIONAL IMMEDIATE	INITIALS		

DIR INFO. CITE MEXI 7115

OPFLOOR

1. REPORTED 27 NOV AFTER SILVIA DURAN FIRST ARREST WAS PUBLIC KNOWLEDGE THAT THERE GREAT DEAL DISCUSSION OF THIS IN EMBASSY. SHE BACK IN OFFICE 25 NOV AND SEEMED QUITE PLEASED WITH HER PERFORMANCE. HER ACCOUNT INTERROGATION CONTAINED LITTLE NEW EXCEPT POLICE HAD THREATENED HER WITH EXTRADITION TO U.S. TO FACE OSWALD. SHE HAD NO FEAR OF CONFRONTATION. DESCRIBES HER AS VERY INTELLIGENT AND QUICK WITTED.

2. OF ASSASSINATION ITSELF SAID THERE ALMOST NO DISCUSSION IN EMBASSY. STAFF MEETING 23 NOV VERY SHORT AND SOMBER WITH GENERAL IMPRESSION BEING ONE OF SHOCK AND DISBELIEF. HEARD NO EXPRESSIONS OF PLEASURE.

3. SEEN NIGHT 27 NOV HAD NOTHING TO ADD TO ABOVE. INDEED VERSION MUCH LESS DETAILED. NEITHER OR HAD ANY PERSONAL KNOWLEDGE OSWALD PRESENCE CUBAN EMBASSY AT ANY TIME.

196-628

09009

COORDINATING OFFICERS

SECRET

WCCURTIS

3P

DISPATCH | PROCESSING ACTION: XXXX MARKED FOR INDEXING

TO: Chief, Western Hemisphere Division

INFO: Chief, WH/COG

FROM: Chief of Station, Mexico City

SUBJECT: ███ The ███ Operation

ACTION REQUIRED - REFERENCES: FYI

Reference: HMMA 31977

1. Forwarded as Attachment One under separate cover are reports prepared by ███ on the activities of ███, dated 9, 13, 22, 23, 25, 26 and 27 May 1967. Forwarded as Attachment Two, also under separate cover, are photocopies of correspondence exchanged between ███ in Mexico City and Paz ESPEJO in Havana. Forwarded as Attachment Three herewith, is a pamphlet obtained by ███ which contains the text of the message allegedly sent the Tri-Continental organization by Ernesto "Che" GUEVARA.

2. There is little question that ███ must often ask himself just where his association with ███ is taking him and must speculate about just what ███ is after. There are obviously times when, left to conjectures and suppositions, ███ must feel like "quitting." Yet, the ascendancy gradually developed by ███ over ███ has reached the point where ███ is unwilling to go back to the drab, uninteresting life he lived before meeting ███. The result of ███'s "second thoughts" has up to now been a desire, in the end, to collaborate even more closely with ███. ███'s report dated 13 May, and more particularly, ███'s scribble attached to that report, give an indication of the confusion which exists in ███'s mind as a result of the contacts he maintains at ███ urging with the Cubans, Guatemalan rebels, and various shades of Mexican and Central American leftists.

CONTINUED...

Attachments:
#1 - Reports s/c para 1 USC
#2 - Correspondence s/c para 1 USC
#3 - Pamphlet s/c para 1 HEREWITH

Distribution:
2 - C/WHD w/atts
1 - C/WH/COG w/o atts
4 - FILES

3 ATT

201-795301

CONTINUATION OF DISPATCH | SECRET/KAPOK | HMMA-32243

In addition ███ finds himself involved in the development of a commercial venture, an undertaking for which he is ill equipped. This shortcoming requires very close guidance by ███ and, in turn, makes ███ even more dependant on his case officer. Thus, while ███ occasionally thinks of returning to ███ and develops qualms about taking money from ███ for what he considers to be little result, ███ keeps involving himself deeper and deeper in activities of interest to ███.

3. The above does not mean that ███'s activities should not be subjected to every operational control possible, on the contrary. ███'s story concerning the manner in which birth certificates can be obtained in Northern Mexico to secure valid Mexican passports continues, for example, to be suspect. It now appears, on the other hand, that "GARCIA" of the Guatemalan FAR exists ███ and that he does not want ███ to come in contact with other Mexico residents connected with the Guatemalan guerrillas such as the alleged FAR propaganda representative at the UNAM University. ███ is convinced he can lay on a meeting with GARCIA in advance so that ███ can have a look at the Guatemalan. In spite of GARCIA's cautiousness, such a meeting has to take place sooner or later. The Station is ready.

███

4. ███'s recent efforts to develop ███'s potential regarding ███ staff) paid off ███ 201-818542

███ It already appears that ███, an experienced hand in ███'s overt business, will be given quite a bit of responsibility in that office. It is hoped that by becoming quasi indispensable she will be asked to remain at ███ ███ while very much in love with her husband, has a mind of her own, a great liking for ███ and, according to ███ himself, an intelligence much superior to his. She is also gifted with Oriental type patience. With ███'s knowledge, ███ has started to make small payments to ███ to provide separate financial incentive and help her pay for furniture and other items she purchased on credit some time ago.

5. The sketch mentioned in the last paragraph of ███'s report dated 26 May was retained by this Station. ███ used this sketch to discuss with ███ the layout of ███. The statement made at the end of paragraph 4 of the report dated 27 May is in error. ███ has two telephones. What ███ took for a third phone in the back room of that section is in reality an intercom unit.

6. Headquarters attention is called to paragraphs 3 through 5 of ███'s report dated 26 May. The fact that Silvia DURAN had sexual intercourse with Lee Harvey OSWALD on several occasions when the latter was in Mexico City is probably new, but adds little to the OSWALD case. The Mexican police did not report the extent of the DURAN-OSWALD relationship to this Station.

201-289245
201 740 720

for Willard C. CURTIS

SECRET/KAPOK

26 May, 1967

Subject: [redacted] Meeting with [redacted]

SECRET/KAPOK

1. [redacted] met with [redacted] at the safehouse from 1800 until about 1930
on 25 May, 1967. [redacted] reported that as yet he had not heard from Garcia
and would stand by for the next two days in the hope that Garcia would reappear at his home. [redacted] agreed to invite Garcia, once he did appear,
to coffee or lunch at a restaurant on 29 or 30 May so that [redacted] could get
a look at him. [redacted] also reported that [redacted] had been working part-
time, in the mornings, [redacted] and that her rapport with the loca
staff was improving. [redacted] suggested that it might be the right time to gi
[redacted] some compensation for her efforts. [redacted] agreed and promised to
ask [redacted] to be at the safehouse at 1000 on 27 May, so that [redacted] could
again talk privately with her and give her the money ([redacted] suggested 500
pesos, and [redacted] agreed that this would be adequate).

2. [redacted] reported that [redacted]'s resumption of contact had begun to pay
off better than he had thought possible. He explained that she had found an
opportunity on the afternoon of 23 May to chat with Abelardo Curbelo and ha
returned home with some interesting information concerning the Cuban attitu
toward [redacted] himself. According to [redacted] [redacted] said that Curbelo
told her that he was happy that she [redacted] in close contact
the Consulate. In commenting on [redacted] Curbelo in a more or less joking
stated that [redacted] must understand that the "revolution is surrounded by
provocations" and that many persons on the outside, such as [redacted], have b
come innocent victims of organizations such as [redacted], that are constantly
sending provocations against the revolution. Curbelo stressed that he did n
feel that [redacted] fell into that category, but [redacted] must understand th
precautions that have to be taken by the revolution. He concluded that he
hoped [redacted] would not take offense (tomarlo a mal) and would feel free to

3. [redacted] then stated that he was doing his best to keep active certain
contacts he had had in the past that were on the periphery of the official
Cuban circle. He mentioned specifically the case of Silvia and Horacio Durá
that then explained the background of the relationship with them. He relate
that Silvia Durán worked as receptionist at the Consulate in 1963-64 and wa
on duty when Lee Harvey Oswald applied for a visa. She had been recommended
to the Cubans by Teresa Proenza, the Press Attaché from 1959 until 1962. [redacted]
[redacted] described Teresa Proenza as a Cuban [illegible] aged about 5?, a Lesbian,
and a member of the Communist party of Cuba, who was currently in jail in

SECRET/KAPOK

11 of 63

DATE 11/9/94

SECRET/KAPOK

Cuba as the result of a conviction for espionage on behalf of [redacted]. [redacted]
[redacted] recalled that during his last visit to Havana, a friend of his [redacted]
[redacted] informed him of Teresa Proenza's present situatic
and advised [redacted] in the event he was asked, he deny that he had known
Teresa Proenza or had had anything to do with her. [redacted] continued that
just the other day Silvia Durán had telephoned [redacted] and that [redacted]

4. [redacted] continued that Silvia Durán [redacted] had first met
Oswald when he applied for a visa and had gone out with him several times si
she liked him from the start. She admitted that she had sexual relations wit
him but insisted that she had no idea of his plans. When the news of the assassination broke she stated that she was immediately taken into custody by
the Mexican police and interrogated thoroughly and beaten until she admitted
that she had had an affair with Oswald. She added that ever since then she h
cut off all contact with the Cubans, particularly since her husband Horacio,
who was badly shaken by the whole affairs, went into a rage and
has forbidden her to see them. She added that she felt certain that her telephone was tapped by the Mexican police, or, more probably by [redacted], since
tapping was an expensive proposition and the Mexicans wouldn't be able to afford it for so long a period.

5. [redacted] counseled [redacted] against any further contact with the Duráns on
the ground that it might put him under some sort of suspicion either in the
eyes of the Mexican police or the Cubans. He pointed out that little or nothi
was to be gained from such a contact.

5. [redacted] then produced, at [redacted]'s request, a sketch of the Consulate and
Embassy premises, copy of which is attached. [redacted] commented that to his
knowledge Cepeda did not have an office, at least not on the first floor. His
other comments appear on the sketch as reproduced by [redacted]

SECRET/KAPOK

12 of 63

OFFICE OF THE DIRECTOR

TOP SECRET

Commission No. 1359

UNITED STATES DEPARTMENT OF JUSTICE

FEDERAL BUREAU OF INVESTIGATION

WASHINGTON 25, D. C.

June 17, 1964

BY COURIER SERVICE

REVIEWED BY FBI/JFK TASK FORCE
ON 12/7/94 EB
☒ RELEASE IN FULL
☐ RELEASE IN PART
☐ TOTAL DENIAL

Honorable J. Lee Rankin
General Counsel
The President's Commission
200 Maryland Avenue, Northeast
Washington, D. C.

DECLASSIFIED BY 5170 HBB/GAT
ON 11-6-93 (JFK)

Dear Mr. Rankin:

Through a confidential source which has furnished reliable information in the past, we have been advised of some statements made by Fidel Castro, Cuban Prime Minister, concerning the assassination of President Kennedy.

In connection with these statements of Castro, your attention is called to the speech made by Castro on November 27, 1963, in Havana, Cuba, during which Castro made similar statements concerning this matter. The pertinent portions of this speech are set out in the report of Special Agent James J. O'Connor dated May 8, 1964, at Miami, Florida, beginning on page 30.

According to our source, Castro recently is reported to have said, "Our people in Mexico gave us the details in a full report of how he (Oswald) acted when he came to Mexico to their embassy (uncertain whether he means Cuban or Russian Embassy)." Castro further related, "First of all, nobody ever goes that way for a visa. Second, it costs money to go that distance. He (Oswald) stormed into the embassy, demanded the visa, and when it was refused to him, headed out saying, 'I'm going to kill Kennedy for this.'" Castro is alleged to have continued and asked, "What is your government doing to catch the other assassins?" and speculated, "It took about three people."

The source then advised that Castro's speculation was based on tests which Castro and his men allegedly made under similar conditions with a similar rifle and telescopic

TOP SECRET
Group 1
Excluded from automatic
downgrading and
declassification

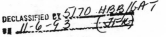

TOP SECRET

Honorable J. Lee Rankin

sight. Castro is said to have expressed the conclusion that Oswald could not have fired three times in succession and hit the target with the telescopic sight in the available time, that he would have needed two other men in order for the three shots to have been fired in the time interval. The source commented that on the basis of Castro's remarks, it was clear that his beliefs were based on theory as a result of Cuban experiments and not on any firsthand information in Castro's possession. In this connection, it should be noted that the FBI Laboratory firearms experts made tests and determined that three shots could be fired with the kind of rifle and sight used by Oswald in the five to six seconds which were available. The Laboratory noted, however, that the timing did not begin until after the firing of the first shot.

It will be noted that the information furnished by our source at this time as having come from Castro is consistent with and substantially the same as that which appears in Castro's speech of November 27, 1963, and which is referred to above.

This additional material is set forth for the Commission's information and no further action is contemplated by this Bureau concerning it.

Sincerely yours,

J. Edgar Hoover

- 2 -

TOP SECRET

Notes

Introduction

1. For those interested in pursuing particular theories about the case, more information is available from two Washington-based organizations: The Assassination Archives Research Center 918 F St. Rm. 510 NW, Washington, D.C. 20004; and the Committee on Political Assassinations, P.O. Box 722, Washington D.C. 20044-0772.
2. See *HSCA Report,* p. 196.
3. See *HSCA Report,* p. 196.
4. The House Select Committee on Assassinations (HSCA), Report of the Select Committee on Assassinations, U.S. House of Representatives (Washington D.C.: U.S. Government Printing Office, 1979) pp. 199–200; hereafter referred to as *HSCA Report*. Here is the remainder of the section on James Wilcott:

   He further testified that he was told that Oswald had been assigned a cryptonym and that Wilcott himself had unknowingly disbursed payments for Oswald's project. Although Wilcott was unable to identify the specific case officer who had initially informed him of Oswald's agency relationship, he named several employees of the post abroad with whom he believed he had subsequently discussed the allegations.

   Wilcott advised the committee that after learning of the alleged Oswald connection to the CIA, he never rechecked official Agency disbursement records for evidence of the Oswald project. He explained that this was because at that time he viewed the information as mere shop talk and gave it little credence. Neither did he report the allegations to any formal investigative bodies, as he considered the information hearsay. Wilcott was unable to recall the agency cryptonym for the particular project in which Oswald had been involved, nor was he familiar with the substance of that project. In this regard, however, because project funds were disbursed on a code basis, as a disbursement officer he would not have been apprised of the substantive aspects of projects.

   In an attempt to investigate Wilcott's allegations, the committee interviewed several present and former CIA employees selected on the basis of the position each had held during the years 1954–64. Among the persons interviewed were individuals whose responsibilities covered a broad spectrum of areas in the post abroad, including the chief and deputy chief of station, as well as officers in finance, registry, the Soviet Branch and counterintelligence.

None of these individuals interviewed had ever seen any documents or heard any information indicating that Oswald was an agent. This allegation was not known by any of them until it was published by critics of the Warren Commission in the late 1960's. Some of the individuals, including a chief of counterintelligence in the Soviet Branch, expressed the belief that it was possible that Oswald had been recruited by the Soviet KGB during his military tour of duty overseas, as the CIA had identified a KGB program aimed at recruiting U.S. military personnel during the period Oswald was stationed there. An intelligence analyst whom Wilcott had specifically named as having been involved in a conversation about the Oswald allegation told the committee that he was not in the post abroad at the time of the assassination. A review of this individual's office of personnel file confirmed that, in fact, he had been transferred from the post abroad to the United States in 1962.

The chief of the post abroad from 1961 to 1964 stated that had Oswald been used by the Agency he certainly would have learned about it. Similarly, almost all those persons interviewed who [p. 200] worked in the Soviet Branch of that station indicated they would have known if Oswald had, in fact, been recruited by the CIA when he was overseas. These persons expressed the opinion that, had Oswald been recruited without their knowledge, it would have been a rare exception contrary to the working policy and guidelines of the post abroad.

Based on all the evidence, the committee concluded that Wilcott's allegation was not worthy of belief.

5. *HSCA Report,* p. 197.
6. Even though the *HSCA Report* went along with the CIA's official story about Oswald, that view was not entirely shared by some HSCA researchers who were closely associated with this part of the investigation. Even a closer look at the *Report* leaves one with some ambiguity:

   For example, personnel testified to the committee that a review of Agency files would not always indicate whether an individual was affiliated with the Agency in any capacity [p. 197]. . . . Nor was there always an independent means of verifying that all materials requested from the Agency had, in fact, been provided. Accordingly, any finding that is essentially negative in nature—such as that Lee Harvey Oswald was neither associated with the CIA in any way, nor ever in contact with that institution—should explicitly acknowledge the possibility of oversight [p. 197]. . . . One officer acknowledged the remote possibility that an individual could have been run by someone as part of a ''vest pocket'' (private or personal) operation without other Agency officials knowing about it. But even this possibility, as it applies to Oswald, was negated by the statement of the deputy chief of the Soviet Russia clandestine activities section. He commented that in 1963 he was involved in a review of every clandestine operation ever run in the Soviet Union, and Oswald was not involved in any of these cases [p. 198, footnote 5].

Chapter One

1. Richard Snyder, interview with John Newman, February 26, 1994.
2. Interviews with Jean Hallett, July 8, 1994, and with Carolyn Maginnis (formerly Carolyn Hallett), also July 8, 1994. For Oswald on the "showdown," see Oswald, Historic Diary, Commission Exhibit 24, Vol. XVI, p. 96.
3. Ned Keenan, interview with John Newman, July 21, 1994. Keenan later became dean of the Graduate School of Arts and Sciences, Harvard University.
4. Richard Snyder, interview with John Newman, February 26, 1994.
5. Oswald, Historic Diary, CE 24, Vol. XVI, p. 96.
6. Oswald, "Diary Embassy Meeting," October 31, 1959, Warren Commission, CE 101, Vol. XVI, p. 440.
7. Interviews with Jean Hallett, July 8, 1994, and Carolyn Maginnis (formerly Carolyn Hallett), also July 8, 1994.
8. Richard Snyder, interview with John Newman, February 26, 1994.
9. CE 909, Vol. XVIII, p. 97. Undated, the note read as follows:

    I, Lee Harey [sic] Oswald, do hereby request that my present citizenship in the United States of America, be revoked.

    I have entered the Soviet Union for the express purpose of appling [sic] for citizenship in the Soviet Union, through the means of naturalization.

    My request for citizenship is now pending before the Supreme Soviet of the U.S.S.R.

    I take these steps for political reasons. My request for the revoking of my American citizenship is made only after the longest and most serious considerations. s/Lee H. Oswald
10. Richard Snyder, interview with John Newman, February 26, 1994.
11. Oswald, Historic Diary, CE 24, Vol. XVI, p. 96.
12. Richard Snyder, interview with John Newman, February 26, 1994.
13. John McVickar, memo to Thomas Ehrlich, special assistant to the legal advisor, Department of State, April 7, 1964, CE 958, Vol. XVIII, p. 332.
14. Testimony of John A. McVickar, WC, Vol. V, p. 303.
15. See WC, Vol. XXVI, p. 156, CE 2769. Three of the most commonly used Helsinki travel agencies were investigated, and the normal visa processing time was seven to fourteen days. Oswald's took just two days.
16. Richard Snyder, interview with John Newman, February 26, 1994.

17. Oswald, Historic Diary, CE 24, Vol. XVI, p. 96.
18. FSD-234, pp. 1–2.
19. Researchers will note that the address written on the picture in Oswald's passport which appears as CE 946, Vol. XVIII, p. 161, has been excised and Robert Oswald's Davenport street address written in above the excised address. In his contemporaneous reporting of the events in 1959 to the State Department (cable 1304 and FSD 234) Snyder did not mention this. I asked Snyder in 1994 why he did not mention this address in 1959. Snyder's reply was that Oswald had probably written the Davenport address in after Snyder gave Oswald his passport back in 1961 (Newman interview with Snyder, August 21, 1994).
20. FSD-234, p. 2
21. Richard Snyder, interview with John Newman, February 26, 1994.
22. Richard Snyder, CE 909, Vol. XVIII, p. 101, Snyder statement, cable 1623, to State Department from American Embassy in Tokyo, November 27, 1963.
23. McVickar, memo to Thomas Ehrlich, November 27, 1963, WC, CE 941, p. 2., Vol. XVIII, p. 154.
24. FSD-234, p. 2.
25. John A. McVickar, June 9, 1964, testimony to WC, Vol. V, p. 301.
26. Richard Snyder, interview with John Newman, February 26, 1994.
27. Richard Snyder, interview with Scott Malone and John Newman, September 1, 1993.
28. Richard Snyder, interview with John Newman, February 26, 1994.
29. Ned Kenean, interview with John Newman, July 21, 1994.
30. Richard Snyder, interview with John Newman, February 26, 1994.
31. Oswald, Historic Diary, CE 24, Vol. XVI, p. 97.
32. Richard Snyder, interview with John Newman, July 4, 1994.
33. See Edward Jay Epstein, *Legend: The Secret World of Lee Harvey Oswald* (New York: McGraw-Hill, 1978), p. 96. Epstein is not specific enough in his use of footnotes to pin down whether Snyder gave him the room number and Snyder does not remember.
34. Oswald, Historic Diary, CE 24, p. 4, Vol. XVI, p. 97.
35. Oswald, Historic Diary, CE 24, p. 4, Vol. XVI, p. 97.
36. Robert Korengold affidavit taken by Consul James A. Klenstine at the American Embassy in Moscow, September 8, 1964, CE 3098, p. 2, Vol. XXVI, p. 708.
37. Robert Korengold affidavit taken by Consul James A. Klenstine at the American Embassy in Moscow, September 8, 1964, CE 3098, p. 2, Vol. XXVI, p. 708.
38. Oswald, Historic Diary, CE 24, p. 4, Vol. XVI, p. 97.
39. CIA document 624-823, March 26, 1964.
40. Aline Mosby, interviewed by FBI in Paris, September 23, 1964; see CIA document DBA82118. Mosby had a CIA 201 number—201-252591, in which her 1964 FBI interview was filed.
41. Aline Mosby, CE 1385, Vol. XXII, pp. 701–710; Mosby in this recollection fails to distinguish between her two visits; the entrance and walk to

Oswald's room must have been the same on both occasions, but the initial introductions must have been on her shorter, first visit.

42. Oswald, Historic Diary, CE 24 p. 4, Vol. XVI, p. 97.
43. Aline Mosby, CE 1385, Vol. XXII, pp. 701.
44. UPI, October 31, 1959; see FBI HQ File 105-82555-2.
45. UPI, October 31, 1959; see FBI HQ File 105-82555-2.
46. CIA internal memo, Soviet Russia Division, Counterintelligence Branch, June 4, 1964; CIA document 861-374. The document is to Cordelia [nfi] from Lee [nfi].
47. UPI-16, October 31, 1959; see FBI HQ file 105-82555-2.
48. Robert Oswald, testimony to WC, February 20, 1964, Vol. I, p. 321.
49. See "Tries to Keep Him from Going Red," datelined Fort Worth, but obviously from a newspaper other than the *Star Telegram*, this from ONI/NIS files NARA, box 1.
50. NARA JFK files, State, Preassassination file, State Department cable 00081 to Moscow, November 1, 1959.
51. Kantor Exhibit No. 4, WC, Vol. XXII, p. 412. Kantor erroneously describes this call as taking place in "1960"—no further date is given. It is obvious that Kantor's account describes what took place on November 1, 1959, the day after Oswald's defection. Otherwise, Kantor's account seems reasonable.
52. Marie Cheatham memo to Richard Snyder, November 2, 1959. See WC Exhibit No. 2659, Vol. XXVI, p. 13.
53. Marie Cheatham memo to Richard Snyder, November 2, 1959. See WC Exhibit No. 2659, Vol. XXVI, p. 13.
54. See Hoover memorandum to J. Lee Rankin, May 4, 1964, WC Exhibit No. 834, p. 1, Vol. XVII, p. 804.
55. For the FBI list of what the Bureau says it had in their files on Oswald prior to the assassination of Kennedy, see CE 834, Vol. XVII, pp. 804–813.
56. FSD-234, p. 2.
57. McVickar, memo to Thomas Ehrlich, November 27, 1963, WC Exhibit No. 941, p. 3, Vol. XVIII, p. 155.
58. McVickar, memo to Thomas Ehrlich, November 27, 1963, WC Exhibit No. 941, p. 3, Vol. XVIII, p. 155.
59. Richard Snyder, CE 909, Vol. XVIII, p. 101, Snyder statement cable 1623 to State Department from American Embassy in Tokyo, November 27, 1963.
60. Richard Snyder, interview with John Newman, February 26, 1994.
61. Epstein, *Legend*, p. 96.
62. Testimony of John A. McVickar, WC, Vol. V, p. 301.
63. Testimony of Richard Snyder, WC, Vol. V, p. 265.
64. Richard Snyder, CE 909, Vol. XVIII, p. 101, Snyder statement, cable 1623 to State Department from American Embassy in Tokyo, November 27, 1963.
65. Snyder cable 1304 to State Department from American Embassy in Moscow, October 31, 1959. Snyder had later to go to Acting Chargé d' Affaires Freers's apartment to get the latter's authorization, and then walk the cable

back to the embassy communications center (Snyder interview with John Newman July 4, 1994). The cable left the comm center sometime that same Saturday afternoon, and therefore arrived early Saturday morning in Washington—in fact at 7:59 A.M.

66. Lee Harvey Oswald, letter to the American Embassy, dated November 3, 1959. See WC Exhibit No. 912, Vol. XVIII, p. 108.
67. Snyder letter to Oswald, dated November 6, 1959, see WC Exhibit No. 919, Vol. XVIII, p. 117. The fact that it was sent "registered return receipt" on November 9 was recorded on the bottom of the letter in handwriting.
68. See WC Exhibit No. 920, which is the embassy account of the letter to the State Department, in Vol. XVIII, pp. 118–119.
69. USNLO Moscow 2090, 1704Z, November 3, 1959, to chief of Naval Operations, routed by Hamner and checked by RE/Hediger. The other defector was Robert Edward Webster.
70. USNLO Moscow 2090, 1704Z, November 3, 1959, to chief of Naval Operations, see Navy copy and ONI copy. The ONI copy is distinctive because it is the only copy that shows Oswald's FBI number, 105-82555. "Hamner" may be a typographical error for "Hammer," the same Lt. J.G. Hammer who was on watch in ONI the moment that Kennedy was shot.
71. CNO 22257 to ALUSNA MOSCOW, 041529Z NOV 59.

Chapter Two

1. Moscow embassy cable 1304 to State Department, October 31, 1959.
2. UPI, dateline Moscow, October 31; see NARA FBI headquarters file, 105-82555-2.
3. UPI, dateline Moscow, October 31; see NARA FBI headquarters file 105-82555-2. Researchers note: You must turn over the original copy in the FBI HQ file in the National Archives to see the date-time and name stamps. This practice of stamping the reverse side of documents and cover sheets was also common at the CIA.
4. See E. B. Reddy memo to A. H. Belmont, FBI HQ file 105-82555-2.
5. See E. B. Reddy memo to A. H. Belmont, FBI HQ file 105-82555-2B.
6. UPI, dateline Moscow, 31 October; See NARA FBI headquarters file, 105-82555-2. Researchers can also locate the UPI ticker by consulting NARA JFK Identification Form number 124-10010-10003.
7. Goldberg interview by the FBI, August 4, 1964; WC, Vol. XXVI, pp. 99–100. Researchers should note that Goldberg thinks he got to Oswald before Mosby that weekend; this is unlikely since, by his own story, he did not go to Oswald's room until the New York AP alerted Goldberg based on a Texas newspaper story (probably the *Star Telegram*). Thus, the earliest Goldberg could have seen Oswald would have been Sunday, and this is borne out by the fact that the first AP story on the event was, in fact, Sunday, November 1.

8. AP, *New York Mirror*, final edition, November 1, 1959; see also FBI New York field office file 105-38431-4. Researchers should note that the Goldberg AP story of November 1, 1959, began an erroneous account of what happened in Snyder's office on Saturday, which was later picked up (probably inadvertently) and used in internal CIA postassassination analyses. The AP story read: ''A 20-year-old Texan strode into the American Embassy today, slapped down his passport on the consul's desk and said: ''I have made up my mind. I'm through.'' This story is mirrored in Coleman-Slawson memorandum (see NARA JFK RIF 157-10002-10432) of March 6, 1964, to Lee Rankin, Chief Warren Commission Counsel, p. 4, which said Oswald ''threw his passport on Snyder's desk.'' In fact, Oswald calmly handed his passport to receptionist Jean Hallett.
9. *Washington Post*, November 1, 1959, ''Ex-Marine Asks Soviet Citizenship''; see also CD 692, p. 104; and CIA document 591-252A.
10. *Washington Post*, November 1, 1959, ''Ex-Marine Asks Soviet Citizenship''; see also CD 692, p. 104; and CIA document 591-252A.
11. John E. Donovan testimony to the Warren Commission, May 5, 1964, Vol. VIII, p. 293.
12. Nelson Delgado testimony to the Warren Commission, April 16, 1964, Vol. VIII, p. 240.
13. J. Edgar Hoover letter to J. Lee Rankin, Warren Commission, April 6, 1964; see CE 833, Vol. XVII, p. 787.
14. See E. B. Reddy memo to A. H. Belmont, FBI HQ file 105-82555-2. Besides Belmont, copies were also sent to Mr. Trotter, Mr. Brannigan, and Mr. Scatterday.
15. *Washington Post*, November 1, 1959, ''Ex-Marine Asks Soviet Citizenship''; see also CIA document 591-252A.
16. For the FBI list of what the Bureau says it had in their files on Oswald prior to the assassination of Kennedy, see CE 834, Vol. XVII, pp. 804–813.
17. *Corpus Christi Times*, October 23, 1959, ''Goodbye,''; FBI headquarters file 105-82555. The placement of this article in the Oswald file might also have been a mistake: someone has written, ''No—not Oswald,'' next to a sentence which was probably referring to another American navy defector, Robert Webster.
18. *Conducting Research in FBI Records* (Washington D.C.: Research Unit, Office of Congressional and Public Affairs, Federal Bureau of Investigation, 1984), p. 14.
19. The next stamp after De Loach's 10:36 A.M. entry is Alan Belmont's at 3:32 P.M.
20. John Mayly (Church Committee) interview with Sam Papich, May 25, 1975, Senate Select Committee on Intelligence (SSCI) Box 265-14; see also NARA JFK RIF 157-10005-10078.
21. The original, CIA document 592-252B, appears to have been changed, with ''Mr. Papich'' having been whited out and the initials ''RBI'' placed in the space; see NARA JFK RIF 180-10092-10380. The real document with Papich's name was released in 1993 in the CIA's 201 file. That

Papich had made the "oral" request to CIA's Counterintelligence Liaison element is recorded in the CIA 1993-released documents list.

22. Summers, Anthony *Official and Confidential* (New York: Putnam, 1993), p. 229.
23. ONI Op-921D1/r1, November 2, 1959, memorandum for the file by J. M. Barron, see NARA JFK RIF 124-10010-10005.
24. Brannigan memo to Belmont, November 4, 1959, Oswald FBI headquarters file, 105-82555-3, p. 2; see also NARA JFK RIF 124-10010-10006.
25. It is in paragraph 3: "Birth: 18 October 1959 at New Orleans, La. Religious Preference: Lutheran. OSWALD entered the Marine Corps at Dallas, Texas, on 24 October 1956 to serve three years. He was released to inactive duty at MACS, El Toro, California, on 11 September 1959 and has obligated service until 8 December 1962. He speaks, reads and writes Russian very poorly. His next of kin, his mother, resides at 3124 West 5th Street, Fort Worth, Texas. At the time he entered service, subject gave his address as 4936 Collinswood Street, Fort Worth, Texas. While in service, he attended the Aviation Fundamental School and completed the aircraft Control and Warning Operator's Course. Subject's record has been sent to Records Facility, Glennwood, [sic] Ill."
26. See E. B. Reddy memo to A. H. Belmont, FBI HQ file 105-82555-2. The handwriting appears at the end of the typed text.
27. ONI Op-9211D1/rl, November 2, 1959, memorandum for the file by J. M. Barron, see NARA JFK RIF 124-10010-10005.
28. USNLO Moscow 2090, 1704Z, November 3, 1959, to chief of Naval Operations, routed by Hamner and checked by RE/Hediger.
29. See E. B. Reddy memo to A. H. Belmont, FBI HQ file 105-82555-2 (see back of memo for date-time stamps).
30. DST 1304 from American Embassy in Moscow to State Department, October 31, 1959; for the FBI copy see FBI headquarters file 105-82555; also see NARA JFK RIF 124-10010-10004. Snyder explained his stalling tactic by referring to the recent Petrulli defection case. In this case, the embassy had successfully stalled, as the Soviets had let Petrulli languish in his hotel room without a visa and then asked him to leave. Petrulli returned to the U.S. still an American citizen.
31. Moscow embassy cable 1304 to State Department, October 31, 1959.
32. The only other words underlined were "4936 Collinwood [sic] St., Fort Worth Texas," his mother's former address and the very same one which was in Barron's ONI memo of the previous day and which someone also wrote by hand on the Reddy FBI memo.
33. We will revisit the problem of when the CIA received these early Oswald documents, as well as their internal handling, in Chapter 4.
34. Rankin's request to Helms was written on September 11, 1964, and Helms's reply was on September 18, 1964. See CE 2752, Vol. XXVI, pp. 131–132.
35. Lists of CIA documents for release, NARA JFK Document ID No. 1993.08.04.08:00:780053; in another location in the National Archives one can find one of these lists appended to the proper memo, entitled "Re-

sponse to HSCA Request of 9 March 1978, Item 1''; see document ID No. 1993.07.02.13:25:25:180530. This second location also conveniently has a Helms memorandum to the Warren Commission of March 6, 1964, ''Information in CIA's Possession Regarding Lee Harvey Oswald Prior to November 22, 1963.''

36. USNLO Moscow 2090, 1704Z, November 3, 1959, to chief of Naval Operations, routed by Hamner and checked by RE/Hediger. Besides the FBI and CIA, this cable was also rerouted to ''CMC'' (Commandant Marine Corps), to ''09M,'' and to ''INS'' (the Immigration and Naturalization Service). This rerouting instruction was followed by the notation ''11/04/59/EW/.''
37. CIA document 592-252B. ''Mr. Papich was advised that we had no info on subject. 4 Nov. 59.''
38. ONI Op-921D1/rl, November 2, 1959, memorandum for the file by J. M. Barron; see NARA JFK RIF 124-10010-10005.
39. W. A. Brannigan memo to A. H. Belmont, FBI, November 4, 1959. See FBI HQ file 105-82555; see also NARA JFK RIF 124, 10010-10006.
40. FBI HQ file, 105-82555-6B.
41. CNO cable to ALUSNA Moscow, 04/1550Z, November 1959.
42. John E. Donovan testimony to the Warren Commission, May 5, 1964, Vol. VIII, p. 298.
43. List of CIA documents for release, NARA JFK Document ID No. 1993,08.04.08:00:780053. See entry number 8.
44. ''Response to HSCA Request of 9 March 1978, Item 1,'' NARA JFK files, document ID No. 1993.07.02.13:25:25:180530; see entries for October 31 and November 1, 9, 16, and 26, 1959.
45. CNO cable to ALUSNA Moscow, 04/1550Z, November 1959.

Chapter Three

1. Samuel D. Berry, interview with John Newman, July 10, 1994.
2. Donald L. Athey, interview with John Newman, July 10, 1994.
3. Samuel D. Berry, interview with John Newman, July 10, 1994.
4. Donald L. Athey, interview with John Newman, July 10, 1994.
5. The author is indebted to Richard C. Thornton, who made available his forthcoming manuscript, ''Exploring the Utility of Missile Superiority, 1958.''
6. NARA JFK records, January 1994 (''five brown boxes'') release.
7. CIA, DDS&T interim reply to HSCA request, May 8, 1978, OLC 78-1573.
8. S/A Berlin interview of Eugene J. Hobbs, March 10, 1964, NARA JFK records, NIS, Box 1.
9. ''Memorandum for the Assistant General Counsel (Manpower), Department of Defense, Subject: Information for President's Commission on the Assassination of President Kennedy; Your Request For,'' May 22, 1964, p. 4. See NARA JFK files, HSCA, RG 233. Oswald's unit traveled back

aboard the *Wexford County*, LST 1168, arriving at Atsugi on March 18, 1958.

10. Epstein, *Legend*, pp. 72–78.
11. John Donovan, interview with John Newman, July 19, 1994.
12. John Donovan, interview with John Newman, July 19, 1994. See also CD 6, p. 138.
13. John Donovan, interview with John Newman, July 19, 1994.
14. John Donovan, interview with John Newman, July 19, 1994.
15. Possibly to demonstrate that Khrushchev would not aid China in a confrontation with the U.S.
16. Epstein, *Legend*, p. 101.
17. Epstein, *Legend*, p. 101.
18. For a different interpretation, see Mark Lane "The Assassination of President John F. Kennedy: How the CIA set up Oswald" in *Hustler*, October 1978, p. 94.
19. John Donovan, interview with John Newman, July 19, 1994.
20. Mark Lane in "The Assassination of President John F. Kennedy: How the CIA Set up Oswald" *Hustler*, October 1978, p. 94.
21. O'Neal refused to answer any questions at all. To their credit, most all former CIA employees have at least been kind enough to grant interviews.
22. FSD 234, November 2, 1959; received November 6 at the State Department. We know it was in the FBI by at least November 12 because of an FBI date stamp on the ONI copy (see also FBI HQ file 105 82555-4).
23. Lists of CIA documents for release, NARA JFK Document ID No. 1993.08.04.08:00:780053. See entry number 8.
24. Lists of CIA documents for release, NARA JFK Document ID No. 1993.08.04.08:00:780053. See entry number 8.
25. John Donovan, quoted in "Oswald in Russia: Did He Tell Our Military Secrets?" *New York Journal American,* December 2, 1963. See also NARA FBI New York Field Office file 105-38431, and NARA JFK RIF 124-10160-10438.
26. S/A Berlin interview of Eugene J. Hobbs, March 10, 1964, NARA JFK records, NIS, Box 1.
27. CIA, DDS&T interim reply to HSCA request, May 8, 1978, OLC 78-1573. See NARA JFK records, January 1994 release.
28. Allen Dulles, *The Craft of Intelligence* (New York: Harper & Row, 1963), p. 58.
29. Richard C. Thornton, Chapter IV, "Exploring the Utility of Missile Superiority, 1958," forthcoming manuscript.
30. Charles J. Murphy, "The Embattled Mr. McElroy," *Fortune*, April 1959, p. 242.
31. McGeorge Bundy, *Danger and Survival: Choices About the Bomb in the First Fifty Years* (New York: Random House, 1988), pp. 343, 350.
32. Eisenhower speech to the U.N. emergency session of the General Assembly, August 13, 1958; see Eisenhower, *Public Papers*, 1958, p. 607.
33. Richard C. Thornton, Chapter IV, "Exploring the Utility of Missile Superiority, 1958," forthcoming manuscript.

34. Charles J. Murphy, ''Khrushchev's Paper Bear,'' *Fortune*, December 1964, p. 227.
35. Francis G. Powers, *Operation Overflight* (New York: Tower, 1970, p. 364.
36. John Donovan, quoted in ''Oswald Was a Troublemaker,'' *Washington Evening Star*, December 2, 1963. See also NARA JFK records, NIS, box 1.
37. John Donovan, quoted in ''Oswald in Russia: Did He Tell Our Military Secrets?'' *New York Journal American*, December 2, 1963. See also NARA FBI New York Field Office file 105-38431, and NARA JFK RIF 124-10160-10438.
38. John Donovan, quoted in ''Oswald Was a Troublemaker,'' *Washington Evening Star* December 2, 1963. See also NARA JFK records, NIS, box 1.
39. Testimony of John E. Donovan to the Warren Commission, May 5, 1964, Vol. VIII, p. 297.
40. Testimony of John E. Donovan to the Warren Commission, May 5, 1964; Vol. VIII, p. 297.
41. CIA memo, name of drafter still classified, December 1, 1963, re telephone call of John E. Donovan. See NARA JFK files, 1993 release.
42. CIA memo, name of drafter still classified, December 1, 1963, re telephone call of John E. Donovan. See NARA JFK files, 1993 release.
43. John Donovan, interview with John Newman, July 19, 1994.
44. N. V. Schultz, ONI-921D4F, ''Memorandum for the File,'' December 3, 1963; NARA JFK files, NIS/ONI, box 1.
45. John Donovan, interview with John Newman, July 19, 1994.
46. Norman Mailer, *Oswald's Tale,* extract printed in *New Yorker,* April 10, 1995, p. 60.

Chapter Four

1. See HSCA Final Report, p. 200.
2. See CIA *Clandestine Services Handbook*, 43-1-1, February 15, 1960, Chapter III, Annex B, ''PERSONALITIES—201 and IDN NUMBERS,'' p. 43; NARA JFK Files, January 1994 release, box 13, folder 29.
3. In a later chapter which deals with the end of 1960, we will revisit the 201 issue and attempt to solve the riddle of the late opening.
4. Dan Hardaway notes on conversation with Ann Egerter, March 21, 1978. See NARA JFK Files, RIF 180-10089-10462.
5. See HSCA Final Report, note 27, p. 628, and note 29, p. 629. These notes reference ''JFK Classified Document 014863,'' pp. 5 and 48.
6. See HSCA Final Report, p. 201 (a propitious page number for this subject!).
7. See HSCA Final Report, p. 202.
8. Helms deposition to the HSCA, September 25, 1978. See, NARA JFK Files, 1993 release.
9. See HSCA Final Report, p. 200.
10. See HSCA Final Report, notes 29 and 35, p. 629. The HSCA refers in

note 29 to a "classified staff summary re opening of Oswald's 201 file, December 15, 1978, House Select Committee on Assassinations (Classified JFK Document 014839)." In note 35 the HSCA also refers to "HSCA requests for explanations," March 20, 1979, p. 4226 (JFK Document 015018).

11. See HSCA Final Report, p. 201.
12. The superstitious will be amused at how fitting it seems, in retrospect, that the story of Oswald's threat to give the Soviets "something of special interest" arrived at the CIA on Friday the 13th.
13. See HT/LINGUAL notecards on Oswald in NARA JFK Files, Oswald 201 file, preassassination folder. It is the first card, dated November 9, 1959.
14. CIA "Response to HSCA Request of 15 August 1978, Item 3," in NARA JFK files, January 1994 release. This document has moved about in the five big brown boxes which comprise the January 1994 release, but its approximate original location in the larger collection might have been in or near box 11, folder 10. Researchers who have trouble locating it can also obtain a copy from the Assassination Archives Research Center (AARC), 915 F. Street, N.W., Suite 510, Washington D.C., 20014.
15. CIA "Response to HSCA Request of 15 August 1978, Item 3," in NARA JFK Files, January 1994 release.
16. There is a conflict, however, with the 12-451 on Marina's November 26, 1963, HT/LINGUAL card, although the number "4" is somewhat indistinct.
17. Our view of that file is the result of the CIA document lists on Lee Harvey Oswald, prepared by the Agency for the 1978 House Select Committee on Assassination investigation.
18. October 31, 1959. It was also Saturday, and Halloween.
19. CIA response to HSCA, March 9, 1978; Oswald documents lists; NARA, JFK files, RIF 1993.07.02.13:25:25:180530.
20. Robert L. Bannerman, interview with John Newman, August 8, 1994.
21. CIA response to HSCA, March 9, 1978; Oswald documents lists; NARA, JFK files, RIF 1993.07.02.13:25:25:180530.
22. Paul Garbler, interview with John Newman January 30, 1994.

Chapter Five

1. Richard Snyder, interview with John Newman, July 15, 1994.
2. Priscilla Johnson McMillan's (hereafter referred to as Priscilla McMillan) CIA files were released in January 1994 in what I refer to as the "five brown boxes" release. They are both at the National Archives and the AARC. For this item see CIA cable, Director Cite 16955, dated April 10, 1958, to a station whose name is blacked out but is probably its station in Paris. This we may surmise from the information line which has WE [Western Europe]/4 in it—so we know it is probably to a station in Western Europe—and also because Priscilla was in Paris at the time. The

headquarters cable also references a cable, probably from Paris, number 37145.

3. The processing of Priscilla McMillan's application was long and convoluted, but, given the controversy surrounding her history and the JFK case, it is appropriate to set down the details chronologically here. All documents are located in the CIA January 1994 "5 brown boxes" release. On October 3, 1952, a request was submitted for a security clearance as an "Intelligence Officer, GS-7," to work in OSO, SR division. On January 21, 1953, this was changed to a request for a security clearance to work as an "Intelligence Officer, GS-7," in Operations, FDD Division, USSR Branch. A March 10, 1964, CIA document says that "Johnson was security disapproved for staff employment in 1953 based upon her questionable associates, her activities in the United World Federalists and the League for Industrial Democracy." But that is not quite the way it happened. Actually, on February 10, 1963, a "Cancellation of Applicant Processing" was put in her file because of "declination by applicant" on January 21, 1953. But the CIA continued to process her security investigation. This is evident from a February 17, 1953, memo from W. A. Osborne to Chief, Security Division, saying Johnson "is now being considered for employment in ORR, where she will need SI clearances." Osborne, who was the chief of the Security Branch, noted that "she's active politically (i.e. interested in domestic and international politics) but is not and has not been tied in with subversive groups." Osborne continued. "While a member of UWF, she does not appear to be objectionably internationalistic." Osborne concluded: "Recommend approval." One week later, on February 24, 1953, the Project and Liaison Section sent a memo on Johnson (identifying her CIA number as 71589) to Deputy Chief, Security Division, requesting that her "case be reviewed from a CE [counterespionage] aspect." On the same day, Bruce L. Solie responded that Johnson had "declined employment on 21 January 1953" and was "no longer an applicant." A formal cancellation had been put in her file on February 10, he said, and therefore "it is not believed there is any CE interest in subject case." Then, on March 23, 1953, our same W. A. Osborne evidently had a eureka experience, because he suddenly changed his mind about Johnson. In a memo to the security officer Sheffield Edwards, Osborne said:

> The most serious question raised by investigation and research is that of her associates. It is felt that these associations being considered in the light of her activities in the United World Federalists, her attendance at questionable schools and her activities in the League for Industrial Democracy raise a question regarding her eligibility which should be resolved in favor of the Agency. It is, therefore, recommended that she be disapproved.

On April 13, Sheffield Edwards followed this recommendation and wrote "security disapproved" below Osborne's signature. A handwritten note by Mr. O'Rourke at the bottom of the memo said, "Advised Mr. [name redacted], PPD, X+[telephone] 3439, that subject has been disapproved. No written notice is required, as no official action is pending." O'Rourke added something that gives a clue to Osborne's reversal: "Above decision was rendered on a verbal request for it."

4. Priscilla McMillan, interview with John Newman, July 15, 1994.
5. See NARA JFK files, January 1994 "five brown boxes" set for "approval request," from Chief, CI/Operational Approval and Support Division, to the deputy director for security, Attn: Mr. Rice, August 8, 1956. Johnson's CIA number was given as 52373. In the remarks section is written: "Please withhold [two to three words redacted] pending favorable assessment. When appropriate, CSN 10-27 memo will be submitted."
6. See NARA JFK files, January 1994 "five brown boxes" release, memo dated August 23, 1956, for the signature of Robert A. Cunningham (someone whose initials might be VAS possibly signed for him) from the deputy director of security, Investigation and Support, to CI/Operational Approvals, referencing the August 8 request for Security Office and FBI record checks on C-52373, #P-276, Priscilla Johnson.
7. See NARA JFK files, January 1994 "five brown boxes" release, CIA Form 937, January 25, 1957, from SR/10, telephone extension 8352 to Chief, CI/OA on C-52373 (Priscilla Johnson).
8. Strangely, neither Priscilla has the middle initial R.
9. Priscilla McMillan, interview with John Newman, July 15, 1994.
10. Priscilla McMillan, interview with John Newman, July 15, 1994.
11. NARA JFK files, CIA January 1994 "five brown boxes" release. They are both at the National Archives and the AARC. For this item see CIA cable, Director Cite 16955, dated April 10, 1958, to a station whose name is blacked out but, as stated above (see footnote 2), this cable was probably sent to the CIA's station in Paris.
12. Priscilla McMillan, interview with John Newman, July 15, 1994.
13. See NARA JFK files, 1994 "five brown boxes" release, "Request for Cancellation of Approval," from Chief, CI/OA to deputy director for security, attn: Mr. Grignon, on C-70300. We know this was Johnson because of a later March 10, 1964, document (same location in NARA JFK files), which stated:

    4. Priscilla Johnson, #71589, was proposed for clearance as [one half line redacted] on 6 May 1958. A summary of derogatory information was furnished [one to two words redacted] and the request for clearance was canceled according to [one to two words redacted] memorandum date 27 June 1958. Johnson's biographic data reflects that from December 1955 to April 1956 she worked in the U.S. Embassy in Moscow as an employee of the Joint Press Reading Service (although other sources show employment variously as "freelance" translator, U.S. Embassy; North American Newspaper Alliance; *New York Times*) and during 1958 to 1960 she was employed in the U.S.S.R. by the North American Newspaper Alliance (NANA). Years later, rumors would surface that NANA was associated with the CIA. NANA was run by Ernie Cuneo and Priscilla's editor was Sydney Goldberg. Priscilla had no inkling of any NANA-CIA relationship at the time. Today she too has heard such rumors.

14. See NARA JFK files, 1994 ''five brown boxes'' release, June 6, 1958, internal CIA handwritten memo on SO #71589 by unidentified author.
15. See NARA JFK files, 1994 ''five brown boxes'' release, memo dated March 10, 1964, from deputy chief, Security Research Staff, Office of Security, to deputy director of security.
16. See NARA JFK files, 1994 ''five brown boxes'' release, CIA form 937, dated August 28, 1958, on C-52373 #P-276 (Priscilla Johnson) from SR/10 to chief, CI/OA. In the space ''Reason for Cancellation,'' it has: ''SR/10 has no further interest in subject. Please cancel.''
17. ''Notes of an Interview of Lee Harvey Oswald Conducted by Aline Mosby in Moscow in November in 1959''; see CE 1385, Vol. XXII, pp. 701–710. Again, researchers must cope with Mosby's account running together the first, shorter October 31 visit, and the longer November 13 visit. My own method was to cull out that material which appears to be what would happen when two people see each other for the very first time and treat it as the October 31 visit, and to treat all the rest as pertaining to the November 13 visit.
18. Robert Korengold statement for the Warren Commission, taken in Moscow by Richard A. Frank, September 14, 1964; see CE 3098, Vol. XXVI, pp. 707–708.
19. ''Notes of an Interview of Lee Harvey Oswald Conducted by Aline Mosby in Moscow in November in 1959''; see CE 1385, Vol. XXII, pp. 701–710. For a number of reasons, not the least of which is that Mosby's notes fail to distinguish between her first and second visits to Oswald's room at the Metropole, Korengold's version seems more likely to approximate what really happened.
20. Albert Newman, *The Assassination of John F. Kennedy: the Reasons Why* (New York: Clarkson N. Potter, Inc., 1970), p. 183. See also Slawson and Priscilla Johnson's comments during the latter's testimony to the Warren Commission, Vol. XI, p. 457.
21. FSD-234, p. 2
22. ''Notes of an Interview of Lee Harvey Oswald Conducted by Aline Mosby in Moscow in November in 1959''; see CE 1385, Vol. XXII, pp. 701–710.
23. FSD-234, p. 2.
24. ''Notes of an Interview of Lee Harvey Oswald Conducted by Aline Mosby in Moscow in November in 1959''; see CE 1385, Vol. XXII, pp. 701–710.
25. Priscilla McMillan, interview with John Newman, July 14, 1994.
26. See Priscilla McMillan testimony to the Warren Commission, July 25, 1974, Vol. XI, p. 448.
27. See Priscilla McMillan testimony to the Warren Commission, July 25, 1974, Vol. XI, p. 450.
28. Testimony of Priscilla McMillan to the HSCA. The transcript is still classified. For this comment, see the final report, p. 213.
29. Snyder interview with John Newman, July 15, 1994.
30. Priscilla McMillan interview with John Newman, July 14, 1994.
31. ''Priscilla Johnson's Recollections of Interview with Lee Harvey Oswald in Moscow, November 1959,'' December 5, 1963, Warren Commission, Johnson (Priscilla) Exhibit No. 5, Vol. XX, p. 294.

32. "Priscilla Johnson Exhibit No. 1," Warren Commission Vol. XX, p. 277.
33. "Priscilla Johnson Exhibit No. 1," Warren Commission Vol. XX, p. 278; in Priscilla's 1963 recollection "released" had been changed to "told people."
34. "Priscilla Johnson's Recollections of Interview with Lee Harvey Oswald in Moscow, November 1959," December 5, 1963, Warren Commission, Johnson (Priscilla) Exhibit No. 5, Vol. XX, p. 294–295.
35. He incorrectly cites November 15, but, as explained earlier in this chapter, we know that this interview was on Friday, November 13.
36. Testimony of Priscilla Johnson, July 25, 1964, Warren Commission, Vol. XI, p. 453.
37. Priscilla McMillan, interviews with John Newman, July 14, 21, and 24, 1994.
38. Testimony of Priscilla Johnson, July 25, 1964, Warren Commission Vol. XI, pp. 453–454.
39. Priscilla McMillan, interview with John Newman, July 14, 1994.
40. It turns out there were no further interviews in any case.

Chapter Six

1. "Note for Oswald File," John McVickar, November 9, 1959, WC, Vol. XVIII, CE 942, p. 156.
2. Marguerite and Ed Pic were divorced on June 28, 1933; see WC, Vol. XXIII, CE 1958, p. 780.
3. See Cable 1448, American Embassy Tokyo to American Embassy Moscow, November 9, 1959; see NARA JFK files, CIA 201 file on Oswald, boxes 1 and 2.
4. Richard Snyder, interview with John Newman, July 19, 1994.
5. Priscilla McMillan, interview with John Newman, July 14, 1994.
6. Richard Snyder, interview with John Newman, July 19, 1994.
7. Richard Snyder, interview with John Newman, July 19, 1994.
8. John McVickar, "Memo for the Files," dated November 17, 1959. See WC, Vol. XVIII, CE 911, pp. 106–107.
9. John McVickar, "Memo for the Files," dated November 17, 1959. See WC, Vol. XVIII, CE 911, pp. 106–107.
10. John McVickar, "Memo for the Files," dated November 17, 1959. See WC, Vol. XVIII, CE 911, pp. 106–107.
11. John McVickar, "Memo for the Files," dated November 17, 1959. See WC, Vol. XVIII, CE 911, pp. 106–107.
12. John McVickar, "Memo for the Files," dated November 17, 1959. See WC, Vol. XVIII, CE 911, pp. 106–107.
13. WC, Johnson (Priscilla) Exhibit No. 5, Vol. XX, p. 298.
14. Priscilla McMillan, interview with John Newman, July 14, 1994.
15. HSCA Final Report, p. 213.
16. Priscilla McMillan, interview with John Newman, July 15, 1994.
17. Priscilla McMillan, interview with John Newman, July 14, 1994.

18. Richard Snyder, interview with John Newman, July 19, 1994.
19. American Embassy cable to State Department, C-241, December 1, 1959; see NARA JFK files, CIA DDO 201 file on Oswald, box 1. See also WC, CE 921, Vol. XVIII, p. 120.
20. Priscilla McMillan, interview with John Newman, July 15, 1994.
21. Tom Mangold, *Cold Warrior; James Jesus Angleton: the CIA's Master Spy Hunter* (New York: Simon and Schuster, 1992), p. 250.
22. Mark Reibling, *Wedge: The Secret War Between the FBI and CIA* (New York: Knopf, 1994), p. 155.
23. Tom Mangold, *Cold Warrior; James Angleton; the CIA's Master Spy Hunter* (New York: Simon and Schuster, 1992), p. 250.
24. Tom Mangold, *Cold Warrior; James Jesus Angleton: the CIA's Master Spy Hunter* (New York: Simon and Schuster, 1992), pp. 249–250.
25. Anthony Cave Brown, *Treason in the Blood: H. St. John Philby, Kim Philby, and the Spy Case of the Century* (New York: Houghton Mifflin, 1994), p. 553.
26. Mark Reibling, *Wedge: The Secret War Between the FBI and CIA* (New York: Knopf, 1994), p. 181.
27. Clare Petty interview with Dick Russell, in *The Man Who Knew Too Much,* (New York: Carroll & Graf, Richard Gallen, 1992), p. 470.
28. David Martin, *Wilderness of Mirrors* (New York: Harper & Row, 1980), p. 105.

Chapter Seven

1. John E. Donovan testimony to the Warren Commission, May 5, 1964, Vol. VIII, p. 293.
2. See Fain report, May 12, 1960, p. 4; a copy may be found in WC Vol. XVII, p. 703.
3. See also FBI report: DL 100-10461, Fain 7/10/62, CE 823, Vol. XVII, p. 727.
4. *Fort Worth Press,* June 8, 1962. See also NARA JFK files, FBI Dallas FBI file, 100-10461-23.
5. "Historic Diary," CE 24, WC Vol. XVI, p. 100. The material in this section on "Alfred" in Minsk was brought to the author's attention by Professor Peter Dale Scott.
6. CE 32, WC Vol. XVI, p. 152.
7. CE 3140, WC Vol. XXVI, p 822; FBI (Boguslav and Heitman) interview of Marina, December 20, 1963.
8. CE 1824; WC Vol. XXIV, p. 484; FBI (Heitman) interview of Marina, January 31, 1964.
9. PLH/#DLB.37.3.
10. WC Vol. V, pp. 406–07 (Marina's testimony, June 11, 1964.)
11. Warren Report, p. 271 (photos): "Oswald and Alfred (last name unknown), a Hungarian [sic] friend of Anita Ziger [sic]" CE 2612 (same photo); WC Vol. XXV, p 884 "Lee Harvey Oswald and Alfred (last name unknown)."

CE 2616 (photo with same background); WC Vol XXV, p 886: "Anita Zieger and Lee Harvey Oswald in Minsk."

12. CE 2955, WC Vol. XXVI, p. 434; see also May 21, 1964, FBI report, Washington Field Office file 105-37111 at NARA, JFK files, RIF 157-10002-10112.
13. WC Vol. XXI, pp. 631–632 [Stuckey Exhibit No. 2].
14. WR p. 689. For Oswald's passport application see also WC Vol. XXII, pp. 77–78.
15. See CIA Oswald documents lists prepared in 1978 for the HSCA, NARA, JFK Records, January (five brown boxes) release. We cannot be sure of when this *Post* article was placed in Oswald's security file, but it is reasonable to assume it was on November 2 or 3, 1959.
16. See CE 2863 in WC Vol. XXVI, pp. 304–305, and CE 825 in WC vol. XVII, p. 765. The FPCC was officially closed on December 31, 1963; see Vincent T. Lee testimony in WC Vol. X, p. 87.
17. WC Vol. XXVI, CE 2863, p. 304, and Vol. XXVI, CE 3081 p. 689.
18. WC CD 1085a3, p. 1; *New York Times,* November 20, 1960.
19. Nelson Delgado testimony to the Warren Commission, April 16, 1964, Vol. VIII, p. 240.
20. Ray Rocca, CIA memo reviewing Castro, Cuba, Oswald, and the Kennedy assassination, presumably May 30, 1975. See Anthony Summers, *Conspiracy* (1989 ed.) p. 562; also see NARA, JFK records, RIF 1993,08.12.17:47:45:370039.
21. Warren Commission Report, p. 687.
22. Nelson Delgado testimony to the Warren Commission, April 16, 1964, Vol. VIII, pp. 240–241.
23. For a discussion of this point, see Morris H. Morley, *Imperial State and Revolution: The United States and Cuba, 1952–1986* (Cambridge: Cambridge University Press, 1987), p. 115.
24. Nelson Delgado testimony to the Warren Commission, April 16, 1964, Vol. VIII, p. 241.
25. Nelson Delgado testimony to the Warren Commission, April 16, 1964, Vol. VIII, p. 241.
26. Ray Rocca, CIA memo reviewing Castro, Cuba, Oswald, and the Kennedy assassination, presumably May 30, 1975; NARA, JFK records, RIF 1993.08.12.17:47:45:370039.
27. Nelson Delgado testimony to the Warren Commission, April 16, 1964, Vol. VIII, p. 241.
28. Nelson Delgado testimony to the Warren Commission, April 16, 1964, Vol. VIII, p. 242.
29. Ray Rocca, CIA memo reviewing Castro, Cuba, Oswald, and the Kennedy assassination, presumably May 30, 1975; NARA, JFK Records, RIF 1993.08.12.17:47:45:370039.
30. Hemming letter to Major General C. V. Clifton, military aide to the president, February 12, 1963; NARA JFK files, CIA January 1994 (5 brown boxes) release.

31. Hemming's 1960 debriefings can be found in NARA JFK files, CIA January 1994 (5 brown boxes) release, and in NIS boxes 1-3.
32. Memorandum for chief, Security Analysis Group, from Jerry G. Brown; Subject: Hemming, April 8, 1977 (Hereafter referred to as "Brown memo"), NARA, JFK files, RIF 1993.06.28.17:12:27:150360.
33. CIA memorandum from Jerry Brown to chief, Security Analysis Group, June 11, 1976; NARA, JFK files, RIF 1993.06.29.15:26:50:400280.
34. CIA memorandum; Subject: Hemming, October 19, 1967; NARA, JFK files, CIA 1992 release.
35. For example, an October 31, 1960, CIA Intelligence Report said this:

    > Source is a twenty-three-year-old ex-Marine who spent the period from February 1959 through July 1960 serving in the Cuban Army and the Cuban Air Force. He obtained his discharge from the Cuban Air Force in June 1960 and returned to the U.S. via Mexico City on 30 Aug. 1960. According to source, he had been nominated by the Marine Corps to enroll in the Naval Reserve Officer Training Corps at a U.S. university even though he had not finished his high school education. He reportedly did not accept this offer because he was much more interested in Special Forces–type activity, and this led to his decision to leave the Marine Corps and a short time later to enlist in the Cuban Army. He appears to be a keen observer. While source's plans are indefinite, he should be available for further interview during the next few weeks (mid-October–November 1960.)

    NARA, JFK files; the 1960 IRs are in several locations: See NIS boxes 1–3; see CIA 1994 (5 brown boxes) release, and see also documents located with or near RIF 1993.06.28.17:20:46:150360.
36. April 8, 1977, Brown memo. The memo contained this helpful explanatory note:

    > 1. Reference is made to the attachment which is a copy of a memorandum contained in Subject file dated 7 November 1960 from Chief/Contact Division/00 to Chief/Personnel Security Division/Office of Security, captioned "Jerry P. Hemming, Jr., Ex-Marine who served in Cuban Army and Air Force 00-A-3170536," a copy of which was sent to WH Division and CI staff. It is apparent that the Henning referred to therein is identical with Gerald Patrick Hemming.
37. April 8, 1977, Brown memo.
38. April 8, 1977, Brown memo.
39. April 8, 1977 Brown memo.
40. April 1976 *Argosy* article.
41. Feb. 1959–June 1960 CIA biographical sketch of Hemming.
42. Gerald Patrick Hemming, January 6, 1995, interview with John Newman.
43. Gerald Patrick Hemming, January 6, 1995, interview with John Newman.
44. CIA memorandum for chief, WHD; Subject: Viola June Cobb, June 1, 1960; NARA, JFK files, CIA January 1994 (5 brown boxes) release, Cobb papers.
45. Attachment, "Viola June Cobb," to CIA memorandum for chief, WHD;

Subject: Viola June Cobb, June 1, 1960; NARA, JFK files, CIA January 1994 (5 brown boxes) release, Cobb papers; the same attachment appears alone, i.e., without the base document, and with different redactions, in the CIA August 1994 microfilm release, reel 10, folder E, RIF 1994.03.11.13:45:14:320005.

46. CIA memorandum for chief, WHD; Subject: Viola June Cobb, June 1, 1960; NARA, JFK files, CIA January 1994 (5 brown boxes) release, Cobb papers.
47. Attachment to CIA June 1, 1960 memo on Cobb, NARA, JFK files, CIA August 1994 microfilm release, reel 10, folder E, RIF 1994.03.11.13:45:14:320005.
48. CIA memo for the record; Subject: June Cobb (216-264), February 21, 1975; NARA, JFK files, CIA January 1994 (5 brown boxes) release; "Box 40A."
49. CIA memorandum for chief, SB/1, from acting deputy chief, Support Branch, June 7, 1960; NARA, JFK files, CIA January 1994 (5 brown boxes) release, Cobb papers.
50. CIA memorandum for chief, SB/1, from acting deputy chief, Support Branch, June 7, 1960; NARA, JFK files, CIA January 1994 (5 brown boxes) release, Cobb papers.
51. CIA routing and record sheet to CSCI 3/762466, November 1, 1960, CIA 1994 microfilm release, reel 11, folder C, RIF 1994.03.08.14:03:26:750007.
52. CIA operation log, New York Field Office, Case 216264, October 23, 1960, Boston Massachusetts. NARA JFK files, CIA January 1994 (5 brown boxes release) Cobb papers, see "Box 40A."
53. Synopsis of June Cobb's telephone calls in New York City, October 19-25, 1960, file 216264. NARA JFK files, two CIA locations: January 1994 (5 brown boxes release) Cobb papers.
54. Mark Lane, *Plausible Denial* (New York: Thunder's Mouth Press, 1991), pp. 288–302.
55. Doug Gentzkow, 1994 interview with John Newman.
56. CIA domestic contacts report to chief, Contacts Division; Attention: Support (Mayo Stunz), and chief, New York office, from Jay B. L. Reeves, OO,3,3,289,019, January 22, 1964; NARA JFK files, CIA January 1994 (5 brown boxes) release, Pawley-Gentzkow papers; see F81-0351-D0547.
57. *The Declassified Eisenhower,* p. 722.
58. *The New York Times,* January 8, 1977.
59. See CIA memorandum for director of Central Intelligence, July 13, 1954, NARA JFK files, CIA January 1994 (5 brown boxes) release, Pawley papers; see pages numbered 18491 and 18493.
60. See CIA memorandum from acting chief, Support Branch, to chief of SB/1; Subject: William Pawley, October 6, 1959; NARA JFK files, CIA January 1994 (5 brown boxes) release, Pawley papers; see document F81-0351-D0371.
61. CIA memo from [3-4 letters redacted] to chief, WH Division, April 6,

1960; NARA JFK files, CIA 1994 microfilm release, reel 10, folder E, RIF 1994.03.11.13:45:14:320005.

62. June Cobb, April 3, 1995 interview with John Newman.
63. CIA memorandum to chief, WH/4; Subject [redacted] June Cobb, aide to Juan Orta, June 3–5, 1960, from: [redacted]; NARA, JFK files, CIA January 1994 (5 brown boxes) release, Cobb papers. Filed under Cobb's 201 file (278891).
64. June Cobb, March 27, 1995, interview with John Newman.
65. CIA operation log, New York field office, Case 216264, November 3, 1960, Boston, Massachusetts. NARA JFK files: January 1994 (5 brown boxes) release Cobb papers.

Chapter Eight

1. The author is indebted to Richard C. Thornton, who made available unpublished material to the author.
2. A speech Khrushchev delivered to the 20th Congress of the Communist Party of the Soviet Union on [date] 1956.
3. See Foreign Relations of the United States–Cuba (hereafter referred to as FRUSC), Vol. VI, document #456, Memorandum of Discussion of the 435th Meeting of the National Security Council, February 18, 1960, p. 792.
4. Secretary of State Christian Herter, telephonic remarks to President Eisenhower on August 25 1960, in FRUSC-VI, p. 1062. Herter was referring to Mikoyan's February 1960 visit to Cuba.
5. Memorandum from Assistant Secretary of State for Inter-American Affairs (Rubottom) to the Assistant Secretary of State for Policy Planning (Smith), Document #519, FRUSC-VI, p. 917. The document Rubottom described, which is apparently no longer extant, was dated May 11, 1960, and was written by a "Mr. Morgan," probably George A. Morgan, Deputy Assistant Secretary of State for Policy Planning.
6. Mario Lazo, *Dagger in the Heart*, (New York, Twin Circle Publishing Co., 1968), p. 333.
7. A. Newman, *The Assassination,* p. 196. Newman states Castro attended 9/18/60.
8. E. Howard Hunt, *Give Us This Day*, p. 39.
9. Letter from President Eisenhower to Prime Minister Macmillan, July 11, 1960, FRUSC-VI, document #551, pp. 1000–1005; see p. 1003 for quoted material.
10. Secretary of State Herter, Circular Telegram From the Department of State to Certain Diplomatic Missions in the American Republics, July 11, 1960, Document #552, FRUSC-VI, pp. 1006–1007. Cable
11. FRUSC-VI, document #410, Memorandum of Discussion at the 429th Meeting of the National Security Council, pp. 703–706; see especially pp. 705–706.
12. FRUSC-VI, Document #408, Memorandum of Discussion at the 428th

Meeting of the National Security Council, December 10, 1959, pp. 698–700; see especially p. 698.

13. FRUSC-VI, Document #410, Memorandum of Discussion at the 429th Meeting of the National Security Council, December 16, 1959, pp. 703–706; see especially p. 704.
14. *Alleged Assassination Plots* Involving Foreign Leaders, Interim Report of U.S. Senate Select Committee to Study Governmental Operations, 1975, pg. 92.
15. CIA 1329-484 C. referring to March 2, 1967 broadcast.
16. Report of Inspector General, CIA, May 1967.
17. This sentence in the I.G. Report could be summarized in this interesting way: Bissell recalled his part of the seminal Castro assassination discussion as having occurred during the Nixon White House, while King recalled it as having occurred during the Kennedy White House.
18. May 23, 1967 memorandum for the record from Inspector General CIA (Cover to I.G. Report)
19. *Alleged Assassination Plots*, p. 74; see also p. 92.
20. *Alleged Assassination Plots*, p. 74; see also p. 92.
21. Footnote 3 page 92, *Alleged Assassination Plots*, which points out that this document was not made available early on in their investigation. The report adds this note:

    The Committee received this document on November 15, 1975, after printing of this Report had begun. As a consequence, there was no opportunity to question either King or Bissell concerning the meaning of ''elimination,'' what consideration was in fact given to Castro's ''elimination,'' and whether any planning resulting from this document in fact led to the actual plots. In this regard it should be noted that Bissell had a ''dim recollection'' of a conversation prior to early autumn or late summer 1960 with King (the author of the above memorandum) concerning a ''capability to eliminate Castro if such action should be decided upon'' (Bissell, 6/9/75, p. 19).

22. Peter Grose, *Gentleman Spy*,: the life of Allen Dulles, Houghlin Mifflin, 1994. p. 494.
23. Richard Nixon *RN: The Memoirs of Richard Nixon*, (New York: Grosset & Dunlap, 1978), pp. 202–203.
24. FRUSC-VI, Document #410, Memorandum of Discussion at the 429th Meeting of the National Security Council, December 16, 1959, pp. 703–706; see especially pp. 704–705.
25. FRUSC-VI, Document #410, Memorandum of Discussion at the 429th Meeting of the National Security Council, December 16, 1959, pp. 703–706; see especially p. 705.
26. On August 28, 1960, Thomas C. Mann replaced Roy R. Rubottom as Assistant Secretary of State for Inter-American Affairs. On the same day, Frank J. Devine was promoted from Staff Assistant, Bureau of Inter-American Affairs, to Special Assistant to the Assistant Secretary of State for Inter-American Affairs. See FRUSC-VI, List of Persons, pp. xxi-xxvii.
27. FRUSC-VI, Document #410, Memorandum of Discussion at the 429th

Meeting of the National Security Council, December 16, 1959, pp. 703–706; see especially p. 705.

28. FRUSC-VI, Document #410, Memorandum of Discussion at the 429th Meeting of the National Security Council, December 16, 1959, pp. 703–706; see especially p. 705.
29. Richard Nixon, *RN*, p. 203. New York: Grossett, & Dunlap, 1978.
30. *Alleged Assassination Plots*, p. 93.
31. Church Committee files, ''Minutes of Special Group Meeting, January 13, 1960.''
32. Church Committee files, ''Minutes of Special Group Meeting, January 13, 1960.''
33. Church Committee files, ''Minutes of Special Group Meeting, January 13, 1960.''
34. Card index: Special Group Meeting January 13, 1960. Also Interim Report of the SSCIA, *Alleged Assassination Plots Involving Foreign Leaders*, Report 94-465, U.S. Government Printing Office, 1975, p. 93.
35. Peter Grose, *Gentleman Spy*, p. 494.
36. FRUSC, Vol. VI, Document #423, Memorandum of Discussion at the 423d Meeting of the National Security Council, January 14, 1960, pp. 740–746. For this remark by Merchant, see p. 742. Nixon said he ''believed we should look at Latin America as a single area from an investment point of view, so that anything which hurts investment in one part of Latin America hurts investment throughout the area.''
37. Church Committee files, Memo for the Record, March 9, 1960.
38. Church Committee files, ''Minutes of Special Group Meeting, March 10, 1960.'' Alleged Assassination Plots, pg 93.
39. For a more complete account of the minutes of the March 10, 1960, NSC meeting, see FRUSC-VI, Document #474, pp. 832–837.
40. Church Committee files, ''Minutes of Special Group Meeting, March 15, 1960.''
41. ''A Program of Covert Action Against the Castro Regime,'' paper prepared by the 5412 (Special Group) Committee, March 16, 1960, FRUSC-VI, Document #481, pp. 850–854.
42. Church Committee files, ''Minutes of Special Group Meeting, March 15, 1960.
43. Church Committee files, ''Minutes of Special Group Meeting, March 15, 1960.
44. Memorandum of a Conference with the President, White House, March 17, 1960, FRUSC-VI, Document #486, pp. 861–863.
45. Dulles biographer Peter Grose, in his book *Gentleman Spy*, p. 495, has a different perspective of Eisenhower and the Covert Program. Grose writes, ''Eisenhower had made clear his scorn for the gimmicks that delighted the little-boy mentality of the clandestine services, so Bissell rephrased the various subversive ploys into a formidable 'Program of Covert Action Against the Castro Regime' for approval by the 5412 [Special Group] committee.''

46. Memorandum of a Conference with the President, White House, March 17, 1960, FRUSC-VI, Document #486, pp. 861–863.
47. Memorandum of a Conference with the President, White House, March 17, 1960, FRUSC-VI, Document #486, pp.861–863.
48. For other interesting references to President Eisenhower's March 17, 1960, authorization to begin the training of Cuban refugees, see *Farewell America* (Hepburn), p. 316, and *Bay of Pigs* (Johnson), p. 30. In his memoirs, *RN*, p. 203, Nixon recalls: "I was present at the meeting in which Eisenhower authorized the CIA to organize and train Cuban exiles for the eventual purpose of freeing their homeland from the Communists." The training of these exiles began in Guatemala. On June 22, 1960, the first 28 anti-Castro Cubans were taken to Guatemala from Florida (see Johnson, *Bay of Pigs*, p. 38). In August 1960, President Miguel Ydigoras Fuentes of Guatemala opened a CIA airstrip at CIA training base at Retalhuleu (see Ross and Wise, *Invisible Government,* p. 28). On October 30, 1960, a Guatemala City newspaper, *La Hora* printed a report on CIA Cuban exile training, describing a training camp and invasion preparations under way (see Johnson, *Bay of Pigs*, p. 49).
49. E. Howard Hunt, *Give Us This Day*, p. 22.
50. The CIA cryptonym for the project was "PB/Success." See Burton Hersh, *The Old Boys*, pp. 342–343.
51. E. Howard Hunt, *Give Us This Day*, pp. 22–23.
52. Prior to this assignment, Esterline had been serving as the CIA station chief in Caracas, a job he had held since 1957. Later, in 1964, Esterline would move from Chief WH/4 to Chief WH/OPS.
53. E. Howard Hunt, *Give Us This Day*, pp. 24–26.
54. E. Howard Hunt, *Give Us This Day*, p. 27.
55. E. Howard Hunt, *Give Us This Day*, p. 38.
56. See the Inspector General's Report, p. 10.
57. "The case officer testified that he and the Cuban contemplated only requiring intelligence information and that assassination was not proposed by them." *Alleged Assassination Plots*, p. 72.
58. According to p. 73, fn. #1, of the SSCIA report *Alleged Assassination Plots*:

    > The duty officer testified that he must have spoken with King because he would not otherwise have signed the cable "by direction, J. C. King." (Duty officer, 8/11/75, pg. 16.) He also would "very definitely" have read the cable to Barnes before sending it, because "Barnes was the man to whom we went . . . for our authority and for work connected with the [Cuban] project." (Duty officer, pp. 4, 25.) Since King at that time was giving only "nominal attention" to Cuban affairs, the officer concluded that a proposal of the gravity of an assassination could only have "come from Mr. Barnes." (Duty officer, 8/11/75, p. 24.).

59. *Alleged Assassination Plots*, p. 73.
60. The case officer avoided the word "assassinate."
61. FRUSC-VI, p. 1022.

62. E. Howard Hunt, *Give Us This Day*, pp. 39–40.
63. E. Howard Hunt, *Give Us This Day*, p. 40.

Chapter Nine

1. WC Vol XVI, p. 825.
2. U.S. Secret Service interview with Marguerite Oswald, November 25, 1963. NARA JFK records, RIF 124-10062-10049.
3. See CE 206, Vol. XVI, pp. 594–95.
4. See CE 1138, Vol. XXII, p. 118.
5. State Operations Memorandum to American Embassy Moscow, March 21, 1960. See CE 922, Vol. XVIII, p. 121.
6. William Macomber letter to Congressman Wright, March 21, 1960. See CE 923, Vol. XVIII, p. 122.
7. See CE 3111, Vol. XXVI, p. 746.
8. Handwritten note from "GWM" to "Miss Waterman," undated. See CE 927, Vol. XVIII, p. 127.
9. For the refusal sheet, see CE 962, Vol. XVIII, p. 356. See also Bernice Waterman testimony to the Warren Commission, June 9, 1964. See WC Vol. V pp. 350–351.
10. See CE 3111, Vol. XXVI, p. 746.
11. See Bernice Waterman testimony to the Warren Commission, June 9, 1964. See WC Vol. V pp. 350–351.
12. See CE 3111, Vol. XXVI, p. 746.
13. Bernice Waterman testimony to the Warren Commission, June 9, 1964. See 5 H, pp. 350–351.
14. See CE 3111, Vol. XXVI, p. 747.
15. See CE 3111, Vol. XXVI, p. 747.
16. State to American Embassy Moscow, March 28, 1960. See CE 929, Vol. XVIII, p. 129.
17. American Embassy Moscow Operations Memorandum to State Department, March 28, 1960. See CE 927, Vol. XVIII, p. 126.
18. See CE 207, Vol. XVI, p. 596; see also CE 1138, Vol. XXII, p. 118.
19. Letter from Professor Casparis to Lee Harvey Oswald, March 22, 1960. See NARA JFK files, 1994 CIA release, "Five Brown Boxes." See also CE 229, Vol. XVI, p. 626.
20. We know of Marguerite's April 6 response from Casparis, reply of April 26. See letter from Professor Casparis to Lee Harvey Oswald, April 26, 1960. See NARA JFK files, 1994 CIA release, "Five Brown Boxes."
21. American Embassy Moscow Operations Memorandum to State Department, March 28, 1960. See CE 927, Vol. XVIII, p. 126.
22. Dallas FBI field office report of John W. Fain, Dallas serial 105-976, dated May 12, 1960. See NARA JFK files, RIF 157-10006-10213.
23. Commander, Marine Air Reserve Training to Private First Class Lee H. Oswald, April 26, 1960. See CE 204, Vol. XVI, p. 590.

24. State Department Operations memorandum to American Embassy in Moscow, May 10, 1960. See CE 928, Vol. XVIII, p. 128.
25. Marguerite Oswald to U.S. Marine Corps, letter of June 10, 1960. See CE 204, Vol. XVI, p. 592.
26. Marguerite Oswald letter to Mr. Haselton, June 8, 1960. See CE 208, Vol. XVI, p. 597.
27. Marine Corps letter to Marguerite Oswald, June 17, 1960. See CE 204, Vol. XVI, p. 589.
28. The Hoover cover note on ONI is dated May 25, 1960, and the FBI transmittal of Fain's report to ONI was recorded on ONI routing slip GG-71228, received May 26, 1960; this routing slip also records the subsequent forwarding of the Fain report to DI09ND under DNI serial 014167F92 of May 1960. The processing for discharge by the Marine Corps Reserves was being handled at 9ND (Ninth Navel District). See NARA JFK files, NIS-ONI box 1.
29. FBI New York field office (105-6103) to Bureau (100-353496), May 23, 1960. NARA, JFK files, RIF 124-10010-10010.
30. Hoover letter to Security Office, Department of State, June 3, 1960, FBI, Bureau file 105-82555, CD 1114.
31. Memo, Boster (typed by Anderson) to Adams, July 11, 1960. See NARA, JFK files, CIA 201 preassassination file, box 1.
32. State Department operations memorandum to American Embassy in Moscow, June 22, 1960. See CE 925, Vol. XVIII, p. 124.
33. State Department to Marguerite Oswald, June 22, 1960. See CE 209, Vol. XVI, p. 598.
34. American Embassy Moscow operations memorandum to State Department, July 6, 1960. See CE 926, Vol. XVIII, p. 125.
35. State Department letter to Marguerite Oswald, July 7, 1960. See CE 210, Vol. XVI, p. 599.
36. Marguerite Oswald letter to State Department, July 16, 1960. See CE 211, Vol. XVI, p. 600.
37. Request of Miss Vann, July 19, 1960. See CE 964, Vol. XVIII, p. 359.
38. George Haselton confidential note to John T. White, July 20, 1960. See CE 964, Vol. XVIII, p. 358.
39. State Department letter to Marguerite Oswald, July 21, 1960. See CE 212, Vol. XVI, p. 601.
40. See ONI "Status Check," September 6, 1960, NARA, NIS-ONI files, box 1; see also NARA, CMC notification to ONI, in FBI headquarters file 105-82555-12, November 15, 1960. CE 2751 WC, Vol. XXVI, p. 130.
41. See letter from Professor Casparis to Marguerite Oswald, September 3, 1960. See NARA, JFK files, 1994 CIA release, "Five Brown Boxes."
42. See Paris Legal attache to Hoover letter to Security Office, Department of State, June 3, 1960, FBI, bureau file 105-82555. See also the initial response (almost completely redacted) from Paris, in FBI headquarters file 105-82555-8, dated July 27, 1960.
43. See Special Agent Kenneth P. Haser memo to SAC, WFO file 105-37111-1, August 9, 1960.

44. See Special Agent W. Dana Wilson memo to SAC WFO file 105-37111-2, September 12, 1960.
45. Paris 105-1067 to Bureau 105-82555, September 27, 1960 (almost wholly redacted), and Paris 105-1067 to Bureau 105-82555, October 12, 1960 (also almost wholly redacted). On October 10, 1960, the FBI inquired through liaison channels at Albert Schweitzer College in Switzerland about LHO. See CE 2918 WC Vol. XXVI, p. 92.
46. Paris 105-1067 to Bureau 105-82555, November 3, 1960.
47. FBI, Dallas field office report of John W. Fain, Dallas file 100-10461, dated July 3, 1961. See also CE 1127, Vol. XXII, p. 102.
48. State Department A-127 to American Embassy in Moscow, February 1, 1961. See CE 930, Vol. XVIII, p. 130.
49. FBI report of November 20, 1963. See CE 1805, Vol. XXIII, p. 443.
50. Warren Commission Report, p. 697.
51. CE 24 WC Vol. XVI, p. 98.
52. See WC p. 697; on Oswald's feelings about Rosa, see CE 24, Vol. XVI, pp. 99 and 101.
53. CD 1, p. 51. This FBI report also reports Oswald's arrival by train in Minsk, and the date.
54. Historic Diary, p. 6; see CE 24, Vol. XVI, p. 99.
55. As Oswald later described it, the shop in which he worked, called ''experimental shop 572,'' employed 58 workers and 5 foremen. It was located in the middle part of the factory area in a two-story building made of redbrick.
56. See WR p. 697; also see CE 1128, WC Vol. XXII, p. 104 and CE 1109, WC Vol. XXII, p. 67
57. According to Marina Oswald, he worked on a lathe. See 5 H 616 (Marina Oswald).
58. See WR p. 697; see also 8 H 360 (Bouhe), 8 H 385 (Anna M. Meller), 5 H 407-8 (Marina Oswald), CE 1401, Vol. XXII, p. 750, and CE 24, Vol. XVI, p. 99. Oswald said that he started work in the Minsk radio and TV factory for 90 rubles per month, and his workbook agrees; see WC Vol. XVIII, p. 137.
59. WR p. 698; see also CE 24, VOl. XVI, p. 99.
60. Oswald wrote that he studied Russian with Rosa during ''Jan-May 1960''; see CE 93, Oswald note, ''Russian,'' Vol. XVI, p. 340.
61. Historic Diary, p. 6; see CE 24, Vol. XVI, p. 99.
62. In March or April, Oswald met Pavel Golovachov, a radio technician and coworker at the factory, when he described as intelligent and friendly; see CE 2609, VOL XXV p. 271.
63. Historic Diary, p. 7; see CE 24, Vol. XVI, p. 100.
64. Historic Diary, p. 7; see CE 24, Vol. XVI, p. 100.
65. WC Vol. I, pp. 14, 328; CE 1402 WC Vol. XXII, p. 764; CE 1964 WC Vol. XXIII, p. 805; CE 2007 WC Vol. XXIV, p. 407; CE 2770 WC Vol. XXVI, p. 156.
66. Historic Diary, p. 7; see CE 24, Vol. XVI, p. 100.

67. See CE 2759, Vol. XXVI, p. 144; for a photograph of Ella, see CE 2609, Vol. XXV, p. 883.
68. See 2606, Vol. XXV, p. 881.

Chapter Ten

1. January 5, 1960 (Tuesday)—Marguerite Oswald received $20 check back, with note from Oswald asking for cash. (WC Vol. XXII, pp. 101, 704) CD 8, p. 7.
   January (on or about Tuesday the 5th), 1960—Marguerite Oswald sent $20 bill to Oswald and it was returned 2/25/60. (WC Vol. XXII, p. 101; CD 8, p. 7): Stamped on reverse side of envelope "Retour Departe" "MOCKBAN NOYTANT, Moscow, Russia 1/18/60 MEX AYHAPOAKO."
   January 18, 1960 (Monday)—This date was stamped in Moscow on the letter enclosing $20 which Oswald's mother sent to him. She received it back 2/25/60. (WC Vol. XXII, p. 101).
   January 22, 1960 (Friday)—Marguerite Oswald bought $25 money order at First National Bank, Fort Worth, #142,688 (CD 8, p. 7) and sent it air mail to Oswald, Hotel Metropole, Moscow. (WC Vol. XXII, p. 101; CD 8, p. 7.).
   April 27, 1960 (Wednesday)—FBI agent John Fain interviewed Oswald's brother Robert. (WC Vol. I, p. 423; WC Vol. XXVI, p. 92). On 12/4/63, Secret Services said LHO "is FBI #327 925 D." (CD 87: SS 449, p. 3; CD 87: SS 451, p. 2).
   April 28, 1960 (Thursday)—FBI interviewed Marguerite Oswald (WC Vol. XXVI, p. 92) at Methodist Orphans Home, 1111 Herring, Waco, Texas. (CD 8, p. 2) LHO: 5' 10"", 165#, blue eyes, light brown, wavy hair (per his mother). (CD 8. p. 4).
2. NARA JFK files, FBI Dallas file 105-976, report of John W. Fain, May 12, 1960, p. 4; WC Vol. XVII, p. 703.
3. CE No. 833, FBI report entitled "Lee Harvey Oswald," April 6, 1964, Vol. XVII, pp. 789–90.
4. See CE 1127, p. 7; WC Vol. XXII p. 101, an FBI report which provides a record of all three mailings; see also Marguerite's testimony, WC Vol. I, p. 204.
5. Marguerite Oswald letter to Secretary of State Herter, March 7, 1960, CE Exhibit No. 206, Vol. XVI, p. 595.
6. CE No. 833, FBI report entitled "Lee Harvey Oswald" April 6, 1964, Vol. XVII, p. 789.
7. FBI New York field office 65-6315 to headquarters 65-28939, February 26, 1960; released to Dr. Paul Hoch pursuant to his FOIA request.
8. We have seen this practice used for other documents in Oswald's FBI files.
9. The serial 105 is for "counterintelligence" files, and the serial 100 is for "internal security" files.

10. See CE 834, Vol. XVII, pp 804-813. The Fain Report should have been item number 12 or 13. See pp. 805-806.
11. Oswald applied for this passport on Sept. 4 at Santa Ana one week before he was discharged from the USMC. He used a Uniformed Services Privelèges Card as identification instead of the normal birth certificate. This card was not issued until Sept. 11, the day following issuance of the passport on Sept. 10, 1959. (WC Vol V, pg 266, WC Vol XVI, pg 601)
12. See Warren Commission Report, p. 690.
13. FBI New York field office memo (105-6103) to Dallas field office, March 9, 1960; released to Dr. Paul Hoch pursuant to his FOIA request.
14. FBI New York field office memo (105-6103) to Dallas field office, March 9, 1960; released to Dr. Paul Hoch pursuant to his FOIA request.
15. See Mark Riebling, *Wedge* (New York: Knopf, 1994), pg 155.
16. See CE 918, Vol. XVIII, p. 116.
17. Ed Jeunovitch, 28 Dec 1994 interview with John Newman.
18. Horton memo to Bissell, November 18, 1960, NARA JFK files, CIA Oswald 201, Box 1.
19. Bissell letter to Cumming, November 21, 1960, NARA JFK files, CIA Oswald 201, Box 1.
20. American Embassy cable to State Department 1304, October 31, 1959, CE 2750, Vol. XXVI, p. 126. See also American Embassy dispatch to State Department 234, November 2, 1959, CE 908, Vol. XVIII, p. 87, and CE 2749, Vol. XXVI, p. 124.
21. American Embassy cable to State Department 1358, November 9, 1959, and CE 2683, Vol. XXVI, p. 42.
22. ALUSNA Moscow to CNO, November 10 1959, ONI files, ONI-139, 921ACT/922-14-N. The dispatch mentioned, i.e. 184, actually referred to Khrushchev's visit to China.
23. *Washington Post*, UPI, "Rebuffed," November 16, 1959.
24. OSI Report of John Cox, Subject: John Edward Pic, File 33-476, January 27, 1960.
25. Marguerite Oswald letter to Jim Wright, March 6, 1960. WC Vol XXII, pg 118; CD 1122
26. Marguerite Oswald letter to Secretary of State Herter, March 7, 1960, CE 206, Vol. XVI, p. 594; CD 1122
27. State Department operations memorandum to Moscow Embassy, March 28, 1960, CE 929, Vol. XVIII, p. 129.
28. Moscow Embassy operations memorandum to State Department, March 28, 1960, CE 927, Vol. XVIII, p. 126.
29. FBI, Dallas field office, 105-976, Fain report of May 12, 1960, CE 821, Vol. XVII, pp. 700–702.
30. FBI, Dallas field office, 105-976, Fain report of May 12, 1960, CIA copy, NARA, JFK files, Oswald 201 file, Box 1.
31. CIA XAAZ35612, "Index cards found in the DDO records system on Lee Harvey Oswald at the time of the assassination." See NARA JFK files, CIA Document 2-524.
32. FBI New York field office (105-6103) AIRTEL to Bureau headquarters

(100-353496), May 23, 1960. Note that this telegram was also placed in the 105 counterintelligence headquarters file on Oswald but was "unrecorded."

33. ONI routing slip GG7122B, dated May 26, 1960, and referencing headquarters Bureau file 100-353496.
34. Hoover letter to Security Office, Department of State, June 3, 1960, FBI, Bureau file 105-82555, CD 1114.
35. Marguerite Oswald letter to Haselton, June 8, 1960, CE 208, Vol. XVI, p. 597; CD 1122.
36. Blocker letter to Marguerite Oswald, June 22, 1960, CE 209, Vol. XVI, p. 598.
37. White letter to Marguerite Oswald, July 7, 1960, CE 210, Vol. XVI, p. 599; Cd 1122.
38. Memorandum from FBI SA Kenneth J. Haser to SAC, WFO. 9 Aug 1960; Paul Hoch item 468; See also NARA JFK files FBI Records WFO 105-37111.
39. Memorandum from FBI SA W. Dana Carson to SAC, WFO, 12 Sept. 1960; Paul Hoch item 469; See also NARA JFK files FBI Records WFO 105-37111

Chapter Eleven

1. See Chapter Four, "I Am Amazed."
2. See CIA response to Church Committee re questions by Paul Hoch, April 9, 1975, by E. H. Knoche, p. 11. NARA, JFK files, RIF 157-10004-10140.
3. CIA Memorandum for the Executive Assistant to the DDO, from Chief, CI Staff, George T. Kalans, CI 315–75, EX 10931, 18 September 1975; NARA, JFK files, RIF 1993. 07.02–13:52:25:56030.
4. Letter from Hugh Cumming to Richard Bissell, October 25, 1960, NARA, JFK files, CIA 201 file on Oswald, box 1.
5. Robert L. Bannerman, interview with John Newman, August 8, 1994.
6. Robert L. Bannerman, interview with John Newman, August 8, 1994. "Jim Angleton was in on this and we were calling in all the people in all the areas who might have something," Bannerman recalled in this interview.
7. Memorandum from Marguerite D. Stevens to Chief, Security Research Staff, October 31, 1960, NARA, JFK files, 1993 release. This document was released in the first wave of 51 CIA boxes that were sent to the National Archives in the spring of 1993, before the RIF numbering system became effective. Unfortunately, the author's handwritten reference to the box number became detached.
8. Marguerite Stevens's memo responded to Bannerman's request for information on American defectors to the Soviet Union, China, and Soviet-satellite countries. Bannerman had specifically asked Stevens for information covering the previous eighteen months.
9. The CIA stated that Martin and Mitchell, both NSA employees, were KGB agents (see CIA response to Church Committee re questions by Paul

Hoch, April 9, 1975, by E. H. Knoche, p. 11. NARA, JFK files, RIF 157–10004–10140). A month after Oswald defected to the Soviet Union, Martin and Mitchell—against NSA regulations—flew to Cuba, where, NSA Chronicler James Bamford reasons, "most likely, they got in touch with Soviet officials. It would be interesting to know if the CIA had learned about the trip and also what, if anything, either of them might have known about the U-2 program. For more on these two men, see James Bamford, *Puzzle Palace* (New York: Houghton Mifflin, 1982), pp. 133–150.

10. Memorandum from Marguerite D. Stevens to Chief, Security Research Staff, October 31, 1960.
11. NARA, JFK files, CIA 1994 microfilm release, reel 7, folders I–J, Joseph Dutkanicz.
12. Bissell letter to Cumming, November 3, 1960, NARA, JFK files, CIA Oswald 201, box 1.
13. Horton memo to Bissell, November 18, 1960, NARA, JFK files, CIA Oswald, 201, box 1.
14. Bissell letter to Cumming, November 21, 1960, NARA, JFK files, CIA Oswald 201, box 1.
15. NARA, JFK files, CIA 1994 microfilm release, reel 7, folders I–J, Joseph Dutkanicz.
16. NARA, JFK files, CIA 1994 microfilm release, reel 7, folders I–J, Joseph Dutkanicz, and reel 17 folder J, Vladimir Sloboda.
17. Report of the Select Committee on Assassinations, U.S. House of Representatives, 1979 (hereafter referred to as *HSCA Report*), p. 200.
18. *HSCA Report,* p. 200.
19. *HSCA Report,* p. 201.
20. George T. Kalaris memo, subject: "Lee Harvey Oswald," dated September 18, 1975. See NARA, JFK files, RIF 1993.07.02.13:52:25:56030. A more redacted version of this document was released earlier as CIA document # 1187–436.
21. The *HSCA Report,* p. 201, added this:

> This statement was corroborated by review of a State Department letter which indicated that such a request, in fact, had been made of the CIA on October 25, 1960. Attached to the State Department letter was a list of known defectors; Oswald's name was on that list. The CIA responded to this request on November 21, 1960, by providing the requested information and adding two names to the State Department's original list.
>
> Significantly, the committee reviewed the original State Department list and determined that files were opened in December 1960 for each of the five (including Oswald) who did not have 201 files prior to receipt of the State Department inquiry. In each case, the slot for "source document" referred to an Agency component rather than to a dated document.

22. CE 245, Vol. XVI, p. 685. For more on the missing Oswald letter of December 1960, see WC Vol. XVIII pp. 133, 135.
23. WR, p. 701.

24. For a complete version of Oswald's February 1961 letter to the American Embassy, see CE 245, Vol. XVI, p. 685, and CE 932, Vol. XVI, p. 133.
25. Snyder testimony, WC, Vol. V, p. 277.
26. NARA, JFK files, RIF 157–10002–10432, report by William T. Coleman, Jr., and W. David Slawson to J. Lee Rankin, subject: Oswald's trip to the Soviet Union and his contacts with the U.S. Department of State, March 6, 1964. Part A is a single 46-page document entitled "Oswald's Trip to, and Stay in, the Soviet Union (September 4, 1959 to June 1, 1962). Attached are three documents: a September 4, 1959, notice of Oswald's release from the Marine Corps signed by A. G. Ayers, Jr., 1st Lt., USMR; Oswald's September 4, 1959, passport application Form DSP 11 filled out and signed by Oswald; and the note Oswald wrote requesting revocation of his U.S. citizenship and which he handed to American Consul Richard Snyder on October 31, 1959.
27. This paragraph first gives the date that Snyder received Oswald's 5 February 1961 letter as "13 February 1960." This is clearly a typographical error, since, in the very next sentence the correct date of 13 February 1961 is used.
28. Draft "Chronology of Oswald in the USSR: October 1959–June 1962, 24 January 1964, Amended 16 April 1964." See NARA, JFK files, CIA DDO 201 file on Oswald, boxes 1 and 2, CIA document XAAZ–22409, January 25, 1964.
29. See "Report of the Department of State: Lee Harvey Oswald," CE 950, Vol. XVIII, p. 262.
30. WR, p. 701.
31. This report of December 10, 1963, is based on a six-page interview of Marina by FBI Special Agents Anatole A. Boguslav and Wallace R. Heitman, of the Dallas office, and they filed their report under Oswald's file 199–10461; see WC, Vol. XXII, pp. 772–775.
32. See WC, Vol. XVIII, pp. 133, 135.
33. See Journal Graphics, transcription of ABC NEWS NIGHTLINE #2740 air date: November 22, 1991, entitled "An ABC News Nightline Investigation: The KGB Oswald Files."
34. Interviews with former CIA employees Ed Jeunovitch (July 14, 1993), and Don Deneselya (August 13, 1993), who both worked in the Soviet Russia Division at the time, and Ray Rocca (August 11 and 20, 1993—Rocca died in October) and Scotty Miler (September 16, 1993), who both worked in Counterintelligence. Jeunovitch later rose to the position of CIA acting deputy director of Plans during the Reagan administration. From interviews by William Scott Malone and John Newman during work on the WGBH FRONTLINE documentary "Who Was Lee Harvey Oswald?"
35. This person probably worked in Counterintelligence—perhaps in CI/R&A.
36. Memo for the record December 5, 1966, from CI/MRO, subj: American defectors to the USSR. NARA, JFK files, CIA 1994 microfilm release, reel 7, folders I–J, Joseph Dutkanicz.
37. Dutkanicz had tried to return to the U.S. on March 22, 1962. The Russians told his wife he had been found in a drunken state and placed in a hospital

in Lvov, where he died in November 1963. HSCA Vol. XII, p. 444; also CIA 976–927AV. (It is interesting that Dutkanicz died in Lvov and the other defector from Army Military Intelligence, Sloboda, was born in Lvov.)

38. Memo for the record December 5, 1966, from CI/MRO, subj: American defectors to the USSR. NARA, JFK files, CIA 1994 microfilm release, reel 7, folders I–J, Joseph Dutkanicz.
39. Memo for the record December 5, 1966, from CI/MRO, subj: American defectors to the USSR. NARA, JFK files, CIA 1994 microfilm release, reel 7, folders I–J, Joseph Dutkanicz.
40. Memorandum from Marguerite D. Stevens to chief, Security Research Staff, October 31, 1960.
41. Noonan (State Department) to Hoover, May 17, 1962, subject: American Defectors: Status of in the USSR, NARA, JFK files, Oswald's CIA DDO 201 file, boxes 1 and 2.
42. Memo for Chief, Security Research Staff, from M. D. Stevens, subject: American defectors, October 31, 1960.
43. Memorandum from Marguerite D. Stevens to Chief, Security Research Staff, October 31, 1960.
44. The possibility that ''MS'' could have been ''Military Service'' was first suggested to the author by Peter Dale Scott in November 1994.
45. Webster (this time she gave his number as EE-18852, whereas two paragraphs earlier she gave the number as EE-18854) had been the subject of a ''OO/C'' (''OO/C'' is a partial [and thus somewhat confusing] acronym for the CIA's Domestic Contacts Division, the Agency element used to contact and/or debrief individuals who possessed information of intelligence value) request for contact on May 29, 1959, but had not been interviewed ''before or after'' his visit to the Soviet Union.
46. Memorandum from Marguerite D. Stevens to Chief, Security Research Staff, October 31, 1960.
47. NARA, JFK files, CIA 1994 microfilm release, reel 17, folder J. Vladimir Sloboda. See Sloboda's notecard, with these numbers on top: 380312* and 01395. There appears to be a number redacted between these two. The text on the card appears to say this:

    POB: subj's statement: Orekhovchnik, Brodak District, Ternopol—Lvov, Uk[raine] SSR, then Poland, DOB: 1927. Nat. US citizen in US Army '58, served as Spec. 5/c, translator, interrogator, doc. clerk 513 MI Grp., Frankfrt., defected from Camp King, Germany 3 Aug 60 to USSR. Claims to have known ''Lypsky, Komaryk, Krul and others,'' at Ft. Bragg. Wife and 1 child Halifax, UK, other 2 in Sov Union with subj. Identified (redacted) YT-1192, 16 Jan 62. 380291 289148 077283 US CIT.

    Note also that the number 289148 contains five digits identical to Oswald's 201 number: 289248. There is also a barely legible stamp at the bottom right which may read ''RIS [Russian Intelligence Service] IMPLANTED.''
48. Memorandum from Marguerite D. Stevens to Chief, Security Research Staff, October 31, 1960.

49. NARA, JFK files, CIA 1994 microfilm release, reel 7, folders I–J, Joseph Dutkanicz, and reel 17 folder J, Vladimir Sloboda. October 2, 1964, memorandum from SR/CI/R to Chief, CI Liaison, subject: Questions Concerning Defectors Joseph Dutkanicz (201–289236) and Vladimir O. Sloboda (201-287527).
50. NARA, JFK files, CIA 1994 microfilm release, reel 7, folders I–J, Joseph Dutkanicz, and reel 17 folder J, Vladimir Sloboda. October 2, 1964, memorandum from SR/CI/R to Chief, CI Liaison, subject: Questions Concerning Defectors Joseph J. Dutkanicz (201–289236) and Vladimir O. Sloboda (201-287527).
51. Internal CIA memo to Scott Miler, CI/OG [illegible], October 12, 1960, NARA, JFK files, CIA 1994 microfilm release, reel folder J. Vladimir Sloboda.
52. NARA, JFK files, CIA 1994 microfilm release, reel 16, folders I, Libero Ricciardelli. See August 9, 1963, CIA memo to Attn: Chief, Personnel Security Division, OS, Mr. Steven Kuhn, Chief, Contact Division, 00; Subject: Ricciardelli, Libero—Permission to Reveal the Identity of a Former US Citizen (now a Soviet citizen) as a source of this Agency to the FBI; Ref: a) Our request for security checks on Subject dated July 11, 1963; b) Mr. Kuhn's oral request on July 15, 1963, regarding FBI interest in information resulting from interviews with the subject.
53. NARA, JFK files, CIA 1994 microfilm release, reel 7, folders I–J, Joseph Dutkanicz. Note on Dutkanicz ''Prepared by CI Staff for State [Department]-Nov. 60.'' The note explained: ''Dutkanicz, who was born in Poland around 1927, was taken to Germany during World War II. After being liberated by the American Army he immigrated to the United States and was then drafted into the Army. His address in the United States was given as Tujanes, California.''
54. NARA, JFK files, CIA 1994 microfilm release, reel 7, folders I–J, Joseph Dutkanicz. October 2, 1964, memorandum from SR/CI/R/ to Chief, CI Liaison Subject: Questions Concerning Defectors Joseph J. Dutkanicz (201–289236) and Vladimir O. Sloboda (201–287527). On this memorandum are two penciled numbers besides Dutkanicz's 201: ''SX-4617,'' and ''200-5-41'' under which it was filed. The ''200'' meant ''miscellaneous international file''; see NARA, JFK Files, SSCI box 265-15, November 14, 1975, memo from Dan Dwyer and Ed Greissing to Paul Wallach. Attached to the Wigren memo is a buck slip with ''HH-6683'' and a note saying the memo ''will not receive further dissemination.'' Elsewhere in this CIA file on Dutkanicz there is a note from Jim Harrison to Ruth Elliff, saying, ''The following OCG records are attached: HH 6683. They contain information on: Joseph *Dutkanicz*.''
55. NARA, JFK files, CIA 1994 microfilm release, reel 7, folders I–J, Joseph Dutkanicz. October 2, 1964, memorandum from SR/CI/R/ to Chief, CI Liaison, Subject: Questions Concerning Defectors Joseph J. Dutkanicz (201–289236) and Vladimir O. Sloboda (201–287527).
56. Field Personality (201) File Request for Lee Henry [sic] Oswald, opened

by Ann Egerter, December 9, 1960. See NARA, JFK files, CIA DDP 201 file on Oswald, boxes 1 and 2.

57. NARA, JFK files, CIA 1994 microfilm release, reel 7, folders I–J, Joseph Dutkanicz. October 2, 1964. Memorandum from SR/CI/R/ to Chief, CI Liaison, Subject: Questions Concerning Defectors Joseph J. Dutkanicz (201–289236) and Vladimir O. Sloboda (201-287527).
58. Note on Dutkanicz ''Prepared by CI Staff for State [Department]-Nov. 60,'' NARA, JFK files, CIA 1994 microfilm release, reel 7, folders I–J, Joseph Dutkanicz.
59. NARA, JFK files, CIA 1994 microfilm release, reel 7, folders I–J, Joseph Dutkanicz. October 2, 1964, memorandum from SR/CI/R/ to Chief, CI Liaison, Subject: Questions Concerning Defectors Joseph J. Dutkanicz (201–289236) and Vladimir O. Sloboda (201–287527).
60. NARA, JFK files, CIA 1994 microfilm release, reel 7, folders I–J, Joseph Dutkanicz. October 2, 1964, memorandum from SR/CI/R/ to Chief, CI Liaison, Subject: Questions Concerning Defectors Joseph J. Dutkanicz (201–289236) and Vladimir O. Sloboda (201–287527). The CIA's Counterintelligence chief, James Angleton, lost no time in putting all this in a November 4, 1964, memo to the assistant chief of staff for Intelligence, Department of the Army, Attention: Director of Security, filed in same location at NARA.
61. CIA Information Report No: CO-3167710; NARA, JFK files, CIA 1994 microfilm release, reel 7, folders I–J, Joseph Dutkanicz. The informant's report also said this:

    3. Dutkanych seemed to be quite familiar with the city and knowing I was a clergyman, suggested I visit a well-known Russian Orthodox church, just up the street. Looking out the window I called his attention to a billboard advertising the latest movie, ''Moscow Souvenir.'' He suggested, however, that I take in another movie that was playing around the corner from the hotel. That afternoon I saw the recommended movie. It was an old war film, depicting the heroism of a young soldier defending his native village from the invading German armies.

62. WC Vol. XVI, CE 24, p. 100.
63. CD 1, p. 52; see also Oswald Historic Diary, CIA document XAAZ 35813, p. 10; WC Vol. XVI, CE 24, p. 100.
64. Warren Report p. 700. Oswald described the manuscript, which amounted to fifty typed pages, as ''a look into the lives of work-a-day average Russians.'' After his return to the U.S., he hired a stenographer to type a draft from his notes.
65. FBI Dallas, report of Wallace Heitman and Hayden Griffin, September 8, 1964, Dallas 100–10461; WC, CD 1546.
66. The FBI report explained:

    Marina exhibited the following photographs which were obtained from Lellie May Rahm at Ketchikan, Alaska, on August 4, 1964. Rahn is the mother of Anita May Setyaeva. These photographs were described as follows:

1. Wedding photo of Marina (last name unknown). At far left is head of Marina's mother, Anita May Setyaeva (Setyaev), nee Zuggef, and her son, Kostia Henkin; unknown woman, Marina (last name unknown) and Vashi (last name unknown), who is Marina's husband, unknown man, woman, man and woman.

2. Head photo of Anita May Setyaeva.

3. Full-length photo of Anita May Setyaeva in Moscow.

4. Full-length photo of Antia May Setyaeva at Moscow University.

5. Photo of Radio Moscow personnel, taken December 27, 1957, left to right—Lucy Pravdina, Anita May Satyaeva, Sergei Rudin, Joe Adarov and sitting, Nikolai Sergeyev.

6. Photo of Radio Moscow personnel, taken September 9, 1960, left to right—Joe Adakov, Anita May Setyaeva, Annabella Ducar, Sergei Rudin.

7. Photo of Radio Moscow personnel—Sergeio Rudin and Anita May Setyaeva; standing—Lucy Pravdina, Joe Adamov, Nikolai Sergeyev.

8. Photo of Radio Moscow personnel—Sergei Rudin, Anita May Setyaeva, Joe Adamov, Lucy Pravdina, Nikolai Sergeyev.

9. (First name unknown) Henkin, Anita May Renkina, now Setyaeva (Setyaev), and Kostia (Bunny) Henkin, taken June 1, 1957.

10. Photo of Radio Moscow personnel, left to right—Sergei Rudin, Lucy Pravdina, Joe Adamov, Anita May Satyaeva, Nikolai Sergeyev, taken December 28, 1958.

Marina could identify none of the individuals appearing in these photographs. When the above-described photographs were examined by Marina Oswald in the presence of interviewing Agents, no unusual reactions were noted.

67. HT-LINGUAL soft file, Document No. 1994.04.13.14:53:55:500005, May 1, 1994, memorandum, subject: HT-LINGUAL items relating to the Oswald case. [''Material from this Operation is handled on a need to know basis within this Agency and such of the material that is given to the FBI receives special handling and limited distribution within the the Bureau.'']
68. WR, p. 691
69. NARA, JFK files, CIA box 6, folder 6, document 05806.
70. CIA memo to FBI, August 27, 1964; NARA, JFK files, CIA Document Number 806–351.
71. Peter Wronski, 1991 interview with Setyaev, in ''Oswald in the USSR: A Preliminary Report from a New Investigation,'' *Third Decade,* May 1992, p. 33.
72. Peter Wronski, June 1991 interview with Ella German. Peter Wronski did some unique and valuable work in the former Soviet Union in 1991; it is reported in *Third Decade,* May 1992.
73. Peter Wronski, 1991 interview with Setyaev, in ''Oswald in the USSR: A Preliminary Report from a New Investigation,'' *Third Decade,* May 1992, p. 34.

74. WC, Vol. XVI, CE 315, p. 871.
75. See *The Trial of the U2* (Chicago: Translation World Publisher 1960), pp. 89–90.
76. CIA Document Disposition Index, documents 1187–436, 1189–1001, and 1190–1002, pp. 270–271.
77. Church Committee interview with Sam Papich, May 29, 1975, p. 13; NARA, JFK files, RIF157–10002–10152.
78. Peter Wronski, 1991 interview with Setyaer, "Oswald in the USSR: A Preliminary Report from a New Investigation," *Third Decade,* May 1992, pp. 33–34.
79. CIA LINGUAL item 60F240; NARA, JFK Files, CIA Document Number 1572–1115–L.
80. Peter Wronski, 1991 interview with Setyaer, "Oswald in the USSR: A Preliminary Report from a New Investigation," *Third Decade,* May 1992, p. 34.

Chapter Twelve

1. August 18 White House meeting on Cuban policy FRUSC-VI, document 577, pp. 1057–1060.
2. Memorandum of a meeting with the president, White House, August 18, 1960, USFRC-VI, document 577, pp. 1057–1060.
3. August 18 White House meeting on Cuban policy FRUSC-VI, document 577, pp. 1057–1060.
4. Memorandum of a meeting with the president, White House, August 18, 1960, USFRC-VI, document 577, pp. 1057–1060.
5. Memorandum of a meeting with the president, White House, August 18, 1960, USFRC-VI, document 577, pp. 1057–1060.
6. Church Committee, *Alleged Assassination Plots,* p. 74. A footnote to this part of the text states: "Although Castro closed the gambling casinos in Cuba when he first came to power, they were reopened for use by foreign tourists in late February 1959, and remained open until late September 1961."
7. Church Committee, *Alleged Assassination Plots,* p. 74. A footnote to this part of the text states: "Although Castro closed the gambling casinos in Cuba when he first came to power, they were reopened for use by foreign tourists in late February 1959, and remained open until late September 1961."
8. Church Committee index card on May 23, 1975, testimony of former CIA director William Colby.
9. *Alleged Assassination Plots,* p. 75.
10. I.G. Report, p. 16.
11. *Alleged Assassination Plots,* p. 75; see also I.G. Report, p. 16.
12. *Alleged Assassination Plots,* p. 79.
13. Church Committee interview with Sam Papich, FBI liaison to the CIA, August 22, 1975; NARA, JFK files, RIF157-10005-10068.

14. Church Committee interview with William Harvey, September 14, 1975, pp. 7–8; NARA, JFK files, RIF157-10011-10124. There is no question, according to Harvey, that this pressure on Bissell continued under the Kennedy White House.
15. WC Vol. XXIII, CE 1697, p. 171.
16. The Kennedy Years, *New York Times,* p. 233. Present at this meeting were the following: President Kennedy, Secretary of State Rusk, Secretary of Defense McNamara, Secretary of the Treasury Dillon, Chairman of the Joint Chiefs of Staff, General Lemnitzer, CIA director Allen Dulles, and CIA's Plans director, Richard Bissell, Senator Fulbright and White House aides Schlesinger and Goodwin also attended.
17. One significant part of the White House today stands as a monument to that tragedy. In June 1961, in a directive resulting from his investigation of the failed invasion, Kennedy ordered that a portion of the White House bowling alley be set aside and that the CIA set up a new operation center where he could keep a close eye on any given situation. The failure at the Bay of Pigs led to the creation of the now famous White House Situation Room. Stuart H. Loory in *Los Angeles Times,* 3/28/69, pp. 1, 10.
18. FBI Report, CD 1, p. 57.
19. WC Vol. XVIII, CE 985, p. 404.
20. WC Vol. XXII, CE 1127, pp. 102, 118; VOL. XXVI, CE 2681, pp. 39–40, 124.
21. For the CIA copy, see NARA, JFK file, CIA DDO 201 file on Oswald, boxes 1-2.
22. WC Vol. XXVI, CE 2681, p. 39.
23. WC Vol. XVI, CE 245, pp 685, 686.
24. WC Vol. V, p. 277 (Snyder); WC Vol. XVI, CE 24, p. 102, entry of February 1, 1961.
25. Oswald's letter was postmarked February 5 at Minsk, February 11 at Moscow, and finally received by the embassy on February 13; see WC Vol. XXII, CE 1138, p. 119.
26. See WC Vol. XVIII, CE 933, p. 135.
27. WC Vol. XVIII, CE 932, pp. 133–134 (dispatch from the American Embassy in Moscow to the State Department, February 28, 1961). Also see WC Vol. XVIII, CE 948, p. 186, which is part of the State Department's May 8, 1964, answers to questions from the Warren Commission.
28. For Snyder's letter, see WC Vol. XVIII, CE 933, p. 135.
29. WC Vol. XVIII, CE 940, p. 151.
30. WC Vol. XVI, CE 24, p. 102, Historic Diary, entry for March 1-16, 1961.
31. WC Vol. XVI, CE 25, pp. 121–122; Vol. V, pp. 407–408 (Marina Oswald).
32. WC Vol. V, p. 278 (Snyder).
33. WC Vol. XXVI, CE 2666, p. 23. Oswald's occasional contact with American tourists possibly increased his determination to return. Every once in a while he would make the acquaintance of one, such as the University of Michigan band member he met on March 10, 1961 (at the time the band was touring in Minsk); Vol. XI, p. 211.
34. On March 12, 1961, Oswald writes to the U.S. Embassy in Moscow. The

embassy received it. On March 20, 1961, the U.S. Embassy, Moscow, received a second letter from Oswald again stating he wanted to leave and needed permission; See WC Vol. XXII, CE 1085, p. 33. On March 22, 1961, Oswald wrote to the embassy; see Vol. XVI, CE 213, p. 602; Vol. XVIII, CE 950, p. 262; Vol. XXVI, CE 2766, p. 24.

35. WC Vol. V, pp. 352–354 (Bernice Waterman); Vol. XVI, CE 94, pp. 367–368; Vol. XVIII, CE 940, 970, 971, pp. 152, 367–368; Vol. XXII, CE 1074, p. 24.
36. State Department cable to the American Embassy in Moscow, April 13, 1961, WC Vol. XVIII, CE 971, p. 368.
37. Marina thought that the date was March 4. WC Vol. I, p. 90 (Marina Oswald); VOL. XVI, CE 24, p. 102, entry of March 17, 1961; Vol. XVIII, CE 904, p. 600; Vol. XXII, CE 1401, p. 748; Vol. XXIII, CE 1792, p. 407.
38. WC Vol. XXII, CE 1138, p. 120.
39. Later that same evening, Marina learned that Oswald was an American; WC Vol. XXII, CE 1401, p. 261; CE 994, p. 5. The Commission learned that it would have been unusual for Oswald to have become so proficient in Russian given the length of his stay; see WC Vol. II, p. 347; Vol. XVIII, CE 994, pp. 596, 600; Vol. XXII, CE 1041, p. 745; *Life* 2/21/64. George deMohrenschildt was reportedly amazed by Oswald's Russian proficiency; see WC Vol. IX pp. 226, 259. The Oswald who visited Mexico City in the summer of 1963, however, was not so proficient, perhaps because by that time he had lost the facility. It is more likely, as discussed in Chapter Eighteen, that person speaking Russian in Mexico City was not Oswald, but an impostor.
40. WC Vol. XXIII, CE 1789, p. 402.
41. WC Vol. XXII, CE 1041, p. 753.
42. WC Vol. XVI, CE 24, p. 102, entry of March 17, 1961. Marina testified that she told Oswald that she might see him at another dance, but did not give him her telephone number. WC Vol. I pp. 90–91 (Marina Oswald); Vol. XXII, CE 1401, p. 267; Vol. XVIII, CE 994, p. 7
43. WC Vol. I, p. 91 (Marina Oswald); Vol. XXII, CE 1401, pp. 267–268; Vol. XVIII, CE 993, p. 7.
44. On March 14 and 15, 1961: On November 30, 1963, Marina says that Oswald was admitted to the 4th Clinical Hospital on the outskirts of Minsk, where he stayed for eleven days; WC Vol. XXII, CE 1401, p. 749. Perhaps this hospital was special, but it does seem odd that Oswald was admitted to a hospital in the outskirts of Minsk when he lived in the central part of the city.
45. WC Vol. XVIII, CE 985, p. 450.
46. WC Vol. I, p. 91, (Marina Oswald).
47. WC Vol. XXII, CE 1401, p. 749.
48. WC Vol. XVIII, CE 994, pp. 603–604; WC Vol. II 302 (Katherine Ford).
49. WC Vol. XXII, CE 1401, p. 750, Vol. XVIII, CE 994, p. 9.
50. WC Vol. XXII, CE 1401, pp. 749–750; Oswald's diary puts the date five days earlier. WC Vol. XVI, CE 24, p. 102, entry of April 1–30, 1961.
51. June 1961—Mrs. Dorothy Gravitis, Dallas resident who is Ilya Maman-

tov's mother-in-law and Mrs. Ruth Paine's Russian teacher, says that Marina tells her that they were married in Moscow and then moved to Leningrad. WC. Vol IX, p. 135. Mrs. Thomas N. Ray, resident of Detroit, Texas, meets Marina at Glover's party in 1963 and hears Marina say that they lived in Moscow for a year. WC Vol. IX, p. 31. Paul Gregory, Fort Worth resident who meets the Oswalds in 1962, says that Oswald shows him pictures of Leningrad and Minsk. WC Vol. IX, p. 142.

52. WC Vol. XXII, CE 1401, p. 750.
53. WC Vol. XVI, CE 24, p. 102.
54. WC Vol. XXII, CE 1401, p. 749; but see WC Vol. II, p. 302 (K. Ford).
55. WC Vol. XVI, CE 24, p. 103, entry of May 1, 1961.
56. WC Vol. XVI, CE 24, p. 103, entry of June 1961.
57. Marina's recollection is that she learned of his plan between May and July.
58. WC Vol. XVI, CE 252, pp. 705, 707.
59. WC Vol. XXII, CE 1401, pp. 740–764; HSCA, Vol. II, p. 288.
60. *New York Times,* 12/9/63, p. C-38.
61. The date May 18, 1961, would be indicated, based on 273 calendar days until June Oswald's birth on February 15, 1962.
62. WC Vol. XVII, CE 833, p. 790.
63. Special Agent Kenneth J. Haser, memorandum to the Special Agent in Charge (SAC), Washington, D.C., field office (WFO) of the FBI, August 9, 1960; Subject: Lee Harvey Oswald, Internal Security-Russia. NARA, JFK files, FBI WFO (105-37111), box 1.
64. The ''100'' had clearly been changed from ''105,'' which can still be observed beneath the ''100.'' This raises the possibility of a possible connection to the FBI Headquarters and Dallas field office 100/105 file compartments for different aspects of the Oswald case.
65. Memorandum from Special Agent W. Dana Carson to Special Agent in Charge at Washington field office (105-37111), September 12, 1960. Subject: Lee Harvey Oswald, Internal Security-Russia.
66. Memorandum from Special Agent W. Dana Carson to special agent in Charge at Washington field office (105-37111), September 12, 1960. Subject: Lee Harvey Oswald, Internal Security-Russia. Carson made an error when, talking of the State Department copy of Fain's ''Funds Transmitted to Residents of Russia'' report, he mentioned one of its file numbers as ''Dallas File 100-976.'' This inadvertent slip again draws our attention to Oswald field file: 105-976.
67. ONI routing slip GG 71228/jhl; Subject: Oswald, Lee Harvey; Funds Transmitted to Residents of Russia, originator: FBI, originator file number: BU 100-353496, date of letter: May 12, 1960, addressed to: DNI, date rec'd on: May 26, 1960, enclosures: W/O, ONI copy distribution: 921E2-cleared for FF 11/10/60 WB. NARA, JFK files, NIS 1994 release, boxes 1-3.
68. April 12, 1960, ONI letter to DIO 9ND, OP-921E2/jws, Ser 0236P92; ONI-119, Paul Hoch FOIA files.
69. Raymond M. Reardon, Security Analysis Group/OS, memo to CIA dep-

uty inspector general, February 1, 1977; Subject: Agency Activities in New Orleans; NARA, JFK files, RIF 1993.06.29.15:18:40:030280.

70. Director of Naval Intelligence to officer in charge, District Intelligence Office, Eighth Naval District; Subject: Oswald, date: November 15, 1960; Paul Hoch FOIA documents, ONI-96. The copy for DIO-9ND is indicated on the bottom of this letter.
71. Letter from officer in charge, District Intelligence Office, Ninth Naval District, to officer in charge, District Intelligence Office, Eighth Naval District; Subject: Oswald, date: November 30, 1960; Paul Hoch FOIA documents, ONI-92.
72. NARA, JFK files, RIF 157-1006-10246; letter from F.O.C. Fletcher, Jr., captain, U.S. Navy, officer in charge, District Intelligence Office, Eighth Naval District, 92/922E, Serial: 053; January 11, 1961, to special agent in charge, Federal Bureau of Investigation, Dallas field office, Re: Oswald, Lee Harvey [handwritten:] 105-976-1, p. 17. For DNI (Director of Naval Intelligence) copy, see PLH item 19. According to Paul Hoch's note, this document was not in Oswald's FBI HQ file. On the other hand, it may have been filed at FBI HQ under 100-353496.
73. Letter from F.O.C. Fletcher, Jr., captain, U.S. Navy, officer in charge, District Intelligence Office, Eighth Naval District, 92/922E, Serial: 053, January 11, 1961, to special agent in charge, Federal Bureau of Investigation, Dallas field office, Re: Oswald, Lee Harvey [handwritten:] 105-976-1, p. 17. FBI Dallas field office file, PLH item 968.
74. Letter from F.O.C. Fletcher, Jr., captain, U.S. Navy, officer in charge, District Intelligence Office, Eighth Naval District, 92/922E, Serial: 053, January 11, 1961, to special agent in charge, Federal Bureau of Investigation, Dallas field office, Re: Oswald, Lee Harvey [handwritten:] 105-976-1, p. 17. For DNI (Director of Naval Intelligence) copy, see PLH item 19. According to Paul Hoch's note, this document was not in Oswald's FBI HQ file. On the other hand, it may have been filed at FBI HQ under 100-353496.
75. As a point of interest, in the files of the FBI field office in Dallas, this document became the second of the new file on Oswald, 100-10461. The first document in 100-10461 was Captain Fletcher's DIO 8ND letter.
76. NARA, JFK files, RIF 157-10006-10247. Memorandum from John Edgar Hoover, director, to Office of Security, Department of State, February 27, 1961. Subject: Lee Harvey Oswald; Internal Security-Russia. File No. 105-82555.
77. NARA JFK files, RIF 124-10228-10036; SAC Dallas to SAC New Orleans, Dallas FBI office to SAC New Orleans FBI office, with the slightly different subject line: ''Lee Harvey Oswald, SM-C,'' probably ''security matter, Communist'' or close to it.
78. WC Vol. XXVI, p. 94.
79. Here Fain's memo said ''Refer to 92/922E, Serial 051, DIO file #,'' which was two before Fletcher's 053. Thus far, 051 has not come to light.
80. PPT, March 2, 1961, from SY/E-Emery J. Adams; Subject: Oswald, Lee

Harvey, REF: SY memorandum, June 10, 1960. NARA, JFK files, DOS passport file on Oswald.

81. HSCA Vol. III, p. 575.
82. Lee Oswald letter to Robert Oswald, August 21, 1961, WC Vol. XVI, CE 303, 836.
83. State Department to American Embassy in Moscow, A-273, April 13, 1961. NARA, JFK files, CIA August 1992 release.
84. The cable advised the embassy:

    If and when Mr. Oswald appears at the Embassy, he should be thoroughly questioned regarding the circumstances of his residence in the Soviet Union and his possible commitment of an act or sets of expatriation and, as contemplated by the Embassy, his statements should be taken under oath. If the Embassy is fully satisfied that he has not expatriated himself in any manner and if he presents evidence that he has (appeared) to depart from the Soviet Union to travel to the United States, his passport may be delivered to him on a personal basis only, after being rendered valid for direct return to the United States. For security reasons, the Department does not consider that it would be prudent for the Embassy to forward Oswald's passport to him by mail.

85. State Department to American Embassy in Moscow, A-273, April 13, 1961. NARA, JFK files, CIA August 1992 release.
86. SA Kenneth J. Haser, memo to SAC, WFO (105-37111), April 20, 1961. A "V. Dunn" of WFO filed this document as the 3rd in Oswald's FBI WFO file, 105-37111. NARA, JFK files, FBI WFO (105-37111) box 1.
87. WC Vol. IV, p. 438.
88. NARA, JFK files, RIF 157-10006-10249; from SAC New Orleans FBI office (100-16601) to SAC Dallas FBI office (100-10461), April 27, 1961; Subject: Lee Harvey Oswald; SM-C; (00: Dallas); Re Dallas let 2/28/61.
89. The memo contained the following data:

    File on Oswald reflected an ONI report by SA John T. Cox dated January 27, 1960, File 33-476, captioned John Edward Pic (DOB 17 Jan '32 S Sgt. AF 11313239 USAF Hospital Tachikowa, APO 323 Communist Matters). In brief this report reflected information concerning Pic's reporting to ONI that Lee Harvey Oswald was his half brother. Basis for Pic inquiry was that he heard that Oswald had turned in his United States passport to the American Embassy at Moscow with intentions of removing his American citizenship. This report contains some background information with respect to Oswald and his family. There was only one copy of this report available in the file; however, it was noted that a copy had been furnished to Carswell Air Force base, Fort Worth, Texas.

    Also in this file was a photostatic copy of a telegram from the Department of State, Moscow, Russia, dated October 31, 1959 at 7:59 am carrying Control Number 20261 and another number 1304, which stated in part "Lee Harvey Oswald unmarried, age 20 PP 1733242 issued 9/10/59 appeared at Embassy to renounce his American citizenship following entry USSR from Helsinki 10:15. Mother's address and his latest address in United States 4936 Callinwood Street, Fort Worth, Texas; Says, I have contemplated last two years. Main reason ''American Marxist,''; attitude—arrogant, aggressive; recently discharged Marine Corps. Says, has offered Soviets any information he has acquired as Enlisted Radio Operator.'' This dispatch was signed Freers and apparently directed to the State department, Washington, D.C.

The file also disclosed a photostatic copy of a memorandum report dated November 2, 1959, which was signed Edward F. Freers Chargé d'Affaires, ad interim, American Embassy. This report reflected an interview with Oswald at the American Embassy at Moscow, October 31, 1959; however, the quality of the photostatic copy was so poor that it was impossible to review.

Also in ONI's files was a memorandum dated October 26, 1959, bearing a control Number 1178 concerning Robert Edward Webster. This memorandum which was a photostat furnished information concerning Webster, who appears to have defected to the Russians at about the same time as Oswald. This individual was identified as having been discharged from the United States Navy 1951, USN Serial Number 7917938. Here again the photostatic copy was impossible to review because of poor quality.

There appeared a photostatic copy of a November 3, 1959, article which appeared in a Fort Worth, Texas, newspaper, which showed it was a UPI dispatch. It related to an interview with Robert L. Oswald, brother of Lee Harvey Oswald. Also was an autostatic copy of a newspaper story from the ''Washington Post,'' Washington, D.C., newspaper dated November 16, 1959, which indicated that subject had been informed by the Russians that he would not be granted Russian citizenship but would be allowed to live in Russia as a nonresident alien. A picture of Oswald accompanied this brief article. There was another photostatic copy of a story from the ''Washington Post'' dated November 1, 1959, which had been dispatched by UPI and which related to the defection of subject.

A photostatic copy of a *Washington Evening Star* article dated November 26, 1959, appeared in this file entitled ''U.S. Defects to Reds Determined Marxist at 15.'' This story related to subject and had been written by Priscilla Johnson for the *North American Newspaper Alliance.* This article mainly reflected an interview with the subject.

There was also found in ONI's files a photostatic copy of a ''Speed'' letter dated March 8, 1960, to the Commander Marine Air Reserve Training Command, Naval Air Station, Glenview, Illinois, from Commandant of the Marine Corps, Washington, D.C., and signed A. Larson. It stated as follows:

''Arrangements being made with a Federal Investigation Agency to furnish you report which relates to PFC Lee Harvey Oswald,

Number 1653230 USMCR inactive, CMN, a member of your Command X, upon receipt CMM. You are directed to process PFC for discharge IAWPARA.10277.2.f MACROMANX.''

90. NARA, JFK files, RIF 157-10006-10249; from SAC New Orleans FBI office (100-16601) to SAC Dallas FBI office (100-10461), April 27, 1961; Subject: Lee Harvey Oswald; SM-C; (OO: Dallas); Re Dallas let 2/28/61.
91. NARA, JFK files, RIF 157-10006-10249; from SAC New Orleans FBI office (100-16601) to SAC Dallas FBI office (100-10461), April 27, 1961; Subject: Lee Harvey Oswald; SM-C; (OO: Dallas); Re Dallas let 2/28/61.
92. FBI Memo from SAC Dallas to SAC New Orleans; Subject: Lee Harvey Oswald, SM-C, April 28, 1961; NARA, JFK files, RIF 157-10006-10248.
93. WC Vol. XXII, CE 1127, p. 98.
94. Record number 157-10006010348. Memorandum from special agent in charge at FBI Dallas (100-10461-4) to special agent in charge at FBI New Orleans (16601-3 and 105-82555-54), April 28, 1961. Subject: Lee Harvey Oswald, SM-C, OO-Dallas.
95. NARA, JFK files, FBI, New Orleans (100-10461), April 28, 1961.
96. Memorandum from Special Agent in Charge at the FBI Washington field office (105-37111-4) to the director of the FBI (100-10,461-6), May 23, 1961. Subject: Lee Harvey Oswald.
97. NARA, JFK files, RIF 124-10010-10014.
98. Memorandum from Emery J. Adams, for the director, Office of Security to the Honorable J. Edgar Hoover, director, Federal Bureau of Investigation, Washington 25, D.C. (105-82555-15). May 25, 1961. Subject: Oswald, Lee Harvey.
99. Memorandum from Emery J. Adams, for the director, Office of Security to the Honorable J. Edgar Hoover, director, Federal Bureau of Investigation, Washington 25, D.C. (105-82555-15). May 25, 1961. Subject: Oswald, Lee Harvey.

Chapter Thirteen

1. Exhibit 22, FBI memorandum from D. E. Moore to A. H. Belmont, March 10, 1961, SSCIA hearing, Volume IV, mail opening.
2. CIA letter to Robert Olsen, SSCIA, April 29, 1975, re: answers to questions put to the CIA by Paul Hoch; CIA document 1634-1088.
3. HSCA Report, p. 205.
4. June 22 memo from Deputy Chief, CI/Project to Deputy Chief, CI, HT/LINGUAL-61G10AK, NARA, JFK files, RIF 1994.04.13.14.53:55:500005.
5. CIA HT/LINGUAL notecard on Oswald, November 9, 1959, NARA, JFK files, RIF 1994.04.13.14:53:55:500005.
6. CIA HT/LINGUAL notecard on Oswald, August 7, 1961, NARA, JFK files, RIF 1994.04.13.14:53:55:500005.
7. Embassy dispatch to State #806, date May 26, 1961; NARA JFK files, CIA DDO 201 file on Oswald, boxes 1 and 2.
8. Cable from American Embassy in Moscow (4495881) to the Department

of State, Washington (201-298248), May 26, 1961. Subject: Citizenship and Passports: Lee Harvey Oswald.

9. Cable from American Embassy in Moscow (4495881) to the Department of State, Washington (201-298248), May 26, 1961. Subject: Citizenship and Passports: Lee Harvey Oswald.
10. ''Progress Report: 1962-1963,'' by John Mertz, Chief, CI/Project; NARA, JFK files, CIA January 1994 (5 brown boxes) release. See p. 3 of ''Progress Report.''
11. WC Vol. XXII, p. 754 (Marina said trip was late summer 1961), p. 744 (Marina said trip was July 8,9,10, 1961).
12. WR, p. 705.
13. WC Vol. XVI p. 103, CE 24, entry of July 8, 1961.
14. WC Vol. XXII CE 1401 (p. 278), p. 754.
15. WC Vol. XVIII, p. 137, CE 935; WR, p. 706.
16. WC Vol. XVI pp. 94–98; CE 24, entries of October 16, 1959, through January 4, 1960; CE 908.
17. WC Vol. XXII, p. 702, CE 1385, p. 4; P. Johnson DE 1, pp. 3, 6, 14; P. Johnson DE 2, pp. 1–2; 11 H 456 (P. Johnson); Vol. XI, p. 456 CE 985, document 1C-2, p. 6.
18. WC Vol. XXII, CE 1109, pp. 67–68; CE 1110, pp. 69–72; and CE 1128, pp. 104–109.
19. WR, p. 706.
20. WC Vol. XVIII p. 138, CE 935 p. 2.
21. WC Vol. XVIII p. 144, CE 938.
22. WR, p. 705.
23. WC Vol. XVIII, 139, CE 935, p. 3.
24. WC Vol. V, p. 284 (Snyder); WC Vol. XVIII p. 161, CE 946, pp. 2–3.
25. WC Vol. V, p. 284 (Snyder); CE 946, p. 6.
26. WC Vol. XVIII, CE 944, p. 158; Vol. V, pp. 304–306 and pp. 318–319, (McVickar); Vol. XVIII, CE 959 (p. 6), pp. 335–338.
27. WC Vol. XVIII, pp. 264–266, CE 950; WC Vol. XXII, p. 88; WC Vol. XXVI, p. 123.
28. WC Vol. XXII, p. 121.
29. Cable from Department of State, Washington (No. W-7) to American Embassy, Moscow, July 11, 1961. Subject: Citizenship and Passports: Lee Harvey Oswald.
30. Cable from American Embassy in Moscow to Department of State in Washington, July 11, 1961. Subject: Citizenship and Passports: Lee Harvey Oswald.
31. WC Vol. XVI p. 103, CE 24, entry of July 14, 1961; WC Vol. XVI p. 833, CE 301.
32. WC Vol. XVI p. 103, CE 24, entry of July 14, 1961; WC Vol. XVI p. 833, CE 301.
33. WR, p. 706.
34. WC Vol. XVIII, CE 935, p. 137; CE 985, documents 1B, 2B, 3B, 4B, in WC Vol. XVIII, pp. 403–479; see CE 1401 pp. 227–278, 280, in WC Vol. XXII, pp. 740–764.

35. CE 1122, pp. 2–3, in WC Vol. XXII, pp. 87–88.
36. WC Vol. XVI p. 104, CE 24, entry of August 24–September 1, 1961.
37. WC Vol. XVI p. 104, CE 24, entry of September–October 18, 1961.
38. WC Vol. XVIII, p. 405, CE 985.
39. WC Vol. XVIII pp. 405, 442, CE 985.
40. WC Vol. XXII, p. 9.
41. WC Vol. XVII, p. 720; WC Vol. XVIII, p. 266, CE 950; WC Vol. XXII, pp. 35, 87; WC Vol. XXVI, p. 122—copy.
42. WC Vol. XVII, p. 720; WC Vol XXII, pp. 35, 87; WC Vol. XXVI, p. 122.
43. WC Vol.XVII, pp. 405, 444, CE 985.
44. WC Vol. XXVI, p. 115. Usual procedures and times required discussed in WC Vol. XXVI, p. 102.
45. November 25, 1963, internal CIA memo by "T.B.C." CIA document 435-173A. NARA, JFK files, RIF 1993. 07.17.09:57:50:000150.
46. September 28, 1961, CIA memo, see CIA document 598-252H; see also NARA, JFK files, RIF 1993.07.02.13:25:25:180530.
47. WC Vol. XVII, p. 720; WC Vol. XXII, pp. 35, 88; WC Vol. XXVI, p. 123—copy.
48. Moscow Embassy dispatch 317 to the State Department, October 13, 1961, NARA, JFK files, CIA DDO 201 file on Oswald, boxes 1–2.
49. WC Vol. XXVI, p. 115.
50. WC Vol. V, p. 604, A comparison of the time it took Marina to get an exit visa with other cases. WC Vol. XXVI, p. 140, Marina requested the visa on August 21, 1961, and it was issued on December 1, 1961, or 101 days later. See Ambassador Thompson's statement above—December 1, 1961, that CIA said that, of 11 similar cases, the time required was from 5 months to 1 year; see WC Vol. 26, p. 157. The CIA said of 26 cases, 3—the wife accompanied the husband upon departure; 15—the husband left first; 8—uncertain. Author Isaac Don Levine said it is hard for a pharmacist to get out of the USSR; see WC Vol. II, p. 8. Oswald said USSR had made it difficult for Marina to leave; see FBI Report, CD 1, p. 32.
51. WC Vol. V, p. 572.
52. "Progress Report: 1962–1963," by John Mertz, Chief, CI/Project, April 1964; NARA, JFK files, CIA January 1994 (5 brown boxes) release.
53. February 12, 1963, Hemming letter to Major General C. V. Clifton, President Kennedy's military aide, February 12, 1963. NARA, JFK files, ONI-OSI boxes 1–3.
54. Memo from Jerry G. Brown, Deputy Chief OS/SAG, to Chief, SAG, June 11, 1976; NARA, JFK files, RIF 1993.06.029.15:26:50:400280.
55. NARA, JFK files, Chief CI/Operational Approval and Support Division, to Deputy Director of Security, on c.87424 [Hemming], January 3, 1961. There is a handwritten signature at the bottom: "Thomas Carroll, Jr.," underneath which are the initials "DWK."
56. NARA, JFK files, ONI-NIS (3 boxes) 1994 release. The associated transmittal sheet shows that on March 2, 1961, the CIA requested checks for Gerald Patrick Hemming's name (using the old "Henning" instead of

Hemming) through the records of the FBI, ONI, ACSI, STATE (sy), STATE (passport) and HCUA; NARA, JFK files, ONI-NIS (3 boxes) 1994 release. On the transmittal sheet the file number used for Hemming was ''EE-29229''; same location.

57. NARA, JFK files, ONI-NIS (3 boxes) 1994 release. CIA memorandum, March 31, 1961, subject: Gerald P. Hemming, Jr., Moves to Miami to Engage in Anti-Castro Operations.
58. NARA, JFK files, ONI-NIS (3 boxes) 1994 release. CIA memorandum, March 31, 1961, subject: Gerald P. Hemming, Jr., Moves to Miami to Engage in Anti-Castro Operations.
59. ''It is always possible, on the other hand,'' the March 31 CIA report said, ''that he is still loyal to the Cuban Government and at some future date will attempt to embarrass the US. NARA, JFK files, ONI-NIS (3 boxes) 1994 release; CIA memorandum,. March 31, 1961, subject: Gerald P. Hemming, Jr., Moves to Miami to Engage in Anti-Castro Operations.
60. NARA, JFK files, ONI-NIS (3 boxes) 1994 release. CIA telegram from SAC DFO to Chief Invest. Div. May 10, 1961, subject: GPH JR EE 29229 [Gerald Patrick Hemming].
61. NARA, JFK files, ONI-NIS (3 boxes) 1994 release. CIA telegram from SAC DFO to Chief Invest. Div. May 10, 1961, subject: GPH JR EE 29229 [Gerald Patrick Hemming].
62. NARA, JFK files, ONI-NIS (3 boxes) 1994 release. Memorandum from M. D. Stevens, Security Research Staff, OS to File. 25 July 1961. Subject: Hemming, Gerald Patrick, Jr. EE-29229.
63. NARA, JFK files, ONI-NIS (3 boxes) 1994 release, box 1. ONI status check from OP-921E2 to CMC (ABN), May 25, 1961, Subject: Hemming, Gerald Patrick.
64. NARA, JFK files, ONI-NIS (3 boxes) 1994 release, box 1. Cross-reference sheet prepared by OP921E2/PIERCE, YN1 on May 26, 1961 regarding Gerald Patrick Henning, Robert Wills aka Willis and Dick Watley for an FBI report of May 19, 1961 on Anti-Communist Legionnaires Neutrality Matters. ONI Routing Slip No. GG 89169.
65. NARA, JFK files, ONI-NIS (3 boxes) 1994 release, box 1. Cross-reference sheet prepared by OP921E2/mlb, YN1 on June 16, 1961, from an FBI report of May 23, 1961, subject: Anti-Communist Legionnaires Matters; ONI Routing Slip No. XX 138316.
66. Papa Doc was president of Haiti.
67. Gerry Patrick Hemming, January 6, 1995, interview with John Newman.
68. NARA, JFK files, ONI-NIS (3 boxes) 1994 release, box 1. Cross-reference sheet prepared by OP921E2/mlb, YN1 on June 16, 1961, from an FBI report of May 23, 1961, subject: Anti-Communist Legionnaires Matters; ONI Routing Slip No. XX 138316.
69. ONI mentioned a May 25, 1961, status check on Gerald Patrick Hemming and a May 18, 1961, FBI report on Anti-Communist Legionnaires; NARA, JFK files ONI-NIS (3 boxes). 1994 release, box 1. Memorandum from Director of Naval Intelligence, Commandant of the Marine Corps to Assistant Chief of State G-2, Headquarters USMC (AO-2A) Rm. 2117—Arling-

ton Annex, July 5, 1961, subject: Hemming, Gerald Patrick, 1488247, USMCR, Serial Number 21252P92.

70. NARA, JFK files, ONI-NIS (3 boxes) 1994 release. Memorandum from William Abbott to J. Edgar Hoover, Director, Federal Bureau of Investigation, Attn: Liaison Section, July 6, 1961, subject: Hemming, Gerald Patrick, 1488247, USMCR, Serial Number 21251P92.
71. NARA, JFK files, 173-10011-10063. Status check from OP-921E2 to CMC (ABN), September 19, 1961, subject: Hemming, Gerald Patrick, Jr.
72. NARA, JFK files, ONI-NIS (3 boxes) 1994 release, box 1. Memorandum from William Abbott to J. Edgar Hoover, Director, Federal Bureau of Investigation, Attn: Liaison Section, October 23, 1961, subject: SGT Gerald Patrick Hemming, Jr., USMCR, 1488247 (inactive), Serial Number 28106P92.
73. NARA, JFK files, ONI-NIS (3 boxes) 1994 release. Memorandum from Director of Naval Intelligence to Officer in Charge, District Intelligence Office, Sixth Naval District, October 23, 1961, serial number 015807P92. The ONI letter to 6ND mentioned a Miami FBI report on Eloy Gutierrez Menoya, a Cuban exile leader with whom Hemming was associated. Menoya's Miami FBI case number was 105-2102. See also NARA, JFK files, ONI-NIS (3 boxes) 1994 release. Memorandum from Director of Naval Intelligence to Assistant Chief of Staff, G-2, Headquarters ASMC (AO-2A), Rm. 2117—Arlington Annex, October 23, 1961, subject: Sgt. Gerald Patrick Hemming, Jr., serial number 007630P92.
74. NARA, JFK files, ONI-NIS (3 boxes) 1994 release, box 3. Memorandum from Officer in Charge, District Intelligence Office, Sixth Naval District to Director Sixth Marine Corps Reserve and Recruitment District, Atlanta, Georgia, November 3, 1961, subject: Hemming, Gerald Patrick, Serial Number 01895.
75. NARA, JFK files, 173-10011-10092. Memorandum from Officer in Charge, District Intelligence Office, Sixth Naval District to Officer in Charge, District Intelligence Office, Eleventh Naval District, December 5, 1961, subject: Hemming, Gerald Patrick, serial number: 02028.
76. NARA, JFK files, ONI-NIS (3 boxes) 1994 release, box 1. Cross-reference sheet prepared by "pCarter," Op-921E on August 8, 1961, for an FBI report of July 12, 1961, regarding Cuban Rebel Activities in Cuba. ONI Routing Slip No. XX 141692.
77. NARA, JFK files, ONI-NIS (3 boxes) 1994 release, box 1. Cross-reference sheet prepared by 921E/mlb on August 10, 1961, for an FBI report of July 3, 1961, regarding the Revolutionary Junta of National Liberation. Serial number 105-4050, ONI Routing Slip No. XX 140903.
78. NARA, JFK files, ONI-NIS (3 boxes) 1994 release, box 1. Cross-reference sheet prepared by OP921E2/PIERCE YN1 on August 25, 1961, regarding Gerald Patrick Hemming for an FBI report of July 31, 1961, on Intercontinental Penetration Forces (INTERPEN). ONI Routing Slip No. XX 14425.
79. NARA, JFK files, 1993.06.29.14:52:03:810280. Memorandum of October 4, 1961, marked OO-A-3198214. Subject: Intercontinental Penetration Force (INTERPEN)/CBS-NBC Interest in Cuban Expedition.

80. Origin of report: FBI; Serial number: MM 105-3514; Subject of report: James William Beck, John Clifford Nordeen, etc.; Date of report: November 14, 1961; Classification: Unclassified; ONI Routing Slip no.: XX 151346; NARA, JFK files.
81. FBI Dallas, report of Wallace Heitman and Hayden Griffin, September 8, 1964, Dallas 100-10461; WC, CD 1546.
82. One guess that comes to mind is the name Thomas W. Comier, offered as a possibility by a former CIA employee.

Chapter Fourteen

1. FPCC, document 1.
2. *Alleged Assassination Plots Involving Foreign Leaders: An Interim Report of the Select Committee to Study Operations with Respect to Intelligence Activities,* hereafter referred to as *Alleged Assassination Plots* (Washington, D.C.: U.S. Government Printing Office, 1975) p. 13.
3. *Alleged Assassination Plots.* pp. 13-190.
4. NARA, JFK files, CIA 1994 microfilm release, RIF 1994.03.08.13:30:54:000007; reel 11, folders E-F.
5. CIA document, dated October 28, 1960, ''LA File on Viola June Cobb as Reviewed by Ed Lopez,'' NARA, JFK files, RIF 1994.03.08.13:30:54:000007; CIA 1994 microfilm release, reel 11.
6. CIA document, dated October 28, 1960, ''LA File on Viola June Cobb as Reviewed by Ed Lopez,'' NARA, JFK files, RIF 1994.03.08.13:30:54:000007; CIA 1994 microfilm release, reel 11.
7. CIA memo from chief, WH/4/CI [name redacted] to Jane Roman, CI Staff Liaison Group, March 1, 1961; NARA, JFK files, CIA 1994 microfilm release, reel 11, folder F; RIF 1994.03.09.09:05:37:810007.
8. C/CI/SIG (Birch O'Neal) memorandum, November 22, 1960; NARA, JFK files, CIA 1994 microfilm release, reel 11, folder F.
9. CIA routing slip to CSCI 3/762466, from Jean T. Pierson, WH/4/CI, November 1, 1960; Nara, JFK files, CIA 1994 microfilm release, reel 11, folder F.
10. CIA memo for the record, February 1, 1961, by Kammer, subject: [redacted] #188-74. NARA, JFK files, CIA January 1994 (five brown boxes) release.
11. To: C/EAB/OS; Attn: Mr. Belt; VIA: WH/4/Security; Attn: Mr. Kennedy; February 1, 1961; Subj. Fair Play for Cuba Committee. NARA, JFK files, CIA January 1994 (five brown boxes) release.
12. To: Mr. Jack Kennedy, WH/4/Security; March 8, 1961 ''Please include this statement in my permanent record. Thank you [redacted] WH/4/Registry, phone ext. 2929. NARA, JFK files, CIA, January 1994 (5 brown boxes) release, Court Wood papers.
13. CIA memo to Mr. Jack Kennedy, WH/4/Security, March 18, 1961, NARA, JFK files, CIA January 1994 (5 brown boxes) release.

14. Memo for the director FBI; Attn: Mr. Sam J. Papich; from R. F. Bannerman, acting director of Security, CIA, October 7, 1961; subject: Court Foster Wood; Internal Security—Cuba; NARA, JFK files, CIA, January 1994 (5 brown boxes) release, Court Wood papers.
15. *The Investigation of the Assassination of President John F. Kennedy: Performance of the Intelligence Agencies; Book V, Final Report of the Select Committee to Study Governmental Operations with Respect to Intelligence Activities,* hereafter referred to as *Church Committee,* vol. V, (Washington, D.C., U.S. Government Printing Office, 1976) book V, p. 66.
16. Church Committee, Book V, p. 66.
17. WR, p. 709; the Warren Report continues: ''He told her that he would need about $800 and that she should insist on a gift rather than a loan; he told her not to send any of her own money [for the letter, see WC, vol. XVI, CE 189, pp. 554–556]. Despite his instructions, she requested a loan from the Red Cross [see WC, vol. XXVI, CE 2731, p. 110 and CE 2660, p. 13]. Oswald wrote to the IRC himself on January 13, asking for $800 to cover the cost of travel for two from Moscow to Texas. On January 26, 1961, Oswald wrote to the IRC again, this time asking for $1000; see WR, p. 709.
18. WC, vol. XVI, CE 246, pp. 688–690.
19. WC, vol. XXII, CE 1078, p. 26.
20. WC, vol. XVI, CE 256, pp. 717–718.
21. WR, p. 709; see also WC, vol. XXII, CE 1079, p. 27. A point of interest: Before receiving this letter, Oswald wrote out such a document himself [see WC, vol. XXVI, CE 2692, p. 57] and mailed it to the embassy [see WC, vol. XVI, CE 247, pp. 691–692]. On January 31, the embassy responded that this affidavit might not satisfy the requirement; WC, vol. XXII, CE 1080, p. 28. Later, by March 16, 1962, the embassy changed this position, and decided that Oswald's own affidavit of support for Marina would be sufficient under the circumstances; see WC, vol. XXII, CE 1095, p. 46.
22. WC, vol. XVI, CE 256, pp. 717–718; see also WC, vol. XVIII, p. 270; and WC, vol. XXVI, p. 117.
23. The idea of Marina as some sort of protection for Oswald was first mentioned to the author by David Lifton in 1992.
24. WC vol. XVI, pp. 691–692.
25. WR, pp. 709–710; see also WC, vol. XVI, CE 190, pp. 558–559. On January 24, the embassy acknowledged receipt of this affidavit, but again suggested that Oswald obtain one from someone else; see WC, vol. XXII, CE 1080, p. 28, and CE 1101, p. 51.
26. WC, vol. XXII, CE 1058, p. 10; *Dallas Morning News,* 11/23/63, p. I-5; Vol. XXII, CE 1082, p. 29.
27. WC, vol. XVI, CE 192, p. 562.
28. WC, vol. XVI, CE 222, p. 612.
29. WC, vol. XVI, CE 192, p. 562.
30. WC, vol. XVI, CE 193, p. 564–566.
31. WC, vol. XVI, CE 315, p. 871.

32. WR, p. 711; see also WC, vol. XVI, CE 193, p. 564. Researchers should note that in the retyped version of this letter, the misspelled word ''forwarned'' is erroneously typed as ''forwarded.''
33. WC, vol. XVI, CE 314, p. 865.
34. WC, vol. I, p. 95; see also WC, vol. CE 194, p. 567; WC vol. XXII, CE 1112, p. 75, CE 1401, p. 748; and *Dallas Morning News* 12/2/63, p. 1-5; and *Life* magazine, 2/21/64, p. 74B.
35. WC, vol. XVI, CE 194, pp. 567–569.
36. WC, vol. XVI, CE 315, p. 870.
37. WC, vol. XVIII, CE 994, p. 612. Elsewhere Oswald gives the date of their return from the hospital as February 24, see WC, vol. XVI, CE 316, p. 875.
38. WC, vol. XVI, CE 316, p. 875.
39. WC, vol.XVI, CE 195, pp. 570–571.
40. WC, vol. XVI, CE 316, p. 875.
41. WR, p. 711. WC Vol. XVI, CE 316, p. 875.
42. WC, vol. XVII, CE 823, p. 722; CE 950, pp. 273–274.
43. WC, vol. XXII, CE 1093, p. 40; WC, vol. XXVI, CE 2682, p. 41; see also WC, vol. XVI, CE 248, pp. 693–695.
44. WC, vol. XXII, CE 1086, p. 35, and WR, p. 711.
45. WC, vol. XXII, CE 1058, p. 5; see also *Dallas Morning New,* 11/23/63, p. I-5.
46. WC, vol. XVIII, CE 950, p. 272.
47. *Laredo Times,* 11/24/63.
48. *New York Times,* 11/25/63, p. C9.
49. WC, vol. XVI, CE 191, p. 560.
50. WC, vol. XVI, CE 190, p. 558.
51. The discharge had actually been ''undesirable,'' a less derogatory characterization than dishonorable.
52. WC, vol. XVI, CE 314, p. 865.
53. WC, vol. XVI, CE 314, p.865.
54. Then governor of Texas. It is possible that Oswald thought Connally was still Secretary of the Navy.
55. WC, vol. XIX, Folsom exhibit 1, p. 713.
56. WC, vol. XIX, Folsom exhibit 1, p. 711; WC, vol. XXVI, CE 2663, p. 19.
57. WC, vol. XIX, Folsom exhibit 1, p. 689.
58. WC, vol. XXVI, CE 2686, p. 47.
59. WC, vol. XIX, Folsom exhibit 1, p. 695; see also WC, vol. XVII, CE 823, p. 723–724. This letter appeared to be too polished for Oswald; see WC, vol. XIX, Folsom exhibit 1, p. 695. Oswald's letter to John Connally in January 1962 appeared to be ghost written.'; see WC, vol. XIX, Folsom exhibit 1, p. 713; there is a 12-page opinion that Oswald was dyslexic; see WC, vol. XXVI, CE 3134, pp. 812–817.
60. WC, vol. XXVI, CE 2658, p. 12.
61. WC, vol. XXVI, CE 2661, pp. 14–16; WR, pp. 710–711.
62. WC, vol. Folsom exhibit 1, p. 693.
63. WC, vol. XVII, CE 780, p. 657.

64. WC, vol. XXII, CE 1063, p. 13. See also CE 1103, pp. 55–57; WC, vol. XVI, CE 249, pp. 697–699 and WR, p. 711.
65. WC, vol. XVI, CE 196, pp. 573–574. See also WC, vol. XXVI, CE 2653, p. 3.
66. WR, p. 711.
67. WC, vol. XXVI, CE 2653, p. 3.
68. WC, vol. XVI, CE 196, pp. 573–574.
69. WC, vol. XVI, CE 197, pp. 576–577.
70. WC, vol. XVII, CE 823, p. 724.
71. WC, vol. XVI, CE 317, p. 877.
72. WC, vol. XVI, CE 317, p. 877; WR, p. 711.
73. WC, vol. XVI, CE 249, pp. 697-699; WC, vol. XXII, CE 1083, p. 30; WC, vol. XXII, CE 1088, p. 37; WC, vol. XXVI, CE 2687, p. 47; WC, vol. XXVI, CE 2688, p. 48; WR, p. 711.
74. WC, vol. XXII, CE 1313, p.485.
75. WC, vol. XVIII, CE 985, document 9A p. 435; WC, vol. XXII, CE 1108, pp. 65–66; WC, vol. XXII, CE 1314, p. 486.
76. WC, vol. XXII, CE 1108, pp. 65-66; WC, vol. XXII, CE 1109, pp. 67–68; WC, vol. XXII, CE 1128. p. 107; WR, p. 712.
77. WC, vol. XVIII, CE 985, p. 435; see also WC, vol. XXII, CE 1108, p. 66, CE 1341, p. 486.
78. WC, vol. XVI, CE 318, p. 880.
79. WC, vol. XVI, CE 318; WR, p. 172.
80. HSCA, Vol. II, p. 317; see also *Marina and Lee,* MacMillan, p. 187. The Oswalds went to Moscow and stayed at the Hotel Ostankino first and then moved to the Hotel Berlin; see WC, vol. XVIII, CE 994, p. 614.
81. WC, vol. XVIII, CE 946, p. 165.
82. WC, vol. V, pp. 617–618 (Marina Oswald); see also WC, vol. XXVI, CE 2722, p. 102; and WR, p. 712.
83. WC, vol. XVIII, CE 946, pp. 164, 167; see also WC vol. XXII, CE 1070, p. 22. Note entries for July (1961) 8, 9, 10. Marina was given a visa; see WC, vol. XVII, CE 823, p. 727. In spite of her firm statement that she was not a Communist (see WC, vol. XXVI, CE 2690, p. 52) U.S. Ambassador Thompson thought the Soviet treatment of Marina noteworthy, and he said that it was unusual for the Russians to allow the baby to leave; see WC, vol. V, p. 572.
84. WC, vol. XVIII, CE 946, pp. 160–170; and see also WC, vol. XXII, CE 1401, p. 755.
85. WC, vol. XXVI, CE 2654, p. 4; CE 2662, p. 18; CE 2690, pp. 49-52; CE 2704, p. 75; and CE 2656, p. 11.
86. WC, vol. XVI, CE 29, p. 141.
87. WC, vol. XVI, CE 198, p. 578; see also *Life* magazine, 2/21/64, and *New York Times,* 12/9/63, p. C38.
88. WC, vol. XXII, CE 1098, p. 47.
89. WC, vol.XXII, CE 1099, p. 48.
90. WC, vol. XVI, CE 57, p.198
91. WR, p. 712

92. WC, vol. XVIII, CE 946, pp. 168–169; see also HSCA, vol. II, pp. 288, 310–311. When the Oswalds crossed Poland (WC, vol. XVIII, CE 946, p. 169) they stopped in somewhere "just for a few minutes"; see HSCA, vol. XII, p. 368. For Germany, see WC, vol. XVIII, CE 946 p. 168; and WC, vol. XXII, CE 1401, p. 755. The train made one or two short stops in Germany; see HSCA, vol. XII, p. 368.
93. WC, vol. XVIII, CE 946, 18, p. 166.
94. WC, vol.I, p. 100; see also WC, vol. XVIII, CE p. 615; and HSCA, Vol. II, p. 288; and *Dallas Morning News,* 12/2/63, p. I-5. The Oswalds spent one night in Rotterdam; see HSCA, vol. II, p. 289. They stayed in a boardinghouse-type place, where the landlady brought meals to their room; see HSCA, vol. II, pp. 289, 310; and HSCA, vol. XII, p. 369. Lee left Marina only once "to obtain tickets for this boat"; see HSCA, vol. XII, p. 369.
95. WC, vol. XVI, CE 29, pp. 137–145; WC, vol. XVIII, CE 946, pp. 161–170; WC, vol. XXII, CE 1099, p. 48.
96. On the Maasdam, Marina met only two people—the steward at the dining table and one gentleman whose father was Russian and mother was from Holland; see HSCA, vol. XII, p. 371. The steward was Pieter Didenko; see *Legend,* Epstein, p. 154
97. WC, vol. I, (Marina Oswald), p. 101.
98. WR, p. 712
99. WC, vol. XXVI, CE 2655, p. 8.
100. WC, vol. XXII, CE 1159, p. 204; see also WC, vol. XXVI, pp. 5–11; WC, vol. XVIII, CE 946, pp. 160–170.
101. WC, vol. XXVI, CE, 2655, p. 8. For more on Oswald's arrival, see WC, vol. I, p. 3; WC, vol. XVII, CE 823, p. 727; WC, vol. XVIII, CE 946 p. 167; WC, vol. XX, Isaacs exhibit 1, pp. 216, 225; WC, vol. XXII, CE 1159, pp. 204, CE 1401. p. 755, CE 1444, p. 860; WC, vol. XXIII, CE 1778, p. 383; WC, vol. XXIV, CE 2189, p. 866; WC, vol. XXV, CE 2213, p. 106; *Dallas Morning News,* 12/2/63, p. I-5; *Saturday Evening Post,* 12/14/63, p. 23. On 11/23/63, Oswald said that he arrived about July 1962; see WC, vol. XXIV, CE 1988, p. 19.
102. WC, vol. XXVI, CE 2655, pp. 5–10.
103. WC, vol. XXVI, CE 2655, pp. 5–10; CE, 2657, p.12.
104. WC, vol. XXII, CE 1060, p. 11; WC, vol. XXVI, CE 2718, pp. 92–93.
105. WC, vol. XXV, CE 2213, pp. 106–107.
106. WC, vol. XXVI, CE 2655, p. 8, CE 2657, p. 12.
107. WC, vol. XXV, CE 2213, p. 107.
108. WC, vol. XXVI, CE 2657, p. 12.
109. WC, vol. XXV, CE 2213, p. 109; WR, p. 713.
110. NARA, JFK files, NIS (3 boxes) 1994 release. Cable from CIA field station to headquarters. January 31, 1963. No. R 311635Z ZEA. Subject: Gerald P. Hemming.
111. NARA, JFK files, NIS (3 boxes) 1994 release. Memorandum from Lt. R. L. Wilbar, Temple DB to Sheriff Peter J. Pitchens. January 30, 1962. File no. 3-781,031. Subject: Found gun.

112. NARA, JFK files, NIS (3 boxes) 1994 release. Cable from CIA field station to headquarters. January 31, 1963. No. R 311635Z ZEA. Subject: Gerald P. Hemming
113. NARA, JFK files, NIS (3 boxes) 1994 release. Memorandum from CIA headquarters to special agent in charge, Los Angeles Field Office, February 7, 1962. Subject: Hemming, Gerald P.
114. NARA, JFK files, NIS (3 boxes) 1994 release. Memorandum from deputy chief, Operational Support Division to chief, Support Branch, February 2, 1962. Subject: Hemming, Gerald Patrick.
115. NARA, JFK files, NIS (3 boxes) 1994 release. Memorandum from deputy chief, Operational Support Division to chief, Support Branch, February 2, 1962. Subject: Hemming, Gerald Patrick.
116. NARA, JFK files, NIS (3 boxes) 1994 release. Memorandum from CIA headquarters to special agent in charge, Los Angeles Field office, February 7, 1962. Subject: Hemming, Gerald P.
117. NARA, JFK files NIS (3 boxes) 1994 release. CIA report of February 15, 1962, on Gerald P. Hemming. File no. 29 229.
118. NARA, JFK files, NIS (3 boxes) 1994 release. CIA report of February 15, 1962, on Gerald P. Hemming. File no. 29 229. This report had a new fragment of the gun incident as well: Hemming ''claimed that he left his .45-automatic pistol in Miami when he came to the Los Angeles area several weeks ago, but that one of his colleagues, who arrived in Los Angeles shortly before the police incident, had brought the gun with him. Subject had then left the gun in Dodd's Barber Shop on Valley Boulevard.''
119. NARA, JFK files, 173-10011-10096. Cross-reference sheet prepared by P. Carter, Op-921E on April 24, 1962, regarding Gerald Patrick Hemming, for an FBI report of April 10, 1962, on Robert James Dwyer.
120. NARA, JFK files, NIS (3 boxes) 1994 release, box 1. Cross-reference sheet prepared by 921E/jgr on June 11, 1962, for an FBI report of May 28, 1962, regarding the 30th of November Revolutionary Movement, with serial number 105-92196.
121. HSCA, vol. X, pp. 96–97.
122. NARA, JFK files, RIF 173-10011-10086. Cross-reference sheet prepared by P. Carter, Op-921E on January 16, 1962 from an FBI report of December 6, 1961, *Intercontinental Penetration Forces Interpen Neutrality Matters,* ONI routing slip no. XX 152779.
123. Origin of report: FBI; serial number: 105-6010; subject of report: Larry J. Laborde (this might be Laborde's FBI number at the Miami office); see NARA, JFK files, 173-10002-10078. Cross-reference sheet prepared by 921E/jgr on September 10, 1962, for an FBI report of August 6, 1962, on Larry J. Laborde, with serial number 105-6010.
124. WR, p. 324.
125. NARA, JFK files, NIS (3 boxes) 1994 release. Cross-reference sheet prepared by 921F5 (M. Wesley) on February 6, 1962, for a case history of the Intercontinental Penetration Forces.
126. The author is appreciative of the help provided by Commander Steve

Vetter, U.S. Navy, in procuring a declassified copy of *Office of Naval Intelligence Sectional Organization,* printed on April 15, 1957, and other unclassified notes on changes in 1958, 1959, 1960, and 1961.

127. NARA, JFK files, NIS (3 boxes) 1994 release, box 1. Cross-reference sheet prepared by 921E/jgr on June 11, 1962 for an FBI report of May 28, 1962 regarding the 30th of November Revolutionary Movement, with serial number 105-92196.
128. ''Prior Reference: A memorandum from chief, New Orleans office of Domestic Contact Division, to chief, Domestic Contact Division, July 2, 1962, subject: Proposal Made to New Orleans Refugee Group for the Military Training of a Refugee Group in the State of Louisiana.'' See NARA, JFK files, NIS (3 boxes) 1994 release. Enclosure 14 to memorandum dated August 7, 1967, held in Garrison Investigation of Kennedy Assassination. Subject: Gerald Patrick Hemming, Jr.
129. ''Prior Reference: A memorandum from chief, New Orleans office of Domestic Contact Division, to chief, Domestic Contact Division, July 2, 1962, subject: Proposal Made to New Orleans Refugee Group for the Military Training of a Refugee Group in the State of Louisiana.'' See NARA, JFK files, NIS (3 boxes) 1994 release. Enclosure 14 to memorandum dated August 7, 1967, held in Garrison Investigation of Kennedy Assassination. Subject: Gerald Patrick Hemming, Jr.
130. To: [CIA] ''Internal Component''; Attn: [CIA] ''Internal Component''; [source name redacted and original CIA components redacted, but were presumably Task Force W or Western Hemisphere Division Branch 3 or 4] Subject: Proposal Made to New Orleans Cuban Refugee Group for Military Training of a Refugee Group in the State of Louisiana. See NARA, JFK files, NIS (3 boxes) 1994 release.
131. To: [CIA] ''Internal Component''; Attn: [CIA] ''Internal Component''; [source name redacted and original CIA components redacted, but were presumably Task Force W or Western Hemisphere Division Branch 3 or 4] Subject: Proposal Made to New Orleans Cuban Refugee Group for Military Training of a Refugee Group in the State of Louisiana. See NARA, JFK files, NIS (3 boxes) 1994 release. At the bottom of the document it says: [''CIA Employee''] [''CIA Employee''] Encls: There is also this handwriting at the end of page 2: ''Attachments filed in Laborde 201 since he is probably the leader and most important from . . . [illegible].'' Bartes is the source. The reviewers blacked out his name everywhere in this memo except for paragraph 5, where the name Bartes was left in the clear, apparently by mistake.
132. Request for investigation or name check, from chief, CI/Operational Approval and Support Division, to deputy director for Security January 3, 1961, subject: C:87424 (Bartes); NARA, JFK files, CIA, January 1994 (5 brown boxes) release, Bartes papers.
133. Request for investigation or name check, from chief, CI/Operational Approval and Support Division, to deputy director for Security, September 13, 1965, subject: 201-289885, SO #225714 (both for Bartes); NARA, JFK files, CIA, January 1994 (5 brown boxes) release, Bartes papers.

Chapter Fifteen

1. FBI memorandum from director (105-82555) to SAC Dallas (100-10461), May 31, 1962, NARA, JFK files, FBI, Dallas, 100-10461-20.
2. FBI airtel from director (105-82555) to SAC New York (105-38431), Lee Harvey Oswald, June 14, 1962; NARA, JFK files, RIF 124-10160-10405; see also New York FBI 105-38431, document 9; see also Paul Hoch item 485.
3. FBI memorandum from SAC New York (105-38431) to director, (105-82555), Lee Harvey Oswald, June 26, 1962; NARA, JFK files, RIF 124-10010-10032; for New York copy see RIF 124-10160-10406. The New York report, sent to the Bureau on June 26, also said that FBI special Agent William F. Martin had spoken with INS inspector Frederick J. Wiedersheim, who had talked with Oswald upon his arrival. Oswald said he had been a mechanic in the Soviet Union and had "threatened to renounce his US citizenship but never carried through with the threat," Wiedersheim reported.
4. He also gives his height at 5' 11", which was 2" taller than his true height; CD 571; CD 385, pp. 67, 225–226, are about CD 571.
5. WC, vol. XXVI, CE 2718, p. 93.
6. WC, vol. XVII, p. 728
7. Clarence Kelley, *Kelley: The Story of an FBI Director,* (Kansas City: Andrews, McMeel and Parker, 1987) p 259.
8. Fain Report, July 10, 1962; NARA, JFK files, RIF 124-10010-10033. See the FD-263 sheet, and the dissemination block in the lower left-hand corner.
9. Report of John W. Fain, Dallas FBI office, July 10, 1962; NARA, JFK files, RIF 124-10010-10033; see also Bureau 105-82555, document 28.
10. Kelley *Kelley: The Story of an FBI Director,* p 259.
11. WC, vol. XXII, CE 1127, p. 99.
12. CD 598, A-7, 9 and 13; WC, vol. XXIV, CE 2119, p. 549; CE 2123, p. 685; WC, vol. XXV, CE 2193, p. 17; CE 2563, p.811.
13. WC, vol. XVII, CE 800, pp. 685, CE 823, p. 718, CE 823, p. 728-729; WC, vol. XVIII, CE 1024, p. 792; WC, vol. XXVI, CE 2669, p. 26; *Dallas Morning News,* 11/29/63, p. I-1
14. Clarence Kelley, *Kelley: The Story of an FBI Director,* p. 260.
15. The only remaining part of the interview not covered so far is this concluding passage:

    Oswald stated that his wife, Marina, speaks no English whatsoever. By occupation she is a pharmacist. He advised that they were married April 30, 1961, at Minsk, Russia. He advised that she resided with an uncle and an aunt at Minsk, Russia. He advised that she has a half-brother and two half-sisters in Leningrad, Russia; however, Oswald declined to furnish the names of any of this wife's relatives, stated that he feared that some harm might come to them in the event he revealed their names.

16. WC, vol. XIX, p. 192; WC, vol. XXII, CE 1389, p. 715; WC, vol. XXIII, CE 1891, p. 694. On July 12, 1962, the Texas Employment Commission phoned Oswald about a job opening at Leslie Welding. Mrs. Virginia Hale of the Texas Employment Commission sent Oswald to Leslie Welding to apply for a job. On July 13, 1962, Oswald applied for a job at Leslie Welding Company, 200 East North Visek Street, Fort Worth, which is also known as Louv-r-pak Company, and gives the address of 1501 W. Seventh, PE 2-3245, Fort Worth.
17. WC, vol. XXIV, CE 2189, p. 867. Oswald had to pay for his utilities which Riggs estimated at $12 per month. The house was near Montgomery Ward's large store on Seventh, Fort Worth, about ½ mile from Oswald's work and about 10 blocks from Marguerite Oswald's apartment.
18. WC, vol. XXII, CE 1144, p. 156.
19. WC, vol. XXII, CE 780, p. 660.
20. WC, vol. XXII, CE 1089, p. 37.
21. WC, vol. XXII, CE 1144, p. 156; *Fort Worth Telegram,* 12/1/63.
22. WC, vol. XXII, CE 1144, p. 156.
23. WC, vol. XXII, CE 1172, p. 271–272.
24. WC, vol. XIX, Dobbs exhibit 9, p. 575.
25. WC, vol. XXV, CE 2213, p. 114.
26. WC, vol. IV, p. 454.
27. WC, vol. XIX, Dobbs exhibit 9, p. 576.
28. WC, vol. XIX, Dobbs exhibit 6, p. 571.
29. WC, vol. XIX, Dobbs exhibit 6, p. 570.
30. WC, vol. XXII, CE 1117, p. 84, CE 1147, p. 178.
31. WC, vol. I, p. 426.
32. "Oswald stated contact had been made by letter with the Soviet Embassy in Washington, DC to advise the Embassy of his wife's current address, saying this is something that is required by Soviet law. He stated she would continue to make reports periodically to the Soviet Embassy in instances where they moved to another address."
33. Oswald denied he had on October 31, 1959, or any other time, requested his U.S. citizenship be revoked. He denied he ever took any steps to apply for Soviet citizenship. He advised he never at any time affirmed allegiance to the Soviet Union, or indicated a willingness to do so. This was a lie.
34. Oswald denied he ever told the Soviets at any time he would make available to them information concerning his U.S. Marine Corps speciality.
35. Oswald advised on about May 19, 1961, he became fearful some reprisals might be taken against him for having made the trip to the Soviet Union. He stated he then inquired of the American Embassy in Moscow as to the possible legal complications. He stated the embassy assured him they were aware of no evidence that would warrant prosecution against him should he return to the United States. In this connection, Oswald said the Embassy tried to persuade him to return to the United States, without Marina. He told the embassy he could not do that. This was new, but not to the FBI.

36. Asked to explain a statement which he was quoted in the press as having made to his mother in a letter to the effect his and mother's (and brother's) values had been different, Oswald stated he had written something to that effect as he prepared to leave for Russia or while on the way. He admitted he might have referred to a difference in political ideologies, but he would say no more.
37. During the entire interview, Oswald discounted the possibility the KGB might attempt to use him. Oswald agreed to contact the FBI "if at any time any individual made any contact of any nature under suspicious circumstances with him." Further, "Oswald stated his employer has no government contracts, and is not engaged in any kind of sensitive industry or manufacturing. He stated he could see no reason why the Soviets would desire to contact him; however, he promised his cooperation in reporting to the FBI any information coming to his attention."
38. Clarence Kelley, *Kelley: The Story of an FBI Director.* p. 260.
39. Clarence Kelley, *Kelley: The Story of an FBI Director,* pp. 260–261.
40. WC, vol. XX, Graves exhibit 1, p. 21.
41. WC, vol. XXII, CE 1405, p. 789; WC, vol. IV, p. 379; WC, vol. VII, p. 295; WC, vol. XI, p. 120; WC, vol. XVII, CE 792, pp. 679, CE 820-A, p. 699; WC, vol. XIX, Burcham Exhibit 1, p. 201; WC, Vol. XXII, CE 1144, p. 161; *New York Times,* November 25, 1963, p. c-11; *Washington Post,* December 1, 1963, p. E-5; *Fort Worth Star Telegram,* December 1, 1963; *Fort Worth Star Telegram,* December 4, 1963; *Time,* February 14, 1964, p. 18; *Life,* February 21, 1964, p. 74-B
42. WC, vol. VII, p. 295; WC, vol. XIX, Cadigan exhibit 13, p. 286; WC, vol. XX, Holmes exhibit 4, p. 177; WC, vol. XXII, CE 1160, p. 207, CE 1390, p. 717; *Dallas Times Herald,* November 24, 1963, p. A-1; *Fort Worth Star Telegram,* November 20, 1963; *Dallas Times Herald,* December 1, 1963, p. A-30; *New York Times,* December 9, 1963, p. C-38; *Life,* February 21, 1964.
43. WC, vol. XI, p. 144; WC, vol. XXIII, CE 1957-A.
44. WC, vol. XXIII, CE 1957-A, p. 778.
45. WC, vol. XXIV, CE 2189, p. 878.
46. WC, vol. XI, p. 144.
47. WC, vol. XVI, CE 320, p. 884.
48. WC, vol. XI, p. 80.
49. WC, vol. XI, p. 387; WC, vol. II, p. 343; WC, vol. IX, p. 143; WC, vol. XI, pp. 52, 59, 62; WC, vol. XVIII, p. 625.
50. WC, vol. XVII, CE 834, p. 809.
51. WC, vol. XXII, CE 1172, p. 271.
52. FBI memorandum, SAC New York (97-169) to SAC Dallas, October 17, 1962; NARA, JFK files, RIF 124-10171-10124; see also Dallas 100-10461-33.
53. Clarence Kelley, *Kelley: The Story of an FBI Director,* p. 260.
54. Clarence Kelley, *Kelley: The Story of an FBI Director,* p. 261.
55. Clarence Kelley, *Kelley: The Story of an FBI Director,* p. 262.
56. WC, vol. XXII, CE 1117, pp. 84, CE 1147, 178.

57. WC, vol. XIX, Dobbs exhibit 9, p. 576.
58. WC, vol. XI, p. 209; WC, vol. XIX, p. 578; WC, vol. XXI, Potts exhibit A-2, pp. 142, Turner exhibit 1, 679; WC, vol. XXII, CE 1117, p. 84; WC, vol. XXIV, CE 2003, pp. 277, 350. They address their letter to Box 2915, Dallas (WC, vol. XXIV, CE 2003, p. 341).
59. WC, vol. XI, p. 179; WC, vol. XXI, Twiford exhibit 1, p. 681.
60. WC, vol. XIX, Dobbs exhibit 12, p. 579.
61. WC, vol. 11, p. 209; WC, vol. XIX, Dobbs exhibit 12, p. 579.
62. WC, vol. XXI, Tormey exhibit 1, p. 674.
63. *Fort Worth Star Telegram,* December 1, 1963; *Fort Worth Star Telegram,* December 4, 1963; *Time,* February 14, 1964, p. 18; *Life,* February 21, 1964, p. 74-B. 63WC, vol. VII, p. 295; WC, vol. XIX, Cadigan exhibit 13, p. 286; WC, vol. XX, Holmes exhibit 4, p. 177; WC, vol. XXII, CE 1160, p. 207, CE 1390, p. 717; *Dallas Times Herald,* November 24, 1963, p. A-1; *Fort Worth Star Telegram,* November 20, 1963; *Dallas Times Herald,* December 1, 1963, p. A-30; *New York Times,* December 9, 1963, p. C-38; *Life,* February 21, 1964. 63*13 Days,* Robert Kennedy; WC, vol. XXI, Potts exhibit 1, p. 141, Tormey exhibit 2, p. 677; WC, vol. XXIV, CE 2003, pp. 277, 341, 350.
64. WC, vol. XIX, Dobbs exhibit 2, p. 567.
65. WC, vol. IX, p. 421; WC, vol. XI, p. 207; WC, vol. XXI, Potts exhibit 1, p. 141, Turner exhibit 1, p. 678, Weinstock exhibit 1, p. 721; WC, vol. XXIV, CE 2003, p. 278, 341, 350.
66. (*Assassination of JFK,* A. Newman, pp. 196, 217) [UN speech vs. USA] [March 26, 1962—"Fidel Castro Speaks Against Bureaucracy and Sectarianism."]
67. WC, vol. XXII, CE 1117, p. 84.
68. See WC, vol. XXII, CE 1170, p. 270—*Time* subscription to expire December 1963.
69. WC, vol. XXII, CE 1147, p. 178—overlapping subscriptions January 1963. (See 11/25/62.)
70. WC, vol. XIX, Dobbs exhibit 7, p. 573; *Assassination of JFK,* A. Newman, p. 301.
71. New York Customs received P.O. Form 2153-X from NYC P.O. which is executed by Oswald, Box 2915; CD 60, pp. 2–3; FBI reports Oswald's writing, "I protest this intimidation"; see CD 205, p. 157.
72. CD 7, p. 367; WC, vol. XVII, CE 773, p. 635.
73. WC, vol. XVI, CE 135, p. 511; WC, vol. XXII, CE 1137, p. 116; WC, vol. XXVI, CE 3088, p. 700.
74. WC, vol. XXVI, CE 3088 p. 700.
75. FBI special agent Hosty, April 30, 1964, testimony to the Warren Commission, see WC, vol. IV, p. 444.
76. See FBI report by James P. Hosty, September 10, 1963; WC, vol. VII, CE 829, p. 772.
77. Kelley *Kelley: The Story of an FBI Director,* p. 263; also see FBI special agent Hosty, April 30, 1964, testimony to the Warren Commission, WC,

vol. IV, p. 444. In this 1964 testimony, Hosty uses the date April 25 for when Oswald's Dallas file was reopened.

78. Clarence Kelley, *Kelley: The Story of an FBI Director,* p. 263.
79. Clarence Kelley, *Kelley: The Story of an FBI Director,* p. 263.
80. *Assassination of JFK,* A. Newman, pp. 79 and 301.
81. WC, vol. XXII, CE 1406, p. 789.
82. WC, vol. XXII, CE 1406, p. 789.
83. WC, vol. XXII, CE 1145, p. 163, 165.
84. WC, vol. XIX, Dobbs exhibit 13, p. 580.
85. WC, vol. XIX, Dobbs exhibit 13, p. 580; WC, vol. XX, Moore exhibit 1, p. 635; WC, vol. XXIV, CE 2003, p. 343.
86. Issue was dated 3/11/63, mailed on 3/7/63 and probably arrived in Dallas on 3/13 or 3/14.
87. Issue was dated 3/24/63, mailed on 3/21/63 and probably arrived in Dallas on 3/27 or 3/28.
88. WC, vol. XXI, Shaneyfelt exhibit 13, p. 454.
89. WC, vol. X, p. 87; WC, vol. XX, Lee exhibit 1, p. 511; *New York Times,* December 9, 1963, p. C-38; *Life,* February 21, 1964, p. 76). On November 24, 1963, Oswald says that he first became interested in the FPCC in New Orleans (WC, vol. XXIV, CE 2060, p. 479).
90. WC, vol. X, p. 87; WC, vol. XX, Lee exhibit 1, p. 511; *Life,* February 21, 1964, p. 76.
91. WR, p. 725.
92. WC, vol. IV, p. 446; vol. V, p. 9; WC, vol. XVII, CE 829, p. 773; WC, vol. XXVI, CE 2718, p. 94.
93. See New York FBI office transmittal of the letter to Dallas on July 1, 1963; NARA, JFK files, RIF 157-10006-10245.
94. FBI, Hosty report, September 10, 1963; NARA, JFK files, RIF 124-10171-10133; see also Dallas FBI file 100-10461-42. See also WC, vol. XXVI, CE 2718, p. 94, which contains these two sentences:

    > Information from our informant, furnished to us on April 21, 1963, was based upon Oswald's own statement contained in an undated letter to the Fair Play for Cuba Committee (FPCC) headquarters in New York City. A copy of this letter is included as exhibit 61 in our supplemental report dated January 13, 1964, entitled "Investigation of Assassination of President John F. Kennedy, November 22, 1963."

95. To verify this, researchers must consult the sixth document in the Mexico City field office file 105-3702. See NARA JFK files, RIF 124-10230-10422.
96. For an unredacted cover sheet on Hosty's September 10, 1963, report, see NARA, JFK files, RIF 124-10035-10256.
97. WC, vol. XXVI, CE 2718, p. 94.
98. FBI special agent Hosty, April 30, 1964, testimony to the Warren Commission, see WC, vol. IV, p. 444.
99. FBI Chicago office, report on FPCC by Paul H. Kellermeyer; located in NARA, JFK files, Church Committee records, RIF 157-10008-10145.

100. WC, vol. IX, p. 164.
101. WC, vol. VIII, p. 377; WC, vol. IX, p. 58; WC, vol. XI, pp. 125, 127.
102. WC, vol. IX, pp. 235–236. The other Dallas resident was Igor Voshinin.
103. WC, vol. X, p. 22
104. WC, vol. IX, pp. 235–236.
105. WC, vol. IX, pp. 235–236.
106. WC, vol. IX, p. 237.
107. Tom Bower, *The Red Web: M16 and the KGB Master Coup* (London: Aurum Press, 1989), p. 159.
108. CIA information report, Cuba, Report no. CS -3/537, 594, Subject: Comments on prominent Cubans by Teresa Proenza and a former Cuban government official, date distributed, February 18, 1963; Date of info.: Late December 1962; Place and date acq.: Mexico City, Mexico (December 28, 1962). NARA, JFK files, CIA, January 1994 (5 brown boxes) release; Proenza papers.
109. CIA information report, Cuba, Report no. CS -3/537, 594, Subject: Comments on prominent Cubans by Teresa Proenza and a former Cuban government official, date distributed, February 18, 1963; Date of info.: Late December 1962; Place and date acq.: Mexico City, Mexico (December 28, 1962). NARA, JFK files, CIA, January 1994 (5 brown boxes) release; Proenza papers.
110. CIA information report, Cuba, Report no. CS -3/537, Subject: Comments on prominent Cubans by Teresa Proenza and a former Cuban government official, date distributed, February 18, 1963; Date of info.: Late December 1962; Place and date acq.: Mexico City, Mexico (December 28, 1962). NARA, JFK files, CIA, January 1994 (5 brown boxes) release; Proenza papers.
111. FBI memorandum, to W. C. Sullivan, from D. J. Brennan, November 24, 1963, subject: Lee Harvey Oswald; NARA, JFK files, RIF 157-10008-10141.
112. Brennan's report said: ''On the night of November 23, 1963, Bernard Raichhardt [possibly B. Reichardt, CH/WH/3/Mexico] CIA, furnished the following information to the Liaison Agent.''
113. FBI memorandum, to W. C. Sullivan, from D. J. Brennan, November 24, 1963, subject: Lee Harvey Oswald; NARA JFK files, RIF 157-10008-10141.
114. Silvia Duran, interview with Anthony Summers, 11 January 1995; questions provided by John Newman. Many thanks are due to the unselfish work of Anthony and Robbyn Summers done in support of this project on this and other aspects of the Mexico City story for this book.
115. FBI memo, special agent Vincent K. Antle to SAC Miami, November 27, 1963, 105-8242, document 44; NARA, JFK files, NIS/ONI 1994 release, boxes 1–3, Hemming.
116. FBI report by special agent Dwyer, Miami 105-8342, December 2, 1963; NARA, JFK files, CD 59.
117. FBI memo, special agent Vincent K. Antle to SAC Miami, November

27, 1963, 105-8242, document 44; NARA, JFK files, NIS/ONI 1994 release, boxes 1–3, Hemming.

118. Earl Golz 1978 interview with Fred Claasen; AARC, John Martino file; see also *Vanity Fair,* December 1994, pp. 86–139.
119. WC, vol. XVIII, CE 986 p. 489.
120. Note: This letter was mentioned in Kelley's book (Kelley: *Story of an FBI Director,* p. 260), but not Oswald's May 1963 change-of-address to the Soviet Embassy.
121. WC, vol. XVIII, CE 986, p. 486.
122. WC, vol. XXII, CE 1117, p. 84, CE 1147, p. 178.
123. WC, vol. XXII, CE 1144, p. 156.
124. WC, vol. XVI, CE 29, p. 145; WC, vol. XVIII, CE 986, p. 493.
125. WC, vol. XVIII, CE 986, p. 499.
126. HT/LINGUAL soft file, CIA memorandum, May 1, 1964, see "Item 61G10AK" [July 10, 1961, item AK]; NARA, JFK files, RIF 1994.04.13.14.53:55:500005; this is also CIA document number 1619-1122-Y.
127. HSCA Report, p. 260.
128. "Progress Report, 1962-1963," an April 1964 internal CIA report on the HT/Lingual program, also known as "CI/Project." This document, classified, "SECRET EYES ONLY," has no author, and comes with a cover note from the chief of CI/Project, John Mertz, to a Mr. Hunt, saying, "Attached is an interesting statement which indicates the Project is oriented along operational lines. JCM." Both documents are in NARA, JFK Files, CIA, 1993 release.
129. Angleton memo to Hoover, Attn: Papich November 26, 1963, "SPECIAL HANDLING," Secret Eyes Only, Subject: Hunter report #10815; NARA, JFK files, RIF 1994.04.13.14:56:04:160005.
130. WC, CD 66, p. 91
131. We really need to see the intercept to verify this CIA claim. Even if Mertz was equating "Alek" to "Alex" we still need to know. This particular [presumably] classified mail intercept along with the rest of these kinds of materials should be released and even if the Agency wants to keep them classified. The Assassination Records Review Board could decide to release them anyway.
133. See HSCA final report pp. 205-206
134. See CIA HT/LINGUAL Card on Oswald, dated 7 August 1961; NARA, JFK files, RIF 1193.07.02.11;10;02;560530. Handwriting on this card states, "deleted 28 May '62.

Chapter Sixteen

1. WC Vol. XXVI, pp. 95–96, CD 12, p. 5.
2. FBI letter, April 6, 1964, WC vol. XXVI, CE 2718, pp. 92–99; for Question Number 9, see pp. 94–95.
3. FBI letter from SAC New York (NY-113) to SAC New Orleans, July 5,

1963; NARA, JFK files, FBI headquarters file 105-82555, document 54; see also New Orleans files 100-16601, document 45; RIF 124-10228-10039.

4. It is item 54R in the Oswald FBI headquarters file 105-82555. It is stamped "Received 7.8 63 FROM CSNY 48S; Paul Hoch item #463. On January 1, 1978, Dr. Hoch added this note: "I got this from the Archives long ago. According to Jim Kostman, FBI item 105-82555-54R includes this card, with part of the FBI's notation of the source deleted." Note also that this card eventually became FBI exhibit D-21.
5. Someone has written the number "54" on an entire string of documents in Oswald's headquarters file (105-82555), including this card, and thus its relative position—and thus its probably date—is obscure.
6. WC Vol. XVIII, CE 986, pp. 516–517.
7. FBI memorandum from SAC New Orleans to SAC Dallas; Subject: Lee Harvey Oswald, July 17, 1963; NARA JFK files, Dallas 100-10461 file, document 36; New Orleans 100-16601 file, document 6 (it had earlier been listed as document 5); see also Paul Hoch, item 985.
8. FBI memorandum from SAC New Orleans to SAC Dallas; Subject: Lee Harvey Oswald, July 17, 1963; NARA JFK files, Dallas 100-10461 file, document 36; New Orleans 100-16601 file, document 6 (it had earlier been listed as document 5); see also Paul Hoch, item 985.
9. FBI office memorandum from SAC New York to SAC New Orleans; Subject Lee Harvey Oswald, July 17, 1963, NARA, JFK files, FBI New Orleans file 100-16601, document 8.
10. NARA, JFK files, FBI New Orleans file 100-16601, document 9; see also Paul Hoch, item 505.
11. Included in this material was a copy of Oswald's June 10 letter to the *Worker* in which he used his New Orleans P.O. Box (30061) as his mailing address; see July 5 FBI New York office memorandum to SAC New Orleans: TO: SAC New Orleans FROM: SAC New York SUBJECT: Lee H. Oswald, P.O. Box 30061, New Orleans, La.; Handwritten: "Lee Harvey Oswald 100-16601*" (copies 1-New Orleans (Info); (Encl. 1); (RM); JVW:rmv; (1); Handwritten: "105-82555-54" and "100-16601-45.") This letter must be different from Oswald's change-of-address card which he mailed soon thereafter to the *Worker*. Although the postmark for the change-of-address card is indistinct, a large stamp is over the front of the card, apparently from the FBI, which reads "RECEIVED 7 8 63 FROM CSNY 48 IS 6." Paul Hoch procured this item from the archives and he says: "I got this item from the archives long ago. According to Jim Kostman, FBI item 105-82555-54R includes this card, with part of the FBI's notation on the source deleted. Paul L. Hoch 1/1/78."
12. FBI memorandum from SAC New Orleans (16601) to SAC Dallas (100-10461) to SAC New Orleans (100-16601), July 17, 1963, Paul Hoch, item #985.
13. FBI memorandum from SAC Dallas to SAC New Orleans; Subject: Lee Harvey Oswald and Marina Nikolaevna Oswald, July 29, 1963; NARA

JFK files, New Orleans file 100-16601, document 9; Dallas file 100-10461, document 38; see also Paul Hoch, item 987.

14. FBI memorandum from SAC Dallas to SAC New Orleans; Subject: Lee Harvey Oswald, July 29, 1963, NARA JFK files, FBI New Orleans 100-16601 file, document 9; and Dallas 100-10461 file, document 38; see also Paul Hoch, item 987.
15. FBI memorandum from FBI SA James P. Hosty to SAC Dallas, May 28, 1963; Subject: Lee Harvey Oswald and Marina Oswald. See NARA, JFK files, Dallas FBI file, 100-10461.
16. FBI memorandum from SAC Dallas to director, FBI (105-82555), March 25, 1963; NARA, JFK files, RIF 124-10035-10255.
17. FBI memorandum from FBI SA James P. Hosty to SAC DAllas, May 28, 1963; Subject: Lee Harvey Oswald and Marina Oswald. See NARA, JFK files, Dallas FBI file, 100-10461.
18. Clarence Kelly, *Kelley: The Story of an FBI Director* (Kansas City: Andrews, McMeel & Parker, 1987), p. 265.
19. WC vol. XVII, CE 793, p. 680.
20. WC vol. VII, pp. 418–427.
21. WC vol. XIX, Cardigan exhibit 14, p. 287.
22. Urgent FBI cable from SAC Dallas to director and SAC New Orleans, 10:37 p.m. CST, November 22, 1963; NARA, JFK files, RIF 124-10248-10078.
23. WC vol. VIII, p. 139; Vol. XIX, Cadigan exhibit 3, p. 266.
24. WC vol. IV, p. 378; WC vol. VII, p. 295; WC vol. XVII, CE 794 p. 680; WC vol. XIX, Cadigan exhibit 14, p. 287; WC vol. XXII, CE 1390, p. 717; *Dallas Times Herald,* 12/1/63, p. A-30; *Fort Worth Star Telegram,* 11/30/63.
25. WC vol. VII, p. 295; WC vol. XVII, CE's 791–794, pp. 679–680; WC vol. XIX, Cadigan exhibits 13 & 14, pp. 286–287.
26. WC vol. XX, Lee exhibit 4, p. 521; WC vol. XXI, Turner exhibit 1, p. 678.
27. WC vol. IX, p. 420; Vol. XX, Lee exhibit 3-A, p. 517; WC vol. XXI, Potts exhibit A-1, p. 141; WC vol. XXIV, CE 2003, p. 274.
28. The card was found on Oswald on November 22, 1963. WC vol. IV, p. 440; WC vol. XI, p. 208; WC vol. XXIV, CE 1986, p. 17; WC vol. XXV, CE 2483, p. 681; *Life* magazine, 2/21/64, p. 76.
29. The FPCC sent this letter to Oswald's 4907 Magazine address, which he probably received on May 30 or later. WC vol. XVI, CE 93, p. 341; WC vol. XX, Lee exhibit 3, p. 514; WC vol. XXI, Potts exhibit A-1, p. 141, Turner exhibit 1, p. 678; WC vol. XXIV, CE 2003, pp. 275, 341, 350.
30. WC vol. XVIII, CE 986, pp. 516–517.
31. WC vol. XVIII, CE 986, p. 518. On June 4, the Russian Embassy in Washington, D.C., wrote to Marina Oswald at the 4907 Magazine apartment, New Orleans, asking her reason for wanting to return to the USSR. Soviet Embassy letter to Marina Oswald, June 4, 1963; WC vol. XVI, CE 11, p. 24; WC vol. XVIII, CE 986, p. 518; and WC vol. XXIV, CE 2003, p. 335. Oswald had furnished their address on May 17. We have already dealt with the issue of Marina's desire to return to the Soviet Union. She

did not want to go back to Russia. That she felt this way then is suggested by what she wrote to Mrs. Paine on May 25. Marina said that she wanted to stay in the U.S.A. even without Oswald.

32. See Conrad memorandum, FBI, "Re: Assassination of the President," November 23, 1963; NARA, JFK files, RIF 124-10035-10148.
33. Telephone conversation between the president and J. Edgar Hoover, November 23, 1963, LBJ Library.
34. See vol. XX, pp. 257–259 Johnson (Arnold), exhibit No. 1; CE 826, vol. XVII, p. 753, October 31, 1963, FBI report by SA Milton R. Kaack; and WC vol. XXII, CE 1145, p. 186. For the New Orleans copy, see NARA, JFK files, RIF 124-10228-10039.
35. WC vol. XX, Lee exhibit 3-A, p. 517, 8-A, p. 531; WC vol. XXI, Turner exhibit 1, p. 678.
36. FBI report by special agent Hosty, September 10, 1963; NARA, JFK files, RIF 124-10171-10133.
37. FBI report by special agent Hosty, September 10, 1963; NARA, JFK files, RIF 124-10171-10133.
38. WC vol. IX, p. 420; WC vol. XX, Lee exhibit 3-A, p. 517; WC vol. XXII, CE 1141, p. 141; WC vol. XXIV, CE 2003, pp. 274, 341, 350.
39. FBI report by special agent Hosty, September 10, 1963; NARA, JFK files, RIF 124-10171-10133.
40. June Cobb notes, October 22, 1960, on visit of Richard Gibson. CIA Cobb 201 file, 201-278841; NARA, JFK files, RIF 1994.03.08.13:30:54:000007. See also at NARA, CIA 1994 microfilm release, reel 11, folders A-F.
41. See *Alleged Assassination Plots,* pp. 13–70.
42. An article in the magazine *Confidential* in 1960 inaccurately described June Cobb's relationship with Marita Lorenz at the time she had an abortion. This was previously discussed in Chapter Seven.
43. See Cobb files in NARA JFK files, CIA 1994 microfilm, reel 11, folder E.
44. See dispatch to chief, WH division, May 21, 1963; NARA JFK files, CIA microfilm 1994 release, reel 11, folders E-F. The routing sheet shows the TFW coordination.
45. CIA memo from Victor White to chief, CI/OA, October 17, 1962; NARA JFK files, CIA January 1994 (5 brown boxes) release, Cobb files.
46. CIA memo from Victor White to chief, CI/OA, June 17, 1963; NARA JFK files, CIA January 1994 (5 brown boxes) release, Cobb files.
47. FBI special agent Hosty, April 30, 1964, testimony to the Warren Commission, see vol. IV, p. 444.
48. Clarence Kelly, *Kelley: The Story of an FBI Director,* p. 265.
49. FBI special agent Hosty, April 30, 1964, testimony to the Warren Commission, see vol. IV, p. 444.
50. Oswald letter to the FPCC, sent April 19, 1963; WC vol. XX, Lee exhibit 1, p. 511.
51. FBI memorandum from SAC New York (97-2229) to SAC Dallas; Subject: Fair Play for Cuba Committee, June 27, 1963; NARA, JFK files, RIF 124-10171-10128. More than the late date of this New York memorandum is curious. Handwriting on this document has the missing Dallas FBI serial

105-976. The writing also notes a "page 17." The Fain report of May 1960 is nowhere near this length, so the conclusion that more documents—including one 17 or more pages long—existed in the 105-976 file at some point.

52. Anthan G. Theoaris and John Stuart Cox, *The Boss* (Philadelphia: Temple University Press, 1988) pp. 14–15, and note 49.
53. Oswald letter to the FPCC, dated May 26, 1963; WC vol. XX, Lee exhibit 2, pp. 512–513.
54. Letter to Oswald from FPCC national director V. T. Lee, May 29, 1963; WC vol. XX Lee exhibit 3, CE 2483, p. 515; WC vol. IV, p. 440; WC vol. XI, p. 208; WC vol. XXIV, CE 1986, p. 17; WC vol. XXV, CE 2483, p. 681; and *Life* magazine, February 21, 1964, p. 76.
55. Letter to Oswald from FPCC national director V. T. Lee, May 29, 1963; WC vol. XX, Lee exhibit 3, p. 515; WC vol. IV, p. 440; WC vol. XI, p. 208; WC vol. XXIV, CE 1986, p. 17; WC vol. XXV, CE 2483, p. 681; and *Life* magazine, February 21, 1964, p. 76.
56. WC vol. XXV, CE 2548, p. 773. This printing company is opposite the Reily Coffee Company, where Oswald worked; see WC vol. XXII, CE 1410, p. 796; and WC vol. XXV, CE 2543, p. 770. There is some question as to whether the person ordering these handbills was actually Oswald; the secretary, Myra Silver, at the printing company believed that the person ordering them used the name "Osborne" and not Oswald; see WC vol. XXV, CE 2195, p. 58. Jones recalled that a "husky laborer-type" ordered the handbills, not Oswald; see WC vol. XXV, CE 2541, p. 769. There is no doubt, however, that these are the handbills that Oswald later distributed. The invoice from Jones Printing Company found in Oswald's effects after the assassination was billed to a "Mr. Osborne"; see WC vol. XXIV, CE 2003, p. 341. On balance, it seems probable that it was Oswald who ordered these handbills, using the name "Osborne." This is the conclusion reached by the Dallas office of the FBI after the assassination; see WC vol. XXV, CE 2548, p. 773.
57. WC vol. XXV, CE 2195, p. 58.
58. WC vol. XXII, CE 1411, p. 800.
59. United States Secret Service report of special agent Anthony E. Gerret, CO-2-34, 030, December 1963; NARA, JFK files, RIF 157-10011-10133. "Confidential Informant NO T-1 advised on July 23, 1963, that Post Office Box 30061 was rented by L. H. Oswald on June 3, 1963. He furnished as his address *657 French Street,* New Orleans, Louisiana." This informant was Mr. L. H. Robertson, postal inspector, 2002 Post Office Building, New Orleans; see October 31, 1963 FBI report by Kaack.
60. WC vol. XXV, CE 2195, p. 58.
61. Oswald letter to Vincent Lee, undated; see WC vol. XX, Lee exhibit 4, pp. 518–521.
62. The letter was obviously written after Oswald picked up the handbills, June 4, and before he leafleted the USS *Wasp* on June 15. Oswald said he had "picketed the fleet" in a letter to Lee dated August 1, 1963; see WC vol. XX, Lee exhibit 5, pp. 524–525.

63. Oswald letter to Vincent Lee, undated; see WC vol. XX, Lee exhibit 4, pp. 518–521. For a cleaner retyped version of this letter by the FBI's New York office, see NARA, JFK files, RIF 124-10160-10437. For Vincent Lee's testimony, see WC vol X, pp. 86–95.
64. WC vol. XVI, CE 115, p. 486; WC vol. XXVI, CE 3119, p. 770.
65. WC vol. XVI, CE 115, p. 486.
66. WC vol. XVII, CE 826, p. 753; WC vol. XX, Johnson exhibit 1, p. 257; WC vol. XXII, p. 166.
67. WC vol. XIX, pp. 568–569; and WC vol. XX, Lee exhibit 8-C, p. 532. On July 8, Oswald notified the *Worker* of his new address; see the Kaack report of October 31, 1963.
68. WC vol. XVII, CE 780, p. 658.
69. WC vol. XX, Lee exhibit 4, p. 518; *New York Times* 12/9/63, p. C-38.
70. *Ramparts,* January 1968, p. 47.
71. HSCA vol. X, pp. 128–131.
72. HSCA vol. X, p. 128.
73. HSCA *Report,* p. 219.
74. HSCA *Report,* p. 218.
75. HSCA Vol. X, p. 128.
76. CD 75, p. 222; WC vol. VIII, p. 170; WC vol. X, pp. 54–58; and vol. XXVI, pp. 705–791.
77. CD 75, p. 517.
78. FBI draft message from New Orleans SAC to FBI director, 89-69, document 138; NARA, JFK files, RIF 124-10248-10191.
79. CD 75, p. 699. FBI report, New Orleans office (NO 44-2064, NO 89-69) report, by special agents John W. Smith and Dean S. Lytle, November 26, 1963.
80. WC vol. XXVI, CE 3029, pp. 575–576.
81. WC vol. XXVI, CE 3029, pp. 575–576. The FBI report summarizing a telephone interview with Alderman claims he said the post office box was 30061. While this number was Oswald's true box number, Oswald never used it. Oswald instead used the false number 30016. All extant copies of the handbills and application forms that have a post office box number stamped on them are ''P.O. Box 30016.'' The FBI, not Alderman, probably made the mistake of using the right box number.
82. It would be even stranger if the Tulane FPCC handbill had, as was alleged in the FBI report, ''P.O. Box 30061'' stamped on it.
83. FBI memorandum from supervisor Leon M. Gaskill to SAC New Orleans (89-69), November 26, 1963; NARA, JFK files, RIF 124-10261-10044; see also Paul Hoch, item 1904.
84. The typed version in Gaskill's memo is probably erroneous in that Gaskill added punctuation; it probably read, ''FPCC - A.J. Hidell, P.O. Box 30016.''
85. ONI document dated July 14, 1964, written by ''DCG,'' who is not further identified. See the Church Committee documents in the National Archives; unfortunately, much of the Church Committee documents were erroneously photocopied with the HSCA record group number, 233, superimposed and,

as a result, the author's copies were misfiled as HSCA documents. The National Archives is attempting to relocate the Church Committee copy of the "DCG" memo and the attached report of Patrolman Ray of June 16, 1963. Both of these documents can also be found elsewhere in the JFK files, such as in box 3 of the NIS/ONI boxes released in 1994. The problem, however, is that—so far—the Church Committee copies are the only place where there is a handbill attached.

86. Oswald letter to Vincent Lee, August 1, 1963, WC vol. XX, Lee exhibit 5, p. 525.
87. New Orleans FBI office memo on Lee Harvey Oswald, dated July 22, 1964; WC vol. XXII, CE 1412, p. 805.
88. FBI memorandum from supervisor Leon M. Gaskill to SAC New Orleans (89-69), November 26, 1963; NARA, JFK files, RIF 124-10261-10044; see also Paul Hoch, item 1904. Gaskill also acknowledged that Major Erdrich had dropped off two copies of the handbill on November 26, 1963.
89. See footnote 85, above.
90. FBI New Orleans office memo on Lee Harvey Oswald, July 22, 1964, WC vol. XXII, CE 1412, pp. 805–806.
91. Memo from Patrolman Girod Ray to Chief L. Deutchman, June 16, 1963; NARA JFK files, NIS/ONI box 3. In his 1964 interview with the FBI, Patrolman Ray gave a slightly different account; the man responded that "he did not have permission to do this and felt that he did not need anyone's permission since he was within his rights to distribute leaflets in any area ha desired to do so." See WC vol. XXII, CE 1412, p. 806.
92. FBI New Orleans office memo on Lee Harvey Oswald, July 22, 1964, WC vol. XXII, CE 1412, p. 806.
93. FBI, San Francisco office, report of SA John P. McHugh, June 17, 1964; see WC CD 1204.
94. FBI Houston office, report of May 25, 1964; see WC CD 1033.
95. Note by "DCG," subject: Lee Harvey Oswald, July 14, 1964; NARA, JFK files, RIF 173-10011-10075; see also 1994 NIS 3 boxes release.
96. FBI document, Washington field office 105-37111; WC CD 1484, p. 2.
97. An exhaustive search has so far failed to turn up the location for this copy of Patrolman Ray's report. It is authentic, as discussion with the National Archives staff confirm. This copy has handwriting on it possibly describing Oswald as being 5' 6" to 5'7" tall, 2 to 3" shorter than Oswald.
98. Marina's testimony to the Warren Commission, WC vol. I, p. 44.
99. For the application itself, se WC vol. XXIV, CE 2075, pp. 509–510; for an undated FBI report—probably from the Washington field office—on Oswald's passport his application, see WC vol. XXII, CE 1062, p. 12.
100. See WC vol. XXIII, CE 1969, pp. 817–823.
101. Oswald letter to Soviet Embassy in Washington, July 1, 1963; WC vol. XVI, CE 13, p. 30.
102. Dallas FBI letter to New Orleans FBI office, July 29, 1963; Paul Hoch, item 987.
103. FBI memorandum from SAC New Orleans (100-16601) to SAC Dallas

(100-10461 and 105-1435 [Marina], August 13, 1963; Paul Hoch, item #988.

Chapter Seventeen

1. WC vol. XVII, CE 826, p. 754. Emmett J. Barbe, general maintenance foreman for Reily testified that he fired Oswald; *New Orleans Times-Picayune.*
2. CIA memorandum from Raymond M. Reardon, Security Analysis Group/OS to the CIA deputy inspector general, February 1, 1977.
3. CIA request for investigative check, from chief, CI/Operational Approval and Support Division to deputy director for Security IOS, June 1965; see NARA, JFK files, CIA, January 1994 (5 brown boxes) release; this document may also be associated with RIF 1993.06.29.16:23:07:500150.
4. FBI airtel [air telegram] from SAC, New Orleans (89-69) to director, FBI 62-109060)) March 8, 1967, Subject: Assassination of President John Fitzgerald Kennedy; NARA, JFK files, FBI New Orleans office, 89-68. This March 8, 1967, FBI air telegram from SAC New Orleans to Bureau contains information from an October 3, 1963, report of New Orleans FBI SA Warren C. DeBrueys entitled ''Anti-Fidel Castro Activities.'' This DeBrueys report has not been released to the public.
5. WAVE 8611 to HQS, December 6, 1963, NARA JFK files, number files, boxes 51-53.
6. Noon's CIA request for operational approval, dated September 6, 1961, can be found in the CIA's January 1994 (5 brown boxes) release.
7. The author's copy of this CIA cable was obtained from the National Archives but the exact location is unclear. It is a ''desensitized'' version of WAVE cable 9537 to director CIA. The exact date is also unclear, but this handwriting appears on the bottom of p. 1: ''30 Dec 67.'' A handwritten file number is below the date: ''100-300-17.''
8. FBI airtel [air telegram] from SAC New Orleans (89-69) to director, FBI (62-109060), March 8, 1967, Subject: Assassination of President John Fitzgerald Kennedy; NARA, JFK files, FBI New Orleans office, 89-68. This March 8, 1967, FBI air telegram from SAC New Orleans to Bureau contains information from an October 3, 1963, report of New Orleans FBI SA Warren C. DeBrueys entitled ''Anti-Fidel Castro Activities.'' This DeBrueys report has not been released to the public.
9. Church Committee memorandum to files, from Dwyer and Greissing, Subject: Interview with Carlos Bringuier regarding New Orleans Cuban group and Oswald, January 12, 1976; NARA, JFK files, RIF 157-10007-10121.
10. Testimony of Carlos Bringuier to Warren Commission, April 7–8, 1964, WC vol. X, p. 35.
11. Testimony of Carlos Bringuier to Warren Commission, April 7–8, 1964, WC vol. X, p. 35.
12. Testimony of Carlos Bringuier to Warren Commission, April 7–8, 1964, WC vol. X, p. 35.

13. WC vol. XXVI, CE 3119, pp. 767, 771.
14. Testimony of Carlos Bringuier to Warren Commission, April 7–8, 1964, WC vol. X, p. 35–36.
15. WC vol. X, pp. 35, 76; WC vol. XIX, Burcham exhibit 1, p. 240; WC vol. XXV, CE 2548, p. 773; *Saturday Evening Post,* 12/14/63; *Life,* 2/21/64, p. 76.
16. Testimony of Carlos Bringuier to Warren Commission, April 7–8, 1964, WC vol. X, pp. 36–37.
17. WR, p. 728.
18. CIA memo, CI/R&A, Garrison and the Kennedy Assassination, June 1, 1967.
19. Enclosure 6 to CIA CI/R&A memorandum for the record; Subject: ''Possible DRE Animus Towards President Kennedy.'' April 3, 1967; see NARA, JFK files, RIF 1993.06.28.15:55:39:460280.
20. Enclosure 6 to CIA CI/R&A memorandum for the record; Subject: ''Possible DRE Animus Towards President Kennedy,'' April 3, 1967; see NARA, JFK files, RIF 1993.06.28.15:55:39:460280.
21. CD 11, p. 2; CD 928, p. 18.
22. WC vol. X, p. 37; WC vol. XXVI, CE 3119, p. 768.
23. WC vol. X, p. 37.
24. JFK NARA RIF 124-10062-10049. To chief, from SAIC John W. Rice, New Orleans; Subject: Assassination of John F. Kennedy.
25. JFK NARA RIF 124-10062-10049. To chief, from SAIC Rice, New Orleans; Subject: Assassination of John F. Kennedy.
26. WC vol. XXVI, CE 3119, p. 768; *New Orleans Times-Picayune,* 2/28/69.
27. WC vol. XXV, CE 2210, pp. 90, CE 2548, 773; WC vol. XXVI, CE 2888, pp. 343, CE 3032, p. 578.
28. WR, p. 728.
29. Martello testimony, WC vol. X, p. 61.
30. WR, p. 728.
31. SA Callender to SAC New Orleans August 1963; NARA, JFK files, RIF 124-10228-10044. Note: the Callender memo is cross-filed into deBrueys's FPCC file 97-74; and has a handwritten note at the bottom reading, ''Indices contained no information identifiable with Hernandez or Cruz.''
32. The report stated:

    1. Lee H. Oswald, white, male, age 23, born 10/18/39, New Orleans, residence 4709 Magazine, New Orleans, lower center apt. Oswald informed arresting officer that he is a member of the New Orleans chapter of the Fair Play for Cuba Committee with headquarters at 799 Broadway, New York City. Lt. Galliot informed that Oswald was handing out yellow leaflets with inscription 'Hands Off Cuba, Viva Castro.'

    2. Carlos Jose Bringuier, white, male, age 29, 501 Adele St. Apt 1, New Orleans, who informed he is the Director of the Cuban Student Directorate [DRE] for the New Orleans area. He informed he immigrated to this country on 2/8/61 INS # A125456223 and has a clothing shop at 107 Decatur St.

3. Ceflo Macario Hernandez, white, male, age 47, 519 Adele St. Apt. E. He advised he is a member of the same group as Bringuier.
4. Miguel Mariano Cruz, white, male, age, 18, 2526 Mazant, Apt. C, who advised he is also a member of the Cuban Student Directorate. According to Lt. Galliot, all four individuals were arrested for disturbing the peace when Oswald became involved in an argument with Bringuier, Hernandez, and Cruz and that a crowd developed. Lt. Galliot informed that he had no further information at this time.

33. August 9, 1963 (Friday at 1:15 P.M.)—NO T-6 reports to FBI that she sees Oswald distributing handbills; see CD 12, p. 4. This NO T-6 might have been a Department of Employment security employee.
34. WC vol. XI, p. 328; WC vol. XXVI, CE 3094, p. 705.
35. WC vol. XI, p. 358.
36. WC vol. XI, pp. 343, 356; WC vol. XXV, CE 2477, p. 671; WC vol. XXVI, CE 2902, p. 358.
37. Pena is a white male, DOB; 8/15/23, 5' 8", 140# POB: Colon, Cuba, brothers: Ruperto, 117 Decatur; Andrea, Las Americas Bar, 407 Decatur; see WC vol. XXVI, CE 2902, p. 359. Orestes Pena applied for a passport in New Orleans on June 24, 1963, the same day that Oswald applied. Pena's passport is #92577 and Oswald's is #92526, both issued on June 25; see WC vol. XI, pp. 349, 360; WC vol. XVI, CE 239, p. 666; WC vol. XIX, Cadigan exhibit 10, p. 283; WC vol. XXI, Pena exhibit 1, p. 43; WC vol. XXII, CE 1062, p. 12; WC vol. XXIII, CE 1969, p. 818; WC vol. XXIV, CE 2075 p. 509; WC vol. XXVI, CE 2754, p. 134, CE 2755, p. 136, CE 2787, p. 177 and CE 2902, p. 358. Orestes Pena plans to go to Spain in August 1963, but he postponed that trip and went to Puerto Rico and the Dominican Republic instead (between August 13–27). Orestes Pena went to Spain in May of 1964; WC vol. XI, p. 351; CD 984h, p. 104.
38. Yet later, on 6/9/64, Orestes Pena cannot recall Oswald; See WC vol. XXVI, CE 2902, p. 358.
39. While Orestes Pena was out of the country between August 13 and 27, his brother Ruperto Pena saw the two Cubans in a car. Since Ruperto could not speak English, he told Carlos Bringuier about seeing the two men. Bringuier then reported the sighting to the FBI. Both Penas denied that either of these two Cubans was Oswald's companion at the Habana Bar; however, Bringuier says one of them was Oswald's companion: WC vol. X, p. 45; WC vol. XI, pp. 349, 351, 367.
40. Rodriguez said it was around 2:30 to 3:00 a.m., but he had difficulty remembering the date, variously placing it somewhere between 5 and 12 August. On 5/12/64, Rodriguez described Oswald's companion as a nattily-dressed white male, 32, 5' 7", medium build, spoke Spanish well; WC Vol. XXV, CE 2477, p. 671. Carlos Bringuier, a Cuba refugee leader in the New Orleans Cuban Student Directorate, thought this event occurred between August 15 and August 30; WC Vol. X, p. 45.
41. A transcript of Martello's August 10, 1963, report can be found in WC vol. X, pp. 53–56.

42. WC vol. IV, p. 437; and vol. XVII, CE 826, p. 762.
43. Prior to Magazine, Oswald had lived at 4709 Mercedes in Fort Worth and worked for a sheet metal company for several months; CD 87 SS 449, p. 3. Lie. Moved from 2703 Mercedes, Fort Worth, on 10/8/62. (Newman, at page 45, stresses that *Oswald wants to hide all Dallas connections.*) 10.Two brothers: Robert Oswald in Fort Worth, 27, and John Oswald in Arlington, 32. Lie. Robert is in Arkansas and John Pic is in USAF in San Antonio. 11. SS# 433-54-3937; Sel. Ser. # 41-114-39532 12. Lutheran 13. Worked at Reily Coffee Co. from May until July 17. Lie. Last day was July 19. 14. Prior to Reily, worked at Jackson Brewing Company, New Orleans, for 1-1/2 months. Lie. Did not work for Jackson Brewing Company. 15. Oswald does not reveal his Russian trip; WC vol. IV, pp. 431, 435, 437; WC vol. X, p. 51; WC vol. XVII, CE 826, p. 757; *Dallas Times Herald,* 1/26/64; *Houston Post,* 11/27/63 p. 16. Oswald says that he does not want his family to learn English as he hated USA; WC vol. XXV, CE 2548, p. 773.
44. WC Martello testimony, WC vol. X, pp. 53–56.
45. WC Martello testimony, WC vol. X, pp. 53–56.
46. WC Martello testimony, WC vol. X, pp. 53–56.
47. HSCA memorandum to files, from Dwyer and Greissing, January 12, 1976; see NARA, JFK files, RIF 157-10007-10121.
48. WC Martello testimony, WC vol. X, pp. 53–56.
49. CD 75, p. 517; Quigley interview with Vinson, November 27, 1963, file NO 80-69.
50. WC vol. XXII, CE 1414, p. 831; WC vol. XXVI, CE 3120, p. 783.
51. WC, Lieutenant Martello testimony to the Warren Commission, WC vol. X, p. 56.
52. WC, Lieutenant Martello testimony to the Warren Commission, WC vol. X, p. 56.
53. WC vol. XVII, CE 827, p. 770.
54. On that occasion, Quigley's work became an April 27, 1961, New Orleans report to Dallas. That was before the FBI had learned Oswald had married Marina. See SAC New Orleans to SAC Dallas, April 27, 1961; NARA, JFK files, RIF 124-10228-10036.
55. FBI memorandum from SA John L. Quigley to SAC, August 27, 1963; NARA JFK files, RIF 100-10228-10052.
56. FBI New Orleans, 100-16601-13, SA John Lester Quigley, 8/15/63 summary of his 8/10/63 interview with Oswald in jail. NARA, JFK files, RIF 124-10228-10047.
57. Testimony of John L. Quigley, WC vol. IV, p. 435.
58. FBI New Orleans, 100-16601-13, SA John Lester Quigley, 8/15/63 summary of his 8/10/63 interview with Oswald in jail. NARA, JFK files, RIF 124-10228-10047.
59. This a fact which was apparently from a July 17, 1963, New Orleans report that had as an enclosure a copy of Oswald's April 14 letter from Dallas to the FPCC in New York. See SAC New Orleans to SAC Dallas, July 17, 1963; NARA, JFK files, RIF 124-10228-10040.

60. WC vol. XXVI, CE 2726, p. 105. Marina suggested that Oswald picked this name because ''Hidell'' sounded like ''Fidel.'' See also WC vol. V. p. 402; WC vol. XVII, CE 826, p. 759; WC vol. XXII, CE 1401, p. 753, and CE 1413, p. 822; WC vol. XXIII, CE 1942, p. 737; WC vol. XXIV, CE 1986, p. 17; WC vol. XXV, CE 2548, p. 773; and WC vol. XXVI, CE 2726, p. 105.
61. FBI New Orleans, 100-16601-13, SA John Lester Quigley, 8/15/63 summary of his 8/10/63 interview with Oswald in jail. NARA, JFK files, RIF 124-10228-10047.
62. FBI New Orleans, 100-16601-13, SA John Lester Quigley, 8/15/63 summary of his 8/10/63 interview with Oswald in jail. NARA, JFK files, RIF 124-10228-10047.
63. FBI report, New Orleans office, September 24, 1963; NARA, JFK files, CIA DDP 201 file box 1; see also RIF 124-10160-10408 and RIF 124-10228-10062.
64. HSCA, vol. X, p. 62; from HSCA staff interview with Bartes.
65. FBI report, New Orleans office, September 24, 1963; NARA, JFK files, CIA DDP 201 file box 1; see also RIF 124-10160-10408 and RIF 124-10228-10062.
66. ''Pamphlet Case Sentence Given,'' New Orleans *Times-Picayune,* August 13, 1963, p. 3.
67. FBI report, New Orleans office, September 24, 1963; NARA, JFK files, CIA DDP 201 file box 1; see also RIF 124-10160-10408 and RIF 124-10228-10062.
68. ''Pamphlet Case Sentence Given,'' New Orleans, *Times-Picayune,* August 13, 1963, p. 3.
69. HSCA, vol. X, p. 62; from HSCA staff interview with Bartes.
70. HSCA, vol. X, p. 62; from HSCA staff interview with Bartes.
71. In this case, Bartes was being used as the source on Arcacha Smith being the previous CRC delegate (before Bartes), but it is crossed out and Banister is used instead. The lined-out material however, makes it clear that Bartes was someone ''who has furnished reliable information in the past and whose identity must be protected.'' SAC New Orleans to director FBI, & SAC Dallas, 89-69-138, undated but presumably in the first days after the assassination. See NARA, JFK files, RIF 124-102248-10191.
72. HSCA, vol. X, p. 62; from HSCA staff interview with Bartes.
73. FBI report, New Orleans office September 24, 1963; see also NARA, JFK files, RIF 124-10228-10062.
74. The *Times-Picayune* carried an article on page three, section one, in their 8/13/63 edition captioned ''Pamphlet Case Sentence Given,'' indicating that Lee Oswald, aged 23, of 4907 Magazine, was sentenced to pay a fine of $10 or serve ten days in jail on a charge of disturbing the peace by creating a scene. It was indicated that Oswald was arrested by First District police in the 700 block of Canal while distributing pamphlets asking for a ''fair play for Cuba.'' Police reportedly were called to the scene when three Cubans reportedly sought to stop Oswald from distributing the above pamphlets.

75. Director FBI to SAC New Orleans, August 21, 1963; NARA JFK files, RIF 124-10228-10049.
76. WC vol. X, p. 61; WC vol. XXV, CE 2546, p. 771.
77. CD 165, p. 10.
78. WC vol. X, pp. 41, 68; WC vol. XVI, CE 93, p. 342; WC vol. XXII, CE 1153, p. 187; WC vol. XXIV, CE 2003, p. 283.
79. WC vol. XXV, CE 2545, p. 771, CE 2548, p. 773.
80. WC vol. X, p. 41.
81. WC vol. XXI, Stuckey exhibit 2, p. 626; New Orleans States Item, 11/23/63; CD 897, p. 547 says at 2:00 P.M.
82. WC vol. XIX, Burcham exhibit 1, p. 236; WC vol. XXIII, CE 1191, p. 711. However, in August 1963; according to Illinois Professor Revilo P. Oliver—a political conservative—Oswald applied for a job at the *Independent American,* a conservative New Orleans publication whose editor was Kent Courtney; see WC vol. XV, p. 720.
83. WC vol. X, p. 269.
84. WC vol. XXVI, CE 3119, p. 762; Secret Service report, New Orleans, La., CO-2-34,030, by A. G. Vial, Anthony E. Gerrets, Roger Counts, and John W. Rice, December 3, 1963.
85. WC vol. X, pp. 41, and 270; WC vol. XXVI, CE 3119, p. 771.
86. WC vol. XXVI, CE 3119, p. 762; Secret Service, New Orleans, La., CO-2-34,030 A. G. Vial, Anthony E. Gerrets, Roger Counts, John W. Rice date December 3, 1963.
87. CIA memorandum, circa May 1967; Subject: "CIA Involvement with Cubans and Cuban Groups Now or Potentially Involved in the Garrison Investigation"; see NARA, JFK files, RIF 1993.06.28.15:07:58:030280. We know about this from another location, apparently, by a quirk. A single sheet of paper, misfiled in Frank Sturgis's papers, a portion of which were in the CIA 1994 (5 brown boxes) release. It is entitled simply "Carlos Quiroga (Paragraph 7(C) of reference memorandum," and is undated. It also notes the fact that Quiroga had been a candidate for the "Agency Student Recruitment Program" while at Louisiana State University. The next sentence, however, it still redacted.
88. Eugene Methvin, August 1, 1963 letter to Edward Lansdale, Lansdale Papers, Hoover Institution.
89. FBI New Orleans SAC to file (100-16601-14), August 21, 1963, Subject: Lee Harvey Oswald; NARA, JFK files, RIF 124-10228-10048.
90. FBI New Orleans, 100-16601-1B2, record of property acquisition, re Stuckey interview with Oswald; NARA, JFK files, RIF 124-10228-10035.
91. Oswald letter to Arnold Johnson, August 28, 1963; WC vol. XX, Johnson exhibit 4, p. 263.
92. HSCA, vol. X, p. 85. According to the final report of the committee, Borja said his DRE responsibilities "involved only military operations and he suggested that Jose Antonio Lanusa, who handled press and public relations for the group, knew Clare Booth Luce and had been in contact with her."
93. WC vol. XXIV, CE 2119, p. 549, CE 2123, p. 685; and WC vol. XXV, CE 2193, p. 17, CE 2563, p. 811.

94. CD 598, p.a-7.
95. CD 1160, p. 4.
96. CD 205, p. 170.
97. NARA, JFK files, CIA document number 761-329A.
98. CD 75, p. 573.
99. CD 75, pp. 588 and 652.
100. HSCA *Report,* p. 218.
101. Stephen Schlesinger and Stephen Kinzer, *Bitter Fruit: The Untold Story of the American Coup in Guatemala* (Garden City, New York: Anchor Books, 1983), p. 82.
102. HSCA *Report,* p. 219.
103. July 19, 1963 (Friday)—Oswald worked from 8:22 A.M. to 4:30 P.M. at Reily (WC vol. XXIII, CE 1896, p. 701) Oswald's maintenance book notes. (FBI exhibit D 66) This was Oswald's last day of employment at Reily. (WC vol. XVII, CE 826, p. 754) Emmett J. Barbe, general maintenance foreman for Reily testifies that he fired Oswald. (*New Orleans Times Picayune,*
104. CIA memo for chief, Security Analysis Group, Subject: Hall, 10 September, 1975; NARA, JFK files, RIF 1993.06.28.17:25:01:900360.
105. James Hosty, September 2, 1994, interview with John Newman.
106. James Hosty, September 2, 1994, interview with John Newman.
107. James Hosty, January 1983 interview with Larry Haapanen.
108. James Hosty, September 5, 1994, interview with John Newman.
109. Church Committee, vol. V, p. 65.

Chapter Eighteen

1. WR, pp. 299–301.
2. *Lee Harvey Oswald, the CIA, and Mexico City* (hereafter referred to as the *Lopez Report*), p. 250.
3. Oleg Nechiporenko, *Passport to Assassination: The Never-Before-Told Story of Lee Harvey Oswald by the KGB Colonel Who Knew Him* (Birch Lane Press, 1993) hereafter referred to as *Passport to Assassination.*
4. LBJ Library, LBJ tapes, November 23, 1963, President Johnson, telephone conversation with FBI director Hoover.
5. WC vol. XXV, CE 2195, pp. 37–39, CE 2464, p. 633, and CE 2566, p. 819.
6. WC vol XXIV, p. 598; Vol. XXV, p, 767; and CD 905-C:11.
7. *Lopez Report,* p. 248.
8. 9/27/63 10:30 AM Man calls Soviet Military Attache regarding a visa for Odessa.'' See *Lopez Report,* p. 117.
9. CIA transcript of September 27, 1963, 10:37 A.M., phone call; NARA, JFK files, CIA January 1994 (5 brown boxes release); box 15b, folder 56.
10. *Lopez Report,* p. 250.
11. Nechiporenko, *Passport to Assassination,* p. 76.
12. *Lopez Report,* p. 118, referencing footnote 471 on p. 32 of the notes,

which cites a "Memo to Clark Anderson from Winston Scott, 11/27/63, with seven attachments; LR p. 32 fn. 471.

13. *Lopez Report,* p. 118.
14. Valery for 10 to 15 minutes and then Oleg for 40 to 45 minutes; see Nechiporenko, *Passport to Assassination,* p. 104.
15. Pavel and Valery for more than an hour and then Oleg escorts him away; see Nechiporenko, *Passport to Assassination,* p. 104.
16. The man is later identified as Oswald and the woman is later identified as Duran; the alleged Oswald comes on the line speaking in very poor Russian.
17. *Lopez Report,* p. 192.
18. *Lopez Report,* p. 192.
19. *Lopez Report,* p. 117.
20. Third Call: 1:25 P.M. [LE3] At 1:25 an unidentified man called the Soviet Consulate and asked for the consul. The man was told that the consul was not in. The man outside asked, "When tomorrow?" The soviet official told him that on Mondays and Fridays the consul was in between four and five. This conversation was also in Spanish. See *Lopez Report,* p. 74; and also p. 117.
21. Nechiporenko, *Passport to Assassination,* p. 66.
22. Nechiporenko, *Passport to Assassination,* p. 70.
23. Mexico City CIA transcript, September 27, 1963, 4:05 P.M.; NARA JFK files, CIA documents, Oswald box 15b, folder 56. This material was also included in the CIA January 1994 (5 brown boxes) release.
24. Mexico City CIA transcript, September 27, 1963, 4:05 P.M., NARA JFK files, CIA documents, Oswald box 15b, folder 56. This material was also included in the CIA January 1994 (5 brown boxes) release.
25. NARA, Oswald box 15b, folder 56, CIA January 1994 (5 brown boxes) release. See also *Lopez Report,* p. 76.
26. The English "Attachment C" states: A telephone call to the Cuban Embassy made at 1626 hours on September 27 by an unidentified man in the Soviet Embassy asking for Silvia Duran. They discuss the visa application for the "American" who with his Russian wife wanted to go via Cuba to the USSR. The Soviet [Embassy man's voice] says he has only no reply from [the] Washington etc. See NARA, CIA document number 133 594 ("part of"), and see also box 6, folder 5 of the CIA January 1994 (5 brown boxes) release.
27. NARA, CIA transcript from Mexico City, September 28, 1963, 11:51 A.M., Oswald box 15b, folder 56, CIA January 1994 (5 brown boxes) release.
28. *Lopez Report,* pp. 193-194.
29. NARA, CIA document number 559-243, a CIA memo to Warren Commission lawyer Lee Rankin about Duran, dated February 21, 1964. This report has an incorrect spelling for Alberu; it gives his name as Luis Alveru. His full name was Luis Alberu Suoto (or Soto). Alberu's agent status is given in a July 27, 1962, request for operational approval under the number "101331," a number cross-referenced to Alberu's Security Office number OS-279-089 in an August 20, 1962, security memo to CI/OA (Counterintelligence Operational Approval). OS-279-089 is itself cross-referenced to Alberu's CIA 201 number, 328609, in many files, such as an April 27, 1967, request for operational approval.

30. Winston Scott, *The Foul Foe,* unpublished manuscript, Chapter XXIV, p. 273. NARA, JFK files, HSCA records, Win Scott files. "Box 4" appears on the cover page.
31. Nechiporenko, *Passport to Assassination,* p. 81; see also p. 103.
32. Winston Scott, *The Foul Foe,* unpublished manuscript, Chapter XXIV, p. 273. NARA, JFK files, HSCA records, Win Scott files. "Box 4" appears on the cover page.
33. Nechiporenko, *Passport to Assassination,* p. 74.
34. Nechiporenko, *Passport to Assassination,* p. 74.
35. Nechiporenko, *Passport to Assassination,* p. 76.
36. Nechiporenko, *Passport to Assassination,* p. 77.
37. Nechiporenko, *Passport to Assassination,* p. 79.
38. The only exception is Azcue, who was confused and describes an event as taking place Saturday which clearly was the Friday afternoon blow-up.
39. Mexico City 5448, to CIA, Action: C/WH 5, July 20, 1963. NARA, JFK files, CIA, January 1994 (5 brown boxes) release; see box 1, folder 2.
40. NARA, CIA transcript from Mexico City, September 28, 1963, 11:51 A.M., Oswald box 15b, folder 56, CIA January 1994 (5 brown boxes) release.
41. *Lopez Report,* p. 77.
42. NARA, CIA transcript from Mexico City, September 28, 1963, 11:51 A.M., Oswald box 15b, folder 56, CIA January 1994 (5 brown boxes) release.
43. *Lopez Report,* p. 79, p. 136, pp. 164–165 and p. 170.
44. Nechiporenko, *Passport to Assassination,* p. 79.
45. There are two possibilities: Either the Soviet was genuine or he was an impostor. When added to our matrix, which is already complicated, this creates an even larger matrix of possibilities. However, we should make note of the fact that if the Soviet, too, was an impostor, then the entire call could have been fictitious, a possibility that seems pointless; for what reason would the CIA station deceive its own people or headquarters? It seems more logical to assume the Soviet was genuine, i.e., inside the Soviet Consulate, receiving the call.
46. Nechiporenko, *Passport to Assassination,* p. 79.
47. NARA, CIA document number 509-803, Information Developed on the Activity of Lee Harvey Oswald in Mexico City, 28 September–3 October 1963 (hereafter referred to as CIA Gist of Oswald Mexican City Sources) January 31, 1964.
48. *Lopez Report,* p. 171.
49. Silvia Duran, January 31, 1995, interview by Anthony Summers with questions posed by the author.
50. Nechiporenko, remarks in a special interview with American researchers at the 1993 Assassination Symposium on John Kennedy.
51. Winston Scott, *Foul Foe,* unpublished manuscript, p. 272.
52. Winston Scott, *Foul Foe,* unpublished manuscript, p. 268.
53. *Lopez Report,* p. 88.
54. Winston Scott, *Foul Foe,* unpublished manuscript, p. 267.
55. Winston Scott, *Foul Foe,* unpublished manuscript, p. 273.
56. Mr. T testified on April 12, 1978, and also recognized the four transcripts

from September 28, October 1 and 3 as his work. He also testified that he recognized the 10/1/63 conversation as his work because the name Lee Oswald was underlined.

57. *Lopez Report,* p. 85.
58. *Lopez Report,* p. 85.
59. *Lopez Report,* p. 83.
60. October 1. [LEO: not in LR] In midmorning an unidentified individual speaking broken Russian contacted the Soviet military attaché in Mexico City. He said he had been to the embassy the previous Saturday (September 28) and had talked with a consul, who had said they would send a telegram to Washington: Had there been a reply? He was referred to the consulate for information.[CIA Gist of OSwald Mexican City Sources, p. 9.] [10/1/63 at 10:31 A.M., transcribed by Mr. T; LR p. 82.] [On this transcript, the translator added the notation: ''the same person who phoned a day or so ago and spoke in broken Russian,'' links to marginal notation on 9/28 11:51 transcript: ''broken Russian''; LR p. 121] There are two slightly different transcripts of this conversation, which occurred at 10:30 A.M., on October 1. This is one of them:

    [LE9 contd] A person later identified as Lee Harvey Oswald, speaking in ''broken Russian,'' telephones the Soviet Embassy.

    OSWALD: Hello. I was at your place last Saturday and talked to your Consul. They said they'd send a telegram to Washington, and I wanted to ask you, is there anything new?

    RUSSIAN EMBASSY: Call another number, if you will.

    OSWALD: Please.

    RUSSIAN EMBASSY: 15-60-55, and ask for a Consul.

    OSWALD: Thank you.

    RUSSIAN EMBASSY: Please.

    NARA, CIA transcript from Mexico City, October 1, 1963, 10:30 A.M., Oswald box 15b, folder 56, CIA January 1994 (5 brown boxes) release. The other is not significantly different; it is in the same location at box 3, volume 1. Five minutes later, an ''Oswald'' calls the 15-60-55 number:

    [LE10] In at 1035 hours MO/the same person who phoned a day or so ago and spoke in broken Russian/speaks to Obyedkov.

    MO: Hello, this is Lee Oswald (phon) speaking. I was at your place last Saturday and spoke to a Consul, and they said that they'd send a telegram to Washington, so I wanted to find out if you have anything new? But I don't remember the name of the Consul.

    OBY: Kostikov. He is dark/hair or skin?

    LEE: Yes. My name is Oswald.

    OBY: Just a minute I'll find out. They say that they haven't received anything yet.

    LEE: Have they done anything?

    OBY: Yes, they say that a request has been sent out, but nothing has been received as yet.

    LEE: And what . . . ? [Oby hangs up]

    [NARA, CIA transcript from Mexico City, October 1, 1963, 10:35 A.M.,

Oswald box 6, folder 5, CIA January 1994 (5 brown boxes) release.] No sense asking for answer from Washington because Oswald did not fill out the application forms.

61. *Lopez Report,* p. 117.
62. *Lopez Report,* p. 125.
63. *Lopez Report,* p. 125.
64. Copies of this award recommendation are available in the National Archives; the author is grateful to the JFK Assassination Records Review Board for providing a copy in time for use in this book.
65. This can be seen from her 1963 fitness report and her career award recommendation, copies of which are available in the National Archives; again, the author is grateful to the JFK Assassination Records Review Board for providing a copies in time for use in this book.
66. David Martin, *Wilderness of Mirrors,* (New York: Harper and Row, 1980), p. 121 and p. 127.
67. CIA inspector general's report, May 23, 1967, pp. 92–93; NARA, JFK files, RIF 1993.06.30.17:10:07:150140.
68. For Phillips's comment, see *Washington Post,* 26 November 1976. For the Sigler story, see William R. Corson and Susan B. Trento, *Windows* (New York: Crown, 1989), pp. 266–396. The details of the Sigler story were brought to the author's attention by Professor Peter Dale Scott.
69. *Washington Post,* November 26, 1976; Anthony Summers, *Conspiracy* (New York: McGraw-Hill, 1980), pp. 388–389; Gaeton Fonzi, *Final Investigation* (New York: Thunder's Mouth Press, 1993), p. 285.
70. David Phillips, *Night Watch* (New York: Atheneum, 1987 ed), p. 181; his book was originally published in 1977.
71. CIA cable to JMWAVE and Mexico City from headquarters, DIR 73214, date no longer visible, but obviously just prior to October 7, 1963.
72. Kelley, *Kelley: The Story of an FBI Director,* p. 267.
73. *Lopez Report,* p. 88.
74. *Lopez Report,* p. 232.
75. Memorandum for the files, from Willard C. Curtis (probably a pseudonym for Winston Scott); Subject: June Cobb [handwritten here: "Interview with Elena Paz about June Cobb], November 25, 1964. CIA document 928-927, TX-1925.
76. Letter from S. D. Breckinridge, CIA principal coordinator for the HSCA, to Mr. G. Robert Blakey, chief counsel and director, HSCA, OLC 79-0113/k, March 13, 1979; NARA, JFK files, RIF 1993.07.16.16:28:40:280500.
77. *Lopez Report,* p. 207.
78. On another page in the *Lopez Report,* we see the reference to Cobb's move into Elena's home properly set in 1964. See *Lopez Report,* p. 231. Just prior to moving in, June had been introduced to Elena by Eunice Odio, whom Cobb had met earlier.
79. *Lopez Report,* pp. 206–207
80. June Cobb, March 4, and March 17, 1995 interviews with John Newman.
81. June Cobb, March 4, 1995, interview with John Newman.
82. *Lopez Report,* pp. 207–208; see also "Lee Harvey Oswald and Kennedy

Assassination,'' re Memorandum of Conversation, December 10, 1965, Elena Garro de Paz and Charles Thomas; courtesy of the Assassination Archives Research Center, CIA 1995 release. By using this December 10 memo, it is easy to fill in the associated redactions in the *Lopez Report.*

83. June Cobb, February 23, 1995, interview with John Newman.
84. Memorandum for the files, from Willard C. Curtis (probably a pseudonym for Winston Scott); Subject: June Cobb [handwritten here: ''Interview with Elena Paz about June Cobb], November 25, 1964. CIA document 928-927, TX-1925.
85. James Hosty, September 5, 1994, interview with John Newman.
86. June Cobb, February 23, 1995, interview with John Newman.
87. Memorandum for the files, from Willard C. Curtis (probably a pseudonym for Winston Scott); Subject: June Cobb [handwritten here: ''Interview with Elena Paz about June Cobb], November 25, 1964. CIA document 928-927, TX-1925.
88. According to the *Lopez Report*:

    Attached to the memo was a note from Flannery to the chief of station, Winston Scott, which read, ''Do you want me to send the gist of this to Headquarters?'' Scott then noted that the memo should be filed. The file indications show that the memo went into the Oswald ''P'' file and the Elena Garro ''P'' file.
89. The *Lopez Report* then has this comparison:

    The story is not as detailed as the 10/5/64 version. There is no mention of Deba Garro Guerrero Galvan. The story, perhaps because it is third hand, differs from the previous story in two areas: It states that the party was at the Cuban Embassy as opposed to Ruben Duran's, and that Elena talked to a Cuban Embassy official instead of her cousins about the three Americans.
90. June Cobb, March 4, 1995, interview with John Newman.
91. Memorandum for the files, from Willard C. Curtis (probably a pseudonym for Winston Scott); Subject: June Cobb [handwritten here: ''Interview with Elena Paz about June Cobb], November 25, 1964. CIA document 928-927, TX-1925.
92. Charles Thomas memo, December 10, 1965; CIA MArch 8, 1995, release to the Assassination Archives Research Center.
93. *Lopez Report,* p. 213.
94. *Lopez Report,* p. 215.
95. Charles Thomas memo, December 25, 1965; CIA March 8, 1995, release to the Assassination Archives Research Center.
96. *Lopez Report,* pp. 221–222.
97. *Lopez Report,* pp. 222–223.
98. Silvia Duran, interview with Anthony Summers, January 11, 1995; questions provided by John Newman.
99. Cable from CIA Mexico City station to chief, Western Hemisphere Division; Subject: Cuba, the [redacted] Operation, June 18, 1967; NARA JFK files, CIA document number 1125-1129B; see also CIA January 1994 (5 brown boxes) release, box 7, folder 6, and box 15, folder 55.

100. *Lopez Report,* p. 253.
101. *Lopez Report,* pp. 206–207, and especially p. 255.
102. *Lopez Report,* p. 253.
103. Agent report from Mexico City, May 26, 1967; Subject: [Redacted] meeting with [redacted]. This report is attached to cable from CIA Mexico City station to chief, Western Hemisphere Division; Subject: Cuba, the [redacted] operation, June 18, 1967; NARA JFK files, CIA document number 1125-1129B; see also CIA January 1994 (5 brown boxes) release, box 7, folder 6, and box 15, folder 55.
104. Agent report from Mexico City, May 26, 1967; Subject; [Redacted] meeting with [redacted]. This report is attached to cable from CIA Mexico City station to chief, Western Hemisphere Division; Subject: Cuba, the [redacted] operation, June 18, 1967; NARA JFK files, CIA document number 1125-1129B; see also CIA January 1994 (5 brown boxes) release, box 7, folder 6, and box 15, folder 55.
105. Agent report from Mexico City, May 26, 1967; Subject: [Redacted] meeting with [redacted]. This report is attached to cable from CIA Mexico City station to chief, Western Hemisphere Division; Subject: Cuba, the [redacted] operation, June 18, 1967; NARA JFK files, CIA document number 1125-1129B; see also CIA January 1994 (5 brown boxes) release, box 7, folder 6, and box 15, folder 55.
106. Larry Keenan January 29, 1995, interview with John Newman.
107. Edwin Lopez, January 29, 1995, interview with John Newman.
108. See *Lopez Report,* p. 198. Lechuga's name is redacted, but Scott's manuscript, in this case described in a memo by Warren Commission lawyer W. David Slawson, was obviously referring to that affair.
109. CIA information report, CS-3/537,594, February 18, 1963; NARA, JFK files, CIA January 1994 (5 brown boxes) release, Proenza file.
110. See *Lopez Report,* p. 198.
111. See *Lopez Report,* p. 199.
112. Agent report from Mexico City, May 26, 1967; Subject: [redacted] meeting with [redacted]. This report is attached to cable from CIA Mexico City station to chief, Western Hemisphere Division; Subject: Cuba, the [redacted] operation, June 18, 1967; NARA JFK files, CIA document number 1125-1129B; see also CIA January 1994 (5 brown boxes) release, box 7, folder 6, and box 15, folder 55.
113. *Lopez Report,* p. 200.
114. See Charles Thomas memorandum, December 25, 1965; Assassination Archives Research Center; there appear to be two P numbers on Duran: on page it is indistinct, but possibly 7969 or 4969.
115. Charles Thomas, memo to Secretary of State Rogers, July 25, 1969; NARA, JFK files, RIF 157-10005-10369.
116. See memo for chief, Covert Action Staff, and attached request for approval on use of Thomas dated September 20, 1963; NARA, JFK files, CIA January 1994 (5 brown boxes) release, Charles Thomas papers. It is interesting that Thomas's previous assignment had been in Haiti, from January 8, 1961, until the summer of 1963, after deMohrenschildt's arrival there.

117. Cable to Thomas from CARLONORB, 15 January 1970; this was possibly a Washington-based attorney, Charles Norberg, whose name and address, including the cable address, were in deMohrenschildt's address book. For this and associated materials on the Thomas-deMohrenschildt link in 1969-1970, see NARA, JFK files, RIF 180-10078-10007. Again, the author expresses appreciation to Larry Haapanen for his insightful work on this point.

Chapter Nineteen

1. A possible exception to this was what was passed to the Agency via its AMSPELL (DRE) assets, mentioned in Chapter Seventeen.
2. DDO response to HSCA letter dated August 15, 1978 (Questions 1 & 2), August 24, 1978; NARA, JFK files, RIF 1993.07.10.11:24:36:210470.
3. Page 26 of "List of Documents for Release," [to HSCA]; NARA, JFK files, RIF 1993.08.04.08:21:00:780053.
4. This is the report previously discussed that mentioned Oswald's letter to the FPCC from Dallas, in which he said he had been passing out pamphlets with a pro-Castro placard around his neck. See FBI report by special agent James P. Hosty on Oswald, September 10, 1963; NARA, JFK files, RIF 124-10228-10058. Note also that there is one redacted organization on that routing slip. It is possible that this was an SAS or WH element. Again, we must await the full disclosure of information.
5. Church Committee, Vol. V, p. 65.
6. It is likely that when the September 16, 1963, CIA memo to the FBI is declassified, we will see that Mexico was one of the "foreign countries" the CIA had in mind.
7. Church Committee memorandum from Dan Dwyer and Ed Greissing to Paul Wallach on review of Oswald 201 file, November 3, 1975; NARA, JFK files, SSCI box 265-15, 10091.
8. Page 26 of "List of Documents for Release," [to HSCA]: NARA, JFK files, RIF 1993.08.04.08:21:00:780053.
9. McCord may have been reassigned by 1963.
10. Page 26 of "List of Documents for Release," [to HSCA]; NARA, JFK files, RIF 1993.08.04.08:21:00:780053.
11. Document number 40. CIA response to HSCA request of March 9, 1978; NARA, JFK: files, RIF 1993.07.02.13:25:25:180530.
12. CI/SIG already had Oswald's 201 restricted to Egerter. See Chapters Four and Eight.
13. The FBI was conducting interviews in New Orleans while Oswald was in Mexico City, on October 1, 1963. See October 1, Kaack report; NARA, JFK files, FBI 105-82555, CIA DDP 201 file.
14. Note: Received by CIA/RID October 2, 1963, 4:26 P.M. by AN-6; read by CI/LS Jane Roman, October 4, 1963; read by SAS/CI (Austin) Horn, October 8, 1963; read by SAS/CI/CONTROL, October 10, 1963 "CR"; read by CI/

SI, (prob) October 10, 1962, Ann Egerter; read by CI/IC, date UNK "C7"; read by REDACTED, date UNK; read by CI/STAFF, room 2B03, date UNK; also has date stamp October 3, 1963, 9:36; coded 100-300-11, later lined through and replaced by 201-289248; document number DBA 52355.

15. Mexico City cable 6453 to headquarters October 9, 1963; NARA, JFK files, CIA 201 file on Oswald.
16. CIA cable 74673 to FBI, State Department, and Navy, October 10, 1963; NARA, JFK files, CIA 201 file on Oswald.
17. CIA headquarters cable 74830 to Mexico station, October 10, 1963; NARA, JFK files, CIA 201 file on Oswald.
18. The Agency's attempt to conceal the name of the drafter seems pointless. John Scelso's (may be a pseudonym) name is all over the hundreds of newly released cables between headquarters and Mexico City [see NARA, JFK files, HSCA records, CIA segregated collection, boxes 51–53, the CIA January 1994 (5 brown boxes release) and other locations], as is a B. [probably Bob] Reichardt, and their positions as the chiefs of WH/3 and WH/3/Mexico respectively. The redacted space for both cables in the *Lopez Report* is 11 spaces. Anyone who works crossword puzzles could venture a decent guess at who it probably was.
19. *Lopez Report,* p. 142.
20. *Lopez Report,* p. 143.
21. *Lopez Report,* p. 143.
22. *Lopez Report,* pp. 146–150.
23. Egerter was identified as signing for CI/SPG. Could this stand for "Special Projects Group"?—possibly the same as CI/SIG? Ann Egerter worked in SIG.
24. *Lopez Report,* p. 151; see also footnote 588, on p. 40 of the notes.
25. *Lopez Report,* p. 155.
26. CD 691, p. 3; see also NARA, JFK files, CIA document number 509-803.
27. Might this problem be explained if the 100-300-11 file into which the FBI reports had been directed was withheld from the Mexico City desk? The answer is no. Even if the 100-300-11 file were withheld, we know that the 201 file was furnished to the drafter and that FBI agent Fain's August 8, 1962, report on Oswald was in it.
28. This was the August 8, 1962, Fain report: see NARA, JFK files, CIA DDP 201 file on Oswald.
29. The out-of-date Soviet focus of the cable is underscored by a CIA description of the October 10 cable in a later October 15, 1963, cable as "Attempts of Lee Oswald and wife to reenter U.S." This comment appeared on the bottom of the headquarters copy of a Mexico City station cable dated October 15, 1963, requesting a photo of Oswald be pouched. See NARA, JFK files, CIA 201 file on Oswald.
30. Copy provided courtesy of Jeff Morley.
31. Copy provided courtesy of Jeff Morley.
32. CIA document entitled "Information Developed by CIA on the Activity of Lee Harvey Oswald in Mexico City, 28 September–3 October 1963." January 31, 1964, p. 3; NARA, JFK files, CIA document 509–803, and CIA DDP Oswald 201 file. 1992 release, boxes 1-2. See also WC CD 692.

33. Jane Roman, November 3, 1994, interview with Jeff Morley and John Newman.
34. Jane Roman, November 3, 1994, interview with Jeff Morley and John Newman.
35. Scelso is openly identified as chief of WH/3 throughout the *Lopez Report.*
36. NARA, CIA document number 377-731: C/WH/3 memorandum for the deputy director (Plans). The subject is given as "Plans for the Oswald Investigation." The "Oswald," however, is handwritten over a redacted word, probably "GPFLOOR." GPFLOOR was a cryptonym used for Oswald.
37. CIA document, attachment No. 2 to [redacted] Project Renewal, forwarded in HMMA-25141; NARA, JFK files, CIA January 1994 (5 brown boxes) release; in sequence as 00787 to documents also containing material on cryptonyms AMROD and GPFLOOR (Oswald); see also CIA Monthly Operational Support for Project, October 1963, from Chief of Station Mexico City, to Chief WH Division, HMMA22452, November 7, 1963.
38. *Lopez Report,* p. 181.
39. See NARA, JFK files, CIA document number 64-552. See also *Lopez Report,* p. 185.
40. See NARA JFK files, Department of State airgram from Mexico City, A-631, by D. E. Boster, December 2, 1963; CIA record is DST 28350.
41. See CIA memo to Rankin. February 21, 1964; NARA, JFK files, CIA document XAAZ-22759.
42. Warren Report, p. 735.
43. Warren Report, footnote 1170 to Section XIII (p. 735), p. 868.
44. Helms memorandum to Rankin. February 19, 1964; NARA, JFK files, CIA document XAAZ-36365.
45. Mexican government note to the U.S. Embassy, May 14, 1964, WC Vol. XXIV, CE 2120, p. 569.
46. Memorandum to A. H. Belmont from W. C. Sullivan, December 3, 1963; NARA, JFK files, RIF 124-10003-10417.
47. FBI report from the "Mexico FBI Rep," subject: Activities of Oswald in Mexico City, undated. This document also happens to be one of the rare occasions when the National Archives RIF sheet is misdated, in this case to July 27, 1963. It was probably between November 23 and the end of December 1963. See NARA, JFK files, RIF, 1993.07.17.09:34:53:46010.
48. FBI memo, from A. H. Belmont to Clyde Tolson, November 27, 1963; NARA, JFK files, 157-10003-10396.
49. HSCA, Vol. III, pp. 30–31.
50. HSCA, Vol. III, pp. 49–51.
51. HSCA, Vol. III, p. 59.
52. CIA memo for the record, by John Scelso, November 23, 1963; NARA, JFK files, CIA document number 36-540, TX-1240. See *Lopez Report,* in which Scott is named along with Scelso, pp. 185–186.
53. *Lopez Report,* p. 186; for the flash cable, see DIR849-6 to Mexico City, November 23, 1963, NARA, JFK Files, CIA document number 37-529.
54. *Lopez Report,* p. 187.
55. Warren Report, p. 736.

56. *Lopez Report,* p. 190.
57. CIA document entitled "Information Developed by CIA on the Activity of Lee Harvey Oswald in Mexico City, 28 September–3 October 1963," January 31, 1964; NARA, JFK files, CIA document 509-803, and DDP Oswald 201 file 1992 release, boxes 1-2. See also WC CD 692.
58. *Lopez Report,* p. 175.
59. NARA, JFK files, CIA document number 603-256, XAAZ-27168, March 12, 1964, "Memo for Record on 12 March Meeting of Rankin, Willems, Helms, Murphy, Rocca, etal on CIA Contribution to Commission."
60. NARA JFK files, RIF 1993.07.02.13:52:25:560530. The document is stamped "CI [counterintelligence] 314-75, dated September 18, 1975, and stamped "George T. Kalaris."
61. Kalaris may not have been fully briefed by his predecessor, Angleton, a possibility we might consider if it turns out that this document was inadvertently released. It appears to have been written for the Church Committee investigators who were then probing the Agency's activities. (SSCI Box 265-14, 10076; from Curt Smothers to Rhett Dawson; Subject "Status of Assassination Report," August 1, 1975; NARA, JFK files. RIF [SSCIA;] 157-0005-10076.) We know from a Church Committee document that its investigators were seeking FBI materials on "Lee Harvey Oswald (a.k.a. A. J. Hidel or O. H. Lee)" in the files of Mexico City (Church Committee memo from Paul G. Wallach to Michael E. Shaheen, Jr., November 24, 1975; NARA, JFK files, RIF 157-10003-10233). Oswald used all three names there. He used the name Oswald, Hidel was on his FPCC identification card, and he used O. H. Lee for his bus ticket back to the U.S. The Church Committee investigators were seeking CIA materials on the same three names in the Mexico City files.

    In what may be a coincidence, a register of CIA documents on the Kennedy assassination is annotated with text describing withheld or partially withheld documents. The register contains two items from September 18, 1975, one of which was the Kalaris memo, and two more from September 22, both of which concerned a "compromise" of intelligence information, meaning something was inadvertently released. The first, 1189-1001, was described in the register this way:

    > This document was denied. The document discusses the compromise of some classified intelligence information and the possible consequences in terms of damage to foreign intelligence sources and methods. The release of this document would provide public confirmation of the validity of the information leaked and would make certain the damage which at this point is only problematical. The document is therefore properly classified and denied.

    The second September 22, 1975, document listed in 1190-1002 contains this remark:

    > This document was denied. The document contains a continuation of the discussion of the compromise of the classified information stated in the document listed immediately above. The same consequences would be entailed should this document be released. It is

therefore properly classified and denied. (CIA document register, 1189-1001, September 22, 1975.)

To recapitulate, these two denied documents describe a security compromise we are theorizing might be the Kalaris memo. A firm conclusion must await the full release of pertinent information. Following this security compromise, and possibly related to it, the "security measures" that greeted Church Committee investigators Dan Dwyer and Ed Greissing eleven days later (November 3) were tight. In their memo of November 14, 1975, they explained that the CIA had decreed that "any notes taken by members of the SSCI [Senate Select Committee on Intelligence Activities] will be photocopied at the end of each session's review. Second, briefcases will remain in the custody of the CI [counterintelligence] office while documents are being reviewed." (Church Committee memorandum from Dan Dwyer and Ed Greissing to Paul Wallach on review of Oswald 201 file, November 3, 1975; NARA, JFK files, SSCI BOX 265-15, 10091.)

62. Win Scott, *Foul Foe,* p. 268.
63. Win Scott, *Foul Foe,* pp. 268–269.
64. *Lopez Report,* p. 172.
65. *Lopez Report,* p. 174.
66. The *Lopez Report* found that nearly everyone thought that this information should have been passed on to headquarters, but people seemed divided on whether it actually happened. Only one person interviewed by the HSCA was certain of her recollection that a second cable had been sent. However, it was an important person—the unidentified CIA Woman who identified Goodpasture as the very person who sent such a cable.
67. *Lopez Report,* p. 181.
68. Former director of Central Intelligence, Richard Helms, August 23, 1994, interview with John Newman.
69. Norman Kempster, *Los Angeles Times,* January 1, 1977, p. 1.
70. See, for example, the October 3 headquarters cable to Mexico included in the documents republished with this book. The handwriting is the author's attempt to reconstruct this cable. It is clear that the CIA station was allowed to share some Soviet cases with the FBI, but something very sensitive is not being shared, and it is going on at the time of Oswald's visit to Mexico City. It is possible that this was the Agency's penetration of the Cuban Consulate.

Chapter 20

1. Kelley, *Kelley: The Story of an FBI Director,* p. 268.
2. Kelley, *Kelley: The Story of an FBI Director,* p. 279.
3. Henry Steele Commager, "Intelligence: The Constitution Betrayed," *New York Review of Books,* September 30, 1976, pp. 32–39.
4. Henry Steele Commager, "Intelligence: The Constitution Betrayed," *New York Review of Books,* September 30, 1976, pp. 32–39.

Index